Complex Systems and Human Behavior

Complex Systems and Human Behavior

CHRISTOPHER G. HUDSON

Salem State College

LYCEUM
BOOKS, INC.
Chicago. Illinois

© Lyceum Books, Inc., 2010

Published by
LYCEUM BOOKS, INC.
5758 S. Blackstone Avenue
Chicago, Illinois 60637
773-643-1903 fax
773-643-1902 phone
lyceum@lyceumbooks.com
www.lyceumbooks.com

6   5   4   3   2   1   10   11   12   13

ISBN 978-0-925065-63-6

Library of Congress Cataloging-in-Publication Data

Hudson, Christopher G.
Complex systems and human behavior / Christopher G. Hudson.
p. cm.
Includes bibliographical references and index.
ISBN 978-0-925065-63-6
1. Human behavior. 2. Adaptability (Psychology) I. Title.
HM1033.H86 2010
302—dc22
2008056139

Printed in the United States of America.

About the cover: In the spirit of Christopher Hudson's integrative approach to complex systems theory, noted artist Richard Hull has brought his extraordinary talent to the creation of the artwork for the cover. Geometric and abstract, futuristic and organic, Hull's bright colors and expressionistic planes beautifully illustrate a world full of related structures and people. This artwork, cohesive and coherent in the end, represents the many attitudes and ways of seeing that inform and enrich the social sciences.

For my wife, Barbara

Contents

Foreword

It is with great pleasure that I write a few words about Chris Hudson's brilliant book, *Complex Systems and Human Behavior.* As a consulting editor to Lyceum Books, I read a lot of manuscripts each year, and I can honestly say that this is one of the best manuscripts I have come across in years. I say this not just as a critical reviewer but as a professor, a social worker, and a sociologist who has more than a passing interest in the substance of the human behavior curriculum.

In the departments and schools of social work of which I have been a member, the human behavior area often has been viewed as the substantive or intellectual foundation for studying and assessing people and the key aspects of environment. More specifically, it is assumed that this curriculum area helps shape a social worker's view and understanding of the practice situation; this in turn can shape the logic of subsequent practitioner interventions. While social work as a profession has developed a full range of practice theory and skills relevant to intervention efforts, the range of such theories that social workers can actually use depends on the cumulative contributions of the academic disciplines referred to as the social sciences.

Members of academic disciplines have a basic responsibility to pursue knowledge, even truth (or some aspects of it). Social work professors and professionals have a responsibility to adapt the knowledge gleaned from relevant disciplines and apply it in a variety of intervention efforts. Since professions are correlates of the modern world that presuppose that aspects of the world are knowable and subject to manipulation by professionals, it is not an overstatement to suggest that social work professionals operate in a very challenging ethical arena. Social work professionals must know a broad range of theory emanating from the social sciences, select from specific theories and concepts to guide their rational assessments, and do their best in applying this knowledge in an ethical way.

This combination of responsibilities of knowing, selecting, and applying social science knowledge and theory leads to several important issues for social work educators and practicing members of the profession. They include 1) ensuring that education of the professional includes a broad range of social science material; 2) organizing the social science content so as to maximize the contributions of the relevant social science disciplines; 3) determining the possible interplay of such dynamic forces as culture and political and economic interests in the larger society; and 4) the very organization of the thinking (collective) and doing of the social work profession, including its quest for acceptance and status.

Chris Hudson's book is a major response to all of these issues and, perhaps more important, provides a wide, complex panorama of social science theory and knowledge of particular relevance to the human behavior curriculum and the social work profession. *Complex Systems and Human Behavior* provides a guidebook for social workers to learn, select, and use the contributions of the various social science disciplines in their practice.

While all of the social sciences focus on knowing and explaining how humans act and behave, Chris Hudson's work operationalizes the critical role of two factors: the selection of units of analysis and the nature of key questions. Each of these affect not only the disciplines, but also the subsequent responses of the profession of social work. *Complex Systems and Human Behavior* clearly shows that selection of a unit of analysis can vary from seeing, and noting, individuals, groups, and social structures to possible exchanges and intersections between and among such units. In our culture this selection has often led to the institutionalization of the discipline of psychology as dominant source of substantive knowledge for the social work profession. Chris Hudson shows the dynamic between a focus on individuals and the ensuing explanations tied to personality structure, human growth and development, and maladaptive responses of human beings.

But *Complex Systems and Human Behavior* also shows that the selection of different (read expanded) units of analysis can and does lead to an appreciation of social systems, culture, role and status, socialization efforts, and even institutional functioning. This selection process, in short, greatly influences the subsequent breadth or narrowness of the social work profession itself.

In addition to expressing the richness of the social sciences, Hudson discusses the crucial role of selection not only of units of analysis but also of questions to be fitted to the units of analysis. He discusses the importance of the "why" question at both the individual level and the level of social structures. This consideration of the "why" question in a broader manner helps the profession to see, note, and possibly change structures that are tied to control and oppression and are associated with differential risk and needs of groups.

Complex Systems and Human Behavior also helps the profession to see and note "how" individuals learn to behave, rather than just "why." With this "how" perspective richly embedded in the social behavioral sciences, social work is able to use very specific concepts to structure professional interventions. But as with the "why" question, Hudson is careful to present material on learning as it affects group members and is clearly reflected in the critical role of system functioning and cultural transmission processes.

Hudson has done a wonderful job on a variety of levels. He has presented a wide range of material. His selection of topics and their discussion clearly reflect the richness and complexity of the human experience, both in terms of process and created constructions. And he has organized the material so that it reflects a commitment to tie a key knowledge base to a profession that is attempting to carry out its ethical responsibilities.

Complex Systems and Human Behavior is not necessarily an easy read. It reflects much of the confusion and complexity of thought within and across the disciplines. This is not a shortcoming of the disciplines; instead, in my view, it provides a fertile context for the social work profession to consider the richness of the human experience, of human beings living in social relationships. We can choose to focus on the need for better theory, but we can also choose to see how complex and rich we are as human beings. Chris Hudson's *Complex Systems and Human Behavior* will help social workers, and the profession of social work, achieve both goals.

Peace
Tom Meenaghan, Ph.D.
Professor Emeritus
Silver School of Social Work
New York University
2009

A Note to Readers

The purpose of this book is to provide a launch pad for the ongoing study of human behavior for graduate-level social workers and other human service professionals. It is designed as an integrative review that is best suited for graduate students who have majored in the social sciences as undergraduates. In addition, it updates that content with some of the most recent developments in the relevant fields and explores applications of human behavior theory and research in advanced professional practice.

Several motivations stimulated the development of this textbook over the past seven years. As social work faculty members involved with teaching human behavior courses for graduate students, myself and my colleagues have encountered considerable difficulty locating suitable readings. There are many informative textbooks available, but most of these tend to be written for the undergraduate student, are overly descriptive, and often give short shrift to both theory and research. But most important, even when these texts do include theory, they often emphasize traditional equilibrium and general systems theories, continuously repackaging the same material from prior generations and ignoring contemporary developments.

In recent years, there has been a sea change in many fields in the ways that systems are thought about, mainly as a result of several developments that are variously referred to as complex systems theory, nonlinear dynamics, nonequilibrium theory, or even chaos theory. This new focus represents an emerging multidimensional paradigm. Many of the core assumptions of structural-functionalism, general systems theory, traditional ecological theory, and classical psychodynamic and cognitive theories are no longer tenable. Thus, a central intent of this textbook is to introduce this new paradigm in terms that are both understandable and relevant for the human services practitioner and to explore how the traditional theories are gradually being reframed and refined in the light of these recent developments. Most important is the exploration of the practical implications of this newer paradigm for advanced practice. In this book, exploration of the implications of these developments takes place in relation to the assessment process. It also occurs specifically in relation both to a conception of advanced generalist practice that is grounded in theories of complex systems and self-organization and to evidence-based practice. The exploration emphasizes the critical integration of values and ethical decision making in practice when understood within a dynamical framework.

The title of this book represents a slight departure from the traditional nomenclature of "human behavior and the social environment." The term *human behavior* is retained here, if only because of its recognizability. But its meaning is interpreted broadly to also include the study of consciousness, states of subjective well-being, motivation, culture, and in general, the phenomenological aspects of inner experience, both individual and collective. However, the term *social environment* is dropped for several reasons. As important as social environments are, other dimensions, such as those involving cultural, economic, biological, and physical systems, are also important, and these cannot continue to be neglected. There is no singular environment, even for a lone individual, but rather each person and group transacts business with multiple environments, loosely entangled with one another, some of which may be monolithic and passive, but others of which are variegated and dynamic, oppressive or nourishing, as the case may be. Furthermore, large systems are not just contexts but can be agents and problem solvers in their own right. The term *complex systems* is used partly to be informally descriptive of the challenges that these diverse systems pose, including those that are directly involved in social and psychological functioning, and to highlight the difficulties of working with these systems. But more important, the term is also used to identify the specific theoretical paradigm that is introduced in the first chapter, namely, the newer generation of systems theories, such as nonlinear dynamics, chaos theory, self-organization, and social autopoeisis. More specifically, this textbook is designed to support a model of advanced generalist practice as it is now being taught in a wide range of graduate programs of social work. Reference to advanced generalist practice is left out of the title mainly because of the book's relevance to other approaches to practice, such as various models of advanced clinical practice. There are several additional themes and content areas that characterize the approach of this book, and these are identified in the outlines and introductions of each chapter.

This text aims to strike a balance between a succinct discussion of traditional areas of human behavior content and the emerging paradigms already mentioned. On one hand, the traditional areas range from general systems and ecological theory to the various developmental and life-cycle models; theories of psychopathology; and various theories of group, family, organizational, and community development and dynamics, to name a few. On the other hand, this book addresses the neglect in most texts of some critically important subjects. These include complex systems theories, including self-organization and self-selection, as well as recent developments in the understanding of consciousness, motivation, and personality; critical thought, problem solving, decision making, creativity, and spirituality. Among the other contemporary developments reviewed are ecological psychology, evolutionary psychology, network theory, self-organization, and communities of practice.

The material is organized so that it can be covered in a single integrative human behavior course or as a part of a two course human behavior sequence, perhaps consisting of one course that focuses on microlevel theories and another that covers larger systems. For this reason, the material in this text is organized not by life stage, problem, or theory but primarily by system level.

The content of this text is designed to support all the major areas that the Council on Social Work Education requires in graduate-level human behavior courses. Each program has flexibility in how to do this, but in general terms, these standards require content on human diversity, values and ethics, populations-at-risk, and social and economic justice; theory and research that range from the biological to the psychosocial, cultural, and spiritual; and diverse system levels, from the individual to the societal and economic. Table N.1 is a checklist illustrating the areas that each chapter covers, some in as little as a paragraph or two, but many in substantial portions of the designated chapter. A few of these merit some elaboration here. Historically, the biological dimensions have been neglected in human behavior curricula. Thus, this text infuses this content at multiple points. It includes evolutionary theory in the chapter on change; neurophysiological material in the chapter on consciousness; biological maturation, infant temperament, neurochemical mechanisms, and sexual development in the chapter on development; biological theories of personality and mental illness in the chapters on motivation and personality and on mental disorders; biological theories about skin color differences and interuterine development of homosexuality, as well as the characterization of haplotypes and haplogroups, the major categories of human biodiversity, in the chapter on diversity. Even in the concluding chapter on ethics and spirituality, there is a brief overview of research on the biological underpinnings of values. Discussions of the applications of economic, social, and psychological theories to selected oppressed or at-risk populations, such as Hispanics, African Americans, women, gays and lesbians, East Asians, low-income individuals, and the elderly, are included either in the chapter on diversity

TABLE N.1 CHECKLIST OF CONTENT INCLUDED, BASED ON COUNCIL OF SOCIAL WORK EDUCATION STANDARDS

Chapter	Values and ethics	Diversity	Population at risk	Social and economic justice
1. Assessment of Complex Systems	✓			✓
2. Roots of Social and Personal Change	✓	✓	✓	✓
3. Understanding in Action	✓		✓	✓
4. Study of Consciousness		✓		
5. Personal Development/Life Cycle	✓	✓	✓	
6. Motivation and Personality		✓		
7. Problem Solving, Decision Making	✓	✓		✓
8. Mental Dysfunction	✓	✓	✓	
9. Small Groups				
10. Families as Complex Systems			✓	
11. Dynamics of Organizations			✓	
12. Community Theory	✓	✓	✓	✓
13. Diversity	✓	✓	✓	✓
14. Helping Relationships and Generalist Practice	✓			✓
15. Values, Ethics and Spirituality	✓		✓	✓

Major Themes

Note: This table is based on the education policy and education standards of the Council on Social Work Education (Revised October, 2004). Check marks indicate content that is included, and bold check marks indicate substantial coverage in the designated chapter.

| | Types of Knowledge | | | | | System Levels | | | | | | |
Biological	Psychological	Sociological	Cultural	Spiritual	Individual	Family	Group	Organizational	Community	Societal and economic	Professional issues / practice
✓	✓	✓	✓		✓		✓		✓	✓	✓
✓	✓	✓	✓				✓		✓	✓	✓
✓	✓	✓	✓							✓	✓
✓	✓			✓	✓						
✓	✓	✓	✓	✓	✓	✓					✓
✓	✓			✓	✓	✓					
	✓	✓		✓	✓		✓	✓	✓	✓	✓
✓	✓	✓	✓	✓	✓					✓	✓
	✓	✓	✓				✓				✓
	✓	✓	✓			✓	✓			✓	✓
		✓	✓					✓	✓	✓	
		✓	✓				✓	✓	✓	✓	✓
✓		✓	✓	✓	✓		✓	✓	✓	✓	✓
	✓	✓			✓						✓
✓	✓		✓	✓	✓						✓

or in earlier chapters, as part of either the text or its associated tables and exhibits.

Human Behavior and Complex Systems is written for graduate students, their faculty, and other scholars in various human service professions and associated disciplines, such as social work, community counseling, psychology, or applied sociology masters programs. It is also suitable for use as part of doctoral programs in these fields but is not recommended for most undergraduates, with the exception of advanced honors students. The text is designed to be the primary textbook for required human behavior courses within these programs, either for a single course or for a sequence, or to function as a theoretical review for scholars. In either case, the instructor has considerable flexibility in picking or reordering chapters, but most students will find those chapters in part I, especially chapter 1, to be particularly important early in their study for the understanding of complex systems concepts that are more briefly revisited or applied in later chapters. Each chapter should be treated as a jumping-off point for further study, with the instructor delving into only the material that is most pertinent to the objectives of his or her course. Depending on whether the textbook is for a single course or a sequence of courses, the instructor may also wish to provide supplemental material to explore in greater depth specialized topics of high priority. For example, an instructor teaching the first of two human behavior courses, one that focuses on theories having to do with the individual person, may want to assign supplemental readings in the areas of human development. This might involve particular life stages or more in-depth material in the area of psychopathology or on groups or families.

Finally, an important caveat needs to be noted. Because of the breadth of this text, its focus on theory, and its introduction of emerging areas not covered in most undergraduate courses, it is not light reading. As with any difficult subject, students will need to grapple with the material, and sometimes reread sections, check the glossary at the end of the text, or study the supplemental materials: those listed at the end of each chapter, in the references, or identified by the instructor. Students are encouraged to also study the supplemental materials in the various tables, figures, and exhibits that illustrate content in the text. Throughout their study, students should be challenged to read actively and critically, constantly asking, What is being said? What is the basis of this or that theory? What are its practical implications? Early in students' study, it is recommended that the instructor review for students the various criteria for critically evaluating theories, and this may be done through exhibit 3.3 in chapter 3, "Criteria for the Assessment of Theory." Instructors are also encouraged to supplement this textbook with audiovisual materials, small-group tasks, case examples, class discussions, and the like.

Acknowledgments

This book would not have been possible without the support and input provided by many people and institutions. My employer, Salem State College, has provided direct and indirect support. Colleagues at Salem State who have read and critiqued chapters or provided other forms of support include the following faculty members and administrators: Philip Amato, Neal DeChillo, Marc Glasser, Diane Lapkin, Robert McAndrews, Barbara Nicholson, Marguerite Rosenthal, Cheryl Springer, Shelley Steenrod, and Yvonne Vissing. My graduate assistant, Matt Stillman, kindly assigned to me by Salem State College's graduate school, also provided substantial help.

I received some very important assistance during my sabbatical in the 2002–2003 academic year: financial support from the William J. Fulbright Commission, in collaboration with the City University of Hong Kong, specifically, its Department of Applied Social Studies. I would like to thank the following faculty and administrators at City University for their critique of chapters or other help: David Chan, Kate Fung, Joseph Kwok, Sik Hung Ng, Vincent Tse, and Yue Xiandong.

Other colleagues, friends, and family have also provided important help, typically reading and providing suggestions on various chapters: Kasumi Hirayami, Lutheran College in Tokyo; Carolyn Jacobs, Smith College; Thomas Meenaghan, New York University; John McNutt, University of Delaware; Leroy Pelton, University of Nevada at Las Vegas; Keith Warren, The Ohio State University; David Moxley, University of Oklahoma; Wendy Haight, University of Illinois; Patricia O'Brien, University of Illinois at Chicago; Jerry Finn, University of Washington at Tacoma; Agathi Glezakos, California State University, Long Beach; and Ralph Woehle, University of North Dakota. From Lyceum Books, David Follmer, Nina Nguyen, and Katherine Faydash have all provided invaluable assistance at the various stages of this project. Also of considerable support have been my friends Richard and Cynthia Griffin, from Salem, MA, and Kenneth Lux, from Rockland, ME.

I would particularly like to thank my children, Daniel and Elisabeth, for their help. And finally, I would especially like to thank my wife, Barbara, for all the support and assistance that she has provided.

PART I

The Framework

CHAPTER 1

The Assessment of Complex Adaptive Systems

We live our lives inscrutably included within the streaming mutual life of the universe.

—Martin Buber

I. Introduction

This textbook and this chapter in particular introduce an emerging theoretical framework for assessment and intervention in the multiple personal and social systems that human service professionals are regularly asked to help with. The framework includes elements of several perspectives that became popular in the latter half of the twentieth century, including the traditional structural-functionalist, general systems, and ecological theories. However, the framework goes well beyond those to incorporate several newly developed paradigms that have been collectively termed *complex systems theory,* which includes chaos, self-organization, and autopoietic theories. Unlike the earlier theories that focus on understanding the conditions for maintaining stable or equilibrium conditions, complex systems theories concern systems that function in far-from-equilibrium conditions. In this respect, they aim to clarify the dynamics of systems, or the processes and means by which systems move from one state to another and how they disintegrate or develop greater levels of adaptability and creativity. The theories covered here are a part of an overarching framework or metatheory of practice, which, in subsequent chapters, is applied to particular areas, such as psychopathology, diversity, and community dynamics.

These newer theories have supplemented, not replaced, the earlier general systems model that now describes a special type of system embedded in a broader array of social phenomena. Both general and complex systems theories involve several themes that this chapter, and the greater text, will explore, including the following:

Systems: Much of human service professionals' work involves systems, which are collections of interrelated parts that typically function as a unit and change in concert. The term *system* has a wide variety of meanings and connotations that range from cultural, political, and bureaucratic to family and personal psychological functioning, to biological entities.

Holism: Systems, it is often said, are greater than the sum of their parts. They cannot be understood adequately through reductionism, which refers to the inappropriate and simplistic application of theories pertinent to one level of analysis, such as the biological, to another level, such as the psychological. In any holistic approach, analytical methods involving the examination of parts of a system must always be secondary to multidimensional efforts to understand the whole system.

Emergence: Similarly, as systems and other phenomena develop, they take on characteristics that are not predictable, at least in any simple fashion, and are based on the characteristics of earlier or component systems.

Interdependence: Causation involves multiple and interactive relationships in which the condition of each part depends on other parts. This is a modern restatement of John Donne's observation that "no man is an island"—whether considering families, communities, or nations, the welfare of each depends on the welfare of the other—and this is becoming increasingly clear in this era of globalization.

In addition, the new generation of systems theories concerns itself with the dynamics of complex and nonpredictable systems that operate at the edge of chaos and are often characterized by consciousness, including the intentions and aspirations of individuals and groups. Some of the most central concepts in complex systems theory are the following:

Dynamics: Although the study of the processes of change is not new, complex systems theorists have raised dynamics—whether of psychological, family, or political functioning—to the forefront of investigation. Unlike the older equilibrium theories that regard change as the exception, change is universal and typically "irreversible" in complex systems theory (see Prigogine & Stengers, 1984). This study has, in addition, moved beyond the traditional focus on linear or tit-for-tat relationships to emphasize nonlinear dynamics.

Complexity: Many clients, and some human service professionals, yearn for simple solutions, magic pills. However, human service professionals are increasingly recognizing the sobering reality of intractably complicated systems, which sometimes do not seem to operate according to any apparent rhyme or reason. Formally, complex systems are defined as "those [systems] formed by a large number of discrete elements that are highly interconnected in non-trivial forms" (Miramontes, 1995). Complexity is more than a system with lots of parts; it also involves interconnections that are typically nonlinear. Yet despite any apparent complexity, it has often been found that simple rules and principles generate complex systems.

Nonpredictability: Findings emerging out of chaos theory demonstrate the impossibility of predicting the long-term evolution of complex systems. Chaos theory is in part based on the principle of sensitivity to initial conditions, or the idea that very small differences in initial conditions can result in wildly divergent outcomes.

Edge of Chaos: It is increasingly recognized that the creative functioning of both individuals and larger social systems requires a delicate balance between stable and chaotic processes, which is usually referred to as the "edge of chaos."

Consciousness: At the same time that many general systems theorists attempt to approach the study of systems through the perspective of the detached, external observer, complex systems theorists are increasingly considering the perspective of the participants, their purposes, values, beliefs, and consciousness. Karl Popper foreshadowed this shift of perspective when he distinguished three perspectives: the objective (*it*), the subjective or psychological (*I*), and the cultural (*we*) (Popper & Eccles, 1977).

The foregoing are a few of the core themes and concepts that define and characterize complex systems theory and its applications. This chapter explores these ideas in a discussion of the major complex systems concepts that are particularly relevant for human service professionals.

Work on systems theory has progressed on several fronts. In its inception and in its continuing development, complex systems theory uses an extensive array of mathematical and modeling techniques. However, human service professionals and researchers infrequently use these techniques, and typically any applications they do use are conceptual and metaphorical. Few human service professionals have the needed quantitative skills, let alone the extensive data, required for such applications. Many have criticized an exclusively metaphorical approach to the subject, pointing out misunderstandings and misapplications of the fundamental ideas. Thus, it is critical that any applications of these ideas go beyond philosophical speculations but also stay grounded in both empirical research and phenomenological research. Nonetheless, the metaphorical and conceptual level is an important starting point. According to the philosopher of science Max Black, most scientific models are systematically developed metaphors (as cited in Barbour, 1974). Whether the atom is imagined as a miniature solar system, the brain as a computer, or society as a biological organism, such metaphorical images make the abstract concrete and suggest new lines of inquiry, but sometimes they lead into conceptual traps. In both the physical and the social sciences, metaphors are routinely used in theoretical work, but then they are operationalized, quantified, and tested.

Much of case assessment in the human services also involves the generation of theories, specifically theories about the origins and dynamics of client difficulties. The hypotheses often cannot be tested through rigorous scientific means, yet given the pressing demands for service, evidence for their validity can often be developed through the process of delivering services. Thus, the final part of this chapter will explore the applications of complex systems theory to the assessment process, to the collection of pertinent information through both qualitative interviewing techniques and quantitatively oriented assessment instruments, and to the conceptualization of the dynamics of client systems and their environments.

II. Equilibrium Theories

A. Early History

The idea of a system in equilibrium and the requirement that it be understood from a holistic perspective has been traced back to Aristotle (Spruill, Kenney, & Kaplan, 2001). However, it was not until the Enlightenment that such ideas gained increasing attention. A dominant theme at that time was the "harmony of an interlocking order of being" (Wilber, 2000, p. 137). Examples that have been cited include Adam Smith's invisible hand, involving the beneficial effects of individual self-interest on collective economic well-being, and the notion of a "vast harmonious whole of mutually interrelated beings" (Wilber, 1995, p. 137). Alexander Pope epitomized this perspective in his comment, "Such is the World's great harmony, that springs from Order, Union, full Consent of things; Where small and great, where weak and mighty, made to serve [one another], not suffer; strengthen, not invade; Parts relate to Whole; All served, all serving; nothing stands alone" (as cited in Roscoe, 1947). Auguste Comte, regarded by many as the founder of sociology, similarly compared society to a vast organism (Appelbaum, 1970).

B. Structural Functionalism

The ideas of Aristotle, Pope, and Comte are counted among the roots of functionalism, which in turn contributed to the development of systems theory. Functionalism was initially developed in England in the early 1900s as a theoretical framework and methodology in such fields as sociology, anthropology, and philosophy. It consists of examining the relationships between parts and wholes, and it focuses on the functioning of social institutions. Its central idea is that social systems are best understood in terms of the functions or the needs that they fill. It directly incorporated Comte's metaphor of society as a kind of biological organism. Although the members of a society can be thought of as cells, and its institutions as organs, the functioning of each is best understood to the extent that each helps maintain the whole organism. The most critical part involves the macro pattern of roles and interrelationships. Some functionalists argue that while any number of particular individuals or groups may occupy those roles at a given time, they are replaceable when it comes to the overall functioning of the system.

In anthropology functionalism is often associated with Bronislaw Malinowski and A. R. Radcliffe-Brown, the originators of its two principal schools. Malinowksi (1944), who introduced psychological or biocultural functionalism, argued that social institutions and cultural traits developed to serve the needs of individuals, typically biological needs such as nutrition or reproduction. In contrast, Radcliffe-Brown (1952) introduced the structural-functionalist orientation, which focused not on individuals but on social behavior and institutions in maintaining the larger social structure, mainly through interactive feedback loops. Similarly, Émile Durkheim argued that social phenomena constitute a domain of functioning that is independent of psychological or biological facts (Broce, 1973). Both schools deemphasized the role of evolution and history, considering them of secondary importance compared with current needs, functions, or purposes. The sociologist Robert Merton (b. 1910–d. 2002) later clarified the concept of function by distinguishing between latent and manifest functions. While latent functions involve consequences of social behaviors that are not intended or recognized, manifest functions are those that are intended and officially recognized (Merton, 1957).

Working in the field of sociology, Talcott Parsons (b. 1902–d. 1979) proposed one of the better-known applications of structural functionalism, a commonly cited version of equilibrium theory. According to Appelbaum (1996), Parsons viewed "society [as consisting] of specialized systems and their subsystems, each engaged in a series of boundary exchanges with the other and with other 'environments' external to the social system itself. . . . All of these changes pose problems for the systems, forcing the system to specialize in one or another of the four functional prerequisites for existence—adaptation, goal attainment, integration, and latent pattern maintenance [AGIL]" (p. 69).

These AGIL functions are analyzed on multiple systems levels, which Parsons referred to as "action systems": organismic, personality, social, and cultural. To the extent that he considered social change, Parsons regarded it as consisting of changes in controls at the highest levels of society (e.g., Karl Marx's superstructures). Under Parsons's assumptions, major social changes originate outside of the system, if they take place at all (Appelbaum, 1970).

Parsonian functionalism dominated sociology from the 1950s into the 1970s, when it met with increasing criticism. Like functionalism in general, it was considered teleological, tautological, static, untestable, and conservative (Bailey, 1994). Despite these limitations, functionalism has contributed substantially to the assessment of client systems, maintaining a focus on current changeable conditions in contrast to unchangeable historic and developmental causes, such as early childhood traumas. As functionalism reached its zenith, a closely related perspective—general systems theory—grew in popularity.

C. General Systems Theory

Social workers and other human service professionals have long been attracted to the notion of understanding the so-called total situation of their clients, a term that the social worker Ada Sheffield (1937) first coined. For this reason, they not only have been influenced by structural functionalism but also have been drawn to the concepts of holism and systems. Ludwig von Bertalanffy (1974) defined a system as "a complex of components in mutual interaction.... Concepts and principles of systems theory are not limited to material systems, but can be applied to any [whole] consisting of interacting [components]" (p. 1100). This definition laid the foundation for the development of general systems theory (GST) and its applications in the human services.

General systems theory attempts to integrate the perspectives and findings from such diverse fields as the organismic social theories of the nineteenth century, the social survey movement, human ecology, information theory, and cybernetics (Leighninger, 1977; Siporin, 1980). Although the concept of GST was initially presented in 1937 and first published in English in 1950 (Bertalanffy, 1950), it was not until the mid-1950s that James G. Miller (1955) popularized it in psychology, and later in the late 1960s Gordon Hearn (1969) introduced it to social work. Shortly thereafter, general systems attained a level of popularity in social work, mostly through the contributions of family systems therapy and the community mental health movement (Siporin, 1980). The 1970s saw a substantial growth in the applications of GST in the profession, as numerous social work texts began to include the perspective. What follows is an overview of some of the central concepts of GST.

General systems theory conceptualizes systems as collections of entities that influence one another and change as a whole. Virtually all systems of concern to human service professionals are open systems, which are understood in terms of three primary stages of activity: input, process, and output (see figure 1.1). First, systems, whether of individuals or organizations,

FIGURE 1.1: SYSTEMS AS SETS OF INTERACTING PROCESSES THAT TRANSFORM INPUT INTO VALUED OUTPUTS

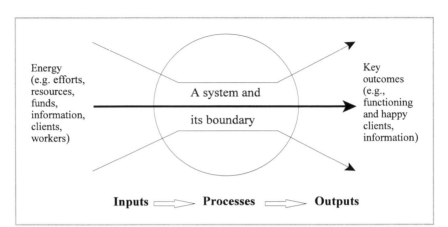

Energy (e.g. efforts, resources, funds, information, clients, workers)

A system and its boundary

Key outcomes (e.g., functioning and happy clients, information)

Inputs ⟹ Processes ⟹ Outputs

regularly take in resources, information, energy, and other inputs from their environments. Second, systems process these inputs, or transform them through a variety of means: clients are assigned to workers, staff members are oriented and paid, administrators work out budgets, and workers provide services to their clients. Third, outputs of the processes include workers leaving for better opportunities, clients overcoming difficulties, and reports by administrators or researchers, to mention only a few.

An integral part of the definition of any system involves its boundaries, or the ways that it delimits itself from its environment and controls its inputs and outputs. Although the boundaries of physical systems are easily identified, complexity and ambiguity often characterize the boundaries of social systems. Are there different levels of membership—perhaps formal and informal? Are there competing rules for defining who is part of the family, organization, or community? Most typically, boundaries are assessed in terms of how closed, permeable, or open they are. However, such a continuum needs to be applied differentially. For example, the same system that is relatively closed to new members may be somewhat more open to the flow of information.

Central to the notion of systems as organized processes is the energy that drives the processes. Both physical and biological open systems depend on the constant input of energy, whether it be radiant, electrical, or nutritional. When the notion of energy is applied to psychological and social systems, it becomes a metaphor for a wide variety of empowering resources, such as money, in-kind resources, encouragement, a sense of commitment, and even certain types of information. If energy is the ability to undertake meaning-ful work or action, then any of the elements of energy (e.g., motivation, competence, resources such as money or information) are types of energy, whether potential or active, when it comes to the analysis of complex social systems. System dynamicists who develop models of biological and social systems differentiate between stocks and flows of energy. A stock is any re-serve of accumulated energy or resources: money in a bank account, a sense of self-esteem, or a body of knowledge. The stocks are then processed and expended, perhaps by being devalued or dated. Flows are the transforma-tions of inputs into output stocks. Figure 1.2 illustrates a transactional sys-tem involving heroin arrests and consumption, and their mixed effects on supply, price, and the extent of importation. This primary cycle has ancillary effects on both costs and crime. The boxes and nodes in figure 1.2 represent stocks; the lines represent flows or processes, with each involving either a

FIGURE 1.2: EXAMPLE OF CAUSAL-LOOP DIAGRAM OF THE BASIC MECHANISMS OF THE HEROIN-CRIME SYSTEM

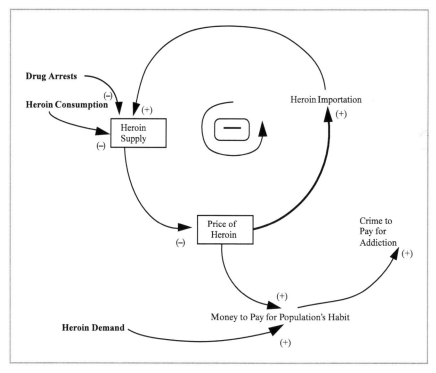

Source: Albin, S. (1997, June). Building a system dynamics model. MIT System Dynamics in Education Project.

positive (+) or a negative (–) relationship between the input and output of the particular activity or process.

The internal processes of almost all systems also have some structure or organization. A critical dimension of this structure is its degree of differentiation, or specialization of function. Does everyone do a little of everything, or are jobs highly specialized? Another element of structure is the degree of hierarchy. Hierarchy refers not only to centralized control but also to multiple levels of organization. Ken Wilber (2000) has generalized this dimension, reconceptualizing it as a system's "holarchy" and the parts as "holons." Wilber points that each part of a system is simultaneously a part and a whole. As a whole, it is concerned with its identity and autonomy, and as a part, it is concerned with its relationships with other parts. Systems are characterized by smaller systems within larger systems, one nested within another like Russian *matryoshka* dolls. Whether we look at biological organisms such as cells and individual humans or social units such as organizations, states, or nations, parts couple together into larger systems, and they become increasingly interdependent on one another for their various inputs and outputs. The specific types of units, the numbers of levels involved, the degree of centralized or decentralized control, among other features of a systems organization, vary dramatically from one type of system to another.

Often it is mistakenly assumed that a degree of clarity characterizes each level of multiple-level systems. Organizational charts and family trees, for instance, usually suggest little ambiguity in this regard. However, one level often blends into the next when we consider the actual functioning of such systems. A worker in a nonsupervisory position may informally exercise more influence than administrators because of his or her respected level of expertise. Family therapists identify parentified children, who precociously assume the role of parent, or transactional therapists talk about pig parents, who emotionally function as children but pretend to act like parents. Amitai Goswami (1995), a quantum physicist, argues that such "entangled hierarchies" (a term originally coined by Douglas Hofstadter [1979]) are ubiquitous throughout evolution, and thus should be considered in the assessment of any system. Many of M. C. Escher's paintings depict the entanglement of multiple hierarchical levels (see figure 1.3).

Related to the idea of structured system processes is the notion in GST that systems regularly gravitate toward equilibrium, homeostasis, or the steady state. Hearn (1979) argues, "After any disturbance, a system tends to reestablish a steady state, and a system can also establish another steady state if and when the disturbing external condition is prolonged" (p. 336). Life becomes a succession of steady states, a struggle to constantly maintain

FIGURE 1.3: M. C. ESCHER'S PAINTING *WATERFALL*

Many of Escher's drawings incorporate an ambiguity regarding hierarchical levels. In the case of this drawing, water flows over the waterfall and continues to flow down until it unexpectedly ends up at the top of the waterfall, symbolizing an entanglement of hierarchical levels.

balance. This assumption that organisms seek equilibrium is fairly wide-spread and ignores findings from chaos theory that most complex adaptive systems are far from equilibrium and can never exactly repeat themselves. The assumption of equilibrium is a limitation of GST, one that in part rests on a lack of knowledge of the complex dynamics of feedback loops. *Homeo-stasis* and *steady state* are terms used more often in biology and physics, whereas the social sciences prefer the term *equilibrium,* which connotes a more complex or dynamic form of balance or stability.

Perhaps one of the most important ways that systems are organized is through feedback loops, or circular causal relationships that structure both the internal and the external processes of physical, biological, and social sys-tems. Most commentators present a fairly clear picture of negative feedback loops, which operate something like a thermostat that constantly brings the target variable of temperature within acceptable bounds (Compton & Galaway, 1994; Hearn, 1979). Depending on the extent to which we see the world as consisting of such deviation-counteracting feedback loops, life will appear to be a succession of steady states punctuated by occasional distur-bances. However, commentators often give short shrift to or even misreport the opposite type of feedback loop, which is positive or deviation-amplifying feedback. For example, Compton and Galaway (1994) mistakenly define the concept as follows: "Positive feedback is generally held to indicate that the system is behaving correctly in relation to its goals and that more behavior of the same quality is called for" (p. 123). *Positive feedback,* as the term is ordinarily used in systems theory, carries no normative implication; it is neither good nor bad. Rather, it is positive because it is deviation-amplifying (Hearn, 1979; see also Maruyama, 1968). A common example is when a microphone is too close to a speaker; there is a sudden surge in noise as the speaker's output becomes continual input back through the microphone and is amplified. No doubt breakdowns, such as psychotic regressions ("When it rains, it pours"), or even happy occasions ("It takes money to make money"), exemplify this kind of process. In either case it represents a process that feeds on itself and breaks out of old bounds, creating either precipitous breakdown or seemingly sudden leaps to higher levels of functioning or creativity. Whereas negative feedback helps us understand stability, positive feedback is a key means for understanding change and growth.

System processes are also characterized by equifinality, the idea that di-vergent means may produce similar ends, and multifinality, or the notion that similar processes can result in divergent outcomes. System theorists, thus, have a deep appreciation for the often-paradoxical outcomes of the best-laid plans and the unintended consequences of many well-intentioned policies. Commonsense thinking is often linear in nature and leads people to believe that outputs will be proportional to inputs, whereas in reality the optimal input is often at some intermediate value and contingent on a complex interplay of many conditions.

A central but fairly controversial notion involving the outcome of system processes is that of entropy, derived from the second law of thermodynamics. Entropy is the idea that all energy tends to flow toward maximum disorganization and homogeneity, or the most probable state. Many use this concept to attempt to explain the driving force of human evolution and behavior and to suggest that any tendency toward greater organization and complexity is merely an anomalous or statistical fluke that inevitably takes place as part of the more pervasive tendency toward disorganization (Rifkin, 1981). Others argue that there are equally fundamental tendencies in physical, biological, and social systems that drive toward greater order. These tendencies have been variously termed *negentropy* or *self-organization.* Although most contemporary theorists have rejected some of the earlier theories, such as Henri Bergson's élan vital, or "vital force," other formulations, such as self-organization, show considerable promise in both their explanatory power and their practical applications, and these will be discussed in the section "Self-Organization" of this chapter.

By the late 1970s, many were increasingly airing their discontent on the wholesale and often uncritical adoption of GST, especially by many educators (Drover & Schragge, 1977; Leighninger, 1977; Siporin, 1980). While complaints included the argument that GST is far too abstract to inform practice, the usual defense was that systems theory is actually a metatheory, intended to guide the selection and application of more specific theories such as ego psychology or learning theory. This defense is not entirely convincing, as the traditional repertoire of concepts taught as part of GST provide few criteria for ordering relations among systems (Drover & Schragge, 1977). Similarly, Drover and Schragge complain about the limited explanatory power of GST and suggest that the difficulties that diminish its power include problems in optimization, ideological assumptions, the assumption that most systems are the same, and a high level of abstraction. For this reason, it has been suggested that unintended and negative consequences too commonly result from programs of planned systemic change (Siporin, 1980). These problems in many respects reflect a failure of many to move beyond the broad conceptual application of the theory to a range of practical techniques for investigating and simulating systems, such as those used in the field of system dynamics.

Another common criticism of GST is assumed equilibrium (Leighninger, 1977), which refers to a tendency of many GST proponents to overemphasize system maintenance functions and negative feedback loops, as exemplified by the action of the thermostat, in perpetuating current modes of adaptation. The equilibrium assumption is by no means fundamental to GST. However, when its proponents focus on the maintenance of equilibrium, they tend to look outside systems rather than inside systems, whether individuals or organizations, for the challenges and sources of change and growth. For this reason, Kahn (1973) pointed out, "Proponents of decentralization, community, and participatory control could find their activities in conflict with a systems emphasis" (p. 43).

Because assumed equilibrium and a lack of operationalized theory mar most human service renditions of GST, it is not surprising that many complain of the limitations of the theory in dealing with change and growth (Drover & Schragge, 1977; Halasz, 1995; Loye & Eisler, 1987) and in generating directions for practice. Drover and Schragge (1977) point out that GST promotes a technical role for the practitioner that depoliticizes practice and thereby promotes conservative and individualistic tendencies in the profession. Still others view GST as reinforcing individual practice and promoting the primacy of transactional, goodness-of-fit, and equilibrium-based solutions between individuals and their social environments (De Hoyos & Jensen, 1985).

D. Ecosystems Theory

In the 1980s, criticism of GST, from both the Left and the Right, undercut but failed to extinguish interest in systems theory. By the mid-1980s, many theorists began integrating GST concepts with ideas from human ecology and related approaches such as ecological psychology and ethnology. This approach has been most commonly associated with Carel Germain, as well as with Max Siporin, and it has been traced to Kurt Lewin's (b. 1890–d. 1947) field theory (see Lewin, 1951; theory example 1.1). The approach focuses not so much on change but on the abilities of individuals to negotiate and compromise with their social environment (De Hoyos & Jensen, 1985). A central theme of ecosystems theory—person-environment transactions—reinterprets many of the long-standing concepts of the social sciences and human services, such as adaptation, stress, competence, coping, and self-esteem (Germain & Gitterman, 1980). The focus of analysis is on the goodness of fit between individuals and their respective environments. When such a fit is lacking, a key question is whether the focus of any intervention should involve changing the nature of the transactions, the environment, the individual, or some combination.

Ecosystems theory is concerned with developing a comprehensive picture of the behavioral repertoire of individuals and their contexts

THEORY EXAMPLE 1.1: KURT LEWIN'S FIELD THEORY

OVERVIEW: Kurt Lewin (b. 1890–d. 1947), whom many consider the founder of social psychology, laid the foundations for such fields as group work, human relations theory, and contemporary social work. His field theory was based on the idea that human behavior (B) is a function of both the person (P) and his or her environments (E), which is expressed in the following equation:

$$B = f(P, E).$$

As such, behavior is determined by the total field of an individual's situation, which Lewin (1951) defined as "the totality of coexisting facts which are conceived of as mutually interdependent" (p. 240). He argued that all behavior is based on purpose, that "we live in a psychological reality or life space that includes not only those parts of our physical or social environment that are important to us but also imagined states that do not currently exist" (Tesser 1995, p. 340).

Three central features of Lewin's field theory have been summarized as including the following:

- Behavior is a function of the field that exists at the time the behavior occurs,
- Analysis begins with the situation as a whole from which are differentiated the components, and,
- The concrete person in a concrete situation can be represented mathematically. (Hall and Lindzey, 1978, p. 386)

APPLICATIONS: Lewin applied field theory to the understanding of group dynamics. In a classic article, "Reflections on Field Theory," Malcolm Parlett (1991) identifies five principles that characterize field theory and its application to groups:

1. **The principle of organization:** The notion that "meaning derives from the total situation, the totality of co-existing facts" (p. 71).
2. **The principle of contemporaneity:** The idea that the constellation of conditions in the current field account for contemporary behavior.
3. **The principle of singularity:** The principle that no two situations are alike, or as Parlett observes, "Circumstances are never quite the same and each of several persons inevitably has a different perspective or vantage point, even if they appear to be located in the same time and place" (p. 72).

THEORY EXAMPLE 1.1 (CONTINUED)

4. **The principle of changing process:** The group field is always changing; nothing is ever the same. The group field refers to that part of the total field that is relevant to understanding a particular group of interest.
5. **The principle of possible relevance:** No part of the field is less important than any other part. Even seemingly trivial or obvious aspects of the field need to be attended to so as to gain a holistic understanding of the group field.

(Allen-Meares & Lane, 1987). It draws on a wide variety of notions of person-environment interaction, such as George Stern's (1970) need-press model. This model conceives of behavior as an outcome of the interaction of a person's needs with environmental "presses," or challenges. Anne Hartman (1995) introduced the popular technique of ecomaps to portray ecosystems, particularly those involving families (see figure 1.4).

Some authors emphasize the phenomenological aspects of ecosystems theory as a humanizing antidote to the impersonal side of GST. For instance, Tyler (1992) argues, "The ecosystemic approach can be seen as a form of structured phenomenology in that it avoids mechanistic perspectives and is focused on the beliefs, values, and meanings of individuals within the system" (p. 4). Similarly, Germain (1999) suggests that the environment needs to be understood in terms of culture and the symbolic meanings that people attribute to it. Allen-Meares and Lane (1987) point out that the ecosystems approach incorporates an ethnological approach. Ethnology is the anthropological study of social knowledge and stresses, or the development of shared understandings based on social transactions. However, they also emphasize the systemic nature of human behavior and the extent to which relationships are "orderly, structured, lawful, and deterministic" (p. 518).

Too often those whose primary interest is to stabilize individual dysfunction rather than to facilitate ongoing growth of individuals and communities have co-opted the ecosystems approach. The integration of the ecological perspective with GST in some ways perpetuates this co-optation; at the same time, it sets the stage for important new theoretical developments in complex systems theory, largely outside of the human services. Despite this limitation, the integration of systems and ecological theory is an important advance, especially because it appears to ameliorate the problem of assumed equilibrium (see Siporin, 1980).

FIGURE 1.4: SAMPLE ECOMAP OF A CLIENT FAMILY AND THEIR ENVIRONMENTS

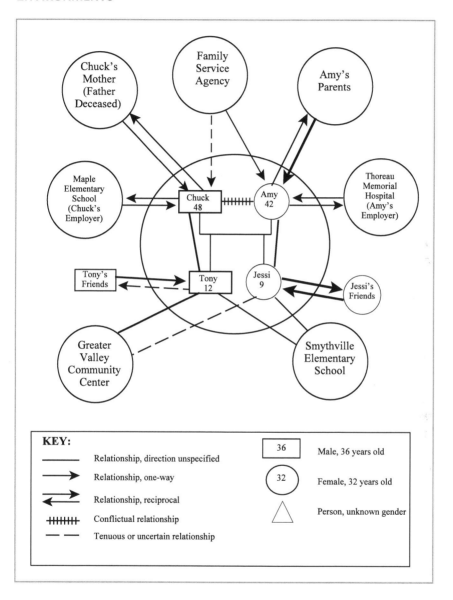

E. Deep Ecology

At the same time that ecological thought has been integrated with GST, systems theory also has been amalgamated with phenomenological and even spiritual perspectives through the deep ecology movement. In 1973 the Norwegian philosopher and mountaineer Arne Naess coined the term *deep ecology* to refer to an understanding of the multiple dimensions of consciousness and spirituality that underlie concerns involving physical ecology. Although the roots of the ecological movement can be traced to Henry David Thoreau, it was the publication of Rachel Carson's book *Silent Spring* in 1962 that launched the environmental movement. However, it was not until the early 1970s that growing dissatisfaction with the exclusive focus on the physical aspects of ecology led to Naess's (1973) articulation of this expanded vision. He contrasted this new, "long-range deep ecology movement" with the "shallow ecology movement" (p. 97), which promoted easy technological fixes, such as recycling and increased automotive efficiency.

Perhaps the most central feature of deep ecology is its appreciation of the intrinsic value of all living beings (see exhibit 1.1). Whereas so-called shallow ecology is considered anthropocentric and views nonhuman life forms instrumentally (i.e., in terms of their value to humans), deep ecology is considered biocentric or ecocentric, concerned with maintaining the well-being and diversity of all life forms for their own sake. Deep ecology is also considered a postmodern philosophy that contrasts with the instrumentalism of modernity, which emphasizes the rational matching of ends

---

EXHIBIT 1.1

I am soil
I am water
I am air
I am sun
I am mountain, river, sea
I am cloud, rain
I am living on planet earth
I am spirit
I am alive
I am flesh and blood
I am forest.

Source: Bragg (1996, p. 93).

EXHIBIT 1.2: PLATFORM OF THE DEEP ECOLOGY MOVEMENT

1. The well-being and flourishing of human and nonhuman life on earth have value in themselves. . . . These values are independent of the usefulness of the nonhuman world for human purposes.
2. Richness and diversity of life forms contribute to the realization of these values and also values in themselves.
3. Humans have no right to reduce this richness and diversity except to satisfy vital needs.
4. The flourishing of human life and cultures is compatible with a substantial decrease in human population. The flourishing of non-human life requires such a decrease.
5. Present human interference with the nonhuman world is excessive, and the situation is rapidly worsening.
6. Policies must therefore be changed. These policies affect basic economic, technological, and ideological structures. The resulting state of affairs will be deeply different from the present.
7. The ideological change is mainly that of appreciating life quality rather than adhering to an increasingly higher standard of living. There will be a profound awareness of the differences between big and great.
8. Those who subscribe to the foregoing points have an obligation directly or indirectly to try to implement the necessary changes.

Source: Foundation for Deep Ecology, http://www.deepecology.org/platform.htm.

and means. It has promoted a vision of divine stewardship that humans have in relation to nature. Deep ecology has also spawned the controversial Gaia hypothesis, associated primarily with James Lovelock (1972; Lovelock & Margulis, 1974). Lovelock hypothesized that Earth's biosphere functions as a single organism, actively transforming the physical environment. He cites several examples, including the control of atmospheric content by living organisms, observing: "We now see that the air, the ocean and soil are much more than a mere environment for life, they are part of life itself. . . . The air is to life just as is the fur to a cat or the nest for a bird" (Lovelock, as cited in Gore, 1992, p. 264).

In 1984 Arne Naess and George Sessions formulated what they characterized as the platform of the deep ecology movement (see exhibit 1.2). Like many platform statements it is intentionally very general, so as to include the support of people with a variety of philosophical and spiritual perspectives.

At the same time that deep ecology is concerned with the sustainable, interdependent functioning of diverse life forms and their associated systems, it is particularly concerned with the ability of humans to recognize their affinity with other life forms. This has been referred to in such concepts as the biophilia hypothesis or the ecological sense of self (Spitzform, 2000). Whatever it is called, the common concern is bringing about an expanded consciousness to support the sustainability and diversity of all life forms. Thus, both technological and ethical concerns take a backseat to the discovery of a kind of consciousness that is ecocentric rather than anthropocentric.

An offshoot of deep ecology is the development of the field of ecological psychology, or ecopsychology, which is interested in issues of the ecological self. A considerable literature has developed on this subject, using such terms as *ecological selving, ecological self-experience,* and even *ecological unconscious.* On the basis of an extensive review of this literature, Bragg (1996) characterizes the ecological self as an "expansive or transpersonal sense of self," describing it in the following terms:

A.   Ecological self is a wide, expansive or field-like sense of self, which ultimately includes all life-forms, ecosystems and the earth itself.
B.   Experiences of ecological self involve:
  1.   An emotional resonance with other life forms
  2.   A perception of being similar, related to, or identical with other life-forms
  3.   Spontaneously behaving towards the ecosphere as one would towards one's small self (with nurture and defense)
C.   It is possible to expand one's sense of self from the personal to the ecological. (p. 95)

Others emphasize the transpersonal or spiritual dimensions of the ecological sense of self. Some have drawn on the Buddhist concept of mindfulness to understand the ecological self. Mindfulness has been defined as "the energy to be here and to witness deeply everything that happens in the present moment, aware of what is going on within and without" (Hanh, 1995, p. 204). Brinkerhoff and Jacob (1999), for instance, surveyed back-to-the-landers about their ecological, religious, and spiritual orientations, and they concluded that adherents of deep ecology are more disposed to ecological sustainability and mindfulness than are adherents of formal religious traditions.

The visions and values of the ecological movement have thus evolved in several directions, becoming progressively integrated with not only GST but also constructivist, phenomenological, and spiritual perspectives. In this respect, the ecological movement has become a critical backdrop and foundation for both complex systems theory and its application in the human services.

III. Complex Systems Theory

A. Overview

The traditional equilibrium theories—structural-functionalist, general systems, and ecological—have provided many insights into the functioning of social systems, despite their limitations. However, in the final years of the twentieth century several new approaches were developed, collectively referred to as theories of complex systems, complex adaptive systems, or nonequilibrium theories; these provide a far richer source of models for understanding human behavior, and thus will constitute a central theme of this text. These theories focus on systems that often function far from equilibrium. The best known of these are nonlinear dynamics and chaos theory. However, also of central importance are self-organization and autopoietic theory, as well as the theories of bifurcation, self-organized criticality, and emergent computation.

Defining complex adaptive systems is not an easy task and doing so typically requires considering GST as an essential backdrop (see the section "General Systems Theory"). A fairly generic definition is that of Varela and Coutinho (1991), who define complex systems as "those formed by a large number of discrete elements that are highly interconnected in non-trivial forms." In contrast, Ahl and Allen (1996) characterize complex systems as "those that require fine details to be linked to large outcomes" (p. 11). Such views emphasize both the substantial number of interacting units or subsystems and the emergent nature of the global properties of the systems, which are not predictable in any simple way because of the characteristics of their components.

An important characteristic of complex systems is their capacity for self-organization. Self-organization is the apparent spontaneous development of organized patterns of functioning with minimal or no external control. It is often associated with the adaptive capacities of complex systems, which demonstrate emergent computation or natural problem solving directed toward system maintenance and change or growth. Whereas a factory production line or a personal computer may exemplify a general but not-so-complex or adaptive system, an individual person, family, or other group of people frequently exhibits the range of features associated with complex adaptive systems, and therefore they are best understood with the aid of self-organization theory. A hallmark of self-organized systems and many complex adaptive systems is the concept of self-similarity, in which similar patterns or themes spontaneously appear on a variety of system levels.

The field of complex system theories encompasses approaches that cover nonadaptive and adaptive, equilibrium and far-from-equilibrium, periodic and nonperiodic, and sparsely connected and highly interdependent systems, as well as those that move toward and away from order. Although the complexity of these systems involves both the multiplicity of their component parts and their interactive nonlinear relationships, their adaptability involves their ability to self-organize and replicate.

B. Nonlinear Dynamics

Complex systems theories are based on an understanding of system dynamics, or the study of the ways that systems change (Devaney, 1992), including their processes and patterns of transformation. Given specified conditions and forces, what are the expected sequences of states that will follow? How can dysfunctional sequences be affected to generate growth or to resolve problems? The field of dynamics has a long history in the natural sciences. Early concepts include Marquis de Pierre Laplace's (b. 1749–d. 1827) vision of the universe as a clocklike machine that, when wound up or initialized, runs in an entirely predictable manner. Generations of physical and social scientists have implicitly subscribed to this classical paradigm, consistently excusing their failure to predict by citing the lack of sufficient data on initial conditions. Jules Henri Poincaré (b. 1854–d. 1912), regarded as the founder of nonlinear dynamics, demonstrated toward the end of the nineteenth century that systems with three or more moving objects, even planetary orbits, involve unsolvable equations and thus are inherently unpredictable.

Dynamical systems are based on temporal relationships between variables that may be related on either a linear or a nonlinear (or curvilinear) basis. There are many relationships that are not temporal. For example, an association between two conditions may be fully explained by a third variable that influences both of the others. Consider this hypothetical example: An association has been found between ice-cream sales and drownings at certain beaches, but on closer examination, this relationship turns out to be spurious: one that does not involve a temporal or causal relationship but is instead based on the temperature and resultant number of beachgoers.

A further analysis of ice-cream sales at these beaches might show that for every one-degree increase in temperature, there is an average $75 increase in ice-cream sales. If this were the case, then we could say that we have identified a simple linear or straight-line relationship. Linear relationships postulate a proportionate tit-for-tat change in an outcome variable (here, ice-cream sales) for each change in a predictor or stimulus variable (here, temperature). In this case, the linear relationship is described by the equation *IC sales = temp × $75.*

Most research in the social sciences that attempts to examine causal relationships uses assumptions and statistical methods that involve linear relationships. However, a closer examination of just about any real-life situation reveals that even if we can identify a linear relationship, it usually exists within only a limited range of values. For example, closer examination of the beach example might reveal that when the temperature passes 95 degrees, there is a $150 increase in sales for each further degree increase in temperature. In this case, the relationship would be nonlinear.

Typically, nonlinear relationships can be plotted on a graph with various types of curves, often described by equations containing terms that are squared, cubed, or raised to various powers. Even though most real-life relationships are not linear, there are many who continue to defend the practice of assuming straight-line relationships, arguing that this simplifies analysis and provides approximate or good-enough solutions. But in the human services, this practice is usually not good enough. If a little of something is a good thing, simply increasing it does not necessarily make it better. For example, although a modest level of stress (i.e., eustress) may provide a needed challenge, excessive stress is usually shown to be fairly unhealthy. Or with psychotherapy or medication, there is usually an optimal level of treatment outcome beyond which one reaches a point of diminishing returns, perhaps when a therapeutic dose is increased too much and becomes a lethal dose. Figure 1.5 illustrates the difference between linear and nonlinear and recursive and nonrecursive relationships.

Traditional evaluations of human services typically examine changes in some condition of interest after an intervention or service has been provided. In contrast, nonlinear dynamicists are interested in the process of change, in the many steps that a person or social system passes through before, during, or after an intervention. These are typically understood as consisting of various types of feedback loops and other interactions. Clients, with continuing feedback, attempt to approximate desired behaviors. Such multistep processes are often modeled using the mathematical technique of iteration. The term *iteration* usually refers not only to the general processes of repetition, feedback, or approximation but also to a mathematical

FIGURE 1.5: ILLUSTRATION OF RELATIONSHIP AMONG LINEARITY, NUMBER OF VARIABLES, AND NONRECURSIVENESS (ITERATION)

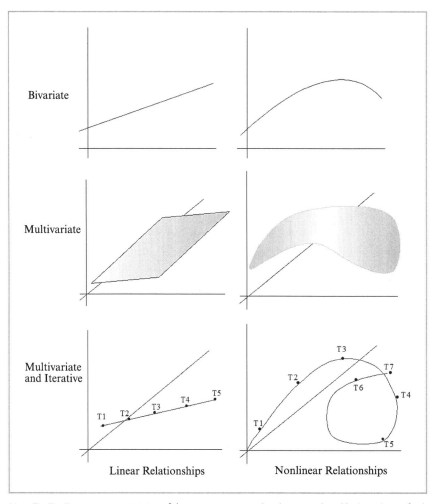

Note: T1, T2, T3, . . . represent states of the system at successive times, produced by iteration or feedback of the results of prior processes as inputs into those that follow.

technique of feeding back the results of solving an equation that describes a relationship into a repeated calculation of the same equation for subsequent time periods.

In the example of ice-cream sales at the beach, it may be that there is no simple relationship but one in which the previous day's sales influence the subsequent day's sales. The original equation, *IC sales = temp × $75*, might then be expressed as *IC sales$_{tn}$ = (temp × $30) + (IC sales$_{tn-1}$)*. This would mean that ice-cream sales in a given period ($IC sales_{tn}$) would be some function of a combination of the day's temperature and the previous day's ice-cream sales ($IC sales_{tn-1}$). The result of the equation for day 1 is then fed into a repeated calculation for day 2, and this is repeated or iterated over any number of periods to arrive at a prediction of sales for some future date. Thus, mathematical iteration is used as a modeling technique to understand naturally occurring processes involving repetition, feedback, or approximation (see figure 1.5). Most computer models of complex systems are based on such techniques, even when they involve games such as "SimCity" or "SimDate." These iterative models result in a wide range of results, from systems that settle into one or alternating equilibriums to those that exhibit periodic or chaotic behavior.

Nonlinear dynamics are the source of many very difficult and intractable analytical and conceptual problems in understanding complex systems. These problems typically entail many variables, changes over time, and interactive and nonlinear relationships. It is for this reason that the field of nonlinear dynamics has been not only the foundation but also the driving force behind the development of the various types of complex system theories, such as chaos and self-organization theories.

C. Chaos Theory

At its heart, chaos theory is a collection of conceptual, mathematical, and geometric techniques that allow one to understand complex systems characterized by periodic, nonlinear, dynamic, and transitional elements (Çambel, 1993). The theory was developed to deal specifically with systems characterized by the mathematical notion of chaos, or systems at an intermediate point in the continuum from the completely periodic and predictable to the totally random, and in which there is a type of order that never exactly replicates itself. More exactly, mathematical chaos has been defined as exhibiting three features: (1) sensitivity to initial conditions, in which small differences in initial conditions lead to dramatically different results; (2) patterned processes, in which behaviors are repeated but only within general bounds; and (3) nonrepeating processes, in which exact trajectories are never repeated. Chaos has been shown to result from at least one positive and one negative feedback loop, at least one of which is nonlinear. Examples of such systems include weather; healthy electroencephalogram patterns; stock market behavior; and many social systems, such as families, organizations, and communities.

As chaos theory has developed, it has been regularly applied to a range of complex, dynamic, and nonlinear systems that do not technically qualify as representing the narrow mathematical notion of chaos. Although chaotic processes are believed to take place in all major categories of systems—conservative (closed), dissipative (open), and quantum (see the glossary at the end of this book)—most work has focused on the occurrence of chaos in dissipative systems, of which biological and social systems are prime examples (Çambel, 1993). It is important to note that, while not all complex systems and nonlinear phenomenon are chaotic, it has been hypothesized that all chaotic systems are inherently nonlinear.

Poincaré foreshadowed chaos theory with mathematical studies of the stability and dynamics of the solar system and discovered that the most important features of the required differential equations were not their solutions in numbers (Galatzer-Levy, 1995) but the qualitative properties of their solutions. Poincaré discovered the limit cycle and the notion of the equilibrium point (Halasz, 1995). Other predecessors included Kurt Lewin, with his notion of freezing and unfreezing structures (Loye & Eisler, 1987); René Thom, the founder of catastrophe theory (Galatzer-Levy, 1995) (see theory example 1.2); and most significantly, Edward Lorenz, who in 1962 discovered the existence of chaotic structures, technically known as "strange attractors," in weather patterns (Lorenz, 1963; Loye & Eisler, 1987). The field of chaos theory, however, did not develop its identity until the eminent mathematician and biologist Robert May (1976) pointed out that certain seemingly simple equations may represent very complicated dynamics, popularizing the work of the mathematicians Li and Yorke (1975), who were first to introduce the mathematical term *chaos* in their now-classic paper "Period Three Implies Chaos."

Central to chaos theory is the notion that fairly simple mathematical equations characterize complex systems (Mandell & Selz, 1995). These are typically iterative equations, based on feedback, as described in the foregoing section (Heiby, 1995). By using iteration or feedback, fairly simple relationships often are found to underlie what appears to be complex or chaotic behavior. For instance, the complex behavior of flocks of birds or crowds of people can be characterized through the repetitive application of simple decision rules that each individual uses: "global structure emerges from local activity rules, a characteristic of complex systems" (Lewin, 1992, p. 47). Chaos theorists have also developed a wide range of graphic techniques, such as phase diagrams and fractals, to characterize and explore such systems (Hilborn, 1995). But the central methodology involves the analysis of time series (Haynes, 1995).

Just as in GST, feedback is central to chaos theory, especially when it results in nonlinear relationships. Feedback processes may be either negative or positive, deviation reducing or deviation amplifying, or some combina-

THEORY EXAMPLE 1.2: RENE THOM AND CATASTROPHE THEORY

OVERVIEW: One of the earliest examples of a nonlinear dynamical theory is that of the French mathematician René Thom (b. 1923–), who applied techniques from the field of mathematical topology to understand processes that exhibit sudden discontinuities or catastrophes. Catastrophes arise from the loss of stability in a dynamic system—and are defined as bifurcations or splits between different conditions that control the system of interest—they are categorized on the basis of the number of variables that control the changes. Catastrophe theory is based on Thom's classification theorem, which proposes that the stationary-state behavior of all systems has up to four control parameters or input variables (an associated function and one of seven elementary catastrophes).

For instance, two control variables may generate the most common type of catastrophe: the cusp catastrophe. Control variables are considered fast or slow depending on the speed of their effect on change processes; however, a fast variable may be associated with slow changes depending on the total constellation of forces in the system.

EXAMPLE: The figure here illustrates the cusp catastrophe as applied to employee turnover, modeled as a function of the behavioral variables of emotional withdrawal, organizational commitment, and job tension or stress (see Sheridan & Abelson, 1983). Instances of job termination are a pathway across a cusp, or a sudden dynamic discontinuity.

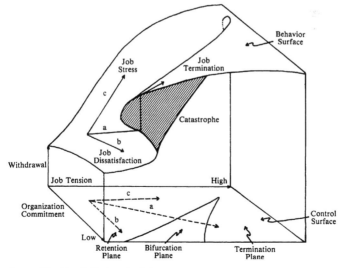

Source: Sheridan & Abelson (1983).

Theory Example 1.2 (continued)

CURRENT STATUS: Catastrophe has been incorporated into the body of non-linear and complex systems theories. Other applications include phase transitions and capsizing in physics; evolution, morphogenesis, and sleep-wake cycles in biology; revolutions, prison riots, hijackings, and committee behavior in sociology; and anorexia and bulimia, bipolar condition, and decision making in psychology.

tion of those. Such amplification may result from the operation of a single variable or the combined effects of several. In any case, time series (i.e., a series of sequential measurements that settle down to a regular linear or periodic pattern) are often characterized by negative feedback, whereas positive feedback processes likely characterize those that never settle into a completely predictable pattern (see Arthur, 1990). Feedback processes may involve two or more variables. Whereas certain attitudes or the availability of resources may become part of positive feedback loops, intolerance or resource constraints may become part of negative feedback loops that maintain the status quo.

One of the concepts most closely associated with chaos theory in the social science literature is that of sensitivity to initial conditions (Galatzer-Levy, 1995; Heiby, 1995; Krippner, 1994; Mandel, 1995; Richards, 1996; Robinson & Yaden, 1993; You, 1993). This notion originates in Lorenz's (1993) discovery concerning the unpredictability of weather patterns. Despite Lorenz's success in mathematically characterizing convection patterns (a pattern similar to boiling) with three simple differential equations, he found that the equations could not be used to predict the weather beyond a short range because the effects of the smallest discernible errors in the measurement of initial conditions became so magnified over time as to nullify any ability to predict. This sensitivity, which is characteristic of all chaotic systems, is the basis of what has been called the butterfly effect, based on the idea that a butterfly flapping its wings in Sumatra can result in a five-degree-centigrade change in temperature in Atlanta eight days later, or a tornado in some other part of the world (Lorenz, 1972; see also Galatzer-Levy, 1995). Small initial errors or perturbations sometimes endlessly magnify, through positive feedback loops, to create major changes. Although such sensitivity is an additional nail in the coffin of Laplace's vision of a mechanical and predictable clockwork universe, it does not suggest that the general form or overall pattern of dynamical processes cannot be predicted, assuming that chaotic structures (or strange attractors) can be identified. It shows only that

FIGURE 1.6: ILLUSTRATION OF A STRANGE ATTRACTOR: LORENZ'S BUTTERFLY

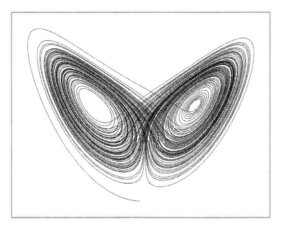

Note: Generated using Chaos Pro 2.0.

the specifics of future behavior can never be precisely defined, especially those in the distant future.

There has been much speculation on the significance of sensitivity to initial conditions in the social sciences. Stanley Krippner (1994) suggests that "chaos theory holds that through amplification of small fluctuations, it can provide natural systems with access to novelty" (p. 53). Similarly, Duke (1994) aptly points out that sensitive dependence leads to the understanding that small things can have major repercussions; that we can not over emphasize large traumatic events. Even a single act of kindness or particularly well-timed intervention on the part of a social worker can have major repercussions, usually beyond his or her appreciation.

Central to chaos theory is the concept of the attractor. According to Roger Lewin (1992), most complex systems exhibit what mathematicians call attractors or states or patterns that the system eventually settles into: "the network at some point hits one or a series of states around which it cycles repeatedly" (p. 20). Until the work of Lorenz, it was presumed that chaotic systems tended toward stable equilibrium (fixed point) or periodic attractors (state cycles) (Krippner, 1994). However, Lorenz discovered that some systems, though falling into a familiar pattern, never exactly repeat themselves, and it has been mathematically shown that if they are iterated ad infinitum, they will never repeat themselves (Devaney, 1989). Thus, in addition to the traditional fixed point, limit cycles, and torus attractors, there are strange attractors (see figure 1.6).

Important but less used concepts from complex systems theory are entrainment, slaving, or mode locking. These terms refer to the tendency of periodic patterns, when sufficiently replicated, to create a threshold effect that then spreads to other systems (Gleick, 1987). This has been observed for hundreds of years in clock shops: despite an initial asynchronous ticking of the clocks, all the clocks tend to fall into unison. Such a phenomenon can be used to understand both the pernicious effects of mental hospitals on their patients, as manifested by institutionalism, and the possibilities of positive behavioral change emerging from programs that provide a minimum required threshold of input and support.

Also rarely mentioned in the social sciences but critical to the science of chaos is the theory of bifurcation (Hilborn, 1995). Hilborn (1995) defines a bifurcation as "a splitting into two parts. The term bifurcation is commonly used in the study of nonlinear dynamics to describe any sudden change in the behavior of the system as some parameter is varied. The bifurcation then refers to the splitting of the behavior of the system into two regions: one above, the other below the particular parameter value at which the change occurs" (p. 13).

Typically there is a series of successive bifurcations that together generate some of the key routes to chaos. As a key parameter increases further— but to a lesser degree—additional splits occur; typically after three to five splits, a chaotic regime ensues involving multiple and conflicted processes. A universal number, one of the most important discoveries in chaos theory, is the Feigenbaum constant (4.6669202 . . .), which governs the successive levels at which bifurcations occur in many natural systems (Çambel, 1993). It may be that as levels of such conditions as expressed emotion increase above certain thresholds in families with schizophrenic members that the psychological and biological processes associated with schizophrenia undergo key alterations.

In addition to strange attractors and bifurcations, the structures of chaotic and other complex systems are also studied through the concept of self-similarity. Besides the principle of sensitivity to initial conditions, this is one of the most widely used concepts from chaos theory in the social sciences. It refers to the observation that "complex systems often involve structures that repeat basic features on several different levels of observation" (Galatzer-Levy, 1995, p. 1095). Whether we examine a coastline or a snowflake close up or from a distance, certain key features repeat themselves at each level of magnification. In the same way, some psychoanalysts have pointed out that important patterns repeat themselves in patients, whether in the micro process of the therapy interview, the overall process of analysis, or in lifelong patterns (Galatzer-Levy, 1995). Similarly, the popular notion of parallel process exemplifies this phenomenon in a different way, as

FIGURE 1.7: ILLUSTRATION OF THE MANDELBROT FRACTAL

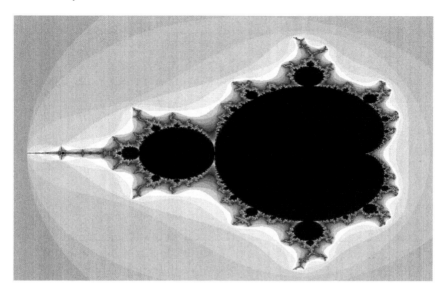

Note: Computed and printed with Chaos Pro 2.0.

key dynamics of a case may play out in staffing or at higher organizational levels. In the same way, interorganizational dynamics may replicate at the staff and the client levels. One of the techniques that chaos theorists have used to study chaotic processes is fractals. Fractals are typically abstract and colorful visual representations of some of the same iterative mathematical calculations used to characterize chaotic processes (see figure 1.7). Strange attractors, when visually represented, are fractal; stated differently, a fractal is the spatial expression, residue, or result of a temporal chaotic growth process, whether this involves the structure of a tree and its leaves or some social process. A key feature of many fractals is the self-similarity of form that is found sometimes on any possible level of magnification. Yet, usually, the patterns are never exactly replicated (see Çambel, 1993; Devaney, 1989; Levinson, 1994).

Many fractals contain boundary regions between periodic and random areas in which highly intricate chaotic structures are found. Several authors have focused on such boundary phenomena in both natural and biological systems, referring to such regions as the "edge of chaos" (Lewin, 1992; Packard, 1988; Richards, 1996; Waldrop, 1992). Lewin (1992), for example, argues: "The edge of chaos is where information gets its foot in the door in the physical world, where it gets the upper hand over energy. . . . Being at the transition point between order and chaos not only buys you exquisite control—small input/big change—but it also buys you the possibility that information processing can become an important part of the dynamics of the system" (p. 51).

Others, such as the psychologist Ruth Richards (1996), argue that the ability to function at the edge of chaos is one of the most important conditions for creativity and effective problem solving. Because chaotic processes never repeat themselves, they are an endless source of novelty. The ability to maintain creative growth in nonequilibrium systems, combine negative and positive feedback, and balance periodic and chaotic structures at the edge of chaos is no doubt a phenomenon that proponents of the now-dated GST are liable to miss without the insights and tools of chaos theory.

D. Self-Organization Theory

Perhaps the person most closely associated with self-organization theory is Ilya Prigogine, who in 1977 won the Nobel Prize for his discovery that self-organization occurs in dissipative structures, or most natural systems. Self-organizing systems are those that exist at far-from-equilibrium conditions and do not follow the general rules of the classical sciences (Bütz, 1997). There have also been several biologists since then who have identified what they consider the "spontaneous appearance of organized structure throughout biological evolution and social development" (Hayles, 1990, p. 21). Stuart Kauffman (1995), for instance, argues that self-organization is the "great undiscovered principle of nature" and that it and natural selection are the twin engines of the biosphere (n.p.).

A review of commonly used definitions of self-organization suggests that it has three primary components that distinguish it as a particular type of emergent phenomenon. First, characteristic structures or organizations are created: "Self-organization is a process whereby, in effect, components at one level interact and amalgamate to create a structure at a higher level. Components at that higher level interact and combine to again create an even higher level" (Merry, 1995, pp. 172–174). Second, such creation occurs with a minimum of external interference: A system is defined as self-organizing "if it acquires a functional, spatial, or temporal structure without specific interference from the outside" (Haken, 1988, p. 11). Third, the foregoing happens with apparent spontaneity: "self-organization [is a] spontaneously formed higher-level pattern of structure or function that is emergent through the interactions of lower-level objects" (Flake, 2000, p. 443). Although self-organization is commonly associated with nonconflictual processes, it encompasses both cooperative and competitive processes. What is perhaps most characteristic of self-organization is the interaction of local units according to identifiable rules, which results in the spontaneous formation of a higher-order structure, whether or not this interaction involves cooperation or conflict.

The literature contains several explanations for the underlying dynamics of self-organizing processes: (1) dissipative structures, (2) edge-of-chaos phenomena, (3) the operation of local activity rules, and (4) the structural coupling of lower-order systems. Some theorists have also emphasized the need for a minimum level of redundancy and reliability, the presence of noise or the amplification of random fluctuations, semipermeable system boundaries, and systemic correlation or coherence (Goldstein, 1995).

Prigogine established that the importation of energy into and its passage through dissipative systems is a prerequisite for self-organization (see Çambel, 1993). The most commonly cited example of a dissipative structure is the whirlpool, in which energy is sucked in from the environment, becomes organized, and is dissipated or dispersed at a higher or lower level. For example, Zohar and Marshall (1994) explain: "Self-organizing systems are like whirlpools. They take material or information from the surrounding environment and form it into a dynamic pattern. In the case of biological systems, they take material and form it into patterns of tissue or organism. In the case of mind, information is formed into patterns of thought, patterns of meaning" (p. 198).

Several authors have hypothesized that the edge of chaos is another precondition necessary for or conducive to self-organization (Lewin, 1992; Packard, 1988; Prigogine & Stengers, 1984; Richards, 1996; Waldrop, 1992). For instance, Prigogine (1997) points out that many natural systems spontaneously organize themselves while on the border between order and chaos. He argues that the maintenance of organization in nature cannot be achieved through "central management," only through self-organization: "Self-organizing systems allow adaptation to the prevailing environment . . . and [make] the system extraordinarily flexible and robust against perturbations from outside conditions" (Prigogine, 1997, p. 71). Elsewhere, Prigogine and Stengers (1984) explain that in those open systems that are at far-from-equilibrium conditions, and through which there is a sufficient flow of energy, minor perturbations become aggregated and transformed, partly as a result of systemwide information transfers, into self-organized structures.

Just as global properties can emerge from rules governing the interactions of the parts of a system, global structures can be demonstrated to self-organize on the basis of the operation of local activity rules. The *V* shape of a flock of birds can be shown to occur not so much because of some overall plan on the part of the birds, but because each bird follows simple, instinctive rules concerning how one bird should follow another.

FIGURE 1.8: STRUCTURAL COUPLING: TWO OUTCOMES

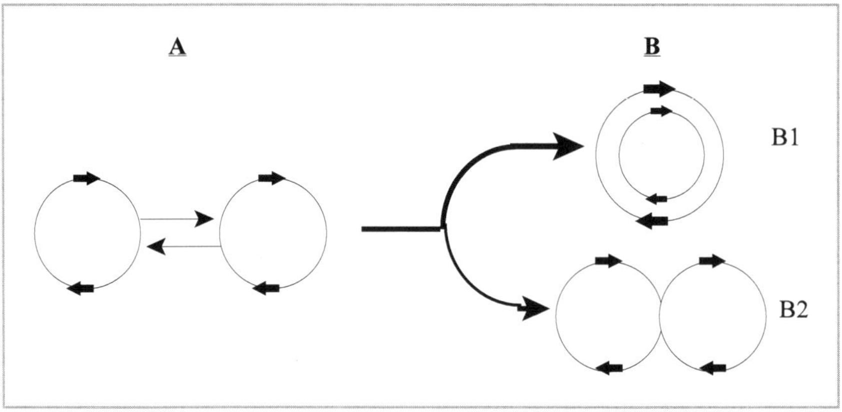

Notes: A. Two systems in mutual interaction. B. When interaction becomes sufficiently strong or recurrent, either (B1) one system incorporates the other, or (B2) the two systems link together to form a single system but preserve the identity of the component systems. Adapted from Maturana & Varela (1987).

A commonly cited dynamic, one that contributes to many self-organizing systems, is structural coupling, or the linking of lower-order systems (Maturana & Varela, 1987; Merry, 1995). Although Margulis (1981) is well known for her identification of such processes in cellular evolution, Laszlo (1996) extensively cites examples of the linkage of lower-order systems, which he suggests is a function of the lower bonding energies that exist at more complex system levels (see figure 1.8).

Most approaches to understanding self-organization emphasize interactions between local or adjacent parts of systems as the basis for emergent forms of organization. Although there are theories about how and why this happens, such as Kauffman's (1995) ideas involving an optimal level of component interrelationships (k) in relation to the number of components (n), the exact principles remain elusive. Much self-organization is no doubt a function of local interactions, but one of the great discoveries of quantum theory is the phenomenon of nonlocality, which involves relationships in which characteristics of systems change in concert with one another without any external or local interactions (see Goswami, 1995). Even if nonlocality takes place only on the microphysical level (e.g., within the neurons of the human brain), commonly observed dynamic feedback processes, characterized by sensitivity to initial conditions, can be expected to amplify, in parallel fashion, nonlocal processes that first manifest on the microphysical level to larger-scale self-organized patterns. Such nonlocal self-organization, in combination with the better-known instances of local self-organization, most likely represent some of the central dynamics governing transitions from disorder to order in psychological and social systems.

E. Autopoiesis Theory

Self-organization has been identified in a wide range of physical, biological, psychological, and social systems. Both biologists and social theorists have, however, narrowed the concept, isolating a particular kind of self-organization known as *autopoiesis* or *social autopoiesis.* Humberto Maturana (b. 1928) and Francisco Varela (b. 1946–d. 2001) classified complex systems into those that are allopoietic and autopoietic (Maturana & Varela, 1987). Unlike allopoietic systems, which are preprogrammed, autopoietic systems—of which most life forms are examples—are self-organizing and self-regulated. They exhibit the ability not only to alter their internal instructions to adapt to new conditions but also to self-produce and to replicate. Thus, while chaos and self-organization theories are concerned with transitions either into or out of disordered states, autopoiesis theory focuses on the maintenance of order, but only in a dynamical sense of the term. Although Maturana and Varela applied autopoiesis theory to biological organisms and human cognition, they were uncertain about its application to society.

Niklas Luhmann (b. 1927–d. 1998), however, has done extensive work in the development of a theory of social autopoiesis, applying it to such diverse areas as the law and social ecology (Bailey, 1997). Luhmann (1990) argued that social systems manifest primarily through the linguistic domain and that their character is a function of interactions among their members, especially their frequency, extent of connectivity, and types of memberships. The influence of the system as whole on its members, and vice versa, is considered recursive and iterative, realized primarily through patterns of communication. Luhmann (1986) addressed the problem of applying autopoiesis to society, specifically the problem of defining what it means for a social system to self-produce. As did Maturana, he argued that the essential components or units of a society are not individual people but communications. He suggested that communications are self-producing as well as self-referential. For example, in his extensive analysis of law as a social system he points out that law is a self-referential system that maintains and replicates itself: "For a theory of autopoietic systems, only communication is a serious candidate for the position of the elementary unit of the basic self-referential process of social systems. Only communication is necessarily and inherently social. Action is not. Moreover, social action implies communication. . . . Therefore the theory of autopoietic social systems requires a conceptual revolution within sociology; the replacement of action theory by communication theory as the characterization of the elementary operative level of the system" (Luhmann, 1986, pp. 177–178).

Luhmann emphasizes the circular, tautological, and self-referential aspects of systems of meaning, within which each element defines the other elements but none has independent meaning outside of the particular system under consideration. As self-referential processes, communication systems define, maintain, self-produce, and replicate themselves, much as living organisms do. Predating Maturana and Varela's work, the work of R. D. Lang (1961) on the communication patterns associated with schizophrenia clearly exemplifies the self-referential character of many complex meaning systems, or how communications define one another in a circular fashion.

In recent years, the theory of social autopoiesis has been applied to various domains. Several theorists have used it to understand cognition, organizational dynamics, accounting, narrative therapy, and family dynamics, to mention a few examples. As a relatively recent addition to the array of complex systems theories, social autopoiesis fills an important gap because it focuses not only on higher-level systems but also on their phenomenology, especially as its participants experience it internally through its self-referential systems of meaning.

IV. Case Assessment Based on Complex Systems Theory

Complex systems theory refers to a general perspective or metatheory, a collection of subtheories and a collection of methodologies. Because of its wide-ranging applications to the understanding of patterns of human breakdown, recovery, and problem solving, it is an integral part of the conceptual foundations of generalist practice in the human services. This section therefore introduces a few of these applications (chapter 14, on advanced generalist practice, will revisit these and explore them in greater depth). Although complex systems theory has a variety of direct applications to all phases of the helping process, this section concentrates on its usefulness in the assessment of client systems, as it is primarily through assessment that intervention goals and strategies are formulated, tasks that inform the entire helping process. Assessment refers to the process of workers and clients developing a mutual understanding of client difficulties, motivations, and abilities, all within the context of the relevant environments.

As a metatheory, the complex systems perspective has both direct and indirect applications to the assessment process (see figure 1.9). Direct applications involve the use of its concepts, especially typical dynamical patterns,

FIGURE 1.9: DIRECT AND INDIRECT USES OF COMPLEX SYSTEMS THEORY IN ASSESSMENT AND GENERALIST PRACTICE

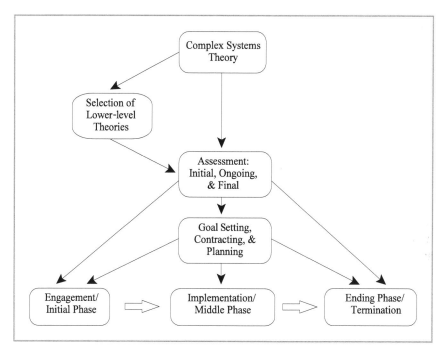

in conceptualizing and building theories about the origins, development, functions, and likely outcomes of client problems. Knowledge about types of feedback loops, periodic or strange attractors, the effects of accumulating bifurcations, conditions conducive to self-organization, or the self-production of autopoietic systems are a conceptual toolbox for building hypotheses about the organizational, family, or intrapsychic dynamics of particular client concerns and systems. It is insufficient for human service professionals to merely collect disconnected items of information about clients using the standard assessment outlines. The purpose of this information goes substantially beyond diagnostic classification to develop an in-depth and dynamic understanding, and to do this, a variety of conceptual tools, both specific and general, are needed to find ways to connect the dots.

The primary indirect application of complex systems theory is that it constitutes a framework for the selection and use of midlevel or content-specific theories. For example, whether the focus of assessment is on understanding staff relationships in organizations or the issues that a small therapy group faces, very different theories will be indicated. Some of the theories will be formulated either partially or fully in complex system terms, and to the extent that they are, this will be one of these central criteria for their selection when all else is equal. Examples of such theories range from ego psychology to family systems theory and organizational theories of goal displacement. Just as with complex systems concepts, propositions gleaned from these theories may be used to guide the assessment process, influencing questions asked and conditions observed, as well as in formulating hypotheses about how they interrelate and suggesting avenues for problem resolution. What follows is a discussion of some of the major considerations and principles involving the assessment process rather than a particular set of instructions or an outline of required information. The particular protocols will be determined first and foremost by the nature of the client problems, and then by the agency context, its mission, its needs, and its culture.

A. The Process of Assessment

Assessment is not a discrete stage of the helping process, one that precedes intervention in the same way that diagnosis precedes treatment in the medical model. Instead, it is an ongoing professional responsibility that is an integral part of intervention, from first contact through termination. This notion, now firmly established in several of the human services such as social work, arises out of a recognition that there can be no truly objective, detached diagnostic process, but rather that understanding and helping both constitute a complex, interactive feedback system. Intervention arises out of our understanding, just as understanding arises out of our helping, in iterative and ongoing transactions. Formulations of client difficulties are hypotheses that are partly confirmed or disconfirmed and continuously revised throughout the helping relationship. Observation, to some extent, actualizes the conditions under consideration, whether these involve strengths or pathologies.

Thus, assessment naturally plays a crucial role at the beginning stages of the helping relationship and is of central importance in engagement, goal setting, intervention planning, and contracting. But even at this early stage, the seasoned professional strives to seamlessly incorporate assessment into the helping process and avoid burdening clients with extensive demands for data collection. By listening to and observing both the clients' strengths and difficulties, these are brought to the surface and clients are thereby aided in bringing to bare their strengths on the challenges and difficulties at hand.

Many who subscribe to systems or ecological perspectives often emphasize the importance of assessing the whole person in relation to his or her environment, and rightly so. Assessment protocols developed on this basis, however, require extensive data collection, including information on service history, childhood conditions, multigenerational family relationships, various psychological functions, and various environmental conditions, to mention just a few of the areas to be covered. Holistic assessment is an ideal that cannot be faulted, but there is an important proviso: the client may come in for perhaps only a few visits around some fairly circumscribed problem and have little time or patience to reveal his or her entire life history to the assigned worker. Thus, it is critical that assessment is appropriate to the presenting problem, whether or not this is the most important difficulty from the viewpoint of the worker, and that the worker only then delve into the various facets of the individual and his or her environments as it is immediately relevant to the issue. As the presenting problem is understood and worked with, a relationship builds, and opportunities for understanding underlying problems emerge in an organic fashion. Unless the worker tempers the ideal of achieving a holistic understanding of the client with sensitivity to the immediate problem and the helping process, it will be the worker who ends up with all the information, while the client terminates with all of his or her problems unresolved. Although it is important to work toward the goal of holistic understanding, it is also important to recognize the difficulty of achieving anything that can even approximate this ideal and to balance it with an understanding of the immediate, here-and-now experience and interests of the client.

Achieving a meaningful focus in the helping relationship is a perennial concern of both novice and experienced professionals, one that directly ties in with the assessment process, which is concerned with clarifying the most salient problem (see chapter 14). This clarification is often achieved through identifying the point of intersection of (1) the client's motivation and capacities for achieving valued ends, and both (2) the mission of the sponsoring agency and (3) the interest and skills that the worker brings to the relationship, as well as (4) other environmental resources and supports. Of primary importance is the client's motivation: What is he or she asking for? How does he or she see the problem? Understanding the client's struggles, yearnings, struggles, and fears is no small task, as the client often has an incomplete understanding of these. Also of some importance is the mission of the sponsoring agency, including its capabilities and supports. For example, the mission of schools is first and foremost education, and thus schools are generally able to assist only partially with complex psychosocial struggles, and usually only to the extent that they directly interfere with academic learning. To overstep these limitations potentially undercuts the helping relationship, and for this reason, when professionals work for human service or other organizations, they need to be aware of the history, mission, and policies of these institutions and to be able to interpret them to their clients.

Finally, professionals have their own limitations, with respect to education, skills, and emotional preparedness as regards certain types of clients. On the one hand, it is important that professionals not be too quick to assume that they are unprepared to work with a difficult client, for example, a person who abuses the elderly. On the other hand, it is also a critical responsibility that professionals recognize their limitations and call on the assistance of colleagues and other institutions either to resolve uncertainty about such matters or to provide supplemental or alternative services. Failure to refer can be a basis for malpractice and litigation against a human service professional, or in some instances, it may violate reporting statutes. For example, a psychotherapist who assumes that a client's complaints of recurrent headaches is psychosomatic and fails to refer to a physician might later learn that the client had a brain tumor that might have been successfully removed had he or she been referred in a timely manner. Thus, out of the various concerns and priorities that the client brings to the table, professionals can achieve some degree of focus by considering both the institutional context and what they themselves have to offer. It is around this salient problem that assessment and the beginning helping relationship will revolve.

The principle of sensitive dependence on initial conditions establishes the strategic importance of beginnings—beginnings of relationships, of interviews, of other events. For many years it has been part of the practice wisdom of human service professionals that impressions form early in relationships, and these impressions take on a life of their own, leading to interactive patterns that are difficult to change for better or for worse. There is a certain imprinting that goes on as a result of initial impressions. For this reason, it is critical that in initiating interviews, workers are careful to support clients in communicating their agendas first, whether directly or through the metaphors involving play or small talk. Too often when professionals have their pet theories or diagnoses, hesitant clients, fearful of revealing their own concerns, are content to play along with the worker, providing any red herrings as their ticket to a relationship with a professional and thus undercutting the professional's ability to understand the client and assess the most salient, pressing concerns that he or she brings. An appreciation of the principle of sensitive dependence in the assessment process calls for considerable care in listening to and understanding the initial communications that clients bring both at the beginning of relationships and at the start of each interchange.

B. Assessment Content

At the same time that process is critical in the conduct and integration of the assessment into the professional helping relationship, there are a wide variety of areas in which information potentially needs to be collected. For example, one assessment protocol first asks the worker to collect information on the following six areas: (1) the presenting problem; (2) symptomatology; (3) salient environmental factors and the current situation; (4) medical and psychiatric conditions and history; (5) family status and relationships; and (6) psychological strengths, conflicts, and deficits. The relationships among these are then formulated into an assessment statement or systemic or ecological summary. This formulation is often accompanied by a diagnostic classification, intervention goals, and an intervention plan or recommendations. The institutional context influences the particulars of such outlines, such as whether the sponsoring agency is a school system, psychiatric hospital, child welfare agency, or medical facility.

Paula Allen-Meares and Bruce Lane (1987) have proposed a more generalized framework for determining required assessment content. They recommend that, to the extent possible, assessment should cover all relevant ecosystems, as well as multiple system levels involving both the person and his or her situation. The ecosystems typically covered include the home, community, and work or school setting. They categorize the person variables into physical, behavioral, and cognitive-affective groups, and situation variables into the physical environment, behavioral or psychosocial environment, and historical-normative environment. This ambitious plan should be understood as an ideal that can be approximated only in limited situations.

When only minimal information can be collected for an assessment, the motivation-opportunity-capacity framework of Lillian Ripple (1969) is particularly useful. She advises that every assessment should minimally involve three areas: (1) What does the client want? (2) What are the environmental opportunities for potentially achieving these ends? and (3) What psychological, social, vocational, or other capabilities does a client have for taking advantage of the identified opportunities? The plan that emerges from such an assessment may focus on enhancing motivation, environmental opportunities, or abilities, but more typically it focuses on bringing these areas into a more direct and synergistic relationship with one another.

Although older theories—such as the structural-functionalist, general systems, and ecosystems perspectives—are useful in determining the content of needed information in the assessment process, they usually provide little guidance in the integration or synthesis of this information. Complex systems theories include a variety of perspectives, concepts, and tools that supplement these now-traditional approaches. Of central importance is the assessment of interactive feedback loops or patterns in the relationships between key members of relevant social systems. Are these positive or negative feedback patterns? Are these two-step or multistep processes? Are they simple periodic interchanges, or are they constantly changing, evolving processes, suggestive of the strange attractors of chaos theory? What are the underlying rules implicit in the individual interactions among a system's members? Are there sufficient interdependencies and other interactions between these and members to support structural coupling and self-organization of higher-level structures? These are a few examples of the dynamic patterns that the human service professional needs to listen and observe for in the effort to formulate individualized assessment theories about the origins and dynamics of client difficulties and needed services.

V. Summary

This chapter has introduced systems theory and reviewed some of the key principles governing its application to the assessment of client systems. It has distinguished several of the traditional approaches to systems from the newer generation of complex systems theory. The earlier approaches, including structural functionalism, general systems theory, ecosystems perspective, and deep ecology, focus on the maintenance of equilibrium, whereas complex systems theories have been most concerned with systems far from equilibrium and with understanding how they change and adapt for better or for worse. Complex systems theory does not replace or negate the contributions of the earlier approaches but rather incorporates them in a larger, more inclusive, and informative framework.

Complex systems theory builds on the earlier approaches and focuses on systems with large numbers of parts that are interconnected in nontrivial ways and that are not understandable in terms of the characteristics of the components. It also directly builds on the field of nonlinear dynamics, which studies how systems change when processes are iterated or repeated and when the impact of input on outcomes is not proportionate. Complex systems theory is actually a collection of theories that has been categorized on the basis of the degree of periodicity of change, the level of interconnectedness, and the direction of change. For example, while chaos theory involves systems in which disorder develops out of order, self-organization theory seeks to understand how order spontaneously emerges out of disorder, with few external influences.

The final part of the chapter reviewed key principles involving the assessment of client systems from a complex systems perspective. It emphasized the need to integrate assessment throughout the helping process and to balance the ideal of holistic assessment with the need to understand the presenting problem. It is very important that the assessment of individuals and small groups, in relation to their environments, be embedded in the assessment of the larger systems that they are part of, including the relevant helping systems.

For Further Reading

Allen-Meares, P., & Lane, B. A. (1987, November). Grounding social work practice in theory: Ecosystems. *Social Casework, 68,* 515–521.

Bailey, K. D. (1997). The autopoiesis of social systems: Assessing Luhmann's theory of self-reference. *Systems Research and Behavioral Science, 14*(2), 83–100.

Bütz, M. R. (1997). *Chaos and complexity: Implications for psychological theory and practice.* Washington, DC: Taylor & Francis.

Çambel, A. B. (1993). *Applied chaos theory: A paradigm for complexity.* San Diego: Academic Press.

Haynes, S. N. (1995). Introduction to the special section on chaos theory and psychological assessment. *Psychological Assessment, 7*(1), 3–4.

Kauffman, S. (1995). *At home in the universe: The search for the laws of self-organization and complexity.* New York: Oxford University Press.

Krippner, S. (1994). Humanistic psychology and chaos theory: The third revolution and the third force. *Journal of Humanistic Psychology, 34*(3), 48–61.

Lewin, R. (1992). *Complexity: Life at the edge of complexity.* New York: Macmillan.

Luhmann, N. (1986). The autopoiesis of social systems. In F. Geyer & J. van der Zouwen (Eds.), *Sociocybernetic paradoxes: Observation, control and evolution of self-steering systems* (pp. 172–192). London: Sage.

Prigogine, I. (1996). *The end of certainty: Time, chaos, and the new laws of nature.* New York: Free Press.

Warren, K., Franklin, C., & Streeter, C. L. (1998). New directions in systems theory: Chaos and complexity. *Social Work, 43*(4), 357–372.

CHAPTER 2

The Roots of Social and Personal Change: Self-Organization, Natural Selection, and Entropy

For nothing is fixed, forever and forever and forever, it is not fixed; the earth is always shifting, the light is always changing, the sea does not cease to grind down rock. Generations do not cease to be born, and we are responsible to them because we are the only witnesses they have. The sea rises, the light fails, lovers cling to each other, and children cling to us. The moment we cease to hold each other, the sea engulfs us and the light goes out.

—JAMES BALDWIN

I. Introduction

A. The Core Issue

On the one hand, James Baldwin's epigraph to this chapter is an eloquent reminder of what we all know. Everything changes; change is one of the most universal of our experiences. Even those things that appear unchanging are simply slower-moving processes. Astrophysicists now agree that even the universe and time itself, until recently thought to be eternal, have a beginning and an ending. On the other hand, change may be something so ubiquitous and unsettling that many still prefer to cling to sources of equilibrium, stability, and predictability. This is particularly true for many theorists in the social sciences. Functionalists such as Talcott Parsons sought to understand role performance within virtually unchanging social structures. Many traditional developmental theorists assumed that personality development was completed in early childhood and that the adult personality remains fairly fixed. More recently, geopolitical theorists have argued that with the end of the cold war and the spread of a supposedly mono-ideological and universal Western culture that we have arrived at the end of history (Fukuyama, 1989). But Samuel Huntington (1996) points out that most civilizations arrive at a point where they become blinded by the "mirage of immortality," and he warns, "Societies that assume that their history has ended, however, are usually societies whose history is about to decline" (p. 301).

Change may be good, bad, or indifferent. Some natural processes, such as childbirth, we embrace and celebrate, but others, such as sickness and death, we deal with or mourn. A perennial question is whether there are underlying driving forces or purposes that direct change. Alternatively, is change simply driven by chance or by other local, physical forces that are indifferent to our professed values? Is there any meaningful direction to the observed pathways of physical, biological, and social development? Or does this great chain of being, the ideal of progressive evolutionary development, merely present us with a mirage of purpose and direction? Do physical law and chance allow for human motivations, purposes, and choices? There are many who cynically believe that our purposes are merely individual or social narratives we construct to deal with an essentially random, purposeless, unjust world.

This chapter provides an overview of selected theories of change, considering the central issue of whether the various discrete theories of evolutionary, macro-social, and personal change represent parts of a broader developmental process. To the extent that the human service professional is able to comprehend both local and global patterns of change in the clients and communities served, he or she most likely is able to identify strategic points of intervention, even if the long-term outcomes of those services may not be predictable. But before considering particular theories of change, we will first review the notion of emergence. This will help integrate these diverse perspectives and answer the core issue of the nature of change, and thus the possibilities for planned action on the part of human service professionals.

B. Emergence as an Overarching Framework

Determining the particular processes that drive change in complex adaptive systems has been a contentious and largely unresolved problem. It has often been argued that as complex systems develop out of the interactions among their component parts, they also develop characteristics that their precursor or component systems cannot reduce or explain: the whole is greater than the parts. Although emergence has become a central feature of complex system theory (Lewin, 1992), it is a notion that has been around for many years and can be traced back to the British emergentists of the nineteenth century, the best known of which was John Stuart Mill (see McLaughlin, 1992). This school attempted to provide an alternative solution to the mind-body problem, which rejected René Descartes' dualism while avoiding the pitfalls of physical reductionism. This traditional variation of the theory proposed that the fundamental entities of psychological and social processes are material. However, the emergentists also argued that "when processes reach a certain level of structural complexity, genuinely novel properties emerge to characterize the structural aggregates" (Markič, 1999, n.p.). Nonemergent properties are those that are simple functions of the qualities of the underlying components, whereas emergent properties cannot be accounted for in such a fashion. Figure 2.1 illustrates emergence as

FIGURE 2.1: ILLUSTRATION OF MULTILEVEL CAUSATION

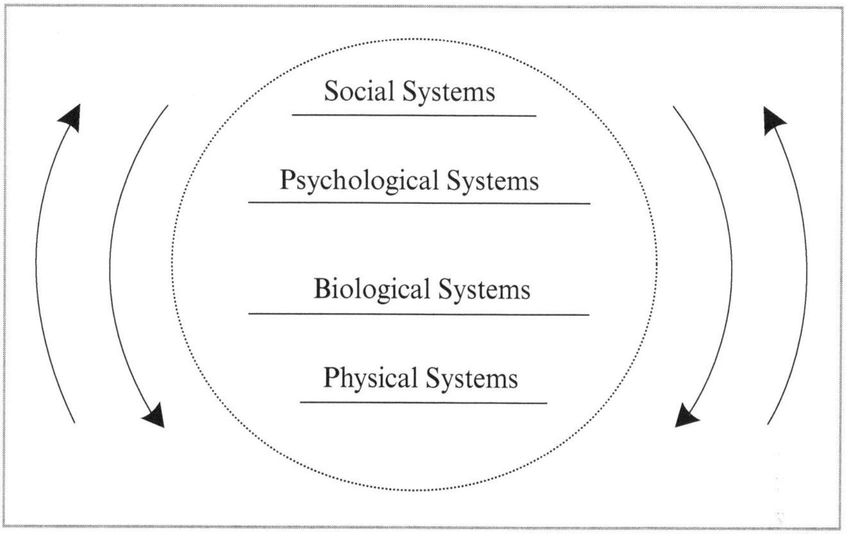

Social Systems

Psychological Systems

Biological Systems

Physical Systems

Notes: Upward arrows indicate bottom-up causation (i.e., emergence). Downward arrows indicate top-down causation (i.e., backaction).

a kind of bottom-up causation (upward arrows), which is supplemented by downward causation or back action, to provide a comprehensive multilevel understanding of transactional causation between various system levels, such as the social, psychological, and biological.

A wide range of views on emergent phenomena have developed since the nineteenth-century emergentists, and these can be divided into weak and strong versions of emergentism. Weak versions typically assert only that properties on the more complex system levels are not explainable from the lower levels and are in some sense novel. For example, a definition from the Web site Dictionary of Philosophy of Mind asserts that "properties of a complex physical system are emergent just in case they are neither (i) properties had by any parts of the system taken in isolation or (ii) resultant of a mere summation of properties of parts of the system" (Eliasmith, 1998, n.p.). Such weak versions have been popular among physical epiphenomenalists, or those who view mental experience as arising out of and determined by, but not strictly reducible to, underlying physical processes.

Strong versions, however, go further and include the idea that, on more complex levels, the emergent properties may become independent of the particular units on the lower levels in that these may be replaceable. Even more controversial is the idea that their properties may attain a causal power to influence underlying components. Independence can easily be argued by citing the example of a computer program that can operate on diverse computers and maintain its essential characteristics, or an organization that maintains its same identity and functions despite a complete turnover of personnel. A small but vocal group of scholars reject the causal power of the more complex levels to influence lower levels, sometimes called downward causation or back action. This group includes some in the cognitive and behavioral sciences who consider mental experience essentially epiphenomenal and reflective of underlying biological processes; choice is a convenient fiction (e.g., Bargh & Chartrand, 1999). For example, one author claims that "there are no independent mental causes with respect to physical effects. This principle is one of the basic scientific principles and it seems that rejecting it would be too high a price" (Markič, 1999, p. 6). When human service professionals minimize choice, they minimize motivation and instead tend to emphasize an interventionist approach, perhaps one that is behavioristic.

Unlike self-organization (see chapter 1), which focuses on the development of particular structures out of simpler components, emergence is a broader concept involving any properties apparently unique to complex systems. Typically—but not necessarily—those who use theories of self-organization subscribe to one or another variation of strong emergence. The continuum of weak to strong positions reflects alternative levels of development of system complexity, with the higher levels more resistant to traditional methods of analysis. Currently, weak versions of emergence are popular in the cognitive sciences, and stronger forms are part of the core assumptions of some social scientists.

Many proponents of complex systems theories, but not all, actively draw on the idea of emergence. For instance, both John Holland (1998) and Robert Axelrod (1997) have done extensive work to model the development of cooperative social relationships using computer simulations that effectively demonstrate the emergence of higher-order cooperative structures out of interacting units governed by simple interactional rules. Just as Axelrod (1997) defines emergent properties of a system as resulting from "the large scale effects of locally interacting agents" (p. 4), Holland defines emergence in generated systems as "persistent patterns with changing components" (1998, p. 225). In contrast, Chris Langdon, of the Santa Fe Institute, adopts a decidedly strong version of emergence as reflected in his statement: "from the interaction of the individual components . . . emerges some kind of global property . . . which turns back to influence the behavior of the individuals" (as cited in Merry, 1995, p. 138).

C. The Emergence of Evolutionary Drivers: Some Definitions

Each discipline conceptualizes the origins of change in different terms. Physicists draw on notions of fundamental forces, such as gravity or the electroweak force, and lawful interactions among them, to explain states of equilibrium or disequilibrium. Biologists, in contrast, emphasize organizing principles, such as natural selection, or evolutionary drivers, such as meiotic, chromosomal, or mutational drives (Campbell, 1985). Psychologists emphasize needs, drives, and motivations, whereas sociologists, economists, and political scientists refer to diverse sources of change, such as cultural values and aspirations, role functioning, rational calculations of economic interests, and power conflicts and imbalances.

This seeming intellectual tower of Babel illustrates what can be characterized as an evolution of evolutionary drivers. Not only do complex structures emerge out of their component parts, but also complex and multiple-layered dynamics of growth and change result from permutations of simpler, lawful forces. It is well known that laws, principles, and even forces themselves evolve. At the most elemental levels of physical evolution, gravity and the electromagnetic forces did not initially exist as such, but instead came to exist as separate forces only when the early universe cooled down sufficiently and early symmetries were broken. Biological principles, such as natural selection, had no meaning before the development of life, and likewise, psychological concepts of motivation presuppose complex neurological and mental functioning, which came with the development of some animal species and humans.

Lower-level forces and evolutionary drivers form a constraining context within which higher-level motivations and interests operate, and at the same time, they operate in and through the higher-level drivers as their components and functions. Some basic definitions illustrate the interrelationships among the various sources of change (see exhibit 2.1). Unlike physical forces, such as gravity, sources of biological and psychological change include drives, needs, and motivations and actually represent complex systems of interacting forces, with their own inputs and outputs.

The drivers of change in living and social systems, thus, are multilevel dynamic configurations that, at least on the human scale, consist of systems of linked perceptions; aspirations; appraisals; and in general, a range of interacting ideas and feelings. Although physical forces and biological drivers both form a constraining context and provide some directive influence, it may be that psychological and social drivers increasingly transcend these constraints and even show some evidence of modifying their physical and biological substrate. For the professional, this suggests that motivations

EXHIBIT 2.1: DEFINITIONS OF EVOLUTIONARY DRIVERS FROM DIVERSE DISCIPLINES

1. **Forces:** Forces create change. In physics, force is defined as that which has a propensity to change the momentum of an object with mass, specifically as a proportion of the rate of change of momentum. A more generic understanding points to force as the effect of any type of energy in bringing about changes in observed reality. Physicists traditionally identified four fundamental forces of nature: Gravitational, electromagnetic, weak, and strong forces, but in recent years the electromagnetic and weak forces have discovered to be versions of the electroweak force.

2. **Organizing principles:** Sometimes referred to as laws, organizing principles entail the regular and identifiable effects of the operation of multiple forces in systems, typically involving the creation or dissolution of organization. Examples include natural selection, self-organization, or entropy.

3. **Needs:** Conditions in living beings that require external inputs to avoid pain, discomfort, or in general, a breakdown or diminution of normal functioning. The concept of need is often associated with biological imperatives (e.g., eating, breathing, reproduction), but it also applies to psychological and social needs (e.g., respect, sense of belonging). A "need" means that the required input exists but is not necessarily available. One might argue that there are needs for things that don't exist as of yet, such as a warp drive or time travel, or things not even imagined.

4. **Drives:** Drives are enduring propensities of living beings to meet needs. Minimally, they involve simple behavioral protocols for meeting such needs, which are acted on consciously or unconsciously. Drives may involve biological, psychological, or social needs, and they may or may not be genetic.

5. **Motivations:** Motivations are the tendency of conscious living beings to invest effort toward attaining valued ends, whether the expression of drives or the accomplishment of nonbiological ends. Motivations are complex mental systems that typically involve goals, conscious appraisals of the self, expectations of feasibility, and the sequencing and planning of complex actions on the part of one or more parties.

cannot be assumed and understood in simplistic terms but require exploration in the context of the professional-client relationship.

D. Roots of Change: Self-Organization, Natural Selection, and Entropy?

The precise relationships among physical forces, biological organizing principles, and psychosocial needs and drives are not known, and in each discipline there has been controversy as to what the fundamental forces, principles, or drives are, especially approaching the human scale. However, this book is based on the theory that three principles—self-organization, natural selection, and entropy—are the central driving forces of biological evolution, social change, and personal development. Whereas self-organization accounts for much of the spontaneous emergence of order, natural selection theory is particularly effective in explaining the incremental adjustment of biological and social systems to their relevant environments. And entropy, which refers to the dissolution of order or the transition from less probable to more probable states, represents a kind of periodic pruning of systems. In short, these three principles entail the creation, maintenance and fine-tuning, and dissolution of living systems. It is the complex ongoing interactions among these organizing principles or evolutionary drivers that are the foundations for the emergence of consciousness (see chapter 4). First we will turn to a review of evolutionary and social change theories. The generalization of evolutionary theory beyond the original and somewhat simplistic notion of survival of the fittest to a more complex and sophisticated understanding of physical, biological, and social evolution that incorporates other drivers of change is a pivotally important foundation for a more comprehensive understanding of the motivations of human behavior.

II. Evolutionary Theory

A. Background

Of the various developments in the history of science, perhaps none has been more influential in social change theory than that of evolutionary thought. Specifically, Charles Darwin's (1859/1900) theory of natural selection and its application to social change theory through the social Darwinian legacy of Herbert Spencer (1874) has had a major but controversial impact on how we understand social and personal change. Although it is now well known that Darwin did not originate the theory of evolution, he developed the version based on natural selection. It has been proposed that his work was the culmination rather than the initiation of evolutionary thought (Degler, 1991). The earliest variations of evolutionary theory go back to the Greeks and to the Hindu Vedantic tradition (Laszlo, 1996). Others versions originated during the eighteenth-century Enlightenment. Immanuel Kant, for instance, suggested that the universe developed over eons (Degler, 1991). Perhaps most relevant to this discussion is the pre-Darwinian evolutionary theory of the French naturalist and philosopher Jean-Baptiste Lamarck (1809), who argued that behavioral adaptations drive evolutionary processes. In his first law, Lamarck theorized that the use or disuse of an organ or other biological function, because of changing environments and needs, would lead to its strengthening or disappearance over several generations. Lamarck's second law expressed his belief that offspring could then inherit those changes. An example often cited is that of the long neck of the giraffe, which followed the increasing need to eat from higher treetops. This is, however, a position that most contemporary biologists have largely rejected.

B. Darwin and Natural Selection

According to Charles Darwin, the engine of evolution is natural selection, which operates on variation among organisms. This variation, which is considered to have its primary origins in both sexual reproduction and chance mutation, is constantly subjected to the struggle for survival. Darwin's (1844/1977) quotation in his "Essay of 1844" of the Swiss botanist Alphonse De Candolle that "all nature is at war, one organism with another, or with external nature" (n.p.) epitomizes his emphasis on such struggle. This is part of the legacy of Reverend Thomas Malthus (1798/1971), who argued that each species inevitably reproduces more quickly than food supplies can expand, leading to an unrelieved struggle for existence within and between species. On the basis of this belief, Malthus went so far as to recommend eliminating the poor laws and actually increasing the mortality rate among the indigent. Specifically, he proposed: "Instead of recommending cleanliness to the poor, we should encourage contrary habits. In our towns we should make the streets narrower, crowd more people into the houses, and court the return of the plague, and particularly encourage settlements in all marshy and unwholesome situations" (Malthus, 1798/1971, pp. 411–412).

The theory of natural selection was based on the notion that the struggle for survival is inevitable and whichever adaptations survive will reproduce at a faster rate and become dominant. The subtitle of Darwin's *Origin of the*

Species epitomizes this perspective: *The Preservation of Favoured Races in the Struggle for Life* (1859/1900).

Darwin believed that those chance variations and sexual pairings that increase the chances for survival also fuel evolutionary developments. The incremental accumulation of many small changes, according to Darwin's theory of natural selection, results in the gradual development of new and often more complex species. Darwin himself preferred the notion of natural selection and avoided the phrase "survival of the fittest," which his contemporary, the sociologist Herbert Spencer (1874), had introduced. Darwin eventually relented in adopting Spencer's more popular phrase (Degler, 1991). Yet in Darwin's theory it was never clear whether organisms survived because they were fit or whether they were fit because they survived. An independent definition of fitness has been elusive. As a tautology, the phrase explains little and has been a reason for the uncritical application of principles of natural selection to theories of social change.

Although natural variation, conflict, and survival play important roles in both evolution and contemporary society, most agree that many other motivations are of critical importance in understanding individual and social behaviors. Beyond the definitional problems, there have been persistent criticisms of the theory of natural selection that its proponents have not effectively countered. One such criticism is a question of probabilities. Statistical studies over the years show an extreme improbability that new species could develop incrementally, with the complex synchronization of various new features that would be required (see Cohen, 1984; Kauffman, 1995). For instance, computer simulations show that about 80 percent of random mutations are lost within ninety generations. About one-fifth (18 percent) persist and come to be shared by 50 percent of the population (Guastello, 1995).

Another problem is the tendency of fossil records to show long periods of stability and few of the changes required for accounting for the transition from one species to another. The popular neo-Darwinian Stephen Jay Gould (b. 1941–d. 2002) attempted to address this problem through the theory of punctuated equilibrium. In this theory, species compete, and when one disappears or when other catastrophic changes take place, the surviving species undergo very rapid change through both natural selection and other processes to fill the new niche (Gould & Eldredge, 1977). Perhaps the most compelling challenge to evolutionary theory's exclusive reliance on natural selection comes out of the field of microbiology. Michael Behe (1996) provides extensive and persuasive documentation of the irreducible complexity of microbiological processes—Darwin's black box—such as the immune response, blood clotting, and cellular propulsion, showing that, in many instances, until multiple and highly unlikely processes are simultaneously linked, there is no survival advantage to the incremental accumulation of the components of complex biological systems.

Setting aside creationists' rejection of the very notion of evolutionary development, it should be noted that the debate has not been about whether natural selection takes place but rather about how central it is to evolution. Most contemporary biologists, who are classified as neo-Darwinians, believe that a somewhat expanded version of natural selection is the primary, if not exclusive, engine of evolution and change. Other biologists, such as Stuart Kauffman, who can be considered post-Darwinians, believe that additional dynamics, such as self-organization, work alongside natural selection to drive evolutionary change. Kauffman (1995) states that natural selection and self-organization are the "twin engines" of the biosphere (n.p.). It has been suggested that natural selection may function as a screen for incremental adjustments in biological mechanisms that have already developed through other means (Baum, 1986).

C. Social Darwinism

Since Darwin introduced the theory of natural selection in the mid-nineteenth century, the theory has undergone considerable transformation. One of the most immediate of those involved its application to social change by the conservative English philosopher and sociologist Herbert Spencer (1874). Social Darwinism, based also on the laissez-faire economics of Adam Smith and the infamous population theory of Thomas Malthus, suggested that virtually any kind of mutual support or social welfare serves only to perpetuate unfit individuals and degrade the human race. Others, such as William Graham Sumner and Thomas E. Huxley were also effective popularizers of the doctrine of natural selection (see Leading Edge, 1995a).

Although the science of genetics did not exist when Darwin proposed his theory, its later development, beginning with Gregor Mendel, provided considerable support for natural selection. In fact, its impact included the delivery of a near-fatal blow to the earlier Lamarckian theory of evolution, which involved the impact of acquired behavioral characteristics on biological development (Lamarck, 1809). As early as 1889 the embryologist August Weisman offered purported scientific disproof of Lamarckism when he showed that no matter what kind of changes occurred in an animal's body or behavior during its lifetime, none appeared in its offspring. He concluded that there was a fundamental disjunction between heredity and environment and that only changes in the germ plasma could be passed on to future generations (Degler, 1991). At the same time that biologists concluded that genetic rather than any behavioral successes or failures controlled evolutionary change, others, such as Francis Galton, argued for the application of principles of social Darwinism to society by means of the eugenics movement, which sought to engineer humanity's genetic legacy (see Rutledge, 1995). Each of these developments—the discrediting of Lamarckism, the development of genetics, the application of genetics in the eugenics movement to society, and its final perversion in the so-called applied biology of the Nazi era—contributed to a fundamental split between the social and biological sciences.

D. Early Alternatives

Most social scientists at the time rejected social Darwinism, including social workers such as Amos Warner, who pointed out in 1894: "if acquired characteristics be inherited, then we have a chance permanently to improve the race independently of selection, by seeing to it that individuals acquire characteristics that are desirable for them to transmit" (p. 120). It has been argued that although Darwin may have made some statements sympathetic to Spencer's approach, there was nothing in his theory that precluded changes in behavior from being inherited and, thereby, altering over time the racial characteristics of populations (Degler, 1991).

Many have pointed out fundamental flaws in social Darwinism, especially its inability to account for the existence of altruism and cooperation that are central to society in general and to the human services in particular. In both human and nonhuman populations, altruism confers a considerable survival advantage for those individuals and groups that exhibit such qualities (see Guastello, 1995; Lux, 1990). Another flaw in social Darwinism is the tendency of unregulated economic competition to result in monopolies, which diminishes the belief that economic competition (a type of social selection) should be the primary engine of social development. Most biologists currently reject Malthus's doctrine. For example, the biologist Lewis Thomas (1995) writes in *The Lives of a Cell,* "Most of the associations between the living things we know about are essentially cooperative ones, symbiotic in one degree or another; when they have the look of adversaries, it is usually a standoff relation, with one party issuing signals, warnings, flagging the other off" (p. 7). An early theory of evolution developed by Peter Kropotkin (1902/1972) in Russia in the latter part of the nineteenth century also emphasized natural selection but argued that the ability to engage in mutually cooperative actions confers the greatest survival advantages. This theory of mutual aid, though eclipsed by Darwinism, in recent years has received renewed attention from evolutionary scholars (Gould, 1997). Kropotkin argued that "under any circumstances sociability is the greatest advantage in the struggle for life. Those species which willingly or unwillingly abandon it are doomed to decay; while those animals which know best how to combine, have the greatest chances of survival and of further evolution" (p. 68).

E. Neo-Darwinism and the Evolutionary Synthesis

By the middle of the twentieth century Darwin's theory of natural selection was integrated with the new science of genetics, as well as with a range of other developments in the biological sciences. This launched what has been called the evolutionary synthesis, or more commonly, neo-Darwinism (Behe, 1996). J. B. S. Haldane (1932), along with Ronald A. Fisher and Sewell Wright, were its initial proponents. In response to their work, a series of meetings was organized in 1947 at Princeton University among leading scientists in genetics, paleontology, comparative anatomy, embryology, and other areas that formalized many of the tenets of neo-Darwinism (Behe, 1996; Leading Edge, 1995b). The impact of this synthesis was that it added random events and both spontaneous mutations and recombination to natural selection—and dropped adaptive responses to environmental changes—as the driving forces of evolutionary change. Since then, neo-Darwinians have also included environmentally induced random responses, such as radiation effects, to the repertory of evolutionary causes. The earlier abandonment of the role of acquired characteristics and adaptive responses to environmental changes in evolutionary thinking may have been a stimulus for the eugenics movement in the early 1900s (Degler, 1991).

F. Post-Darwinism and the Social Sciences

In recent years post-Darwinian biologists have identified additional mechanisms of evolutionary change. Sober and Wilson (1998) propose a multilevel version of evolutionary theory involving not only individual level but also group- and species-level competition and cooperation to account for altruism and social change. Taking a somewhat different approach, Lynn Margulis (1981) received widespread acclaim for her endosymbiotic theory of evolution, the theory that mitochondria, the energy sources for plant and animal cells, evolved from a separate bacterial organism that then developed a symbiotic relationship with eukaryotic cells and were eventually completely incorporated in them. She emphasizes cooperation and symbiosis, rather than competition and other forms of conflict, as critical evolutionary processes. To the extent that cooperative social action and mutual aid are important in social change, work with larger systems—groups, families, organizations, and communities—is a critical strategy for human service professionals.

Recent studies also challenge the conventional wisdom that behavioral changes can have no impact on the course of evolutionary change and have sought to demonstrate the existence of directed or nonrandom mutations. Other developments include the work of Stuart Kauffman (1995) at the Santa Fe Institute, who demonstrates the role of self-organization in the development of complex adaptive systems. A recent development is the work of several scientists who have found evidence that subcellular quantum-level processes, associated with the emergence of consciousness in evolution, may have generated directed or nonrandom mutations based on the enormous information-processing potentials of quantum computation (Ogryzko, 1999). Laszlo (1996) proposes a general theory of evolution that integrates physical, biological evolution, and social change processes using elements from complex systems theory. Others emphasize coevolutionary processes involving the constant interplay between evolving individuals and species, a type of biological arms race that guarantees that any equilibrium is temporary.

It is perhaps no coincidence that at about the same time that biologists developed their neo-Darwinian evolutionary synthesis in the mid-twentieth century, which excluded most theories emphasizing either environmental factors or those intrinsic to the organism, many in the social sciences came to subscribe to what Tooby and Cosmides (1992) have dubbed the "standard social science model" (SSSM), in which social development proceeds largely independently of, or under only general constraints of, the long leash of biology. Many social scientists, thus, have felt free from any obligation to consider the impact of biology on their models, and vice versa, yet they borrow the metaphors of natural selection and the struggle for survival as the driving force of social change, careful to avoid any obvious application of social Darwinism. In *The Descent of Man,* Darwin (1871/2007) argued for the continuity of animal and human development. In contrast, social scientists have sought to establish their independence from many of the traditional sciences, including biology, and to reject any hint of reductionism, thereby creating an artificial split reminiscent of Descartes' separation of mind and body. The evolutionary synthesis and the SSSM, no doubt, have been key contributors to the growing divide between the biological and social sciences. One result of this divide has been the stagnation of social change theory.

Although few social scientists openly endorse social Darwinism, many consider themselves Darwinians. In the final years of the twentieth century, the many advances in biology—from research in ethology to the Human Genome Project and developments in the neurosciences—have profoundly challenged the divorce of the social from the biological sciences. One part of this rapprochement is sociobiology, which developed out of the work of Edward O. Wilson (1975) and Richard Dawkins (1986). This patently reductionistic approach attempts to explain many of the details of human behavioral patterns in terms of genetically encoded carryovers from prehuman ancestry, minimizing the many instances in which more recently developed human functions, such as language and culture, have an independent impact on behavioral and social change. Wilson (1998), in *Consilience,* proposes that even ethics and religion may ultimately be explainable in terms of biology. Similarly, Dawkins (1986) argues that genes have an independent life of their own. He has gone as far as using the metaphors of genetic action and natural selection to characterize the spread of ideas and other elements of culture, which are now referred to as memes. Wilson (1975) echoes this view and proposes that there may be a gene that explains cooperative human action. The impact of both Wilson and Dawkins is vividly illustrated in the recent and widely cited works of Herrnstein and Murray (1994), *The Bell Curve* (1994), and of Steven Pinker (1997), *How the Mind Works.* These works openly endorse the direct application of principles of natural selection to social and psychological development. Herrnstein and Murray, for instance, argue that the allegedly fixed spread of IQs between whites and blacks has a genetic basis and that compensatory education is, therefore, a waste of both time and public resources. This clearly echoes the sentiments of Herbert Spencer. Others such as William Calvin (1999) use natural selection in the theory of neural Darwinism to explain individual cognitive functioning as involving competition and selection among the most dominant or fittest groups of neurons. Critics of sociobiology and psychobiology include Gould and Richard Lewontin, who have denounced the efforts to seek an evolutionary basis for all human actions.

At the same time that many biologists continue their work along neo-Darwinian lines, emphasizing the selection of the fittest individuals on the basis of conflict and competition, others have pursued a post-Darwinian theory of evolution. Such theorists as Margulis, Kauffman, and Laszlo emphasize behavioral adaptation, cooperation, and self-organization and have identified a rich repertory of processes for social theorists to draw on in understanding the mechanisms of social change. As the theory of evolution has been generalized to incorporate principles of self-organization in complex systems, its relevance to human systems and for the human services has become increasingly apparent, and for this reason there has been an explosion of efforts in recent years to apply evolutionary theory throughout the social sciences to such areas as learning, organizational dynamics, politics, and in general, social change theory, a subject to which we will now turn.

III. Social Change Theory

A. Overview

For the first half of the twentieth century, the major efforts in sociology involved the study of social structure. It was not until the middle of the century that efforts shifted to understanding social change. The study of social structure tended to portray change as an aberration or disruption rather than an ongoing natural condition of life (Hallinan, 1997). Both evolutionary incrementalism and the study of social structure created for many the sense that social change, to the extent that it exists, is very gradual, and for this reason, stability and homeostasis are emphasized. Darwin (1859/1900) pointed out, "As natural selection acts solely by accumulating slight, successive, favourable variations, it can produce no great or sudden modifications; it can act only by short and slow steps" (p. 282). That physicists and astronomers believed the universe eternal and unchanging—until Edwin Hubble made his discovery of the expanding universe—was certainly an important backdrop, lending support to both creationism and the incrementalism of Darwinians. Those who either ignored change or portrayed change as an incremental process, as many social scientists have done, leaned toward models in which external conditions determined internal organization, change, and growth. Free will and human purpose, as well as chance and accident, have not been so easily modeled and are often discounted (see chapter 3). Assumptions that change is incremental, continuous, and deterministic tend to undermine efforts to understand social movements and revolutions on the macro level and deviant behaviors on the micro level and, thus, undermine efforts of human service professionals to intervene in a systematic manner. For example, when people with serious mental illnesses are cast as chronic or process schizophrenics, mental health professionals too often ignore these people or provide services designed merely for maintenance and control.

It is argued here that the assumptions and metaphors of social Darwinism pervade and undermine efforts to formulate useful theories of social change, at the same time that social scientists seek to divorce their efforts from biological research. The concepts of variability, conflict, and selection of the fittest underlie the earlier evolutionary or organismic social change theories, such as that of Auguste Comte (1876), as well as the cyclical and macro-conflict theories and several more recent efforts to resolve differences between these perspectives, such as ecosystems theory and some of the community and organizational change theories that this chapter briefly introduces. Two pervasive themes that characterize these approaches are (1) the emphasis on external conflict, especially competition for resources, status, or survival, and (2) the identification of the drivers of change as external to the system of interest. Both the conflict and the resulting selection may take place on either the micro level or the macro level, or some combination of those, typically as a result of external environmental changes. These approaches are characterized by a tendency to minimize cooperation, interdependency, and self-organization, and instead emphasize externally induced change. It has been in only recent decades that there have been concerted efforts to model cooperative action in social change processes (see the introduction to chapter 11) and only since the 1980s that internally generated change or self-organization has been actively investigated. Because of a decline of interest in social change theory, to date there have been only sporadic efforts to apply post-Darwinian approaches to the understanding of social change.

B. Evolutionary and Organismic Theories

Auguste Comte (b. 1798–d. 1857), widely regarded as the father of sociology, often used the metaphor of the biological organism to characterize society. This has been an image that has proved to have great durability among those classified as evolutionary theorists (Appelbaum, 1970). Proponents of this position have typically viewed social change as naturally smooth and continuous (Hawkinshire & Liggett, 1990), based not so much on large-scale conflict and selection between classes or nations but between ideas and individuals. Change is considered a function of increasing adaptability that results from a process of structural-functional differentiation, specialization, and increasing complexity (Appelbaum, 1970). Most of the original evolutionary theories, including theories of modernization, have tended to be unilinear in that they treat Western and industrialized societies as singular end products of social evolution. In addition to Comte, theorists associated with this tradition include Spencer (1874), Toennies (1964), Steward (1964), Smelser (1968), and less commonly Weber (1964) and Durkheim (1964a).

Émile Durkheim (1964a) worked within the organic tradition as he focused on the role of increasing social complexity and interdependency. Despite his many differences with the social Darwinist Herbert Spencer, Durkheim also emphasized the role of competition in social survival. For instance, he argued, "There are a number of circumstances where different functions enter into competition. Thus, in the individual organism, during a long fast, the nervous system is nourished at the expense of the other organs, and the same phenomenon is produced if cerebral activity develops too considerably. It is the same in society. In time of famine or economic crisis, the vital functions are obliged, in order to maintain themselves, to support themselves at the expense of less essential functions" (Durkheim, 1964b, p. 271). Although functionalists such as Durkheim shared some of the assumptions of the social Darwinists, they began to emphasize cooperative social relationships and thus are precursors to the self-organization theorists considered in the next section of this chapter.

Many evolutionary theorists have characterized development as unilinear, as proceeding through a fairly well-defined set of stages; however, there are important exceptions. Those who have espoused multilinear theories of social evolution include Sahlins and Service (1960) and Steward (1964). Sahlins and Service argue that social development moves simultaneously in two ways. On the one hand, specific evolution is based on historical transformations in multiple directions and dependent on particular cultures. On the other hand, general evolution is "the passage from less to greater energy transformation, lower to higher levels of integration, and less to greater all-around adaptability" (1960, p. 38).

C. Cyclical Theories

Proponents of cyclical models of social change, such as Spengler (1939), Toynbee (1939), and Sorokin (1962), can be regarded as adherents of multilinear evolutionary theory. However, they differ from the evolutionary theorists in that they minimize the cumulative impact of these developments and instead view them as patterned and recurrent. Cyclical theorists typically consider societal events as passing through three stages: growth, maturity, and decline (Hallinan, 1997). Toynbee's theory of challenge and response treats societal change in essentially evolutionary terms (see Laszlo, 1996). Similarly, Spengler treats cultures as organisms and world history as their collective biography. He argues, "Each culture passes through the age-phases of the individual man. Each has its childhood, youth, manhood, and old age" (1964, p. 21). In contrast, for Sorokin the emphasis is on supersystems that integrate diverse cultural elements. These supersystems are based on the most "general of all ontological principals, namely, the one defining the ultimate nature of reality and value" (Sorokin, 1947, p. 590). Societies can be characterized as incorporating sensate systems, based on the sensory validation of beliefs; ideational systems, based on supernatural validation of beliefs; and idealistic systems, based on validation by both sensation and the supernatural. Societies, therefore, tend to oscillate among science, rationalism, and religion, with rationalism being the intermediate form (Sorokin, 1962). Similarly, Max Weber (1964) characterized societies as alternatively using three types of authority: (1) charismatic, (2) transitional, and (3) rational, none of which he considered stable. As did the evolutionary theorists, he also emphasized increasing rationalization and bureaucratization in a variety of institutional arenas, especially in economic development in the West. In some respect, these theorists are an offshoot of the evolutionary or organic school and can be treated separately only to the extent that change is considered multilinear and cyclical. Just as was the case with the evolutionary theorists, conflict and the survival of the fittest—in these cases the fittest societies, nations, institutions, or belief systems—are regarded as the driving forces of social change.

D. Conflict Theories

Conflict theories originated from the dialectical materialism of Marx and Engels (1932). In contrast to organismic theories, change was assumed to be pervasive and ubiquitous, and specifically discontinuous and often disruptive (Hawkinshire & Liggett, 1990). Although most versions of organismic theories emphasized conflict, such conflict was regarded as primarily involving individuals, unlike in conflict theory per se, which focuses on clashes among interests, classes, or other large groups. Marx and Engels claimed that "without conflict, no progress: this is the law which civilization has followed to the present day" (1959, p. 21). In addition to Marx and Engels, proponents of variations of macro-conflict theory have included Simmel (1964), Brinton (1952), Coser (1956), and Dahrendorf (1964). Impressed with Darwinism, Marx and Engels also incorporated Hegel's evolutionary theory of the history of ideas, involving the spiraling of theses, antitheses, and syntheses into ever-higher levels of development, as part of their theory of dialectical or historical materialism. They cast development in terms of class struggle over the control of the means of production. Similar to unilinear evolutionary theorists, they considered technology central to determining the organization of production processes: technology enables the separation of the control of capital from the means of production through the exploitation of the working class. In their theory, conflict and change are a function of inherent contradictions that arise under the centralized authority system required by evolving technologies and the resulting impact on the ownership of productive property (Appelbaum, 1970). All other social realities, such as institutions, values, and beliefs, are secondary superstructures that overlay the separation of capital from the means of production.

There have been numerous criticisms of Marxist social theory, many of which have been an outcome of historical developments over the course of the twentieth century. Societies have often failed to polarize as Marx predicted, especially given that working classes have become considerably more varied in their interests than he expected. Marx also failed to distinguish among the functions of ownership, control, and technical expertise in the leadership of corporations. He did not consider the functions of bureaucracy or other social groups in mediating and resolving conflict (Appelbaum, 1970). Similarly, Dahrendorf (1964) has criticized Marx for restricting the resolution of class conflicts to violent upheaval. Such critiques have led to the development of various post-Marxist conflict theories, such as elitism and pluralism, which are more palatable to current political philosophies. However, in both its Marxist and its post-Marxist versions, conflict theory is a close cousin of social Darwinism: it emphasizes conflict between and survival of the most powerful interests, classes, elites, or interest groups as the driving force of social change.

In recent years there have been many applications of conflict theory, by both those on the Left and those on the Right, to understandings of global patterns of change. Jared Diamond (1997), in his widely acclaimed study of the driving forces in human history—*Guns, Germs, and Steel: The Fates of Human Societies*—argues that it is has not been the differences among peoples, such as their genetic makeup, but differences in physical environments that account for the disparate levels of development in contemporary societies. So-called ultimate factors that he identifies include the presence of an east-west continental axis permitting the rapid diffusion of innovations and a variety of wild plants and animal species suitable for domestication; while proximate factors include early success in the conversion from a hunting-gathering to an agricultural economy and the development of immunities to contagious diseases conferred from the long-term exposure of Eurasians to domesticated animals (see figure 2.2). The transition to settled agricultural societies permitted the development of food surpluses, and thus larger stratified societies, and ultimately technology, including metallic weaponry and oceangoing ships. He contends that development arises from conflict between societies at varying levels of development, and the resulting survival and diffusion of those at more advanced levels based on environmental advantages. As such, while not a Marxist, his work has been cited by neo-Marxists as critical evidence for such a vision of history involving the primacy of the forces of production (Carling & Nolan, 1998) and criticized by others for failing to consider the feedback effects of varying

FIGURE 2.2: FACTORS DRIVING WORLD HISTORICAL DEVELOPMENTS

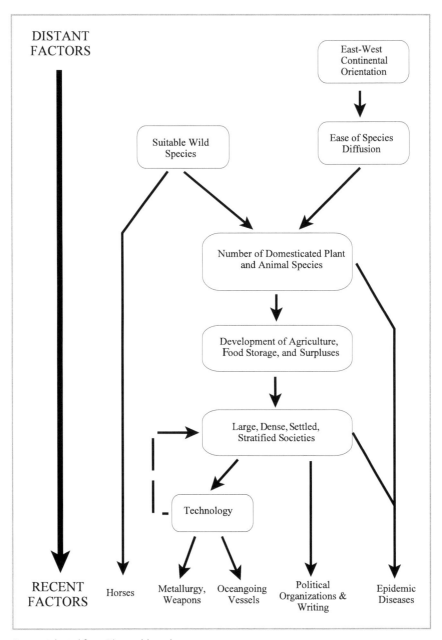

Source: Adapted from Diamond (1997).

environments on genetic transmission of favorable traits, such as intelligence and industriousness, as an explanation for uneven patterns of economic development throughout the world (Levin, 1998).

Another recent application of conflict theory has been the effort of Samuel Huntington (1996), in his work *The Clash of Civilizations: Remaking of World Order,* to understand the geopolitical dynamics of the post–cold war era. Huntington argues that as a result of both the end of the cold war and broader trends, the central conflicts are no longer between nation-states or coalitions of mature states but instead between civilizations, which he regards as primary cultural entities. While drawing heavily on traditional sources of political and economic conflict in his analysis, he argues that increasingly the central conflicts involve those of religion, ideology, and culture. The closest he comes to defining any central driving force in history is when he argues that population migration is the "motor of history" (p. 198). For the most part the development and outcome of civilizational conflicts reflect particular proximate circumstances. However, Huntington draws on the work of Carroll Quigley (1979), who, in the tradition of the cyclical theorists, argued that civilizations typically pass through seven stages: mixture, gestation, expansion (migration), an age of conflict, a universal empire, and finally decay and invasion. Unlike Diamond, Huntington takes a broader view of the sources of conflict and includes culture and values but is less successful in identifying any longer-term dynamic forces driving historical change. And both Diamond and Huntington fail to fully consider the role of cooperation, cultural synthesis, and self-organization in their theories, opting instead for a vision of conflict and survival of the fittest groups as a basis for understanding the broader patterns of social change.

E. Equilibrium Theories

At about the same time that biologists adopted the neo-Darwinian synthesis, which banished environmental and behavioral factors from evolutionary theory, social scientists moved away from the explicit use of evolutionary theory and biological metaphors. Instead they focused on equilibrium and downplayed social change. It has been pointed out that in some respects equilibrium theory is a direct legacy of earlier evolutionary theory, in that it posits slow and continuous change as the norm. For example, Smelser (1968) explained change as a complicated series of equilibrium processes and held that factors that governed these processes would dominate during a given period (Hallinan, 1997). The focus became homeostasis, and the metaphor of choice became the thermometer, exemplifying the

Theory Example 2.1: The Social Entropy Theory of Kenneth Bailey

OVERVIEW: Kenneth Bailey's theory of social entropy argues that the equilibrium of systems is a special case of entropy and—its opposite—negentropy. He defines entropy as the tendency for systems to move to greater disorder or uncertainty in the relationships among variables. Bailey argues that entropy is not specific to any particular type of content, such as energy. For example, it can consist of disorder and uncertainty in the relationships between means and goals in a social system. Entropy can be positive or negative; it can increase, decrease, or remain the same (see Bailey, 1990, 1994).

The social entropy theory has multiple levels: it considers, simultaneously, the relationship between the whole and its parts. Societies are characterized and studied in terms of the operation of several critical variables, categorized in three groups:

1. Global variables (PILOTS)
   Population (P), of persons
   Information (I), both informal and formal
   Level of living (L) (e.g., quality of life, social functioning)
   Organization (O), positions in formal or informal organizations
   Technology (T), processes that support the level of living
   Spatial area (S), or total area of a population
2. Immutable variables (GRA)
   Gender (G)
   Race (R)
   Age (A)
3. Mutable Variables (LOTIS)
   Individual achievements or achieved statuses, vis-à-vis global variables
   Level of living (L)
   Organization (O)
   Technology (T)
   Information (I)
   Space (S)
   Mutable distributions, formed for the population and based on individual achievements
   Income (L)
   Jobs (O)
   Skills (T)
   Education (I)
   Residence (S)

THE ROOTS OF SOCIAL AND PERSONAL CHANGE

THEORY EXAMPLE 2.1 (CONTINUED)

ANALYSIS: Social entropy theory proposes analysis of the interactions of the foregoing variables to understand how social systems accomplish their goals and satisfy needs. It achieves this, in part, through both what he calls Q-analysis of variations in objects or units and R-analysis that focuses on variables.

---

operation of negative feedback loops. Positive feedback loops, or processes that feed on and amplify themselves, were rarely considered in the sudden transitions to more or less favorable conditions.

Variations of equilibrium theory include cybernetics, general systems theory, functionalism, and some of the most recent incarnations of these approaches, such as social entropy theory, living systems or the ecosystems approach, and cultural transformation theory. Each has unsuccessfully tried to reconcile differences between the earlier micro and macro theories of social change. At the same time, each has preserved the legacy of natural selection through an emphasis on change as resulting from attempts to resolve micro-level conflict and maintain equilibrium in response to external influences. Parsons's (1951) functionalism, discussed in chapter 1, was one of the earlier versions of equilibrium theory.

A more recent effort to correct some of the problems in equilibrium theory, and one that is specifically sociological in its focus, is Bailey's (1994) social entropy theory (see theory example 2.1). The theory postulates that there are three sets of conditions relevant to the analysis of social change: (1) global conditions, having to do with society as a whole, such as population, level of living, organization, technology, and spatial area; (2) immutable characteristics of individuals, such as sex and race; and (3) mutable characteristics of individuals involving both individual achievements and changeable distributions of jobs, skills, education, and the like. It employs what it refers to as Q-analysis among objects and R-analysis among variables to understand how the three types of conditions interact to maintain suitable levels of entropy in society. The theory is presented as a nonequilibrium perspective; nonetheless, it emphasizes equilibrium and regards change as an anomalous deviation from a steady state of energy flow.

The proponents of the various equilibrium theories sought to achieve a grand unification of the earlier approaches to social change, but they have often ended up closer to the traditional organismic or evolutionary approaches than to macro-conflict theories. Although recently there has been a rapprochement with the biological sciences, as reflected in the living and ecosystems versions, this tradition has, on the whole, been based on a strict separation of social and biological change processes (e.g., the SSSM model). An effect of this split has been that many social change theorists have failed to stay abreast of recent developments in post-Darwinian biology and complex systems theory. In addition, they often borrow tacitly from the traditional metaphors of natural selection—survival, conflict, and selection—at the same time that they eschew any overt association with social Darwinism. The obvious contradictions of such a stance, however, are easily camouflaged by the highly abstract language of these theories, which unfortunately has contributed to the stagnation of social change theory in the last third of the twentieth century.

F. Recent Applications: Modernization and Cultural Lag Theory

A direct extension of the evolutionary change theories are the various twentieth-century theories of modernization. These have typically emphasized developing technology, including increasing specialization, centralization, bureaucratization, urbanization, nucleation of the family, democratization, and secularization as key causes, correlates, or outcomes of the process of modernization (see Appelbaum 1970; Hawkinshire & Liggett, 1990). A more recent generation of theories, inspired by the work of Daniel Bell (1973), is in many respects a direct extension of the earlier evolutionary social change theories. Such theories focus on the transition from industrial to postindustrial societies, that is, the shift from the production of goods to the production of knowledge, sometimes referred to as the "information economy" or "globalization." Often-cited features of globalization are increasing economic specialization among nations and the reduction of trade and other barriers to free competition (Bartos, 1996; Bell, 1973; Morris-Suzuki, 1988; Toffler, 1990). The linkage between these perspectives and unilinear evolutionary theories of social change is the idea that societies follow a singular line of development driven by technological innovation. Appelbaum's (1970) suggestion that the principal link between evolutionary thought and functionalism is the concept of differentiation is, thus, especially relevant to current theoretical and societal developments. By *differentiation,* Appelbaum means the development of societal structures that serve specialized functions, such as the military or justice systems.

Even before the decline of functionalism, there was an effort to develop more operational and specialized models of social change processes, such as cultural lag theory. William Ogburn's (1922) original cultural lag theory attempted to account for crises in social development as reflecting lags between the rates of technological and cultural development. A recent application of cultural lag theory is that of the Nobel laureate Robert Fogel (2000), of the University of Chicago, who argues that most of the major transformations in American history can be understood as the result of technological developments outpacing cultural norms, leading to a variety of reform movements, often religious in origin, which eventually become secularized and institutionalized. In addition, over the years there has been a wide variety of applications of social change theory to understand change within the context of organizations and communities (for a review of several of these theories, see chapters 11 and 12).

IV. Implications for Theories of Personal Change

One of the central questions of the preceding sections concerns the forces that drive or motivate social change, whether these involve geopolitical relationships, communities, or organizations. Addressing this same question about individuals has been a fundamental challenge of psychology and, in fact, of a wide range of the cognitive and social sciences. This section, thus, sketches out a few of the concepts that are particularly pertinent to the question of the sources of personal change, and it proposes a reformulation of some of them, one that will be explored in greater depth in several of the chapters of the second part of this book.

Whereas the previous sections focused mostly on biological and large-scale social change, this section departs from the macro level to concentrate on individual change, not only within this larger context but also within the person's more immediate social environment. But to talk about the environment, or even the multiple environments, leaves much unsaid. An individual's changing environments can be said to have two general types of effects on his or her ability to grow and change: constraining effects and directive effects. Environments are usually thought of as providing constraints on behavior and as providing a structure, norms, standard rewards and sanctions, and the like, within which individuals live their lives on the basis of their individual choices, personal histories, accidents, or biological inheritance. In contrast, the directive effects of environments on individual behavior often involve the active initiation or facilitation of individual changes. Young men are drafted into the military, children are socialized to pursue unrealized dreams of their parents, and families are forced to flee persecution. Another type of directive effect is opportunities, whether they be economic, social, psychological, or spiritual. There may be no rigid line dividing constraining and directive environmental effects; rather, some environmental effects broadly channel behavior, and some guide behavior so narrowly that a person loses any sense of personal choice. In addition, while many in the human services assume one-way causation from the environment to the individual, a growing view in the field is that this is a two-way street: changes in one or many individuals feed back to and affect their various environments, thus generating new challenges and opportunities. Societies define individuals and individuals define their societies in what is ultimately a self-referential and self-organizing process. Understanding individual clients means understanding the challenges and opportunities inherent in their relevant environments, whether physical, social, or cultural, and how people, individually and collectively, can change them.

Personal change is typically theorized to result from not only external environmental conditions but also internal factors. Internal factors most typically center on motivation, as well as a range of psychological capabilities, expectations, and attitudes, including a sense of efficacy, hope, and trust. External environmental conditions involve threats, supports, opportunities, and challenges, whether material, social, or cultural. Most theories offer dramatic simplifications. For example, Martin Ford (1992), in his theory of motivation, proposes the following formula: *achievement-competence = motivation × skill × responsive environment.*

Any of those concepts might be broken down into a number of other subconcepts, or other obvious ones might be added, for example, individual choice, self-image, or cultural considerations. There are hundreds of theories of personal change that are expressed through almost as many different vocabularies. These theories come out of such fields as personality and human development theory; the personal change literature; psychopathology; decision making, problem solving, and creativity; motivation theory; the broader field of the cognitive sciences; and so forth. Each of these theories typically emphasize one, or perhaps a combination, of the following dimensions: environmental selection, personal self-organizing developmental processes, personal self-organizing intentional processes, or social entropy or the processes of personal or social disintegration. These can be thought of as both alternative patterns of personal change or as contrasting models for understanding personal change.

The theories that focus on the environment also tend to emphasize what are essentially evolutionary processes of conflict and social selection of the winners. Individuals change because they, or their behaviors or beliefs, are either selected or reinforced by their environments. The traditional social learning theories tend to fall in this category. Individual choices, beliefs, and skills are minimized, and to the extent that they are acknowledged, they are considered an outcome of prior selection or differential rewards. An extreme version of this position is Pavlovian learning, exemplified by a dog that mindlessly learns to salivate at the sight or sound of an object associated with food. Individuals change because they or their behaviors are successfully selected or reinforced, or extinguished, perhaps because their skills or other personal characteristics are no longer relevant in a changing world. A key question is whether individuals are proactive in guiding this process or are passive pawns, like Pavlov's dogs. Can people pull themselves up by their bootstraps or just say no despite punishing environments?

Two types of theories of personal change emphasize what are often self-organizing processes involving development across the life cycle (see chapter 5, section III) and intentional problem solving (chapter 7, section II). Many of the theories of motivation, personality (see chapter 6), and development assume that personal change is primarily a function of the complex developmental history of the individual (see Caspi, 1998). They conceptualize change in terms of the interplay between various psychological functions, and only secondarily, if at all, as the intentional response to environmental constraints and opportunities. In particular, developmental theorists have proposed a number of stage theories of general psychosocial development or of more particular lines of cognitive, moral, libidinal, or spiritual development (e.g., Carpendale, 2000; Fowler, 1996), to name just a few examples. Change is conceptualized typically as the result of the successful or unsuccessful passage from one stage to another, or as a reflection of arrests, regressions, and the like. Perhaps most useful are those who consider the interrelationships among these various lines of development and the lags that might occur, for instance, between different levels of cognitive, ego, or moral development. A key issue here is the extent to which such dynamical interactions are best characterized in conflict terms, as outcomes of the selection of the fittest psychological functions, or as outcomes of self-organization. For example, traditional Freudian theories typically used hydraulic metaphors to characterize internal or interpersonal conflicts, and for this reason they were based on the assumption of the primacy of conflict (see Maddi, 1996). Many of this first group of theories emphasize processes that can be regarded as either partially or fully self-organizing, whether these involve conflict or cooperative and synthetic processes. Most such theories view change as an outcome of long-term socialization and/or psychodynamic processes that entail little meaningful choice on the part of the individual involved.

The other group of personal change theories emphasizes conscious choices and associated decision making, problem solving, and other creative capacities (see chapter 7). Theories of intentional personal change range from those that focus on rational, linear, processes of goal setting and evaluation of alternative means to those that give greater weight to integrating unconscious and intuitive capacities. Personal change happens, in this

Theory Example 2.2: Intentional Personal Change: The Transtheoretical Model of Velicer and Prochaska

OVERVIEW: The transtheoretical model aims to understand how individuals are able to decide on and successfully carry through with changes in their behavior, especially behaviors involving unhealthy habits (e.g., smoking, alcohol abuse, lack of exercise). It is a stage model, which hypothesizes that individuals pass through prototypical steps as they successfully change. The steps involve changes in cognitions, feelings, and behaviors. The model identifies ten independent variables, or change processes, that facilitate success, and it proposes the use of particular outcome scales, such as a decisional balance sheet with perceived pros and cons (see Cancer Prevention Research Center, n.d.; Velicer, Prochaska, Fava, Norman, & Redding, 1998).

STAGES OF CHANGE: The stages are organized in the following manner:

1. **Precontemplation:** In this initial stage, the individual has no conscious intention of changing within the next six months. Such individuals often deny or minimize their difficulties and are frequently characterized as resistant or unmotivated. They consider change only occasionally.
2. **Contemplation:** In this stage, the individual actively considers changing within the following six months and tries to muster the motivation or figure out some way but also chronically procrastinates.
3. **Preparation:** At this stage, the individual has largely figured out a plan and is planning on undertaking it in the immediate future. There is hope but ambivalence.
4. **Action:** The individual actively engages in some systematic efforts to eliminate unhealthy behaviors and/or develop healthy behavior.
5. **Maintenance:** Change has largely occurred and the focus has shifted to relapse prevention.

THEORY EXAMPLE 2.2 (CONTINUED)

PROCESSES OF CHANGE:

EXPERIENTIAL	BEHAVIORAL
1. Consciousness raising, increasing awareness	1. Stimulus control (reengineering)
2. Dramatic relief (emotional arousal)	2. Helping relationship (support)
3. Environmental reevaluation (social reappraisal)	3. Counterconditioning (substituting)
4. Social liberation (environmental opportunities)	4. Reinforcement management (rewarding)
5. Self-reevaluation (self appraisal)	5. Self-liberation (committing)

model, as an outcome of choice, planning, concerted action, and the like, or as a consequence of its failure. As with the previous group of theories, these may involve conflict, but a greater emphasis is placed on synthesis and integration, as these are so critical to successful intentional action. And for this reason, many of these patterns of intentional change can also be characterized through the lens of self-organization theory. A popular theory based on the role of personal intentions, developed to understand to the stages in the adoption of healthy behaviors, is the transtheoretical personal change theory proposed by Prochaska, Velicer, DiClemente, and Fava (1988). This theory suggests that individuals typically pass through several predictable stages—precontemplation, contemplation, preparation, action, and maintenance—before they become sufficiently committed to successfully replace unhealthy behaviors with healthy ones (see theory example 2.2).

Finally, only a few theories have delved into the role of entropy (e.g., Bailey, 1994). In the hard sciences *entropy* refers to transitions from less likely and more ordered to more likely and less ordered states. But in the social sciences the term *entropy* is used in a more generic sense to refer to personal or social disintegration, to the tendency for social systems to lose their coherence and break down into progressively smaller, independently functioning units. A certain degree of entropy or disorder in a social system is considered healthy. In the psychoanalytic tradition, regression in the service of the ego, involving activities such as creative expression, play, and sexuality, may exemplify this. But when the level of disorganization and free energy becomes too great or too little, problems occur. The level of optimal entropy provides positive opportunities, for new learning, for starting over, or for resolving fears of death and the like. Neuroscientists have shown the pruning of unnecessary brain cells as a part of growth, and others have emphasized the value and necessity of a degree of forgetfulness as permitting the individual to focus on new tasks. In one case entropy may be dysfunctional, and in another it may be particularly useful.

Most theories have failed to consider the value of entropic processes in growth, regarding them instead as a dark shadow to healthy patterns of growth and problem solving. But entropy, under certain conditions, sets the stage for social learning as well as intentional or unintentional self-organizing patterns of personal change. It may clear away antiquated structures and relationships to permit new growth. Popular but questionable applications of the idea includes the notion of hitting bottom, which is popular among Alcoholics Anonymous members, or the tough-love movement.

These three approaches to understanding personal change focus on three of the most fundamental principles of biological and social development: (1) self-organization, (2) evolutionary processes of competition and social selection, and (3) entropy. Self-organization, as it applies to both human development and to intentional behavior, is particularly useful for understanding the development of new behaviors, so often sought by the human service professional. However, social competition and social selection, with their differential rewards and sanctions (carrots and sticks), is most applicable to understanding how behaviors and social structures, once developed, are fine-tuned and adapted to changing conditions. And social entropy is particularly useful in understanding patterns of social disintegration that may set the stage for possible renewal.

Central to theories of personal change are alternative views on the nature of the underlying drives and motivations that fuel change, whether or not conscious and intentional. Over the years a wide variety of core motivations have been proposed, from Freud's Eros (love) and Thanatos (death wish) (1920/1990), to White's (1963) notion of competence or efficacy, Frankl's (1993) search for meaning, and Maslow's (1943) hierarchy of needs, involving safety, security, self-esteem, self-actualization, or self-transcendence (for a critique, see Wahba & Bridwell, 1976; for elaboration, see chapter 6, section III.D.). The three themes identified here, or candidate motivations, permeate the earlier formulations and are proposed as a theoretical framework for understanding the underlying forces driving personal change. First is the drive for power or a sense of efficacy or power, over either one's environment or even the self. Second is the drive for knowledge, for meaning, for understanding. Third is the drive for feeling, whether this is sought after in pleasure, joy, or bliss. The three drives roughly correspond to what several of the world's spiritual traditions view as the three fundamental aspects or attributes of consciousness: (1) power, (2) knowledge, and (3) bliss. Although power can mean crude control of others or physical resources, it can also mean a more subtle sense of individual control of oneself. Similarly, knowledge and bliss are sought in many graded forms. Any of these may be an individual's primary motive or serve as secondary motives. For instance, knowledge may be sought to obtain power or pleasure, or power may be sought to provide opportunities for research and knowledge development or to bring pleasure and happiness to one's family.

Most often individuals pursue experiences of efficacy, knowledge, or feeling externally through manipulation of their social environments, believing that these are externally dependent. But as individuals grow, these experiences may become progressively internalized, which results in a sense of partnership with others, of not having to obtain these qualities or experiences through others, and it creates a need to share them in reciprocal relationships. And some exceptional individuals may develop such a clear sense of these qualities within themselves that their primary interest is in transmitting their knowledge, their power, or their happiness and joy to others, with little regard to what might be provided in return.

The combined effects of self-organization, social selection, and entropy structure the dynamic interplay of these motivations and their progressive transmutation. The recurrent creation, fine-tuning, and dissolution of social and behavioral patterns, resulting from the operation of these three principles, perhaps is what allows the emergence of these dynamic motivational structures, those involving the drives toward efficacy, knowledge, and feeling. Such motivational structures refer to complex systems of interrelated and enduring values, beliefs, feelings, memories, self-appraisals, environmental assessments, and expectancies. These build on and yet transcend the fundamental physical forces and biological drives that they emerged out of.

V. Summary

The central concern of this chapter has been social and personal change and the ways that change has been conceptualized. It concerns the question of whether there are any underlying forces driving social change, especially any involving human intentions. A wide range of disciplines draw on seemingly disparate concepts to answer this question, including ideas about fundamental physical forces; biological drivers and change principles; and human needs, motivations, and the like. These represent the emergence of new evolutionary drivers that are progressively more intentional in character. Much of the chapter focuses on three fundamental processes believed to drive change in multiple systems: (1) natural selection, (2) self-organization, and (3) entropy.

The chapter reviewed the problems and contributions of evolutionary theory, specifically of Charles Darwin's theory of natural selection, as well as its subsequent refinements and recent applications in the social sciences. While the neo-Darwinian theories retain many of the same original assumptions about the primacy of conflict, several more recent post-Darwinian theories, such as that of Stuart Kauffman, deemphasize natural selection and suggest that it is useful not so much for their explanations of the development of new forms but for their fine-tuning, once developed as a result of self-organization. The chapter next considered theories of social change in the context of developments in evolutionary theory. A key shift in recent years has been from those theories that emphasize equilibrium in systems beset with conflict, such as the structural-functionalist school of sociology, to theories that assume nonequilibrium conditions, such as social entropy theory.

The final part of this chapter explored implications of theories of social change for personal change. It is noted that the theories of societal, community, and organizational change concern the environment for personal change. These environments may exert a constraining or directive influence on personal change; however, the distinction between these is a matter of degree. Most theories of personal change usually emphasize some combination of external conditions (e.g., opportunities, social supports, and internal attitudes and motivation, expectations) as the elements that collectively explain or govern personal change.

This final section also identified and commented on four approaches to personal change: (1) those that emphasize the environment and social learning, ones that are usually based on notions of competition, conflict, and social selection (i.e., survival of the fittest); (2) developmental and related personality theories, which emphasize the internally generated emergence and self-organization of new behaviors; (3) theories of intentional social change, involving decision making, problem solving, and creativity, many of which also assume some degree of self-organization; and (4) entropy, involving the breakdown and disintegration of personal and social organization, and its healthy as well as unhealthy consequences. The chapter concludes with a discussion of self-organization, social selection, and entropy as representing three fundamental processes, involving the creation, fine-tuning, and dissolution of behavioral patterns.

For Further Reading

Bailey, K. D. (1994). Talcott Parsons, social entropy theory, and living systems theory. *Behavioral Science, 39,* 25–45.

Baum, R. F. (1986). *Doctors of modernity: Darwin, Marx and Freud.* Peru, IL: Sherwood Sugden.

Degler, C. N. (1991). *In search of human nature: The decline and revival of Darwinism in American Social Thought.* New York: Oxford University Press.

Diamond, J. (1997). *Guns, germs, and steel: The fates of human societies.* New York: Norton.

Fogel, R. W. (2000). *The fourth great awakening and the future of egalitarianism.* Chicago: University of Chicago Press.

Guastello, S. J. (1995). *Chaos, catastrophe, and human affairs: Applications of nonlinear dynamics to work, organizations, and social evolution.* Mahwah, NJ: Erlbaum.

Hallinan, M. (1997, February). The sociological study of social change. *American Sociological Review, 62,* 1–11.

Inglehart, R., & Baker, W. E. (2000). Modernization, cultural change, and the persistence of traditional values. *American Sociological Review, 65,* 19–51.

Kauffman, S. (1995). *At home in the universe: The search for laws of self-organization and complexity.* New York: Oxford University Press.

Kezar, A. J. (2001). *Understanding and facilitating organizational change in the twenty-first century: Recent research and conceptualizations.* San Francisco: Jossey-Bass.

Laszlo, E. (1996). *Evolution: The general theory.* Cresskill, NJ: Hampton Press.

Midgely, J. (1993). Ideological roots of social development strategies. *Social Development Issues, 15*(1), 1–13.

Pinker, S. (1997). *How the mind works.* New York: Norton.

Sober, E., & Wilson, D.S. (1998). *Unto others: The evolution and psychology of unselfish behavior.* Cambridge, MA: Harvard University Press.

CHAPTER 3

Understanding in Action: The Role of Theory in the Human Services

*We are the bees of the invisible. We madly gather the honey
of the visible to store it in the great golden hive of the invisible.*

—RAINER MARIA RILKE, "LETTER TO HULEWICZ"

I. Introduction

This chapter completes part 1 of this book, "The Framework," by exploring
the use of theory as a core strategy of knowledge building in the human services. It first examines the context of professional practice and an evolving
consensus concerning some of its most essential elements. These include
the expectation that human service professionals critically use and add to
their profession's knowledge base, which consists of theory, the results of
research, and their field's practice wisdom. After an overview of some ways
to define theory and how it is used in professional practice, the chapter
takes a broader look at how evolving conceptions of knowledge building in
philosophy and the sciences—including the field of epistemology—have
influenced the use of theory in the social sciences and the human services.
This discussion sets the stage for what is the heart of the chapter: the role
and applications of theory in practice. After an overview of a metatheory of
practice, the chapter provides a detailed framework for evaluating particular
theories and for selecting and using them in generalist practice. The chapter
concludes by developing the notions of understanding and wisdom as part
of an integrative vision for guiding the use of theory, research, and other
forms of knowledge in practice.

The central thesis of this chapter is that the most important role of theory
in the human services involves both a cyclical and a developmental process of theorizing, testing, and application through a wide range of practice methods, based on a diversity of perspectives, tools, and both objective
and subjective means of observation. It is a process that moves from the
many sources of raw data to the generation of information, knowledge, understanding, and—one dare hope—a kind of wisdom that transcends the
boundaries of the personal and the professional.

A. The Context: Human Services and Professional Practice

Knowledge building in the human services is guided and informed by
its institutional contexts and professional cultures, and especially by the
service mandates and values that undergird those systems. Contemporary

societies often strive to approximate the ideal of the welfare state, but only imperfectly. Such societies use diverse systems to transfer resources from those who are economically better off to those who are less well off. Such resources include monetary payments; various goods and services; and less tangible privileges, rights, and statuses. At the same time that such transfer systems strive to embody the values of social justice, interdependency, caring, and mutual support, the mandates must constantly be balanced against competing values, such as the provision of fair and equitable rewards for individual initiative and productivity, as well as societal expectations for controlling those who may be dangerous, be markedly different, or otherwise make unpopular demands.

Specifically, the term *social welfare* usually refers to cash or in-kind transfers to people who need support because of physical or mental illness, poverty, age, disability, or other defined circumstances or conditions (Chatterjee, 1996). It includes natural helping systems, such as families, religious groups, work organizations (e.g., unions, professional associations), the formal systems of income transfer (e.g., income maintenance, progressive taxation), and the formal human services. The human services consist of overlapping service sectors, such as child welfare, community action, mental health, the elderly, juvenile justice, health care, and education. These systems are defined by type of problem, stage of life, method, purpose, or some combination of those. Both within and between these sectors there is typically a hodgepodge of diverse service systems, each having evolved during distinct historical eras, each with its particular practice models and philosophies, and each representing an aborted and often incomplete response to the problems that stimulated its development.

People from several professions and occupations typically staff the public and private organizations that make up service systems. In some contexts, there may be a single dominant or host profession, such as social work in child welfare or medicine in health care. In other cases, such as community mental health (or what remains of it), a more truly interdisciplinary model prevails in which several professions collaborate on an equal basis.

The notion of a profession is distinct from the broader ideas of an occupation or a discipline. Whereas occupations comprise fields of work undertaken for a living—whether plumbing, secretarial work, or financial advising—most sociologists of the professions typically identify several additional features that are either always or often characteristic of professions. Perhaps the most critical of these are the notion of a calling and the ideal of service. Professionals commit their careers to a line of highly skilled work, one that is rooted in a sense of calling; mission; or, in the East, dharma or one's lifework. It is also characterized by service, or placing the needs of one's clients, in some respect, above one's own needs. Professions are also characterized by a type of formal membership, extended educational preparation, and codified ethical standards. And, most pertinent to this text, professional practice is based on a common, agreed-upon knowledge base, one that in modern societies is at least partly supported by socially sanctioned methods of scientific investigation and critical analysis. Sociologists of the professions, using these criteria, have developed a range of classifications of various professions, placing only a few—such as medicine and law—as so-called true professions, others as near professions, others as would-be professions, and the like. Almost a hundred years ago, in 1915, a renowned authority on professional education, Dr. Abraham Flexner, delivered a speech to the National Conference on Charities and Corrections in which he declared that social work was (at that time) not yet a profession. Flexner (1915/2001) argued that the new field lacked its own knowledge base—and "possesse[d] a technique communicable through education" (p. 157)—and thus could not yet claim the mantle of professional status. Since then, social work has come to be recognized as one of the preeminent professions in the human services.

Professions such as social work are distinct from the academic disciplines that they draw on. Disciplines such as sociology or anthropology are primarily concerned with the generation of new knowledge, not with its professional application. However, there are some fields, such as psychology, that can claim to be both professions and academic disciplines.

Only a few professions, such as medicine and law, can argue that they possess their own knowledge base. Most fields, including the various human service professions, such as social work, necessarily draw on knowledge from a wide range of academic disciplines. There has been ongoing debate as to whether the human service professions possess unique knowledge bases or whether this is even feasible or desirable. Such questions about the foundational knowledge of the human services are, thus, central to any study of human behavior theory. For this reason, before focusing on the particular type of knowledge that is referred to as "theory," it is first necessary to explore what is meant by the notion of a professional knowledge base.

B. The Knowledge Base

The term *knowledge base* in the human service professions refers to the body of theory, empirical research, practice wisdom, and procedures that are widely recognized and used in a given profession (see figure 3.1). Certainly, a particular professional will draw on knowledge commonly used in his or her specialty or field of practice and may not even recognize some

FIGURE 3.1: COMPONENTS OF A PROFESSION'S KNOWLEDGE BASE

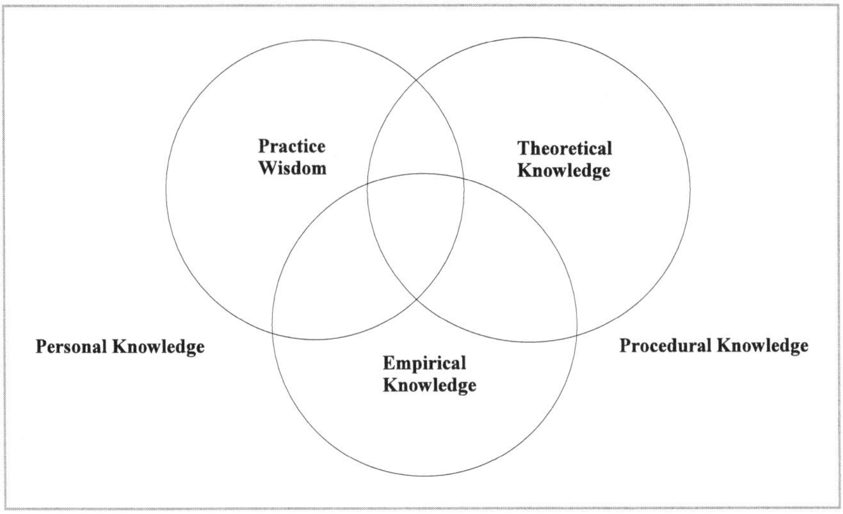

Source: J. D. Hudson (1997).

of the theories in other specialties with which the profession is involved. Nonetheless, as professionals gain experience and move between specialties, they tend to develop a consensus as to what constitutes relevant theories, research, or principles for practice. Much of this knowledge is not exclusive to a particular profession. Many fields, for example, actively use various psychotherapeutic practice models, such as the cognitive-behavioral or psychoanalytic models. In this respect, there is considerable overlap of the knowledge bases of the various human service professions, such as social work, psychology, or psychiatry. Although most commentators typically identify three overlapping components to a profession's knowledge base— theoretical knowledge, empirical research, and practice wisdom—Julie D. Hudson (1997), an Australian social worker, proposes that the knowledge base also includes procedural and personal knowledge.

Theoretical knowledge includes not only formal theories but also the more inclusive paradigms, perspectives, and conceptual frameworks, as well as the more specific models that operationalize formal theories. Theories, in this general sense, refer to either formal or informal explanations that a profession develops to account for the causes, dynamics, and consequences of phenomena of interest, often social problems or conditions, or intervention strategies.

In contrast, empirical knowledge is the knowledge generated from various types of formal, systematic research, whether involving experiments, large-scale surveys, or case studies. Some of the most critical defining features of such knowledge are that (1) it is based on direct observation; (2) the procedures are specified sufficiently such that other researchers can replicate and validate them; and (3) recognized procedures are used to maximize the reliability, validity, and generalizability of the findings to the extent possible, considering the purposes and limitations of the particular study. Although most of this knowledge is published in professional journals and summarized in texts and other books, some of it is found only in the professions' so-called gray literature, or unpublished reports, memoranda, and other materials that agencies and governmental bodies issue. Such empirical knowledge is often associated with recognized theories, but not necessarily.

Practice wisdom is typically regarded as the body of practice principles, rules of thumb, and tricks of the trade that are a central part of a profession's culture and are typically passed down from supervisor to supervisee. "Start where the client is at" and "If you can't choose between two differential diagnoses, focus first on the less severe" are two typical examples. Although many of these principles can be codified into practice theories and tested in empirical research, many are not. Many of them may be discussed in practice texts or articles, but some may never be written down. Much of this "wisdom" is unsubstantiated, but it represents a rich source of hunches and hypotheses for theory and research.

Procedural knowledge refers to the agreed-on steps—a type of protocol or algorithm—for undertaking some valued activity, such as referring clients to services, hospitalizing an acutely ill patient, or placing a child with a foster family. These procedures are often specific to an agency, a service system, or a profession. Julie Hudson (1997) defines such knowledge as also including "knowledge about the organizational, legislative, or policy context within which social work operates" (p. 38). Examples of procedural knowledge include the typical steps of program development and grant writing, and knowledge of the decision-making procedures in executive or legislative bodies. Much of this knowledge is published, if at all, only in agency manuals or materials issued by advocacy associations.

Finally, although it is debatable whether personal knowledge is part of a profession's knowledge base, it is clear that personal knowledge is an invaluable source that professionals regularly draw on. Julie Hudson (1997) argues that such knowledge includes intuition, common sense, and cultural knowledge. Any form of knowledge, especially practice wisdom and personal knowledge, may be what Michael Polanyi (1966) referred to as "tacit knowledge": knowledge that is so internalized that it is not conscious but nonetheless accessible, such as the knowledge of how to ride a bike or interact socially. A critical part of tacit and personal knowledge is intuition, which Hudson defines as "a spontaneous process of awareness that lies outside of a person's immediate consciousness and is largely based on instinct or feeling" (p. 40) (see chapter 7).

A given concept or proposition can simultaneously be part of a formal theory, supported by a body of research, and be a recognized truth in one's professional culture. It may also have been incorporated into recognized procedures and into one's personal knowledge. And it is not unusual for the holder of such knowledge to forget where it came from in the first place and to assume that it is his or her original insight. The practice has been for human service professionals to overemphasize the use of practice wisdom, procedural knowledge, and personal knowledge, and to neglect empirical and theoretical knowledge in their work. When this happens, the professional forgoes an important integrative tool that exists in the critical use of theory: a bridge between, on the one hand, the plethora of impressions, facts, propositions, and ideas that the professional confronts on a daily basis and, on the other hand, the development of understanding. But before discussing the role of understanding and wisdom in knowledge development, we will delve further into the question of what constitutes theories and how they are used.

C. Defining Theory

In a nutshell, theories are the formal and informal conceptual frameworks with which we organize our beliefs and knowledge in a communicable, testable, and potentially useful manner. *Theory* can be defined either narrowly or broadly, depending on the degree of formality and systematization that one expects of a theory, as well as the degree that research has validated the theory. A typical definition emphasizing the formality of theories is that of Tripodi, Fellin, and Meyer (1969): "Theory consists of an interlocking set of hypotheses that are logically related, and it seeks to explain the interrelations among empirical generalizations" (p. 13). Bomben (2002) comments: "In science, a theory carries a great deal of weight. Theories are backed by an incredible number of facts. As Webster implies, to dismiss evolution as 'only a theory' is to grossly abuse the language. That is like claiming Thomas Jefferson was 'only a farmer'" (para. 18).

In contrast, a popular and broad use of the word *theory* treats it as mere hypothesis, conjecture, or guess. Although most professionals are not nearly this inclusive when they discuss theory, many do treat it very broadly. For instance, Schuman and Schwartz (1998) comment, "For our purpose, we will loosely define theory and model interchangeably as a set of interrelated concepts that explain or predict some behavior" (p. 90). In short, a conceptual framework may be a set of interrelated propositions that may be stated as an explanation or a narrative, especially if one chooses to treat theory in such a manner. Theories are also distinguished from paradigms, which are overarching and often unarticulated frameworks or perspectives that generate a range of particular theories, conceptual frameworks, and hypotheses (see Kuhn, 1970).

A theory may include either knowledge or simply belief. The fundamental stuff of theories are concepts, or ideas, and these may be abstract or concrete (e.g., anxiety, stress, resilience, race, height and weight). These building blocks are then combined into statements or propositions that interrelate them, in terms of either their causal relationship or their logical relationship. An example that explains the impact of various levels of challenge on personal response is the following proposition: When challenge is too low relative to skill, boredom is experienced; when challenge is too high, anxiety results. This statement interrelates the concepts of challenge, skill, boredom, and anxiety in a single proposition, one that is part of a more comprehensive theory of the experience of flow, or successful engagement in task attainment, which Mihaly Csikszentmihalyi (1990) and his later followers developed (see chapter 6). If such propositions have been researched and empirical support for them is forthcoming, we regard them as involving some type of knowledge. In other cases, the propositions may be unsubstantiated beliefs, perhaps merely hypotheses, conjectures, and guesses. The originators of many theories in the social sciences often do not label them as theories. They simply discuss a phenomenon and, unfortunately, do not always distinguish between what is fact and what is conjecture. A key question in examining such materials is whether they represent an integrated, cohesive explanation of some phenomenon of general interest.

Theories vary considerably. A critical dimension for human services is the question of whether a theory simply explains a phenomenon, which is useful for the purposes of assessment, or whether it is a practice theory (i.e., the kinds of intervention strategies, methods, and skills that are useful under various circumstances). Although a theory can be either of those, theories are typically developed first to explain some condition, problem, or behavior, and then they may be extended to become practice theories. Although psychoanalytic theory was originally a theory of psychological functioning, Sigmund Freud and his successors wasted little time in extending it to various theories of psychological treatment such as psychoanalysis and psychodynamic psychotherapy. Table 3.1 overviews the various theories and chapters in this text as they relate with both system levels and the assessment or intervention focus.

TABLE 3.1: THEORIES AND CHAPTERS, CATEGORIZED BY SYSTEM LEVEL AND FOCUS

SYSTEM LEVEL AND FOCUS	ASSESSMENT		INTERVENTION
CROSSCUTTING: ALL LEVELS AND ALL FOCI	3. Understanding in Action: The Role of Theory in the Human Services 13. Cultural Diversity: Problems, Challenges, Opportunities 15. Values, Ethics, and Spirituality in the Human Services		
MACRO: POLICY	2. The Roots of Personal and Social Change		
MEZZO: ORGANIZATIONAL AND COMMUNITY	11. The Dynamics of Organizations 12. Community Theory, Dynamics, and Assessment		
MICRO: INDIVIDUAL AND SMALL GROUP	4. Recent Advances in the Study of Consciousness 5. Maturation, Learning, and Personal Development through the Life Cycle 6. Motivation and Personality: Conflict, Consistency, and Fulfillment Models 8. Theories of Mental Dysfunction 9. Small Groups and Their Processes 10. Families as Complex Systems	1. The Assessment of Complex Adaptive Systems 7. Decision Making, Problem Solving, and Creativity	14. Models of Generalist Practice in Complex Systems

Notes: The placement of chapters is approximate. In several cases, theories will be covered that apply to more than one system level.

D. The Functions of Theory in the Human Services

Although many in the human services emphasize the importance of theory, its use in practice has been found to be scant, at least the application of formal theories per se. Studies have documented only a minimal association between the theories that practitioners subscribe to and what they actually do (Rosen, Proctor, Morrow-Howell, & Staudt, 1995). Yet if theory is understood broadly, then it is difficult not to use theory. The statements "Engage the client in a helping relationship" and "Helping the client express his or her feelings will improve problem solving" not only are part of the helping profession's practice wisdom but also are incorporated into various practice theories, such as the problem-solving and generalist models. Perhaps one of the best-known proponents of theory is Kurt Lewin (1951), who was known for his comment, "There is nothing so practical as a good theory" (p. 169). He argued not only that theory is a guide to practice but also that developing new theory is a central responsibility of the practitioner (Marrow, 1969). At the other end of the spectrum are the family therapist and the theoretician Carl Whitaker (1976), who introduced his essay "The Hindrance of Theory in Clinical Work" with the remark: "I have a theory that theories are destructive" (p. 154). He argues that theory has a "chilling effect" (p. 155) on intuition and creativity, and that it tends to make the elimination of symptoms the exclusive objective of therapy. As a substitute for theory, he suggests: "The accumulated and organized residue of experience, plus the freedom to allow the relationship to happen, to be who you are with the minimum of anticipatory set and maximum responsiveness to authenticity and to our own growth impulses" (p. 163). It is clear that although the obsessive use of theory, especially as a device for distancing or mystification, is often counterproductive in the human services, the notion that it is desirable, or even possible, not to use theory—broadly conceived—is highly questionable and certainly a minority view.

Although theories can be thought of as particular kinds of intellectual objects, ones that can be encapsulated in a list of bullet points, a figure, or a chapter in a textbook, they should also be considered processes of critical thought involving such ongoing activities as definition and clarification, application and testing, and revision and reformulation. The Noble laureate Ilya Prigogine (b. 1917–d. 2003) proposed that science is a "dialogue between mankind and nature" (1997, p. 157). Thus, theories in the human services are the sentences and paragraphs in the ongoing dialogue between practitioners and their clients, colleagues, profession, and society as a whole. They are the explanations and stories that we continuously frame and reframe in collaboration with others. When practitioners engage a client in the beginning phases of their work together, they also assess the client's difficulties. As part of this process, clients tell their story, and practitioners listen and inevitably reframe the material, developing an assessment or theory of what is involved in the client's situation. That theory will, to various degrees, draw on the many formal theories in the social sciences that have influenced individual practitioners, or perhaps theories that practitioners have consciously forgotten. The selection of goals and interventions—whether a particular form of psychotherapy, some kind of community action such as a public education campaign, or program development—will in turn be molded by theories of what is possible and the means to accomplish such ends. And the success or failure of the intervention provides rich, yet often inconclusive, evidence about the validity of the original assumptions and theories employed in the assessment. These theories and the activities associated with their development and testing are not just personal ones, or even ones unique to a given profession; instead, they exist as part of the development of society's conceptions of knowledge and how it might be built. It is to this topic that this chapter now turns.

II. Knowledge Building: Its Possibilities and Limitations

A. Epistemology and Its Ongoing Dilemma

The way that knowledge is developed in the human services has been molded by more than two thousand years of debate about what, in general, we can know and how we best acquire knowledge. The study of knowledge is known as epistemology, which has been a branch of philosophy since the time of the classical Greeks. However, nonphilosophers in most academic and professional fields are regularly involved in the study of epistemology, referring to their particular subspecialties with such diverse terms such as *evolutionary epistemology, quantum epistemology, feminist epistemology,* and *genetic epistemology.*

One of the most central issues throughout the history of epistemology has been the debate between empiricists and rationalists. Empiricists emphasize observational knowledge, which is believed to mirror an external reality. This approach has also been called the reflection-correspondence theory of truth. In this view, knowledge results from "a kind of mapping or reflection of external objects, through our sensory organs, possibly aided by different observation instruments, to our brain or mind" (Heylighen, 1993, n.p.).

In contrast, rationalists emphasize the use of logic and reason to derive statements about the world that are consistent with one another.

Traditionally, these statements have been based not on observation but on beliefs and assumptions, for example, theological ideas passed down from one generation to the next. This second approach has been known as the coherence theory of truth. In contrast to the empirical approach, the coherence theory often begins with propositions derived from either authority or assumptions and values regarded as self-evident. In this respect, adherents of the coherence theory tend to subscribe to a type of traditional foundationalism, or the view that knowledge can be deduced from certain key pieces of infallible knowledge, such as "I think, therefore I am" or the sanctity of human life. Although there are obviously many perversions of such foundational approaches to knowledge building, the accomplishments of fields such as mathematics exemplify the obvious usefulness of such approaches when confined to an appropriate domain.

B. Evolving Conceptions of Knowledge

Throughout history, the rational and empirical theories of knowledge have been progressively developed beyond their initial extreme versions, and at the same time, there have been repeated attempts to integrate the best of each approach (see figure 3.2). Efforts in the twentieth century have had to contend with a widening array of approaches to knowledge building in the context of both the massive accomplishments of scientific investigation and the repeated demonstrations of the impossibility of achieving irrefutable, consistent, and comprehensive knowledge.

1. EARLY HISTORY

Many of the earliest Greek approaches to knowledge building were responses to the position of the Sophists of the fifth century BCE, who argued that "nothing really exists, that nothing can be known, and if knowledge were possible, it could not be communicated" ("Gorgias," 2001, para. 2). Plato (b. 428 BCE–d. 347 BCE) and his teacher Socrates (b. 469 BCE–d. 399 BCE) developed the rationalist response to this position: there is, in fact, a world of eternal ideas or truths that exists independent of physical reality but nonetheless can be known. Every physical object is an imperfect representation of its eternal essence.

In contrast, Aristotle (b. 384 BCE–d. 322 BCE) developed the foundations of the empirical or correspondence model of truth in his position that all knowledge is gained from experience. Yet he shared the Socratic vision of abstract knowledge as being of the highest type of knowledge and the importance of logic, and especially deductive reasoning through syllogisms. An important contribution of Aristotle's was his differentiation of the various

FIGURE 3.2: MAJOR CONTRIBUTORS TO EPISTEMOLOGY

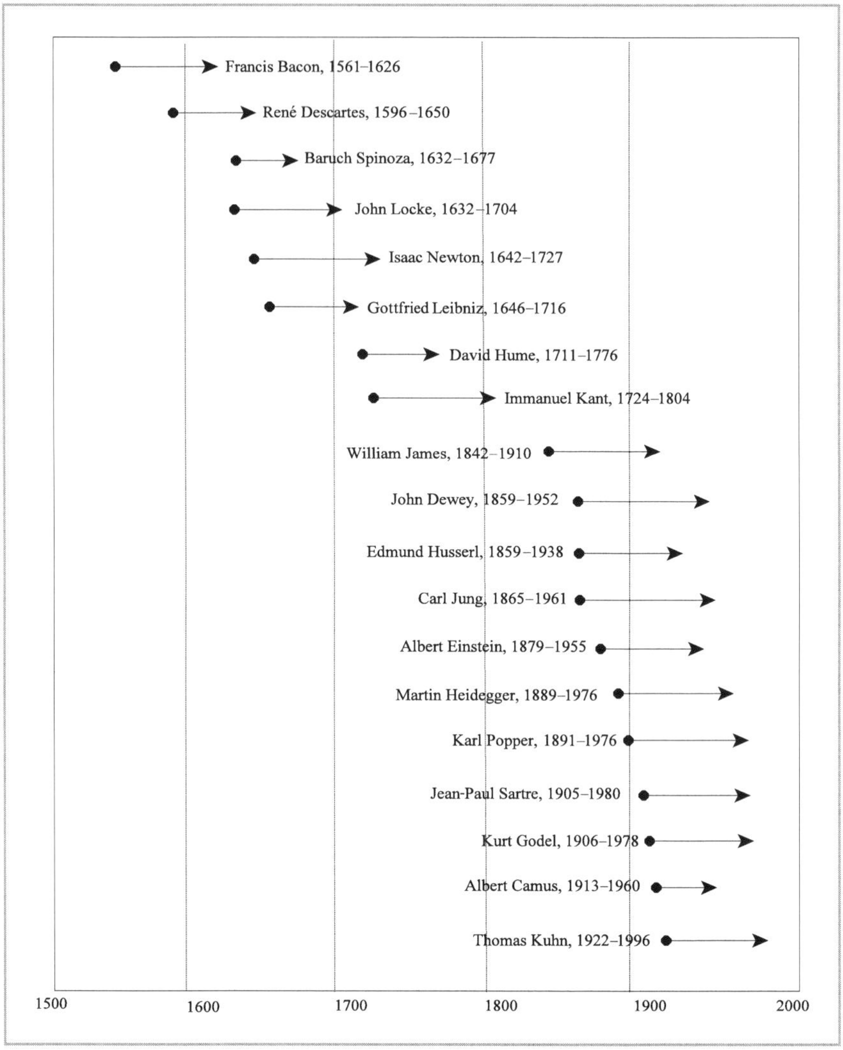

Francis Bacon, 1561–1626

René Descartes, 1596–1650

Baruch Spinoza, 1632–1677

John Locke, 1632–1704

Isaac Newton, 1642–1727

Gottfried Leibniz, 1646–1716

David Hume, 1711–1776

Immanuel Kant, 1724–1804

William James, 1842–1910

John Dewey, 1859–1952

Edmund Husserl, 1859–1938

Carl Jung, 1865–1961

Albert Einstein, 1879–1955

Martin Heidegger, 1889–1976

Karl Popper, 1891–1976

Jean-Paul Sartre, 1905–1980

Kurt Godel, 1906–1978

Albert Camus, 1913–1960

Thomas Kuhn, 1922–1996

1500   1600   1700   1800   1900   2000

Note: Living contributors to the development of epistemology are not included in this graph.

types of causes, all of which constitute elements of a theory or explanation of a given phenomenon: (1) the material cause, or the material or substance out of which an object is formed; (2) the efficient cause, in contrast, is the means by which an object or event is brought about; (3) the formal cause is an idea, plan, or design that comes to be expressed in the object or event; and (4) the final cause is the purpose, end, or function that brought all the foregoing elements together to produce the object or event to be explained. In the human services, allocated funds for a program might be considered a material cause; the intervention efforts of staff, an efficient cause; various practice principles, work plans, proposals, or procedures, a formal cause; and the goal of successfully helping clients live outside of institutions, the final cause for the success or failure of a program of, for example, deinstitutionalization (Copleston, 1974). Other precursors to the modernist views include Thomas Aquinas, René Descartes, David Hume, and Immanuel Kant.

2. TWENTIETH-CENTURY DEVELOPMENTS

One of the first and most influential approaches to knowledge building in the twentieth century is the school of pragmatic epistemology, associated with William James (b. 1842–d. 1910) and John Dewey (b. 1859–d. 1952). Although James and Dewey acknowledged that, in a sense, knowledge needs to mirror an external reality, they argued that this begs the question of the exact criteria for the correspondence. Their solution was to emphasize the successful application of knowledge in problem solving as a critical criterion for its validity.

William James (1909/1997), for instance, argued: "Pragmatism asks its usual question 'Grant an idea or belief to be true,' it says, 'what concrete difference will its being true make in any one's actual life? What experiences [may] be different from those which would obtain if the belief were false? How will the truth be realized? What, in short, is the truth's cash-value in experiential terms?'" (p. ix). James, who was both a philosopher and a psychologist, is often referred to as the father of modern psychology, and he continues to be influential.

John Dewey, a philosopher regarded as the founder of the progressive education movement, was, like James, a pragmatist. He believed that the rationalists and empiricists had too sharply distinguished between knowledge and the domain of facts that knowledge is intended to refer to. Foreshadowing the evolutionary epistemologists, he envisioned knowledge development as an adaptive response to disturbances in the interaction between organism and environment. Specifically, he believed that the world is never passively perceived but known only through its active manipulation (see Field, 2002).

Logical positivism, an offshoot and extreme version of the pragmatic approach, was developed in the initial years of the twentieth century by a group known as the Vienna Circle. This group argued for a type of verificationism in which only statements that referred to observed realities were regarded as meaningful; thus, ideas in ethics, metaphysics, and religion must be regarded as meaningless. Logical positivism has been characterized by eight major propositions: (1) the preeminent need for verification, (2) the reliance on observation, (3) a deemphasis on the analysis of causes, (4) the downplaying of explanation, (5) minimized use of theory, (6) the rejection of ethics and metaphysics, (7) the use of logical analysis, and (8) the assessment of probability (Yu, 2001).

Despite the fact that both scientists and philosophers have almost universally rejected logical positivism for more than fifty years, several textbooks have mistakenly characterized logical positivism as the prevalent approach to knowledge building in the human services (Feldman, 1998). Such textbooks typically mistakenly equate logical positivism with the use of quantitative research methods. However, it has been persuasively argued that logical positivism is better understood as a type of naive empiricism that downplays the use of theory, regardless of whether a qualitative or quantitative methodology is used (Yu, 2001). The generalizations derived from observations are to be verified by further observations rather than falsified or disconfirmed, as is the case in the prevailing approach, known as fallibilism, which Karl Popper (1963/1974) promoted. Even the philosopher Alfred J. Ayer, one of the founders of logical positivism, came to disavow logical positivism. In 1979, when asked about what he considered the main problem of logical positivism, he replied, "I suppose the most important . . . was that nearly all of it was false" (as cited in Hanfling, 1981, p. 1). Logical positivism attempted to apply principles of the natural sciences to the social sciences. These principles were borrowed from the Newtonian worldview and assumed a deterministic, atomistic universe and the possibility of completely objective observation. At the same time, revolutionary developments in science and mathematics were supplanting this older view and starkly demonstrating the limits of human knowledge. These included Albert Einstein's theory of relativity, quantum physics, and developments in mathematics. Einstein (b. 1879–d. 1955) launched these developments by demonstrating that there was no preferred or absolute frame of reference defined by a set of Cartesian x and y coordinates but that time and space could vary under diverse circumstances. For example, he showed that space can be curved, and that time can speed up, slow down, or even come to a stop.

Then, in the 1920s, quantum physics was developed, revolutionizing our understanding of the microphysical world and, in the process, establishing both limits of the ability to predict phenomena and a profound interdependency of existence. One of the most significant contributions of quantum physics at this time was the Heisenberg uncertainty principle, a proof that it is possible to know the position or momentum of a particle, but never both at the same time; and that the more exactly one knows one variable, the less exactly is it possible to know the other variable. The relationship between position and momentum is only one example of the uncertainty principle; there have been shown to be many other instances of quantum uncertainty.

Quantum theory also served to popularize the notion of probability. While quantum theory demonstrated that complete predictability is impossible, it also showed that relative predictability is both possible and useful. Thus, both the theory of relativity and quantum physics introduced a new understanding of the impossibility of complete knowledge of physical realities. However, in doing so, both theories demonstrated unheard-of levels of accuracy in the prediction and understanding of physical reality. The two theories are among the greatest achievements in the history of science, paving the way for modern electronics, photonics, nuclear energy, and computerization, to mention only a few of many fields. In recent years, quantum theory has opened up new avenues in the study of consciousness and brain functioning, for example, in helping explain the subjective qualities of consciousness. It also addresses the binding problem, which refers to the difficulty of traditional models in explaining how diverse cognitions and perceptions are integrated in a coherent experience (see chapter 4 and the appendix).

At the same time that developments in the sciences were dramatically demonstrating the power of theory in knowledge building, several postmodern philosophers were developing existential phenomenology. Although phenomenology had been developed by such nineteenth-century thinkers such as G. W. F. Hegel and Søren Kierkegaard, its popularity was greatly enhanced by its integration with existentialism in the twentieth century, as well as by widespread disillusionment with both science and scientism. This disillusionment resulted partly from experiences during the Second World War of Nazi perversions in evolutionary and genetic theory, as well the use of nuclear energy for destructive purposes, especially the bombings of Hiroshima and Nagasaki, and the nuclear arms race. Existential phenomenology minimizes both the use of theory and any attempt to identify causes. Instead, it is a type of radical empiricism in which an attempt is made to understand phenomena descriptively, purely in terms of direct experience. The philosopher Edmund Husserl (b. 1859–d. 1938) is generally regarded as the founder of existential phenomenology. His best-known contribution is his method of phenomenological analysis: eidetic reduction. With this method, one identifies and brackets off all unessential elements of a phenomenon—of time, anguish, or even a physical object such as a cup—until its bare essence is isolated:

> Look at the cup on your desk. Discard all that is not really a part of "cupness." My cup is ceramic but ceramic is not a significant portion of cupness. My cup had a handle but cups can be cups without

a handle . . . Japanese tea-cups don't have handles. My cup is beige
and brown but cups can be any color or have none at all. My cup is
about 8 oz. but cups can be bigger or much smaller . . . is there ever
a point at which a cup becomes too big or too small to be a cup. . . .
No! Size is not the essence of cupness . . . keep on going until you get
to the real, irreducible eidos of cupness then tell me what you have.
(Young, 2002, sec. C3)

Existential phenomenology was further developed by Husserl's student
Martin Heidegger (b. 1889–d. 1976), as well as by a wide range of thinkers such as Jean-Paul Sartre (b. 1905–d. 1980) and Albert Camus (b. 1913–
d. 1960). Because of its attempt to stay close to experience, phenomenology
has had considerable influence in the fields of philosophical psychology and
psychotherapy, through the efforts of Victor Frankl, Eugene Gendlin, and
others, who were interested in developing clinical methods for helping clients develop a sense of meaning and better connect with and process their
own immediate experience through active listening and focusing.

The shift from the rationalism of the modern era to postmodernism was
exemplified in the development of social constructivism, an offshoot of existential phenomenology. This theory of knowledge building originated largely
in the humanities, which although superficially similar to phenomenology
is very different from it. Unlike the radical empiricism of phenomenology,
social constructivism is a type of radical coherentism. Constructivists often,
but not always, reject the notion of an external reality that truth can correspond with. They also reject any kind of axiomatic or foundational principles that traditional coherentists build their knowledge on. Instead, social
constructivists believe that knowledge is socially constructed, and if there
are any criteria for its validity, they are usefulness, viability (not truth), or the
level of consensus or agreement that the knowledge commands. Social constructivists argue that knowledge is not what individuals believe but rather
what knowledge communities subscribe to (see Bruffee, 1993). This position
is similar to what some psychologists refer to as the "ecological validity of
knowledge," which emphasizes the social rather than individual ecology or
context of knowledge. What appears to be individual knowledge building
and thought is understood as a type of internalization of social conversation.
Only after a child learns the "social struggle between contending interpretations" (Bruffee, 1993, p. 114) does he or she develop the ability to conduct such
conversations (or thoughts) in the privacy of the mind (Vygotsky, 1978).

Social constructivists emphasize the analysis, taking apart, or deconstruc-
tion of existing theories and systems of knowledge. This involves the identification of their underlying assumptions, biases, and class interests, followed

by the formation of alternative systems with as much coherence, agreement, or viability as possible. This process is often understood as a hermeneutical dialogue. Hermeneutics traditionally involved interpretation of and dialogue about the meaning of religious texts and, as a result of this dialogue, continuous updating of the interpretations (or theories) (Ross, 2002). In a similar fashion, social constructivists see interpretation, dialogue, and the use of narratives as central to both knowledge building and therapy. Understanding clients' stories or narratives of their difficulties and helping them reformulate those narratives is considered a central part of the application of social constructivism in human services practice.

Perhaps one of the best-known applications of social constructivism is the classic 1970 work of Thomas Kuhn (b. 1922–d. 1996), *The Structure of Scientific Revolutions*. In this book, Kuhn argues that science advances not so much through the incremental accumulation of new truths but through the competition of dominant and alternative paradigms. When the dominant paradigm accumulates too many inconsistencies—when its coherence breaks down—new paradigms emerge through a "social struggle between contending interpretations of intrinsically ambiguous evidence" (Ross, 2002, para. 7).

Another more recent application of social constructivism is feminist epistemology, which focuses on the ways that traditional approaches to knowledge building systematically oppress women and on the identification of alternative approaches. According to the *Stanford Encyclopedia of Philosophy*, feminist epistemologists argue that traditional approaches to knowledge building affect women through the following means: (1) exclusion of women from inquiry, (2) undermining of legitimacy, (3) minimization of feminine cognitive styles, (4) development of theories that portray women in a demeaning fashion, (5) development of theories that make women and their relationships invisible, and (6) production of scientific knowledge that is not useful to women or that maintains dominant power structures (see Anderson, 2002). Among the most central ideas in feminist epistemology is that of the situated knower, and thus situated knowledge, which maintains a relationship with its subject and in which context is not stripped away. Feminist epistemologists are also particularly interested in the ideals of objectivity and rationality, and the ways that those have been used to maintain the interests of dominant groups. Some of the specialties within feminist epistemology are standpoint theory, feminist postmodernism, and feminist empiricism (Anderson, 2002).

Just as phenomenologists and social constructivists were testing the limits of the empirical and coherence approaches to knowledge building, perhaps one of the most significant attempts to reconcile the diverse approaches in the twentieth century has been the work of Sir Karl Popper

(b. 1902–d. 1994), whom many regard as the most important philosopher of science since Francis Bacon. In his early work Popper was known for his devastating critique of inductivism, or naive empiricism, in which he showed that simply generalizing from observations, without any theory to guide this process, is hopelessly misleading. In *The Logic of Scientific Discovery* (1959), he argues that scientific discovery never advances by direct confirmation or verification of scientific theories but only through their falsification. He points out that when one attempts to verify a theory by the accuracy of its predictions, one may commit the fallacy of affirming the consequent. For example, if it rains, the floor becomes wet; the floor is wet, and therefore it rained. There is a parable about a chicken scientist who observes the farmer who regularly comes to feed it, concludes that the farmer is concerned about the chicken's welfare, and predicts such continued generosity (Deutsch, 1997). There are other possible theories to explain the farmer's behavior, not the least of which is that the farmer wants to fatten the chicken for his next meal. Thus, Popper rejects such inductivism as futile, as there are usually many contradictory theories that can explain the same data equally well. Instead, he argues for a problem-solving approach that begins with the identification of a problem and a theory about it, followed by systematic attempts at its falsification (Deutsch, 1997) (see exhibit 3.1). A key part of this approach is that one tries not to confirm or verify theories but instead to falsify or disconfirm them.

Although Popper's early work on the problem-solving process has been widely accepted throughout the sciences, perhaps equally significant is his

EXHIBIT 3.1: INDUCTIVISM AND THE ALTERNATIVE OF SCIENTIFIC PROBLEM SOLVING

INDUCTIVISM

1. Observation of phenomena of interest
2. Generalization and theory building
3. Further observations and data collection
4. Validation of theory

SCIENTIFIC PROBLEM SOLVING

1. Identification of a problem
2. Formulation of possible solutions or theories
3. Testing of solutions through critique and experiments
4. Modification of solutions and theories
5. Identification of new problems

Source: Deutsch (1997, pp. 59 & 65).

later work on evolutionary epistemology.* Popper argues that knowledge development not only parallels the process of evolution but also is, in a sense, a direct continuation of it; that is, evolution is knowledge development. Like evolutionary theory, Popper considers knowledge development a social adaptation to changing environments. And similar to natural selection, knowledge generation happens through "unjustified variation and selective retention" (DeRoos, 1990, p. 281). Model construction is viewed as a trial-and-error undertaking in which only those models that are adaptive are retained (Heylighen, 1997).

The sociobiologist Richard Dawkins, who introduced the notion of memes and the field of memetics, introduced a variation of evolutionary epistemology. Knowledge is transmitted from person to person and is continually reproduced, something like a biological or a computer virus. And while ideas spread, they are continually revised, redefined, and a process of natural selection is applied to the ideas themselves, causing them to lose any connection with a particular person or group (Dawkins, 1989). This theory of knowledge is particularly relevant to understanding popular culture—whether myths, urban legends, folklore, or practice wisdom—and perhaps less relevant to more formal types of empirical or theoretical knowledge.

Although Popper's problem-solving method and his evolutionary epistemology attempt to integrate the empirical and the rational, they also acknowledge, albeit indirectly, the importance of hunches and, thus, of transrational forms of knowledge. There have been many others, however, who have specifically pursued theories that emphasize the importance of intuition, tacit knowledge, empathy, and the like, in generating new knowledge or at least new hypotheses. Perhaps best known is Michael Polanyi (1966), who coined the term *tacit knowledge* to refer to unarticulated, preconscious knowledge, which is nonetheless accessible. Others, such as the French philosopher Henri Bergson, emphasized intuition as a type of immediate consciousness (see chapter 7, section V). In contrast, the proponents of Heinz Kohut's self-psychology emphasize empathy as a critical alternative to the more detached, objective, and external ways of theoretically understanding human experience. Likewise, proponents of transpersonal psychologies, such as Abraham Maslow (Maslow & Lowery, 1998), Roberto Assagioli (1965), and Ken Wilber (1997), emphasize alternative, often transcendental, and spiritual states of awareness. Simultaneous with attempts to emphasize

---

* The late educational psychologist Donald Campbell, who made major contributions in research methodology in the human services, coined the term *evolutionary epistemology* (see Campbell, 1974).

the reflective-correspondence (or empirical) and rational (or coherentist) approaches to knowledge building, or to somehow integrate the two through approaches such as Popper's approach to problem solving, new transrational sources of knowledge have been increasingly emphasized. And it is perhaps appropriate to note that a convincing and fully practical integration of all these approaches to knowledge building is yet to be achieved.

C. Integration, Current Status, and New Directions

The foregoing review of the development of epistemology or knowledge building is the backdrop to a long-term debate about the proper role of theory in the social sciences and the human services. Although empiricists usually minimize the use of theory, viewing it as, at best, a long-term outcome of extensive data collection and analysis, others, such as supporters of Popper's problem-solving approach, place theory in a pivotal position in knowledge formulation.

1. Overview of Application of Theory in Social Sciences

Lars Mjøset (2002), a Norwegian sociologist, has identified five types of uses of theory in the social sciences. Mjøset identifies the deductive-nomological approach (as well as the lawlike notion of theory), which focuses on theory testing; the idealizing notion, on modeling; the constructivist position, on theory formation; and critical theory, on ethical grounding. He contends that each is a critical part of the process of theorizing and knowledge development.

The traditional and perhaps best-known position is the deductive-nomological notion of theory. This approach borrows heavily from the experimental natural sciences and the use of logical deduction to identify hypotheses that are candidates for universal laws. Data are collected to test the extent to which a hypothesis corresponds with external observed realities.

An offshoot of the preceding is the law-oriented notion of theory. The rarity of universal laws in the social sciences has led many to focus instead on regularities or lawlike behavior that occur in particular social contexts. The sociologist Robert Merton (1968), for example, emphasized middle-range theories involving discrete, local phenomena. Many have followed Merton's lead and have produced work that has been weak on generalizability and parsimoniousness but strong with respect to contextual explanations.

Another modification of the deductive-nomological approach is the idealizing notion of theory. Proponents of this approach point out that, because it is often impossible to specify all the conditions for a given phenomenon, one must instead concentrate on the ideal or perhaps typical case. Much of

the work of both Max Weber and Émile Durkheim came out of this orientation, as have more recent attempts to generate computer models and simulations of social phenomena.

In the constructivist notion of theory there is the idea that social science theories are in principle no different from other constructions, such as
myths of tribal societies. The approach emphasizes the analysis of human
behavior in terms of both motive and context, and thus it has resisted the depersonalization and decontextualization of some other types of theorizing.
These theories are not parsimonious and are often accused of relativism, in
that they minimize any correspondence with external realities and focus on
the impact of dominant groups in defining the prevailing theories.

Finally, like the constructivist approach, proponents of critical theory
reject the deductive-nomological approach. However, critical theorists part
ways with the constructivists in their emphasis on the need for a strong ethical foundation. For instance, Jürgen Habermas, a chief proponent, argues for
consensus rather than correspondence with external realities as a criterion
for the legitimacy of a theory. He distinguishes among the action sciences
(much of the human services) and the empirical-analytical natural sciences
and the historical-hermeneutical sciences. He points out that different interests drive these, such as technical dominance in the natural sciences and the
development of social consensus in the historical sciences.

2. THE CHALLENGES OF CHANCE, FREE WILL, AND HISTORY

Although decisions regarding the appropriate use of theory in the social
sciences, as well as criteria for determining their validity, are significant
problems, they are by no means the least of the difficulties that theorists face
in the human services. The search for meaningful explanations of problems
can easily be side-tracked by the unending search for predictable patterns
or regularities. The deductive-nomological approach has rarely achieved its
goals of identifying truly universal laws, especially in the case of human
behavior, and for this reason the various alternative strategies have been
pursued. Three major problems that have thwarted social theorists in this
quest have been chance, free will, and history.

Chance may appear to be the most manageable of the three, as probability theory and social statistics provide a variety of tools to model the
likelihood of various events, including an assessment of both the chance
errors involved in the measurement of social phenomena and the ability
to assess the generalizability of conclusions from samples to larger populations. While determinists treat chance as merely the aggregate effect of
all variables that we are presently unable to measure or model (i.e., those
that are sometimes modeled using an error term), others argue that many

events are fundamentally undetermined. Whichever is the case, we know from chaos theory that even single, fairly minor chance events often have effects that become dramatically magnified through negative feedback loops and sensitive dependence on initial conditions (see chapter 1). Although the aggregate effects of multiple chance events often are predictable, occasionally unique events have effects that grow exponentially and overwhelm all efforts at prediction, thereby defeating the best of theories. Often, the best we can do is to simply identify and acknowledge the degree of error in the ability of our theories to predict outcomes.

A more serious problem for theory is the possibility of free will. For many, of course, this is not a problem, as they believe that free will is only a convenient "story" we tell ourselves, that such impersonal forces as genetic or biochemical processes, unconscious psychological drives, class interests, or economic forces in fact determine our lives (Bargh & Chartrand, 1999). Perhaps the most fundamental objection to the notion of free will comes from those who believe that the law of conservation of matter and energy prohibits anything nonphysical, such as the mind or consciousness, from having an effect on the physical world (Markič, 1999). Although it may be true that many of our choices are reflexive, automatic outcomes of biology, past learning, or economic incentives, and that we overestimate our ability to make genuine choices, there remain considerable philosophical arguments and empirical evidence for free will. Many people assume that an individual's choices may not be predictable, if for no other reason than his or her free will, but many of the same people argue that, in aggregate, either choices of multiple individuals or multiple choices of a single individual can be explained and modeled. Others believe that any explanation of the regularities of free choices necessarily implies a type of determinism. The prevalent approach is to acknowledge some limited free will and to use theory to understand patterns in the outcomes of choices, as unpredictable as they may be, on the aggregate or population basis. Although this works up to a point, occasionally tragic or great decisions that people make have effects that overwhelm all the lawful regularities that social scientists so cleverly identify. An example of a theory that takes free will seriously is the theory of planned action (see theory example 3.1), which is based on the notion that the most important human behaviors are more accurately regarded as human actions, characterized not so much by external behaviors but by the underlying intentions, choices, and rules that govern them. Although social scientists have traditionally focused on Aristotle's efficient or immediate causes in their explanations, often the most persuasive explanations of many actions involve their formal cause, or the goals or purposes that motivate people to choose to do certain things.

THEORY EXAMPLE 3.1: THE THEORIES OF REASONED AND PLANNED ACTION

ORIGINATORS: Icek Ajzen, Ph.D., professor of psychology, University of Massachusetts, and Martin Fishbein, Ph.D., professor in the Department of Psychology, University of Illinois at Urbana-Champaign.

PURPOSE OF THEORY: To explain the motivations that underlie behaviors that are under volitional control; to predict diverse behaviors, including interpersonal, consumer, or political actions; and to identify strategies for affecting such behaviors (see Ajzen, 1991; Brown, 1999; Fishbein & Ajzen, 1975).

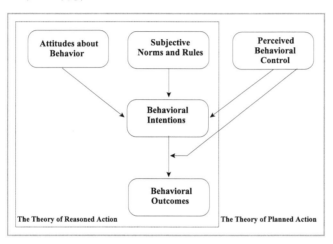

KEY PROPOSITIONS

- The most important determinants of behavior are people's intentions; the stronger the intentions are, the more effective the behavior will be in achieving valued goals. However, the longer the time between the intention and the behavior, the greater is the probability that unforeseen events will alter the intended behavior.
- Intentions are formed primarily by people's attitudes about the positive or negative consequences of the envisioned behavior.
- Intentions are also a function of subjective norms in that people are likely to perform behaviors that significant others approve of and to avoid behaviors that they disapprove of.
- The theory of planned action extends the original theory of rational action to situations that are not fully under volitional control. The essential idea is that intentions are also determined by the degree of control that a person perceives in the anticipated action, and this

THEORY EXAMPLE 3.1 (CONTINUED)

is a function of the degree of perceived opportunities, resources, and capabilities (i.e., internal, psychological factors and external conditions).

CENTRAL CONCEPTS

- **Behavior:** The implementation of intentions in actions
- **Behavioral intention:** The extent of effort that an individual is willing to expend to undertake a behavior
- **Attitude:** The way that a person perceives a possible behavior as a means for accomplishing some valued end
- **Subjective norm:** Perceptions of the social acceptability of an envisioned behavior, heavily influenced by the approval or disapproval of significant others
- **Perceived behavioral control:** An individual's beliefs about the feasibility of the envisioned action, usually a function of an assessment of motivations, opportunities, capacities, and other resources

LIMITATIONS OF THEORY: The theory heavily relies on assumptions that behavior is a function of rational, utilitarian calculations of costs and benefits, and it minimizes unconscious and transrational motivations, including altruism. It is applied primarily to the behavior of individuals and is of less value in understanding the behavior of groups or situations in which multiple actors hold divergent attitudes, values, subjective norms, and assessments of behavioral control. Also, the theory pays minimal attention to environmental and demographic influences on the formation of behavioral intentions.

Finally, there is the problem of history. Are history and life "just one damned thing after another"? This was reputed to be Winston Churchill's characterization of history, inferring the ceaseless succession of unique events that history appears to be and that seems to defeat any attempt achieve a general theoretical understanding.[†] What if the asteroid 65 million years ago missed Earth and failed to wipe out the dinosaurs? Would we be around to theorize about it? Many believe that, had the dinosaurs not become extinct, our mammalian progenitors would have continued to be food for the dinosaurs and would have failed to evolve into what we are

---

[†] Variations of this saying have been variously attributed to several other historical personalities, including Elbert Hubbard, Frank O'Malley, and Mark Twain. Its original source is debatable.

today (Gould, 1989). And what if the bullet had missed Archduke Francis Ferdinand—would the First World War have occurred? History, whether concerning nations or individuals, is the aggregate effect not only of the predictable needs, crises, and psychosocial processes that can be theoretically modeled but also of those chance events—encounters, accidents, lottery winnings—and personal choices that we and others make. Some would even throw another monkey wrench into the works—spiritual grace and intervention—but we need not pursue this matter here.

Considering both the epistemological problems of our limited ability to know, as discussed earlier (e.g., relativity, quantum theory), and the problems of chance, free will, and history, it is perhaps not surprising that there have been so many different approaches to the use of theory, as well as so many people who simply give up attempts to develop any general understanding of human needs and ways to address those needs and instead rely exclusively on some comfortable combination of common sense, intuition, and habitual modes of thought and action.

3. NEW DIRECTIONS

One thing that hardened empiricists, phenomenologists, and many practitioners have in common is the view that, although theory may be a good thing, it is usually something that must wait for additional observations. Those who subscribe to this view consider theory a type of add-on, an eventual outcome of data collection and observation that has few immediate consequences, that is, the caboose on the knowledge-building train. In contrast, the prevailing view holds that theory—broadly conceived—is the starting point, the engine that drives both knowledge development and professional practice. Popper recommends that we begin with our best understanding of a phenomenon—whether a formal theory (if available) or simply some hypotheses and speculations—and then attempt to falsify them through both critical analyses and experiment. If we are unable to do so, we provisionally use them as the best available theory. But, as significant as Popper's problem-solving method is, there are many problems identified in the foregoing review that the method does not solve. For this reason, there is a dire need to broaden our understanding of both theory and the process of theorizing. Although most of this section has focused on the problems and limitations inherent in what is a decidedly precarious process of knowledge building, the following list focuses instead on some of the possibilities:

Broadening of Types of Theory and Methods Used: Theories need to address problems that a diversity of constituencies identify, such as the funders and overseers of human services, but also problems that any one group identifies, such as practitioners, clients, and their significant others. Although some theories seek to explain universal patterns, it is sufficient that most theories instead focus on particular problems, groups, or even a single client. A worker's psychosocial assessment should contain his or her theory, developed collaboratively with the family, of the problems that the client faces and should draw on elements of various formal theories of families and related systems.

Broadening of the Sources of Experience and Data: Although formal theories often call for standardized testing methods to collect observational data, these should be complemented with a variety of other sources of data, including self-reports, participants' observational experiences, focus groups, and the like. Especially in the formative stages of theory development, the collection of information on people's intuitions, beliefs, hunches, and general impressions can provide a rich source of informal theories that can then be used to guide more formal approaches to knowledge development.

Broadening of the Types of Causes Considered: Most theorists prefer to focus on fairly immediate causes, often the efficient cause of a phenomenon. However, there are several lines along which the types of causes should be broadened. Very important is the consideration of other types of causes as identified by Aristotle: material, formal, and final. Of particular importance are final causes, or the goals, purposes, or reasons that motivate many actions, some of which may be conscious and others of which may be preconscious or unconscious. A distinction between types of causes involves the difference between originating and sustaining causes (Cowan & Rizzo, 1996). A crisis that initiated some interpersonal conflict may be very different from the factors that sustain it. While most people understand that many phenomena of interest have multiple interacting causes, fewer theorists understand the breadth of possible causes.

Broadening of Knowledge Development: One of the most significant contributions to our understanding of knowledge development is Popper's theory of evolutionary epistemology, which places knowledge in an evolutionary context. Yet the theory suffers from some of the same limitations of Darwinian and neo-Darwinian theories of evolution, in that it is overly reliant on competition and natural selection as the driving forces of change. Certainly theories of competition and selection of the fittest are important dynamics, but also important to an understanding of the evolution of both biological and knowledge systems is the notion of self-organization, as theorists such as Stuart Kauffman (1990) and Ilya Prigogine (1997) have so effectively argued. Self-organization refers to the spontaneous development of order, often through cumulative effect of the rules governing local interactions (C. G. Hudson, 2000b).

Just as biological evolution is multilevel and multilinear, characterized by multiple and simultaneous lines of development (including occasional devolution), knowledge building is also characterized by multiple lines of advancement, some of which reach dead ends. This wide diversity of biological and social developments has led many to question the existence of any great chain of being that involves progressively higher forms of evolution (Gould, 1989). Nonetheless, it is proposed here that knowledge development includes the following levels of comprehension. First, at the most basic level are data, which typically are the accumulation of various signs and symbols—whether numbers, letters, graphic symbols, or information expressed through other media—that are intended to record or communicate information. Second, however, data do not become useful information until they are decoded and defined. For example, a matrix of numbers comprises data, but when the rows and columns are labeled, and other definitional and contextual explanations are added, the matrix then becomes a comprehensible table of information. Third, in contrast, knowledge typically involves supported conclusions about relationships—causes and effects and their various specifications—among various concepts. Using the example of the matrix, the overall pattern of relationships between the row and column variables may be summarized in a formula or in a single sentence as a proposition that relates some concepts (e.g., "Marital therapy results in better communication skills than does individual psychotherapy"). Fourth, just as knowledge includes and builds on data and information, understanding builds on knowledge but goes beyond it. Understanding not only is more inclusive than single propositions, usually building on a system of propositions or a theory about a phenomenon, but also includes in many instances an empathic understanding and an integration of the knowledge with one's skills, or tacit knowledge. In short, understanding is a type of knowledge that is broader, more integrated, and even affectively deeper than the types of statements that are typically classified as cognitive knowledge. Simple theories, if they have held up to testing, constitute knowledge, but other more comprehensive theories make understanding possible. Finally, wisdom is understanding that is effectively integrated with

---

Exhibit 3.2: Level of Knowledge Building

1. **Data:** Collections of signs and symbols—whether numeric, alpha-numeric, graphic, or audiovisual—intended to represent ideas, feelings, or the external world.
2. **Information:** Data organized in a useful manner, including appropriate definition and context.
3. **Knowledge:** Information of a general summary nature, typically involving overall patterns, relationships, and causes and effects—and including some empirically supported theories of a basic level.
4. **Understanding:** Knowledge of both a general and a comprehensive nature that is integrated with related areas of knowledge, apprehended from several perspectives, involving such forms of intelligence as verbal, mathematical, interpersonal, or intrapersonal—and including some more fundamental and/or comprehensive theories.
5. **Wisdom:** Understanding that is integrated with and grounded by a person's ethical, philosophical, or spiritual values and perspectives.

---

an ethical, philosophical, or spiritual perspective (see exhibit 3.2). Not only do we understand someone's suffering or the struggles of some cultural group, but also we understand them in relation to certain core values and beliefs about life and the universe. Of course, what qualifies as wisdom is a matter of interpretation. However, there may be any number of external indicators, such as equanimity, wholeheartedness, contentment, or compassion that point toward such attainment.

III. The Role of Theory in Practice

For most of the human service professions practice is not a technology but an art, albeit one that is scientifically informed and evidence based. It is an art based on the best research and theory about what *is*—that is, on the nature, extent, causes, and consequences of the many different types of challenges, environments, and other conditions that clients face. But practice also addresses inherently value-based questions about what should be, and it draws on critical analysis of the just and ethical means to achieve such ends. Social science and other theories and research relevant to individual or social dynamics can provide invaluable information about what is or is not likely or possible, and thus can point toward certain choices regarding values or ethical principles. For instance, they can demonstrate the possibilities of overcoming divisive group differences and the feasibility of integrated social structures; ultimately, though, decisions to implement procedures that promote a given value are value-based choices that draw more from our basic assumptions, worldviews, philosophies, and spirituality than from any empirically based knowledge. When professionals make a decision, often in collaboration with clients, to work toward particular ends, then the results of theoretical and empirical knowledge are invaluable in identifying critical information about the nature of the problem at hand and what is the most effective means to achieve some desired outcome. The art involves the process of determining these ends and the unique manner or style in which a particular method or practice model is implemented. This will typically be in a manner that draws on a professional's conscious use of self, or the thoughtful use of his or her personal qualities—such as empathy, intuition, analytical skill, and emotional reactions—in tailoring the generic method to the particulars of the client's concerns.

A. A Metatheory of Practice

Chapter 14 outlines in greater detail an advanced generalist model of practice that bridges the underlying knowledge base of the various human services with day-to-day practice. Figure 3.3 previews a few of the multiple dimensions involved in this model. At its foundation is the interplay between knowledge building and value development. Instead of regarding knowledge and values as things—as discrete nouns—they are more accurately viewed as processes of living, breathing beings. More important than discrete values are the processes of clarifying and refining our values; specifying them; envisioning their realization; and consciously deciding to retain, modify, or change them. Ultimately, the most critical part of value development is value implementation. Many question whether a particular value—social justice, caring, mental health, money—means anything if it is merely a felt value rather than one that actively influences our behaviors, our devotion of efforts to promote its realization. The two lines in figure 3.4 connecting value development with knowledge building express the notion that the relationship between the processes is interactive: (1) the values we pursue influence the knowledge we decide to develop, and

FIGURE 3.3: AN OVERVIEW OF HUMAN SERVICES PRACTICE AND ITS FOUNDATIONS

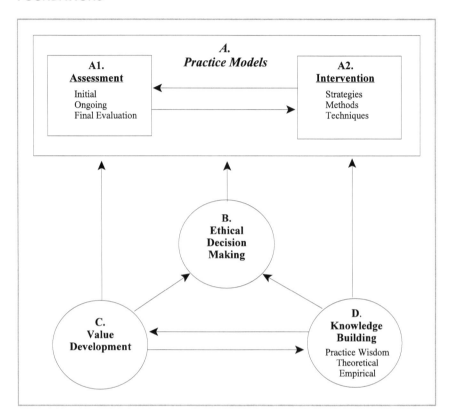

(2) the knowledge we acquire, especially when it involves defining what is or what is not possible, affects the values we decide to pursue and our vision of their eventual realization.

Whereas knowledge focuses on what *is* and values focus on what should be, processes of ethical decision making typically concern the movement from what is to what should be. In many cases, the decisions are so routine that we hardly think of them as involving ethical decision making. But increasing complexity and diversity are causing a wider variety of decisions to emerge as ethical dilemmas that require thought; study; consultation; and in short, an increasingly extensive and deliberative process. Institutional review boards, bioethical review committees, and ethical audits are a few of the means that have been developed to aid human service workers in making these decisions.

Value development, knowledge building, and ethical decision making are perhaps the three most critical processes that are the foundations of professional human service practice. Practice is a complex concept, referring to the implementation of not only the most formal and general intervention models and procedures (or protocols) but also a wide range of principles or heuristics, such as "Treatment begins the moment the client walks in the door" or "Monitor progress toward your goals" (see chapter 7). Many of these principles cut across both assessment and intervention, two of the core processes in most practice models, which often proceed concurrently. Assessment of the client (whether an individual or an organization) and relevant opportunities, abilities, and motivations is a task that often predominates at the beginning of a practice relationship and is the foundation for the interventions that follow. Just like the relationship between value development and knowledge building, the relationship between assessment and intervention is an interactive one. The ongoing outcomes of interventions provide invaluable information about the initial assessment, which is then modified on a continuing basis. While some professions, such as nursing, have fairly well-defined protocols and techniques of intervention, other professions, such as social work, historically have relied more on general strategies and methods, which are implemented using a few generic techniques.

The ongoing multiple interactions between assessment and intervention take place, consciously or unconsciously, in the context of the professional's efforts to develop his or her values and knowledge, and to make the most ethical decisions possible. It is within this context that the professional needs to constantly update his or her theoretical knowledge of human behavior and its relevant systems. Many have promoted an empirical model of practice that emphasizes the systematic incorporation of research results; recently, this has come to be referred to as "evidence-based practice" (Gambrill, 1999). This approach involves "integrating individual practice expertise with the best available external evidence from systematic research as well as considering the values and expectations of clients" (Gambrill, 2000, p. 46) and emphasizes the "search for the best available external, evidence related to the client's concerns and an estimate of the extent to which this applies to a particular client" (Poertner, 2001, p. 97). Information used in assessments is diverse, ranging from that derived from clinical observations and interviews, rapid assessment tests and surveys, and reviews of records to that from published databases, research journals, and theoretical reviews. Evaluation of this information, in this approach, is based not so much on attempt to confirm initial suspicions but instead on active efforts to disprove one's preferred theory. For this reason, the ability to assess theory, whether one's own or that of others, is of central importance in human service practice, and it is to this subject we now turn.

B. A Framework for the Critique of Theory

Because all theories are provisional, the assessment of any theory must take place within the context of established and alternative theories. Assessment is, thus, comparative. Any theory that generally improves on its best competition is the one that should be used. If it is superior in only some areas and inferior in others, then the question becomes one of whether the competing theories can be combined or whether one or the other can be revised to incorporate the best of each competing model. Another major consideration in evaluating any theory is the intent or goal of its proponents: Is it meant primarily to describe? To explain the causes or current dynamics of some problem or condition? Is it proposed as a means to predict the future or past functioning of some system? Is it meant to account for a fairly discrete condition, such as posttraumatic stress disorder or psychopathology or personality functioning generally? Of course, if someone proposes a theory involving a fairly specific phenomenon, such as the reasons why people go to the movies, but a theory already explains entertainment choices generally, then all else being equal, one would naturally opt for the more general theory. The assessment of theory within a comparative framework that takes into account the intent or goal of the proposed theory are two of the most critical crosscutting criteria that influence the consideration of the various specific criteria (see exhibit 3.3).

Although it would be simple enough to incorporate the criteria in exhibit 3.3 into a quantitative rating instrument, they are inherently qualitative criteria: some have more central importance, and others (e.g., parsimoniousness and elegance) have secondary relevance. The criteria emphasized are largely a function of the limitations of existing theories, the intent of the proposed theory, and the needs of its potential users.

C. Strategies for Using Theory

Although theory has a wide range of applications throughout the intervention process, from initial engagement to final evaluation, its most important use is in the assessment phase. Professionals may struggle to understand an individual client, a treatment group, a dysfunctional organization, or a community, and in this undertaking, they hear, observe, and otherwise collect a wide variety of information on facets of a client that may or may not be readily apparent. The use of theory in assessment is essentially a method of connecting the dots and determining what to ask about or observe. This is done by developing a case-specific theory or set of hypotheses about what the client systems struggle with, or how particular events,

Exhibit 3.3: Criteria for the Assessment of Theory

1. **Value base:** Is the theory, including its assumptions and implications, congruent with core human values, such as mutual support, free will, or social justice? Because some groups may not accept such values or have unusual interpretations of them, it is difficult to use these as absolute, make-or-break criteria. Rather, the analysis and explication of the fit of a theory with such core values should be considered a fundamental responsibility of users of theory in the human services.

2. **Relevance:** The relevance of theory goes beyond its congruence with core values to consider the actual or potential usefulness of the theory for accomplishing the many activities and ends involved in a field such as the human services, including general understanding of diverse populations and the facilitation of helping relationships.

3. **Comprehensiveness:** Does the theory apply to a wide range of phenomena, or does it focus merely a single problem or condition, forcing its users to draw on an unnecessarily wide variety of theories for their many needs? Does it attempt to accomplish too much or too little?

4. **Clarity:** Is the theory easily comprehensible and communicable both orally and in writing? Are its definitions, key relationships, propositions, and predictions clearly explained? Can they be explained with sufficient specificity to permit the theory to be tested and used? Are the relationships sufficiently specified, with respect to both their direction and their form?

5. **Reasonableness:** Are the theory's assumptions kept to a minimum, and are they truly self-evident or generally acceptable? If the theory's predictions are counterintuitive, are the steps that go into deriving them reasonable? If the theory predicts the obvious, then it may not be very useful, but if its predictions go against common sense, then the foundations of the predictions must be solidly defensible.

6. **Coherence:** Is the theory internally consistent? Or is it so inconsistent or vague that it can be used to justify opposing conclusions or predictions? Many theories suffer from a lack of logical independence between presumed causes and effects. Does the definition of a cause logically entail a given effect? For example, if one defines empathy as the ability to be aware of another's state of mind, and then predicts that as empathy increases, the

EXHIBIT 3.3 (CONTINUED)

ability to understand others likewise increases, then one is restating the obvious and adding little to knowledge.

7. **Parsimoniousness:** This involves explaining the most effects with the fewest possible assumptions, initial conditions, and causes. Einstein's $E = Mc^2$ is a classic example involving an exact specification of the convertibility of matter and energy, with only five symbols. But Einstein also said that, while it is important to keep things simple, they can not be any simpler than necessary for the desired explanation. Most theories in the social sciences are more complicated or cannot be mathematically expressed in a formula. The elegance of a theory is related to parsimoniousness. Temporarily lacking empirical data, one may opt for a theory that satisfies a sense of elegance or intellectual beauty.

8. **Empirical basis:** While theories can be proposed without an empirical basis, any theory worth its salt needs to have some of its propositions or predictions supported by, or at least consistent with, evidence that has been collected through systematic, scientific means. There are usually important parts of theories that are not empirically supported. In fact, an advantage of theory is that it permits us to extrapolate or predict phenomenon beyond immediately known facts. The critical question is, of course, has the theory been falsified? Has it withstood repeated attempts at its disconfirmation? How adequate have the tests been?

9. **Explanatory ability:** Does the theory go beyond simply explaining effects in terms of various causes to provide a plausible and even accurate account of the specific means or dynamics of influence? In the social sciences and human services, this often involves identifying multiple sources of causation, including— immediate or efficient causes—and underlying causes involving purposes and plans.

10. **Predictive ability:** Can the theory be used to generate testable, accurate, and useful predictions? Predictions involve not only future phenomena but also current or past conditions. For example, Hudson (1998) proposed an interdependency theory of homelessness to predict the numbers of homeless people in U.S. counties, and the results were then successfully compared with independent surveys of homeless populations. Others have used various theories to "postdict" various social or historical conditions of past eras.

11. **Usefulness:** While understanding is inherently useful, the human services place a premium on the ability of a theory to improve

> **EXHIBIT 3.3 (CONTINUED)**
>
> people's lives by being able to identify the sources of problems
> and predict which interventions will provide the most help with
> the least trouble. Thus, if a theory helps people avoid ineffective
> treatments, improves the ability to target resources to where the
> problems are the greatest, or identifies when they are able to
> continue to progress without professional help, then it has dem-
> onstrated its usefulness.
>
> 12. **Heuristic value:** Does the theory suggest new lines of inquiry
>   or generate new research and theory? Although the theory may
>   not, in itself, provide convincing explanations, does it success-
>   fully suggest questions for the practitioner to ask that success-
>   fully lead to useful theories?

traumas, choices, personality patterns, policies, and community trends have come together to produce the anguish, dysfunction, or other concern requiring intervention. Most theories are collections of statements about a wide variety of things—from A to Z—that might transpire and consequences that might follow. The application of theory in the assessment process typically puts aside much of the abstract language and says that, in this particular situation, it is primarily P and Q, or perhaps Y and Z.

Any theory worth its salt will help practitioners identify manipulable variables, or conditions that can be practically changed. A theory may help a therapist recognize that, although a bygone traumatic event cannot be changed, there are current beliefs, attitudes, and feelings about the event that treatment can affect. Practitioners sacrifice the generality of the formal theory to develop a formulation that is specific to the client in the context of relevant environments, one that is increasingly precise and useful. Typically the theory is applied to a single individual, group, organization, or community and may not be immediately testable through formal social scientific methods. However, the theory is constantly fine-tuned as additional evidence is accumulated, and the results of its use are observed in interventions. In most situations, this developing understanding is a collaborative one with the client, not merely something that happens in the privacy of the practitioner's mind.

When practitioners identify conditions in their clients or environments that are likely candidates for change—whether attitudes, dysfunctional interactional patterns, community power structures, or oppressive social policies—the focus then shifts to the use of relevant practice theories and methods. Theories of community organization, family therapy, or behavioral desensitization are then drawn on to select from both possible goals and the means to achieve those goals. These may be comprehensive theories, specific procedures, or particular practice principles that may or may not be embedded in a larger practice theory. For example, community organizers seeking to alter dysfunctional power structures have been advised to first consider collaborative strategies; if these don't work, then campaign strategies; and as a last resort, methods involving contest and confrontation. Thus, as one moves from a primary concern with assessment to intervention planning, one shifts from theories involving individual or social problems to associated theories of practice, however formal and comprehensive or informal and focused they may be.

Throughout this process, theory is used merely as one aid to understanding, one that complements and grows out of fundamental human processes of listening, observing, sharing, and responding. While an important function involves letting all the abstractions fall by the wayside and entering directly into the immediacy of the current experience, an equally important function involves the need to periodically step back to develop a general perspective, one that is independent of the demands impinging on the professional.

A story has been told of Greek octopus fishermen. These men work in pairs. When one spots an octopus from a boat, the partner dives into the creature and lets it catch him. His partner, in turn, from the safety of the boat, then pulls him out by his feet and, in the process, pulls up the octopus. In the same way, as professionals let go of the safety of theory and react in an immediate fashion to a client's difficulties, they may successfully engage the client, but they often lose perspective. The professional's partner—or his or her own observing and theorizing alter ego—in turn steps back to develop a general understanding of the situation, thereby bringing to light hidden and dysfunctional patterns. This ability is developed only as professionals gain experience, emotional maturity, and self-awareness. Although the metaphor can be used most easily to understand how cotherapists work with families, with some imagination it applies to a wide variety of problems, contexts, and involved professionals.

D. Practice Wisdom as an Integrative Strategy

Currently there is considerable debate about the role of knowledge development and application in the helping process. Most commentators emphasize the centrality of both knowledge development and its systematic application. Nonetheless, debate has come to focus on the types of knowledge that can legitimately be called on; whether these should be limited to formal theory and research; and whether they should be extended to include forms of personal, tacit, or intuitive forms of knowing. Similarly, there is considerable debate about the acceptable methods of knowledge development, to what extent these should include qualitative methodologies, and the responsibilities for frontline practitioners to contribute to this process.

A central theme of this chapter has been that we need to draw on a wide variety of knowledge sources, both intellectual and tacit, and that theory plays a central role in integrating diverse sources of knowledge and serves as a stepping-stone to deeper and more comprehensive forms of knowledge, commonly referred to as "understanding" and "wisdom." This position is not dissimilar to what others advocate. For instance, Klein and Bloom (1995) comment, "Practice wisdom is reconceptualized as an integrating vehicle for combining the strengths and minimizing the limitations of both the 'objective' or empirical, practice model, and the 'subjective' or intuitive-phenomenological, practice model in the development of efficacious knowledge in social work" (p. 799). They go on to suggest that practice wisdom fulfills four roles in empirically based practice: (1) it fills in when knowledge is missing from formal research, (2) it serves as a means for the ongoing evaluation of one's practice, (3) it provides information for use in practice, and (4) it supports the emergence of new theories.

But what exactly is practice wisdom? Earlier it was mentioned that practice wisdom is typically understood as consisting of that body of rules, practice principles, and tacit knowledge that a profession implicitly accepts as its foundational knowledge; often it is not written down, but rather passed informally from one generation of practitioners to the next. Donald A. Schon (1983) argues that it consists of the combination of both knowing-in-action and reflection-in-action. Knowing-in-action consists of all those internalized or tacit practice principles that practitioners use but often cannot articulate. In contrast, reflection-in-action consists of the ongoing "conscious evaluation of action during the course of action" (Schon, 1980, as cited in DeRoos, 1990, p. 283). He maintains, "Practice wisdom is truly meaningful only at this second level of knowing. If knowing-in-action refers to our practice habits, reflecting-in-action refers to our ability to recognize the uniqueness of each situation and to adjust our problem solving action accordingly" (Schon, 1980, as cited in DeRoos, 1990, p. 284).

It is easy to take a jaundiced view of practice wisdom. Many consider it haphazard and disorganized (DeRoos, 1990) or of questionable validity (D. Scott, 1990). A few others have conducted research that suggests that its "usefulness may exceed its reputation" (Zeira & Rosen, 2000, p. 119; see also Carew, 1979). This chapter points out that practice wisdom is integrative and builds on descriptive information on clients and their environments, theoretical and empirical knowledge of causal relationships, and an understanding of their larger context and their ethical and value dimensions. In addition, the foregoing are integrated with practitioners' philosophical, existential, and spiritual understanding of life and its purposes, which, one would hope, engenders a sense of perspective and meaning, justice, and compassion. Unlike information or theoretical knowledge that can, to an extent, be objectively tested, the validity of practitioners' understanding and practice wisdom is strictly a matter of interpretation but nonetheless is able to be expressed through public actions that can be assessed for their consistency with values held in common by a profession and in society.

IV. Summary

This chapter has reviewed the role of knowledge generally and theory specifically in the actions of human service professionals. It began by discussing the context of knowledge building in the human services, pointing out that it is an integral part of the very notion of professionalism. Most professions have identifiable knowledge bases, though these may overlap. Essential components of the knowledge base of a profession include empirical knowledge, practice wisdom, theoretical knowledge, and procedural knowledge. Although many professionals avoid the use of theory, in its broad sense, theory is unavoidable and, in fact, essential. Theory is defined here as the formal and informal conceptual frameworks with which we organize our beliefs and knowledge in a communicable, testable, and potentially useful manner.

The chapter discussed the development of epistemology, or theories of knowledge, as an essential context for human service practice. A theme that cuts through most of this development is the debate between proponents of the correspondence theory of truth (i.e., truth needs to mirror external reality) and the coherence theory (i.e., truth needs to be consistent within itself or in relation to certain self-evident truths), as well as recurrent efforts to reconcile these positions. That section concluded with a review of Karl Popper's approach to knowledge development as a problem-solving process involving the attempt to falsify the best current theories, one that takes place in an evolutionary context. The chapter critiqued this promising approach as minimizing alternative or transpersonal ways of knowing and of being subject to some of the same limitations as evolutionary theory. It also discussed the notions of chance, free will, and history as three fundamental challenges to efforts involving theoretical understanding. It suggests that, despite the difficulties, theoretical understanding has an essential role in the development of knowledge, understanding, and even wisdom.

The final section applied the foregoing review to an understanding of practice. After previewing a model of practice as rooted in both theoretical empirical knowledge and ethical analysis, it presented a framework for the critique of theory. This framework always takes into account the intent or purpose of the theory, competing available theories, and the needs of potential users. The section then considered various levels of integration of theory with practice, strategies for its use in practice, and the notion of practice wisdom as a proposed way to bridge some of the divisions in the field.

For Further Reading

DeRoos, Y. S. (1990, June). The development of practice wisdom through human problem-solving processes. *Social Service Review, 64*(2), 276–287.

Gambrill, E. (1999). Evidence-based practice: An alternative to authority-based practice. *Families in Society: The Journal of Contemporary Human Services, 80*(4), 341–350.

Goldstein, H. (1999). The limits and art of understanding in social work practice. *Families in Society: The Journal of Contemporary Human Services, 80*(4), 385–395.

Gomory, T., & Thyer, B. (2001). Special point/counterpoint on the role of theory in research on social work practice. *Journal of Social Work Education, 37*(1), 9–66.

Kuhn, T. S. (1970). *The structure of scientific revolutions* (2nd ed.). Chicago: University of Chicago Press.

Lewis, H. (1982). *The intellectual base of social work practice.* New York: Haworth Press.

Polanyi, M. (1966). *The tacit dimension.* Garden City, NY: Doubleday.

Popper, K. (1990). *A world of propensities.* Bristol, U.K.: Thoemmes Antiquarian Books.

Robbins, S. R. (1999). Theory, knowledge, and social work practice: Ongoing debates and fresh perspectives. *Families in Society, 80*(4), 325–326.

Zeira, A., & Rosen, A. (2000, March). Unraveling "tacit knowledge": What social workers do and why they do it. *Social Service Review, 74*(1), 103–123.

PART II

The Person

CHAPTER 4

Recent Developments in the Study of Consciousness

The whole drift of my education goes to persuade me that the world of our present consciousness is only one out of many worlds of consciousness that exist.

—WILLIAM JAMES, 1902

I. Introduction

Systems, how they change, and the ways that knowledge is developed about them are of great importance in comprehending human behavior. However, this understanding is of limited value if we neglect the pivotal reality of the individual person, his or her development and functioning, and especially consciousness within larger social and cultural systems. What does it mean for us to claim to be aware, sentient beings, endowed with a sense of our existence, with the seeming ability to make choices? More than a century of work in the cognitive and social sciences has done much to clarify how the mind functions—how we see, remember things, and make decisions—yet there has been scant progress on the so-called hard problem of consciousness:

> that of giving an intelligible account of why experience exists at all, and also of why it is found in intimate association with individual physical systems such as the nervous systems of human beings and other sentient creatures. Why should a physical system, no matter how complex and well-organized, give rise to experience at all? Why is it that all this processing does not go on "in the dark," without any subjective quality? The hard problem as articulated above is that of how colourless, soundless, feelingless spatio-temporal structures could ever generate our consciousness with the qualia that fill them so richly. (Shear, 1994, p. 54; see also Chalmers, 1995a)

This chapter reviews recent developments in the study of consciousness in the context of the long-term struggle with the mind-body problem, especially the hard problem. It concludes with a discussion of the prospects for a truly integrated theory of consciousness, one that includes its biological, psychological, and phenomenological dimensions. The particular understanding of consciousness that is adopted has a profound impact on how one understands the sources of human development and motivation, strategies of problem solving and decision making, and—when these fail—some of the key sources of psychopathology. To the extent that motivation arises out of and is an expression of the nature of the underlying consciousness, strategies of change cannot simply rely on external behavioral or social modifications; they also need to facilitate underlying changes in the consciousness of the individuals or groups of concern.

A. The Emergence of Consciousness Studies

Since the early 1990s there has been an explosion of interest in the study of consciousness. An estimated thirty thousand articles and books were written on consciousness from 1992 to 2002, but fewer than 1 percent of these have attempted to elucidate the hard problem (Carter, 2002). There is much speculation about the source of this newfound interest. For many decades, because of the impact of behaviorism, functionalism, and the earlier generations of cognitive science, consciousness was a taboo subject, something no self-respecting psychologist or social scientist would risk broaching. Given this neglect and pent-up demand, many researchers started entering the field in the late 1980s and early 1990s, perhaps because of the holistic focus of the new sciences on complexity and an emerging interest in bridging the biological and social sciences. The director of the National Institute of Mental Health coined the 1990s the Decade of the Brain, as it featured dramatically expanded brain-imaging capabilities, such as functional magnetic resonance imaging (fMRI). These capabilities led to a new optimism that it might be possible to identify the neurological correlates of consciousness (NCCs).

The various fields involved in consciousness studies range from neurophysiology to philosophy and linguistics, and they can be placed into four primary groups (see Wilber, 1995):

- Psychological and phenomenological approaches consist of introspectionism and phenomenology, social psychology, and developmental psychology.
- Cognitive science has come to include such specialties as neuropsychology, neuroscience, artificial intelligence, linguistics, and the philosophy of mind. It is based on an understanding of mental representations or maps, which may be either conscious or unconscious and mediate between psychological and brain functioning.
- Clinical approaches attempt to apply theories and research derived from the foregoing areas to practice, including the application of data derived from clinical practice to consciousness research. These areas include individual psychotherapy, clinical psychiatry, and psychosomatic medicine.
- Alternative approaches include the study of nonordinary states of consciousness, such as dreams, near-death, and psychedelic experiences. Such studies sometimes draw on Eastern and other mystical traditions. Included here are those interested in research on various subtle energies (generally considered a fringe area). Perhaps

one of the most promising of the alternative lines of research and theory involves the application of quantum theory to the study of consciousness.

B. Key Positions in the Philosophy of Mind

Given the various professions that are involved in the study of consciousness, as well as the diverse philosophical positions with which researchers have approached the subject, it is not surprising that there has been so little agreement on the fundamental problems of consciousness (see exhibit 4.1). Although consciousness itself is a fairly modern concern, the philosophy of mind dates back to the ancient Greeks. The pivotal issue in the philosophy of mind has consistently been the mind-body problem, and competing ontologies, or beliefs about the nature of reality, have mostly driven the debate. Are there one, two, or many separately existing substances or realities? Is this matter and energy? Is it mind, information, or consciousness—or God? If there are multiple realities, how do they interact, if at all? There have been two primary perspectives—dualism and monism—along with several variations of each. Plato, who advanced the notion of a world of ideal forms that is distinct from the outer world of shadows and appearances, is often regarded as the first dualist. In contrast, Aristotle was one of the first monists who believed that both mind and matter arose from a single underlying substance (Eliasmith, 1998). For close to two thousand years, debate on the mind-body problem largely took place on a philosophical level, as little data could be brought to bear on the problem. Thomas Nagel (1974) lamented, "Without consciousness the mind-body problem would be much less interesting. With consciousness it seems hopeless" (p. 166).

Dualism assumes that both matter and mind are primary and coexisting realities, neither reducible nor explainable one in terms of the other. Gottfried Wilhelm Leibniz (b. 1646–d. 1716) proposed parallelism, a classical and rather extreme form of dualism that suggested that the two realms never interact but rather operate independently in parallel dimensions. Although this eliminates the problem of having to explain how something material can interact with something immaterial, parallelism created so many new problems that few take it seriously. The most popular form of dualism is interactionism, which suggests that somehow mind and matter are constantly influencing each other. Although this is intuitively plausible for many, materialists argue that even if mind were to exist, it would violate the law of the conservation of matter and energy to suppose that an immaterial mind or soul might influence physical reality. Another less common but emerging position, proto-panpsychism, suggests that consciousness and

EXHIBIT 4.1: KEY POSITIONS ON THE MIND-BODY PROBLEM

I. **Dualism:** The idea that there are two fundamental realities in the universe—matter and/or energy and mind or consciousness. There are two positions that can be schematically represented:

A. **Parallelism:** the notion that the two realms operate independently but parallel to each other, thereby creating the appearance that they interact.

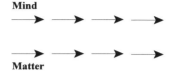

B. **Interactionism:** the theory that mind and matter constantly influence each other and proceed on the basis of their own inner logic.

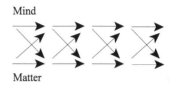

II. **Monism:** The notion that there is a single underlying reality out of which everything else is built or emerges from.

A. **Materialism and related theories** (e.g., eliminative materialism): Everything is ultimately reducible or explainable in terms of material reality.

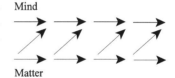

B. **Monistic idealism:** Physical reality, ultimately, is a manifestation of a universal mind or consciousness.

C. **Protopanpsychism:** This refers to the belief that an incipient form of consciousness is ubiquitous through the universe. One version of this view suggests that there is a single underlying reality, such as information, of which mind and matter are manifestations.

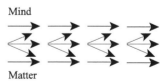

Notes: The schematics represent the passage of time from left to right. Arrows represent causal influences. Solid lines reflect actual, real, or fundamental realities and influences; dashed lines indicate only apparent or illusory lines of causation.

physical reality both exist, and that mind is a fundamental characteristic of physical reality and emerges from it. The idea is that consciousness pervades the universe but typically is found in only an incipient, latent, or rudimentary (proto) form (see Chalmers, 1996).

Monism, in contrast, assumes that there is a single, underlying substance or reality that constitutes all of the phenomenal world. Everything—matter, energy, mind, consciousness—consists of this primal stuff. At one end of the monistic spectrum are materialists who believe that ultimately only matter and energy can be said to be real. All else is a derivation of physical processes. One school of materialists—physical epiphenomenalists—believe that consciousness is really only a brain process, the apparent residue or secretion of some type of neural activity that cannot possibly have any influence on those processes or on any other physical realities. A less extreme form of materialism is represented by those weak emergentists and functionalists who believe that consciousness is an emergent quality of physical brain processes but is not fully explainable by them.

At the other end of the spectrum are those who subscribe to monistic idealism, or the idea that physical reality is an outgrowth or reflection of a single underlying reality involving consciousness, the mind of God, or some other notion of an ultimate reality. This is an ancient idea that is central to many spiritual traditions; however, in philosophy it is most commonly associated with George Berkeley (b. 1685–d. 1753). The quantum physicist Amitai Goswami (1995) presents a contemporary version of this philosophy in his book *The Self-Aware Universe.* What might be characterized as a compromise position, a type of simple monism, proposes that both matter and consciousness are different forms or views of one underlying reality. The philosopher David Chalmers (1996) suggests that this may be information. Others, such as David Bohm (1996), hypothesize that the difference is merely one of viewpoint. Finally, there are the so-called mysterians, who believe that consciousness, and consequently its relationship with physical reality, is unknowable—that as humans we lack the mental capabilities required for this task in the same way that a dog is unable to understand calculus.

One position on the mind-body problem that does not fit neatly into the continuum of monism and dualism is functionalism. Functionalists may either say that they do not know what is more primary or sometimes take a position. What they are most interested in are questions about the functions—biological, psychological, or social—that various mental capabilities perform for individuals. Through what processes are inputs converted into outputs for particular mental capabilities, such as perception, memory, and decision making? What role do these processes play in the larger system? The reality of mental functioning lies in how the parts fit into the overall pattern, not in the substance or medium that it takes place in. Some proponents of artificial intelligence—the hard AI school—propose an extreme variation of functionalism. They believe that it makes no difference whether a mental system is implemented in a living brain, silicon chip, or any other medium. Because a computer program can be represented in diverse media—on a disk, in a memory chip, in a book, or even on a piece of toilet paper—they suggest that consciousness may not be much different: the reality is in the informational pattern and its transformation or functioning, not in any particular substance. Although many functionalists profess a kind of agnosticism when it comes to the mind-body problem, others are overtly materialistic, and only a few could be characterized as monistic idealists.

The philosopher John Searle (1980) attacked functionalism by asking one to imagine someone locked in a room with no knowledge of Chinese but equipped with a codebook. Questions in Chinese would be passed into the room, and the subject would look up Chinese answers in the codebook to these questions, and then pass them back out, with no understanding whatsoever of what the questions or answers were. Functionalists, especially those of the hard AI school, try to argue that this Chinese room—as a whole—is conscious in some sense, even though the individual subject has no understanding of what he or she is saying, but Searle suggests that the individual and his or her Chinese room is the equivalent of an unconscious zombie or automaton. He suggests that a system—the Chinese room or a zombie—may have the inputs and outputs of what looks identical to a conscious state, but that such functional equivalence does not constitute consciousness.

These positions on the mind-body problem are unproven hypotheses for which there is mixed evidence. Francis Crick (1994), in his provocative book *The Astonishing Hypothesis,* takes this stance, preferring a strictly materialistic hypothesis: "The Astonishing Hypothesis is that 'You,' your joys and your sorrows, your memories and your ambitious, your sense of personal identity and free will, are in fact no more than the behavior of a vast assembly of nerve cells and their associated molecules" (p. 3). Concepts such as mind and consciousness, as well as matter and energy, are all reifications of diverse and fragmentary sources of experience and evidence of whatever it is that constitutes reality. The representation that we construct probably has an imperfect relationship with the world as it is. Thus, although it makes sense to take a position on such issues, it is critical that we treat this as mere hypothesis. Otherwise, we are liable to become blinded to an increasingly rich body of empirical and experiential evidence. The problem that we confront is reconciling the apparent reality of the physical world, specifically our bodies and brains, with the apparent reality of our thoughts, feelings, and consciousness, and with the common impression that these somehow influence one another.

C. Historical Background

A lack of clarity in terms such as *mind* and *consciousness* has often complicated the mind-body problem. Whereas mind is an ancient concept that has typically referred to a wide range of capabilities involving thought, feeling, decision making, planning, and the like, consciousness is a more recent concept, much more ambiguous and constantly changing. Its many meanings will be explored at greater length subsequently, but here it is sufficient to note that the word *consciousness* first appeared in the English language in 1632. According to Antonio Damasio (1999), the term comes from the word *conscience,* which was blended with *inwit,* which means "interior" or "mind" and with the prefix *con-,* which means "gathering" or "coming together." Thus, *consciousness* originally connoted the coming together of knowledge for moral self-reflection. But as culture and language have evolved, more mental functions have been separated out of the terminology of consciousness. Some contemporary languages still do not distinguish between consciousness and conscience, or among other mental functions.

At about the same time that the term *consciousness* appeared in the English language, the philosopher René Descartes (b. 1596–d. 1650) popularized the notion of a mind-body dualism. Descartes (1640/1996) declared, "Cogito, ergo sum," which is translated as, "I think, therefore I am" (p. 68). He arrived at this through his method of hyperbolic doubt, of doubting everything until there is nothing left to doubt. He concluded that only the fact of doubting, or of thinking and being conscious, cannot be doubted. Then, on the basis of this foundational truth, he attempted to build knowledge back up. He concluded that the mind is fundamentally immaterial and distinct from the brain, and merely functions through it. He went so far as to propose that the soul perceives the world through the pineal gland, as an observer that has been characterized as a kind of little man or homunculus in the brain, observing the world through the Cartesian theater. Among its various problems, this theory displaces the question of the origins and functions of consciousness in the brain to that of the homunculus, creating a problem of potentially infinite regress (Dennett, 1991). An unfortunate effect of Descartes' dualism is that it mystifies mind and consciousness, causing many to reject the notions altogether and others to claim that these are beyond the realm of rational investigation and discourse.

Although he was not the first, the most influential of the early psychologists in the study of consciousness was William James, who considered consciousness a central concern of psychology (see profile 4.1). He is best known for his notion of stream of consciousness: "The first and foremost concrete fact which every one will affirm to belong to his inner experience is the fact that consciousness of some sort goes on. 'States of mind' succeed each other in him. If we could say in English 'it thinks,' as we say 'it rains' or 'it blows,' we should be stating the fact most simply and with the minimum of assumption. As we cannot, we must simply say that thought goes on" (1892, p. 152).

James went on to identify four essential characteristics of consciousness: (1) every state is a part of a personal consciousness, (2) the states are constantly changing, (3) yet are perceived as continuous, and (4) they display intention in generating a focus of attention and a resulting periphery. In 1904 James scandalized psychology in the provocatively titled article "Does 'Consciousness' Exist?" In that piece, he argued that consciousness does not exist as an independent entity but only as a function of the flow of particular experiences; that consciousness and its object must always be considered simultaneously. His work established not only the foundations of pragmatic psychology but also the foundations of introspectionism and phenomenology. James's best-known application of his phenomenological approach to consciousness was his 1902 book *The Varieties of Religious Experience.*

At about the same time, Sigmund Freud (b. 1856–d. 1939) launched the psychoanalytic movement, focusing primarily on the origins of psychological conflict and the nature of mental functioning. Freud's theory of consciousness (see Solms, 1997) has never been clearly defined. He regarded consciousness as a kind of internal organ for the viewing of selected mental functions. Thus, some have characterized his theory as a spotlight theory of consciousness. Freud considered consciousness as representing the subjective side of brain functioning, his so-called omega processes. He proposed that the mind consisted of three types of processes: (1) phi, which involves sensation; (2) psi, which is responsible for memory; and (3) omega, which is responsible for integrating these in consciousness (Freud, 1895). Freud is also known for his topological theory of consciousness, which divides mental functioning into conscious (Cs), preconscious (Pcs), and unconscious systems (Ucs). On the whole, Freud deemphasized the role of consciousness and viewed it as largely determined by unconscious mental processes. In this respect, he was a functionalist, and one who avoided tackling the hard problem head-on, equivocating among dualism, physical epiphenomenalism, and other positions on the mind-body problem.

In the early twentieth century, the field of psychology rejected James's introspectionism and Freud's analytic efforts in an effort to establish itself as a scientific discipline. This hiatus in work on consciousness happened under

Profile 4.1: William James, 1842–1910

William James grew up in an affluent and cosmopolitan New York family. His father, Henry Sr., was a deeply religious man with wide interests in philosophy and the humanities, devoted to providing the best conceivable upbringing for his five children. In addition to William, the family included the renowned novelist Henry and their sister Mary, also a writer. Henry Sr. spared no expense in employing the best tutors and in sending his children to elite finishing schools in the United States and Europe. The James household saw regular visits from the likes of Henry Thoreau, Ralph Waldo Emerson, Nathaniel Hawthorne, and J. S. Mills. As a teenager, James was interested in studying painting, but despite the reluctant support of his father, he eventually decided not to pursue it as a career. At the start of the Civil War, he entered the Lawrence Scientific School at Harvard University. He and Henry succeeded in avoiding the draft at that time, pleading a range of maladies, including, on William's part, neurasthenia and depression.

Because the family fortune had diminished, William reluctantly decided to take up medicine, and he finished his graduate studies at the Harvard Medical School at the age of twenty-seven. He also had toyed with the idea of pursuing botany and accompanied Louis Agassiz, the renowned naturalist, on an expedition to the Amazon.

For the first three years after school, William lived at home as he fought bouts of depression and thoughts of suicide. His emergence from that period coincided with struggles with basic philosophical issues, especially that of free will. He concluded that biology did not absolutely determine life and that free will existed: "My first act of free will shall be to believe in free will." Shortly thereafter, William's neighbor and former instructor, and the president of Harvard, offered him a job as an instructor of physiology. William would spend the remainder of his career at Harvard, proving himself as an inspiring teaching and prodigious writer, loved and respected by students and colleagues. He was Harvard's first psychology professor and also taught philosophy. At the age of thirty-seven, William married Alice Gibbens, introduced to him by his father. William warned her about his mental condition, but that did not dampen her commitment.

William James's contributions were extensive and profound. At the age of forty-eight, he published the first psychology textbook, *The Principles of Psychology,* which was, despite its literary character, well received. The

PROFILE 4.1 (CONTINUED)

longest chapter in this book, "The Consciousness of the Self," reflected his interest in consciousness and introspectionism. He went so far as to argue that psychology should "admit" the idea of the soul. At times he referred to himself as a radical empiricist, as he pursued knowledge building through the study of not only perceived realities but also the mind, including one's own experience. In this respect, he laid the foundations of phenomenology. Perhaps his most famous phenomenological study is that of religion, *The Varieties of Religious Experience*. But he was also considered the father of pragmatism, arguing that a key criteria of knowledge is its practical usefulness. Functionalism formed a central part of his study of consciousness: he saw consciousness as an adaptive, enabling form of self-regulation.

Despite his acknowledgment as the father of both American psychology and pragmatism, James and his contributions were initially eclipsed by the onslaught of logical positivism and behaviorism in the early 1900s, two orientations that James disapproved of. However, in more recent years, as the study of consciousness has reemerged, his extensive contributions have been rediscovered, especially his work on the phenomenology of consciousness (for biographical information on James, see Pajares, 2002).

both the influence of the Vienna circle of logical positivists (see chapter 1) and John Watson's introduction of behaviorism in 1924. The behaviorists argued that it would be feasible to study only the inputs and outputs of mental functioning, not the intervening black box of the mind or consciousness. Watson (1930) remarked, "Behaviorism claims that consciousness is neither a definite nor a usable concept . . . [and] holds, further, that belief in the existence of consciousness goes back to the ancient days of superstition and magic and is useless. The behaviorist asks: 'Why don't we make what we can observe the real field of psychology?'" (p. 2). It was not until such figures as Donald Hebb (1949) and Noam Chomsky (1959) decisively challenged behaviorism in the 1940s and 1950s that psychology lost its ability to keep internal mental processes out of the field of psychological investigation. Both critics, founders of the cognitive movement, stressed the role of internal mental representations. Hebb (1949), for instance, hypothesized that thoughts were the activity of reverberating assemblies of neurons.

It was the cognitive movement, often regarded as arising out of the 1956 Symposium on Information Theory, that set the stage for the contemporary revival of interest in consciousness (see Gardner, 1985). The cognitive sciences consist of such diverse fields as psychology, anthropology, linguistics, artificial intelligence, neuroscience or brain science, and the philosophy of mind. It is no coincidence that the field developed at the same time as the digital computer, as its central metaphor for the mind has been the computer. The brain is equated with the hardware (or wetware), and the mind is treated as its software. Just as various different physical computers made of silicon or other materials can process software, so the mind is viewed as functionally independent of the brain, theoretically operable in alternative systems. The most central concept of the cognitive vision is that of mental representations or maps. Mental representations are models constructed in the mind of the body, the self, or external environments or objects that guide thought and behavior and operate on an intermediate level or link between conscious experience and the physical brain. Also central is an interest in thought, specifically information processing, as a central explanatory concept for the panoply of mental functions, including feeling and emotion, intuition, and the like. Cognitive scientists often view the mind as composed of various loosely connected modules, each specialized in a particular computational task, such as vision, planning, valuing, or decision making. Although cognitive scientists are interested in an internal mental world of maps and information processing, they view these functions as largely unconscious, thereby minimizing or rejecting the role of conscious experience.

Since its inception in the late 1950s, the cognitive movement has undergone considerable changes. In its first two decades, cognitivists such as Marvin Minsky, Noam Chomsky, and Herbert Simon, who were interested primarily in highly abstract models of cognition that had little relation to neurobiological functioning, dominated the field. Beginning in the late 1970s, the movement shifted its focus to connectionism, which most typically involves the modeling of mental functioning based on systems that superficially resemble the human brain, specifically, neural networks, rather than the serial digital computer. These involved programs that display rudimentary abilities to learn from experience rather than rely on prewritten programs. Because of the artificiality and limitations of these systems, during the past decade the focus has shifted not only to integrating the various models of mental processing but also to understanding them in the context of information processing in the body and in the environment, an approach referred to variously as enactment or embodiment theory (discussed in the next section).

Concurrent developments in biology, including brain imaging, complex systems theory, the phenomenology of mind, and the psychology of emotion and feeling, have created a remarkably rich environment of ideas that has sparked the current explosion of interest in consciousness studies. This has largely been an interdisciplinary movement concerned with the integration of these diverse perspectives, both to solve the various specialized, or easy, problems of mental functioning and to come to terms with the hard problem of what consciousness is in itself. Thus, we now revisit the question of definition.

D. Defining Consciousness

It is usually assumed that to study some phenomenon, it first needs to be defined. Preferably one begins with a definition that identifies the specific essential or unique characteristics of the subject; that is, characteristics that nothing else shares. Failing this, the second-best approach is usually to approximately identify the most probable features, though these may not be unique. In addition, the definition should not define the phenomena in terms of itself—this would be tautological, or circular—but should instead use specific and commonly understood terms. Defining consciousness, using these or just about any criteria, has been one of the great Gordian knots of the cognitive sciences, one that many argue is impossible or should be deferred until there is a better understanding of the subject. Yet most investigators have attempted either implicitly or explicitly to achieve some kind of clarity about their subject (for a few examples of these efforts, see exhibit 4.2).

It has been persuasively argued that a definition of consciousness using its essential features is both impossible and unnecessary, as each person who comes to the subject has some direct experience of it, and thus a definition needs to be only suggestive rather than logically definitive (Peters, 2000). Most efforts at a definition attempt to distinguish different meanings of the term, different types of consciousness, or different understandings of the nature of consciousness, often obscuring which of those is of central concern. There have been multiple attempts to distinguish the dimensions that characterized the different definitions. For example, Chalmers (1996) distinguishes between phenomenal consciousness and psychological consciousness, which reflects the nebulous boundary that exists between any definition and its associated theory. In fact, it may not be possible to fully separate the two.

Definitions of consciousness typically refer to the one or more themes or dimensions, such as simple alertness, a sense of existence, feeling or qualia, knowledge, intention, internal narrative, or the capacity for self-reflection.

- Waking, alert, or aware state: Although these definitions are inherently circular, they employ slightly more familiar terms but often

EXHIBIT 4.2: SELECTED DEFINITIONS OF CONSCIOUSNESS FROM THE LITERATURE

The waking state of the mind: The knowledge which the mind has of anything that is being experienced; awareness; thought.
—*CHAMBERS DICTIONARY*, 1994

The state of being conscious; knowledge of one's own existence, condition, sensations, mental operations, acts, etc. Consciousness is thus, on the one hand, the recognition by the mind or ego of its acts and affections ... the self-affirmation that certain modifications are known by me, and that these modifications are mine.
—SIR W. HAMILTON.

Mind is the capacity for thought, consciousness is a present activity of thought, and thought itself is an activity of the brain.
—DONALD HEBB

Consciousness is the tutor who supervises the education of the living substance and leaves his pupil alone for all those tasks for which he is already sufficiently trained.
—ERWIN SCHRODINGER

We can define "conscious" in the basic sense as follows: to be conscious is, inter alia, to perceive, to feel emotions and sensations, to have images and recollections, and to have desires, intentions, and thoughts.
E. O. EVANS

The consciousness that we speak of is the immediate experience, that sentience of the mind, by means of which everything we see and feel has reality.
EVAN WALKER

By "consciousness" I mean those states of sentience or awareness that typically begin when we wake up in the morning from a dreamless sleep and continue throughout the day until we fall asleep again.
—JOHN SEARLE

Consciousness is the subjective state of being currently aware of something, either within oneself or outside of oneself.
—G. W. FARTHING

obscure important distinctions. For example, one may be aware while asleep and dreaming (especially during lucid dreaming) but not particularly alert.

- Sense of existence: Very closely associated with the previous dimension are those definitional elements that stress the need for there to be some sense or awareness of existing for consciousness (Baruss, 1986–1987). This also contains an element of circularity, but its appeal is its intuitive understandability.
- Feeling or qualia: Many definitions stress the presence of some kind of feeling, sensation, or qualia. McCarthy (2003) explains qualia as "the subjective qualities of conscious experience. Examples of these are, the way coffee tastes to you, the way a violin sounds to you, the way it feels when you hit your finger with a hammer without reference to particular properties of either hammer or finger" (n.p.).
- Knowledge: Many definitions emphasize thought, knowledge, or information processing. Although it is easy to point out that many of these things may happen without any awareness, it is difficult to imagine consciousness without at least some rudimentary level of knowledge.
- Intention: Although intentionality and decision making are less frequently mentioned, many emphasize this dimension nonetheless, which suggests that an essential function of consciousness is to make selections, if only on what to focus on, and that consciousness may have evolved to deal with novel situations that are not amenable to already-developed routines.
- Thought, self-talk, and internal narrative: There are many who argue that language-encoded thought, self-talk, or narratives constitute or are required for consciousness. However much language may amplify (or restrict) consciousness, there is much neurobiological and phenomenological evidence to suggest that there are a range of conscious states that have little association with internalized language.
- Self-reflection: Some definitions suggest that consciousness is uniquely associated with higher-level capacities for self-reflection, introspection, or reflexive thought. Certainly such capacities often amplify consciousness, but to suggest that they are required for consciousness seems a bit anthropomorphic. Just because my dog does not seem to be very introspective does not disqualify her as a conscious being.

Antonio Damasio (1999) differentiates between core and extended forms of consciousness. Whereas core consciousness involves a basic sense of awareness, body consciousness, and a sense of existence, extended consciousness connotes active processes of thought, self-reflection, conscience, and the like. He argues, "It may be that conscience and extended consciousness are incompletely understood only because core consciousness is inadequately understood" (p. 233).

Thus, in the working definition proposed here, awareness and a sense of existence are a common denominator of the other dimensions in a single definition of human consciousness: Consciousness is a sense of existence or awareness accompanied by knowledge, feeling, and intention, however minimal. This awareness or sense consists of the ability to recognize, register, or otherwise apprehend something—an aspect of self, or some object or objects, or another state, whether material or immaterial. This capacity includes knowledge or information processing, however complete or incomplete, consistent or inconsistent, accurate or inaccurate. At the same time, it involves some feeling and/or sensation (e.g., qualia such as anger, bliss, redness, coolness, happiness) associated with the knowledge or information. It also involves some intention or choice regarding the preceding (e.g., observe, attack, embrace, deny, consider, research, enjoy).

Consciousness may involve any foci, including the self, feelings, thoughts, or sensations associated with physical phenomena. It may or may not be structured according to the categories of subject and object. Examples range from a vague sense of awareness, with minimal knowledge, feeling, and intention, to highly self-reflective forms of language-mediated thought. This chapter builds on this perspective and now turns to a review of recent developments in consciousness studies. It will focus on both theoretical and research contributions made during the past two decades: those in a specifically phenomenological or psychological orientation—the neuropsychological that encompasses brain functioning—and alternative and emerging approaches that aim to synthesize these contributions.

II. Cognitive and Phenomenological Theories

Although there has been declining interest in theories that exclude brain functioning, a range of approaches still draw primarily on first-person accounts and observations of cognitive or linguistic functioning. Many of these refer to brain functioning to some extent; however, they do so only secondarily and in a general manner. After reviewing a few such approaches that purport to be theories (but are rather descriptive frameworks of theories), this section discusses several overlapping themes of interest for contemporary psychological theories: dynamics of competition; modularity and hierarchization;

integrative mechanisms; internalized language; and the physical and cultural environment of conscious functioning, or enactment theory.

A. Selected Frameworks

David Chalmers (1995b) created a sensation with his *Scientific American* essay "The Puzzle of Conscious Experience." In it he concludes that subjective consciousness continues to defy all materialist explanations, and he emphasizes the irreducibility of conscious experience; consciousness is a fundamental and ubiquitous reality throughout the universe. He argues that information has two basic aspects, physical and experiential: "Wherever we find conscious experience, it exists as one aspect of an information state, the other aspect of which is embedded in a physical process in the brain" (p. 85). Chalmers also distinguishes between phenomenal and psychological consciousness. Whereas the former concerns the subjective aspects of consciousness, its qualia, the latter involves its functioning as an element of mental life, for example, in decision making. Thus, phenomenological approaches tend to focus primarily on the experiential dimensions of consciousness, and psychological theories emphasize its role in information processing and the like.

The transpersonal psychologist Ken Wilber (1997) applauds Chalmers's work and elaborated on it in his own "An Integral Theory of Consciousness." Wilber (1997) extended Karl Popper's (1972) distinction between the worlds of phenomenology (I), culture (we), and objective science (it), and proposes a four-quadrant model of consciousness that distinguishes among its intentional (I), behavioral (you), cultural (we), and social dimensions (it). He argues that all holons have not just two, but rather four, fundamental and irreducible aspects; that every information state actually and simultaneously has an (1) intentional, (2) behavioral, (3) cultural, and (4) social dimension. He goes on to categorize the various theories of consciousness under the four general rubrics, but unfortunately he does not elucidate the specific areas of agreement or disagreement. Somehow, he suggests, it all fits together. He contends that his "all-quadrant, all-level" (1997, p. 71) approach is the minimum degree of sophistication that is needed for an integral theory of consciousness.

Both of the frameworks are descriptive theories of the relevant types of consciousness and of the kinds of theories that can be brought to bear on consciousness itself. Because of their generality, the theories have limited explanatory ability. Nonetheless, they provide a global road map for some of the more detailed theories that follow, especially in the section on neuropsychological theories.

B. The Dynamics of Competition

An increasing number of theorists have used competition as a central organizing concept for understanding consciousness. For instance, Daniel Dennett (1991) proposes the multiple-drafts model of consciousness, which suggests that only those ideas or other mental contents that survive in the intrapsychic competition become conscious. The process of a percept, idea, or other content emerging into consciousness involves constant revision and amalgamation with other ideas. Some features of the content undergoing revision will persist through the various drafts; others are so transitory as to elude notice altogether. Only those that are successfully revised and combined with others become conscious. This is notwithstanding Dennett's argument that consciousness, as well as qualia, cannot be said to have any meaningful existence. David Rosenthal (1995) describes how Dennett diminishes the value of any first-person accounts by pointing out, "Reporting our experiences may seem to be the last word on this matter, much like publishing a text. But even publication fixes a text only relative to a social context; post-publication revision can and does occur." (p. 360). Dennett has little to say about why or how the survival of the fittest mental contents should see the daylight of consciousness, other than his proposal that consciousness is a type of internalized language (discussed in a subsequent section). Dennett's psychological Darwinism is intended to be analogous with theories of neural Darwinism (see Calvin, 1999), in which consciousness is believed to arise out of the spreading (or surviving) activation of large neural assemblies and systems.

C. Modularity and Hierarchization

An important focus of many contemporary theories is the emphasis on the structure of consciousness, which potentially corresponds with brain structure. A central theme of the cognitive sciences is that the human mind consists of various interacting modules that specialize in particular tasks or functions, such as vision or language. Among others, Ray Jackendorff (1987) also subscribes to the notion of the modularity of mental functions, especially with respect to language. The most distinctive aspect of his approach is an intermediate-level theory of consciousness rather than a central-level theory in which conceptual structure is the integrative mechanism of consciousness. He suggests that there is a top-down influence of the higher levels of consciousness on lower-level maps in short-term memory. It is at this intermediate level that memory and sensation interact and, in turn, are coordinated with various other modular functions of the mind. Jackendorff's notion of modular functions derives in part from Fodor's (1983) concept of the modularity of the mind.

Many psychological and neurological theories of consciousness are built on the notion of hierarchies of mental functioning. Just as Dennett's (1991) multiple-drafts model presupposes a hierarchy of levels of mental functioning, most theories assume that the sensory contents build up as they permeate the various levels of consciousness, until they represent multimodal three-dimensional models with ideas and values attached to them.

D. Theories of Integrative Mechanisms

Many psychological and functional theories associate consciousness with the mind's integrative functions. This is true for most of the traditional analytical theories, such as those of the ego psychologists. Ego psychologists believed that consciousness is most typically associated with the functioning of ego, which acts as a ship's ballast in stabilizing mental life. For instance, Heinz Hartmann associated consciousness with a type of neutralized libido (Hartmann, Kris, & Lowenstein, 1949). Ego psychologists believe that consciousness involves cognitive, executive, and integrative capabilities such as perception, decision making, and conflict resolution. Current theories do not reject this perspective but provide reformulations that their creators hope are more compatible with developments in the neurosciences. Bruce Buchanan (1997), for instance, proposes that consciousness involves integrative functions of the evaluation of experience, thus permitting purposeful behavior. He also argues that consciousness entails the regulation and feedback of information, linking perception and behavior, and thus enabling specific adaptations. Like many cognitivists, Buchanan believes that processes outside of awareness— as well as feeling, memory, and conceptual thought—affect consciousness. He believes that conflict and novelty most specifically activate consciousness.

One of the most influential theories that involves integrative mechanisms is Bernard Baars's (1988) global-workspace model of the mind. As do other theorists, Baars believes that sensations and ideas compete with each other, with the most salient (or fittest) emerging through a complex system of mental modules and hierarchical levels. However, these do not become conscious until they enter the global workspace, a kind of theater of consciousness, which simultaneously has access to the entire system of mental modules. This global workspace both controls access to consciousness on the part of competing unconscious processors and integrates the multimodal representations or maps contained in those processors that gain transitory access to the global workspace. The model assumes that consciousness is nothing more than a form of information processing, and according to some commentators such as Chalmers, it does nothing to explain why consciousness should be associated with such an integrative mechanism. Computers have integrative mechanisms and general workspaces in memory, but few suggest that they are conscious.

E. Consciousness as Internalized Language

One group of theorists believe that consciousness is primarily a function of language. Lev Vygotsky (1962) and Don Tucker (1981) were among the first to propose that internalized speech is critical to thought, and perhaps to consciousness. Tucker suggested that thought develops during childhood as a left-hemisphere function based on the "internalization of self-directed talk" (p. 43). This is believed to result only when nerve pathways connecting major brain structures mature sufficiently.

Dennett (1991) also incorporated the internalized speech theory into his approach to his multiple drafts model of consciousness. In *Consciousness Explained,* Dennett points out that as soon as the serial structure of natural language brings about the control and integration of competing mental modules, consciousness arises. Adaptionist and functionalist approaches to consciousness often flounder on the binding problem: if there is no little person or homunculus in the head, and no central unit in the brain that integrates the diverse modules, how does experience usually have the sense of being integrated or whole? Dennett, and many of those who hold similar representational theories of consciousness, argue that internalized serial language is the thread that holds it all together.

In recent years, the debate on language-based representational theories has involved higher-order experience (HOE) theories. Such theories suggest that consciousness exists not because we represent the world in our minds, but because we create representations of our representations. There are two variations of these theories: Armstrong's (1981) higher-order perception (HOP) theory and Rosenthal's (1991) better-known higher-order thought (HOT) theory. Both suggest that a person's awareness of his or her mental state involves representing that state on a second-order basis. The HOP model contends that this is done partly on a perceptual basis, whereas the HOT model suggests that having a verbal thought about the primary state is sufficient to bring about consciousness, as long as this thought arises directly out of the first-order representation or mental map.

Higher-order experience theories, especially those involving language and metacognition (see chapter 7), have made a significant contribution to consciousness studies, especially to problems involving cognitive functioning as it relates to the role of language in psychodynamic processes. However, they fail to address the hard problem of conscious qualia and are unconvincing in their treatment of the binding problem of the integration of conscious experience.

F. Enactment Theory

An insight to emerge out of the slow progress of the artificial intelligence field in simulating human cognition is that, no matter how sophisticated the computer programs that are developed or how well-trained neural nets become, they lack many capabilities of children, including common sense. It has been proposed that much of this common body of knowledge evolves from humans sharing similar bodies and environments, and that these form critical parts of our cognitive systems, and thus of our consciousness. For this reason, numerous investigators have recently emphasized the sensorimotor, physical, and environmental contexts of cognition.

Among the best known of these theories is that of Francisco Varela, a Chilean biologist, who originated the theory of autopoiesis (see chapter 2). After ten years of concerted work, in 1991 Varela, Thompson, and Rosch published the now-seminal *The Embodied Mind,* in which they argued that cognition is not based so much on representations—as in the standard cognitivist position—but instead emerges from "recurrent sensori-motor patterns to enable action to be perceptually guided" (p. 173) in embodied behavior in environments that are not preestablished but enacted and co-originated "through the history of structural coupling" (p. 200). They attack cognitivism because they believe that the traditional theories are not grounded in neurobiological data and ignore human experience in favor of largely unconscious information-processing functions.

Their theory, also known as embodied or situated cognition, regards consciousness as an activity structured by the body and its situatedness in its environments (i.e., as an embodied action). They explain, "To say that cognition is embodied means that it depends upon the perceptual and motor capacities of our body, and that it is intertwined with the environment. What recent cognitive science has begun to show is that the embodied mind is intersubjective at the most fundamental levels. Human self-consciousness, for example, emerges from a primordial and preverbal proprioceptive sense of self that is inseparably coupled to the perceptual recognition of other human beings" (Varela et al., 1991, p. 173).

Varela treats perception as a type of perceptually guided action. He points out that, for instance, our eyes move to frame the visual field and to focus on areas of that field; similarly, our heads move to maximize biaural localization. This behavior emerges from extensive feedback mechanisms of sensory and motor control modules in the brain. Thus, he suggests that cognitive structures develop out of the repeated sensorimotor patterns that guide perception in the context of locally situated actions.

Varela et al. (1991) take the middle ground between the demands of objectivist science, which emphasizes the role of mental representations of external realities, and extreme constructivists, who deny any external reality: "We reflect on a world that is not made, but found, and yet it is also our structure that enables us to reflect upon this world" (p. 3). They strongly argue for an integration of phenomenology with neurology, and they reject notions of consciousness that place it purely in the head or in language. Given their interest in Buddhist mindfulness, they also reject the association of consciousness with the Western idea of a stable, immutable ego or self: "The existential concern that animates our entire discussion in this book results from the tangible demonstration within cognitive science that the self or cognizing subject is fundamentally fragmented, divided, or non-unified" (xvii). The work of Varela exemplifies the efforts of an increasing number of investigators to move behind the highly theoretical and disembodied models of the early functionalists and cognitivists to an understanding of subjective consciousness in externally observable brain structures and in the physical body and its material, social, and cultural environments.

III. Neuropsychological Theories

At the same time that psychologists and other social scientists have felt an increasing need to ground their theories in biology, neuroscientists have struggled to generate theories that are relevant to phenomenological and psychological approaches. Neuropsychological theories usually focus on overall brain structure, functioning at the level of the neuron or neuronal assemblies, and recently, there has been increasing interest in intracellular functioning, a topic discussed in the next section. Many of the particular theories introduced in the preceding section and those reviewed in this section are not mutually exclusive, and in fact are consistent with one or another version of the now-prevalent theory that certain types of activity in the extended reticular thalamic activating system (ERTAS) are the most salient NCCs. As promising as this theory may be, this section concludes by reviewing a few of its limitations, ones that may require fundamentally new approaches to the problem of subjective awareness or consciousness.

A. Brain Structure

A central issue in the study of brain structures is the specificity of their functioning. Is consciousness a global property of the entire system, or does it reside in one or a few locations in the brain? Do single brain structures perform particular psychological functions, such as attention, control of emotions, decision making, vision, or conscience, or are they implemented at multiple locations, perhaps redundantly? With the accumulation of a large body of evidence from many types of brain damage, as well as the results of scanning technologies, a consensus is emerging that the answer to this question depends on the particular function. Some, such as fear, are associated with a single brain structure such as the amygdala. Others, such as core consciousness or basic awareness, are associated with interactions of a small number of discrete structures, whereas others, such as self-reflective or extended consciousness, are widely distributed and redundantly implemented. This discussion of neurocognitive theories does not assume that consciousness is simply an epiphenomenon or outcome of brain processes, even though many theorists may assume exactly this. Much can be understood about the associations—the NCCs—without making premature conclusions about causal relationships.

One of the most global divisions in the brain is between the left and right hemispheres of the cortex. The hemispheres appear to be mirror images of each other, but careful examination reveals that they are highly specialized regions that perform different functions (see table 4.1). Much of our understanding of the hemispheres is attributable to Roger Sperry (1966), who worked with people who, because of surgery or accident, had lost one or the other hemisphere or had had them separated. The left hemisphere controls the ability to express oneself in language. In more than 95 percent of right-handed people, the left hemisphere dominates for speech. The rate is somewhat lower for left-handers but still high at approximately 70 percent. The left hemisphere controls our logic, our reasoning, and our analytical thought processes. It can focus on details; however, it has difficulty comprehending the whole picture. In contrast, the functions of the right hemisphere are more specialized, such as the processing of space and geometrical shapes and forms, and in general, material presented at the same time, unlike the sequential nature of language. The right hemisphere is usually considered the creative half of the brain, as it can often grasp the whole out of the parts. The right hemisphere also performs a critical function in the processing of emotions. In one experiment in which subjects saw pictures of faces with intense expressions on them, the right hemisphere grasped the expression more accurately than did the left hemisphere. In another

TABLE 4.1: FUNCTIONS OF BRAIN HEMISPHERES

HEMISPHERE	LEFT	RIGHT
THINKING	Abstract, linear, analytical	Concrete and holistic
COGNITIVE STYLE	Rational, logical	Intuitive, artistic
LANGUAGE	Rich vocabulary, good grammar and syntax	No grammar, syntax; prosody, poor vocabulary, metaphoric, verse
EXECUTIVE CAPACITY	Introspection, will, initiative, sense of self, focus on trees	Low sense of self, low initiative, focus on forest
SPECIALIZED FUNCTIONS	Reading, writing, arithmetic; sensorimotor skills; inhibits psi	Three i's, music, rich dream imagery, good face and gestalt recognition, open to psi
EXPERIENCE OF TIME	Sequentially ordered, measured	"Lived" time, primitive time sense
SPATIAL ORIENTATION	Relatively poor	Superior, also for shapes, wire figures
PSYCHOANALYTIC ASPECTS	Secondary process, ego functions, consciousness; superego?	Primary process, dream work, free association; hallucinations?
IDEAL PROTOTYPE	Aristotle, Appollonian mode, Marx, Freud, Koestler's commissar	Plato, Dionysian mode, Nietzsche, Jung, Koestler's yogi

Source: Ehrenwald (1984, p. 16).

experiment, subjects listened to verbal messages expressed with various emotions. The messages were spoken separately to each ear, as each ear is connected with the opposite hemisphere. When the messages were spoken to the left hemisphere, the subject responded more accurately as to manifest content. However, the right hemisphere more accurately picked up on the emotional feeling of the voice (Springer & Deutsch, 1989).

A critical structure for the integration of the two hemispheres of the brain is a thick bundle of nerves known as the corpus callosum. In the 1970s Julian Jaynes (1976) proposed that consciousness arose only rather recently in history, and he identified evidence to suggest that the corpus callosum had become thick enough only at that time to permit the right and left hemispheres to adequately communicate with each other, thus permitting the full internalization of speech. Prior to this period, he suggests, people experienced thoughts as coming from outside, as voices attributed to super-natural beings. More recent brain-scan studies have supported this hypothesis, as they have found that a significant difference between the brains of people with and without schizophrenia is that the corpus callosum of the former is thinner than expected, perhaps accounting for the lack of integration between cognition and affect associated with schizophrenia (Woodruff, McManus, & David, 1995).

The brain has also been divided up into three major parts: (1) the cerebral cortex, (2) the midbrain (including the limbic system), and (3) the hind brain. The cerebral cortex, a thin layer of cells surrounding the core of the brain, is the most recently developed and has been associated with many cognitive functions believed to be unique to humans. The midbrain and limbic system, including such structures as the thalamus, hypothalamus, and hippocampus—sometimes referred to as the mammalian brain—are deeply involved with control of emotion and memory, whereas the hind brain, including the brain stem, is the most ancient part (sometimes called the reptilian brain) and focuses on control of basic bodily functions (see figure 4.1; see also Carter, 2002).

The cerebral cortex includes the frontal, temporal, parietal, and occipital lobes. Probably the most important structure of the cerebral cortex for extended consciousness is the prefrontal cortex, which is part of the frontal lobe. This structure, located just above and behind the eyes, is considered vital to abstract thought, decision making and planning, and the formation of questions. It is in part an extension of the limbic system, and thus integrates emotions with action planning. Research has revealed that people with lesions in this area of the brain are unable to solve many cognitive tasks because they are unable to ask themselves the right questions when needed in their thought process. Many types of mental illness have been associated with particularly low levels of metabolic activity in the prefrontal cortex. In addition, some recent studies have found that extensive playing of computer games suppresses activity in this part of the brain. Other parts of the cerebral cortex serve as centers for speech, vision, and hearing, and often association centers. Often several distant areas may be involved in the performance of separate parts of a function such as vision or speech, but how these results integrate to produce unified experiences is not yet understood.

While extended or higher-level consciousness is associated with the cerebral cortex, especially the prefrontal area, core consciousness or basic awareness is associated with deeper structures in the midbrain and hind brain, such as the thalamus, reticular activating system, and brain-stem structures.

FIGURE 4.1: MAJOR STRUCTURES OF THE HUMAN BRAIN

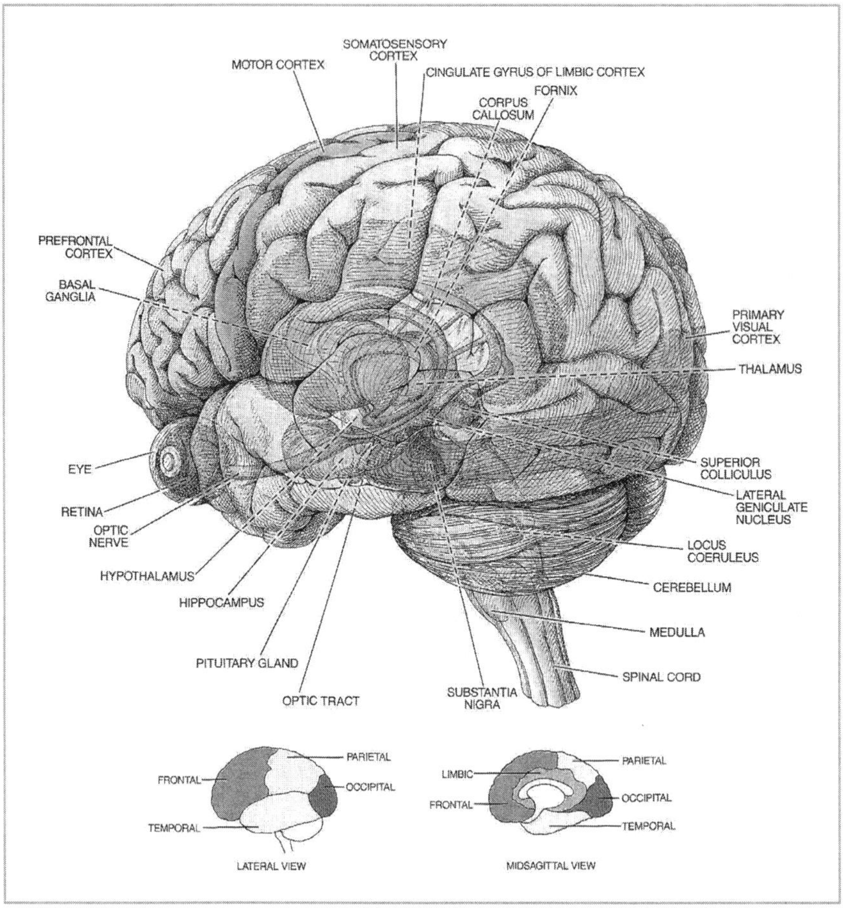

Source: Fischbach (1992). p. 51.

One part of the limbic system, the hippocampus, controls emotional responses having to do with the 4 Fs: fighting, fleeing, feeding, and f—ing (Newman, 1996). Of central importance is the thalamus, a complex structure at the center of the brain that traditionally was believed to relay impulses between the senses and the cerebral cortex but recently has been hypothesized to also activate the various cortical structures. Particularly critical for core consciousness is the reticular activating system, best known for its control of sleep and waking. Another structure critical to consciousness is the posterior parts of the brain stem; which, when damaged, results in coma (Damasio, 1999).

Within these various structures are approximately 100 billion brain cells, or neurons. Many believe that the neuron is the basic functional unit of the brain. Neurons are complex cells (see figure 4.2) that consist of branches, called axons, which receive impulses, and dendrites, that transmit them to other calls. The impulses are electrochemical transfers of energy and information. Between the axons and dendrites of adjacent neurons are small gaps, called synapses, within which the transfer is typically a chemical one that uses a variety of complex macromolecules called neurotransmitters. Within the neurons, transmission is both chemical and electrical. Neurons may fire, activating one or many additional neurons, or by firing, they may inhibit the activity of other cells. In this way, they both transmit and modify information, not entirely unlike the circuits and transistors of a computer. There is, however, increasing controversy over whether neurons are the fundamental unit of information processing in the brain. Some neuroscientists propose that the basic units may be cell assemblies, that is, systems of cells. Others argue that considerable information processing goes on inside each neuron; that the cells are better compared with computers in themselves than with simple on-off transistors (see the appendix).

B. Neurological Functioning

Discovering how the various brain structures function together is a formidable challenge, but the difficulty of identifying how this functioning, or some aspects of it, is associated with consciousness is a virtually intractable problem. We are looking at a problem involving approximately 100 billion cells, each connected with up to 80,000 other cells, and each representing a complex system in itself (Scott, 1995). These cells communicate with one another through neurochemical transmission at the synaptic junctions and through direct electrical connections called gap junctions, long-range diffusion of neurotransmitters, hormones released through the bloodstream, and other means. Several themes have dominated efforts to understand brain functioning: the spotlight theory of consciousness, synchronic interactivity of reentry loops in the key systems, neural Darwinism, and the role of memory in its interaction with perception.

Although the use of the metaphor of consciousness as a spotlight goes back to Freud, Francis Crick (1984) reintroduced the metaphor as the searchlight hypothesis. Crick suggested that there is an internal attentional searchlight that is controlled by the reticular complex of the thalamus. This refers to patterns of activation of cell assemblies in the cortex that represent various aspects of attended objects. In general, spotlight theories propose that attention illuminates whatever falls within a given region of the brain. The related zoom-lens

FIGURE 4.2: COMPONENTS OF THE NEURON

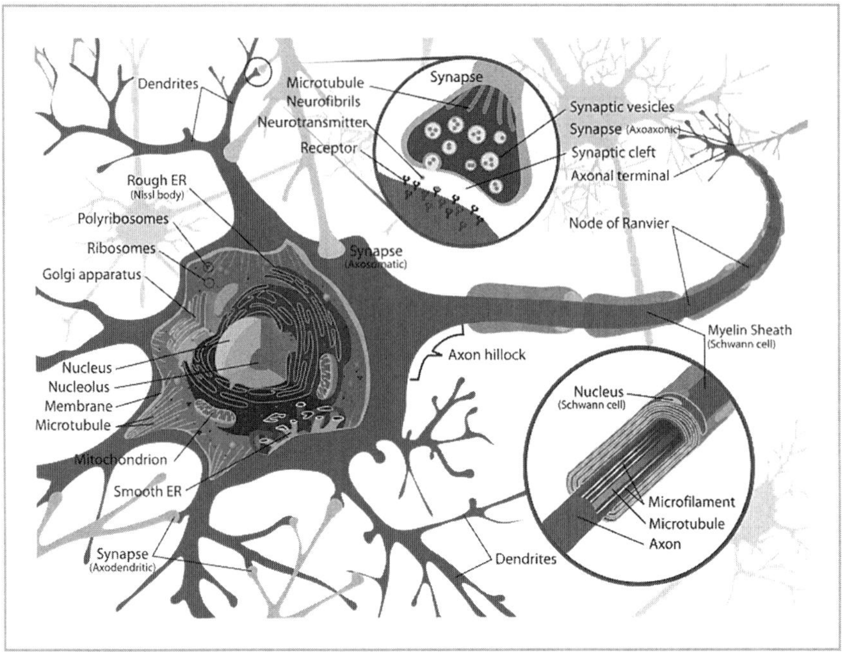

Source: Wikimedia Commons (http://www.commons.wikimedia.org).

model proposes that attention can be directed at broad areas with little detail or focused on small areas with fine detail (Eriksen & St. James, 1986). As such, searchlight or spotlight models are a way of bracketing off the hard problem of consciousness, associating consciousness with areas of the brain that are activated but saying little about how or why the association exists.

Another limitation of spotlight models is that they fail to explain how the brain solves the binding problem, that of integrating various aspects of experience. For example, some neurons specialize in visually recognizing lines, others color, and others motion, and these may be in separate areas of the brain. The most common explanation for integration are feedback loops between the related areas, in which patterns of activation cycle back and forth through reentry loops. Such loops are a central element of Gerald Edelman's (1989) theory of consciousness. He explains, "Since reentry to and from mapped receiving areas correlates the various signals emerging from an object ... there is no homunculus 'looking at the image'" (p. 155). Feedback loops also form an important part of Crick's theory. However, Crick argues that the presence of such loops and their coordinated firing at approximately forty times per second (or 40 hertz) are associated with conscious experience. This hypothesis is applied to vision through the idea that "neurons responding to the separate features of an object are bound into temporary cell assemblies by semi- synchronous oscillations (in the 40–70 Hz range). The binding is brought about by means of attentional mechanisms such as the cortico-thalamic feedback loops. . . . External input is transmitted from the retina via the thalamus to the cortex, where distinct features of objects are processed in separate areas. When features processed in these areas are conspicuous, feedback to the LGN [lateral geniculate nucleus] enhances the output of corresponding locations there" (Crick & Koch, 1990, as cited in Ellis & Newton, 2009, n.p.).

Others have extended this model beyond vision to incorporate other senses and motor control. David LaBerge (1995), for instance, proposes that object directed attention becomes conscious when combined with attending to a representation of the self. LaBerge explains that awareness occurs when an experience becomes "my" experience. He suggests that attention is an event in the brain consisting of simultaneous activity in three areas of the brain, interconnected by a triangular circuit. The sites correspond to three aspects of attention: (1) expression, (2) enhancement mechanism, and (3) control (LaBerge, 1998).

Another theme in the efforts to understand brain functioning is Darwinian selection, which determines which cells thrive, which synaptic junctions develop, and which activation patterns reach the level of consciousness. Such researchers as William Calvin (1999) and Gerald Edelman (1989) have championed this approach. Edelman (1989), for instance, explains that his theory of neural group selection is that two different intracerebral evolutionary processes produce our brains. One is a developmental process consisting of Darwinian competition between groups of neurons that is only partly constrained by genetics. The other is a learning process driven by a faster but less permanent process that strengthens or weakens and prunes neuronal circuits only temporarily. This pruning is brought about by interactions between maps composed of neuronal groups organized by the first selection process.

The extent to which the neural activation associated with consciousness is organized primarily by reverberatory feedback loops or a process of Darwinian competition is still an open question. In either case, most theorists believe that activation involves interactions between current perceptual inputs and memory. For instance, some of the feedback or reentry loops are believed to involve the iterated comparison of perceptions with value-laden memories. The memories provide feedback, helping to organize the perceptual activation before it emerges into consciousness. Damasio (1999), for example, proposes, "In effect, primary consciousness results from the interaction in real time between memories of past value-category correlations and present world input as it is categorized by global mappings (but before the components of these mappings are altered by internal states)" (p. 155).

C. Integrative Efforts

Efforts to understand how the various brain structures and processes collectively function to support consciousness have typically involved variations of a theory on regions of the brain known as ERTAS. One of the first to propose such a theory was Bernard Baars. Recently, Baars, Newman, and Taylor (1998) have attempted to integrate psychological and neurological versions of this theory using the global-workspace or theater metaphor. Whereas the active bright spot on the stage represents the consciousness inherent in working memory, contextual systems that reside backstage shape consciousness. The audience represents the various unconscious mental modules, for example, long-term memories or motor automatisms. In terms of neurology, they propose that the active bright spot is associated with the sensory projections areas, supported by the thalamus, basal ganglia, hippocampus, and brain stem. The reticular activating system, specifically, is a selective attentional mechanism, a system that functions to control awakeness. The audience of specialized modules that shape consciousness is found in the frontal cortex, hippocampus, basal ganglia, and other parts of the limbic system and amygdala. The modules are connected to the global workspace between the anterior and posterior cortex, between the hemispheres, and from the cortex to the thalamus and back. Specifically, Baars et al. hypothesize that the neural basis for the global workspace to be the complex of connections between the reticular system, thalamus, and cortex. The interconnections involve the interactive comparison of current perceptual inputs with memories and competition between modules for input into the global workspace or ERTAS system (Baars et al., 1988).

Others such as Edelman and Damasio have proposed variations of this theory. Gerald Edelman proposes that inputs from the self, through the brain stem and hypothalamus, are integrated with external inputs, via the sensory cortices, in the hippocampus and related structures, then fed into the frontal, parietal, and temporal cortices. Primary consciousness is associated with the cyclical interactions of this information in the sensory and linguistic modules of the cortex (see figure 4.3).

Antonio Damasio presents one of the better-developed accounts of the ERTAS theory in *The Feeling of What Happens: Body and Emotion in the Making of Consciousness* (1999). He distinguishes core consciousness, which is a basic sense of awareness, from extended consciousness, which involves higher cognitive capacities, and from the autobiographical self, or a sense of historical identity. Core consciousness, he explains, "occurs when the brain's

FIGURE 4.3: GERALD EDELMAN'S MODEL OF CONSCIOUSNESS: AN EXAMPLE OF ERTAS THEORY

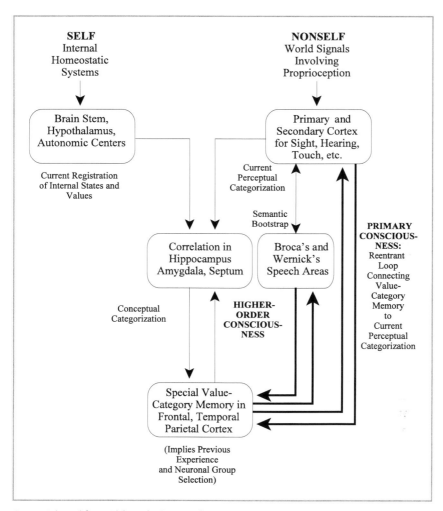

Source: Adapted from Edelman (1989, p. 132).

representation devices generate an imaged, nonverbal account of how the organism's own state is affected by the organism's processing of an object, and when this process enhances the image of the causative object, thus placing it saliently in a spatial and temporal context" (p. 169). Core consciousness is generated in pulses, each pulse triggered by an internal memory or idea or an external sensory object. Unconscious cognitive processing generates maps of the object, the self at that instant, and the self as modified by the object. Then, second-order conscious maps are generated of the collective process of the object affecting the self, and this enhancement generates the pulses of core consciousness.

In contrast to core consciousness, Damasio portrays extended consciousness as placing the transient pulses of core consciousness on the broader canvas of past and future. Its secret, he contends, is that the autobiographical memories, which form its context, are also its objects. As such, these objects also generate pulses of core consciousness. Extended consciousness relies on two tricks. One is the buildup of autobiographical memories and facts, each of which forms the context for and enhances core consciousness. The other is "holding active, simultaneously and for a substantial amount of time, the many images whose collection defines the autobiographical self and the images which defines the object" (p. 198). It involves the ability to generate a sense of perspective, ownership, and agency. Damasio theorizes that extended consciousness relies on continuously activated convergence zones located in temporal and frontal higher-order cortices, as well as in the subcortical nuclei. He believes that the thalamus paces this activation, and he agrees that Baars's global-workspace model, including the ERTAS theory, describes some of the key elements of extended consciousness. Whether one considers the formulations of Baars, Newman, Edelman, or Damasio, there has developed remarkable consensus about how the major brain structures function together to support consciousness. Yet there remain substantial problems with this emerging model.

D. Limitations of Neuropsychological Models

Theories about brain functioning typically assume that the brain works as a massively parallel computer, or that consciousness is a global property that emerges out of the activity and complexity of several of its component systems. There is, however, a growing awareness that, as much as ERTAS theories contribute to understanding the neurological correlates of consciousness, they leave much unexplained. The following are some of the critiques of such approaches that have been discussed in the literature (see Hameroff, 1998):

- There is considerable skepticism about whether reentry loops solve the binding problem. One line of argument against is statistical and computational: there is insufficient computing power in even the 100 billion neurons to explain how continuously integrated visual field can be computationally assembled.
- The mathematician and physicist Roger Penrose (1994) has advanced a more fundamental critique. In his a now-classic work *Shadows of*

the Mind, he argues that much human cognition is noncomputable, an argument based partly on a mathematical discovery known as Godel's incompleteness proof. While many reject his claim, those who believe that human cognition can be fully modeled using traditional computational means have yet to demonstrate the successful simulation of many basic pattern recognition problems that even children typically solve.

- A strictly connectionist view leaves no room for free will. Most cognitivists believe that all important decisions are simply the result of unconscious information processing, which the individual then imagines are his or her free choices. Experiments of Benjamin Libet and his colleagues (Libet, Wright, Feinstein, & Pearl, 1979) are often cited to support this view. Libet detected brain activity that occurred routinely a fraction of a section before decisions on the part of subjects to move their fingers. Yet Libet himself points out that the experiments pose no problem for free will, as they also showed that individuals had the ability to follow through or block the emergent impulse picked up through physiological measurements.
- These approaches are particularly limited in their ability to account for creativity and intuition, as well as such phenomena such as psi and the range of altered states of consciousness reported in the literature.
- Connectionist approaches often assume that the neuron is the fundamental unit of information processing, but it has been amply demonstrated that considerable information processing occurs in each cell. Hameroff (1998) points out that single-cell organisms, such as paramecia with no nervous system, demonstrate rudimentary problem solving and goal-directed behavior. This processing has been attributed to a complex internal system of microtubules in such organisms.
- There is considerable neurological data that traditional models do not account for. These models ignore direct electrical and electron-tunneling junctions between cells. They say nothing about the 80 percent of the brain that consists of glial cells or about the diverse means that neurons communicate with one another, factors that make a traditionally computational model of consciousness questionable.
- Finally, although connectionist and neurological models have much to contribute to understanding mental functioning, they tend to bracket off and minimize the problem of accounting for qualia, or the subjective aspect of consciousness. They assume that somehow certain types or patterns of neural activity account for the experience of being conscious, but they pretty much leave it at that.

Although these critiques do not negate the significant contributions of neurological and connectionist theories to the understanding of mental functioning, they force us to step back from the claims that they are theories of consciousness to a more modest claim that they are theories of mental functioning, some of which is conscious.

IV. Discussion

Despite the intense interest and progress in the study of consciousness, no truly comprehensive theory has been developed. Yet there is a growing consensus regarding some of its key elements. Early theories were primarily psychological in focus and ignored biological realities; perhaps for that reason, the development of such theories had slowed, at least until the recent developments in brain-scanning technology. Most contemporary activity has involved efforts to formulate models of the neurological and physical correlates of consciousness, and only secondarily to identify how these articulate with the traditional psychological models.

The various ERTAS models typically hypothesize that awareness and higher forms of human consciousness are associated with a series of reverberatory or feedback loops in the brain that connect the cortex, limbic system, thalamus, reticular system, and brain stem. These theories differ from one another in the particular structures that are emphasized and in the primary source of activation associated with conscious experience. As the specific functions of each structure and their interconnections are better understood, the task of relating them with psychological models will be simplified. The ERTAS model is consistent with notions of a global workspace, the interactive comparison of memories with sensations, and the emergence of consciousness from this self-organizing and competitive process. It is congruent with various psychological theories involving higher-order thought; enactment theory; and even with Freud's original ideas of phi, psi, and omega.

If one takes the materialist position that consciousness is a kind of incidental secretion of the brain, then one will probably assume that NCCs are fairly limited—confined to particular brain structures and probably to those at a fairly general level of organization. However, if one believes that consciousness is somehow a fundamental and pervasive part of the universe, then one will probably look for the NCCs in a wider range of brain structures and on a lower or finer-grained level of organization, such as within the information processing that goes on in neurons.

This second approach does not contradict but includes and extends the former one. Several lines of theory, such as quantum theory, quantum computation, and microbiology, have all converged in recent years to fuel these efforts (see the appendix). The best developed of these theories, Hameroff and Penrose's (1996) orchestrated objective reduction (Orch-OR) theory, is of considerable heuristic value in this regard. Although far from confirmed, there is a growing body of evidence supporting the importance of intracellular computation, perhaps within the cytoskeletal structures of neurons, that capitalize on quantum phenomena. These processes may be particularly valuable for understanding the substrate or the qualia of consciousness—the sense of depth, wholeness, and choice so pervasive in human experience—rather than overall patterns of problem solving and mental functioning that may be better understood through the global patterns of activation that operate between the major brain structures.

The reverberation of thalamic cortical feedback loops, especially those operating at 40 Hertz, is undoubtedly important for understanding many types of consciousness. However, cross-level feedback loops between neuronal and intraneuronal functioning may be critical. The cortical feedback loops may help orchestrate coherent superposed quantum states in cells, and in turn organize the global patterns of activation and feedback on the results of choices, intuitions, and feelings to the larger structures.

Many believe that, given hundreds of millions of years of evolution, the brain can be expected to have evolved all available means of computation, including serial and parallel; electrical, chemical, and photonic; and classical and quantum. Some have even gone so far as to relegate the biological brain to a mere input-output device for the mind, permitting access to thought and consciousness that takes place more fundamental levels of reality than is visible through the senses. It seems likely that the variety of reported states of consciousness correlates with an equally wide range of biological, classical physical, and even quantum processes. For example, depending on the species and the individual involved, Baars's global workspace may be highly integrated and built on a rich foundation of multiple levels of conscious processing, or it may be fragmented and undergirded with few such substrate experiences. What may be more important than a single global workspace is the globality of the workspace, as well as its depth within finer-grained structures of biological and physical information. Perhaps it will require a theory that links consciousness with a variety of interrelated physical processes, on multiple levels ranging from the structural on down to the intracellular and quantum levels, to understand the multiplicity of manifestations of consciousness in human beings (see exhibit 4.3) and in other life forms.

EXHIBIT 4.3: ALTERED STATES OF CONSCIOUSNESS: A WINDOW INTO THE MULTIPLE DIMENSIONS OF CONSCIOUSNESS

The study of consciousness includes not only a wide array of everyday core and extended states of consciousness but also less typical altered states of consciousness. Alternative states may be functional, dysfunctional, or purely neutral. Examples of such states include the following:

1. Lucid dreaming is the experience of being alert during and able to control the course of a dream. Many people report being able to cultivate this experience. During lucid dreaming, the contents of the dream are often experienced with far greater detail and realism than typical dreams. Sometimes the dreams occur spontaneously as hypnogogic or hypnopompic dreams just after falling asleep or prior to awakening.

2. Near-death experiences have been reported by thousands of people who have recovered from accidents, surgery, or illnesses involving the temporary stoppage of life functions. Researchers have reported many commonalities in such experiences, such as a sense of bliss, light, a tunnel, contact with departed loved ones, and the viewing of one's body from afar.

3. Psychopathologies, such as schizophrenia, are known to produce radically altered and often painful states, including perceptual alterations (e.g., two-dimensionality, a sense of unreality, intense elation).

4. Dissociative states include a variety of alterations of consciousness, including the sense of derealization, depersonalization, and multiple identities.

5. Alterations attendant on neurological deficits include such disturbances as "blindsight," the ability to access and use information from the senses without being conscious of it; anosognosia, or obviousness of physical disorders, such as amputation or stroke; and asomatognosia, or the inability to feel or experience one's own body.

6. Drug-induced states include intense euphoria, sedation, perceptual alterations, and pseudoinsight, to mention a few that are a function of the combination of particular drugs, the characteristics of the individual, and context.

7. Flow is particularly intense absorption in a challenging task that is meaningful and highly satisfying, such that all sense of time is suspended (see chapter 6).

EXHIBIT 4.3 (CONTINUED)

8. Hypnosis, although controversial, can involve an intense reliving of past experiences.
9. A wide variety of transpersonal, spiritual, and mystical experiences are radical alterations in everyday consciousness. These include mindfulness, intense feelings of bliss and light, a sense of pervasive peace and unity with the universe or God, intense love, inexplicable knowledge or insight, or a sense of overarching control or surrender of control. These may be transitory peak experiences or ongoing states that last indefinitely. They may be experienced internally only, as if in another dimension, or in the context of the everyday world. They may be highly unbalancing, involving such states as the so-called God intoxication of *masts* in India (Donkin, 1969), or extremely facilitative of integration into the responsibilities of society.

The phenomenology of these and many other altered states of consciousness provides an invaluable window to understanding the multiple dimensions of consciousness, but one that needs to be supplemented by rigorous research of cultural, psychological, and neurological correlates and that requires theoretical guidance.

Theories of consciousness based on quantum theory (see the appendix) may be an important extension of the classical approaches, such as the ERTAS models. Quantum theory, which has established itself as one of the two master theories of physics, focuses on microphysical phenomena, showing that at least on this level, there are multiple simultaneous realities that are superposed, and that causation involves local interactions and nonlocal associations between separated systems, unexplainable through hidden variables or laws based on Newtonian physics.

There have been multiple applications of quantum theory to the understanding of the problem of consciousness. The early ones did not consider the details of biology and assumed that superposed quantum processes could exist on relatively large scales. However, more recent theories, such as the Orch-OR theory, propose specific biological mechanisms that are believed to capitalize on quantum computational processes in the structure of each individual neuron. These involve the cytoskeletal structure of microtubules that previously were thought to have only a structural function but more recently have been implicated in information processing and the control of neural activation.

V. Summary

This chapter has two primary aims, to introduce the field of consciousness studies and to review some of its more recent developments. Its focus is on the hard problem, that of understanding qualia, or the subjective aspects of consciousness, including their sense of wholeness, depth, and choice. The introductory section of the chapter reviewed some of the underlying philosophical positions fueling these efforts, including dualistic positions such as interactionism, emergentism, proto-panpsychism, and monistic philosophies such as materialism and idealistic monism. Key themes in the approaches are the presence of an awake or alert state, a sense of existence, feeling or qualia, knowledge or information processing, intentionality, language and internalized self-talk, and self-reflection. That section proposed that consciousness is most universally characterized by a sense of existence or awareness accompanied simultaneously by some level of knowledge, feeling, and intention. Each characteristic of consciousness holds profound implications for the understanding of human development, motivation and personality, problem solving, and their failures.

After reviewing the historical background of consciousness studies, the chapter then considered psychological and phenomenological approaches to the study of consciousness. Several organizing concepts reviewed include the dynamics of competition, modularity and hierarchization, integrative mechanisms, internalized language models (e.g., HOE), and Varela's enactment theory of the bodily and environmental contexts of mental functioning. The chapter concluded with a discussion about some ways in which the diverse approaches might be integrated, in part by drawing on theories involving the application of quantum theory to consciousness. It is suggested that there are far more commonalities than differences among the seemingly diverse approaches; that the more recent quantum models of consciousness do not invalidate but supplement the earlier psychological and neurological theories, especially given their ability to address the hard problem.

For Further Reading

Carter, R. (2002). *Consciousness.* London: Weidenfeld & Nicolson.

Chalmers, D. J. (1995b, December). The puzzle of conscious experience. *Scientific American, 273,* 80–86.

Damasio, A. (1999). *The feeling of what happens: Body and emotion in the making of consciousness.* New York: Harcourt, Brace.

Gardner, H. (1985). *The mind's new science: A history of the cognitive revolution*. New York: Basic Books.

Hameroff, S. R. (1998). "Funda-Mentality": Is the conscious mind subtly linked to a basic level of the universe? *Trends in Cognitive Sciences, 2*(4), 119–127.

Penrose, R. (1994). *Shadows of the mind: A search for the missing science of consciousness* Oxford: Oxford University Press.

Scott, A. (1995). *Stairways to the mind: The controversial new science of consciousness.* New York: Springer-Verlag.

Stapp, H. P. (1993). *Mind, matter, and quantum mechanics.* Berlin: Springer.

Varela, F. J., Thompson, E., & Rosch, E. (1991). *The embodied mind: Cognitive science and human experience.* Cambridge, MA: MIT Press.

Walker, E. H. (2000). *The physics of consciousness.* Cambridge, MA: Perseus Books.

Wilber, K. (1997). An integral theory of consciousness. *Journal of Consciousness Studies, 4*(1), 71–92.

CHAPTER 5

Maturation, Learning, and Personal Development Through the Life Cycle

I. Introduction
   A. Background
   B. The Field of Human Development
   C. Current Issues
II. Lines of Development
   A. Biological Maturation
      1. The Role of Genetics
      2. Neurochemical Mechanisms
      3. Infant and Childhood Temperament
      4. Sexual Development
   B. Cognitive Development
      1. Piaget's Genetic Epistemology
      2. Vygotsky's Sociocultural Theory
      3. The Development of Multiple Intelligences
   C. Behavior and Learning Theory
      1. Classical and Operant Conditioning
      2. Social Learning Theory
   D. Psychosocial Development
      1. Psychosexual and Drive Development
      2. Attachment Theory
      3. The Sense of Self and Identity
      4. Ego Development
      5. The Relational Perspective on Women's Development
   E. Moral and Spiritual Development
      1. Kohlberg's Theory of Moral Development

The only "good learning" is that which is in advance of development.

—LEV VYGOTSKY

I. Introduction

The previous chapter considered consciousness as a central dynamic of human change and growth. This chapter, in contrast, is concerned with the ways that conscious strivings, especially those expressed through learning, translate into particular lives and distinguishable patterns of growth and development. It builds on chapter 1 in its understanding of human development as a self-organizing system, often poised at the edge of chaos and embedded in a variety of complex biological and social systems. It also delves into theories of personal change, introduced in chapter 2, and considers human development, in part, an expression of personal knowledge building, as discussed in chapter 3. Thus, this chapter reviews key theories of human development in relation to complex systems, change, knowledge building, and consciousness.

The study of human development is the study of a particular type of change that has been defined in various ways. Common definitions suggest that development is "the biosocial process of orderly and adaptive change from conception to death and is a product of both biological maturation (nature) and environmental learning (nurture)" (Romig, 1997, p. 1) or a "selective age-related change in adaptive capacity" (Baltes, Lindenberger, & Staudinger, 1998, p. 479). In contrast, Meacham (1997) regards development as change that is at once orderly and predictable, yet generates results that are "both irreversible and novel" (p. 43). This chapter reviews theories of childhood and adult development that assume only partly predictable patterns and demonstrate the spontaneous self-organization of biological, cognitive, psychological, and moral changes in individuals and in their social and physical environments. This self-organization acts on the products of natural selection, social selection, and self-selection, including a combination of cooperative and competitive relationships on the group, personal, and intrapsychic levels.

A. Background

Approaches to human development have emerged from the major movements in the development of psychological thought. Abraham Maslow (b. 1908–d. 1970) characterized these as consisting of three forces, and later four (see Cassel, 2001). The first force is primarily behaviorist. Its assumptions are firmly grounded in modernism, with a belief in the possibility of objective understanding of a physical universe, governed by local, atomistic interactions among its component parts. This force assumes that external conditions primarily drive change, with mechanistically interacting component parts, including individuals, having little intrinsic direction other than movement to the lowest available level of homeostasis. In this view, young people's minds are essentially tabulae rasae, or blank slates, ready for family and society to write on. The second force involves the psychoanalytic schools of thought, commonly associated with Sigmund Freud, Alfred Adler, and Carl Jung. These approaches regard development as driven by conflict, either among components of the personality or between the personality as a whole and the needs and wishes embedded in the social environment. In contrast, the third force, which represents the humanistic and existential psychologies, emphasizes the role of consciously held human values, aspirations, and free will in guiding development. It regards the primary sources of development as intrinsic to the individual rather than extrinsic or the result of a combination of internal and external forces. Later in his career, Maslow also introduced the notion of the fourth force, which is transpersonal and emphasizes advanced levels of development, including self-actualization and spiritual awakening. Maslow's typology leaves out the cognitive sciences, which is a fundamental departure from each of these four forces. Although the first force has had little direct impact on the study of human development, most current studies draw heavily on later developments of the psychoanalytic tradition, such as ego or self psychology; on some of the humanistic psychologies of the third force; or on the cognitive-developmental tradition.

B. The Field of Human Development

Theories of human development can be characterized using several typologies, two of which are discussed here. Merriam and Caffarella (1999) classify human development theories in mainly disciplinary categories:

biological, psychological, sociocultural, and integrative. The biological perspective focuses on issues of maturation and the physical components of the aging process. It is concerned with the complex interplay among genetic, hormonal, and other physical factors. From the psychological perspective have emerged theories of ego development, cognitive and intellectual development, moral reasoning, spiritual transformation, the role of life events and transitions, and the development of relationships. In contrast, the sociocultural perspective is primarily concerned with the impact of social, cultural, and historical conditions on the succession of roles. For example, Neugarten (1985) suggests, "Every society is age-graded, and every society has a system of social expectations regarding age-appropriate behavior" (p. 16). Finally, with the increasing use of complex system theories, there has been a growing interest in an integrative perspective, popularly referred to as the biopsychosocial approach. Clark and Caffarella (1999) rightfully point out that most such studies remain in the conceptualization stage.

Pulkkinen and Caspi (2002) propose an alternative typology of human development theories and identify three approaches: (1) growth models, (2) life-span models, and (3) life-course models. Growth models derive from the psychoanalytic and humanistic traditions. Some of the best known include those of Erikson (1963), Loevinger (1976), Piaget (1953), and Levinson (1994). These are typically models of psychosocial and individual development that involve stages of task achievement, with each stage a prerequisite for successful progression to successive stages. Such models also tend to focus on particular areas of functioning, such as psychosexual maturity, cognitive abilities, or moral reasoning. Life-span models, in contrast, take a broader view and are concerned with both childhood and adult development, as well as three major sources of influence: (1) age-graded influences (e.g., education), which shape development in normative ways; (2) history-graded influences, which mold behavior on the basis of unique circumstances (e.g., wars, depressions); and (3) nonnormative influences, such as accidents or unexpected actions of particular individuals (see also Baltes et al., 2006). Thus, development is viewed as resulting from the cumulative impact of ongoing and discontinuous processes. The unfolding of expected stages continuously interacts with the effects of chance, history, and individual decisions. Some have criticized such models as reflecting a Western cultural bias that overemphasizes individualism and free will (Kagitcibasi, 1996).

Finally, life-course models tend to take an even broader sociocultural perspective than life-span models (see Elder & Shanahan, 2006). Elder and Shanahan explain that the life course consists of "a series of socially-defined, age-graded events and roles that defines, in large measure, the contours of biography" (p. 667). Unlike growth and stage theories, which focus on the temporal order of life stages, life-course models emphasize interactions between social roles and societal systems encountered at various stages and in various historical eras. They are interested primarily in developmental trajectories and are based on personal and social conditions, such as choice, the timing of life events, the linkage of lives within and between generations, and cultural and historical changes.

C. Current Issues

The human development field has seen few radically new theories in recent years. Most activity has involved the critique and refinement of traditional theories and attempts to reconcile some divergent approaches. Recent work has focused on understanding emotion, biological factors in development, cognition, and relationships. Interest in emotion has involved the ways that mental and biological factors interact, which has spawned such new fields as psychoneuroimmunology. Much of the newfound interest in emotion pertains to questions about the regulation of emotions. Closely related with the emerging interest in emotion is interest in the biological basis of socioemotional development. For example, Coie and Dodge (1998) examine how biological and environmental factors generate observed differences in the sexes in aggressive behavior. However, they argue that there is not sufficient data to support the role of genetics in explaining differences between the sexes in physical aggressiveness among adults.

In recent years, the study of cognition has focused on whether cognition plays a primary role in development, generating various emotional and behavioral patterns, or whether it is mostly reactive, and emerges only after the fact, generated by underlying feelings. For example, research on moral development often assumes that cognition is central. Turiel (1998) argues that cognition is as important as emotion, if not more important, in moral development. Interest in the role of relationships has also been significant. Some theorists, especially feminist theorists, have sought to recast developmental theory primarily in relational terms (Jordan, Kaplan, Miller, Striver, & Surrey, 1991). The topic of attachment has received attention as well, especially the question of the long-term impacts of early disruptions in attachments with caretakers. There also has been much effort to reinterpret traditional theories using some of the terminology and insights of complex systems theory. For example, some have used the notion of dynamic attractors, especially strange attractors (see chapter 1), to explain psychological complexes, personality patterns, and development trajectories, among other phenomena (see Thelen & Smith, 2006).

The field of human development has made considerable progress in formulating a more multidimensional vision than that which the various stage theories can encompass. Much of this research, drawing on life-span and life-course models, has grown out of a few long-term longitudinal research programs, such as the Berkeley Growth Study and the Oakland Growth Study, at the University of California, Berkeley; the Dunedin Multidisciplinary Health and Development Study, at the University of Otago, New Zealand; the Fels Longitudinal Study, at the Fels Institute in Yellow Springs, Ohio; and the National Child Development Survey, at the Institute of Education, London. Nonetheless, there are many unresolved issues that require continued work. One is resiliency (see chapter 5), or the ability to spring back or rebound, to successfully adapt in the face of adversity, and to develop social competence despite exposure to severe stress (Rivkin & Hoopman, 1991). Many have observed the unpredictable recovery of individuals from childhoods of severe deprivation and trauma—thus, the interest in the sources of resiliency.

Resiliency has been studied from several different angles. One has focused on understanding how childhood temperament is related to adult personality patterns. Temperament has been defined as "constitutionally-based individual differences in reactivity and self-regulation, influenced over time by heredity and experience" (Rothbart, 1989, p. 59). While reactivity refers to excitability, responsiveness, or arousal, self-regulation connotes "behavioral processes that modulate this reactivity" (Clark & Watson, 1999, p. 399). Although the relationship between childhood temperament and subsequent adult personality is generally assumed, it is remarkably difficult to establish a definitive connection. One reason for this is the lack of consensus regarding the appropriate typologies for describing childhood and infant temperaments and adult personality (Clark & Watson, 1999).

In addition, it is particularly difficult to relate adult personality with patterns of development, and it is much less clear whether there is any simple association. To what extent does adult personality determine subsequent developmental trajectories? Conversely, is personality the outcome of those trajectories? The belief in developmental contextualism, predominant in life-span and life-course models, suggests that personality is marked by a greater degree of plasticity than many have assumed, especially those who emphasize the evolutionary basis of behavior. Traditional social scientists assume that genetics and evolutionary inheritance provide only broad constraints for behavior, with considerable leeway. This contrasts with sociobiologists, who believe that there is, in some sense, a core human nature that all humans share.

II. Lines of Development

Much of the research on human development has explored discrete lines of development, particular aspects of the individual, such as biological maturation, cognitive abilities, ego strengths, sense of self, relational skills, and moral reasoning. This section reviews some of the key theories in each area. There is much debate about how developmental lines interact. Is there a minimum level of ego development needed to achieve a desired level of moral reasoning, or vice versa? To what extent can growth in one area (e.g., cognitive development) compensate for lack of development in another area (e.g., poor relational skills)? The answers to such questions partly depend on the individual's social and cultural environment, as significant others will support or reject individuals on the basis of their own values and prejudices. The less supportive the social environment is, the greater is the need for strong integrative and executive ego functions that capitalize on strengths in other areas. This review of the multiple lines of development begins with the biological dimension, which in many respects is a foundation for the others.

A. Biological Maturation

1. THE ROLE OF GENETICS

Maturation is a process of unfoldment in which various structures and functions come to operate in a predictable sequence, based on the successful emergence of previous stages and genetic instructions. Romig (1997) defines maturation as any relatively permanent change in behavior or ability that primarily results from genetics or biological causes. The environment is usually viewed as playing a secondary or supporting role in maturation. There is controversy over whether biological maturation simply provides the necessary structures and overall constraints for psychological and social development or whether it controls the development of particular temperaments, personalities, or behavioral patterns. Nonetheless, there is evidence that the blank slate of inherited predispositions is not nearly as blank as earlier generations of social scientists had imagined. Caspi (1998) studied identical twins who had been raised apart, and he found that genetic effects account for between 22 percent and 46 percent of total variation in the personality traits of extraversion, agreeableness, conscientiousness, neuroticism, and openness to experience. Most of the remaining variance is a function of environmental influences unique to each individual, as well as gene-environment interactions and errors of measurement. Sharing an environment with siblings or larger groups accounts for only minimal variance.

Even in the same family, different individuals (e.g., the oldest and youngest children) experience markedly different environmental influences.

The ongoing nature-nurture debate between those who emphasize genetics and those who emphasize the environment and social learning has often obscured the complex interrelationships between processes of biological maturation and social learning. Each individual's genotype—the corpus of genetic information encoded in genes—is only one factor, though an important one, in determining phenotype, or the actual biological individual who develops. It is generally believed that multiple genes are implicated in the more enduring behavioral patterns, and that each gene may have different patterns of influence on the final outcome. Rarely does a particular gene, or even a system of genes, have a deterministic influence on personality. A gene may create a propensity for a behavioral pattern (e.g., through the development of a cognitive deficit) that then has secondary or tertiary behavioral effects depending on the responses from others who are significant in the social environment. Genes may sensitize individuals to particular environmental conditions that they may or may not actually encounter. Genetic effects may influence individuals to seek out particular environments or even to create new environments, thereby generating complicated feedback loops. In general, most genetic effects on behavior are no doubt fairly indirect and operate through complex chains of influence (e.g., through their effect on initial brain structure and its subsequent development).

2. NEUROCHEMICAL MECHANISMS

Neurochemical mechanisms are an important part of an individual's biology. There is substantial evidence of three primary emotional systems with genetic and neurochemical roots. First, the behavioral inhibition system of the brain's septal and hippocampal circuits has been linked to the omission or termination of rewards and the ability to inhibit behavior. Second is the better-known fight-or-flight system, rooted in the amygdala, hypothalamus, and central gray areas of the brain. Threatening or aversive events, such as pain, activate this system and lead to escape or aggression. Third, the behavioral approach system of the basal ganglia, which accompanies dopaminergic tracts and parts of the thalamus, is activated by events associated with reward or the termination of punishment, and it generally elicits approach behaviors (Gray, 1991).

Central to these systems and to the brain as a whole is the functioning of neurotransmitters. There are hundreds of neurotransmitters, but only a few are of central importance (Kagan, 1998). Kagan (1998), for instance, reports that norepinephrine, has been found to increase the signal-to-noise ratio in sensory areas, causing sensitivity to sensory events. It is also important for the functioning of the sympathetic nervous system. Boys with conduct disorder have been found to have lower-than-average heart rates, associated with low levels of norepinephrine, which in turn is associated with insensitivity to environmental cues. Impulsivity has also been associated with low levels of dopamine, also considered critical for the control of motor behavior. Above-average levels of endorphins have also been implicated in children's blunted sympathetic reactions to challenge, whereas lower-than-average endorphin levels may bring about exaggerated reactions. Serotonin is associated with a sense of well-being, but at low levels it can result in states of excitation, anger, or depression. However, in each instance, it has been nearly impossible to determine whether abnormal levels of these neurotransmitters are the cause or the consequence of the associated mood, or whether both are an outcome of some other underlying process, either physical or mental.

3. Infant and Childhood Temperament

Biological processes are known to have specific and substantial impacts on infant development. The unfoldment of standard reflexes, such as the startle response, hiccups, or yawns, appear with remarkable regularity and little variation. Likewise, there is a high level of agreement between the timing of the emergence of object permanence, fear of strangers, separation fear, language acquisition, and symbolic play (Kagan, 1998). There has been much research to identify infant and childhood temperaments, the presumed precursors to adult personality patterns. One of the best-known efforts is that of Mary Rothbart (1989), who isolated two dimensions of infant temperament. On the one hand, infants can be characterized on the basis of their ease of arousal with respect to motor activity, affect, and autonomic or endocrinal responses. On the other hand, infants can be characterized on the basis of their degree of self-regulation. Such processes modulate reactivity, such as attention, approach or withdrawal, and the ability to self-soothe. Both sets of characteristics are stable behavioral patterns during infancy. These concepts are not without problems, as they represent fairly generalized patterns that can have different meanings according to context. For example, ease of arousal can involve either happy or sad affects. Thus, when affect is used to characterize infant temperament, it is important to specify tone, context, and objects. Other proposed dimensions of infant temperament include level of irritability, smiling, activity, and attention span.

The extent to which infant temperament affects subsequent development is controversial. For example, infants with a tendency to smile may invite considerably more care and nurturing than those who are irritable. Several researchers (e.g., Caspi, 1998) have categorized the kinds of relationships that infants and children have with their social environments along the following lines. First, reactive transactions are those made in response to the actions of significant others. Second, evocative transactions (e.g., smiling) invoke standard responses from others. Third, proactive transactions are those in which the subject selects, seeks out, or creates environments on his or her own. This last type of transaction presupposes the highest level of maturity of the three (which may well emerge from the second transaction), the ability to evoke desired reactions from others.

Temperamental patterns identified for children older than two resemble infant patterns but are more diverse and complex. Bates's (1989) typology identifies several key dimensions. Negative emotionality is the display of distress, fear, and anger. Related are difficultness or irritability, sensitivity to stress, and demandingness. Adaptability to novelty is the tendency to approach unfamiliar events or situations. Reactivity is similar to Rothbart's (1989) ease of arousal. Attention regulation is the ability to focus and shift attention as appropriate. Finally, sociability and positive reactivity reflect the extraversion dimension found in many adult personality tests (Bates, 1989).

Although there are only nominal correlations between infant temperamental patterns and adult development, there is considerably more evidence linking childhood and adult patterns. Measures of difficultness are predictive of internalizing and externalizing adult tendencies. In addition, childhood inhibition or unadaptability has been found to be associated with adult tendencies to internalize problems, and with attention difficulties (Caspi & Silva, 1995; Hirshfield et al., 1992).

4. Sexual Development

An important part of biological maturation is sexual development, a process that occurs throughout the entire life span. Even infants have demonstrated sexual responses such as erections or vaginal lubrication (Masters, Johnson, & Kolodny, 1982). Early forms of masturbation appear as soon as the age of two and a half or three years old. Beginning at about three years old, children begin to learn about genital differences. Sexual play takes place throughout childhood; however, it becomes more covert around the ages of six to nine. During the preadolescent years of eight to twelve, children have a "homosexual" social organization, based on the division of children into groups of boys and girls (DeLemater & Friedrich, 2003). This is also a period during which children gain greater experience with masturbation. Marking the transition from preadolescence to adolescence (typically between ten and fourteen years old) is puberty, or the sudden enlargement and maturation of the gonads, other genitalia, and secondary sexual characteristics (e.g., breasts, pubic hair). Many boys masturbate more frequently at this time; however, the start of masturbation among girls tends to be more gradual. Between the middle and end of adolescence, approximately 48 percent of girls and 52 percent of boys in the United States experience heterosexual intercourse for the first time (DeLamater & Friedrich, 2003).

During young adulthood, sexuality is increasingly integrated into ongoing relationships or expressed through a wide variety of sexual preferences and lifestyles. Following childbearing age, women usually pass through menopause anywhere between the age of forty and sixty, with the decline in estrogen leading sometimes to uncomfortable changes in the female genitalia. At about the same time, men undergo what has been referred to as andropause, or a decline in testosterone levels, which can lead to slow erections and a long refractory time, or the period between orgasms during which erections cannot occur (Verma, Mahajan, & Mittal, 2006).

This section has introduced a few of the many biopsychosocial dimensions of maturation. Other important areas are the development of fine and gross motor coordination, speech production, development of disease resistance, changes in sensory acuity, and important processes associated with old age (see exhibit 5.1). The emergence of each of the many physical capabilities or conditions (e.g., dexterity, sexual pleasure, visual or auditory acuity) facilitates the development of the functions of the personality, which in turn often buffer against the decline of those functions in old age.

B. Cognitive Development

Emerging from biological maturation and the interaction of the child with his or her social environment is cognitive development. The development of cognitive abilities has been both narrowly and broadly defined. On the one hand, it can refer to the specific acquisition of skills in hypothetico-deductive logic. On the other hand, it includes a wide variety of problem-solving skills, such as observation, decision making, and the use of analogies.

1. PIAGET'S GENETIC EPISTEMOLOGY

The most influential theorist in the field of cognitive development is Jean Piaget (b. 1896–d. 1980), a Swiss psychologist best known for his theory of formal operations, but his more important contributions are rational constructivism or genetic epistemology and his rich observations on how children solve problems and learn.

Piaget argued that knowledge serves a biological function and derives from action. He argued that children learn through the active construction of mental representations, or schemes, of the self in relation to its world.

EXHIBIT 5.1: THEORIES OF AGING

The following outline covers some of the most prominent theories on the biological basis of the aging process, as well as some of the social and psychological ways people respond to these changes:

I. Biological Theories of the Aging Process
   A. Developmental-Genetic Theories
      1. **Hayflict limit theory:** The maximum number of times that cells can replicate, which Hayflict found to be about fifty. It is believed that this upper limit determines the maximum possible life span.
      2. **Free radical theory:** Highly charged ions—known to be damaging to cells. Aging may result from damage created by the proliferation of free radicals.
      3. **Immunological theory:** The decline of the immune system, especially as the T-cell function also declines with age. The breakdown of the immune system leads to increased susceptibility to disease and to the development of various autoimmune conditions.
      4. **Theory of intrinsic mutagenesis:** Declines in the effectiveness of regulatory mechanisms with age are hypothesized to lead to increase in mutational events and, thus, diseases such as cancer.
      5. **Neuroendocrinal and hormonal theory:** Regulation of many aging processes has been linked to the hypothalamus. Reduced secretions from the gland are suspected to initiate the aging process.
   B. Stochastic Theories
      1. **Error theory:** The accumulation of random errors in the synthesis of proteins is believed to lead to physical breakdown.
      2. **Somatic mutation:** Exposure to radiation and other environmental conditions is believed to cause genetic damage and result in degraded physical functioning.
      3. **Transcription theory:** Random errors in the copying of genetic information lead to mutations or other deleterious changes.
II. Psychosocial Theories Involving the Response to Aging
   A. **Disengagement theory:** A natural process of withdrawal of the individual and society, each from the other. Older adults

EXHIBIT 5.1 (CONTINUED)

> step aside and make room for younger people, which in turn enhances the diversity and vitality of the species and society.
>
> B. **Continuity theory:** Successful adaptations used earlier in life often should continue, as a person's traits, habits, values, associations, and goals often remain stable, regardless of life changes.
>
> C. **Activity theory:** Life satisfaction depends on maintaining involvement with life by developing new interests, hobbies, roles, and relationships appropriate to the new stage of life.

Piaget, Inhelder, and Weaver defined schemes as "the structure or organization of actions as they are transferred or generalized by repetition in similar or analogous circumstances. Thus schemes are habits of thought or action" (1969, p. 4). Piaget believed that the development of knowledge is at its root a biological process, a matter of an organism's adaptation to an environment. Some of his assumptions are the idea that schemes can be understood by observing behaviors during the solution of cognitive problems; that the construction of knowledge takes place in ongoing transactions with the physical, social, and linguistic milieu of children; and that both the needs and the processes of organization and adaptation motivate growth.

Organization is the achieving or maintaining of an internal coherence toward one's various schemes. Piaget, however, paid considerably more attention to the second process, adaptation, which consists of two tasks: assimilation and accommodation. Assimilation is the adaptation of one's perceptions and environment to existing schemes. When this is not possible (e.g., in a novel situation), one then has to accommodate either by adjusting existing schemes to the new situation or by creating new schemes. While infants and young children make greater use of assimilation, older children rely more on accommodation. The use of both types of adaptation constitutes the process of reflecting abstraction, by which children find a balance between the maintenance of internal organization or coherence of their schemes and the demands of their environment. Thus, Piaget's theory of formal operations is an equilibrium theory in that it envisions growth as driven by conflict or departures from equilibrium that must be dealt with through adaptation and equilibration.

Schemes can be mental representations of static physical objects, but more important they are representations of processes or operations. For example, children develop an understanding of the principle of conservation of the volume of a liquid as it is poured from one container to another or of the continued existence of an object when it is out of sight. At an older age, children learn principles of classification. Piaget might have shown a child six toy dogs and three toy cats, and asked, "Which are there more of—all of the animals or just the dogs?" A younger child would often say, "More dogs." In contrast, children age six and older would answer that there are more animals and be able to justify their answers. Although he deemphasized stages, Piaget theorized that rational schemes or constructions are acquired in four major stages or periods (with possible further stages).

1. Sensorimotor period (0–2 years old): During this thinking-in-action period, thought is almost entirely enacted and a type of egocentrism that merges the self with the surrounding world. The period culminates with an understanding of permanent objects and the ability to imitate others from memory alone.
2. Preoperational period (2–7 years old): This period is characterized by the ability to anticipate consequences of actions before carrying them out. The semiotic function of speaking and understanding language as well as pretend play also appear.
3. Concrete operations (7–11 years old): During this period, the ability to hierarchically classify objects develops, as does seriation, or the ability to order things in terms of some other variable (e.g., height, weight, conservation of physical quantities, simple mathematical operations). In this stage, children are still very limited in their ability to test hypotheses and to consider problems from multiple perspectives.
4. Formal operations (11 years and older): Formal thinking is characterized by the ability to solve problems with a broader range of possibilities by considering multiple perspectives, including abstract ones. Unlike concrete operations that involve first-order operations on physical objects, at this stage second-order operations are used to conduct operations on operations. For example, adolescents are at this time able to move from learning simple arithimetic to algebra, and they are able to distinguish logic from truth and to understand that statements may be logically true but untrue or even ridiculous.

Piaget also is known for his notions of horizontal and vertical decalage. Horizontal decalage is the tendency of people to rely on the most highly developed abilities during a given period of development to scaffold development of other less developed abilities. In contrast, vertical decalage is the partial appearance of a new cognitive structure during a stage before it is ordinarily encountered.

There have been numerous criticisms of Piaget's theory, some of them common to all stage theories. For example, many point out that there is considerably greater variability in the age that various cognitive abilities appear than Piaget believed. In particular, the appearance of the ability to engage in formal operations may appear in some preadolescents, but in many cases it does not manifest even in adulthood. Piaget has also been criticized for overemphasizing the role of formal logic, overestimating people's abilities to rationally problem solve, and neglecting other forms of problem solving. In addition, Piaget's approach is limited by the assumption that change and growth originate in the external environment; that without conflict and external challenge to create disequilibrium, there would be no motivation to adapt, equilibrate, and construct more rational cognitive structures.

2. VYGOTSKY'S SOCIOCULTURAL THEORY

In recent years, the work of Lev Vygotsky (b. 1896–d. 1934) has been recognized as a broader sociocultural alternative to Piaget's genetic epistemology. Since the demise of the Soviet Union, there has been a surge of interest in the work of Vygotsky, a developmental psychologist who has often been called the Mozart of psychology. As did Mozart, Vygotsky died very young, but he was a prolific writer. He proposed a cultural-historical theory of child development that emphasized children's interactions with their social environment and with significant objects (e.g., books, toys), which he referred to as artifacts. As did Piaget, Vygotsky viewed children as active participants in interactions, constructing knowledge, skills, and attitudes. Vygotsky proposed that maximal learning occurs through the integration of speech with action, and that most higher mental processes are first enacted in the social arena and then internalized. Movement is usually from the interpersonal to the intrapersonal. He also emphasized the role of formal education and its ability to stimulate development if it occurs in the child's zone of proximal development (ZPD) (Leong & Bodrova, 2001). Vygotsky (1978) defines the ZPD as "the distance between the actual developmental level as determined by independent problem solving and the level of potential development as determined through problem solving under adult guidance or in collaboration with more capable peers" (p. 86).

Closely associated with ZPD is the Vygotskian tutorial, or a learning situation (often a dyad) in which a slightly more experienced peer assists a child in the ZPD. Vygotsky also emphasized the role of play in supporting development in social and cognitive development, and he suggested that "a child's greatest achievements are possible in play, achievements that tomorrow will become her basic level of real action" (Vygotsky, 1933/1978, p. 92). Although Vygotsky's work is often promoted as an antidote to the more narrowly conceived cognitive focus of Piaget, there are many points of overlap between the two, not the least of which is their rejection of some of the more traditional deficit-based models that compare children with adult norms (Gillen, 2000). Vygotsky's work is the seminal source for the development of contemporary sociocultural theories of development (see Cole, 1996; Rogoff, 2003).

3. THE DEVELOPMENT OF MULTIPLE INTELLIGENCES

Central to the study of cognition is intelligence. However, intelligence paradoxically has not been a central concern of human development researchers. Traditionally, intelligence has been conceived of as a general unitary factor (the "g factor"), which is believed to be common to multiple domains of functioning and unchanging over development. Statistical interpretations of psychometric data suggest that individuals who solve one kind of problem well tend to be good at solving other types of problems. Furthermore, in such global theories of intelligence, relative intelligence has shown remarkable stability over various developmental stages. Especially in the United States, intelligence is popularly considered a genetic inheritance, hardly amenable to improvement. This is in marked contrast to Asian cultures, which often assume that there is little natural difference in intelligence among people and that what counts is individual effort.

However, an increasing number of researchers have advanced a more developmentally based understanding of intelligence. Several early investigators such as Thurston (1938) and Guilford (1967) proposed theories of multiple dimensions of intelligence. Howard Gardner (1999), an educational psychologist at Harvard, has most effectively pursued the idea that there are multiple, independent dimensions of intelligence. Gardner (1999) defines intelligence as a "biopsychological potential to process information that can be activated in a cultural setting to solve problems or create products that are of value in a culture" (p. 34). He bases his theory on traditional psychometric analyses and on psychoneurological studies, evolutionary data, and sociological and other studies. According to Gardner, there are at least seven distinct types of intelligence that vary independently both within and between people and that range from the logico-mathematical to the intrapersonal (see exhibit 5.2).

C. Behavior and Learning Theory

While cognitivists emphasize the development of various intelligences, and in general the ability to process information and construct mental models

---

EXHIBIT 5.2: GARDNER'S SEVEN DIMENSIONS OF INTELLIGENCE

1. **Logico-mathematical intelligence,** or the ability to solve problems through formal logic and mathematics
2. **Linguistic intelligence,** or the ability to use spoken and written language or to learn languages and use language to achieve desired ends
3. **Musical intelligence,** or skill in performing, appreciating, or composing musical patterns and the ability to solve problems in integrating harmonies, scales, tones, melodies, and the like
4. **Bodily-kinesthetic intelligence,** or the ability to use the physical body and motion to solve practical, athletic, or artistic problems—a form of intelligence important to craftspeople, magicians, stunt artists, athletes, and dancers, among others
5. **Spatial intelligence,** or the ability to perceive spatial relationships and manipulate their representations to solve problems, whether an architect's arrangement of rooms in a, a surgeon's planning of a delicate brain operation, or an archaeologist's reconstruction of an ancient village
6. **Interpersonal intelligence,** or the ability to understand human relationships, including others' motivations and ways they might engage in an undertaking—of particular importance for those in the human services and a variety of other fields
7. **Intrapersonal intelligence,** or the ability to understand oneself, to perceive oneself accurately, forgive oneself, and to regulate one's emotions and activities. There has been considerable interest in this area because of Daniel Goleman's (1995) best seller *Emotional Intelligence.* Goleman's emotional intelligence combines Gardner's interpersonal and intrapersonal intelligences.

---

of the self and the environment, behaviorists and social learning theorists regard behavioral inputs and outputs as central. They have not proposed stage theories of development but instead argue that understanding the component processes of learning, and how learning can be externally induced, is of primary importance.

1. CLASSICAL AND OPERANT CONDITIONING

The behaviorists of the early 1900s, such as Ivan Pavlov (1927) and John Watson (1930), promoted an approach that has come to be known as classical behaviorism or classical conditioning. Pavlov discovered in experiments that dogs would begin to salivate when an experimenter entered the room around mealtime. The dogs came to associate an unconditioned stimulus (i.e., food) with a neutral stimulus (i.e., the experimenter's entry), which became a conditioned stimulus. The dogs' salivating—an unconditioned response—then became paired with the conditioned stimulus of the experimenter's entry, regardless of the actual presence of the food. This is also referred to as a type of stimulus response, or S-R learning, which is the creation of associations between naturally occurring and intentionally introduced stimuli and responses. Other concepts central to classical conditioning include discrimination, or the ability to distinguish between cues; generalization, or the ability to carry over learning from one situation to others; extinction, or the interruption of the association of conditioned and unconditioned stimuli; and spontaneous recovery, the reappearance of a conditioned response after a rest period or period of weakened response.

In contrast to S-R learning, behaviorists later focused on operant conditioning, associated with Burrhus F. Skinner (b. 1904–d. 1990). Operant conditioning is a type of R-S learning in that it relies on a stimulus that reinforces a prior response. This idea originates in Edward Thorndike's law of effect (see Herrnstein, 1970): when some satisfactory state of affairs follows a behavior, the chances of the behavior reoccurring are greater. Skinner distinguished between reinforcement and punishment, and between positive and negative forms of those. Whereas reinforcement is the provision of something desirable to increase the probability of a target behavior, punishment is the provision of something bad to diminish the probability of a behavior. In positive reinforcement, a reward is given to promote a target behavior. In negative reinforcement, an undesirable state of affairs is removed to encourage a behavior (e.g., the discontinuation of an adolescent's grounding). With a positive punishment, some unpleasant sanction is delivered to discourage a behavior, whereas negative punishment involves the removal of a positive condition (e.g., allowance) to discourage a behavior.

Skinner found that learning is best stimulated through schedules of partial reinforcement, and often reinforcement delivered at variable times. Another principle of Skinner's operant conditioning is the shaping of discrete behaviors into larger patterns, often through the successive approximation of the desired state. Both classical and operant conditioning have been used to understand cognitive and social learning processes, but they have been largely ignored in recent years as excessively narrow, as they reject cognitive and emotional processes of learning and development and, in general, all the intervening processes in the mental black box between stimulus and response.

2. SOCIAL LEARNING THEORY

Eventually, social learning theories came to supplant classical and operant behavioral approaches. The person most commonly associated with
social learning is Albert Bandura, who identified several additional forms of
learning based on notions of self-efficacy and observation. Bandura, Ross,
and Ross (1961) conducted several studies known as the Bobo doll experiments. They found that children who observed adults playing calmly with
the doll also played calmly with it, and children who saw adults hitting
and abusing the doll tended to do the same. This led Bandura to propose
three principles of social learning (Bandura, 1977). The first two involve the
principles of radical behaviorism (e.g., conditioning, reinforcement, generalization), or the idea that behaviors can be acquired, maintained, and extinguished through stimulus-response and operant conditioning. The third
involves the ways that people learn through methods that the classical or
operant conditioning theorists did not consider:

1.   Observational or vicarious learning (sometimes called latent learn-
     ing), in which people can observe behaviors and implement them
     at a later time.
2.   Self-reinforcement, in which individuals reward themselves or de-
     velop a sense of pride or pleasure in the pursuit or accomplishment
     of some goal through various internal feedback mechanisms. This
     can also involve the impact of observing others being reinforced.
3.   Anticipatory control, another means of learning, is the expectation
     of reward or the fear of punishment.
4.   Motivation, which social learning theorists consider critical in
     moderating how individuals evaluate and respond to externally
     imposed reinforcements or sanctions and in driving the learning
     process in the absence of any external controls.
5.   Reciprocal determinism, which Bandura defined as the interaction
     among cognitive factors (e.g., motivations, beliefs, perceptions,
     values, emotions), environmental conditions (e.g., rewards, pun-
     ishments), and the behaviors themselves.

Over the years, Bandura progressively incorporated new elements from
the cognitive sciences into his theory of social learning; by 1986, he had
renamed it the *theory of social cognition.* Several themes have pervaded his
work. One is modeling, or people's ability to learn through identification
with significant others in their social environment. Another is self-efficacy,
which Bandura views as the foundation of human agency. He argues that
self-efficacy should not be equated with a type of excessive individualism

or pitted against the social interdependency that collectivist cultures stress. He suggests that there are three types of self-efficacy: (1) personal, (2) proxy, and (3) collective. Individuals can develop a sense not only of personal efficacy but also of being able to have an indirect impact through the help of others. Very important is the sense of collective efficacy, which enables groups to have sufficient faith in their ability to take action to pursue valued ends. Bandura also has emphasized the role of self-regulation in learning, which involves self-observation, judgment processes, and self-response or self-reinforcement. On the whole, Bandura's work is a generalization of behavioral learning theory integrated with cognitive theory. His most recent work recognizes the importance of the cognitive dimension and the role of nonlinearity, reciprocal relationships, self-organization, and complex systems in social and cognitive learning.

D. Psychosocial Development

Biological, cognitive, and behavioral development concerns particular, albeit critical, aspects of personality. Each of these lines of development comprises elements that affect the overall development of the personality and its evolving relationship with society, an area referred to as psychosocial development. Chapter 6 explores theories of motivation and personality in greater depth, but this section introduces a few of the leading theories on the development of the personality, including self-psychology, object relations theory, and the stage theories of ego development. Approaches to psychological development have shifted only gradually from those that emphasize intrapsychic functions to those that place development in a social context. Classical Freudian approaches are intrapsychic in that they assume that the primary conflicts are between personality structures, that only social relations influence development during infancy and early childhood, and that thereafter such influences are internalized for better or for worse. Contemporary approaches, in contrast, consider the relationship between the individual and society to be more truly transactional and extending over the entire life cycle.

1. Psychosexual and Drive Development

The classic analytic understanding of psychological development is that it is primarily driven by psychosexual development, particularly the development of the sexual and aggressive drives, and secondarily by anxiety, object relations, and defense mechanisms (see table 5.1). Freud considered the sexual or libidinal drive (Eros) of central importance in very young children, where it is expressed mainly through the mouth, then the anal region, and

TABLE 5.1: THE CLASSICAL PSYCHOANALYTIC THEORY OF PSYCHOSEXUAL DEVELOPMENT: DRIVES, ANXIETIES, AND DEFENSES

| | Drive Development | |
APPROXIMATE AGE	SEXUAL (LIBIDINAL) DRIVES	AGGRESSIVE DRIVES
Birth to about 7–12 months	Primary narcissism	Primary masochism
6 months to 3 years	Oral	Oral sadism
2–4 years	Anal	Anal sadism
3–6 years	Phallic-Oedipal	Phallic sadism and competitiveness
5–12 years	Latency	Aggressive sublimated in learning and competitive games
11–13 years	Puberty	
12–25 years	Adolescence	Competitiveness for heterosexual partner
21–65 years	Adult genital	Aggressive sublimated in work and recreation

Note: This rendition of classical psychosexual drive theory has been adapted from an earlier table of unknown origin.

DEVELOPMENT OF ANXIETY	DEVELOPMENT OF DEFENSES
Diffuse anxiety from traumatic states of undischarged drive tension	Stimulus barrier; denial
Separation anxiety	Introjection and tension discharged by impulsive action
Ego-ideal anxiety: shame	Reaction formation, undoing, and isolation
Castration anxiety	Repression, displacement, and avoidance
Superego anxiety: guilt	Intellectualization, rationalization, and beginning sublimation
Resurgence of superego anxiety, shame, and guilt	Disruption of defenses
Gradual reduction of fear, shame, and guilt	Intellectualization, idealization, and asceticism; gradual reestablishment of former defenses
Realistic fears	Sublimation and realistic adaptations

finally the genitals. Likewise, the aggressive drive gradually transforms from oral sadism to anal and phallic sadism as well as competition for sexual partners, and eventually it may be expressed in a healthy manner through work and recreation. Later, Freud also hypothesized the existence of a death wish, which is referred to as Thanatos.

Freud conceived of the drives as inherently threatening because, when unrestrained, they bring the individual into conflict with others, or at least with his or her own conscience. Thus, at each stage of development, he identified various types of signal anxiety with respect to the individual's reaction to the potential emergence into consciousness of the drives and their feared consequences. For example, during the oral period, separation anxiety is of central importance, and subsequently shame and guilt become more salient. As the individual matures, these anxieties give way to more realistic fears. To deal with the various forms of anxiety, the individual develops progressively more sophisticated layers of defense mechanisms that hide the true threat of the underlying drives while expressing or discharging them in a safe manner. Earlier stages feature the mechanisms of denial, repression, and projection; however, these prove counterproductive and give way to more adaptive defenses such as intellectualization and sublimation.

2. ATTACHMENT THEORY

As children develop various psychological structures and defenses, they develop a capacity for relationships, initially through their relationships with a mother or other primary caretaker. Whereas traditional drive theorists regard pleasure seeking as the primary motivation for relationships, object relations theorists assert that individuals seek other people first and pleasure only secondarily.

The psychoanalyst Margaret Mahler (b. 1897–d. 1985), a founder of object relations theory, took an empirical approach to the study of early infant development. Mahler is best known for her theory that a child's sense of self results from the process of separating from the mother. If separation proceeds normally, then the child is able to internalize an image of his or her mother and achieve object constancy, or a sense of the mother's existence even when she is not present, as well as the ability to unify good and bad split object parts or partial images of the mother. If this does not happen, major mental disorders may develop, such as childhood psychosis or borderline personality disorder, in which the individual cannot simultaneously comprehend both good and bad aspects in a psychological object. Specifically, Mahler identified the following stages of childhood development in her classic work *The Psychological Birth of the Human Infant* (Mahler, Pine, & Bergman, 2000):

1. Normal autism (0–1 months): A half-asleep and half-awake state
    in which the infant perceives the mother as part of him- or herself.
    The infant's central task is to achieve homeostasis with the envi-
    ronment.

2. Symbiotic phase (1–5 months): The child becomes aware of his or
    her mother but still needs to develop a sense of individuality. The
    infant experiences fusion with the mother, as well as a boundary
    between them and the rest of the world.

3. Separation and individuation (6–24 months)

    a. Differentiation (6–10 months): The infant begins to crawl
        and "hatch" from his or her relationship with the mother. The
        infant develops a more alert sensorium and begins to scan
        the environment for what is and is not mother. As a result,
        stranger anxiety emerges.

    b. Practicing (10–18 months): Free upright walking begins; how-
        ever, the infant periodically needs to return to the mother for
        sustenance. Separation anxiety develops, as does the child's
        assertion of his or her ability to say no.

    c. Rapprochement (18–24 months): The child begins to accept
        separation and master separation anxiety, and develops an
        interest in sharing various new skills with the mother. This
        subphase begins with the rapprochement crisis, an intensified
        need for the mother and for being soothed, yet not without
        considerable difficulty in accepting such care (e.g., this has
        been symbolized by the child standing at the threshold of a
        door and being unable to decide whether to pass through it
        or return).

4. Emotional object constancy (24–36 months): The child develops
    the ability to play independently and to cope with the absence of
    the mother because her image is now internalized.

Some of the most important initial insights into the role of object relations are found in the work of the British psychiatrist John Bowlby and
the American developmental psychologist Mary Ainsworth (1991). In direct
observations of infants, they found that there is a fundamental drive that
causes people to seek out caretaking objects. They conceptualized attachment through an ethological framework, developed through natural selection as a genetically based drive. They also identified the phenomenon of
filial imprinting, in which infants at very early stages attach to caretakers,
often regardless of many of the presumed requirements, such as oral stimulation and feeding.

Bowlby and Ainsworth's work (1991) drew on the experiments of Harry Harlowe (1962), who demonstrated that baby rhesus monkeys would attach even to surrogate mothers made from wire frames covered with terry cloth. Their attachment to the surrogates, although most easily influenced by the softness of the terry cloth, could also be influenced by the presence of milk, being rocked, or warmth, which demonstrates an innate drive to attachment that depended only marginally on the particular characteristics of the object.

Bowlby and Ainsworth (1991) identified three styles of attachment that they found carried over into adult relationships with significant others, each of which partly depends on the type of response the infant received from his or her mother. Most people (about 62 percent) are able to experience secure attachments with others, which are associated with loving and responsive maternal relationships. However, about a quarter (23 percent) of adults can be characterized as avoidants (i.e., they actively avoid or are detached from others), and such adults were typically denied physical contact with their mothers as infants. A smaller group of people, about 15 percent of the population, falls into the anxious/ambivalent group: they are anxious, clinging, and insecure in their relationships with others, and generally experienced inconsistent caretakers.

Although attachment theory may appear to state the obvious, it represents a major departure from the classic drive perspective that treated the infant as a kind of blank slate whose evolving psychological makeup was passively impressed on him or her by the mother, whose quality of care was considered almost entirely responsible for whether pathology or health developed. Attachment theory, while still identifying an important role for the caretaker, shows that the intensity of the infant's own drive to attach also plays a critical role.

3. THE SENSE OF SELF AND IDENTITY

An essential part of psychosocial development—largely ignored by the classical psychoanalytic tradition—is the development of a sense of self, identity, and self-esteem. This is an area, however, of increasing interest for psychological theorists. One of the most notable such developments is the work of Daniel Stern, who extended Heinz Kohut's work on self-psychology (see theory example 5.1). In Stern's 1985 book *The Interpersonal World of the Infant,* he argues that infants never experience a primary narcissistic or autistic-like phase, as Mahler and others theorized.

Stern found that, from the start, the infant organizes the world around a rudimentary feeling of self, which he refers to as the emergent self. This phase, lasting for the first two months of life, involves episodic, loosely

THEORY EXAMPLE 5.1: SELF-PSYCHOLOGY: THE THEORY OF HEINZ KOHUT

OVERVIEW: Heinz Kohut (b. 1913–d. 1981) departed from the classical psychosexual drive theory to argue for the centrality of relationships, specifically, empathic relationships. His two-person psychology conceives of two lines of development: that of a cohesive self with its internalized guiding ideals and that involving the capacity for empathic relationships. Kohut (1984) defined empathy as the "capacity to think and feel oneself into the inner life of another person" (p. 82). He also saw it as the main therapeutic agent, the source of theoretical knowledge, and a model for social conduct (Kohut, 1977).

CENTRAL CONCEPTS: The central notion is the self-object, which refers to the experiences of another, specifically, the experience of an impersonal function that another person provides and is often incompletely integrated or internalized as part of oneself.

Growth arises from a two-step process: (1) basic empathic attunement between the self and its self-objects sets the stage for, and is followed by, (2) transmuting internalizations, whereby small or manageable failures are experienced in either one's sense of self or one's idealizations of significant others. Such small failures permit the individual to develop a more realistic and cohesive sense of self, psychological structure, and a more empathic relationship with significant others. These may occur as part of therapeutic relationships or transferences or as part of the natural course of development.

When such growth processes fail, what is often seen is split-off narcissism or grandiosity becomes unconscious, often manifesting as a sense of inner depletion—the narcissistic personality is characterized by such symptoms as directionlessness, fear of death, desire to merge with idealized objects, repressed rage, fear of dependence, and a sense of inner emptiness.

Kohut (1971) hypothesized three types of relationships with self-objects that typically need to be worked through and resolved:

1. **Idealizing transference,** or the tendency to project one's grandiosity on to another. The resolution of this transference permits the internalization of guiding ideals or values.
2. **Mirroring transference,** in which the individual reacts to a self-object "only insofar as it contributes to (or interferes with) the maintenance of the analysand's narcissistic homeostasis" (p. 122)
3. **Twinship or alter-ego transference,** in which the self-object is similar but separate from the self—when worked through, this is the basis for many types of social relationship

THEORY EXAMPLE 5.1 (CONTINUED)

CRITIQUE: While Kohut can be commended for moving beyond the narrow psychosexual focus of the classical or id psychologies, and for his contributions to the study of empathy, his theory remained narrow and highly intrapsychic, minimizing rational and conscious functions, complex relationships, and the larger society and culture. An exception is Christopher Lasch's application of self-psychology to an analysis of American culture (1978).

connected experiences and at least four primary abilities: (1) the seeking of sensory stimulation, (2) the demonstration of preferences for some types of stimulation over others, (3) the testing of hypotheses about the surrounding world, and (4) participation in affective and cognitive processes. These abilities develop in the context of a relationship with a primary caregiver. After the first two months, the emergent self gives way to the core self, which involves self-agency, or "a sense of authorship of one's own actions" (1985, p. 71); a sense of being a nonfragmented physical whole; self-affectivity with inner feelings; and self-history, or the feeling of the continuity of existence. Following the core self, at about seven to nine months, the subjective self develops. In this phase, the infant participates in deliberately sought sharing: both the infant and caretaker share attention, intentions, and affective states. It is a period in which the infant seeks what has traditionally been referred to as mirroring or empathic resonance. Stern refers to the caretaker's ability to empathize and respond to the infant as a type of affect attunement. Finally, during the second year, the verbal self develops. In addition to the ability to verbalize about the self, children begin to develop gender identity, empathy, and the ability to objectify themselves. Later, Stern added a fifth phase, the narrative self, which involves the ability of the child to conceive of and tell a story about him- or herself. He referred to this ability as a laboratory for self-identity, which sets the stage for the evolution of the sense of self throughout the life cycle.

Other theorists have focused on the development of self-identity, a more circumscribed function built on the sense of self that most actively develops during adolescence. Harold Grotevant (1987), for instance, proposed a process model of identity formation that involves both the exploration of alternatives and the commitment to choices between those alternatives. Exploration consists of gathering information and testing hypotheses about oneself and one's roles and relationships, and commitment depends on the degree of coherence that the individual can achieve, based on such factors as flexibility, self-esteem, self-monitoring, openness, and cognitive abilities. Michael Ber-zonsky (1993) extended Grotevant's model and characterized identity seekers as self-theorists, involved in the process of theorizing about themselves. He distinguishes three styles of self-theorizing: (1) scientific, (2) dogmatic, and (3) ad hoc. Scientific self-theorists systematically explore alternatives and test individual inclinations, while dogmatic self-theorists are self-serving in their tendency to conform to expected roles. In contrast, ad hoc self-theorists move among many alternatives but are never able to settle on one.

Berzonsky's styles of self-theorizing parallel the better-known model of James Marcia (1966), who hypothesized that adolescents and young adults experience four identity statuses (see figure 5.1). Ad hoc theorists are most likely to have what Marcia refers to as a diffused identity status. Dogmatic theorists, in contrast, have a foreclosed status, one that cuts short necessary exploration, and scientific theorists are in moratorium, are actively seek-ing resolution, or have achieved a sense of identity. Self-identity commonly entails both affective and cognitive commitments to such areas as vocation, political and religious identification, and sexual preference, though not nec-essarily all of these.

4. EGO DEVELOPMENT

Probably the most significant efforts to understand psychosocial de-velopment have been undertaken by proponents of stage theories of ego development. Freud identified the ego, or "I," as one of three major psy-chological structures, along with the id, or unconscious, and the superego, or conscience. The ego is that part of the personality that integrates and resolves conflicts between the drives and the conscience, and between the individual as a whole and society. It functions like the ballast of a ship, pro-viding stability and continuity and a platform for consciousness and its vari-ous problem-solving activities. Traditional ego psychologists identify three major functions of the ego: (1) cognitive, (2) executive, and (3) integrative. The cognitive involves both perception and problem solving; the executive, the ability to make and carry out decisions; and the integrative, the ability to harmonize the various problem-solving efforts and reconcile them with basic values and social demands.

Best known among the ego psychologist is Erik Erikson (b. 1902–d. 1994) (see profile 5.1), whose theory differed from the classical analytic view in several important respects. Erikson deemphasized the role of psychosexual development and the unconscious and instead regarded the individual as a rational, moral agent. He also believed that development continued through adult life and depended integrally on the individual's relationship with soci-ety as a whole, rather than on only a few significant caretakers during early

FIGURE 5.1: IDENTITY STATUSES: DEVELOPMENTAL PATHWAYS AND A DECISION TREE FOR THEIR ASSESSMENT

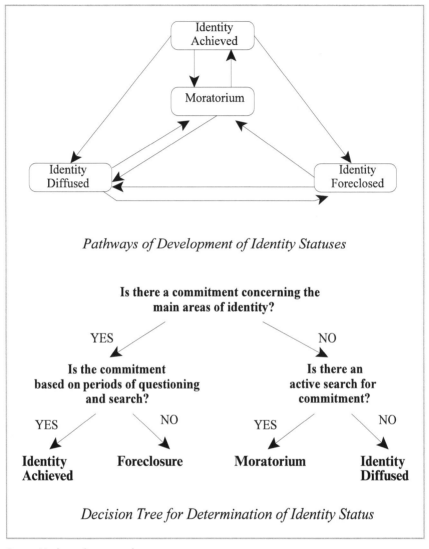

Pathways of Development of Identity Statuses

Decision Tree for Determination of Identity Status

Source: Moshman (1999, p. 73).

childhood. He characterized his theory of development with an epigenetic perspective borrowed from biology, which he explained in the following terms: "anything that grows has a ground plan, and that out of this ground plan the parts arise, each part having its time of special ascendency, until all parts have arisen to form a functioning whole" (Erikson, 1968, p. 92). He

Profile 5.1: Erik Erikson

Erik Homberger Erikson (b. 1902–d. 1994) was born to a single Jewish mother, Karla Abrahamsen, whom his biological father had abandoned. She later married her son's Danish pediatrician, Dr. Theodor Homberger, who adopted the young child. As a child, Erikson's Jewish neighbors rejected him for his Nordic appearance, and his classmates teased him for being Jewish.

After high school graduation, Erikson's initial aspiration was to become an artist. He took art classes, visited museums, and wandered around Europe, often sleeping under bridges. By the late 1920s, he was teaching art in Vienna and studying with Anna Freud, who was also his analyst at the Vienna Psychoanalytic Institute. At that time, he met Joan Serson, a Canadian dance teacher, whom he married and later had three children with.

When the Nazis came to power, Erikson left Vienna for Copenhagen, and in 1933, he immigrated to the United States to become Boston's first child psychoanalyst and a professor at Harvard's Medical School. He subsequently held positions at Yale, Berkeley, the Menninger Foundation, the Center for Advanced Study in the Behavioral Sciences at Palo Alto, and the Mount Zion Hospital in San Francisco. During the McCarthy era in the early 1950s, Erikson resigned from a post at Berkeley rather than sign a loyalty oath. He then spent a decade working and teaching in a clinic in Massachusetts before returning to Harvard, from where he retired in 1970.

It was in Erikson's initial book, the Pulitzer Prize–winning and National Book Award–winning *Childhood and Society* (1950), that he divided the life cycle into eight psychosocial stages of development. The book also included his study of Native American children, which permitted him to correlate personality development with social conditions; analyses of Maxim Gorky and Adolf Hitler; his reflections on the American personality; his views on Freudian theory; and his introduction of the concept of identity crisis, which he considered central to adolescence.

Erikson's work was profound and far ranging. He was interested in combat crises of American soldiers in World War II, child-rearing practices among the Sioux and Yurok, social behavior in India, troubled adolescents, and patterns of play among both normal and emotionally disturbed children. He wrote about a wide variety of social issues, including the generation gap, racial tensions, delinquency, sex roles, and nuclear war. His later work, in general, concerned ethical issues confronting the modern world.

viewed development as a series of conflicts or crises, each with one of the pivotal ego strengths pitted against its opposite. The progressive development of each strength depends on the successful resolution of each of the proceeding psychosocial stages and their associated crisis; as such, growth is a process of cumulative unfoldment. The crises of each stage have also been characterized as general tasks that require extended periods of time for completion as well as particular environments and significant others. For example, a child in elementary school needs to learn how to be industrious, something that he or she can master only through the complex interrelationships of child, school, and family (Erikson, 1963).

The first of Erikson's stages takes place from infancy to approximately the first year of life (see table 5.2). The child's task is to develop trust without completely forgoing the ability for mistrust. The second stage is associated with the traditional anal-muscular stage of early childhood, from about eighteen months to three or four years old, and involves achieving a degree of autonomy while minimizing shame and doubt. Nevertheless, minimal shame and doubt is not only inevitable but also beneficial; without them, Erikson points out that impulsiveness might develop. From three to about five or six years old, the task for each child is to learn initiative without experiencing too much guilt. Initiative entails a proactive response to life's challenges, the taking on of responsibilities, the learning of new skills, and being purposeful. The fourth stage is latency, which applies to school-age children from about six to twelve years old. The task in this stage is to become industrious while avoiding an excessive sense of inferiority. Too much industry may lead to the tendency known as narrow virtuosity, which is seen in children who are not allowed to "be" children (e.g., child actors, athletes, musicians, prodigies). An alternative negative outcome is inertia, or the tendency to resist change.

The fifth stage, adolescence, begins with puberty and ends at about eighteen to twenty years old. The task here is achieving ego identity and avoiding role confusion. Ego identity refers to an individual knowing who he or she is and how he or she fits in with society. It also involves developing a unified self-image that is also acceptable to the community. After adolescence, young people confront the sixth stage, the tasks of young adulthood, from about eighteen to thirty years old. The task during this phase is to be able to be intimate (i.e., close to others, as lovers or friends) rather than remain in isolation. The seventh stage of middle adulthood includes the period during which people are actively involved in raising children. The task at this time involves cultivating the proper balance of generativity (i.e., the investment of love and effort in future generations) and stagnation. The final stage of late adulthood or maturity begins at about the time of retirement. For Erikson,

TABLE 5.2: ERIK ERIKSON'S STAGES OF PSYCHOSOCIAL DEVELOPMENT

AGE	PSYCHOSOCIAL STAGE	EGO STRENGTH AND ANTIPATHY	IMPORTANT ACTIVITY
Birth to 12–18 months: Infancy	Basic Trust vs. Basic Mistrust	Hope vs. Withdrawal	Feeding
18 months to 3 years: Toddler Years	Autonomy vs. Shame, Doubt	Will vs. Compulsion	Toilet Training
3–6 years: Early Childhood	Initiative vs. Guilt	Purpose vs. Inhibition	Independence
6–12 years: Latency	Industry vs. Inferiority	Competence vs. Inertia	School
12–18 years: Adolescence	Identity vs. Role Confusion	Fidelity vs. Role Repudiation	Peer Relationships
19–40 years: Young Adulthood	Intimacy vs. Isolation	Love vs. Exclusivity	Love Relationships
40–65 years: Adulthood	Generativity vs. Stagnation	Care vs. Rejectivity	Parenting
65 to death: Old Age	Ego Integrity vs. Despair	Wisdom vs. Disdain	Review of and Acceptance of One's Life

Source: Erikson (1950).

reaching this stage is a major achievement; not reaching it suggests that earlier issues inhibited development. The task entails the development of ego integrity with minimal despair. Ego integrity is the acceptance of one's life, with its successes and failures, and thus acceptance of death. A maladaptive outcome of this last stage is presumption, which takes place when a person presumes ego integrity without having actually worked through the issues of old age. A similarly negative tendency is disdain, by which Erikson means a contempt of life, either one's own or anyone else's. The impact of Erikson's work has been substantial: he not only introduced the concept of identity and psychosocial crises but also stimulated a variety of applications of his theory, such as Gail Sheehy's (1991, 1995) work on adult development (see theory example 5.2).

In recent years, Jane Loevinger (1976) has advanced the preeminent approach to ego development. Her model has been placed in the traditions of

THEORY EXAMPLE 5.2: PASSAGES AND PATHFINDERS: THE PERSPECTIVE OF GAIL SHEEHY

OVERVIEW: Gail Sheehy has conducted several large-scale surveys to examine American adult development, building on Erikson's psychosocial stages and other theories of life-course development. She is particularly interested in the transitions between age-graded phases, or "passages," and their interactions with historical and cultural developments and with individual strengths.

PASSAGES: The term *passages* refers to the predictable crises or turning points that usher in a new life stage. Although a passage might be an event such as marriage, childbirth, a first job, or the empty nest, Sheehy (1995) defines a passage as an "underlying *impulse toward change* that signals us from the realm of mind or spirit. The inner realm is where we register the *meaning* of our participating in the external world" (p. 11). The following are some examples:

- **Pulling up roots (18–22):** Beginning separation from family of origin
- **Trying twenties (23–27):** Initial attempts to establish a provisional career identity, cultivation of a capacity for intimacy, and proving oneself unique
- **Catch-30 (28–33):** A crisis involving reevaluation of the efforts of the prior decade
- **Deadline decade (35–45):** First crisis of mortality, acceptance of limitations, renewed commitments to family and career
- **Comeback decade (46–55):** Concern with balance between work and play, and intensified efforts toward previous commitments
- **Freestyle fifties:** A central task is "giving permission to oneself to do not only the things one should, but also the things one likes to" (1981, p. 51).
- **Selective sixties:** A paring down of activities and renewed commitment to others, and deciding how long one wants to live
- **Thoughtful seventies:** Bringing enjoyment and new independence or stagnation
- **Proud-to-be eighties:** Balancing giving and taking aid and comfort

GENERATIONS: The common experience of various generations—the World War II generation (born between 1914 and 1929), the silent generation (born between 1930 and 1945), the Vietnam generation (born between 1946 and 1955), the "me" generation (born between 1956

THEORY EXAMPLE 5.2 (CONTINUED)

and 1965), and the endangered generation (born between 1965 and 1980)—molds the experiences with the foregoing passages.

PHASES OF A SUCCESSFUL PASSAGE:

1. **Anticipation:** Imagining oneself in the next stage of life
2. **Separation and incubation:** Letting go of an outlived identity
3. **Expansion:** Deliberate intervention in life conflict and risk taking
4. **Incorporation:** Reflection on and integration of one's new aspects; and dormancy, for rest, reward, and play to offset stress of change (Sheehy, 1981).

CHARACTERISTICS OF A SUCCESSFUL PATHFINDER

1. Sense of meaning and direction
2. Ability to handle transitions creatively
3. Willingness to take risks
4. Sense of justice, goodness, and trust in life
5. Ability to attain long-term goals
6. Ability to grow
7. Ability to love
8. Ability to maintain friendships
9. Ability to maintain cheerfulness and perspective
10. No oversensitivity to criticism
11. Lack of major fears (Sheehy, 1981)

both ego psychology and cognitive developmentalism, and is considered an attempt to integrate the two. Unlike Piaget, who regards the process of equilibration as driving development, Loevinger deemphasizes the need to maintain equilibrium and instead considers the drives to mastery and meaning as two central driving forces of growth. She also emphasizes two principles that guide development. The first is a dialectic of personal growth that involves, among other things, the internalization of relationships with significant others that come to serve as models for internal differentiation. The second is the reversal from the passive to the active voice, which includes achievement of mastery by actively repeating that which an individual experienced passively, formerly referred to as the repetition compulsion. She regarded the extent and type of growth as characterized by four dimensions: (1) impulse control and/or character development, (2) independence and autonomy, (3) conscious preoccupations, and (4) tolerance for ambiguity (see Blasi, 1998).

At each developmental stage there are progressively more sophisticated forms of impulse control, interpersonal mode or style, and conscious preoccupations (see table 5.3). During the initial three stages, though, individuals are impulsive, self-protective, or conformist. Most Americans have been found to have achieved an intermediate level of ego development, either the self-aware or conscientious stages (Hy & Loevinger, 1996). The self-aware stage involves recognition of the discrepancies between one's ideal self and one's real self, and the beginning of the ability to self-reflect. In contrast, the conscientious stage involves the ability to internalize self-evaluated standards and the capacity for inner-directedness. The next level, the individualistic stage, brings about a sense of individuality and an appreciation of individual differences, as well as the ability to understand psychological causation. At the subsequent autonomous stage there is "a high toleration for ambiguity and a recognition of paradoxes.... The conscientious person's striving for

TABLE 5.3: JANE LOEVINGER'S STAGES OF EGO DEVELOPMENT

	Characteristics		
LEVEL	CONTROL OF IMPULSES	INTERPERSONAL MODE	CONSCIOUS PREOCCUPATIONS
Impulsive	Impulsive	Egocentric, dependent	Bodily feelings
Self-Protective	Opportunistic	Manipulative, wary	Trouble, control
Conformist	Respect for rules	Cooperative, loyal	Appearances, behavior
Self-Aware	Exceptions are allowable	Helpful, self-aware	Feelings, problems, adjustment
Conscientious	Self-evaluated standards; self-critical	Intense, responsible	Motives, traits, achievements
Individualistic	Tolerant	Mutual	Individuality, development, roles
Autonomous	Coping with conflict	Interdependent	Self-fulfillment, psychological causation
Integrated		Cherishing individuality	Identity

Source: Adapted from Hy & Loevinger (1996, p. 4).

achievement is transmuted into a search for self-fulfillment" (Hy & Loevinger, 1996, p. 6). The final stage, integration, is ill defined, and less than 1 percent of the U.S. population is believed to have achieved this stage; however, it is similar to Erikson's final stage of integrity, which involves self-acceptance (see Hy & Loevinger, 1996). Loevinger's stages echo Erikson's in that individuals require a clear sense of themselves before they can form truly intimate relationships with others. However, she concluded that because most people spend a lifetime developing this ability, an individual's psychological clock, not age or environment, determine progression from one level to the next.

5. THE RELATIONAL PERSPECTIVE ON WOMEN'S DEVELOPMENT

Another recent development is the relational perspective, which originated with a group of psychologists affiliated with the Stone Center at Wellesley College. Judith Jordan (1997) points out that most traditional theories of human development derive from the study of male development, and thus excessively emphasize the ability to separate, to become independent, and to individuate. Jordan (1997) concludes that "Increasing self-control, a sense of self as origin of action and intention, an increasing capacity to use abstract logic, and a movement toward self-sufficiency characterize the maturation of the ideal Western self" (p. 9). The Stone Center theorists instead propose that the fundamental human drive or need is to relate with others, and that "relational capabilities and processes exist from the time of birth and develop over the course of one's life" (Jordan 1997, p. 21). For this reason, the development of women involves not so much the transition from dependence to independence but rather increasing levels of connection, empathic attunement, and caring. Although the group is particularly critical of traditional Freudian theories, its proponents also believe that neo-Freudians, attachment theorists, and self-psychologists, among others, fall into many of the same traps of overemphasizing individualistic modes of development. In recent years, the group has attempted to generalize its model to take into account the diverse cultures in which women develop, as it had been criticized for perpetuating an upper-middle-class Western bias. Although the proposed theory remains more of a general perspective, given its lack of specificity and explanatory ability, it nonetheless has made a significant contribution to relational values and to the understanding of women's development.

E. Moral and Spiritual Development

A line of development that mainstream developmental theorists have traditionally neglected is moral decision making and spirituality. However, newer developments as diverse as postmodernism, phenomenology, and the cognitive sciences have set the stage for theorists such as Kohlberg, Fowler, and Wilber to address moral and spiritual development.

1. Kohlberg's Theory of Moral Development

The development of the ability to make decisions consistent with ethics is the focus of the emerging field of moral psychology. As might be expected, definitions of moral development are controversial, especially Lawrence Kohlberg's (1981) definition. Kohlberg built on Piaget's theory of cognitive development to propose his now-classic theory of moral development. In his view, moral development is the increasingly sophisticated ability to intellectually apply principles of justice to the solution of moral dilemmas (see table 5.4). Part of this consists of the ability to assume multiple perspectives on the problem at hand, as well as the ability to deductively reason from general principles to particular situations, something that Kohlberg believed develops in an invariant stagelike fashion.

Kohlberg hypothesized that moral development progresses from what he referred to as preconventional stages to the conventional and

TABLE 5.4: KOHLBERG'S STAGES OF MORAL DEVELOPMENT

LIFE STAGE	STAGE OF MORAL DEVELOPMENT
Infancy	
Early Childhood	Preconventional: punishment and obedience
Middle Childhood	Preconventional: instrumental exchange
Older Childhood	Conventional: interpersonal relations/conformity
Adolescence	Conventional: social order/laws
Early Adulthood	Postconventional: social contract/utility
Middle Adulthood	Postconventional: universal rights/principles
Older Adulthood	

Note: Under "Stages of Moral Development," the final three stages represent uncertain or exceptional progression.

postconventional. Each of the three levels has two substages. In the first preconventional substage, punishment and obedience, the child conceives of morality as unquestioning obedience to authority and the avoidance of punishment by not breaking rules. In contrast, instrumental exchange, the second preconventional substage, is characterized by a more utilitarian view of rules that calls for following them depending on whether they contribute to individuals' welfare. In the first conventional substage, interpersonal relations and conformity, morality is viewed in terms of meeting the needs of the majority. In the second conventional substage, social order and laws, the maintenance of order becomes a central concern.

In contrast, in the postconventional levels of moral development, the idea of principled reasoning, which only a minority of adults achieve, assumes central importance. The first substage, social contract and utility, involves the upholding of rules because they are part of a social contract. In the second substage, universal rights and principles, moral development reaches a level at which moral decision making is internalized and the individual fully understands that what is legal and what is ethical are not necessarily the same. The movement in individuals is from particularistic to universal principles.

Kohlberg's stages have been criticized from several perspectives. Carol Gilligan (1998), for instance, points out that his emphasis on justice tends to undervalue expressions of morality among many women who have an ethic of relationship, care, and mutual support. Even though Kohlberg studied only men, he speculated that women were unlikely to advance past the third stage. Others criticize Kohlberg's focus on cognitive, and specifically deductive, forms of rational decision making and his assumption that there are universal principles of justice (Arnold, 2000). Others, such as Blasi (1995), suggest that a conception of the self is missing from Kohlberg's model, and that consistency in moral decision making may be a function of the coherence of the self. Similarly, some suggest that emotion may play a critical role in moral decision making (see Damasio, 2003). In any case, Kohlberg should be credited with elevating moral decision making to a process that develops systematically over time and with rejecting the once-popular notion that morals were simplistically imparted from one generation to the next, as if by osmosis.

2. APPROACHES TO SPIRITUAL AND TRANSPERSONAL GROWTH

While the development of moral decision making serves an integrative function in ego development, a potentially broader, more inclusive type of development is spiritual or transpersonal. Carl Jung (1921) characterized this process as individuation, which he believed began most commonly in the second half of life with the process of reconciling and integrating split-off and unconscious aspects of the personality (which he referred to as the shadow) with the conscious ego. In contrast, James Fowler (1996), a Christian theologian, views spiritual development as one of faith development, and he incorporated elements of Piaget's genetic epistemology and Kohlberg's stages of moral development. He defines faith broadly as a "pattern of our relatedness to self, others, and our world in light of our relatedness to ultimacy" (p. 21). Faith serves to ground ego functioning and moral decision making in the individual's relationship with whatever it is that he or she considers of ultimate significance. Fowler conceives of spiritual or faith development as progressing from fantasy and a mythic-literal understanding of religion during childhood to a conventional faith grounded in the attitudes of peers and, for some adults, an individuative-reflective faith involving critical reflection. A few adults are believed to progress to either a conjunctive or a universalizing faith that is nonjudgmental, transcendent, and inclusive.

Others, such as Ken Wilber (2000), have drawn on Eastern mystical traditions to envision spiritual growth as a movement from the pre-egoic to egoic and transegoic levels of awareness to increasingly inclusive levels of integration, culminating in what he terms *unitary consciousness*. Depending on how one conceives of spirituality—as attitudes of faith, ethical behavior, a relationship with the divine, the quality of everyday life, or inner experience—resultant stage theories will take wildly divergent forms. Thus, these models should be regarded as only suggestive of possible avenues of individual development (for further discussion of spiritual development, see chapter 15).

III. Complex Systems and Human Development

Traditional stage theories, as well as life-span and life-course models, have all contributed much to understanding some of the normative developmental patterns, at least in modern societies. A key limitation of such models, though, is their inability to go beyond description to clarify the forces that drive long-term patterns of change and generate their simultaneous coherence and unpredictability. Most models point to conflict, whether micro or macro—or intrapsychic, interpersonal, or cultural—as the primary motivator for change. For example, in Piaget's theory of cognitive development, disequilibrium forces response and adaptation on the part of the individual and drives growth. Freudian theories of human development assume not only that conflict is central but also that the major thrust is to discharge libido or psychic energy to the lowest available state, to satisfy biologically rooted needs. While there is certainly evidence that conflict and the effort to reestablish equilibrium initiate change, there is also much evidence that at least some individuals and systems have sufficient control over immediate problems such that they are able to act proactively, either to solve long-term problems or to seek out new challenges and discover novel problems that require no particular reaction or adaptation. Some growth is reactive, but much is not externally driven. Development from a complex systems perspective involves the reciprocal interaction of the individual with key environmental conditions that select for particular behaviors and characteristics. This interaction, depicted in the top-left circle of figure 5.2, is nested within

FIGURE 5.2: DEVELOPMENT AS AN OUTCOME OF THE MULTIPLE EFFECTS OF SELECTION, ADAPTATION, AND SELF-ORGANIZATION: SOME KEY RELATIONSHIPS

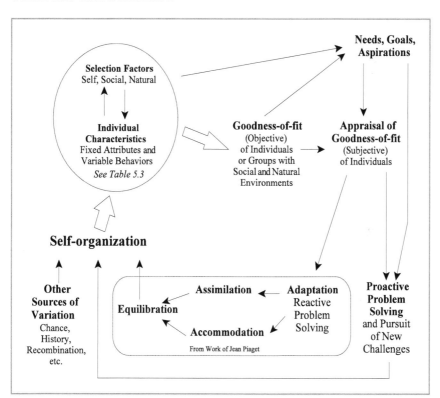

Notes: The above reflects only a few of the important relationships between self, social, and natural selection; individual goals; reactive and proactive problem solving; and self-organization in human development. It is the iterative or repeated looping around this causal chain, both within lives and between generations, on the intrapsychic, personal, and group levels that is expected to produce the developmental patterns we experience and observe.

Source: Hudson (2004).

a larger interactive system consisting of the extent of the goodness of fit between the individual and his or her environments, including individuals' subjective appraisal of the fit in the light of needs, goals, aspirations, and values, as well as the reactive adaptation to any lack of fit and proactive problem solving based on aspirations and values. The results of multiple reactive and proactive efforts are then self-organized, and perhaps given a certain critical mass of activity, into new sets of characteristics, behaviors, and ultimately selective factors. The relationships portrayed in figure 5.2 represent a few of the key ways that self, social, and natural selection are nested within the larger problem-solving efforts of the individual and the ways that these are self-organized to create observed developmental patterns.

A. The Role of Natural, Social, and Self-Selection

In evolutionary biology, selective factors include conditions in the physical environment, other species, and other members of the same species. The power of environmental factors to favor or disfavor the propagation of particular attributes (e.g., the stripes of a zebra, the swiftness of a cheetah) explains the biological evolution of such attributes. However, when evolutionary principles are applied to human behavior, it is necessary to consider these principles in the context of society and culture, and of individual consciousness and choice. While humans continue, albeit less frequently, to be subject to selective factors in the natural environment (e.g., viruses), social change is becoming increasingly based on social and self-selection. Table 5.5 provides examples of each of these types of selection and how they affect behavior and physical attributes.

Of greatest importance in understanding human behavior is self-selection, which refers to the propensity of humans to select for particular relationships, activities, occupations, or life courses. Of course, people may not actualize many of their selections, and it is not unusual that preferences of the family and larger community take precedence (e.g., those with severe mental illness may live in institutions, in lonely flophouses, or on the street). Perhaps the most powerful selections are those that represent agreements between the selections of the self and the larger social systems.

It is particularly important to keep in mind that selective factors can operate on seemingly fixed individual attributes and on behaviors and attitudes. It would seem that the sex or race of individuals can not changed by social selection, but we know that the gender or racial composition of groups is often dramatically affected by recruitment, admissions, promotion, and discharge practices, as well as by the tendency of many individuals to select themselves in or out of particular groups on the basis of such

TABLE 5.5: SOURCES OF SELECTION AND EXAMPLES OF THEIR IMPACT ON VARIATIONS IN INDIVIDUAL CHARACTERISTICS AND BEHAVIORS

Selection / Variation		Type of Selection		
		SELF	SOCIAL	NATURAL
CHARACTERISTICS THAT SELECTION ACTS ON	SOCIAL, BEHAVIORAL, CULTURAL	• Commitment to a personal identity • Rejection of self based on behavioral or cultural stereotypes • Decisions of average students not to apply to the most competitive colleges	• Recruitment of individuals with outgoing personalities into various clubs or careers • Selection of human service professionals for positions based on their perceived interpersonal skills or their maturity • Greater likelihood for survival during wars of people who can cooperate with one another	• Survival of people in floods based on ability to swim • Survival during epidemics based on ability to maintain hygiene and to cooperate with one another • Increased chance for living a long life, based on exercise, social support, access to health care, etc.
	PHYSICAL (e.g., age, gender, race, height)	• Decisions of individuals to undergo arduous migrations based on an assessment of their own health or strength • Tendency of many to select themselves out of certain career options based on their gender	• Exclusion of individuals from social opportunities based on sexism, racism, ageism, physical disability • Competition of strippers for jobs based on sexual attributes	• Survival of individuals with strong immune systems during epidemics • Better ability for heavier people to survive life in extremely cold conditions

Note: Each of the above are illustrations of the impact of self, social, or natural selection on individual lives, specifically, on factors that enhance or detract from their well-being and survival, as well their support of other's well-being and survival.

Source: Hudson (2004).

physical attributes and the reception that they anticipate in an envisioned group. Environmental selective factors are usually thought to primarily affect the individual rather than vice versa. However, figure 5.2 depicts this relationship of the selections and individual as a two-way relationship: once selection takes place, the new set of individual characteristics modifies the selective factors. Much of this relationship may operate through the system portrayed, through adaptive and proactive action, but some feedback is more immediate. For example, a company that discriminates against anyone older than forty in its hiring may later be forced to reverse course when key areas of experience are discovered to be missing or when age-discrimination lawsuits become prohibitively expensive to defend against.

The individual's response to their fit or lack of fit with the environment — and the ability to carry over these responses from one life phase to another, or from one generation to the next — affects the outcome of the interaction of selective factors, which typically involve environmental challenges and opportunities. In evolutionary biology, this transmission is believed to operate primarily through the transmission of genes from one generation to the next. To the extent that a characteristic or a behavioral pattern is genetically linked, this is a relevant avenue of intergenerational propagation. But when it comes to behavior and culture, many other means of transmission are available, including imitation, family socialization, and formal education. This transmission may be functional or dysfunctional. For instance, problem-solving methods that worked in an earlier stage of life or for one generation may become destructive in a new context. Adaptive responses of individuals to traumas experienced during childhood may become dysfunctional when carried over into adult life.

B. Selection and Self-Organization

Progression through the various developmental stages is an interplay between self-organization (with self-selection as one of the most central processes) and the selective influence of the social and physical environments. Although the environment has a considerable impact on nourishing or thwarting development, and on creating challenges, it also plays an increasingly reactive role in the direction inherent in the individual's self-organizing tendencies. As development progresses, with an increasingly wider array of individual capabilities coming into play, the relative importance of the various lines of development change. At the earlier stages, biological, cognitive, and emotional lines of development assume particular importance, but as these become established, their integration becomes particularly important. For this reason, ego, moral, and spiritual development become increasingly critical as the personality develops and becomes more complex and engaged with a wider variety of environments. The assessment of development, thus, entails not only judgments about which stages have been achieved in the various lines of development but also, and more important, judgments about how the different capabilities support or conflict with one another. Are interpersonal skills used to compensate for a lack of ability to feel empathy? Are a person's cognitive skills (e.g., intelligence) engaged in the supporting the solution of difficult moral dilemmas? Are a person's spiritual beliefs used to find a balance between a difficult-to-implement universal moral principle and the demands of an immediate practical situation? Do certain functions missed during earlier periods, such as the development of a cohesive sense of self, now undermine the unfoldment of other capabilities, such as a sense of identity during adolescence?

C. Assessment from a Developmental Perspective

The extent to which human services professionals are able to fully assess the breadth and depth of developmental dynamics involved in a given problem is contingent not only on their skill and knowledge but also on the mandate of the employing agency, the available assessment tools, and the interest and openness of the clients in engaging in such exploration. The various problems that clients bring to human service professionals unfortunately preclude any standard assessment protocol. Thus, staff in particular settings (e.g., schools, developmental centers, hospitals) need to use protocols appropriate to the types of clients they see most commonly. In some assessments, such as those involving children, the evaluation of developmental accomplishments and problems is a concern. However, in adults, the assessment of developmental stages is somewhat less central, and developmental issues are treated as part of the context for the examination of the presenting difficulties (e.g., a mental illness, a financial emergency). The assessment protocol draws on information from some mix of interviews, tests, observations, historical records, and other suitable sources of information. The assessment of human development is performed in a wide range of contexts, including schools, hospitals, correctional centers, developmental programs, and general counseling programs for children, adults, and families. Although there is no single protocol that can be used, there are several general principles that guide assessments in many of these contexts:

1. Be clear about the purposes of the assessment (e.g., to decide on admission to a program, to determine classroom placement, to develop a therapeutic intervention, to recommend exceptions from

legal sanctions). Part of this involves clarity regarding confidentiality, including the development and distribution of reports.

2. Assessment should be a collaborative undertaking to the extent possible, focusing on concerns and needs of those being assessed and including them in the collection and interpretation of information.

3. Assessment should draw on multiple sources of information and perspectives. For example, in a school setting it should include the viewpoints of the child, family, teachers, and any other personnel involved, and it can include informal interviews, tests, observations, and structured tasks.

4. Those conducting assessments need to find a balance between focusing merely on presenting problems and engaging in protracted but sometimes necessary assessments of multiple lines of development. Secondary areas examined should have a reasonable connection with the presenting concerns.

5. When tests or other protocols with known reliability and validity are available to measure some area of development they should be used and administered by professionals trained to do so.

6. Assessment protocols should be used whenever possible but should not substitute for professional judgment, which must guide their flexible application and interpretation.

7. Procedures and tests should be culturally and linguistically appropriate for the subject and should have age and other norms developed for them using appropriate populations.

8. Assessments should focus, whenever possible, on those difficulties that are possibly or potentially remediable. The process should be presented as a part of and in the context of a helping relationship.

9. Assessment should be ongoing and integrated with any services provided.

10. Assessments go beyond diagnosis to shed light on the dynamic processes involved in client difficulties, and identification of types of changes can realistically facilitate improvement in areas of concern.

11. Those conducting assessments need to understand the ways that assessment affects those being assessed, the emotional stress created, and the possibility of reinforcing any areas of weakness, as well as the therapeutic benefits. There is the saying, "If you assess what you value, others will value what you assess." For these reasons, assessment should also focus on areas of strength whenever

possible, including ways to employ these strengths to address any areas of difficulty.

12. Results of assessments and recommendations should always be shared and discussed first with the subject of the assessment.

13. The assessment process and results should be adequately documented.

14. Not only should the confidentiality of all records be assiduously protected, but also the privacy of the assessment process needs to be guarded (e.g., children in school should not be called for special education testing by a school's loudspeaker system).

IV. Summary

This chapter has introduced human development and some of the ways that it can be understood through complex systems theory. It has reviewed theories involving biological maturation, social learning, psychosocial development, and moral and spiritual growth. In its introductory section, it considered growth, life-span, and life-course models of human development and reviewed several of the current issues in the field, including psychophysiological aspects of growth, the role of emotion, temperament and its relationship to adult personality, and resiliency.

Various lines of development were each reviewed in discussions of the leading theories in each area, including biological maturation, cognitive development, theories of learning, and psychosocial and moral development. The discussion of biological maturation included several of the major ways that genetic instructions translate into behavior, such as the role of neurotransmitters. The section also examined Rothbart's work on infant temperament and its relationship with temperamental patterns of older children and the personalities of adults. The review of theories of cognitive development included Piaget's genetic epistemology, Vygotsky's sociocultural theory of development, and Gardner's theory of multiple intelligence. Although learning theorists have been reluctant to propose any stage theories of development, the progression of work in this area illustrates broader thinking in this field and an attempt to bring learning theory into line with the complexities of human cognition.

The discussion of psychosocial development identified several component avenues of development, including classical psychosexual theories of the development of the drives, anxiety, and defenses; the sense of self and identity; the ability to attach to and relate with others; and ego development.

Two leading approaches to ego development were presented, those of Erik Erickson and Jane Loevinger. While Erikson's has work focused on the development of a series of strengths through age-specific crises involving the relationship of the self and the social environment, Loevinger has sought to integrate ego psychology with the cognitive tradition, especially with Piaget's theory of cognitive development.

Finally, the review of theories of moral development built on the prior sections in that it treated moral and spiritual development as inclusive of and transcending the prior lines considered. It began by considering Kohlberg's somewhat narrow view of moral development and several of its critiques. It then presented an example of a theory of faith development, that of James Fowler, and the alternative approach of Ken Wilber, which draws on various Eastern spiritual traditions.

The chapter concludes with a discussion of the role of self-organization in development and its relationship with the various types of selection— natural, social, and self—that form the backdrop of development. It emphasizes that self-organization operates on each of these sources of internal and external selection, as do both chance and historical events, to generate observed patterns of development. The section also discusses a few of the principles that guide the application of developmental theory, from a complex systems perspective to the process of professional assessment in the human services.

For Further Reading

Blasi, A. (1998). Loevinger's theory of ego development and its relationship to the cognitive-developmental approach. In P. M. Westenberg, A. Blasi, & L. D. Cohn (Eds.), *Personality development. Theoretical, empirical, and clinical investigations of Loevinger's conception of ego development* (Chap. 1). Mahwah, NJ: Erlbaum.

Bowlby, J., & Ainsworth, M.D. (1991). An ethological approach to personality development. *American Psychologist, 46,* 333–341.

Caspi, A. (1987). Personality in the life course. *Journal of Personality and Social Psychology, 53,* 1203–1213.

Erikson, E. (1963). *Childhood and society.* New York: Norton.

Fowler, J. W. (1996). *Faithful change: The personal and public challenges of post-modern life.* Nashville, TN: Abingdon Press.

Gardner, H., Krechevsky, M., Sternberg, R., & Okagaki, L. (1994). Intelligence in context: Enhancing students' practical intelligence for school. In

K. McGilly (Ed.), *Classroom lessons: Integrating cognitive theory and classroom practice* (pp. 105–128). Cambridge, MA: MIT Press.

Jordan, J. V. (Ed.). (1997). *Women's growth in diversity. More writings from the Stone Center.* New York: Guilford Press.

Kagitcibasi, C. (1996). *Family and human development across cultures: A view from the other side.* Hillsdale, NJ: Erlbaum.

Lerner, R. M. (2006). *Handbook of child psychology: Vol. 1. Theoretical Models of Human Development.* New York: Wiley.

Rothbart, M. K. (1989). Temperament in childhood. In G. A. Kohnstamm, J. E. Bates, & M. K. Rothbart (Eds.), *Temperament in childhood* (pp. 59–73). New York: Wiley.

Sheehy, G. (1995). *New passages: Mapping your life across time.* New York: Ballantine Books.

Stern, D. (1985). *The interpersonal world of the infant.* New York: Basic Books.

CHAPTER 6

Motivation and Personality: Conflict, Consistency, and Fulfillment Models

*The happiness and unhappiness of men depend as much on
their turn of mind as on fortune.*
                    —LA ROCHEFOUCAULD (B. 1613–D. 1680)

I. Introduction

This chapter explores the relationships among three pivotal features of
human functioning: happiness, motivation, and personality. It begins by
considering the theory and research on subjective well-being, reflected in
a person's happiness, resiliency, and mental health. The things that give us
pleasure or happiness, and the many flavors of such experiences—whether
love, knowledge, social inclusion, power, sexuality, avoidance of suffering,
or service—are ultimately the things that motivate us. Conversely, the fulfillment of our motivations contributes to the levels and types of happiness
that we experience. At the same time, our sense of well-being and our enduring motivations, which are elaborated on and refined through various developmental phases, become the foundations of our personality. Thus, states of
well-being, motivation, and personality display complex interactive relationships and are both cause and consequence of each other (see figure 6.1).

After reviewing the research on subjective well-being and motivation, this
chapter begins by exploring personality theory through some of the major ways
that individual personality differences have been identified and described empirically. It then moves to a discussion of theories about why such differences
exist. These theories are based on one of several competing assumptions about
the sources of personality differences, specifically about the ways individuals
handle conflict, live out an inner drive to actualize or fulfill inherent potentials,
and attempt to achieve cognitive coherence or consistency (see Maddi, 1996).

A. Some Definitions

There have been just about as many definitions of personality as there
have been researchers on the subject. Derlega, Winstead, and Jones (1999),

FIGURE 6.1: MAJOR DIMENSIONS OF PERSONALITY AND THEIR RECIPROCAL RELATIONSHIPS

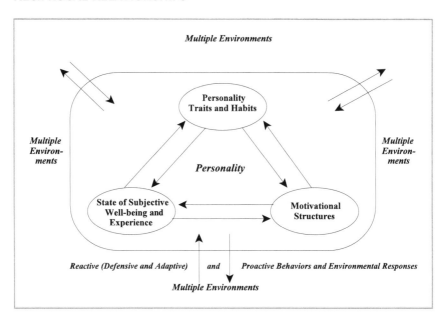

for instance, define personality as "the system of enduring, inner character-istics of individuals that contributes to consistency in behavior" (p. 22). Sim-ilarly, Gordon Allport (1937), a founder of the field of personology, derived the following definition from an analysis of fifty others that were available at the time: "personality is the dynamic organization within the individual of those psychophysical systems that determine his unique adjustments to his environment" (p. 48). In general, most researchers regard personality as involving two essential characteristics: (1) regularities and consistencies in personal behavior and (2) the synergistic effect of these characteristics, or the way that they operate collectively as a system or dynamic organization.

The study of personality involves an essential distinction between traits and states. Traits are enduring characteristics of a person's mental or be-havioral functioning, such as insightfulness, gregariousness, or docility. A personality includes but is more than a collection of traits. In contrast, a state is a temporary and context-specific personality condition or feature, often one that is broader than a particular trait, such as conditions of agita-tion, elation, or boredom. Traits may predispose individuals to particular states; conversely, states may accumulate to generate new traits. In general, the term *personality* connotes the enduring organization of an individual's behavioral and mental traits and recurrent or typical states, including the ways they function together, positively or negatively, to fulfill needs, desires, and aspirations.

Personality differs from the two related concepts of temperament and character (see Livesley, 2001). The concept of temperament, introduced in chapter 5, refers to underlying biological predispositions toward particular types of mental and behavioral functioning. Although some people may be fearful in general, others may have temperaments oriented toward novelty and exploration. Thus, a person's temperament is the ground out of which his or her personality grows. In contrast, the term *character* refers to a person's tendency to engage in virtuous or moral action, and to forgo the opposite. Honesty, courage, thoughtfulness, loyalty, industriousness, kindness, and the like, are usually regarded as traits that define a commendable character. Personality and character are overlapping concepts but, most important, represent two different frameworks for viewing the same questions: the scientific, What is? and the ethical, What should be?

B. Background

The term *personality* originated in the Greek theater, and comes from *persona,* or "mask" (Millon & Davis, 2000). Thus, the term originally connoted the mode or style of a person's public appearance and only recently has come to refer to a person's more private and global manner of functioning. Although the scientific study of personality is a fairly recent phenomenon, it is not without historical precedent. The Greek physician Hippocrates (c. 460–370 BCE) believed that four fluids or humors made up the human body: blood, black bile, yellow bile, and phlegm. The Roman physician Galen (c. 129–210) expanded this theory and proposed that temperament resulted from an excess of at least one of these humors. Those with an excess of blood were sanguine or hopeful; too much black bile was associated with melancholy or sadness; yellow bile, with a choleric or hot-tempered disposition; and phlegm, with being phlegmatic or apathetic. This remained a popular theory for close to two thousand years, until the late 1600s when Thomas Willis developed detailed chemical explanations for various mental and physical disorders. Willis believed that blood was the primary substance, and that all others were derivative of blood (Powell, n.d.). Although the founders of the psychoanalytic tradition, such as Sigmund Freud, Carl Jung, and Alfred Adler, introduced some of the first dynamic theories of mental functioning, it was Gordon Allport in the 1930s who launched in earnest the scientific study of personality.

The early research on personality used a lexical approach. Allport and Odbert (1936) identified almost eighteen thousand terms descriptive of personality from Webster's dictionary. They categorized these into traits, states, evaluations, and other, and then undertook statistical analyses to determine which of the terms people commonly treated as identical, similar, or distinct from one another. This effort resulted in typologies of traits and groups of traits that they referred to as dimensions of personality. Many researchers have focused on discovering what the critical dimensions of personality are, and there is particular focus on determining whether there are three or five dimensions. Others who are more theoretically inclined have been working to develop theories about why the differences exist in the first place and how people function with respect to personality.

II. Happiness and Well-being

A. Recent Research

Since the early 1990s there has been a surge of interest in happiness or subjective well-being. This is a broad field that encompasses states of happiness; related feelings such as self-esteem and hopefulness; and a range of capabilities such as resiliency and hardiness, decision making, and intrinsic motivation, each of which is believed to be an element of mental health. Martin Seligman, the president of the American Psychological Association, recently referred to this new field as "positive psychology" (Seligman & Csikszentmihalyi, 2000). However, he makes no claims that the study of happiness is an original area of investigation.

B. Major Dimensions

What are positive mental states, such as happiness? Happiness is an enduring and underlying feeling of contentment, and even joy, which transcends the daily fluctuations of good and bad moods. One theory suggests that there are three components of happiness, otherwise referred to as subjective well-being (SWB): (1) overall life satisfaction (or happiness), (2) the presence of positive mood, and (3) the absence of negative mood (Ryan & Deci, 2001). A review of the research in this field reveals two competing conceptions of SWB. The hedonic view holds that happiness is essentially composed of enduring feeling states; the eudaemonic view regards happiness as arising out of a sense of meaning, of living according to one's inner daemon, or true self (Waterman, 1993). However one chooses to define happiness, it is clear that there is no monolithic state of happiness but a variety of possible states—often intermingled with one another—that reflect many kinds of affect and cognition. These no doubt result from the expression and inter-mingling in the consciousness of states of bliss, power, and knowledge.

C. Self-Reports of Happiness

Researchers typically rely on self-report, usually surveys or interviews, to gauge levels of happiness. A review of this body of research concluded that more than 80% of the general population consider themselves more satis-fied with life than dissatisfied. No more than 33% reported being lonely, bored, or depressed. There have been few alternative methodologies to self-report in studies of happiness. One may wonder, though, Who is in a better position to judge a person's happiness than that person him- or herself?

Yet it is well known that many survey questions receive biased answers due to the tendency of people to provide socially desirable replies to bolster their image, either to others or themselves. One survey (Asakawa & Csik-szentmihalyi, 2000) used experiential sampling methods in which Asian American and Caucasian college students received survey questions on a pager at random times and replied throughout the day. This is a relatively re-liable method that does not require reports of global feeling states, just what one is experiencing at the selected moment. The study found that the Asian American and Caucasian respondents reported similar levels of happiness. In contrast, with conventional and less reliable survey methods, Westerners report considerably higher levels of happiness than do East Asians, possibly because of a more a pronounced norm of personal fulfillment in the West. These findings are of particular significance for those in the human services, because they suggest that human service professionals, who are constantly confronted by human suffering, often develop a fairly skewed and jaded view of human well-being, one that often can only lead to undue pessimism about the prospects for clients to live satisfying and meaningful lives.

D. Key Findings

Reviews and meta-analyses (a type of statistical summarization) of the research on SWB have revealed unexpectedly high levels of happiness when the usual demographic predictors are controlled for, including sex, age, hav-ing children, geographic location, race, and income (see Myers, 1992). Not more than 1% or 2% of the variation in happiness can be attributed to any one of these variables. There is also a remarkable consistency in levels of happiness within individuals over their life course: people who report them-selves as happy at one time regularly do so decades later. Life events, even major ones, can have dramatic impacts on short-term levels of happiness, but people typically revert to their characteristic level of happiness, a kind of set point, within six months to a year. This is not to say that there are not important variations. For example, 80% of both men and women report leading satisfied lives, but when they do not, suffering manifests quite differently, as women experience considerably higher levels of depression than men (see Myers, 1992).

Income also has a fairly modest impact on happiness (Csikszentmihalyi, 1999). Low income has a strong impact, but as soon as people reach a modest threshold of subsistence, it makes little difference whether they have average or high levels of income. This same type of nonlinear relationship has also been found between levels of socioeconomic status (SES) and mental illness (Hudson, 2005). Although SES and mental illness are strongly and negatively correlated, the relationship mainly results from the effect of extreme financial hardship; above a modest SES level, one's risk for mental illness does not vary much according to socioeconomic status.

E. Predictors of Happiness

The sparsity of demographic predictors does not mean that there are not other important predictors of happiness. Some regularly identified predictors are obvious, such as an individual's self-esteem, sense of efficacy, social support, physical health, and feeling of relatedness with others—primarily because many of these variables are conceptually related with happiness. What would it mean to be happy but to have low self-esteem or to feel powerless or disconnected from others? Such a combination is unlikely: happiness tends to be regarded in terms of feeling good about one's self, having a sense of efficacy, and being socially included. Other predictors include involvement in a loving relationship with a significant other, personality traits such as extraversion and openness, community involvement, optimism, lack of neuroticism, and a spiritual or religious orientation (see Myers, 1992).

F. Theories about Happiness

In addition to describing levels of happiness and their various predictors, research has increasingly formulated more dynamic theories about the processes that generate states of subjective well-being. Traditional approaches emphasized need fulfillment and personality. For instance, Deci and Ryan's (2000) theory of self-determination posits that happiness results from the fulfillment of fundamental needs involving autonomy, competence, and relatedness. In contrast, Costa and McCrae (1980) propose that highly extraverted and less neurotic personalities experience the highest

FIGURE 6.2: THE SELF-CONCORDANCE MODEL OF SHELDON AND ELLIOT

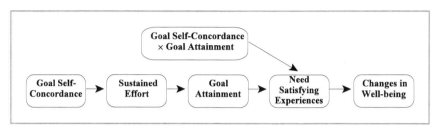

Source: Sheldon & Elliot (1999, p. 483).

levels of happiness. A popular notion is that of adaptation, in which positive or negative events usually have only a short-term impact on happiness because people become habituated to them, and in which each person has an internal set-point, determined largely by inherited temperament, that moods gravitate toward (Headey & Wearing, 1992).

There are several theories that have emphasized the importance of goals and values (see chapter 15) for happiness. According to goal theory when people progress toward their goals in a way that is consistent with their values, they are most likely happy. A variation on this theme is Sheldon and Elliot's (1999) self-concordance theory, in which not just sustained effort toward and attainment of one's goals but also attainment of goals that are self-concordant (i.e., consistent with fundamental needs and values) are important for generating need-satisfying experiences and positive changes in well-being (see figure 6.2). Diener, Suh, Lucas, and Smith (1999) attempt to integrate several of the prevailing approaches and propose that the happiest people have a positive temperament, are optimistic and avoid ruminating over negative events, live in economically well-off circumstances, have close relationships, and possess adequate resources and capabilities to pursue meaningful goals.

G. Flow, Hardiness, and Resilience

The search for the wellsprings of happiness has led to the identification of several abilities, such as experiencing a sense of flow and confronting life in a hardy or resilient manner. The research of Mihaly Csikszentmihalyi (1990) has stimulated a substantial body of research on everyday experience, one that focuses on understanding the conditions in which people partake in a type of optimal experience that he calls "flow" (see theory example 6.1). Flow refers to the ability to become fully absorbed in some personally

THEORY EXAMPLE 6.1: MIHALY CSIKSZENTMIHALYI'S THEORY
OF OPTIMAL EXPERIENCE, FLOW CHARACTERISTICS, AND
CONDITIONS OF THE FLOW EXPERIENCE

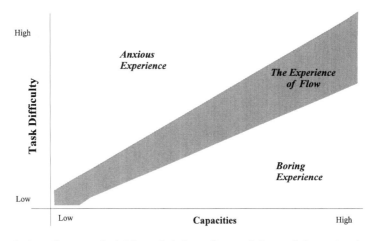

Mihaly Csikszentmihalyi (1991) defines *flow* as follows: "The optimal state of inner experience is one in which there is *order in consciousness*. This happens when psychic energy—or attention—is invested in realistic goals and when skills match the opportunities for action. The pursuit of a goal brings order in awareness because a person must concentrate attention on the task at hand and momentarily forget everything else" (1990, p. 6).

1. The experience of flow assumes a challenge that requires skill. For the most part, flow is found while conducting tasks that have clear goals, methods, and rules, and that cannot be accomplished without skill (e.g., reading, socializing, artistic activity, surgery, mountain climbing).

2. Flow assumes a matching of skills with meaningful challenges: too great a challenge leads to anxiety, and too little challenge in relation to skills creates boredom.

3. Flow is accompanied by the merging of action and awareness. People cease being aware of themselves as separate from their actions—it entails spontaneity and seemingly effortless movement.

4. Flow involves intense concentration on the task at hand, control over actions, and the loss of self-consciousness.

5. Flow is characterized by the transformation of time and the sense of timeless absorption in meaningful activity.

meaningful and challenging activity (e.g., a hobby, sport, or profession). This engagement involves both self-forgetfulness, obliviousness to time and extraneous matters, and absorption in the task at hand. It involves, says Csikszentmihalyi, the merging of action and awareness; people cease being aware of themselves as separate from their actions. Spontaneity and effortless movement prevail. Research with people who have such optimal experiences while engaged in activities as disparate as rock climbing, surgery, or psychotherapy has identified several critical conditions for such experiences: a challenge that requires some skill and often the limit of one's abilities; clear goals and some system of feedback, often from the activity itself; and a personally meaningful activity. While Csikszentmihalyi makes it clear that such optimal experience is not the same as the more generalized experience of happiness or subjective well-being, it is one that both contributes to happiness and tends to emerge out of it.

With respect to personal adaptability, Kobasa and Maddi (1977) advanced hardiness, or the ability to confront change and bounce back, which is related to flow. Hardiness is the "sense of self-in-world that emphasizes commitment, control, and challenge, [and] may reflect a common denominator of mental health" (Maddi & Khoshaba, 1994, p. 272). Hardiness buffers the individual against the effects of stress, thus facilitating maximum adaptability. Commitment is the ability to set goals and invest effort in their accomplishment, and control involves confidence in the ability to achieve those goals and to influence the course of events in the environment. Challenge entails a preference for growth rather than security and routine. These three beliefs are the essential ingredients for hardiness or resiliency. Figure 6.3 depicts how hardiness supports coping, thereby minimizing the strain of stressful circumstances, and the important supportive role of hardy social support and health practices (e.g., exercise, nutrition) in the prevention of mental and physical breakdown.

Whereas the idea of hardiness is based on a more general theory of coping, the notion of resiliency emphasizes coping with situations of considerable stress or even trauma. Siebert (1996) defines resiliency by five essential characteristics: (1) reason, or the ability to set aside panic and engage in logical problem solving, (2) focus, or the ability to focus on the current situation and not be distracted by the past or future, (3) humor, or the ability to poke fun at adversity and take a larger perspective, (4) integration, or the ability to see adversity and its consequences as part of a larger life story and identity, and (5) positivity, or the ability to make lemonade from lemons, or to turn negative experiences into positive outcomes, often through the learning involved.

Siebert (1996) points out that resilient people avoid focusing on stressful

Figure 6.3: The Hardiness Model of Salvatore Maddi

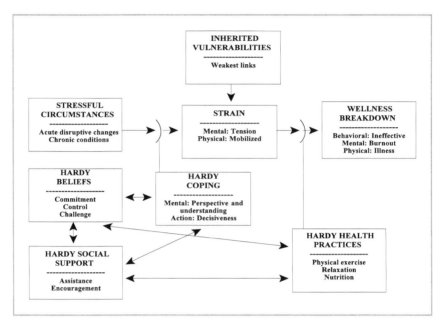

Source: Maddi (1994, p. 5).

circumstances, and instead concern themselves more with their ability to respond to whatever challenges they face. Hans Selye first introduced the notion of the stress reaction, but he later regretted his choice of the term *stress,* as English was not his native language. He explained that what he meant to focus on was strain. Whereas *stress* involves the pressures of the external environment, *strain* is how the organism responds to such pressures. Different people exhibit remarkably different reactions to the same stresses, and by focusing on internal reactions rather than on the external stresses themselves, we avoid the danger of casting individuals as helpless victims of circumstances. To his credit, Seyle identified eustress, or healthy stress that facilitates growth. What is a debilitating stress for one person may be a healthy form of challenge for someone who is particularly hardy or resilient and an opportunity to experience flow.

Interest in flow, hardiness, and resiliency is part of the larger concern with positive mental health. Examples of other such abilities involve coherence (Antonovsky, 1993), ego strength, intrinsic motivation, and optimism (see Maddi, 1999a, 1999b). The challenges of defining and measuring each ability pale in comparison to the task of understanding how a range of such traits and abilities function separately or together to constitute mental health.

H. Conceptions of Mental Health

It is considerably easier to define mental illness than mental health, no doubt because the latter is a more complex phenomenon, reflected in the range of approaches (e.g., subjective, functional, normative, cognitive) to its definition. Many argue that various states of subjective well-being (e.g., happiness, self-esteem, vitality) best epitomize mental health. Adherents of humanistic and positive psychologies often emphasize these approaches. In recent years, though, the predominant approach has been the functional orientation, in which mental health is regarded as the ability to solve life's problems, to exercise control over self and environment, and to successfully relate with others. The normative approach, popular in psychiatry, views mental health primarily as an absence of signs and symptoms of mental illness, as adherence to statistical norms and roles involving of what most regard as average. Finally, some have theorized that mental health is best understood in terms of cognitive traits, such as self-understanding, insight, or individuation.

Perhaps the most famous of all definitions of mental health is that of Sigmund Freud, who remarked that mental health is the ability to love and to work—to enter into loving emotional and sexual relationships, and to engage in productive activity. But he also regarded mental health as the ability to attain intrapsychic equilibrium between the major structures of the personality (i.e., ego, id, and superego) and interpersonal equilibrium with the social environment. Conflict may be endemic, but some lucky ones may attain a type of truce. In addition to this functional orientation, Freud also regarded mental health in cognitive terms as involving the attainment of self-knowledge. He compared the process of making the unconscious conscious with that of draining the Zuider Zee, of claiming land of the conscious from the ocean of the unconscious.

The ego psychologists of the mid-twentieth century refined Freud's views, and emphasized the role of conscious processes involving the ego and its integrative and problem-solving abilities. For example, Heinz Hartmann, Ernst Kris, and R. M. Lowenstein (1949) suggested that mentally healthy individuals have more neutralized psychic energy, or libido, at the disposal of consciousness than do those suffering from mental illness, for whom various unconscious drives and conflicts may overdetermine mental functioning. Other ego psychologists, such as Harry Stack Sullivan (1953) and Karen Horney (1950), cast psychoanalytic theory in social terms. Horney (1950), for instance, posits that people have three fundamental orientations toward others: (1) moving toward, (2) away from, or (3) against. Whereas neurotic individuals often express only one orientation and attempt to suppress or repress the others, mentally healthy people draw on and integrate all three orientations in their personal repertoire, expressing each in appropriate contexts. Horney also regarded mental health as freedom from neurotic "shoulds" and expectations, and especially as the ability to be wholehearted in attending to whatever one needs to do (as in flow).

Several theorists from the psychoanalytic tradition have emphasized various conceptions of psychic integration, wholeness, or sense of self. Carl Jung (1921) spoke about the process of individuation, which occurs mostly in the latter half of life (see profile 6.1). Individuation makes some of the unconscious conscious and integrates opposite and undeveloped features of the self into the conscious ego. An example of this phenomenon is the tendency for some older men develop their feminine sides, and older women, their masculine qualities. Heinz Kohut (1977), the founder of self-psychology (see table 5.3), attempted to update Freud's definition of mental health. He stated that mental health is the "capacity of a cohesive self to avail itself of its talents and skills, enabling the person to love and work success-fully" (p. 284). Kohut posited that the capacity involves the development of empathy, creativity, humor, and even wisdom. He explained, "The establishment of ego dominance in the realm of the two great narcissistic configurations is, however, only the precondition for that total attitude that we call wisdom—it is not wisdom itself. The achievement of wisdom is a feat that we must not expect of our patients, nor, indeed necessarily of ourselves. Since its full attainment includes the emotional acceptance of the transience of individual existence, we must admit that it can probably be reached by only a few and that its stable integration may well be beyond the compass of man's psychological capacity" (1971, p. 327).

In the analytic tradition, the primary orientation toward mental health has been functional, but important subthemes are cognitive understanding and subjective well-being. Interest in the normative orientation has come out of biological psychiatry, but not without some recognition of the functional and subjective dimensions.

Unfortunately for many, mental health is such an elusive, complex, and abstract notion that the focus is instead on the concrete realities of mental illness. However, in this way, the unexamined helping agendas of mental health professionals tend to go underground and become expressed in pernicious forms of social control, for example, the criminalization of many seriously mentally ill people. An ongoing debate has been whether mental health and illness represent points on one continuum or several, or whether they represent qualitatively distinct states or categories. Whereas those who have espoused functional, subjective, and cognitive orientations have emphasized the continuous nature of these phenomena, adherents of biological

PROFILE 6.1: CARL GUSTAV JUNG

Carl Gustav Jung (b. 1875–d. 1961), best known as the founder of analytical psychology, advanced theories that integrated the study of personality with culture and spirituality (see Storr, 1998). Jung was born in the small Swiss village of Kessewil to Paul and Emelie Jung. His parents were well educated and started him on the study of Latin by the age of six. Jung was a reclusive adolescent who, despite his enrollment in some of the best Swiss boarding schools, rejected formal schooling and learned several languages, including Sanskrit, on his own.

Jung's initial career interest was archaeology but he settled on medical school, attending the University of Basel from 1895 to 1900 (see Jung, 1963). Under the supervision of Eugene Bleuler at the Burgholzli Clinic in Zurich, Jung's early work was on the subject of schizophrenia. His well-received papers and book on the subject led to a meeting in 1907 with Sigmund Freud, who for a time considered Jung his heir apparent. For the next seven years their relationship flourished, and Jung became the head of the International Psychoanalytic Society. During that time, he developed the notion of the autonomous psychological complex and the technique of free association. However, by 1914, Jung's rejection of Freud's focus on the role of sexual conflict in neurosis led to a breakdown of the relationship. In his autobiography, Jung reported that Freud said to him, "My dear Jung, promise me never to abandon the sexual theory. . . . [W]e must make a dogma out of it, an unshakable bulwark." When Jung asked what this bulwark was to be directed against, Freud paused and mentioned occultism, not realizing that Jung's doctoral dissertation was on the subject.

Jung later suffered a six-year breakdown but emerged out of it highly productive and founded the analytical school of depth psychology. Jung differentiated Freud's notion of the unconscious, calling it the personal unconscious, from the collective unconscious, or the psychic repository of humanity's memories and dreams, myths, and archetypes. The analysis of archetypes, supported by the study of religion and mythology, became a central part of analytical psychology. About archetypes, Jung (1922) explained:

> The primordial image [or archetype] is a figure—be it a daemon, a
> human being, or a process—that constantly recurs in the course of

PROFILE 6.1 (CONTINUED)

history and appears wherever creative fantasy is freely expressed. Essentially, therefore, it is a mythological figure. In each of these imagines there is a little piece of human psychology and human fate, a remnant of the joys and sorrows that have been repeated countless times in our ancestral history (Vol. 15, p. 127).

The development of the personality, Jung believed, took place throughout the life course—especially in its second half—as a process of individuation in which the individual integrates excluded parts of self into consciousness. These include the anima (for men) or animus (for women), as well as the shadow, which involve disowned parts of a person's identity. In his study of personality, Jung coined the terms *extraversion* and *introversion,* and proposed a typology that involves various combinations of ways that people take in and process information. While information may be obtained either through sensation or intuition, individuals may rely more on thinking or feeling (valuing) to process it, and thus he defined the sensation-thinking, sensation-intuition, intuition-feeling, or intuition-thinking personality types. Jung's interest in the collective unconscious and in archetypes inspired him to study the religions of both the East and West, the history of alchemy, the belief in flying saucers, and the Pueblo Indians. After retiring in 1946, he died in Zurich, on June 6, 1961.

and normative orientations have argued for categorically distinct, qualitative distinctions. For example, a given client may either meet or fail to meet the required criteria for diagnosis with schizophrenia. However, complex systems theory recognizes both the continuities and the abrupt discontinuities between alternative states. For example, some incremental changes in functioning may accumulate until there is an abrupt and catastrophic change as critical thresholds are reached, the entire system becomes reconfigured, and mental functioning becomes reorganized around a radically different and impoverished core.

It is clear that as important as happiness and other subjective states of well-being are, they represent only one dimension of the broader and more complex ideal of mental health and wellness. Mental health is typically regarded as the enduring ability to seek out and confront the challenges of life, with an array of affective, cognitive, and executive skills, rooted in internalized values and ethics, and sensitive to biological, social, and cultural realities. It has been suggested that "'mental health' properly describes a sense of well-being: the capacity to live in a resourceful and fulfilling manner, having the resilience to deal with the challenges and obstacles which life presents" (Ahead 4 Health, 2006). Mental health and physical health are possibly essential elements of a broader conception of existential or spiritual well-being.

III. Theories of Motivation

A. Concept of Motivation

Chapter 2 defined motivation as the tendency of conscious living beings to invest effort in the attainment of valued ends, whether these involve biological, psychological, social, or cultural needs. A commonly used definition (Franken, 1994) is that motivation is an internal state that energizes and directs persistent goal-oriented behavior. This, however, leaves out an appreciation of motivations as complex psychological systems with affective, cognitive, and behavioral elements. Much of this complexity, however, is reflected in the range of theories about the various types of motivations and their underlying dynamics, several of which are introduced in this section. Readers should be aware that there is considerable debate about the actual importance of motivation in behavior. To what extent is motivation a primary or secondary influence on learning and behavior? Do reflexive and need-based reactions to external conditions necessarily entail motivation? This depends on how broadly or narrowly one defines motivation and the extent to which it pertains to conscious goals. Those who lack coherent motivations may nonetheless react in the immediate situation to minimize discomfort or to maximize various states of physiological satiation or states of psychological well-being. Behavior governed by habits is often considered as laying outside the scope of motivated behavior. Many contemporary theorists equate motivation with needs; however, it is more accurate to treat motivation as overlaying and serving needs (Sheldon, Elliot, Kim, Youngmee, & Kasser, 2001). Although most people are motivated to meet basic needs, there are certainly motivations (e.g., altruism) that aim to achieve ends that do not represent any particular need of the subject, as well as needs for which there are no associated motivations (e.g., the needs of depressed or apathetic people).

B. Types of Motivation

Theorists have often categorized the different types of motivation according to one or a combination of factors. Probably the most common is the extrinsic-intrinsic dimension. Ryan and Deci (1999) distinguish between extrinsic motivations that involve doing something because it leads to a separable outcome (e.g., working a boring job for pay) from the activity itself and intrinsic motivations that involve doing something because the activity is inherently enjoyable, interesting, or meaningful (e.g., working as a psychotherapist or community organizer). They go on to distinguish four types of extrinsic motivation. The least autonomous form is external regulation, or behavior purely to satisfy an external demand—this is the most alienating form. In contrast, with introjected regulation external sources influence action on the basis of the perceived need for a person to maintain self-esteem or a feeling of worth. Identification involves a person accepting external influences as legitimate as his or her own. Finally, integration occurs when the identified regulation is fully internalized. Ryan and Deci argue that this still falls short of truly intrinsic motivation because the outcomes are separable from the activity itself. Specifically, they suggest that intrinsic motivation typically involves activities that enhance the person's sense of competence, autonomy, or relatedness with others.

Two closely related dimensions of motivation in the literature are the distinctions between approach and avoidance motivation and between deficiency and growth motivations. Approach-oriented motivations simply aim at some positive outcome, such as maintaining or enhancing one's sense of inclusion or power, whereas avoidance-oriented motivations are concerned specifically with preventing some undesired state, such as isolation or powerlessness. A particular motivation may manifest elements of approach and avoidance depending on the circumstances. The distinction between deficiency and growth motivations is a more specific one involving, on the one hand, the lack of essential resources (e.g., food, shelter, respect) and, on the other hand, the interest in an ongoing process of unfolding or self-actualization. Abraham Maslow (1943), for instance, distinguished between the deficiency motivations involving physiological and safety needs and growth motivations involving aesthetic, self-actualization, or transpersonal needs.

Motivations also vary according to whether they are performance or mastery oriented. The performance orientation refers to achieving some visible benchmark, such as a grade point average, sales volume, or number of points per game. In contrast, those concerned with mastery worry not so much about making the grade and more about understanding the subject, being an effective salesperson, or playing an excellent game. Thus, the mastery orientation represents a greater appreciation of the intricacies and complexity of tasks than does the performance orientation, despite the fact that both are

TABLE 6.1: GOAL ORIENTATIONS AND THEIR APPROACH AND AVOIDANCE STATES

	APPROACH STATE	AVOIDANCE STATE
MASTERY ORIENTATION	Focus on mastering task, learning, understanding	Focus on avoiding misunderstanding, avoiding, and not learning or mastering task
	Use of standards of self-improvement, progress, deep understanding of task	Use of standards of not being wrong, not doing it incorrectly relative to task
PERFORMANCE ORIENTATION	Focus on being superior, besting others, being the smartest or best at task in comparison to others	Focus on avoiding inferiority, not looking stupid or dumb in comparison to others
	Use of normative standards such as getting best or highest grades, being top or best performer in class	Use of normative standards of not getting the worst grades, being lowest performer in class

Source: Pintrich (2000, p. 100).

outcome oriented. Paul Pintrich (1999) suggests that the two orientations toward outcomes, when combined with the approach-avoidance distinction, are the basis for a general typology of motivations (see table 6.1).

C. Content of Motivation

It is also important to understand the specific type or content, the "what" of motivation, and many typologies have been proposed. Freud, for instance, at first theorized that there were two fundamental drives: Eros (sexual love) and aggression. Later, he suggested a third, the death instinct, or Thanatos as it is commonly referred to. Alfred Adler emphasized the will to power or perfection, and David McClelland emphasized achievement and affiliation in addition to power. These proposals stimulated considerable interest in mastery, self-efficacy, and achievement. At about the same time, existentialists such as Viktor Frankl argued that the will to meaning or the striving to find purpose in life may be central, and Gordon Allport identified five fundamental needs: (1) relatedness, or the need for social connection, (2) transcendence, or the need to be separate from other people and things,

(3) rootedness, or the need to have a sense of belonging, (4) identity, or the need to know who and what one is, and (5) a frame of reference, to be oriented to one's world (see Maddi, 1996).

D. Some Typologies

There have been multiple attempts to integrate and synthesize the range of proposals into coherent typologies. The best known of these is that of Abraham Maslow, who based his motivations on a list of primary needs: physiological, safety, social inclusion, self-esteem, autonomy, and self-actualization (see Wahba & Bridwell, 1976). Later, he added aesthetic needs prior to self-actualization and transpersonal needs after it (see figure 6.4). This typology received considerable attention because of the notion of prepotency, or the idea that the earlier, deficiency-based motives, such as the physiological and safety, take precedence until they are met, and then successively the next emerge until they too are eclipsed by a higher need. Despite the immense popularity of this theory, the sequence of emergence of the needs has not been empirically supported, except in that general, deficiency-based motives have been found to take precedence over growth-based needs, until the former are adequately addressed (Wahba & Bridwell, 1976). Social workers attempting to engage homeless people, thus, need to give priority to addressing the obvious problems of concrete needs for housing, physical safety, and nutrition, but also recognize that sometimes such people may have higher-order or even spiritual needs that may need to be addressed simultaneously.

One of the more recently developed typologies deserves note here. Sheldon et al. (2001) reviewed the current literature, paying close attention to both Maslow's hierarchy of needs and Deci and Ryan's self-determination theory of motivation. Their preliminary categorization suggested the following fundamental needs or motivations: autonomy, competence, relatedness, physical thriving, security, self-esteem, self-actualization, pleasure and/or stimulation, money and/or luxury, and popularity and/or influence. On the basis of the only three studies they conducted with college students, they reduced this list to autonomy, competence, relatedness, and self-esteem. Unfortunately, the authors did not consider the needs that children or working and retired adults manifest. Carl Jung and other transpersonal theorists have suggested that self-actualization or individuation most often develop in the latter half of life. Thus, this list of four motivations may better describe contemporary college students than the general population. There continues to be considerable debate about fundamental needs, drives, and motivations. The research required to settle these debates probably will

FIGURE 6.4: ABRAHAM MASLOW'S HEIRARCHY OF NEEDS

The Needs

1. **Transcendence:** This entails developing a relationship with a larger reality than the limited ego and helping others do the same as well as develop their potentials.
2. **Self-actualization:** This involves developing the range of potentials of the individual, both those of a personal and an occupational or professional type.
3. **Aesthetic:** Symmetry, order, and beauty.
4. **Cognitive:** The need for knowledge and understanding.
5. **Esteem needs:** The need for social recognition and approval as well as self-respect.
6. **Belongingness/love:** Relational needs, both to be part of a larger social whole and to have individual loving relationships.
7. **Safety/security:** Protection of harm and other longer-term physical deficiencies, such as lack of a home.
8. **Physiological:** Primary or immediate needs for food, air, water, warmth, and other requirements of life.

The Principal of Prepotency of Needs

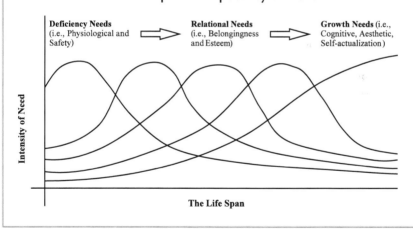

Source: Maslow (1971); Maslow & Lowery (1998).

not be forthcoming until there is some agreement as to definitions (e.g., of needs, drives, and motivations) and the operational criteria for determining the existence of such phenomena.

E. Process Theories

Just as there are various content theories or typologies of the different kinds of motivations, there are a range of process theories that attempt to clarify how systems of motivations actually develop and function. Such theories focus on the different types of mental functioning, including affect and cognition, and their behavioral manifestations. Whereas theories involving the affective or feeling dimensions are concerned primarily with the energizing part of motivation, theories on cognitive dimensions are concerned more with direction or channeling. The behavioral dimension mostly concerns the question of how motivations are maintained or extinguished, though each dimension is known to have reciprocal effects with the others.

Classic psychoanalytic drive theory assumes that motivations are, at root, concerned with reducing or discharging recurrent states of tension. Their goal is to maximize instinctual gratification while minimizing punishment and guilt. The assumption is that states of physiological tension transform into various emotional or feeling states, which in turn energize thought and behavior. For instance, physiological hunger transforms into a craving for food, which in turn elicits thoughts and fantasies about food, including decisions and plans to obtain it, and finally into behaviors such as cooking or locating a restaurant. The underlying motives are both expressed in and hidden from consciousness through multiple layers of internal psychological defenses, such as denial, repression, displacement, sublimation, and the like.

Most recent process theories have focused on the cognitive elements of motivation. An early theory is the cognitive dissonance theory of Leon Festinger (1957), who showed that when there is discrepancy between two or more beliefs or actions, an individual attempts to resolve the conflict and achieve consistency, either by changing a belief to fit a behavior or vice versa. In contrast, attribution theory (Weiner, 1974) proposes that motivation is, in part, a function of whether people's motivations arise from external or internal factors and whether there is stability in their control over external factors. The two dimensions generate four possible attributions that people give for their successes and failures (see table 6.2). Those who are internally motivated and have a sense of control tend to see their successes as arising from ability, whereas in unstable circumstances, they emphasize effort. In

TABLE 6.2: ATTRIBUTION THEORY

	Locus of Control	
STABILITY	INTERNAL	EXTERNAL
STABLE	Ability	Task Difficulty
UNSTABLE	Effort	Luck

Source: Weiner (1974, p. 6).

contrast, those with an external locus of control and stable circumstances emphasize the degree of task difficulty as the primary determinant of success, unlike those with an external locus of control and an unstable environment, who consider luck most important. Human service professionals concerned with enhancing their clients' motivation may need to understand the perceived locus of control and environmental stability (and the resulting attributions that people give for their difficulties) and be prepared to help clients reexamine any such dysfunctional attitudes.

Another cognitive theory of motivation is expectancy theory. Vroom (1964) hypothesized that the extent of motivation for a given activity is a function of the combined interaction of three factors: (1) the perceived probability of success (i.e., expectancy), (2) whether success in the activity is actually linked to desired rewards (i.e., instrumentality), and (3) how much the rewards are actually desired (i.e., valence or value). In short: motivation = expectancy × instrumentality × valence.

Finally, behavioral theories of motivation are concerned mainly with questions of how goal-directed behaviors are enhanced, maintained, or extinguished. Proponents of classical behavioral conditioning theorize that biological responses to stimuli associated with needs facilitate target behaviors, whereas operant conditioning focuses on the application of reinforcements to target behaviors. In both cases, the focus is on extrinsic sources of motivation (e.g., rewards or punishments), as it is assumed that there are few sources of motivation intrinsic to individuals, other than generalized physical and perhaps social needs.

IV. The Multiple Dimensions of Personality

So far this chapter has focused primarily on some of the key components of personality, specifically states such as happiness and mental health, as well as underlying motivations. However, the concept of personality involves the entire mental organization of an individual and is considerably more complex. The remainder of this chapter, therefore, considers the subject of personality more directly. This section is concerned with the problem of describing the plethora of states and traits that make up personality, and the following section considers several theories about these patterns and how they function. Unfortunately, much of the theory has been developed fairly independently of most of the descriptive data considered here. Usually, personality research and theory has drawn on the study of dysfunctional or pathological patterns—especially personality disorders—however, this is a subject that is not reviewed until chapter 8, which covers theories of mental dysfunction.

A. Layers of Personality

Although the notion of personality originally connoted the more external or public manner of a person's presentation of self, the usage of the term *personality* has come to include multiple and hidden levels of functioning. For example, early in his career, Timothy Leary (1957) identified five layers of personality: (1) public communication; (2) conscious communications, or individuals' perceptions of self and the interpersonal world; (3) private perceptions, or the symbolic, fantastic, and preconscious aspects of interpersonal experience; (4) unexpressed or unconscious desires; and (5) values or ego ideals. Most regard personality as consisting of those characteristic or consistent patterns of interpersonal functioning and the less visible area of cognition, including characteristic modes of mental representation and problem solving, as well as values, ethical judgments, and spiritual perspectives.

B. Categorical versus Dimensional Approaches

The description of personality has typically involved either a categorical or a dimensional strategy. The categorical strategy is exemplified by the standard psychiatric nosology, or system of classification and naming (e.g., *Diagnostic and Statistical Manual of Mental Disorders,* 4th revised edition). For instance, dysfunctional personality patterns include borderline, explosive, or passive-dependent personalities. These are discrete categories defined by multiple traits and states, signs, and symptoms that are believed to typically cluster together. For example, a borderline personality is "a pattern of instability in interpersonal relationships, self-image, and affects, and marked impulsivity" (American Psychiatric Association, 2000, p. 629). Most personality theorists, however, have usually favored dimensional approaches. These involve not discrete groups of individuals but groups of traits that are observed in research to covary with one another. For example, one of the most common dimensions is that of extraversion-introversion. Although there are no discrete groups of extraverts or introverts, everyone can be placed somewhere on this continuum (e.g., at low, medium, high, or very high levels of extraversion). Extraverts tend to exhibit similar characteristics, even though there may be no unique or defining combination of such traits. The dimensional approach allows for a considerably greater variety of combinations of features depending on the number of dimensions used. It is also a more dynamic approach and, many believe, more consistent with experience. Categories can always be constructed on the basis of one or several dimensions, in a way similar to how a color category (e.g., blue) is constructed from the thousands of shades of blue defined as part of the typical color wheel. Some claim that dimensional systems are too complicated to use in human services. However, even the current medical model is largely based on the measurement of continuous variables (e.g., glucose levels in blood) rather than of discrete categories. Cutting points are used—based on the dimension of interest—for instance, to differentiate normal, prediabetic, and diabetic glucose levels, similar to depression scale that is scored from 0 to 100, where 30 or lower represents a clinical level of depression.

C. Early Dimensional Approaches

For many years, personality theorists have proposed various dimensions that describe the range of personalities. One of the most common is the extraversion-introversion dimension of Carl Jung (1921). Jung pointed out that the activity of the extravert is oriented toward the external world and that of the introvert focuses on him- or herself. The extravert is typically an active person who is happiest when around other people and expressing his or her feelings. The introvert, in contrast, is usually a more private person who enjoys solitude, ideas, and imaginative pursuits (see Jung, 1921). Another of the original dimensions proposed was that of the German psychiatrist Ernst Kretschmer, who argued that personalities tend to be either schizothymic or cyclothymic, depending on body type. He believed that the stocky, or pyknic, body type is associated with the cyclothymic personality, characterized by mood swings, which as a psychosis manifests as bipolar illness. The asthenic and athletic body types are believed to be associated with the schizothymic personality, which, under stress or conflict, sometimes disintegrates into schizophrenia (see Livesley, 2001). Such continua, however, have largely been discredited, partly because their pathological focus makes them unsuitable for describing most personalities.

D. Three- and Five-Factor Models

Dimensional models have been mostly inductive and empirical models, driven more by data than by theory. They have commonly employed the statistical procedure of factor analysis, which identifies patterns of covariation among a large group of signs and symptoms derived from surveys or other data. Some of the earliest research was based partly on lexical studies of the terms (derived from dictionaries) that people commonly used to describe personalities (Allport & Odbert, 1936). Currently there are two competing lines of research, one initiated by Hans Eysenck (1991), who has identified three dimensions, and another gaining in popularity that relies on five dimensions (Costa & McCrae, 1992). The oldest of the approaches is that of Eysenck, who has drawn on traditional theories, such as those of Carl Jung, to identify the following dimensions:

1. Extraversion: sociable, lively, active, assertive, sensation seeking, carefree, dominant, surgent, venturesome
2. Neuroticism: anxious, depressed, guilt feelings, low self-esteem, tense, irrational, shy, moody, emotional
3. Psychoticism: aggressive, cold, egocentric, impersonal, impulsive, antisocial, unempathic, creative, tough minded (Livesley 2001, p. 21).

Eysenck theorizes that the three dimensions are rooted in three different brain systems. For instance, the level of autonomic reactivity is suspected to be the basis for neuroticism. The model proposes that a personality can be described largely on the basis of the individual's characteristic level at each dimension. Personality disorders are believed to be associated with high levels of all three, with the predominance of the respective dimensions accounting for the particular pattern. Eysenck and others have conducted numerous studies that have validated this model fairly consistently.

An advantage of identifying the multiple dimensions within which personality vary is that it becomes possible to formulate and test theories about the neurobiological underpinnings of the dimensions. Best known among these efforts is that of Cloninger (1986), who theorizes that the three psychological systems are based in the various set points involved in corresponding parts of brain functioning, which involve three major neurotransmitter systems (see figure 6.5). Novelty seeking, he argues, is a function of activity in the dopaminergic system; the propensity to avoid harm, in the serotonergic system; and the dependence on external rewards and relationships, in the noradrenergic system. The various personality disorders,

FIGURE 6.5: CLONINGER'S NEUROBIOLOGICAL THEORY OF PERSONALITY

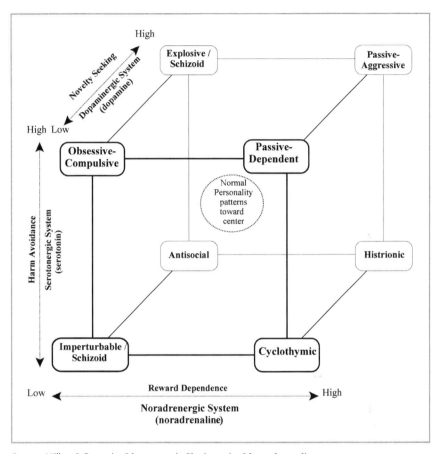

Source: Millon & Roger (1986, p. 19–20); Cloninger (1986, p. 167–226).

he hypothesizes, can be linked to unusually high or low set points for one or more of these systems. For example, the histrionic personality has high dopamine and noradrenaline but low serotonin levels. To the extent that an individual has a balance in each system, that individual tends to have a "normal" personality.

In contrast to Eysenck's three-factor model, the five-factor model has gained considerable popularity in recent years, and the most recent version is that of Costa and McCrae (1992). The approach arose from both the lexical analysis of dictionary terms and a fairly atheoretical or inductive approach to analysis of clinical data. The approach identifies five factors, with each categorized into six subdimensions:

1. Neuroticism: anxiety, hostility, depression, self-consciousness, impulsivity, vulnerability
2. Extraversion: warmth, gregariousness, assertiveness, activity, excitement seeking, positive emotions
3. Openness to experience: fantasy, aesthetics, feelings, actions, ideas, values
4. Agreeableness: trust, straightforwardness, altruism, compliance, modesty, tender-mindedness
5. Conscientiousness: competence, order, dutifulness, achievement striving, self-discipline, deliberation (Livesley, 2001, p. 22).

There is considerable agreement among studies about the existence of the extraversion, agreeableness, and conscientiousness dimensions, but not about neuroticism and openness to experience. This model departs from the original lexical model in that it recasts what was originally considered intellectuality or imaginativeness as openness. Neither of these is consistently replicated, though there is considerable evidence in support of neuroticism as a basic personality dimension.

E. The Circumplex Model

Another approach to assessing the dimensions of personality is an attempt to base the dimensions on social orientations. Karen Horney (1950), theorized that individuals can be characterized on the basis of the strength of their tendencies to move toward, against, and away from others. The most recent such model is Pincus's (1994) circumplex model. This approach evolved from naturalistic observations of patients in group psychotherapy. It identifies two fundamental dimensions in which personalities vary: dominance-submission and hostility-affiliativeness. A given individual may be highly affiliative and submissive, or very hostile and submissive. In addition, any combination of traits may be enacted minimally, moderately, or with great intensity. The various combinations of levels of the two primary dimensions generate the multiple traits plotted around the circular diagram of the circumplex model (see figure 6.6). The distance from the center of the circle reflects the intensity of a given trait, with the most intensely enacted traits appearing near the outer circumference. Many regard this model as a particular operationalization of the five-factor model, as the dominance-submission and hostility-affiliativeness dimensions are viewed as equivalent to the extraversion and agreeableness dimensions of the five-factor model.

FIGURE 6.6: THE CIRCUMPLEX MODEL OF PERSONALITY

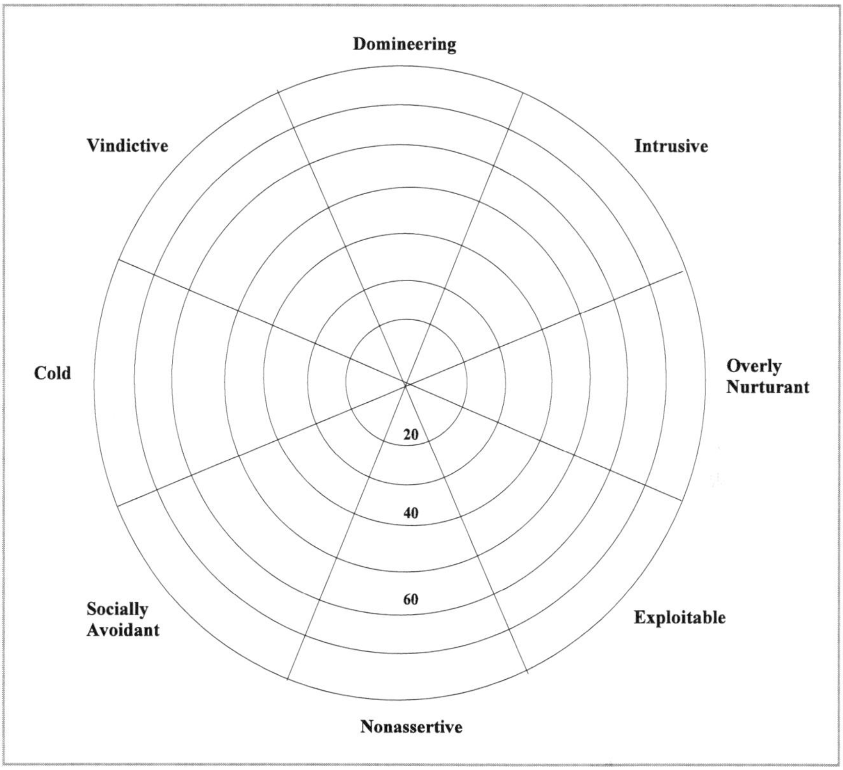

Source: Adapted from Pincus (1994, p. 1130–1131).

F. Gender Differences in Personality

Extensive research has been conducted over the past thirty years to assess the types and magnitudes of personality differences between genders. Several meta-analyses have been conducted (e.g., Hall, 1984; Maccoby & Jacklin, 1974), as well as on data collected through psychometric testing, typically using Costa and McRae's five-factor model (Feingold, 1994). Meta-analysis is a particularly powerful method, though not without its limitations, for statistically combining results from multiple studies. A review of meta-analyses (Feingold, 1994) confirms that males score notably higher on scales of assertiveness, whereas females have appreciably higher levels of anxiety, trust, and tender-mindedness. Females, in addition, are slightly more extraverted than males. However, no overall differences have been found on scales of impulsiveness, activity, ideas, and order. On the whole, the differences noted were not found to vary over ages, educational levels, or countries. The results are consistent with the view that, though men score higher on agentic (or instrumental) dimensions of personality functioning, women have more pronounced communal (or expressive) traits. Comparisons of means and effect sizes, as in these meta-analyses, tend to overshadow an understanding of the considerable overlap between groups on any characteristic (see chapter 13).

Most of the research that has been conducted is primarily descriptive and has been unable to isolate the sources of differences. Multiple theories have been proposed, including biological explanations that assume differences in inherited temperaments, sociocultural theories that emphasize socialization and gender-based stereotypes, and biosocial approaches that try to integrate the two. Although the lack of variability in the findings across educational levels and countries lends some support to a biological interpretation, the data on the modest correlations between childhood temperament and adult personality imply that environmental factors must play a significant role. This should encourage researchers to find new ways to model the interplay between social conditions on the one hand and biological predispositions on the other hand.

Thus, while considerable progress has been made in narrowing the search for the essential dimensions that describe personality, both normal and pathological, much work remains in linking the descriptions with biological and social conditions and in understanding the phenomenology of the associated conscious experience and how this experience is expressed through and modified by the patterns.

V. Personality Theories

Theories about how and why people's personalities differ have for the most part been developed independently of solid research or even basic descriptive data. Often several theories fit the same set of observations equally well, and many are insufficiently specified to be adequately tested. Nonetheless, differences in the many theories reveal something about the fundamental dynamics of personality functioning.

Salvatore Maddi (1996) has proposed one of the more useful typologies of personality theories, which is based on core assumptions about the underlying forces that drive or motivate individuals. He identifies three general types of theories—conflict, fulfillment, and consistency models—and each consists of two versions. Conflict models, such as Freudian theory, assume that the primary motivation is to reduce tension and relieve conflict—between the individual and society (psychosocial version), within the individual, or between different parts of the personality (intrapsychic version). The fulfillment model assumes an overriding drive toward growth and development that exists even without conflict. In the actualization version, this drive is ongoing, with no predetermined end point, whereas the perfection version of the model suggests that there is an end state, which perhaps involves the full development of certain innately defined potentials. Finally, the consistency model emphasizes the centrality of the information that a person obtains through interactions with the external world. This model assumes that individuals develop personalities that maximize the likelihood of their receiving and integrating needed information. Unlike consistency theories, fulfillment and conflict theories emphasize inherent human nature as a component of personality. Both fulfillment and conflict theories, more than consistency theories, suggest that attributes that people express in their behavior mostly mold personality. In addition, consistency theories are largely cognitive theories that assume that the central organizing principle is the need to achieve cognitive coherence or integration. Each broad class of theories emphasizes particular facets of mental functioning, such as the impact of human motivation (fulfillment models), the negotiation of conflict (conflict models), and the achievement of cognitive consistency or integration (consistency models).

A. Conflict Models

For Freud the central conflict of the individual is the problem of maximizing instinctual gratification or relief while minimizing conflict with society and the resulting punishment and guilt. According to Freud, an individual can only deal with this conflict and can never eliminate it. The Freudian theory of personality includes several overlapping perspectives: developmental, topographic, structural, dynamic, and psychosocial (for a discussion of the topographic perspective, see chapter 4; for a discussion of the developmental perspective, see chapter 5; see also figure 6.7).

The structural perspective is based on the notion that the core of the personality involves the development of the ego, a set of psychological capabilities or functions for dealing with conflict between the individual and society. Although Freud believed that this conflict originates in clashes with the external world, that conflict quickly becomes internalized. External prohibitions and ideals become internalized as the superego or conscience, whereas the biological drives are represented in the mind primarily on an unconscious level, in what Freud referred to as the id (sometimes translated as "it"). Freud believed that the id uses primary process thinking, based on

FIGURE 6.7: SIGMUND FREUD, IN 1907

the pleasure principle (involving the seeking of immediate gratification and avoidance of pain), whereas the mature ego draws on secondary process thinking, based on the reality principle (which defers pleasure whenever necessary). Primary process thought is essentially hallucinatory: what is wished for is immediately translated into what seemingly is, in much the same way as in some dreams. Whereas the id and superego are largely unconscious, the ego has been compared to an iceberg, with substantial portions in the unconscious and preconscious, but with a significant component residing in consciousness (see figure 6.8).

The ego consists of positive abilities and adaptations, as well as various defenses. Positive adaptations include cognitive, executive, and integrative functions (e.g., perception, decision making, goal setting, planning, coordinating action). But the functions are never completely successful in resolving the conflicts between individual and society, and that conflict becomes internalized or converted into internal psychological conflict.

The dynamic perspective concerns the operation of psychological conflict. Specifically, Freud suggests that intrinsic motivation typically involves activities that enhance a person's sense of competence, autonomy,

FIGURE 6.8: FREUD'S TOPOGRAPHIC AND STRUCTURAL PERSPECTIVES ON PERSONALITY

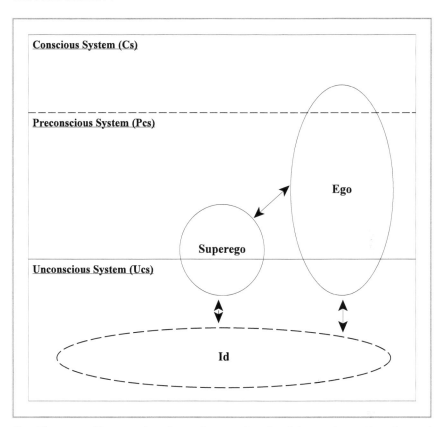

Note: The topographic perspective refers to the respective roles of the conscious, preconscious, and unconscious systems, whereas the structural perspective concerns the configuration of the major psychological structures, specifically, the ego, superego, and id.

or relatedness with others. Psychological conflict typically entails the threat of some instinctual drive breaking into consciousness, perhaps involving sexual or aggressive wishes. The ego, Freud found, uses various defenses to prevent the breakthrough of forbidden wishes, the temptation of illicit actions, and resultant social approbation. Each defense serves to simultaneously mask a desire and express it, just as the Trojans used the gift of a wooden horse to hide and carry out their aggressive intentions. These defenses are primarily directed against the id and only secondarily against the superego or external world. Some of the defenses are considered fairly primitive (e.g., repression, denial), whereas others are viewed as serving

TABLE 6.3: EXAMPLES OF MAJOR PSYCHOLOGICAL DEFENSES

DEFENSE	DESCRIPTION	EXAMPLE
DENIAL	Inability to perceive and/or comprehend the existence of some apparent reality, one that is often anxiety provoking	A patient for the first time hears her terminal diagnosis and can't understand what is being said
PROJECTION	Thinking or perceiving what is inside one to be in the external world	An angry teenager refuses to acknowledge his own anger and assumes others are angry at him
INTROJECTION	Thinking or perceiving what is outside one to be inside oneself	A child feels she is the mother whom she has lost
IDENTIFICATION	A feeling of wanting to be like some admired individual, or affinity with some organization or cause	A young man identifies with his therapist, wishing that he could come across like this admired figure
REPRESSION	Exclusion of an anxiety-provoking thought, feeling, or impulse from both the conscious and the pre-conscious	An employee unable to be aware of sexual feelings he has toward his boss
SUPPRESSION	Effort expended to exclude some thought, feeling, or impulse from consciousness, one that the person had already, if only temporarily, become aware of	An employee attempting to avoid sexual thoughts about his boss
DISPLACEMENT	Expressing impulses in a similar yet less threatening situation	Instead of personally criticizing his boss, an employee expresses negative feelings about the overall organization
RATIONALIZATION	Using the appearance of reason to hide the real reasons for one's anger, to hide some impulse from one's self	A person caught stealing rationalizes the act on the basis of the rationalization that something was owed to that person

TABLE 6.3 (CONTINUED)

DEFENSE	DESCRIPTION	EXAMPLE
REACTION FORMATION	Taking a contrary position to hide, from one's self, one's true desires	A latently suicidal person assiduously avoids or hides knives
SUBLIMATION	Expressing a forbidden desire in a social acceptable manner	A young man sublimates some voyeuristic tendencies by becoming a detective

Note: The above are examples of some of the major intrapsychic defenses and do not consider a wide range of adaptive and proactive problem-solving strategies that individuals use, both internally and in their interactions with others.

adaptive purposes (e.g., sublimation). For Freud, there is little beyond defense and adaptation that involves the creative and proactive pursuit of goals or the expression of any higher self. The inner and unconscious self is essentially a repository of primitive desires, residues from childhood and biological evolution. Table 6.3 outlines the major defenses that are considered layered functions that bolster one another and collectively serve to control conflict and the resulting anxiety but never actually resolve it. The dynamic perspective is concerned with the ongoing interactions among the major structures of the personality—ego, id, and superego—including the interactions among the various adaptations, defenses, wishes, and feeling states as well as the external social environment. The dynamic perspective is very much a hydraulic viewpoint. For example, to counter (or repress) some wish that is threatening to break into consciousness, an equal amount of energy is required to counteract it, and if it were counteracted with a primitive defense, the wish would pop up someplace else, requiring additional defenses.

The Freudian view of mental functioning is the basis for the identification of several personality or character types (see Maddi, 1996), each of which is composed of a particular constellation of traits and defenses, linked to arrests or unresolved issues at certain developmental stages. The oral character—involving mostly defenses of projection, denial, and introjection—originates in unresolved wishes for oral gratification. Typical traits are the alternatives of extreme optimism and pessimism, gullibility and suspiciousness, manipulativeness and passivity, and admiration and envy. For the anal character—involving unresolved wishes from the anal stage of psychosexual development—the major defenses are reaction-formation, isolation, undoing, and intellectualization, and common traits are the alternatives of stinginess and overgenerosity, stubbornness and acquiescence, orderliness and messiness, and precision and vagueness. For the phallic character, repression is central. Individuals with such disordered personalities can be characterized by the alternatives of vanity and self-hatred, pride and humility, blind courage and timidity, and chastity and promiscuity. Because Freud and his followers have viewed the human personality from a clinical viewpoint, believing that unresolved conflict and pathology are all pervasive, they have had little interest in proposing any typologies or theories of normal personality functioning.

While Freud's original viewpoint involved psychosocial conflict, which only secondarily became internalized as intrapsychic conflict, he and many of his successors nonetheless focused on the internalized part of this equation. Although society is an important and real force in people's lives, many in the psychoanalytic tradition have been mostly interested in the relationship between the self and internal objects or representations of others, which may have originated in actual individuals in the person's social environment. For this reason, proponents of this tradition are mostly interested in inner relationships rather than relationships among real people. Actual people and society itself constitute only the backdrop for inner dramas.

Whereas Freud and many ego psychologists, such as Karen Horney or Harry Stack Sullivan, were adherents of the psychosocial version of the conflict model, others in the analytic tradition largely rejected conflict with the external environment as important and instead believed that conflict originates inside the personality and only secondarily translates into social conflict.

B. Fulfillment Models

Unlike the conflict model, the fulfillment model proposes that there is only one central driving force located within the person (Maddi, 1996). Although conflict may be significant, it is not all-pervasive and inevitable and is of secondary importance. In the actualization version, fulfillment is an ongoing process with no fixed end point (e.g., the theories of Carl Rogers [1965] and Abraham Maslow [1943, 1971]). For Rogers, the central driving force is the need to actualize the self with all its inherent potentials. Two subsidiary needs facilitate this force: positive self-regard from others and positive self-regard. The latter refers to the situation in which one finds one's self-perceptions to be consistent with one's conscious self-image.

Rogers, unfortunately, does not have a fully developed system for describing or understanding the details of individual personality functioning, though he does distinguish between the fully functioning and the maladjusted person. The former displays openness to experience (emotional depth and reflectiveness), existential living (flexibility, adaptability, spontaneity, and inductive thinking), organismic trusting (intuitive living, self-reliance, and confidence), experiential freedom (subjective sense of free will), and creativity (the ability to produce new and practical solutions). In contrast, maladjusted people "live according to a pre-conceived plan rather than existentially, disregard their organism rather than trust it, feel manipulated rather than free, and feel common and conforming rather than creative" (Rogers, quoted in Maddi, 1996, p. 509).

Maslow's theory (first discussed in chapter 5) distinguishes between deficiency and growth motivations, placing the latter in a primary position, but one that comes into play only after deficiency motivations are satisfied. As did Rogers, Maslow did little to formulate a developmental theory or a theory of particular personality types. Both theorists were reluctant to categorize behavior in a way that might be used to stereotype individuals. However, Maslow did describe the self-actualizing person as one who is realistic; accepting of self, others, and the natural world; spontaneous but task oriented; independent; spiritual though not necessarily religious; having a sense of identity with mankind; able to experience intimacy with significant others; valuing of democratic ideals; recognizing the difference between means and ends; displaying a sense of humor that is not hostile; and creative and nonconforming.

Another example of the perfection version of the fulfillment model is Erich Fromm's theory of personality (1941). In Fromm's theory, the core tendency is the expression of an underlying human nature. The unfoldment of this unique human potential involves five subsidiary drives: relatedness, transcendence, rootedness, identity, and frame of reference. The way these are expressed generates the various personality patterns or orientations he observed: receptive, characterized by passivity, lack of character, submissiveness, and cowardliness; exploitive, suggested by the traits of aggressiveness, egocentrism, conceit, arrogance, and seductiveness; hoarding, which involves stinginess, unimaginativeness, suspiciousness, stubbornness, and possessiveness; marketing, seen in traits such as opportunism, inconsistency, aimlessness, lack of principle, relativism, and wastefulness; and productive, which involves the useful aspects of the other orientations (e.g., modesty, adaptability, activeness, pride, flexibility, open-mindedness, and experimentalism) (see Maddi, 1996).

C. Consistency Models

In the consistency model of personality functioning, the overriding driving force is the need to achieve and maintain consistency, coherence, or integration of one's various mental schemes, maps, or representations of reality. The theory of cognitive dissonance suggests that this occurs through minimizing inconsistencies or discrepancies between mental representations. McClelland (1988), for instance, suggests that the major core tendency is to minimize the gaps between expectations and perceptions of occurrence, but at the same time to maintain and even maximize small discrepancies between anticipated and actual events to maintain novelty and prevent boredom. Central to this theory is the concept of expectancies, which are the fundamental cognitive units involving the nature of anticipated events. Positive affect tends to be attached to small discrepancies and to lead to approach behaviors, and negative affect tends to lead to avoidant behaviors. McClelland draws on Murray's (1938) identification of achievement, affiliation, and power as critical content areas of these motivations, and he theorizes that there is both an approach and an avoidant version of each. In addition to the motives, which are based on small or large inconsistencies between expectations and occurrence, traits and schemes structure personality functioning. Traits are similar to habits and are not goal-directed behaviors. Schemes, in contrast, are mental representations involving past experience, ideas, values, and social roles, and they are important in determining expectations.

Unlike the cognitive dissonance version of the consistency model, the activation version focuses on the maintenance of an optimal level of mental activation. In Fiske and Maddi's version (see Maddi, 1996), *activation* refers to psychological excitement or tension and to physiological engagement of key brain centers. Each individual is said to have a customary level of activation, a kind of set point, that is the basis for the regulation of activation levels. Maddi explains, "The level of activation at any time is determined by the *impact of stimulation,* meaning the degree of *intensity, meaningfulness, and variety* of stimulation emanating from *internal* and *external* sources" (1996, p. 518). Some people with an activeness trait can proactively anticipate required levels of stimulation in terms of their intensity, meaningfulness, and variety, whereas others with a passiveness trait must correct for unfavorable levels after they occur. In addition, people differ in the extent that they rely on external versus internal sources of stimulation and activation.

Fiske and Maddi (see Maddi, 1996) theorize that there are four types of personalities based on activation levels. First, high-activation people with an external orientation tend to be go-getters, energetic, and voracious, but this may vary according to their needs for variety versus intensity. Second, high-activation people who have an internal orientation seek activation through such activities as thinking, daydreaming, and other mental challenges, and they tend to be subtle and complex. Within this group, people differ from one another according to the extent of their need for meaningfulness, intensity, and variety. Third, low-activation people with an external orientation tend to be conservative and conformist and to have simple tastes. Those who fear meaningfulness may oversimplify problems, or those who fear variety may seek safety in familiar routines. Fourth, low-activation people with an internal orientation tend to be conservative and are "uncomplex and devoid of inconsistencies" (Maddi, 1996, p. 519). They often like to avoid excesses and value the ideal of the golden mean, or the ideal of moderation and balance.

In many respects, the three models of personality functioning, along with their various versions, parallel one another, yet fundamentally depart from one another in their assumptions about the core driving forces of personality. Fulfillment models emphasize a singular evolving and unfolding thrust to personality functioning, which may secondarily lead to conflict and inconsistency. Conflict models take a broad view of conflict as ubiquitous and as involving conflicts either between the individual and society or among major parts of the personality. In contrast, consistency models also focus on conflict but in a much more circumscribed range, namely, within conscious and preconscious mental representations and associated activation levels. To the extent that a simple homeostatic model cannot achieve the consistency, coherence, or integration of mental representations, understanding personality becomes a matter of understanding how conflict is controlled or transformed. This is especially the case when conflict involves such discrepant forces as unconscious instinctual drives, internalized cultural prohibitions, or the external social environment. So, while each model has fundamentally different assumptions, the question becomes, Which one is correct, or does each focus on separate aspects of personality functioning? The parable of the three blind men feeling the trunk, leg, and tail of an elephant and describing the parts as unrelated illustrates the possibility that seemingly distinct assumptions and explanations of how personalities function may mask different but valid approaches to a single phenomenon.

VI. Discussion

A central theme of this chapter is that there is a complex, interactive relationship between a person's states of consciousness—particularly subjective experiences of well-being and happiness—and the motivational systems that energize and direct their behavior. States of consciousness, motivations, and behavioral patterns are a few of the elements that collectively make up personality. Also important are habit patterns and other traits, temperamental predispositions, and the contributions of larger social and cultural systems. But how exactly do all of these elements interact to generate personality? The previous chapters on social change, consciousness, and development all contribute to the answer to this question. Thus, this section draws on a few of those insights to illustrate some of the key processes involved in personality development.

Personality is not only a system but also a highly complex and often adaptive system. It is composed of multiple negative and positive feedback loops. Negative feedback loops, much like a thermostat, maintain the system around some set point that may be biological, involving activation levels; psychological, involving optimal moods; or social, involving acceptable levels of social interaction. Positive feedback loops challenge and sometimes change these set points, forcing the system into new constellations that are either more or less adaptive. This may involve the breakdown of simple structures through repeated splitting of key processes, or the generation of new perspectives, skills, and behavioral patterns through self-organization. A special relationship with a teacher or a spiritual awakening are examples of transformations in consciousness that stimulate positive feedback loops throughout the personality and social relationships, thereby stimulating new aspirations that transform the personality.

Chapter 2 identified three competing processes of change: self-organization, selection, and entropy. These processes collectively mold personality. Self-organization most often consists of the interaction of subsystems (e.g., individual traits, feelings, motivations, ego, id, superego) according to local activity rules to generate the larger system. It involves the dissipative flow of energy, an optimal level of density of interconnections, and a degree of randomness (i.e., activity at the edge of chaos) to generate novel and adaptive structures. Growth spurts, especially during childhood and adolescence, are common examples, during which the elements of one's life may seem to come apart and recrystallize around a new center and new self-selections, hopefully ones based on more mature or adaptive principles and values. But while self-organization may generate new structures, the competition and selections of life either dispose of them or force their revision. Whereas self-selection is central to self-organization, social and natural selection are central to the adaptation of existing or new structures to conditions involving competition and scarcity. Finally, change is also driven, for better or worse, by entropy, which is the tendency of organized systems (e.g., humans) to dissipate energy and move toward less-ordered, more probable states. Entropy provides the element of disorder required for new cycles of self-organization and new opportunities to compete and select the best. However, it also drives toward death in a manner reminiscent of Freud's concept of Thanatos. The three processes of self-organization, selectionism, and entropy that are the broad-brush drivers that both energize and channel the various motivational systems (e.g., moving toward, against, or away from others; aspiring for autonomy, competence, relatedness, or self-esteem).

Several theorists, such as Ken Wilber, Otto Rank, and David Bakan, have proposed that the central issue for both motivation and personality is the balance between achieving communion versus agency; between the desire to be part of the larger whole of society and the universe and fully discovering the whole that one already is; of achieving a sense of individuality, autonomy, and free will. One's approach to this dilemma, whether one moves in one direction or the other or attempts some kind of compromise or integration, has fundamental implications for one's sense of well-being, for the specific motivational structures that one develops, and for one's entire personality. For example, those who value communion are more likely to seek relatedness and social inclusion, whereas those who seek agency lean toward competency and autonomy. Each motivational structure is associated with particular states of subjective well-being. Achieving a sense of competence in a task may generate the experience of flow, whereas seeking relatedness may generate distinctive types of conscious or subjective well-being. When these aspirations are successful, the resulting qualities of experience reinforce the original motivations and push for their integration with the whole of the personality.

Chapter 3 introduced the idea that three motivational structures—aspirations for power, knowledge, and bliss (or subjective well-being)—arise out of the same three aspects of consciousness. Power may mean raw aggressiveness and control over others, or it may mean control over one's self, competence, or self-efficacy. Knowledge likewise may manifest as awareness, expertise in economic planning, or self-understanding. The desire for positive sensory and feeling experiences ranges from that for sexual experience to a feeling of contentment, the enjoyment of a sunset, or spiritual bliss. Although the objects of human motivation might be described along these lines, the orientation toward this content is a different matter. For some, the focus is predominantly on obtaining these experiences through external means, through the manipulation of associated conditions (e.g., money, relationships, symbols). However, to the extent that these experiences are truly integrated into the personality, the sense of their dependence on external conditions is progressively lessened, thus giving way to the realization that they reflect aspects of the self rather than the external world. As this process unfolds, movement is from the effort to obtain to a reciprocal give-and-take of these experiences, and finally to an altruistic concern with giving them, developing understanding in others, enhancing the sense of well-being, or empowering others.

Each individual has values that incline him or her to be mainly concerned with knowledge, power, or finding a sense of subjective well-being, of pleasure or happiness, or some combination of these. When aspirations are suppressed from consciousness, they tend to piggyback onto conscious ones. One's main passion may be in generating useful knowledge, but this might camouflage a desire for control of others. Or perhaps one seeks political, economic, or religious power for access to sexual relationships. A key question in the analysis of any motivational structure and its underlying values is whether a particular interest represents a core value (i.e., something sought for its own sake) or is merely instrumental in achieving some other end, either consciously or unconsciously. One may seek knowledge but mainly to get a job, to obtain power, or to provide for happy life for one's self and family. As the discussion on typologies of motivation illustrated, there are many ways to cut up the pie of human experience, and some ways no doubt provide more comprehensive and balanced views than others.

What is argued here is the importance of understanding the relationship between immediate conscious experience, with its diverse qualities, and personality and motivation; among what has been, what is, and what might be. Personality can be understood as the crystallization or imprint of multiple past experiences, successful and failed aspirations, and the techniques for their attainment. Traits and habits are the residues of past dynamic and living experience. It is the unique and lingering signature of the self-organized stuff of these traits and habits combined with the current living edge of experience and the underlying motivational systems that form what we think of as personality. Based on Abraham Maslow's work, Everett Shostrom (1963) suggested that a central dimension of mental health is "time competence," which he regarded as the ability to live primarily in the present but also to maintain a relationship with the past and future. Doing so involves the ability to draw on the repertoire of past memories and habits, as well as anticipations of the future, without letting either obscure one's ability to live wholeheartedly in the present moment.

VII. Summary

This chapter has focused on alternative approaches to understanding personality by considering two critical areas: states of subjective well-being and motivation. Personality is a complex interplay between the current conscious state, often involving a sense of subjective well-being and motivation, and both positive and negative experiences determine motivations, which in turn, with their associated behaviors, perpetuate or diminish those states. The residue or imprint of this interplay typically generates the constellation of traits and habits that constitute the personality context for continued functioning.

The chapter then discusses research on happiness, which is a much more common state than formerly believed, fairly constant through the lives of individuals, and minimally associated with their demographic characteristics or even financial resources. Important predictors include loving relationships, extraversion and openness, community involvement, optimism, and a spiritual orientation. Theories about happiness and broader states of well-being have often emphasized the importance of attaining meaningful goals that are consistent with underlying values. If this is true, it supports the eudaemonic view of happiness of living according to one's daemon, or essential values, rather than the narrower hedonist view, which emphasizes the predominance of positive feeling states. The chapter then considers a few other elements of positive mental health, such as the sense of flow through engagement in challenging and meaningful activities, as well as hardiness and resilience. All of these and other traits are elements of mental health.

The chapter also reviews a range of approaches to motivation, including the essential dimensions needed to understand motivation: the extrinsic-intrinsic, approach-avoidance, and performance-mastery dimensions, and the generality of the motivational structure of interest. Especially important is the content of motivation, which largely involves its object or aim, whether relatedness, self-esteem, autonomy, or competence. The chapter also reviews process theories of motivation, which involve the question of how cognitive, affective, and behavioral elements dynamically interact to produce motivation. It is proposed here that motivation not only should be regarded as states that energize and direct persistent goal-directed behavior but also involves cognitive-affective systems in their own right.

The chapter then discusses the field of personality theory, beginning with the multiple social and intrapsychic levels of functioning involved. A major issue is the debate between the categorical and dimensional approaches to the description of personality. Practitioners have often favored the former, but most researchers and theorists tend to favor the latter. There is considerable agreement among studies about the existence of the extraversion, agreeableness, and conscientiousness dimensions but less agreement about neuroticism and openness to experience than there is among three and five essential dimensions.

The chapter concludes with a discussion of the problem of understanding how the phenomena—states of well-being, motivation, and personality—interact. More important, it discusses how personality as a whole relates to the notions of complex systems, change, consciousness, and development covered in earlier chapters. For instance, the three principles of change—self-organization, selectionism, and entropy—are fundamental processes that are applicable to understanding the interplay among the development, maintenance, fine-tuning, and dissolution of the patterns of personality functioning. The section concludes with some suggestions about the centrality of knowledge, power, and bliss as themes linking the discussion of consciousness, motivation, and personality.

For Further Reading

Bütz, M. R. (1997). *Chaos and complexity: Implications for psychological theory and practice.* New York: Taylor & Francis.

Diener, E., Suh, E. N., Lucas, R. E., & Smith, H. L. (1999). Subjective well-being: Three decades of progress. *Psychological Bulletin, 125,* 276–302.

Feingold, A. (1994). Gender differences in personality: A meta-analysis. *Psychological Bulletin, 116*(3), 429–456.

King, L. A., & Napa, C. K. (1998). What makes a life good? *Journal of Personality and Social Psychology, 75*(1), 156–165.

Maddi, S. R. (1996). *Personality theories. A comparative analysis.* New York: Brooks/Cole.

Maddi, S. R., & Khoshaba, D. M. (1994). Hardiness and mental health. *Journal of Personality Assessment, 63*(2), 265–274.

Mandell, A. J., & Selz, K. (1995). Nonlinear dynamical patterns as personality theory for neurobiology and psychiatry. *Psychiatry, 58,* 371–390.

Myers, D. G. (1992). *The pursuit of happiness.* New York: Avon Books.

Ryan, R. M., & Deci, E. L. (2001). On happiness and human potentials: A review of research on hedonic and eudaimonic well-being. In S. Fiske (Ed.). *Annual review of psychology* (Vol. 52, pp. 141–166). Palo Alto, CA: Annual Reviews.

Seligman, M. & Csikszentmihalyi, M. (2000). Positive psychology: An introduction. *American Psychologist, 55*(1), 5–14.

Sheldon, K. M., Elliot, A. J., Kim, Y., & Kasser, T. (2001, February). What is satisfying about satisfying events? Testing 10 candidate psychological needs. *Journal of Personality and Social Psychology, 80*(2), 325–339.

Wahba, M. A., & Bridwell, L. G. (1976). Maslow reconsidered: A review of research on the need hierarchy theory. *Organizational Behavior and Human Performance, 15,* 212–240.

CHAPTER 7

Problem Solving, Decision Making, and Creativity

> *Problems cannot be solved at the same level of awareness that created them.*
>
> —ALBERT EINSTEIN

I. Introduction

This chapter turns to the subject of problem solving, one of the most universal activities of human beings. It considers problem solving in its broadest sense to include both individual and collective, as well as rational and transrational processes, including decision making, creativity, and intuition. But the chapter begins by reviewing problem solving in a restricted sense. This involves conscious and deliberate efforts to understand difficult situations and to decide and implement means for achieving valued solutions. In either case, problem solving entails an immense range of problems, including the everyday problems that clients present. Some examples are a battered spouse trying to figure out how to save her marriage without being assaulted again, a person with paranoid schizophrenia trying to get authorities to investigate an imagined plot, or a family member trying to figure out how to keep an aged parent at home and still provide sufficient care and safety. Other examples might involve the challenges of human service professionals trying to figure out how to support these same clients in their problem-solving efforts, administrators trying to figure out how to handle a budget crunch, or policy makers trying to determine how to craft a compromise to gain the votes needed for the passage of a new social program. The chapter focuses mainly on the range of theories and the supporting research concerning how people and groups actually make decisions, and whether they do so in a productive or dysfunctional manner. It also identifies the implications of this work for human service professionals. The chapter takes the position that effective problem solving is not an either-or choice between rational and transrational methods but a both-and opportunity to draw on rational, even technical, procedures and to ground these in creativity and intuition.

As important as problem solving is, not everyone shares an interest in the subject. Psychoanalysts have traditionally assumed that if people develop sufficient self-understanding, problem solving comes naturally. Many cognitivists assume that mental functioning is largely unconscious; thus, some may view conscious problem solving as a quaint ideal of a bygone era. Many social scientists take a reductionist and unidirectional view of causation, understanding most problems of human behavior as reflections of impersonal biological, social, or economic forces. Yet many psychoanalysts, cognitivists, and social scientists take very seriously conscious problem solving and decision making. An emerging theme is that, although there are many problems and decisions that people routinely and sometimes mindlessly confront, problems that are more complex, ambiguous, or novel require conscious, deliberate, and often goal-directed problem solving. This is particularly true for the human services, in which conscious and systematic problem solving that draws on a profession's knowledge base is a defining expectation of professional practice.

The growing diversity and complexity of the postmodern information economy is one of the conditions that have fueled the explosion of research and theory on problem solving in recent decades. The development of complex systems theory, reviewed in previous chapters, has been a critical component in some of the advances made. Yet readers should remember that there is much that involves the functioning of individuals and groups that cannot be easily cast in a problem-solving or decision-making framework.

This chapter builds on the previous chapters. It not only applies complex systems theory to the broad field of problem solving, decision making, and creativity but also specifically considers how both individuals and groups self-organize these efforts. In particular, the theories of creativity and intuition illustrate the power of consciousness to draw on self-organization in unconscious information processing. This chapter links adult problem solving with the various cognitive, psychosocial, and moral developmental processes reviewed in chapter 5. In addition, it considers problem solving in the context of personality (discussed in chapter 6), which includes characteristic styles of conscious functioning as well as temperamental patterns, habits, and styles. This chapter sets the stage for us to specifically consider dysfunctional problem solving with respect to psychopathology in the next chapter.

The terms *problem solving, decision making,* and *creativity* have multiple meanings and can be defined narrowly or broadly, depending on the preferred theories. These terms are best treated as alternative frames or perspectives on problem solving. Figure 7.1 illustrates a few of the relationships among these and other phenomena. At the center of this figure is rational problem solving, defined by the Noble Prize–winning behavioral economist Herbert Simon (1986) to include establishing agendas, setting goals, designing actions, and implementing decisions and evaluating outcomes. Thus, problem solving encompasses cognitive and affective components, values, and actions or behaviors. Decision making, in contrast, typically involves the evaluation and selection of alternative solutions. Any of these activities might be creatively undertaken, but too often they are not. Surrounding and supporting the various protocols and processes of problem solving, decision making, and creativity are various cognitive capabilities for which many terms have been coined: *mindful learning, critical thinking, intuition, multiple intelligences, metacognition,* and *lateral thinking.*

Figure 7.1 does not show the many connecting paths among various functions, as there are no simple or linear progressions for complex problems but instead innumerable permutations of feedback loops, too many to illustrate here. Thus, it is easy to think of exceptions to what is shown in Figure 7.1. For instance, some creativity might not consist of solving a problem per se but instead involve various kinds of creative expression or play. Similarly, we also make decisions about agendas, goals, or plans for implementation. We may make decisions about things that we do not necessarily consider problems (e.g., deciding which CD to play as I write this introduction). This, however, raises the question of problem solving, and it is to this topic that the chapter now turns.

II. Problem Solving

A. Definition and Context

Problem solving is first and foremost a process of individuals or groups achieving difficult ends. A generic definition of a problem is "any situation in which something undesirable or unwanted exists in the opinion of the person calling it a problem" (Agre, 1983, p. 96). Thus, what you consider a problem (e.g., a barking dog) may not be a problem at all to someone else (e.g., the dog's owner). The problem-solving process is usually conceptualized as a fairly rational one of analyzing a situation of concern, determining goals, assessing alternative interventions in terms of those goals, selecting a goal, and then implementing it. Herbert Simon (1986) contends that "the first three of these activities—fixing agendas, setting goals, and designing actions—are usually called problem solving; the last, evaluating and choosing is usually called decision making" (p. 18). Problem solving is both a cognitive and a practical task, though in some fields, such as mathematics, the actual intervention may not involve much beyond elaboration and verification. But in social work, Helen Harris Perlman (1957), who originated the problem-solving approach, suggested: "In sum, the ego's continuous task is that of solving the problems, small or great, posed by what the person wants, what powers of mind, spirit, and body he can harness to his

FIGURE 7.1: RELATIONSHIPS AMONG PROBLEM SOLVING, DECISION MAKING, AND CREATIVITY

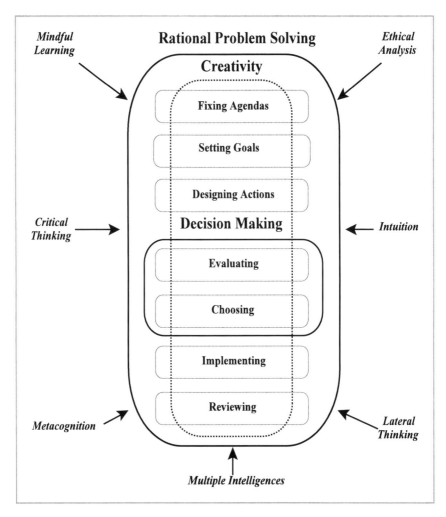

purposes, and what his environment requires, gives, or withholds" (p. 100). In the human services, problems are typically regarded as involving threats to fundamental human values—such as human dignity, caring, mutual support, and social justice—and as involving a breakdown in the goodness of fit among the motivations of individuals or groups to achieve these ends, their opportunities to do so, and their capacities to capitalize on these opportunities (Ripple, 1969).

The emphasis on rational, deliberate, goal-directed problem solving can obscure the fact that much of our behavior may be otherwise; we often operate on automatic pilot or sometimes act impulsively. Mattingly-Scott (2003) distinguishes between knowledge acquisition on the one hand and categorization, action, and problem solving on the other hand, with the former being static and the latter dynamic. Knowledge-acquisition behaviors typically have been either informally or formally learned to become part of the actor's repertoire of possible responses. Many cognitivists argue that much of behavior is habitual, either unconscious or semiconscious, and only intermittently punctuated by motivated and goal-oriented actions in select situations. It is argued that there is a continuous interplay of routine behavior and deliberate action. Between the two are actions that, though conscious and deliberate, may not be particularly goal directed. We make a joke for the immediate pleasure of a good laugh (or to express some hostility), and not necessarily to achieve some future end beyond the action itself. The combined impact of habitual behaviors, immediate non-goal-directed actions, and goal-directed actions has been referred to as the "action competence of a person." This model regards problem solving as a special type of planned action that takes place when a goal is not directly achievable because of some barrier or uncertainty (Mattingly-Scott, 2003).

Other cognitive scientists, such as David Green (1996), make a similar distinction but break it down into four levels of action, each of which successively builds on the former:

Level 1 consists of the ability to make object appropriate actions (e.g., lifting a cup of coffee).

Level 2 entails sequencing these actions into a behavioral routine (e.g., drinking the cup of coffee).

Level 3 adds voluntary control over the automatic sequencing of level 2.

Level 4 involves the integration of the former three levels with cognition, which usually takes place in situations that involve more complex planning and decision making, error correction and troubleshooting, responses that are not well learned, danger or difficulty, overcoming a strong habitual response, or resisting temptation.

Problem solving for human service professionals means considerably more than managing the usual routines of everyday activity; it means helping clients and themselves deal with the often overwhelmingly complex dilemmas of contemporary society. One study compared novices and experts in complex systems and the ways that they think about problems (Jacobson, 2000). The researcher hypothesized that novices would take a reductionist approach to understanding problems, emphasize centralized control, look at single causes, consider consequences proportional to their causes, rely on teleological explanations, and emphasize static structures with predictable consequences. He also hypothesized that those schooled in complex systems theory were more likely to take a holistic approach; emphasize decentralized control, and multiple and disproportional causes; and rely on nonteleological explanations of a dynamic nature. He found that many, but not all, of the hypothesized differences actually characterized his fairly small sample. It is perhaps the recognition that because problem solving typically involves considerable complexity, no standard protocols will ever be sufficient. Instead, problem solving must be supported and supplemented by a variety of cognitive skills, which are listed in the periphery of figure 7.1, and it is this topic that will be discussed in the next section.

B. Cognitive Skills for Problem Solving

In recent years there has been a proliferation of approaches to problem solving, some of which have originated in the self-help tradition and others that have been developed with an eye toward educational or management training or consulting. The approaches assume certain generic cognitive skills that can apply across a broad range of problem situations, often ones that can be systematically developed. The focus is on discrete cognitive tactics rather than on more complex procedures or strategies. The approaches constitute generic competencies that can be used in conjunction with more specialized strategies for creative problem solving and decision making. This section briefly presents examples of a few such competencies, such as critical thinking, mindful learning, lateral thinking, and metacognition (for a discussion of multiple intelligences, see chapter 6).

Critical thinking is among the better known skills. Critical thinking uses several methods of logical and empirical inference, as well as a vigilant avoidance of bias. Gibbs and Gambrill (1999) have identified the following characteristics of critical thinking:

- It is purposeful.
- It is responsive to and guided by intellectual standards.
- It supports the development of intellectual traits in the thinker of humility, integrity, perseverance, empathy, and self-discipline.

- The thinker can identify the elements of thought by linking the previous elements with the problem at hand.
- It is self-assessing and self-improving.
- There is an integrity to the whole system.
- It yields a well-reasoned answer.
- It considers opposing points of view and the need to seek weaknesses in one's preferred position.

Critical thinking relies, in part, on a vigilant avoidance of the cognitive biases found among many professionals, not just among laypeople, such as hindsight bias, framing effects, and the law of small numbers. Hindsight bias is the tendency to recall only correct predictions and to forget incorrect ones. For example, a casework supervisor mentions the tragic case of a client who murders his family and then commits suicide. A manager responds by noting that the client had previously tried to commit suicide and that the situation could have been avoided had he been hospitalized. In contrast, a critical thinker is more careful about jumping to such conclusions.

Framing effects also prompt many premature conclusions. Such effects are well known in survey research. A survey might ask, "Do you favor cutting back on welfare for able-bodied individuals who can work?" or "Do you favor cutting back on welfare for families with young children?" The posing of questions often elicits alternative answers based on corresponding emotional reactions to the issue at hand.

Social service professionals are also vulnerable to biases originating from the law of small numbers, which is the idea that because an expert has intimate knowledge of a few selected cases, he or she presumes to offer expert consultation on a wide range of clients. The indiscriminate use of poignant anecdotes to argue for a policy of a general scope exemplifies this law (see Gibbs & Gambrill, 1999).

Other theorists focus not so much on critical thought about existing information but on the ability to gain new knowledge and skill, a key example of which is mindful learning. Mindful learning is, in part, an application of the Buddhist notion of mindfulness, which is the ability to be fully and wholeheartedly engaged in the present with all of its attendant tasks, and with both care and detachment. Ellen Langer (1997), a Harvard social psychologist and the author of *The Power of Mindful Learning,* explains that, when applied to learning, the notion goes a bit further to assume that the skills are based on successful learning strategies, ones that are consistent with the nature of human learning and problem solving. She identified three characteristics of mindful learning: (1) continuous creation of new categories, (2) openness to new information, and (3) an implicit awareness of more than one perspective. As do many others, Langer emphasizes the importance of the ability to be multiperspectival, to look at problems from diverse angles. She debunks seven myths that undercut mindful learning, myths based on the classical tradition of the correspondence theory of knowledge (see chapter 1):

1. The basics must be learned so well that they become second nature.
2. Paying attention means staying focused on one thing at a time.
3. Delaying gratification is important.
4. Rote memorization is necessary in education.
5. Forgetting is a problem.
6. Intelligence is knowing what is out there.
7. There are right and wrong answers.

Langer points out that "studies suggest that mindfully varying perspective helps us pay attention" (p. 48) and that the ability to forget irrelevant information may be healthy. Her approach, unfortunately, does not say much about the integrative process: how coherence is achieved once one can draw on multiple perspectives. Many assume that this process happens on its own as long as one attends to the phenomenon in a sufficiently focused and mindful manner.

Similar to mindful learning is lateral thinking, a notion from popular self-help literature introduced by Edward de Bono (1967). He deemphasizes the formal use of vertical thought, typically involving methods of deduction and induction, and instead argues for looser horizontal associations that draw on a wide range of seemingly unrelated information and perspectives. This type of thinking requires tolerance for ambiguity because it moves away from predefined concepts and is quite similar to divergent or multiperspectival thought (see Harmon & Rheingold, 1984). De Bono identifies four critical conditions for lateral thinking: (1) recognition that dominant ideas often polarize the understanding of a problem, (2) search for different ways to look at things, (3) relaxation of rigid control of thinking, and (4) use of chance to encourage other ideas.

De Bono recommends that, to get a new perspective on a problem, one can experiment by breaking up the elements of a problem and recombining them in new and creative ways, perhaps even randomly. He contends that more intelligent people are often poor thinkers because of arrogance, defensiveness, and the need to be seen as always clever and right. De Bono speculates that people with greater intelligence generally act more unintelligently. He calls this paradox the intelligence trap and argues that intelligent behavior is primarily a matter of learned thinking skills (see Nordby, 2001). To illustrate lateral thinking, De Bono (1967, as cited in Kearsley, 2003) tells the following story:

> A merchant who owes money to a money lender agrees to settle the debt based upon the choice of two stones (one black, one white) from a money bag. If his daughter chooses the white stone, the debt is cancelled; if she picks the black stone, the moneylender gets the merchant's daughter. However, the moneylender "fixes" the outcome by putting two black stones in the bag. The daughter sees this and when she picks a stone out of the bag, immediately drops it onto the path full of other stones. She then points out that the stone she picked must have been the opposite color of the one remaining in the bag. Unwilling to be unveiled as dishonest, the moneylender must agree and cancel the debt. The daughter has solved an intractable problem through the use of lateral thinking. (p. 11)

De Bono's theory of lateral thinking, though intuitive, is hardly original. Like many entrepreneurial self-help theorists, De Bono appears more concerned with distinguishing his approach from various traditional approaches than with specifically identifying how lateral or multiperspectival thought can be used in conjunction with traditional approaches. The theory is beset with a kind of anti-intellectualism that unduly discounts the role of logical and empirical approaches, including critical thinking.

Another skill of some importance is metacognition, which refers to the ability to step back from one's current problem-solving efforts and think about one's thinking, to review the process of problem solving. Although the capacity for self-reflection has been written about extensively, the particular formulation of metacognition was first advanced by John Flavell (1979) in the late 1970s. He regarded metacognition as a strategy for learning and cognitive problem solving, one that emphasizes the role of executive processes in overseeing and controlling a range of cognitive processes. Flavell distinguished among self-reflection concerning one's knowledge (metacognitive knowledge), one's current behaviors (metacognitive skill), and one's current affective state (metacognitive experience). Metacognition involves stepping back from whatever problem or task one is engaged in and examining how one thinks about and experiences that problem, including any assumptions about it. The notion of metacognition has become popular in such diverse fields as primary and secondary education and management consulting. It emphasizes the use of techniques such as self-assessment, journaling, and process recording of counseling cases. It differs from lateral and multiperspectival thinking in that it promotes consideration of a wide range of alternative formulations and emphasizes an examination of the process of problem solving itself. It assumes that better options and better processes will be generated, but it does not make explicit how this might happen.

C. Strategies for Problem Solving

The problem-solving literature is replete with a wide range of recommended strategies and models. There are several generic approaches: trial and error, creativity and systems thinking, use of formal strategies, and restructuring or reframing (Torre, 1995). The complexity of most problems tends to defeat a strictly trial-and-error approach, given the immense number of possible solutions and the impossibility of trying them all out. Most agree that creativity, systems thinking, and the cognitive abilities discussed in the previous section are all important and do not exclude formal procedures to simplify problem solving.

This section therefore focuses on the use of formal strategies, including restructuring, as they may dramatically reduce the need for trial and error and focus critical thinking and creative processes along the most productive lines. Most proposed formal models do not differ dramatically from one another. They are mostly variations on the process that Herbert Simon (1986) proposed (see figure 7.1): fixing agendas, setting goals, designing actions, evaluating, choosing, implementing, and reviewing. Their critical features are that they compare ends and means, and they determine the means that achieve the desired ends most effectively and at the lowest cost. The process typically aims at what is referred to as optimization: finding the single means or combination of means that achieves the best possible outcome. The various professions have demonstrated a love-hate relationship with the optimization model. Most textbooks extol optimization as the preeminent model of rationality, even in a field such as social work. Yet most authors note its obvious flaws, including the difficulty of deciding on appropriate goals without consensus, forecasting the consequences of various alternatives, and comparing and aggregating the various types of benefits and costs involved. But often the same authors go on to propose variations of the model that are not fundamentally different (see figure 7.2).

Several authors have attempted to clarify the beginning stages of problem solving. Instead of simply fixing agendas, they identify the need to adequately find and represent the problem, to define the domain or context, or to analyze it, all important tasks. Others explain the evaluation and

FIGURE 7.2: EXAMPLES OF PROBLEM-SOLVING MODELS

1. Finding the Problem
2. Representing the Problem
3. Planning the Solution
4. Carrying out the Plan
5. Evaluating the Solution
6. Consolidating the Gains
(Hayes, 1989)

1. I – Identify Problems
2. D – Defining Problems
3. E – Exploring Alternatives
4. A – Acting on a Plan
5. L – Looking at the Effects
(Bransford & Stein, 1984)

1. Identify Problem Evnironment
2. Analyze the Problem Situation
3. Identify the Solution Scope
4. Evaluate the Solution
(Mattingly-Scott, 2003)

1. The Problem is Decided
2. Alternatives are Generalized
3. Solutions are Evaluated
4. Iteration
(Robertshaw, 1978)

For Ill-Structured Problems:
1. Learners articulate problem space and context
2. Identify and clarify alternative opinions, positions, perspectives of stakeholders
3. Generate possible problem solutions
4. Assess viability of alternative solutions with arguments and beliefs
5. Monitor problem space and solution options
6. Implement and monitor solution
7. Adapt the solution
(Jonassen, 1997)

Ethical Problem Solving:
1. Determine whether there is an ethical issue or dilemma
2. Identify key values and principles involved
3. Rank values and ethical principles which are most relevant to issue
4. Develop action plan that is consistent with ethical priorities determined above
5. Implement plan, using most appropriate practice skills and competencies
6. Reflect on the outcome
(Reamer & Conrad, 1995)

Source: Adapted from Torre (1995, p. 183).

selection of alternatives in slightly different terms as a process of generating options, planning implementation, or ranking values. Although some leave out implementation and its review, other theorists emphasize its importance or propose particular tasks, such as the iteration or fine-tuning of the process or the consolidation of gains.

Some approaches have been specifically designed to ameliorate shortcomings in the traditional rational model of optimization or to apply it to particular domains of activity. Jonassen's (1997) model for solving ill-structured problems is one such example. His approach emphasizes paying careful attention to the diversity of perspectives of the various stakeholders, considering pro and con arguments for each alternative, and carefully monitoring and adapting the implementation of the chosen solution.

Complex systems theory has also been used to generate problem-solving strategies. For instance, Carlos Torre proposes a triadic model that emphasizes the parallel and interactive use of cognitive, affective, and pragmatic processes. He cites Mandell's (1980) finding that people alternate between two brain states, one that is layered and based on period and point attractors, and another that is governed by strange attractors (see chapter 2). Thus, they suggest that both linear and nonlinear, as well as cyclical and iterative processes, can be used in conjunction with one another. They simplistically identify analytical cognitive processes as linear and point out that these are most relevant to the statement of the problem, information gathering, and diagnosis and planning. The affective-perceptive processes, they argue, are most relevant to prognosis, the generation of solutions, and decision making. Pragmatic or actional processes are primarily concerned with rehearsal, orientation, mentorship, planning, and implementation. They point out that while some processes may be linear, others are often carried out simultaneously and in an interactive manner. This interaction, they argue, may happen on the basis of activation (positive feedback), restraint (negative feedback), or integration. Although Torre's model draws on important insights, it needs further development, especially in the context of a particular domain of activity. The model exemplifies one of the limitations of many of the skills and models reviewed, namely, the difficulty of identifying universal approaches to problem solving that cut across multiple domains of activity. The focus on decision making, likewise, has faced similar criticisms, but it has advanced further in addressing them, and it is to this topic that we now turn.

III. Decision Making

Decision making is a particular facet of problem solving that consists of the process of selecting from among alternative options to achieve some valued end. It is typically a conscious and deliberate activity and one that involves the interplay of cognitive processes with the social and cultural environment. It is also a rational process, the study of which includes the fields of economics, political science, management, statistics, operations research, and psychology more recently. Cognitive psychology has spawned the field of naturalistic or behavioral decision making, which includes the study of the role of intuition and professional judgment in decision making.

A. The Range of Approaches

As various disciplines have pursued the study of decision making, it should come as no surprise that there are diverse approaches. One of the broader distinctions among types of decision making is between substantive and procedural rationality. The classical approach, originating in economics, involves the problem of optimizing, or of making the best possible choice. Such approaches make unrealistic assumptions that problems are simple, that participants agree on specific goals, that alternatives are few, and that it is possible to forecast the consequences. In contrast, psychologists have been more concerned with developing models that work under more complex real-life conditions, an approach associated with behavioral decision making or procedural rationality (see Shakun, 2001).

B. General Purpose Strategies

Some of the earliest general purpose models focused on large-scale political and institutional decision making and were heavily influenced by economic rationality, the idea that individuals and groups consciously calculate and select the alternative that optimizes their economic utility or other self-interests. This ideal has often been traced to Adam Smith's belief in the beneficial impact of each person freely calculating and pursuing his or her self-interest, a process that serves as an invisible helping hand for the larger social good (see Lux, 1990). The strategies that either exemplify or attempt to correct this ideal vary along several dimensions. The simplicity or complexity of the focal problem has often been thought to determine the feasibility of the traditional rational model. But models also differ in terms of either their reliance on rational and empirical methods or on their inclusion of extrarational procedures, whether political negotiation, intuition, or chance, to mention a few. They also vary to the extent that they call for a single comprehensive decision or promote gradual, incremental, or iterated processes in the making of many small decisions. In addition, the strategies vary depending on the extent of consensus regarding goals. Table 7.1 outlines several of the best-known strategies based on problem complexity and value consensus.

The traditional economic ideal of optimization has also been referred to as the rational-comprehensive model, which is usually applied only when

TABLE 7.1: MAJOR STRATEGIES OF DECISION MAKING

	Goal/Value Consensus	
PROBLEM COMPLEXITY	LOW	HIGH
LOW	Rational-Disjointed (e.g., Satisficing)	Rational-Comprehensive (e.g., Optimizing)
HIGH	Incremental-Disjointed, (e.g., Garbage Can Model, Muddling Through)	Incremental-Comprehensive (e.g., Mixed Scanning)

problems are simple and there is agreement about preferred goals. This model shares many elements with many of the problem-solving strategies previously presented—definition of the problem, setting of goals, determination of alternatives, forecasting of alternatives, and selection of the optimal alternative—except that it applies rational problem solving to large-scale social problems. Its pitfalls are well known. Values influence how the problem is defined, which in turn affects outcomes. Stakeholders often cannot agree on goals and end up with the lowest common denominator. There are often more alternatives than can be imagined, and their consequences rarely can be forecasted with confidence. The time and cost of the search for and testing of alternatives is often prohibitive. Different outcomes may be measured in different metrics or units (e.g., dollars versus lives versus quality of life) that do not convert easily to a common measure. Herbert Simon (1976) commented that people simply don't have "the wits to maximize" (p. xxviii).

In contrast, when problems are complex and there is consensus, an incremental-comprehensive strategy is possible. This approach uses pragmatic methods of solving broadly defined problems and often is found in institutional, political, and personal decision making. For example, Amitai Etzioni's (1967) mixed-scanning model combines incremental processes for routine decisions and rational-comprehensive methods for fundamental issues.

Relatively simple problems for which there is disagreement about values and guiding principles lend themselves to a rational-disjointed strategy. Rational-disjointed decision making is characterized by the application of various types of deductive or inductive rational methods—technical, legal, philosophical, or empirical—in a systematic way to solve narrowly defined problems, often on a case-by-case basis. The best-known variant of this model is Herbert Simon's (1976) satisficing. Simon argues that most decision makers engage in a series of determinations about emerging alternatives, and then they pick the first one that is both satisfactory and sufficient. For example, a social worker looking for a couple to adopt a child does a series of home studies on prospective couples until he or she finds one that meets minimum agency standards. The model takes into account the cost of information search, including forgone opportunities that might result from overly prolonged search and deliberation. The model is particularly useful with complex problems that have a comprehensive impact.

Finally, when problems are complex and there is little consensus, an incremental-disjointed strategy is often used. One of the earliest of the macro models proposed, Charles Lindblom's (1950) idea of "muddling through" is a prime example. Lindblom argued that political decision making in the United States is not only disjointed or fragmented but also incremental. Separate legislative committees may decide the budgets of various state agencies, such as those that work in mental health or with older adults. In addition, those committees consider only proposed budgets that differ slightly from those of the previous year. Lindblom argued that by breaking decisions down in this way, the results are more adaptive and responsive to unique and changing conditions. In addition, such a procedure is more realistic, given the difficulties of obtaining agreement from diverse stakeholders in a pluralistic society. However, many have criticized this approach as inherently conservative and protective of vested interests.

A classic variation of incremental-disjointed model is that proposed by Cohen, March, and Olsen (1972), which they refer to as the "garbage-can model." The authors focused on a class of institutions that they referred to as "organized anarchies," or those characterized by "problematic preferences, unclear technology, and fluid participation" (p. 1) (e.g., universities). Such organizations, they explain, "can be viewed as choices looking for problems, issues and feelings looking for decision situations in which they might be aired, solutions looking for issues to which they might be an answer, and decision makers looking for work" (p. 1). In such institutions, Cohen et al. theorized that preferences are discovered only through action. They regard the organizations as encompassing simultaneous streams of problems, decisions, and problems that somehow (even fortuitously) become linked at critical junctures. Decision makers may look for problems, decision opportunities may attract problems and decision makers, and the like. Decision makers may even work backward from solutions to find problems that match them. As such, this kind of decision making is disjointed and typically incremental. Cohen et al. are very clear in their focus on normative decision making and do not present the situation as ideal in any way. But their analysis of how the process happens is one of the first truly dynamic theories of the decision-making process, though one that is yet to be adequately tested.

C. Contingency Models

Decision-making theorists have increasingly rejected the notion that one size fits all and have sought to develop contingency models that combine the best of several approaches. Typically, they have proposed criteria to determine when two or more models might be used most effectively. The criteria vary widely, but there are three noteworthy approaches.

The first, and perhaps the best known, is the mixed-scanning model proposed by the sociologist Amitai Etzioni (1967). Scanning refers to the search for alternatives, including processing, evaluating, and weighing information. Mixed scanning distinguishes fundamental from operational decisions. Etzioni recommends seeking a rational-comprehensive solution for the occasional fundamental or truly strategic decision. However, for the many operational or routine decisions, he recommends the incremental-disjointed approach: making a series of small decisions based on particular circumstances and gradual changes in conditions. By following this course, Etzioni argues for integrating the best of both approaches—the planful and radical nature of rational-comprehensive change with the adaptive features of incremental adjustments.

Tarter and Hoy (1998) also propose a contingency model, with the following rules. If there is complete information and clear ends, use the classical rational model. If information is incomplete but ends are clear, use Simon's satisficing strategy. With incomplete information and tentative ends, use a modified or adaptive form of satisficing. And if information is incomplete and ends are tentative, use the incremental strategy, at least in the short run. They suggest that a political or negotiated model is rarely appropriate, and they hardly ever recommend the garbage-can model.

There have been several efforts to understand behavioral or naturalistic decision making in view of a contingency approach. One of the first was that of Janis and Mann (1977), who referred to their model as a conflict model of emergency decision making. Their model is particularly valuable for diagnosing the failures of decision making (see table 7.2), as it is based on the notion that the healthiest form of decision making—"vigilant decision making" (p. 333)—involves the systematic application of rational methods of problem solving, previously reviewed, in solving complex problems.

TABLE 7.2: A CONFLICT MODEL OF BEHAVIORAL DECISION MAKING

ORDER OF QUESTION	QUESTION	IF ANSWER IS NEGATIVE, RESULTING DECISION-MAKING PROCESS	RESULTING OUTCOMES
1	Is there danger if emergency action is not taken?	Unconflicted inertia	
2	If action is considered, are the dangers great?	Unconflicted change	Ineffective coping, unexpected, and unfavorable consequences
3	If action is considered, is an optimal solution feasible?	Defensive avoidance	
4	Does ample time exist to develop and decide on an optimal solution?	Hypervigilance	
5	If all of above are answered positively		Vigilance, effective coping, and favorable consequences

Note: If the decision maker(s) sequentially answers the above questions in the affirmative, the succeeding question is then considered, and if all questions are answered positively, Janis and Mann theorize that there is the greatest likelihood for a vigilant decision-making process, one that is often associated with effective coping as well as positive outcomes.

Source: Janis & Mann (1977, p. 71).

They argue that when this takes place, individuals experience the least post-decisional regret, and evidence the highest levels of commitment to follow through and implement difficult decisions despite adversity. However, they also argue that four basic conditions must be met for vigilant decision making to happen; when these are not present, one of the various compromised forms of decision making takes place. They assume that all decisions are responses to some sign of impending danger; thus, they propose a model of reactive or adaptive decision making. The first criterion is the recognition of the need to take protective action; if this is not present, unconflicted inertia, or avoidance and even denial, results. If the danger is recognized, the subject also needs to recognize the risks inherent in taking the most obvious response; if this condition is not met, then unconflicted or thoughtless change results. Another vital condition is that the subject must have a realistic hope for finding a better solution. If the perceived alternatives do not seem favorable, the subject is likely to defensively avoid action. Finally, the subject needs to believe that there are sufficient time and resources available to search for and decide on an acceptable solution. If this does not happen, then hypervigilance or panic is likely to occur. But when all four conditions are satisfied, the subject is likely to be able to engage in a thorough and rational or vigilant problem-solving process, which will result in the best possible solution. The model works best with personal decision making and does not consider sufficiently the decision-making styles of groups or the fit between personal and social styles. In addition, the model does not consider the role of transrational features of decision making, such as creative problem solving and intuition.

D. Specialized Methods

Many recent efforts to understand and develop techniques to improve decision making have eschewed the general problem strategies previously discussed, including contingency models, and instead have focused on discovering discrete rules, systems, or techniques that facilitate decision making in specific fields. These approaches have varied dramatically, ranging from the definition of simple decision rules or heuristics to complex systems for pattern matching, such as pattern languages or case-based reasoning. The field of clinical decision making, most developed in medicine, has attempted to combine the best of several approaches.

Heuristics are usually framed as simple if-then rules or principles that are easy to remember and use but nonetheless allow considerable latitude in their interpretation (for the potentials and pitfalls of such rules, see the examples in exhibit 7.1). The rules may be derived purely from theory or from empirical research, or they may simply reflect the practice wisdom or common beliefs of a profession, whether true or false. Simon (1986) concludes that "research demonstrates that people solve problems by selective, heuristic search through large problem spaces and large data bases, using means-ends analysis as a principal technique for guiding the search" (p. 3). Decision heuristics may prescribe the use of general strategies or be embedded into the structure of a contingency model or may stand alone. Their power is their ability to simplify decision making based on past experience, but their indiscriminate application can create major problems. Currently, the trend in many of the human services to formulate best practices is an

EXHIBIT 7.1: EXAMPLES OF HEURISTICS

Heuristics are simple rules of thumb or practice principles often used to guide decision making in complex problems. Although some are based on formal research or theory, many reflect the accepted practice wisdom of a profession, the validity of which is often untested. Here are some examples of heuristics from the field of behavioral decision making:

- **Representativeness heuristic:** If a set of signs and symptoms are common to two phenomena, the causes and/or effects of each will also be the same. The danger is that prior probabilities are often ignored, and equifinality may be involved, so that the same end may result from different causes (Kahneman, Slovic, & Tversky, 1981).
- **Availability heuristic:** The probability of an event occurring is estimated according to how readily it comes to mind. This is a particular dangerous heuristic, as many factors other than salience influence recall (Kahneman, Slovic, & Tversky, 1981).
- **Anchoring heuristic:** The first values in a series are relied on to estimate the progression of a series of values (Kahneman, Slovic, & Tversky, 1981).
- **Elimination by aspect:** When a choice must be made from among many alternatives, groups of alternatives are progressively rejected if they fail to meet various minimum criteria. This may result in either eliminating too few alternatives, all of them, or focusing inappropriate criteria for a final decision (Tversky, 1972).
- "Do what we did last time if it worked, and the opposite if it didn't" (Janis & Mann, 1977).

Here are a few examples specific to the human services:

- Implement those alternatives for which consensus can be achieved.
- If two diagnoses for the same problem are equally plausible, focus on treating the less severe one, and monitor the outcome.
- Start where the client is at.
- Start working in a collaborative manner—if there is no consensus, then consider a campaign strategy or, as a last resort, a conflict strategy (Warren, 1973).

attempt to codify heuristics, making them explicit for use in education, supervision, training, and research.

When heuristics are sufficiently specified and are interrelated in a logical manner, it is possible to define decision-making protocols or algorithms. These may be presented as decision trees in which one heuristic serves as the precondition for the next (for an example involving child welfare decision making, see figure 7.3). The health-care field, including nursing,

FIGURE 7.3: EXAMPLE OF A DECISION-MAKING PROTOCOL USED IN CHILD PROTECTIVE INVESTIGATIONS

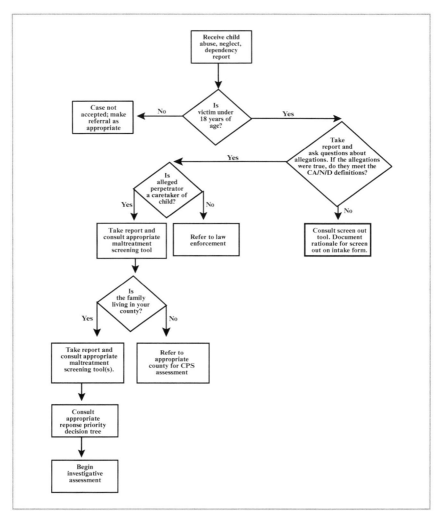

Source: North Carolina Division of Health and Human Services (2009, Chap. VIII).

pharmacology, and psychiatric diagnosis, have done much to define such decision-making algorithms to guide their practice. These algorithms presuppose a fairly limited number of logically interrelated alternatives, the benefits and drawbacks of which are well understood and agreed on. When the number of alternatives is greater and there is more uncertainty about their validity and their relationships, it may be possible to develop what is referred to as an expert system. Expert systems are supported by databases of rules, or knowledge bases, which are logically linked together and implemented in an interactive software program. These can include weighting factors that indicate a level of certainty or importance for relevant decisions.

In many situations, simple if-then rules are inappropriate, as there may be multiple conditions implicit in the "if" part of the statement. If-then rules assume simple situations that can be identified by one or a few criteria (e.g., "If the client is mentally ill and immediately dangerous to self or others, then hospitalize the client"). Even in the preceding seemingly simple example, scores of criteria are actually involved in the definition of mental illness and dangerousness. Thus, much of professional decision making involves complex pattern matching, such as matching the pattern of a patient's presentation of signs and symptoms, as well as strengths and other characteristics, with a known diagnostic pattern (e.g. schizophrenia; see chapter 8). In recent years there have been several promising approaches to pattern matching. Christopher Alexander (1999) has developed one in the field of architecture and urban planning (see exhibits 7.2 and 7.3). The approach has since been used in several other fields, from computer programming to social work. In the approach, a collection of patterns are formulated and written, with each minimally defining a typical problem, context, and solution. Thus, the matching is not only with individual characteristics, such as signs and symptoms, but also with the environmental context and a solution that has previously been developed for the particular kind of problem and context. The patterns also cite other relevant patterns.

The field of clinical decision making has leaned heavily on the combined use of heuristics, algorithms, and informal pattern recognition. Increasingly, behavioral decision-making theorists have been investigating the application of more systematic approaches to uses of algorithms, pattern recognition, and general cognitive skills and problem-solving strategies in order to improve decisions around assessment and treatment planning. One such approach being investigated is case-based reasoning (CBR) (see exhibit 7.4), which calls for the development of a database of cases, or a case base, to recognize patterns. As new cases are encountered, the case base is searched for similar cases using designated criteria and perhaps weights to indicate

EXHIBIT 7.2: PATTERN LANGUAGES AS INTRODUCED BY CHRISTOPHER ALEXANDER

OVERVIEW: An increasing number of fields are developing pattern languages to support decision making, including architecture and city planning, software design, cybercultural studies, ecology, health-care education, communications, and community development. Pattern languages are collections of statements about best practices or recommended solutions for typical problems encountered in practice. They go beyond mere listings of interventions, as they routinely identify a problem or issue and a context for its application. They are often developed collaboratively, using a common template and agreed-on procedures for their development, review, and updating.

- Patterns typically identify a problem, a context, and a solution, and sometimes include background information and a rationale.
- Patterns may specify other patterns that they are part of or can be used in conjunction with.
- Pattern statements can include observable actions, empirical research, hypotheses to be tested theories, or best practices.
- Patterns can be framed in many ways; they can be general or specific in their focus, and can draw on theoretical knowledge or practice wisdom.
- Patterns can also serve a heuristic function in stimulating discussion, research, or advocacy.

Exhibit 7.3 presents an example of a pattern statement developed as part of a collaborative Internet-based effort to develop a pattern language for living communications.

BACKGROUND: The architect Christopher Alexander introduced the notion of a pattern language in his book *Pattern Languages* (Alexander, Ishikawa, & Silverstein, 1977). He explains:

A pattern language consists of a cascade or hierarchy of parts, linked together by patterns which solve generic recurring problems associated with the parts. Each pattern has a title and collectively the titles form a language for design. . . . A pattern is essentially a morphological law, a relationship among parts within a particular context. Specifically, a pattern expresses a relationship among parts that resolves problems that would exist if the relationship were missing. As patterns express these relationships, they are not formulae or algorithms, but rather loose rules of thumb or heuristics.

Exhibit 7.2 (continued)

RECENT APPLICATIONS: Alexander and his colleagues have researched the many pattern languages that they stimulated and identified fifteen deeper properties governing living systems. Those properties are the focus of *The Nature of Order*, by Alexander (2003). That research asked people questions like the following:

- Is your wholeness increasing in the presence of this object? . . . Or this one?
- Do you feel more whole?
- Do you feel more alive in the presence of this thing?
- Do you feel that one is more of a picture of your own true self?

In analyzing the results, Alexander found evidence of universal agreement among humans about the design patterns that support wholeness, coherence, and aliveness. He concluded: "The life that is actually in the thing is correlated in some peculiar fashion with the condition of wholeness in ourselves when we are in the presence of the thing . . . not merely a hunch, but a testable empirical result" (Alexander, 1999). He explains: "At the root of these Fifteen Properties, there appears to be a recursive structure based on repeated appearances of a single type of entity—the primitive element of all wholeness. These entities are what I call 'centers.' All wholeness is built from these centers, and centers are recursively defined in terms of other centers."

relative importance. The research then identifies one or a few similar cases, examines them to find out what worked or did not work in those situations, and extrapolates a plan for the current case. Then, the current case, along with the outcome of the intervention, is added to the case base. Because CBR can be regarded as an extension of Alexander's pattern languages, it does not necessarily involve as much contextual information as those pattern languages. But for the most part, clinical decision making in the human services remains fairly informal and only minimally systematized. Debates continue about the relative importance of professional judgment versus definable heuristics, protocols, and pattern-matching procedures, including formal testing. Although those who favor greater systematization question the reliability of professional judgment, intuition, listening with the third ear, and the like, many psychotherapeutically oriented clinicians argue that such techniques undermine the quality of the relationship; objectify, stigmatize, and disempower clients; and impose an oppressive medical model on them.

Exhibit 7.3: Example of a Pattern from a Communication Pattern Language: Who Speaks for Wolf?

PROBLEM: Much effort and thought goes into decision making and design. Nonetheless, it is often the case that bad decisions are made and bad designs conceived and implemented because some critical and relevant perspective has not been brought to bear. This is especially true if the relevant perspective is that of a stakeholder in the outcome.

CONTEXT: Complex problems such as the construction of new social institutions or the design of complex interactive systems require that a multitude of viewpoints be brought to bear. Unfortunately, this often does not occur. One group builds a "solution" for another group without fully understanding the culture, the users' needs, the extreme cases, and so on. The result is often a system—whether technical or social—that creates as many problems as it solves.

BACKGROUND: The idea for this pattern comes from a Native American story transcribed by Paula Underwood:

In brief, the story goes as follows. The tribe had as one of its members, a man who took it upon himself to learn all that he could about wolves. He became such an expert, that his fellow tribes people called him "Wolf." While Wolf and several other braves were out on a long hunting expedition, it became clear to the tribe that they would have to move to a new location. After various reconnaissance missions, a new site was selected and the tribe moved.

Shortly thereafter, it became clear that a mistake had been made. The new location was in the middle of the wolves' breeding ground. The wolves were threatening the children and stealing the drying meat. Now, the tribe was faced with a hard decision. Should they move again? Should they post guards around the clock? Or, should they destroy the wolves? And, did they even want to be the sort of people who would kill off another species for their own convenience?

At last it was decided they would move to a new location. But as was their custom, they also asked themselves, "What did we learn from this? How can we prevent making such mistakes in the future." Someone said, "Well, if Wolf would have been at our first council meeting, he would have prevented this mistake."

"True enough," they all agreed. Therefore, from now on, whenever we meet to make a decision, we shall ask ourselves, "Who speaks for Wolf" to remind us that someone must be capable

<hr>

EXHIBIT 7.3 (CONTINUED)

and delegated to bring to bear the knowledge of any missing stakeholders.

Technological and sociological imperialism provide many additional examples in which the input of all stakeholders is not taken into account. Of course, much of the history of the U.S. government's treatment of Native Americans avoided inclusion of all the stakeholders.

A challenge in applying the "Who speaks for Wolf" pattern is to judge honestly and correctly whether someone does have the knowledge and delegation to speak for Wolf. If such a person is not present, we may do well to put off design or decision until such a person (or Wolf) can be present.

As a variant of this, a prototype creativity tool has been created. The idea is to imagine a board of directors of famous people. When you have a problem to solve, you are supposed to be reminded of, and think about, how various people would approach the problem. Ask, "What would Einstein have said?" "How would Gandhi have approached this problem?"

SOLUTION: Therefore, provide automated reminders of stakeholders who are not present. These could be procedural (certain Native Americans always ask, "Who speaks for Wolf?" to remind them) or visual or auditory reminders with technological support.

Reprinted with the permission of the author John Thomas.

<hr>

In many instances, these are not mutually exclusive options. The professional's use of his or her self as the primary instrument of practice means using not only feeling and intuition but also the power of rationality, the knowledge base of the profession, and the full array of its decision-making and practice methods.

E. Mezzo and Macro Theories of Decision Making

Often decision making is a group or community undertaking in which individuals participate. Treatment teams meet and agree on clinical plans; a staff member seeking a promotion may need to secure the approval of several individuals, groups, and offices; or a proposal for new program must successfully navigate two or three levels of formal review. Agency accreditation, similarly, involves cumbersome processes of group review and decision making. The assumption is that by combining the knowledge and

EXHIBIT 7.4: CASE-BASED REASONING: A STRATEGY FOR CLINICAL DECISION MAKING

OVERVIEW: Case-based reasoning (CBR) refers to a recently developed set of methods to draw on the results of past clinical decisions to make current case decisions. It was developed during the 1990s from work in the cognitive sciences, specifically from artificial intelligence. It relies on identifying one or more previous cases, recorded in a case base, on the basis of their similarity to the case at hand and then using the previous experience to select or reject potential interventions for the current case (see Riesbeck & Shank, 1981).

BACKGROUND: Case-based reasoning has its roots in Roger Shank's work on dynamic memory as far back as Ludwig Wittgenstein and his critique of a problem generating classical definitions with necessary and sufficient conditions for most phenomena. The first actual CBR system was developed by Janet Kolodner at Yale University in the 1980s and involved the meetings and travels of then secretary of state Cyrus Vance.

MAJOR METHODS: Most approaches to CBR, at a minimum, use the following:

- Collect data and document current case.
- Retrieve from the case base the most similar case(s) relevant to the current problem. Assign weights for each feature according to importance—the case(s) with the highest weighted average serves as the reference case(s).
- Extrapolate solutions from retrieved cases to the current case.
- Adapt the solution to unique features of the current case.
- Include data on the current case and outcome in the case base.

APPLICATIONS: CBR has been used in a wide variety of fields, in health and human services and beyond. The following are a few examples:

- Medical diagnosis
- Help desk and consultation in helping customers problem shoot a product or service
- Legal reasoning
- Social work education (Visser 1996).
- Designing supports for homebound disabled and elderly

TOOLS: The following are a few resources available to support case-based reasoning:

- Software—a variety of commercial and free programs are available (see http://www.ai-cbr.org/tools.html).

EXHIBIT 7.4 (CONTINUED)

- Increasingly, CBR systems are used on the Internet to facilitate large-scale collaborative efforts.

ADVANTAGES AND DISADVANTAGES: CBR is especially useful where the complexity and variety of cases encountered, as well as the demand for individualized response, preclude the use of simpler decision rules or more highly structured decision trees. An important problem involves determining relevant features of cases and some criteria for assessing case similarity. Sometimes multiple precursor cases can be identified, each suggestive of different interventions; conversely, there may be no relevant cases available.

experience of several experts, the quality of the decision making may be improved.

Unfortunately, it is not unusual that the whole may be less than the sum of the parts, especially if they do not work together to amplify the strengths of the individual participants. Irving Janis (1982) investigated this phenomenon, referred to as "groupthink." Groupthink is characterized by the inability of the group to explore differences in perspectives and a tendency to jump on the bandwagon of an idea proposed by a more powerful participant. Janis identified six conditions that tend to create such dysfunctional groups: (1) high group cohesiveness, (2) an authoritarian-style leader interested in pet projects, (3) isolation of the group from the real world, (4) absence of systematic procedures for decision making, (5) inclusion of many members from similar backgrounds, and (6) the feeling among the members that they lack the resources, skills, or time to search for a better solution than that proposed by the leader. Although research has generally supported the theory, results are inconclusive for the first of these preconditions, group cohesiveness. A possible clarification has been offered by Mullen, Anthony, Salas, and Driscoll (1994), who distinguish between task- and maintenance-based cohesiveness. Whereas some groups maintain cohesiveness based on tasks and their accomplishments, others are maintained through attention to relational and other needs. The authors found that the higher a group's maintenance-based cohesiveness, the worse their decision quality tended to be. They also found that authoritarian-style leadership and absence of methodical decision-making procedures were strongly negatively correlated with decision quality. However, the theory has been criticized for failing to provide a more detailed causal analysis of the linkages among input, process, and output variables (Longley and Pruitt, 1980).

It should be pointed out that Janis and Mann did not intend their theory of groupthink to account for all possible failures of group decision making. Other causes might be lack of clarity in roles, insufficient expertise or authority, and unfavorable external conditions, to mention a few examples. Also important is the lack of fit between individual decision-making styles and those of the group. It is, therefore, clear that human service professionals need to engage in complex metacognitive tasks that involve thinking about how they will to think about and make decisions and how they will participate in group decision-making activities, whether they will follow others' lead, collaborate, or take a proactive leadership role.

Just as individual decision making is often embedded in group decision making, so are individual and group decision making nested in community and large-scale political decision making. Over the past fifty years, there have been extensive studies on this subject, especially in the field of political science. One of the debates has been among pluralists, elitists, and dialectical materialists. Pluralists argue that community decision making in the United States is best understood as a consequence of the pushes and pulls and the many conflicts with a multitude of players, both individual and group. Coalitions are formed, compromises and negotiations are made, and in the end, the most powerful combination of interests prevail. In contrast, elitists suggest that the process is largely illusory, that there are typically only a small group of well-connected, privileged actors who, behind the scenes, control the decision-making process, keep some issues off of the public agenda, and force their preferred decisions on others. Dialectical materialists also adopt a conflict model but emphasize that the primary conflict is not between partisan interests or between the elite and out-groups but rather among social classes. It is this economic conflict that secondarily manifests as conflicting cultures and values; that structures decision making, molding both pluralistic and elitist dynamics to serve the interests of the classes that control capital and the means of production.

There have been periodic attempts to resolve the conflict among these perspectives. For example, conflict between the pluralist and elitist perspectives has been clarified by a focus on the distinction between power and influence. Elites often control resource allocation, but they do not always choose to exercise their power in actual acts of influence, thereby leaving many decisions to a pluralistic political process (Magill & Clark, 1975). Instead, they may act to veto decisions that threaten vested interests. The relative roles of these processes also vary by type of community; smaller towns are often more centralized, but centralization also can vary in the same community depending on the domain of decision making involved. In a classic review of this literature, Magill and Clark (1975) conclude that centralized decision structures tend to produce more decisions that favor public goods (e.g., parks, highways), whereas decentralized structures often favor the provision of separable goods and services (e.g., counseling, special projects). While centralized structures are good at generating policies involving fragile or controversial outputs (e.g., affirmative action), decentralized structures rely on the production of popular goods and services, especially those that are not controversial.

The analysis of community decision making involves the immensely complicated interplay among individual, group and institutional, and more formal political and interorganizational protocols for decision making. Human service professionals, with their preference for informal, qualitative, and even intuitive procedures, have often avoided involvement in these larger processes that may seem to them overly formal, legalistic, or rational. Instead, they often rely on specialized advocacy groups and associations to represent their interests.

F. Attempts at Overall Integration

Unlike the contingency models discussed earlier that combine two or more of the general purpose strategies, there are emerging efforts to combine the best of the general purpose strategies with specialized techniques. The most promising such example of a combination model is the recognition/metacognition (R/M) model that Cohen, Adelman, and Thompson (2000) propose. The model is premised on the notion that humans typically combine the strengths of both recognitional and metacognitive or reflective processes, and they explain, "The R/M model implies that the two paths along which expertise develops are intertwined. Reflection increases the power of recognition, but itself gains power as a base of recognitional knowledge is built" (p. 14). Recognitional processing is one of pattern matching; it consists of building a mental model of a situation, matching it against models of similar situations, and selecting an action based on this matching and what has been found to have worked previously. A doctor or therapist cognitively matches a pattern of symptoms with formal diagnostic categories and deduces a treatment based on the profession's past experience with the diagnosis (see figure 7.4). However, there are usually too many possible real-world situations and insufficient historical cases or patterns to match them with. Thus, recognition must be supplemented with critical thought and the application of heuristics, or rules of thumb for decision making (see the rightmost column of figure 7.4). The model includes a quick decision

FIGURE 7.4: COMPONENTS OF THE RECOGNITION/METACOGNITION MODEL OF DECISION MAKING

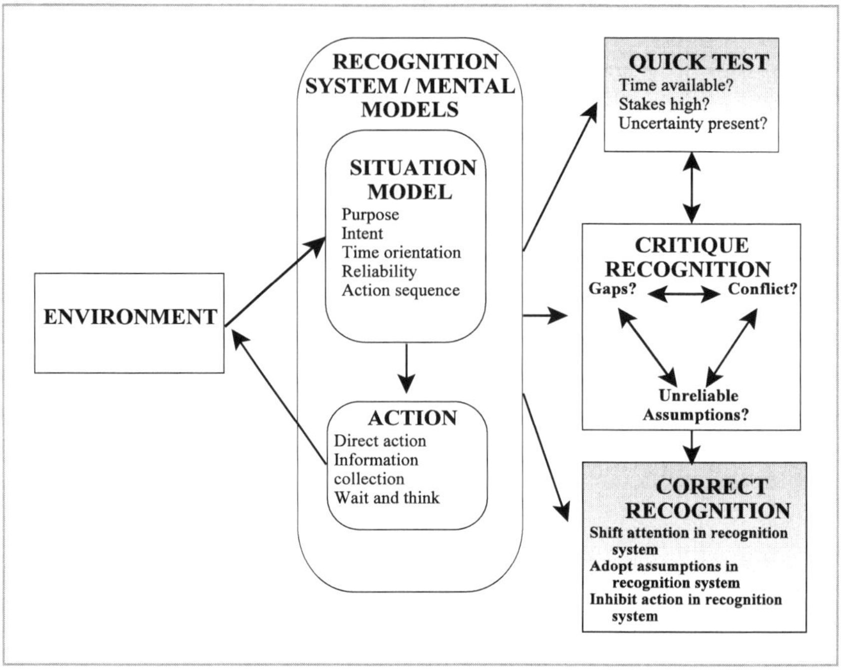

Source: Adapted from Cohen, Adelman, and Thompson (2000).

test to determine whether there is sufficient time and enough at stake to merit further reflection. If so, the decision maker critiques the preliminary model, asking whether there are gaps in the information available, conflicts between what the information suggests, or questionable assumptions, all in an iterative manner. Depending on those results, the decision maker will accept or reject the outcome of the recognitional process or modified it with new models of the problem and the possible interventions. The recognitional process constrains reflection. Reflection, in turn, may control, adapt, or enhance the recognitional process. Thus, this model of behavioral decision making integrates the use of general decision-making strategies with heuristics and pattern matching, including critical thinking, thus illustrating the power of human decision making.

Decision-making theory and research has generated a rich array of models, most of which take as their point of departure the classical ideal of rational optimization, of ends-means analysis. Each contribution to the field has attempted to find a balance between a realistic portrayal of how decisions are actually made and means of improving the quality of decision making, but in the process, this distinction has often been ambiguous. The major thrust of efforts has been to identify the conditions under which alternative approaches are used, or might be used, and these are most commonly referred to as "contingency models." Several contingency models combine two or more general purpose strategies (e.g., Etzioni's [1967] mixed scanning, Tarter and Hoy's [1998] contingency model). Others focus less on global strategies and more on particular techniques, such as heuristics, algorithms, or expert systems, often adapted to specialized domains. Similarly, efforts are increasingly focusing on combining the best of these models into unified approaches. One of the few efforts to date that has attempted to define a contingency model that draws on both global strategies and heuristics (including approaches to pattern recognition and critical thought) is the R/M model of Cohen, Adelman, and Thompson (2000). Others, such as Melvin Shakun (2001), argue that a truly comprehensive model needs to incorporate cognition, affection, and conation as three aspects of consciousness and of decision making, placing these in a complex systems framework. Shakun (2001) points out, "What we normally term decision making is a manifestation of consciousness. As such, the decision process operates through cognition, affection, and conation and is an emergent property. Interaction of unconscious neuronal processors exerts upward control on the decision process while the latter exerts downward control on the former. Downward causation involves conscious processing of the decision problem through cognition, affection, and conation that influences unconscious neuronal processing. Upward causation, i.e. emergence of an evolving decision problem comes from interacting neuronal processors" (p. 104).

G. Concluding Comments

Whichever models or combinations of models have been promoted, the field of behavioral decision making has been hamstrung by the inability to understand the unconscious, irrational, and transrational elements of decision making, as most have assumed that it is only a rational, conscious, and deliberative process. While psychoanalysis and cognitive science have extensively studied the impact of unconscious processes in everything from slips of the tongue to cognitive and perceptual errors, less understood are creative and intuitive processes, which have been missing elements in decision making. Thus, this chapter now turns to the subject of creativity.

IV. Creativity

A. Definitions

Those committed to exclusively rationalistic explanations of problem solving have often overlooked humans' ability to generate novel and meaningful solutions to difficult problems. *Creativity* is a term that covers real-life outcomes generated as solutions to practical social, political, scientific, and ethical problems; novel expressions of beauty or understanding; or other productions of the humanities and fine arts. Carl Rogers regarded creativity as the "ultimate expression of health, fueling ongoing curiosity, growth, and development, and representing at best the fullest expression of the human potential" (see Richards, 1998, p. 620). Although creativity is often spontaneous and original, a critical feature of it is the ability to generate meaningful solutions or expressions. A psychotic person might be spontaneous and original, but the product is usually devoid of shared meaning or usefulness. Spontaneous processes might be regarded as creative, but usually they are of interest only to the extent that they generate outputs—ideas, theories, inventions, paintings, novels, and so on—that others recognize for their originality, value, beauty, or meaningfulness. Thus, the focus of this section is on understanding the psychological and social processes that produce such recognized outcomes.

B. Types of Creativity

Although the creativity of eminent men and women has usually been of most interest to researchers, perhaps no less important are the more modest levels of creativity evidenced in everyday life. Getzel (1964; see also Getzel & Csikszentmihalyi, 1976) similarly distinguished between presented problem solving and discovered problem solving. Presented problem solving involves the ability to creatively solve routine problems that others present and define. In contrast, discovered problem solving is the more unusual ability to seek out and discover new problems that others have not been thought of or conceptualized yet. Creativity in discovered problem solving is usually a more extended process, an ongoing project or series of projects entailing considerable study, preparation, and struggle. Some individuals may demonstrate much insight and creativity in solving everyday problems, perhaps those raised during work meetings or by difficult clients, but be unable to anticipate and formulate the more pervasive and ambiguous problems that are the common denominators to such everyday work problems.

C. Conditions for Creativity

Several researchers have proposed conditions conducive to creativity, specifically to that involving discovered problem solving. Nakamura and Csikszentmihalyi (2001) concluded that such creativity is unlikely to happen under the following negative conditions: an absence of a thorough grounding in at least one symbolic domain (e.g., mathematics, psychology, medicine), an absence of interaction with other experts in the field, an absence of opportunities for relaxation and problem incubation, and a lack of opportunity or interest in testing and elaborating any insights or discoveries. In contrast, some theorists, such as Carl Rogers, have identified positive conditions for creativity to occur. Three inner or psychological conditions are (1) an openness to experience (called extensionality), (2) an internal locus of evaluation, and (3) the ability to toy with the various elements or concepts involved with the problem. In addition, Harmon and Rheingold (1994) identified two outer conditions conducive to creativity: (1) psychological safety and (2) psychological freedom.

D. Stages of the Creative Process

Researchers have regularly reported remarkably consistent results suggestive of several stages to the creative process. One of the first was Joseph Wallas (1926), who identified four stages of the creative process: (1) preparation, (2) incubation, (3) illumination, and (4) verification. Specifically, the stages can be described as follows:

1. **Preparation:** Preparation may involve such tasks as problem identification and formulation, initial study, identification of possible solutions, and assessment of their merits. This is often is a fairly rational process and can involve much tedious work, such as literature review, data collection, accumulation of materials, preliminary attempts at a solution, and the like.
2. **Incubation:** At some point, either by plan or because of competing commitments, or even exhaustion, the efforts are set aside, and the person either attends to other more routine tasks or takes time off to relax or work on a hobby. This stage is called incubation because it is believed that, in some way, the problem is being incubated, perhaps worked on in the person's unconscious. Some have suggested that incubation is more likely to occur when there has been considerable preparation and when the individual has

posed to him- or herself, or even stated, an explicit question or problem.

3. **Illumination:** Illumination is the sudden insight, the aha experience, that may happen after a period of incubation. It may be experienced as a cascade of insights, in which things seem to fall into place. Sometimes it might occur as result of an image from a dream or reverie, or some seemingly unrelated reminder or association. Sometimes even a fairly complete solution, such as a poem, song, or other product, emerges into consciousness, but more often it arrives in installments.

4. **Verification:** Verification involves the elaboration and testing of the results of prior illumination. An insight is elaborated into a theory; a few lines are extended to an entire song or poem. A very important part, though, is verification. Is this theory consistent with the evidence? Is it testable? Does this poem hang together and express one's experience? Is this interpretation of the clinical data defensible?

Since Wallas proposed these stages in 1926, most have stuck with them, but others have tinkered with them and proposed some modifications. In clinical work with clients, preparation can include preliminary case review, problem exploration, and case assessment; incubation can involve simply being with the client or even putting aside the problem of formulating a workable plan while other tasks are undertaken; illumination may involve insight into a novel treatment or intervention plan; and verification can be implementation and testing in the course of work with clients or groups of interest.

Recently, Nakamura and Csikszentmihalyi (2001) developed Wallas's theory further and elaborated on its social dimensions (see figure 7.5). They found that most creative ideas of a discovered kind are the "outcome of multiple cycles of preparation, incubation, insight, and elaboration, with many feedback loops, the end result of which is a solution that may be either final or temporary, in which case the cycle may repeat itself again and again" (p. 344). Discovered problem solving, they emphasize, often means making connections among multiple fields of inquiry. In contrast, presented problem solving may be the outcome of a single cycle, one involving a single field and often one that is highly compressed. It may begin with a few questions, followed by some moments of thoughtfulness (preparation), perhaps some distractions (incubation), an insight (illumination), and some discussion about applicability (verification). Of course, some simple and well-structured problems may be amenable to purely rational, logical, and

FIGURE 7.5: STAGES OF THE CREATIVE PROCESS

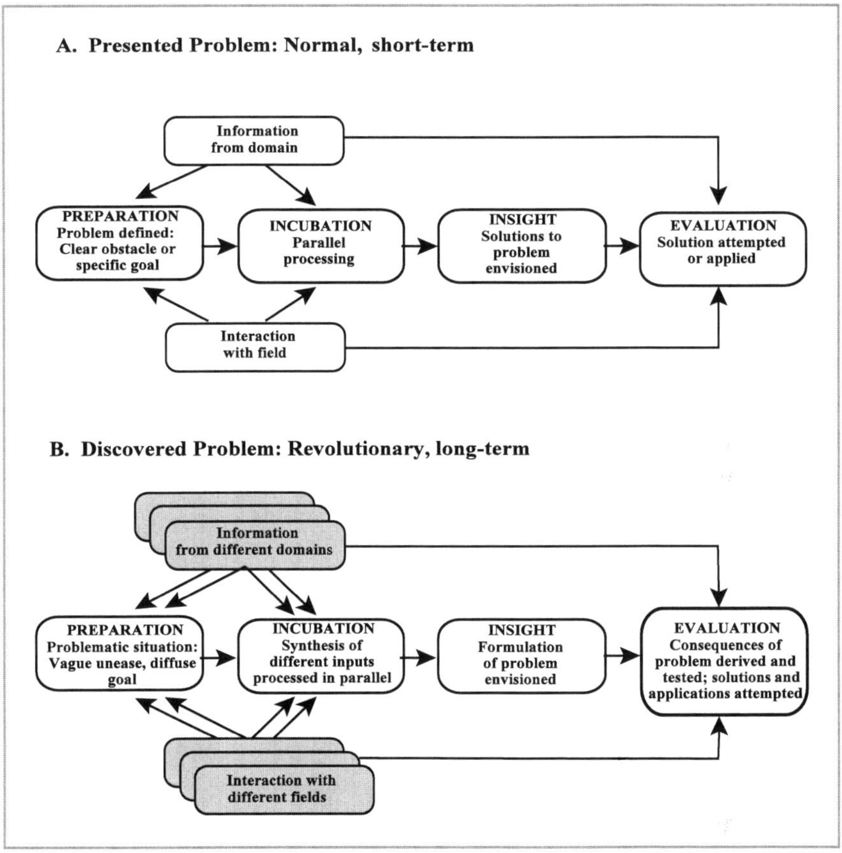

A. Presented Problem: Normal, short-term

B. Discovered Problem: Revolutionary, long-term

Source: Csikszentmihalyi & Sawyer (2001).

algorithmic solutions, and thus do not necessarily not require the incubation stage, but these are exceptional, especially in the human services, which require both rational and transrational creative and intuitive capabilities.

E. Theories of Creativity

On the whole, there is a scarcity of persuasive theories of creativity. In recent years, however, some clarification of the dynamics of creativity has taken place. Freud (1958/2009) took a reductionist approach to understanding culture and the capacities of the conscious ego to engage in creative problem solving. He focused on the role of motivation in creativity, and one of his primary theories is that curiosity is often rooted in a sublimation of a child's sexual curiosity. Of course, while curiosity may be a precondition for many types of creativity, it is not creativity itself, and it is by no means a sufficient condition. In contrast, Carl Jung (1923) believed that creativity could originate in either the personal or collective unconscious. Specifically, he proposed that the unconscious animation of an archetype often generates creativity. A recurrent story or theme becomes a compelling reality for an individual, first in the unconscious, and then becomes expressed or struggled with through conscious preoccupations. The history of art has often been analyzed in a Jungian framework, particularly through the ways that individuals or societies have recurrently expressed the same theme in various ways until the underlying issues are finally mastered. The mother-child or hero archetypes often represent ideational psychic structures that channel and direct conscious creative work. One of the original ego psychologists, Ernst Kris (1952), departed from Freud's and Jung's interest in the role of the unconscious to theorize that creativity is a function of preconscious processes that have greater access to the conscious mind. Contemporary theorists, such as Nakamura and Csikszentmihalyi, also depart from the analytic tradition: they do not reject the unconscious, but they do suggest that it may not be a unitary entity but rather a loosely connected system of mental modules that functions on an unconscious or a preconscious level.

A central theme in many theories of creativity is divergent thinking, an ability not unlike De Bono's lateral thinking, which Guilford (1967) first introduced as part of the structural theory of intellect. Guilford identified 120 different types of intelligence that represent combinations of the dimensions of different types of mental operations, content, and products. He identified five types of mental operation: production, choice, evaluation, memory, and cognition. These are performed on any of four types of content—semantic, figural, symbolic, and behavioral—to produce as many as six different types of products: units, classes, relationships or interactions, systems, changes (or transformations), and implications (e.g., consequences, conclusions), thus generating 120 possible mental abilities. For example, one might involve skill in evaluating figural or numeric propositions to identify groups of similar units, or the ability to produce a variety of semantic or verbal statements to facilitate the development of relationships among disconnected individuals. He points out that any one individual is particularly strong in only a limited number of the 120 abilities. Divergent thought, Guilford theorized, is characterized by fluency of production, indicated by the frequency of thoughts generated in a given unit of time; flexibility, indicated by the diversity of the thoughts produced; the originality of the thoughts; and their elaboration and expression in specific products (e.g., statements, acts, formulas). Thus, divergent thought cuts across mental operations, contents, and products, but it draws heavily on production. In short, it refers to the ability to generate a variety of potentially valuable mental outputs relevant to a particular task. It has been measured by examining the variety of responses that individuals can generate to open-ended questions (Richards, 2000/2001).

Several theorists have drawn from chaos theory in their study of creativity and have emphasized the role of chaos, and especially edge-of-chaos phenomena, in divergent thought (see Richards, 2000/2001). Chaotic processes are those that are sensitive to initial conditions, never repeat themselves, and yet demonstrate a global orderliness (see chapter 2). Edge-of-chaos processes are those that, often because of the multiple splitting or bifurcation of the dynamic patterns, demonstrate areas of chaos that are embedded in and constrained by the orderliness of lower-dimensional point and periodic attractors (see chapter 2). Chaos, thus, guarantees a critical level of variability in many biological and cognitive processes, as these will, given their mathematical definition, never repeat themselves. Richards reports results from her research that show that more creative people not only seek out more challenges but also find higher-dimensional representations more appealing. They also tolerate ambiguity and complexity better than the average person does and are attracted to and engaged by those challenges.

Yet divergent thought is clearly insufficient by itself to ensure creativity. The individual must also have some ability to process, evaluate, select, and integrate the divergent productions in a useful manner. A person with schizophrenia speaking nonsense words or a person in a manic episode are both, in some sense, highly divergent thinkers, but they lack the ability to integrate and transform meaningless outputs to meaningful products. It is this second dimension of creativity, involving convergent, synthetic, or integrative thought, that is much less understood, and it no doubt entails self-organization.

The ability to integrate, although poorly understood, has become an increasing area of study in creativity research. Cognitive developmentalists such as Vygotsky and Piaget have sought to understand the development of the capacity for abstract or conceptual thought. Vygotsky (1962), for instance, found that an important precursor stage on the route to conceptual thought is "thinking in complexes," (p. 112) in which children begin to organize the objects of their worlds "by bonds actually existing between these objects." (p. 112). Bonds are "concrete and factual rather than abstract and logical." Thinking in complexes develops in five substages: (1) association, in which syncretic or visual images serve as rudimentary concepts; (2) identification of collections; (3) thinking in chain complexes; (4) diffuse complexes, and (5) use of pseudoconcepts. These substages involve behaviors, say, the grouping of triangles not by the concept, but by appearance. Pseudocon-cepts, Vygotsky argues, are the main precursors to conceptual and integrative thought (see Richards, 1996).

However, simply acquiring the ability to form and manipulate concepts is a far cry from truly integrative thinking. Several theorists—Silvano Arieti (1976), Arthur Koestler (1989), and Gilles Fauconnier and Mark Turner (2002)—have made significant contributions to this problem. The earliest was Arieti (1976), who made major strides in integrating psychoanalytic theory with the cognitive sciences. He drew on his in-depth study of schizo-phrenic thought to develop a theory of creativity that itself integrates divergent and convergent, or integrative, modes of thought. More specifically, he theorized that creativity involves the ability to simultaneously use secondary rational thought processes with the diverse products of unconscious primary process thinking. He characterized primary process thought as a kind of amorphous cognition that occurs without formal representation in images, words, or actions and is commonly associated with unconscious and hallucinatory wish fulfillment. What is wished for becomes an experiential reality in dream images, hallucinations, and delusions. He referred to the primary units of such paleological thought as endocepts, a type of "primitive organization of past experiences, perceptions, memory traces, and images of things and movements" (Arieti, 1976, p. 54). Paleological thought involves identification based on similarity, an altered relationship between words and their meanings, and the concretization or symbolization of concepts, perhaps through thinking in metaphors. This can be illustrated by the breakup of a stream of verbal thoughts into a stream of dream images as a person falls asleep. Arieti explains that the creative process then takes the inarticulate endocepts and expresses them in consciousness and its products.

For Arieti, creative integration often takes place through a process known as progressive abstraction, or the process of moving toward higher levels of abstraction in formulating a problem. Questions that may be asked as part of such a strategy include the following: What are the essential components of the problem? What purposes are served? What are the barriers to its solution? In contrast, progression symbolization is less obvious and has more than one meaning. It can involve the breaking down of concepts into concrete symbols or the use of symbols and metaphors to move behind the limitations of linguistic modes of thought. Arieti emphasizes the symbolization of similarities or relationships, a more difficult task than recognizing unities, objects, and categories. While language can often express relationships that are embedded in one or two dimensions (e.g., a temporal sequence or two-dimensional table), as more dimensions are added to the problem, the use of metaphors and other symbols become increasingly vital in apprehending such complex relationships. Building representations or models in the usual three spatial and one temporal dimensions is a daunting task that requires both progressive abstraction and progressive symbolization.

In his theory of bisociation, Arthur Koestler (1976; see also 1989) also conceptualizes creativity as depending on the "association of two self-consistent but habitually incompatible frames of reference" (p. 108). He regards creativity primarily as a single illuminative act rather than an incremental process, involving not just the integration of seemingly unrelated concepts but also the integration of discrete frames of reference, each involving multiple concepts. Koestler's (1976) recollection of the reason for his formulation of bisociation—"I have coined the term 'bisociation' in order to make a distinction between the routine skills of thinking on a single 'plane,' as it were, and the creative act, which, as I shall try to show, always operates on more than one plane" (p. 110)—echoes Einstein's epigraph to this chapter.

More recently, Gilles Fauconnier and Mark Turner (2002) have proposed in their book *The Way We Think: Conceptual Blending and the Mind's Hidden Complexities,* a comprehensive theory, not just of creativity but also of human cognition based on research they conducted during the 1990s on conceptual blending. Although previous theorists often regarded such blending as anomalous, Fauconnier and Turner demonstrate that it is a ubiquitous process underlying much of abstract thought, language, and creativity. Fauconnier and Turner (2002) define conceptual blending as the coming together of discrete ideas or images from various contexts, times, or domains to create new concepts and expressions, enabling what Arieti (1978) referred to as "progressive abstraction." (p. 309). This blending, they argue, permits the compression of considerable data, and thus the manipulation of those data in consciousness. Blending assumes various forms and operates below the level of consciousness; thus, its results are taken for granted.

Of particular relevance is a type of blending that Fauconnier and Turner call double-scope blending, in which individual items of information and discrete cognitive frames are blended. They emphasize that blending can be a complex process, involving multiple items of information, frames, times, and modalities, and that it can happen in stages. They theorize that language developed only once the capacity for double-scope blending emerged, about fifty thousand years ago. An example of such double-scope blending is illustrated in the advertisement in exhibit 7.5. The advertisement, which promotes educational funding, merges or blends the image of three schoolchildren with three future heart surgeons, along with the implication for the reader's vital medical care. It notes "Joey, Katie and Todd will be performing your bypass," and thereby establishes the personal implications of inadequate funding for education. The advertisement compresses ordinarily

EXHIBIT 7.5: CONCEPTUAL BLENDING IN A CREATIVE ADVERTISEMENT

TEXT: "Before you know it, these kids will be doctors, nurses and medical technicians, possibly yours. They'll need an excellent grasp of laser technology, advanced computing and molecular genetics. Unfortunately, very few American children are being prepared to master such sophisticated subjects. If we want children who can handle tomorrow's good jobs, more kids need to take more challenging academic courses.

"To find out how you can help the effort to raise standards in America's schools, please call 1-800-96-PROMISE. If we make changes now, we can prevent a lot of pain later on."

Source: The Education Excellence Partnership. Reprinted with permission.

separate items of information into a powerful and persuasive statement, and it shows the integrative role of conceptual blending in a particularly creative way. Thus, although many investigators have emphasized divergent thought in creativity, recent trends suggest that convergent and integrative thought is also a critical and long-neglected feature of the creative process.

F. Social Dimensions

Studies of creativity have mostly ignored the role of the creative individual's social environment. An exception is the work of Nakamura and Csikszentmihalyi (2001), which attempts to systematically incorporate the role of professional groups into the creative process. They note that because creative products are socially defined, they are in part an outcome of ongoing supportive interactions between the individual and his or her profession (see figure 7.6). They point out that a profession can be a catalyst in fostering the work that leads to innovations, but that the most important function of a profession is its selective function, in accepting or rejecting the completed work. Employers, journal reviewers, professional audiences, and funders, to name a few examples, all perform this critical function of social selection. Specifically, they explain: "We contend that a creative contribution is jointly constituted by the interaction of three components of a systems: (a) the symbolic domain that the individual absorbs, works with, and contributes to; and (b) the social field of gatekeepers and practitioners who solicit, discourage, respond to, judge, and reward contributions. It is a model of cultural evolution, with individuals as the generators of variations; the field as the mechanism of selection, determining what gets preserved; and the domain as the mechanism by which innovations are retained and transmitted to the next generation" (p. 337).

Nakamura and Csikszentmihalyi (2001) speak about "concentric circles of evaluation" that serve selective functions (p. 339). Such circles may include feedback loops with immediate colleagues in an agency, as well as feedback from local and even national and international groups, depending on the types of review that the field of practice engages in concerning its members' work. This work can involve case presentations and write-ups, policy reports, and journal articles submitted to diverse groups for their reactions. While Nakamura and Csikszentmihalyi argue for the importance of self-organization—within the individual and between the individual and his or her professional environment—a limitation of their theory is the overly simplified dichotomy of individuals as the generators of variation and the environment as the selective mechanism. The process of creativity involves considerable self-selection (see chapter 6) in which innovators accept or re-ject their own creations, and accept or reject potential contributions from the social environment. Professional environments, including journals, funders, and employers, are themselves selected or rejected by creative individuals, and they often rise or fall on the basis of the creative stars that decide to sign on. It is a two-way street, with negative feedback loops limiting the pros-pects of some potentially creative individuals or organizations and positive feedback loops catapulting others into the limelight.

G. Concluding Comments

This section of the chapter has provided an overview of a few of the highlights of the research and theory on the creative process. Clearly, the most difficult part of understanding creativity is its transrational aspects, often lumped into the stage of incubation, which in itself hardly consti-tutes an explanation. Many researchers have emphasized the importance of divergent thought, or the ability to brainstorm and to generate multiple ideas and especially alternative solutions. This is especially relevant to the preparation stage, but it is also needed in all stages of the creative process. In contrast, several approaches have revealed the critical importance of inte-grative and conceptual thought—Arieti's progressive abstraction and sym-bolization, Koestler's bisociation, and Fauconnier and Turner's double-scope blending—each of which is particularly relevant to the convergent thought that emerges during incubation. Incubation is first and foremost a time of selection and integration of the material already generated during prepa-ration, and it occurs mostly on the unconscious and preconscious levels. There are various views on how this might happen. Csikszentmihalyi (1998) speculates that the various unconscious mental modules try out possible combinations of the contents previously generated, with only the most sa-lient being filtered into consciousness and the rest screened out. In addition, the various mental modules often use types of symbolic compression, often images, which permits associations that would not otherwise be made. It may also be also that the unconscious mental modules engage in system-atic thought processes—whether semantic, figural, or visual, not unlike the conscious mind—and not just the random testing of various combinations of mental contents. Whichever strategies of thought that an individual has developed as part of his or her regular conscious repertoire, simplistic or sophisticated, may be launched as unconscious or preconscious processes under the right conditions. The synergistic interplay between self-selection and social selection on the part of the creator and his or her professional field, especially when amplified through positive feedback loops, serves as a powerful force to drive this process. The transrational dimension of the creative process, especially relevant in the incubation stage, has also been studied through the lens of intuition, and it is to this final aspect of problem solving that we now turn.

V. Intuition

A. Significance and Definitions

The role of intuition in problem solving and creativity is controversial. At the same time that many hard-minded empiricists diminish its importance, pointing out the many different types of errors and distortions than can occur, others regard it as one of the preeminent mental functions. The mathematician and mystic P. D. Ouspensky (1922/2008), for example, regarded intuition as the "highest logic" and defined it as the "logic of infinity or logic of ecstasy" (p. 269). He characterized this intuitive logic as based on the simultaneous occurrence of seemingly contradictory realities: "A is both A and not A," and "A is All" (p. 274). He noted that this view was based on Plotinus's *On Intelligible Beauty*, which says that "everything contains all things within itself . . . so that all things are everywhere, and all is all. . . . And the splendor there is infinite" (*Mystica*, 2003). However one may envision its promises and limitations, intuition is usually regarded as a central element of problem solving, decision making, and creativity.

One dictionary defines intuition as "(1) quick and ready insight; (2a) immediate apprehension or cognition (2b) knowledge or conviction gained by intuition (2c) the power or faculty of attaining to direct knowledge or cognition without evident rational thought or inference" (Merriam-Webster, 2003). Other definitions elaborate on this broad theme. For instance, Philip Goldberg (1983) defines intuition as "anything knowable, including vague hunches and feelings about mundane matters, significant discoveries of concepts and facts and divine revelation" (p. 31). He also emphasizes its spontaneity and immediacy, pointing out that "intuition is the word we use when we know something, but we don't know how we know it" (p. 32). Intuition, he says, might signify an event ("I had an intuition"), represent a faculty of the mind ("She used her intuition"), express an action ("He intuited the danger"), describe a personality attribute ("You are an intuitive person"), or describe a mode of functioning ("He approached the task in an intuitive manner").

B. Types of Intuition

Several authors have attempted to categorize the various kinds of intuition. One approach is to associate intuition with some of the major mental functions. Shallcross and Sisk (1989), for instance, suggest that intuition may be physical, emotional, mental, or spiritual. They equate physical intuition with a type of "jungle awareness," and state that emotional intuition relies on feelings. In contrast, mental intuition relies heavily on images; on the spiritual level, they associate intuition with direct spiritual experience, independent from sensations, feelings, and thoughts. Perhaps a more useful typology is that proposed by Goldberg (1983):

Discovery intuition: The classic "aha" experience, in which diverse bits of knowledge and information cohere or spontaneously self-organize into a general recognition or understanding.

Creative intuition: Similar to discovery intuition, except that is a consideration of a wider range of alternatives and their integration in a more complex product.

Evaluation intuition: Usually presented as a simple dichotomous decision, true or false, present or absent, just or unjust, go or don't go.

Operational intuition: Rather than a simple go-or-don't-go decision, operational intuition presents a map or plan for action.

Prediction intuition: This involves forecasts: if I do x, y will come about. This can manifest as practical business decisions, the avoidance of physical dangers, and the like.

Illumination intuition: This type is said to transcend all the other types, and it typically involves the apprehension of spiritual realities.

C. Functions and Role of Intuition

One of the earlier theories that has served as a point of departure for contemporary theorists is that of Carl Jung. Jung (1921) proposed that, in addition to being extraverted or introverted, humans have two primary ways of processing information, through thought and feeling, and two ways of taking in information, externally through sensation and internally through intuition. Thus, he suggested that, depending on an individual's characteristic ways of taking in and processing information, the individual may be intuitive-thinking, intuitive-feeling, sensing-thinking, or sensing-feeling.

Including the introversion-extraversion dimension, there are eight personality types that he identified. These types were incorporated into the Myers-Briggs personality test and included along with other dimensions such as sensing-judging. Jung (1938/1977) regarded intuition as "a set of perceptions which does not go exactly by the senses, but it goes via the unconscious" (p. 15). The contemporary view is that, like perception, intuition does not represent simply the taking in of information but instead the various ways of unconsciously processing information obtained through several means.

D. Theories of Intuition

Contemporary theories of intuition draw heavily on the cognitive sciences, especially behavioral or naturalistic decision making. One example is the theory of predictive deduction by intuition, which concerns the use of intuition in professional practice. Chris Lang (2003) bases this theory on recognition-primed decision making, discussed earlier. This is another term for pattern matching and its associated logical processes. Lang also bases his theory on the forum model of consciousness, first proposed by Bernard Baar (see chapter 4), and the use of chaotic process in cognitive modeling:

> According to this elaboration, a brain is a forum of players (neural structures) that store and pass data as electrochemical potentials. Assuming that all chaotic systems share this kind of structure (see "Why do you believe that brains are chaotic systems?"), then every brain contains a built-in general model of every chaotic system, just as calculators have built-in arithmetic tables. Thus, when our neural structures accurately imitate the players in the systems we forecast, the resolutions that occur in our brains mirror what would happen in those other systems. In other words, the phases that our brains pass through yield insights into what will (or did) happen outside them. (2003, n.p.)

A substantial portion of this modeling and recognitional process possibly happens unconsciously, with only the results passing along to consciousness, often experienced as intuitions. Lang theorizes that the conclusions of intuition often reflect unconscious logical processes. He suggests a thought experiment: Consider how your father would react if you pinched him— would he lash out, withdraw, make a surprised comment? Then, ask how he would react if you did the same, but only after you had saved his life. The different answers you give reflect the extent to which such predictive intuitions are based on input, especially the context and problem involved. As such, Lang points out that just like memory and other cognitive processes, intuition is subject to much error and is no better than the quality of the inputs and processes involved.

It is, therefore, clear that intuition is not a monolithic capacity but instead a diverse class of mental abilities that range from the mundane to the sublime and draw on diverse sources of information. If nothing else, these involve different types of unconscious cognitive processing, such as pattern matching, logical inference, and various modalities such as the semantic, figurative, or visual. Many of these processes may have initially been developed in consciousness and then internalized into the unconscious in a fashion similar to the way that learning to drive or ride a bike becomes somewhat automatic as the skill is mastered. However, considering a now extensive body of research on psychic (or "psi") phenomena, for which a series of meta-analyses has been conducted, it would be a mistake to simply assume that all intuitive processes represent the functioning of a personal unconscious, as some intuitions may also draw on psi capacities (Radin, 1997). Theories that explain such abilities, as well as how they interrelate with the conscious and unconscious mind, are still in their infancy. Yet it is clear that problem solving, especially when it involves decision making and creative processes, often relies on intuition as a critical supplement to rational thought.

VI. Summary

This chapter has reviewed theory and research on problem solving, both as it is narrowly defined to involve conscious, rational, and goal-directed efforts to address well-understood difficulties, and as it is broadly defined to also encompass decision-making tasks, creativity, and intuition, including some of the minimally understood transrational dimensions. It takes as its point of departure traditional approaches to rational decision making, rooted in classical economics, but it considers their limitations, including the poorly understood process of problem formulation. Problem solving includes decision making as one of its central tasks, and both problem solving and decision making may, under the right conditions, be conducted in a way that generates creative solutions.

Approaches to decision making are even more multifaceted than are those to problem solving. The early models tended to be global strategies, such as economic optimization. These include the rational-comprehensive model, Herbert Simon's satisficing, Lindblom's muddling through, and the garbage-can model. But beginning with Etzioni's mixed-scanning approach, the main interest has been in developing contingency models that combine the best of several general purpose models.

In more recent years, the field of behavioral or naturalistic decision making has generated a wide variety of specialized methods, such as the use of heuristics, algorithms, expert systems, pattern languages, and case-based reasoning. Several of these have been incorporated into clinical decision making. At the same time that the work on individual behavioral decision making has been developing, researchers have also sought to understand group decision making. Recently there have been efforts to combine the best of the general purpose strategies with the more specialized methods of pattern matching, case-based reasoning, and critical thinking, a promising example of which is Cohen and Adelman's R/M model.

Creativity, as reviewed in this chapter, constitutes skill in the generation of products that are novel and either useful or meaningful to others. No less important than the creativity of eminent individuals is that evidenced in everyday life. Creativity can take place in the context of presented problem solving or as a part of discovered problem solving, involving the seeking out, discovery, and formulation of new problems. Most researchers support the stage model originally identified almost eighty years ago—preparation, incubation, illumination, and elaboration—with some proposed variations. Theories of creativity, which often focus on the rather elusive incubation stage, vary widely but often focus on either divergent or convergent cognitive processes.

One of the cognitive skills of central importance in creative problem solving is intuition. Intuition typically involves a spontaneous insight of a useful nature that emerges already formulated into consciousness, though it may arrive in stages. The sources of intuition, likewise, are diverse, but they often involve the functioning of one or several unconscious mental modules, the products of which are screened into consciousness according to the needs embodied in the conscious, rational problem-solving process that may be going on.

For Further Reading

Alexander, C. (2003). *The nature of order* (Vols. 1–4). Oxford: Oxford University Press.

Arieti, S. (1976). *Creativity: The magic synthesis.* New York: Basic Books.

Fauconnier, G., & Turner, M. (2002). *The way we think: Conceptual blending and the mind's hidden complexities.* New York: Basic Books.

Gibbs, L. E., & Gambrill, E. (1999). *Critical thinking for social workers.* Thousand Oaks, CA: Pine Forge Press.

Gigerenzer, G. (2007). *Gut feelings: The intelligence of the unconscious.* New York: Viking.

Langer, E. J. (1997). *The power of mindful learning.* Reading, MA: Perseus Books.

Myers, D. G. (2002). *Intuition: Its powers and perils.* New Haven, CT: Yale University Press.

Nakamura, J., & Csikszentmihaly, M. (2001). Catalytic creativity: The case of Linus Pauling. *American Psychologist, 56*(4), 337–341.

Simon, H. A. (1986). Decision making and problem solving. In National Academic of Sciences (Ed.), *Research briefings 1986: Report of the Research Briefing Panel on decision making and problem solving.* Washington, DC: National Academy Press.

Torre, C. A. (1995). Chaos, creativity, and innovation: Toward a dynamical model of problem solving. In R. Robertson & A. Combs (Eds.), *Chaos theory in psychology and the life sciences* (pp. 123–134). Mahwah, NJ: Erlbaum.

CHAPTER 8

Theories of Mental Dysfunction

Nothing defines the quality of life in a community more clearly than people who regard themselves, or whom the consensus chooses to regard, as mentally unwell.

—RENATA ADLER

I. Introduction

Human service professionals are usually asked to intervene only when some social or personal problem threatens core values, and frequently when the presenting problem entails some kind of mental illness. A recent study by the World Health Organization (2001) concluded that, compared with conditions such as cancer or heart disease, mental illness ranks as the leading cause of disability in the United States, Canada, and Western Europe. The study reported that 25% of all work related disabilities are the result of mental illness. Epidemiological studies suggest that more than a quarter of the U.S. population (26.2%) will have a diagnosable mental illness at some point in the course of a typical year (see Kessler et al., 2005). Yet despite the extent and depth of suffering involved, the various mental illnesses have been largely hidden because of their stigmatization, disempowerment, and mystification by society.

This chapter introduces a framework for thinking about mental illness that draws on key insights from the complex systems literature and provides a foundation for continued study. After clarifying terminology and reviewing some of the crosscutting features of the mental disorders, the chapter considers the phenomenology of mental illness: the subjective experience and the manifest symptomatology, as well as major syndromes that have been identified. The chapter then turns to some of the major theoretical perspectives and the problems of integrating these into a holistic or systemic approach, and finally it applies this material to the practical task of biopsychosocial assessment. It is critical that readers appreciate the need to master the considerable body of knowledge that consists of multiple texts on the biological, psychological, social, cultural, and spiritual dimensions of mental illness, topics that this chapter can introduce only briefly.

A. Definitions and Terminology

The various mental illnesses constitute a broad spectrum of disorders that defies any strict definition and terminology. Most contemporary approaches rely on the *Diagnostic and Statistical Manual of Mental Disorders* (DSM-TR), which defines a mental disorder as "a clinically significant behavioral or psychological syndrome or pattern that occurs in an individual and that is associated with present distress (e.g., a painful symptom) or disability (i.e., impairment in one or more important areas of functioning) or with a significantly increased risk of suffering, death, pain, disability, or an important loss of freedom. In addition, the syndrome or pattern must not be merely an expectable and culturally sanctioned response to a particular event, for example, the death of a loved one" (American Psychiatric Association 2000, xxxi). The manual then qualifies the definition by explaining that, for diagnosis, a disorder must arise out of a problem that is behavioral, psychological, or biological, regardless of its original etiology.

The DSM approach represents an amalgam of conceptions that emphasize abnormal symptomatology, poor functioning, and psychological distress. The focus on disorder or dysfunction is a broad one that makes few assumptions about the causes of mental illness. In contrast, with an emphasis on mental disease or pathology, there is usually an underlying belief that the condition is an endogenous (i.e., internal and biological) process, one that has become largely independent of the social environment and conscious functioning, if it was not always so.

Each set of terms used and the associated assumptions represent alternative views and contain some truth relevant to subgroups of individuals and conditions. Figure 8.1 juxtaposes several of these concepts to propose that mental conditions, such as mild depression (dysthymia), adjustment reactions, or social phobias, are a special subgroup of the challenges and problems of everyday life. Included also in this spectrum of disorders are serious mental illnesses, which involve more recalcitrant forms of suffering, often referred to as psychopathology, and may even involve fundamental deficits, such as inadequately developed psychological structures, genetic defects, or neurophysiological lesions, which are often associated with psychoses. A subgroup of the serious mental illnesses is characterized by the legal notion of insanity, in which an individual has negligible ability to control his or her behavior, appreciate its consequences, and know the difference between right and wrong. Most people with serious mental illness, and certainly all those diagnosed as legally insane, are considered disabled, that is, to lack the capacity to function in one or more arenas of life.

B. Categorical versus Dimensional Approaches

It is commonly assumed that mental health and mental illness are mutually exclusive, regardless of whether they fall on a continuum or represent distinct categories. Yet researchers have increasingly discovered that they are not distinct categories, but rather can coexist in the same individual. Even individuals with severe personality disorders or psychoses experience periods of lucidity, calm, and insight. Thus, an exclusive focus on underlying pathology or the individual's overarching strengths may be a dangerous bifurcation or polarization. The complex systems perspective suggests that human service professionals must simultaneously be sensitive to any underlying pathology and constantly aware of the strengths and humanness of

FIGURE 8.1: THE EMBEDDING OF SERIOUS MENTAL ILLNESS AND DISABILITY WITHIN EVERYDAY LIFE

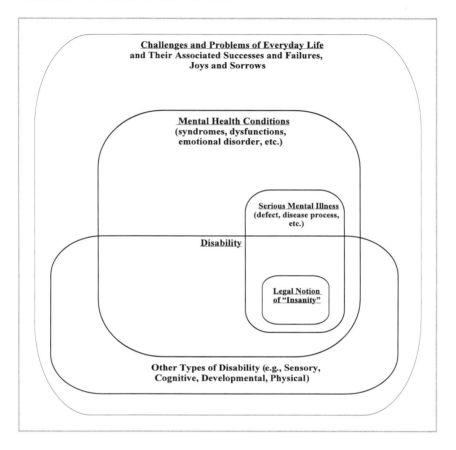

their clients—and they must be able to move back and forth between these. The variety of terms used (e.g., problems-in-living, psychopathology) reflects society's confusion, ambivalence, and discomfort about those who experience mental disorders, and often the impulse is to objectify, dehumanize, distance, and control such individuals.

C. Crosscutting Themes

Although there are probably no universally necessary and sufficient conditions for most mental illnesses, researchers and theorists have identified several crosscutting features:

Apparent failure in development and problem solving: The consistent inability to find satisfactory solutions to the problems of everyday life, such as those involving interpersonal relationships or career choices, accumulate and block psychosocial development. The result may be problems developing specific abilities (e.g., to socialize, to self-sooth, to engage in productive activity), a generalized arrest of development, or even regression. As such, many mental illnesses are extensions of the problems of everyday life as they accumulate over years and decades.

Problems in integration: Just as many forms of mental illness represent an inability to reconcile conflicting interests, needs, and parts of the personality, other forms of mental illness represent an overly rigid or simplistic form of integration and the inability to tolerate an internal diversity of feelings, ideas, or behavioral repertoires. David Bakan (1968) argued that much of mental illness is a type of "telic decentralization," a decentralization or fragmentation of purpose in the personality. Although this is a common phenomenon, the possibility of foreclosure, of premature and forced integration, is also a serious concern for many people.

Too little or too much equilibrium: Increasingly, the issue of structural integration is being redefined in dynamic terms as the lack of an optimal balance between order and chaos. Traditional models conceived of mental illness as an inability to maintain equilibrium, but complex systems theories, especially chaos theory, have demonstrated that human psychological systems thrive at the edge of chaos, where there is a balance of periodic and chaotic attractors. The various states generated at the edge-of-chaos are essential to smooth functioning.

Lack of personal control: A pervasive feature of mental illness is the lack of control, both as it is directly experienced and as others observe it. Individuals complain of involuntary ideas, overwhelming feelings, or inexplicable actions that they find themselves engaged in and unable to resist. Examples include a sense of hopelessness or self-loathing; overwhelming feelings of anger, sadness, or dissociation; and uncontrollable impulses to repeatedly wash one's hands, hide knives, or slash one's wrists.

Lack of relatedness: Whether a cause or a result of mental illness, the inability to connect with others, make friends, and enjoy empathic and loving relationships is characteristic of most mental illnesses. Such inabilities may arise from rejection by others, rejection of oneself, or the inability to simultaneously sense others' mental states while also maintaining some awareness of one's own state of mind. When lack of relatedness is a consequence of mental illness, rather than its cause, it serves to perpetuate the condition and diminish the ability to use treatments, especially psychotherapeutic treatments that rely on the ability to become engaged in an interpersonal helping relationship.

Lack of a sense of self: The inability to feel good about one's self (self-esteem), or even to experience a cohesive identity or a sense of one reality, is also a pervasive feature of various mental illnesses. Again, this may be a cause or a consequence of the condition. Lack of relatedness and lack of a sense of self are often regarded as two sides of the same coin, though one does not necessarily imply the other. A complex systems perspective precludes making assumptions about the primacy of any of these features for a particular individual, and it suggests the need for openness to diverse hypotheses about their dynamic functions.

Time incompetence: Abraham Maslow (1971) proposed that mental health is a function of the ability to live primarily in and enjoy the present, while also retaining a relationship with past and future. Likewise, many mental illnesses represent a distortion in consciousness and in the ability to experience and use time. The depressive individual often lives in the past, while the anxious individual lives in the future—and some people with certain personality disorders or organic conditions live in a narrow and concrete present moment, oblivious of where they have come from or where they would like to go.

D. The Complex Systems Perspective

This chapter not only provides a framework for thinking about mental illnesses but also introduces the application of complex systems theory to the subject. Complex systems theory is the study of multiple levels of organization, where each level has multiple units that are interconnected in nonobvious and usually nonlinear ways (see chapter 1). The human mind has been characterized as a "society of mind," a diverse collection of mental modules, each of which competes and cooperates with others. The hierarchical levels (e.g., memories, sensations, ideas, functions, modules) may be entangled, meaning that the levels may not be discrete. As an open and dissipative system, the mind involves continual inputs, the processing of those inputs in relation to memories and values, and their output in terms of communications and actions. Multiple feedback loops, both internal and external, structure each of those steps. The constant interplay among multiple feedback loops generates new and coherent structures through self-organization. The interaction between these bottom-up, self-organizing patterns and interlevel, environmental feedback processes further tweaks and modifies the emergent psychic structures—the moods and patterns of thought and behavior—that contribute to the phenomenology of conscious experience.

The complex systems perspective assumes that an individual's ability to master the often-overwhelming complexities and ambiguities of their internal and external worlds is a function of a person's complexity of information processing (CIP). Some of the features of CIP include the ability to think abstractly and to appropriately use if-then forms of reasoning. But it also involves the ability to draw on multiple forms of intelligence, and to integrate those with other modes of knowing, such as intuition. A critical feature of one's CIP is the ability to accept and use chaotic and random mental processes to generate novel solutions to problems and to avoid a pathological synchronization of thought, feeling, or action.

Cognitive complexity has also been defined as "the extent to which an individual or organization differentiates and integrates an event. Differentiation is the number of distinctions or separate elements (e.g., factors, variables) into which an event is analyzed. Integration refers to the connections or relationships among these elements" (Streufert & Swezey, 1986). The breakdown of complex thought patterns might be exemplified by a person replacing an intuitive appreciation of the nonlinear aspects of life and the need for dynamically changing balance with simplistic attempts to optimize a single value, in a strictly linear fashion, ignoring competing values and diminishing returns (e.g., "If three units of something feels good, then twice as many units should feel twice as good").

Thus, each of the traditional themes associated with mental health and illness—developmental accomplishment, integration, equilibrium, control, relatedness, sense of self, and the ability to live in the present—are best understood as interrelated dimensions along which individuals find or fail to find a dynamically evolving balance, one that permits them to master the complexities of their internal and external worlds. Thus, mental illnesses are outcomes of failures to solve problems, ones that often originate from a mismatch between the motivations and abilities developed with past and current resources and environmental opportunities and other conditions. Frequently, they are a function of the inability to use internal complexity to model and adequately respond to external complexity. This failure may generate disease processes, which in interaction with the environment, often bring about considerable disability. This chapter directly builds on the immediately preceding chapters on consciousness, human development, and problem solving, conceiving of mental illnesses as some of the predominant manifestations of the breakdowns in these processes and of the quality of life in a given society.

II. Phenomenology of Mental Illness

A. The First-Person Perspective

A key approach to the study of mental illness is based on the first-person accounts of those who are undergoing or who have undergone various forms of mental conflict or breakdown. This approach relies on the use of diaries and journals, as well as relatively unstructured interviews in which interviewees are encouraged to construct and share a narrative of their life situation in their own natural language. Often such interviews are highly interactive and rely on intersubjective processes, a central component of which is empathy. This approach emphasizes understanding the experience of the individual, in his or her own words and in the full context of his or her life, and minimizing preconceived notions, theories, and objective external observation. When such interviews are written up, they often provide highly suggestive findings, but unfortunately, they are rarely replicable or generalizable. Although they may provide valuable case studies for training purposes, they add only minimally to the development of a shared knowledge base.

Fortunately, many such investigators do not stop at this point but seek to combine the understanding generated through their analyses with that gained from more objective means. Francisco Varela urges that we develop "generative passages" between cognitive science and phenomenology that involve a "multi-naturalism that encompasses a plurality of first person, second person, and third person methods of research" (see E. Thompson, 1999). For example, some researchers have sought to correlate audio- or videotapes of such accounts with objective indicators, such as functional magnetic resonance imaging or electroencephalography. The cognitive and social sciences, however, are only beginning to find ways to bridge these various perspectives and methodologies: most researchers focus on only a piece of this larger picture and ignore the others.

A classic work on the phenomenology of mental illness is *The Inner World of Mental Illness* (Kaplan, 1964), a collection of first-person accounts. One contributor recounts her experiences in a state mental hospital, beginning her account with this observation: "Something has happened to me—I do not know what. All that was my former self has crumbled and fallen together and a creature has emerged of whom I know nothing. She is a stranger to me—and has an egotism that makes the egotism I had look like skimmed milk" (p. 31). The various passages chronicle her almost complete regression. For instance, she recalled:

> Sometimes the break comes slowly. A pressure unmarked at the first, but slowly rising. A gnawing discontent; a childish fear that swings onward and outward in an over widening orbit etching itself into the mysterious force called personality. Perhaps it is such a small slow motion when it first begins that the beginning is lost sight of. Then Ruin follows. For Ruin it most surely is: as any know who have stood beside a fellow being strapped hand and foot to save himself and others from his fury. We call it ruin; this collapse of faculties where reason is displaced by daemoniac delusions; where staid and ordered thought gives way and in the "ordered track of reason, a wild disorder reigns and all the senses riot." Ruin. (Jefferson, 1948, qtd. in Kaplan, 1964, p. 31)

Another author explores the experience of depersonalization, or the sense of unreality of the self that many patients experience. A nurse asked the author to explain what she meant by feeling unreal, and when unable to do so verbally, she wrote about her experience:

> In order to explain the feeling of not being real, it is necessary to go into a long unreal definition of the feeling, for it is so far from reality that, in order to be made into a concrete real definition, it has to be described in an abstract unreal way, if it is to be fully understood. . . . [The] feeling itself is one of unworthiness, in the way that a counterfeit bill might feel when being examined by a banker. . . .
>
> It is like a constant sliding and shifting that slips away in a jelly-like fashion, leaving nothing substantial and yet enough to be tasted, or like watching a movie based on a play and, having once seen the play, realizing the movie is a description of it and one that brings back memories and yet isn't real and just different enough to make all the difference.
>
> Even a description of it is unreal and tormenting, for it is horrifying and yet seems mild and vague, although it is acute. It is felt in an unreal way in that it isn't constant torture and yet never seems to leave and everything seems to slip away into impressions. . . . The

important things have left and the unimportant stay behind, making the loss only more apparent by their presence. (Meyer & Covey, 1960, p. 215)

This patient is able to personalize and reflect on her experience, but she is still able to vividly recall the sense of depersonalization. This is one of the paradoxes and limitations of narrative analyses of experience. To engage in such reflection presupposes certain cognitive abilities that are often absent in severe forms of psychotic regression. But most important, it illustrates that such narrative reflection and analysis cannot be regarded simply as a type of objective, scientific reporting; they also are a transforming therapeutic experience that helps build a cohesive sense of identity, to the extent that one can engage in such a process.

In stark contrast with intrapsychic theorists, who emphasize the role of the unconscious, phenomenologists are specifically interested in conscious experience. Although they eschew theory, especially the use of preconceived theories in deductively guiding research, some are open to inductively developing theories out of careful attention to direct experience, typically, through the identification of emergent themes. In sociology this is referred to as grounded theory (see Glaser, 2002).

B. The Second-Person Perspective

Although the foundation for understanding mental illnesses involves the first-person or phenomenological perspective, practitioners must also be able to step back and carefully observe the various signs and symptoms, to conceptualize the manifest difficulties exhibited, as well as the client's values, coping abilities, and other strengths. This is no small task, as workers often cannot rely exclusively on their direct observations and may need to also draw on the client's self-report, or the reports of others, each with its particular biases. One of the most fundamental distinctions is that between symptoms and signs. Symptoms are the client's complaints about him- or herself, such as feelings of depression, tiredness, fearfulness, or frightening voices. Signs, in contrast, are observable things that the client is often unaware of displaying, such as fidgeting, slowed speech, or lack of eye contact. The symptoms and signs of mental illness typically fall into several broad areas. They may be behavioral, involving inappropriate or self-defeating actions; cognitive, involving phenomena such as repetitive or self-defeating thoughts; affective, involving pervasive and painful moods; or physical (or "vegetative"), such as lack of appetite, trouble sleeping, or heavy perspiration.

A fundamental part of assessment is developing a full profile of the client's symptomatology by answering questions such as the following:

- What, specifically, is the client concerned about?
- What does the client mean when he or she uses terms such as *depression* or *anxiety*?
- How long has the problem existed?
- Is it continuous or intermittent? Does it manifest in the morning, afternoon, or evening?
- What is the context of the symptoms—what situations, thoughts, or concerns accompany them?
- How have the client and significant others attempted to respond to the problems?
- What has been the practical impact of the reported symptoms?

The reported symptoms and signs may or may not covary and form a recognizable and meaningful pattern that can be named and understood. Just as is the case with some physical disorders, the same symptoms may be associated with multiple disorders, and conversely, any single disorder or syndrome typically has multiple signs and symptoms—often none is an essential indicator. There is considerable controversy about the extent to which distinct patterns of mental illness exist. Proponents of the traditional medical or diagnostic model argue that distinct patterns exist based on symptom clusters, the course of development, and etiology. In contrast, most psychometricians have taken a dimensional approach, measuring mental illness on one or several continuous dimensions and using only arbitrary cutoff points to separate health and illness.

Whether or not a client's symptomatology adheres to a recognizable pattern, such as those reported in the *DSM-IV*, an important responsibility of the professional is to attempt to understand what the symptoms mean to clients, and how these symptoms function in their inner and outer worlds. Psychodynamic theorists have advanced various hypotheses about the functions of symptoms:

- Retrospective or historical functions: Symptoms are often carry-overs from past development phases, behaviors, or ways of thinking that were once appropriate or functional but no longer serve a useful purpose in a new context.
- Intrapsychic functions: Psychoanalysts have emphasized that symptoms simultaneously hide and express forbidden wishes.

Other intrapsychic functions include self-soothing, controlling anxiety, or compensating for an inability to develop key psychological functions.

- Adaptive functions: Many symptoms help to deal with or control difficult social situations. Depression may be an expression of anger, or passive-aggressive behaviors may exert some control over others. Both symptoms may be a client's way to deal with oppression, and perhaps they are the best response under the circumstances.
- Assimilative functions: Sometimes symptoms function to help individuals maintain a semblance of identity and cohesiveness. A person's aggressiveness may be perceived as strength or self-abasement as humility.
- Restitutive functions: Some symptoms may bridge lost access to the real world; for example, some psychotic symptoms help maintain some minimal relationship with others.
- Communicative functions: Many symptoms function as indirect communications about preferred relationships or other needs; sometimes this is referred to as metacommunication (i.e., communication about communication).

For any particular symptom, one or a combination of these functions may be salient and the others less so. Some signs and symptoms may have limited psychological significance and primarily be manifestations of dysfunctional neurological or biological processes (e.g., the hallucinations of a person experiencing delirium tremens, the vocal tics and coprolalia [i.e., involuntary swearing] of a person with Tourette's syndrome). Symptoms may have either primary or secondary functions, or both. Symptoms with primary functions serve a psychological or internal purpose, such as one of the intrapsychic, assimilative, or restitutive functions just mentioned. Secondary functions typically serve social or practical purposes; they develop after the fact, so to speak. A fear of knives may primarily function to control aggressive or self-destructive wishes, but it may come to serve a social or adaptive function, perhaps exempting the individual from certain responsibilities. Even a neurological symptom, such as vocal tics, may come to serve secondary functions, and thus even these symptoms need to be understood with respect to their psychological and social dimensions, although they may function merely as aggravating rather than causative factors.

To the extent that a client's symptoms retain an integral relationship with his or her conscious repertoire of coping patterns, they can hardly be considered symptoms. However, when these become separated from the self, they come to be considered semiautonomous patterns over which the individual has limited control, and they are conveniently labeled "symptoms." As symptoms proliferate and develop a life of their own, recognizable patterns often emerge, and these are typically referred to as syndromes or disorders. Most mental illnesses can be classified into several broad categories. A traditional distinction is between functional, or psychologically based, and organic, or biologically based illnesses. This is an artificial distinction, as all conditions have both psychological and organic dimensions. However, for some conditions it is very difficult to identify an organic deficit, and the main issues are best conceptualized and worked with on a psychological level, or vice versa. Such splits often obscure the complex interplays between the diverse aspects of a problem, including the multiple systemic levels.

   Another more useful distinction is that between symptom disorders and personality disorders. Symptom disorders involve patterns of identifiable symptoms or complaints that people have about themselves that are usually of a short-term, acute nature and do not pervade personality functioning. In contrast, most personality disorders involve well-entrenched, long-term patterns of dysfunctional behaviors, often ones that the individual may not be concerned about (as such, they are signs of dysfunction). Symptom disorders (e.g., anxiety disorder) often involve symptoms that are ego-dystonic, or ones considered atypical of one's personality. In contrast, personality disorders involve patterns that are ego-syntonic, or ones that are believed to be consistent with the individual's self-concept. Personality disorders often start out as acute symptom disorders that, over time, become entrenched and generalized; thus, they are resistant to many forms of therapy.

   An understanding of the personal complaints that bring an individual to the attention of a mental health professional requires consideration of these concerns in the context of the person's own values and psychological functioning, as well as in larger social and cultural contexts. Although one cultural group may be intolerant of efforts to separate and individuate, other groups may be intolerant of dependence and the lack of initiative, causing them to view and respond to such behaviors in a starkly different manner. Thus, it is critical that symptoms, and the syndromes that they are part of, are assessed in relation to the client's total situation. In this respect, mental illnesses indicate the health of the broader community.

C. The Third-Person Perspective

   The understanding of mental illness rests on both the internal experience of its victims and the direct observations of professionals and significant others. But there is also a third-person perspective, removed from the foregoing viewpoints and representing the collective perspective of many

---

EXHIBIT 8.1: DIMENSIONS OF PSYCHOPATHOLOGY FROM THE *DIAGNOSTIC AND STATISTICAL MANUAL OF MENTAL DISORDERS*

- **Axis I:** Clinical disorders and other conditions that may be a focus of clinical attention
- **Axis II:** Personality disorders; mental retardation
- **Axis III:** General medical conditions
- **Axis IV:** Psychosocial and environmental problems
- **Axis V:** Global assessment of functioning

Source: American Psychiatric Association (2000, pp. 25–31).

---

other parties in the mental health field, including insurance companies. For example, in the DSM-IV-TR, the American Psychiatric Association (2000) uses this system to categorize mental illnesses. For some mental health professionals, the third-person perspective dominates and supplants the first- and second-person approaches. But for many others, it is merely a supplement, one that cannot substitute for empathic understanding and a dynamic and functional assessment. This section provides a bird's-eye view of the third-person perspective and concludes by discussing its major advantages and problems.

The DSM-IV-TR (American Psychiatric Association, 2000) is a multiaxial system in that it calls for characterizing mental illness along five axes. Actually, most of the axes represent groups of diagnostic categories, and only one is a truly continuous dimension (for an overview of the five dimensions, see exhibit 8.1). Axis I, "Clinical Disorders and Other Conditions That May Be a Focus of Clinical Attention," is where the clinician lists the one or several diagnoses of the presenting problem, the one that brings the client to treatment, and which is usually an acute symptom disorder. However, the presenting problem may, on occasion, be noted on Axis II, which focuses on personality disorders and other ongoing problems. Axis III, "General Medical Conditions," calls not for a complete medical profile but for only those medical conditions relevant to the client's mental condition. Axis IV, likewise, lists major environmental problems relevant to the mental disorder (e.g., occupational, educational, housing, economic, legal, health-care-system problems, difficulties with primary support groups). Under Axis V the clinician provides an overall rating of the level of the client's functioning in home, work, and interpersonal contexts. This 0 to 100 scale ranges from "persistent danger of severely hurting self or others or persistent inability to maintain minimal personal hygiene or serious suicidal act with clear expectation of death" at its low end to "moderate symptoms or moderate difficulty in social, occupational or school functioning" at the moderate level and "superior functioning in a wide range of activities; life's problems never seem to get out of hand, is sought out by others because of his or her many positive qualities. No symptoms" at the highest level (American Psychiatric Association, p. 34).

This classification system represents a significant advance over earlier versions of the manual, as it calls for the clinician to think about some of the dynamic relationships between mental disorders and their personal and social contexts. Figure 8.2 illustrates the relationship between the first four axes. At its heart is Axis I, the clinical syndrome or presenting problem, which is invariably embedded in the client's personality, which may or may not be subject to an Axis II personality disorder. Thus, one of the first questions is whether the presenting problems arise out of the client's overall personality functioning, and in turn, how they affect this pattern

FIGURE 8.2: THE RELATIONSHIP OF PERSONALITY, AND BIOLOGICAL AND ENVIRONMENTAL CONDITIONS, IN THE ETIOLOGY OF MENTAL ILLNESS: A MULTIAXIAL PERSPECTIVE

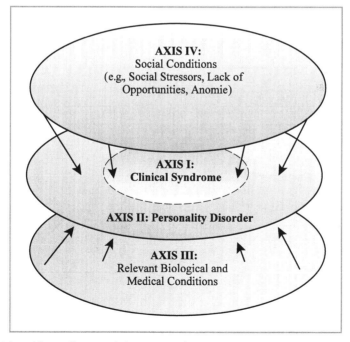

Source: Adapted from Millon & Davis (2000, pp. 8–9).

of functioning as assessed on Axis V. But the individual, along with his or her presenting problems and any personality disorders, also is affected by underling biological conditions (Axis III), whether an under- or overactive thyroid problem or a brain tumor, as well as the surrounding social conditions (Axis IV), such as employment problems, which may be either a cause or a consequence of mental illness. As such, the listing of diagnoses under the various axis presents one possible starting point for hypothesizing about the dynamic processes operative in the client's life, but any such listing, by itself, will never substitute for the deeper understanding required in clinical practice.

The overwhelming preponderance of diagnoses enumerated in the DSM-IV-TR are pertinent only to Axis I. Exhibit 8.2 lists the major groupings of the diagnoses, which cover childhood conditions, such as autism and the pervasive developmental syndrome; states of delirium and dementia, particularly relevant to the field of gerontology; substance-related disorders;

EXHIBIT 8.2: MAJOR DIAGNOSTIC GROUPS IN THE *DIAGNOSTIC AND STATISTICAL MANUAL OF MENTAL DISORDERS*, IV-TR

- Disorders usually first diagnosed in infancy, childhood, or adolescence
- Delirium, dementia, and other cognitive disorders
- Mental disorders due to a medical condition not elsewhere classified
- Substance-related disorders
- Schizophrenia and other psychotic disorders
- Mood disorders
- Anxiety disorders
- Somatoform disorders
- Factitious disorders
- Dissociative disorders
- Sexual and gender identity disorders
- Eating disorders
- Sleep disorders
- Impulse-control disorders not elsewhere classified
- Adjustment disorders
- Personality disorders
- Other conditions that may be a focus of medical attention

Source: American Psychiatric Association (2000, pp. 13–24).

mood disorders, such as depression; psychoses, and particularly schizo-phrenia; sexual, eating, and sleeping disorders; as well as problems with social adjustment. The only Axis II diagnoses listed in the manual are mental retardation and personality disorders. For each disorder, the man-ual typically includes sections on the major diagnostic features, associated features and disorders; specific culture, age, and sex characteristics; and prevalence, course, and familial pattern. An important part of each diag-nostic profile is the section on differential diagnosis, which provides crite-ria for distinguishing the diagnosis from similar conditions. Finally, each section concludes with a summary outline of the major criteria defining the disorder.

Unlike earlier diagnostic systems, the recent DSM manuals have moved away from identifying necessary and sufficient conditions and instead usu-ally require a preponderance of or minimum number of symptoms to be present, perhaps for some specified length of time. An example of such criteria is that for schizophrenia. Exhibit 8.3 summarizes the major crite-ria presented and identifies several primary symptoms, such as delusions, hallucinations, and negative symptoms such as flat affect or avolition (lack of will), as well as impaired functioning, and a six-month minimum for the persistence of the disturbance. In addition, exhibit 8.3 defines exclu-sion criteria. In the case of schizophrenia, the condition must not be due to schizoaffective or mood disorders with psychotic features, substance abuse, or a pervasive development disorder such as autism.

The ambiguities involved in the criteria published in the DSM-IV-TR for various diagnoses and treatment options complicate diagnostic decision making and require a series of contingent determinations. Diagnosticians, for this reason, have developed decision trees to aid both diagnosis and treatment planning. Figure 8.3 provides one such example for depression and its various comorbidities. Other examples that help clarify differential diagnostic issues are found in the appendix to the DSM-IV-TR.

An important part of the DSM-IV-TR is the section on personality dis-orders. The manual defines such disorders as "enduring patterns of per-ceiving, relating to, and thinking about the environment and oneself that are exhibited in a wide range of social and personal contexts" (American Psychiatric Association, 2000, p. 686). Some of the main features of person-ality disorders, originally identified by Theodore Millon (1969), are adaptive inflexibility; the tendency to foster vicious cycles (feedback loops) of protec-tive constriction, perceptual and cognitive distortion, behavioral generaliza-tion, and repetition compulsive; and tenuous stability (1969). Usually clients do not seek help with personality disorders, and many people with such disorders have little awareness of the patterns, and often imagine them as

---

EXHIBIT 8.3: DSM-IV-TR DIAGNOSTIC CRITERIA FOR SCHIZOPHRENIA

A. **Primary symptoms:** At least two of the following, each present for a significant portion of time during a one-month period (or less if successfully treated) (only one criterion A symptom is required if delusions are bizarre or if hallucinations consist of a voice keeping up a running commentary on the person's behavior or thoughts, or two or more voices conversing with each other):
   • Delusions
   • Hallucinations
   • Disorganized speech (e.g., frequent derailment or incoherence)
   • Grossly disorganized or catatonic behavior
   • Negative symptoms (e.g., affective flattening, alogia, avolition)
B. **Social/occupational dysfunction:** For a significant portion of the time since the onset of the disturbance, one or more major areas of functioning (e.g., work, interpersonal relations, self-care) are markedly below the level achieved before onset (or when the onset is in childhood or adolescence, failure to achieve expected level of interpersonal, academic, or occupational achievement).
C. **Duration:** Continuous signs of the disturbance persist for at least six months. This six-month period must include at least one month of symptoms (or less if successfully treated) that meet criterion A (i.e., active-phase symptoms) and may include periods of prodromal or residual symptoms.
D. **Exclusions:** The following conditions need to be excluded as causes to support a diagnosis of schizophrenia:
   • Schizoaffective disorder and mood disorder with psychotic features
   • Substance/general medical condition
   • Pervasive developmental disorder (e.g., autistic disorder)

Source: American Psychiatric Association (2000, pp. 297–316).

---

strengths. But sometimes such individuals seek help with personal issues, typically with emotional crises—perhaps depression, anxiety, or anger—which the individual blames on someone or something in his or her social environment. The American Psychiatric Association has sought to incorporate earlier typologies for personality disorders into the DSM system (see table 8.1; for descriptions of the current DSM-IV-TR personality disorders, see exhibit 8.4).

FIGURE 8.3: EXAMPLE OF A DIAGNOSTIC AND TREATMENT PLANNING DECISION TREE FOR DEPRESSION

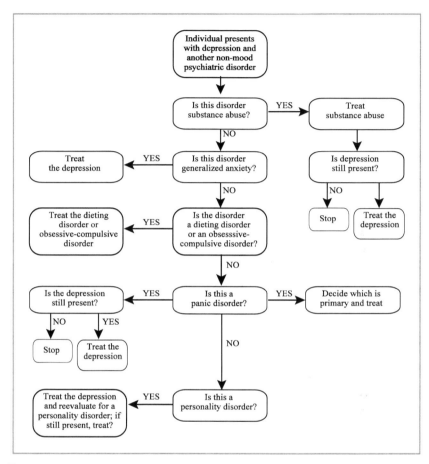

Notes:
—When the depression is treated, the anxiety disorder should resolve as well.
—Choose medications known to be effective for both depression and other disorder as well.
—The primary disorder is the one that is longest, most severe, or runs in patient's family.
—In certain cases (based on history), both depression and substance abuse may need to be treated simultaneously.
—This is for illustrative purposes only and should not be used for current clinical practice.

Source: U.S. Department of Health and Human Services (n.d.)

TABLE 8.1: PERSONALITY DISORDERS, UNDER ALTERNATIVE PSYCHIATRIC NOSOLOGIES

Low Harm Avoidance[1]

	LOW NOVELTY SEEKING		HIGH NOVELTY SEEKING	
	LOW REWARD DEPENDENCE	HIGH REWARD DEPENDENCE	LOW REWARD DEPENDENCE	HIGH REWARD DEPENDENCE
CLONINGER[1]	Imperturbable Schizoid	Cyclothymic	Antisocial	Histrionic
FREUDIAN[2]			Phallic Character	
HORNEY'S NEUROTIC TYPES[3]	Detached Type		Aggressive Type	
FROMM[4]		Distrustful Orientation	Sadistic Orientation	
MILLON[5]	Asocial		Aggressive; Narcissistic	Gregarious
DSM-IV[6]	Schizoid; Schizotypal	Paranoid	Antisocial; Narcissistic	Histrionic

Sources:
1. Categories and Cloninger's own types based on Cloninger (1986, pp. 167–226).
2. Freud (1959).
3. Horney (1945).
4. Fromm (1947).
5. Millon & Davis (2000, pp. 19–20).
6. American Psychiatric Association (2000, pp. 690–730).

High Harm Avoidance

LOW NOVELTY SEEKING		HIGH NOVELTY SEEKING	
LOW REWARD DEPENDENCE	HIGH REWARD DEPENDENCE	LOW REWARD DEPENDENCE	HIGH REWARD DEPENDENCE
Obsessive-compulsive	Passive-dependent, Avoidant	Explosive Schizoid	Passive-aggressive; Avoidant
Anal-retentive Character	Oral-dependent Character	Anal-expulsive Character	
Compliant Type	Compliant Type	Aggressive Type	
Hoarding Orientation	Receptive Orientation		
Conforming	Submissive	Avoidant	Negativistic
Obsessive-compulsive	Dependent	Avoidant	Borderline

Exhibit 8.4: Overview of Personality Disorders from the DSM-IV-TR

1. **Paranoid personality disorder** involves a pattern of suspiciousness of other's motives.
2. **Schizoid personality disorder** consists of both detachment from others and impoverished affect.
3. **Schizotypal personality disorder** is characterized by acute discomfort in close relationships, cognitive misinterpretations of others, and various eccentricities.
4. **Antisocial personality disorder** is associated with disregard for rules and the needs and rights of others.
5. **Borderline personality disorder** includes emotional instability, impulsivity, and the tendency to think in black-and-white terms.
6. **Histrionic personality disorder is** epitomized by extreme emotionality and attention seeking.
7. **Narcissistic personality disorder** entails a "pervasive pattern of grandiosity, need for admiration, and lack of empathy."
8. **Avoidant personality disorder** is associated with social inhibition, lack of self-confidence, and the tendency to be excessively sensitive to criticism.
9. **Dependent personality disorder** is characterized by submissiveness to and extreme dependence on others.
10. **Obsessive-compulsive personality disorder** involves preoccupation with order and control, as well as pathological perfectionism.

Source: American Psychiatric Association (2000, pp. 685–729).

Although there is no definitive theory of the underlying forces that generate personality conditions, there is developing consensus that personality conditions represent fairly stable dynamical patterns (e.g., strange attractors) that result from various combinations of regulatory set points of cognition, affect, and conation, as well as the underlying neurophysiology of the brain. For example, Cloninger (1986) proposes that the patterns are extreme set points of unusually high or low values with respect to harm avoidance, novelty seeking, and reward dependence (see figure 6.5 in chapter 6).

Despite the efforts of the DSM-IV-TR developers to provide a more realistically complex system for describing and understanding the mental disorders, there have been many criticisms of the system. The American

Psychiatric Association has enlisted hundreds of mental health professionals in its efforts, and as such, many outcomes are political accommodations. Although the association has sought to avoid conflict and to set theory aside, diverse theories have inevitably crept in. Some of the disorders are defined merely on the basis of symptomatology; others are based on etiology or course, despite scant understanding of these areas. The multiple diagnoses and criteria have invariably led to the problem of multiple diagnoses or co-morbidity. For example, differentiating between obsessive-compulsive disorder and obsessive-compulsive symptom disorder is no small task. For this reason, some have complained that the system is too complex and requires too many ratings. Others point out that the system minimizes assessment of the environment. Any time descriptive listings of factors are elicited, professionals may be lulled into a sense of complacency that such lists can substitute for any useful or dynamic understanding. Many have criticized the reliability and validity of the diagnoses; however, at this point, the major diagnoses have been demonstrated to have a minimally acceptable level of reliability and are significantly improved over earlier versions.

Other more fundamental criticisms have been advanced, such as the tendency for any such system to mystify and ultimately stigmatize the mentally ill. To the extent that conditions merely are given esoteric names, without any understanding on the part of those who diagnose, then such a result is completely expected. But to the extent that the system provides a foundation of understanding of the problems and practical needs of mentally ill individuals, then a more beneficial impact can be expected. This raises a fundamental issue: to what extent do the diagnoses help identify practical treatments or other interventions? Some clearly do, such as bipolar disorders that point to the use of lithium. Others, such as schizophrenia, anxiety disorder, or phobias have definite but less specific implications for medication and various psychosocial interventions; still others, have few clear implications. To the extent that a diagnostic system helps identify efficacious treatments and contributes to the understanding and, thus, humanization of the mentally ill, then the drawbacks of any categorical system such as the DSM will be minimized. Practitioners will be left to decide whether the use of this system is warranted, and if so, how it can be most effectively and ethically used.

There are also advantages to using the DSM. The system provides a communication shorthand among professionals, both clinicians and researchers. It defines a common language that enables the accumulation of knowledge from one study to the next. This is in contrast to a situation in which each researcher uses different definitions and criteria in studies, which then greatly complicates the ability to aggregate findings. It is useful for ensuring equity in the application of rules for insurance reimbursement, and in some cases, for the identification of treatment options. In some cases, it increases clients' confidence when their difficulties can be associated with a known condition. Perhaps the DSM's strengths are best realized when it is used only in the context of thorough first- and second-person assessments. The use of the DSM, thus, needs to be based on the phenomenology of the client's own experience, the clinician's direct observations, and a broad range of theoretical perspectives, all integrated into a complex systems perspective. It is to this topic that the chapter now turns.

III. Theoretical Perspectives

The fragmentation, ambiguities, and resulting complexities of most mental illnesses have generated a variety of theoretical approaches, each with its distinctive focus. These can be classified on the basis of the system levels involved, whether sociocultural, psychological, or biological, or alternatively on the basis of the particular mental functions emphasized, whether cognitive, affective, or conative. Although most overviews of theoretical perspectives begin with the biological and work their way up from there, the approach here is based on the premise that consciousness, however conceived, is central to understanding mental illness, and that all other system levels and mental functions need to be understood in relation to alterations in consciousness.

A. Existential and Spiritual

Although existential and spiritual perspectives derive from very different yet overlapping traditions, they both emphasize the centrality of consciousness in understanding mental illness. Existential phenomenologists, in particular, have focused on so-called bad faith, which refers to inauthenticity or alienation from the self. Underlying social anomie and isolation is the phenomenon of individuals not being true to their innermost feelings and dreams. This is associated with a sense of futility and despair. Ludwig Binswanger, Rollo May, Abraham Maslow, and Victor Frankl are among the proponents of this approach. Each has emphasized the centrality of choice. Even when there are few apparent opportunities for choice in oppressive environments, individuals can at least choose how they view and respond to circumstances. Although some existentialists reject any suggestion of a religious or spiritual dimension to life, others, such as Søren Kierkegaard, are specifically theistic. Among the most popular of the existential psychologists is Victor Frankl (1993), who developed logotherapy, or the therapy of meaning. Its main thrust is aiding clients in finding and clarifying a sense of meaning and of purpose to life. David Bakan (1968) argued specifically that mental illness is a type of telic decentralization, or a fragmentation of purpose. A landmark study during the 1980s that challenged the notion of the chronicity of schizophrenia found that patients admitted that "the most important ingredient in their improvement—and, and in some cases, their complete recovery—was hope: 'Someone believed in me, someone who told me I might have a chance to recover, and my own persistence'" (Harding, 1995, p. 672).

Central to the phenomenological approach is the notion that mental illness represents an inability to come to terms with one's existence. Ludwig Binswanger (1946), one of the existential psychologists, proposed that to understand the sense of existence, the individual needs to accept it on three levels: the biological (*Umwelt*), the social (*Mitwelt*), and the inner or psychological experience (*Eigenwelt*). *Umwelt* refers to the awareness of physical sensations, such as pain, pleasure, thirst, and warmth. *Mitwelt,* in contrast, pertains to our awareness of social relationships. And *Eigenwelt* is our inner experience, our awareness of our own inner world of feeling and thought. Mental illness is conceived of as an inability to integrate the three dimensions of experience, letting one dominate at the expense of the others or walling each off from the others.

For Binswanger, when individuals are unable to draw on these dimensions of conscious experience, they fail to be true or authentic to themselves, and thus fail to experience what he termed *being-in-the-world.* This inauthenticity leads to ontological anxiety, involving a precarious sense of one's being, the failure to make meaningful connections with others, and ultimately a sense of nothingness. Although existential phenomenologists have not been able to entirely desist from theoretical speculation, they have made a special effort to base their theories as closely as possible on pervasive themes identified in individuals' reports of their direct experience, especially despair and alienation.

Those who have studied psychopathology often have either ignored spirituality or viewed it as a manifestation of underlying pathology. However, in recent years there has developed an appreciation of a far more complex relationship. One approach derives from the notion that mental illnesses develop in the context of a wide range of spiritual beliefs and attainments. This idea originated with William James (1905), who distinguished normal, neurotic, and psychotic religion. Mental conflict and breakdown, thus, can occur given a wide variety of spiritual attainments, and they may be either a cause or a consequence of transformations in the underlying spiritual values and consciousness, a topic explored in greater depth in chapter 15.

Spiritual conditions are perceived differently across cultures. For example, in India many villagers revere and care for *masts* (pronounced "musts"), individuals who appear completely dysfunctional but are regarded as God intoxicated, overwhelmed by the bliss and joy involved in their acute awareness of spiritual realities (see Donkin, 1969). Villagers make a sharp distinction between *masts* and mentally ill people, as they sense an atmosphere of bliss that surrounds the *masts*. In these cases, the integrative functions of the mind, sometimes referred to as the ego, can be overwhelmed whenever there are fundamental changes in the underlying consciousness, including those of a spiritual nature, and these reactions can involve both familiar and unfamiliar forms of mental illness and other altered states of consciousness. The multiple dimensions of spirituality (e.g., integrative beliefs, uplifting affects, guiding ethical principles and behaviors) are no doubt directly linked with the cognitive, affective, and conative aspects of consciousness. As such, the individual's spirituality can paradoxically reflect disturbances in consciousness and provide invaluable personal resources for dealing with such disturbances, which sometimes manifest as mental illness.

B. Sociocultural

Social and cultural theories range from those that emphasize large-scale patterns of social change, migration, and economic stress to mezzo-level theories of institutional and group cohesiveness, and the quality of interpersonal relationships and communication patterns. Traditional researchers in the field of cultural psychopathology treated culture and larger social patterns merely as aggregated individual behaviors, but increasingly researchers in this field have subscribed to the notion that sociocultural patterns can take on lives of their own and generate important feedback loops at the individual level.

This controversy is illustrated in the context of the relationship between socioeconomic status and mental illness. One of the most replicated findings in the social sciences is the negative correlation of socioeconomic status with rates of mental illness: the poorer the socioeconomic conditions, the higher are the rates of mental illness (see Hudson, 1988, 2005). This result has been shown to be the case regardless of the type of indicator used—education, income, or occupational status—and true for virtually every type of mental illness, including organic conditions. Depending on the study, the rates of mental illness in the lowest social strata are anywhere from two times to more than nine times what they are in the highest socioeconomic classes. However, correlations, no matter how strong, do not prove causation. For this reason, there has been considerable controversy around the theoretical interpretation of the relationship. On the one hand, there are those who subscribe to various social causation models, typically that the economic stresses of poverty conditions cause the development of mental illness. On the other hand, people of higher status have better social supports, receive better care, and are less likely to be stigmatized. One theory, proposed by Melvin Cohn (1969), suggests that it is a sense of fatalism and inability to influence the environment among lower-income people that is most important in predisposing such individuals to mental illness. The opposite interpretation is referred to as the social selection or drift model, in which when people develop mental illnesses, typically because of biological or genetic causes, they are unable to replicate the social status of their family of origin, to progress in their careers, and even drift geographically into poor communities.

In recent years there have been several longitudinal studies that could potentially untangle this mystery, but they have shown mixed results, with only a slight preponderance supporting the social causation model and some support for social drift. One such study (Hudson, 2005), tested both hypotheses with a state-level data set of psychiatric hospitalizations over a seven-year period. The author found almost no support for the social drift hypothesis and considerable support for a version of the social causation model, one that emphasizes the role of economic stress on mental illness (see figure 8.4). This finding directly supports a classic 1973 study by Harvey Brenner, *Mental Illness and the Economy,* which found remarkable levels of correlation between unemployment levels and psychiatric hospitalization over 150 years in New York state. Because of such studies, state departments of mental health have in recent years paid increasing attention to psychiatric rehabilitation, and in particular to helping mentally ill individuals find and maintain employment.

A prevailing theory about the relationship between social conditions and mental illness is the diathesis-stress model, independently developed by both Eysenck (1970) and Slater and Slater (1944). The model simply states that, although 40% to 50% of the variation in personality patterns is attributable to genetic factors, genetic factors virtually never entirely determine personality patterns and mental illnesses. Rather, genetic and other biological abnormalities create a predisposition that, for the most part, sensitizes individuals to stressful conditions in the social environment. Thus, the predisposition, referred to as "diathesis," interacts with stresses to generate various disorders. However, both diathesis and stress are complex concepts. What is stressful for one person may be an exciting challenge for the next, depending on each person's temperaments and skills. Likewise, measuring stress has been beset with various methodological difficulties. Typically,

FIGURE 8.4: THE IMPACT OF SOCIOECONOMIC STATUS AND ECONOMIC STRESS ON MENTAL ILLNESS

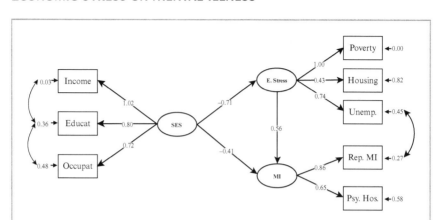

Notes: SES—socioeconomic status; E. Stress—economic stress; MI—mental illness. Numbers on paths are standardized coefficients, indicating the number of standard units of the dependant variable that results from each standard unit change in the independent variable.

Source: Hudson (2005).

individuals are asked to identify events, both good and bad, which have transpired in the previous year (see table 8.2), and a score is computed to reflect the collective impact of the various events. The events are often a cause of various stress-related conditions, but they may be consequences of prior periods of stress; thus, it is difficult to distinguish the role of stress as a cause versus a consequence of mental illness. This is made more difficult by the fact that a stress for one person may be a pleasurable challenge to another, and this varies on the basis of the individual's subjective appraisal of the situation.

Related to these findings is that migration, and social change in general, is associated with higher rates of mental illness. The theory of cultural lag (Ogburn, 1922)—that many of the problems of modernity arise out of the tendency of technology to change more quickly than culture—may be particularly important in understanding mental illness. One of the most significant findings in support of this view is that schizophrenia is somewhat more prevalent in industrialized nations and its course less debilitating in third-world nations. Also, schizophrenia has been found to be more prevalent in urban than in rural areas, though only slightly so. Because it is well known that schizophrenia diminishes an individual's ability to make decisions, to solve problems, and to plan complex actions, it is not surprising that the particular types of challenges and stresses inherent in more complex societies would have an unfavorable impact on vulnerable individuals.

This is also consistent with another body of replicated research that has shown that high rates of expressed emotion in the family environment are predictive of relapse among people with schizophrenia (Kavanagh, 1992). Such individuals are easily overwhelmed by the frequent, intense, and unpredictable emotional reactions of significant others.

Communication theorists have suggested that particular patterns of dysfunctional communication may be to blame for many forms of mental illness. Most famous is the double-bind theory of Bateson, Jackson, Haley, and Weakland (1956). Bateson et al. suggested that some families frequently give conflicting messages, which often revolve around separation issues (e.g., "If we don't stick together, you might die," "You've got to get out and make a life for yourself"). Very importantly, such families disavow the conflicting "damned if you do, and damned if you don't" nature of these messages. Although such communications are obviously stressful, their role as a general cause of schizophrenia is no longer taken very seriously. In fact, many see these as relics of a bygone era when serious mental illnesses were routinely blamed on dysfunctional family patterns, and often on the so-called schizophrenogenic mother. That many health professionals blame such parents or families is particularly unfortunate, as it undercuts the role of the family as a cohesive source of support for mentally ill individuals. The challenge is not to stigmatize families but to collaborate with them in addressing the wide variety of needs of the affected individual, which only occasionally may require realignment of family relationships and behavior. It is also critical that professionals are open to the possibility that some dysfunctional family patterns could be a response to the mentally ill member's difficult behavior rather than a cause of it.

The study of cross-cultural patterns of mental illness is an emerging discipline that is laden with controversy (see Lopez & Guarnaccia, 2000). To what extent are patterns of mental illness unique to particular cultural groups or universal? The approach of many is to assume that the fundamental patterns are universal but that the particular manifestations and content of disorders vary considerably among cultures. The object of paranoid delusions is different in China from in the United States. Nonetheless, the form of the delusions is remarkably similar. Although some cross-cultural researchers have focused on esoteric conditions not seen often in the West, most emphasize that culture also plays critical roles in the more common conditions. An example of such a condition is what Koreans refer to as *hwa-byung,* a disorder that involves both somatic and psychological symptoms. *Hwa-byung,* or "suppressed anger syndrome," is symptomatized by sensations of

TABLE 8.2: THE STRESSES OF MAJOR LIFE EVENTS, AS MEASURED BY THE LIFE EVENTS INVENTORY

1 Death of spouse	93.8
2 Jail sentence	90.2
3 Death of immediate family member	88.4
4 Immediate family member attempts suicide	87.5
5 Getting into debt beyond means of repayment	83.9
6 Period of homelessness	82.5
7 Unemployment of head of household	81.4
8 Immediate family member seriously ill	81.0
9 Divorce	80.8
10 Breakup of family	80.6
11 Immediate family member sent to prison	79.5
12 Sudden and serious impairment of vision or hearing	79.4
13 Death of close friend	79.3
14 Infidelity of spouse/partner	79.2
15 Marital separation	78.3
16 Children placed in care of others	77.1
17 Miscarriage suffered by wife/partner	74.2
18 Serious physical illness or injury	73.4
19 Abortion of child by wife/partner	72.2
20 Unwanted pregnancy of wife/partner	70.9
21 Involvement in physical fight	70.1
22 Trouble/problem behavior of children	69.0
23 Illicit sexual affair outside of marriage	67.8
24 Prolonged ill health	68.1
25 Immediate family member drinks heavily	63.4
26 Breakup of affair	62.2
27 Problems related to alcohol or drugs	61.4
28 Increase in arguments with spouse or partner	60.6

TABLE 8.2 (CONTINUED)

29 Income decreased substantially	60.4
30 Problem related to sexual relationship	59.1
31 Moving house	59.0
32 Sexual difficulties	53.9
33 Marital reconciliation	53.8
34 Increase in family arguments	53.3
35 Trouble with superiors at work	53.0
36 New job in line of work	52.8
37 Increase in family arguments with other family member	50.9
38 Purchasing of house	49.9
40 Conviction for minor violation, such as speeding	49.8
41 Marriage	49.8
42 Pregnancy (or of wife)	49.3
43 Serious restriction in social life	49.2
44 Spouse/partner begins/stops work	47.1
45 Quarrel with neighbors	46.6
46 Death of a pet	45.9
47 Son/daughter left home	43.5
48 Trouble with relatives	42.1
49 Promotion at work	40.7
50 New job same line of work	37.0
51 Gain new family member (immediate)	35.8
52 Change in hours/conditions present job	31.3
53 Retirement	27.2
54 Going on vacation	24.2
55 New neighbors	23.5
56 Income increased substantially	10.0

Source: Spurgeon, Jackson, & Beach (2001, pp. 288–289).

constriction in the chest, palpitations, sensations of heat, flushing, headache, dysphoria, anxiety, irritability, and problems with concentration. Upward of 12% of Koreans have been reported to have this condition (Lin, 1983; Prince, 1989). Although the names and particular symptomatology may vary from culture to culture, along with relative rates of occurrence, there continues to be much controversy about whether these represent fundamentally different types of mental illness or different presentations.

The understanding of mental illnesses also requires a keen appreciation of the complex roles of demographics. Although, overall, men and women develop mental illnesses at about the same rate, the particular types of mental illness vary dramatically between sexes. Whereas women have considerably high rates of depression, men are at greater risk of antisocial personality disorders and other anger-related conditions. There has been some controversy about whether mental illness increases or decreases with age, and recent analysis of the 2001 replication of the National Comorbidity Study suggests that serious forms of mental illness decline with age (Hudson, in press). Whereas African Americans and other minorities of color typically develop higher rates of mental illness, in studies that control for socioeconomic status, the differences among races disappear, thus indicating that the different rates mainly reflect higher levels of poverty among minority individuals. Even when demographics do not play a significant role in the etiology and course of mental illness, they do play a considerable role in society's response to and willingness to support individuals with mental illness. Ageism, sexism, and racism all greatly complicate the problem of engaging significant others, community groups, and society as whole in supporting the mentally ill. The problem is not only of individual attitudes but also of structural patterns that perpetuate the exclusion of such individuals and camouflage the extent to which this takes place (i.e., institutional racism, sexism, ageism; see chapter 13).

Finally, the sociocultural approaches include labeling theory, which emphasizes the recruitment of individuals into dysfunctional roles and the impact of stigmatization. Traditional labeling theorists, such as Szasz (1960), Goffman (1959), or Scheff (1984), generally minimize or reject outright any role of endogenous biological processes underlying the mental illnesses, and instead seek to identify some of the pathways by which individuals are socialized into "careers" as mental patients, typically through typecasting and the impact of negative expectations, known as the Pygmalion effect (Rosenthal & Jacobson, 1992). An extreme version of labeling theory contends that mental illness is a myth: that it is simply a social construction that elite groups impose for the purposes of social control (Szasz, 1960). Few professionals currently believe that such processes can account for a substantial proportion of mental illnesses, but most agree that typecasting, negative expectations, and stigmatization significantly aggravate the course of most mental illnesses and diminish the prospects for social reintegration.

In recent years, sociocultural theories of mental illness have been marginalized in an attempt to assert the primacy of psychodynamic factors and especially biological explanations. Yet there is a vast body of research, introduced in this section only briefly, that provides substantial support for this perspective. Sociocultural theories provide considerable insight into the complex and changing environments that are in constant and reciprocal interaction with individuals' psychodynamic and biological characteristics. Sometimes they affect them positively and negatively, which sometimes occurs before mental illnesses occur and other times only after their occurrence. Conversely, individuals struggling with mental illness transform these environments themselves, for better or worse.

C. Psychodynamic

Psychodynamic theories include both the intrapsychic and the psychosocial. Whereas intrapsychic theories regard mental illness as a function of internal psychological conflict, psychosocial theories posit that the primary conflicts are between the individual and society. The traditional intrapsychic orientation assumes that the most fundamental causes of mental illness are frustrated instinctual drives, most commonly sexuality, which are associated with anxiety and various defensive maneuvers to ward off anxiety and to camouflage the underlying instinctual drive. Mental illness is viewed as arising out of the failure to deal with conflict among the fundamental structures of the personality—specifically, the ego, id, and superego—whereas for the psychosocial orientation, the core conflicts are primarily between personality and society (Maddi, 1996).

Both orientations view mental illness as a specific failure to deal appropriately with conflict and the anxiety that emerges out of conflict. While both healthy and unhealthy functioning emerge out of the operation of the defenses, mental illness entails the predominance of developmentally primitive defenses such as denial, repression, projection, or splitting (see chapter 6, table 6.3). Such defenses include overcompensation and, in general, failure to adapt to difficult conditions; as a result, one unresolved issues snowballs with others. It was Anna Freud, the daughter of Sigmund Freud, who placed psychopathology in a developmental context and developed her father's theories on the role of the various defenses (see profile 8.1).

PROFILE 8.1: ANNA FREUD

While Sigmund Freud was the best known of the founders of the psychoanalytic movement, it was his daughter, Anna (b. 1895–d. 1982), who extended psychoanalytic theory to the study of psychopathology and, in doing so, emphasized the role of the ego. Anna Freud is best known for her book *The Ego and the Mechanisms of Defense* (1937), in which she describes how the defenses work, especially those of adolescents. Anna took her father's earlier work as a crucial foundation but extended it into the more ordinary, practical, everyday world of the ego. In doing so, she applied the theory not only to psychopathology but also to social and developmental issues.

Anna, the youngest of Sigmund and Martha Freud's four children, was raised in Vienna. Although she felt excluded by her older siblings and had a distant relationship with her mother, Freud himself had a particular affection for Anna. She felt overshadowed by her beautiful older sister, Sophie; the family often referred to them as the beauty and the brains (see "Anna Freud, 1895–1972"; Young-Bruehl, 1994).

After finishing school in 1912, Anna began to prepare to become a school teacher but, because of ill health, did not pursue this beyond a few initial employment and volunteer assignments. During those early years, she often assisted her father—initially by translating

> "I was always looking outside myself for strength and confidence, but it comes from within. It is there all the time."
>
> —ANNA FREUD

his work into German. Also during that period, Freud personally analyzed Anna, and he was enamored of her intelligence, dedication, and fidelity to psychoanalytic ideals. He commented that she was "industrious and delightful"; that "she is developing into a charmer, by the way, more delightful than any of the children." After the completion of her analysis from 1918 to 1922, Anna became a member of the International Psychoanalytic Conference. She then had to curtail some of her professional activities to help care for her father; his physical condition had

PROFILE 8.1 (CONTINUED)

worsened. Nonetheless, by 1927, she was able to begin publishing, initially taking issue with Melanie Klein's belief that the conflicts with the superego originated in pre-Oedipal period. Her expertise focused on children, including moral and ethical issues, and included the publication of *Young Children in War Time* (1942) and *Beyond the Best Interests of the Child* (1973).

Anna and her father escaped the Holocaust by moving to London in 1938, where she founded the Hampstead Child Therapy Course and Clinic in London in 1947. She served as its director until 1952, and during this period helped initiate the journal *Psychoanalytic Study of the Child.*

Psychodynamic theorists emphasize the role of fixation and regression in psychopathology. Fixation refers to arrested development that arises from the overinvestment of one's psychic energies in multiple layers of psychological defenses. Regression, in contrast, refers to the breakdown of the defenses that leads to the intensification and generalization of dysfunctional affects, eventually accompanied by a regression to developmentally earlier forms of thought and behavior. For instance, what may be initially perceived as a manageable challenge becomes anxiety producing, and when an individual becomes convinced that a feared loss has occurred, the particular loss gives way to generalized demoralization and perhaps depression. If these reactions begin to threaten the cohesiveness of the self, other symptoms such as hypochondria or dissociation may follow. Regression in extreme cases may lead to psychosis. The essential analytic view is that most of the mental illnesses arise from the failure of the adaptive and integrative functions of the ego, which in turn leads to a replacement of healthy behavior with regressive substitutes. This results in an increasing need to use primitive defenses to control anxiety. The resulting regression involves the following:

- Precipitating factor
- Challenge, stress, and resulting strain (e.g., fear or anxiety, depression, hypochondria)
- Regression, spreading, generalization of affective responses to the internal strain (this often begins on an affective level and then generalizes to behavior)
- Substitution of mature with infantile wishes and objects
- Resulting revival of old conflicts, including those from childhood
- Secondary shame and guilt, and self-punitive measures
- Subsequent conflict and impoverishment of ego functioning

In the psychodynamic tradition, there is considerable divergence of opinion about the nature of the central conflicts. Intrapsychic theorists believe that the critical conflicts are those between the instincts and the superego (or conscience), especially when the ego is too weak to reconcile conflicts. Some of the psychosocial conflict theorists, such as the proponents of object relations, believe that the most fundamental conflicts involve responses to the deprivation of basic relationships, usually with parents or other caretakers, which lack empathy or mirroring (i.e., admiration). Other psychosocial theorists emphasize the role of anxiety—not so much the threatened breakthrough of instinctual wishes but a wide variety of current issues, especially self-identity and efficacy. These theorists include Alfred Adler, who stresses the drive to perfection and the tendency for many to overcompensate for feelings of inferiority, as well as the ego psychologists such as Harry Stack Sullivan (1953) and Karen Horney (1950).

Karen Horney emphasizes conflicts arising from difficulties with counterbalancing the three basic social orientations—moving toward, moving away from, and moving against others—as well as conflicts between the real and the idealized selves. On the one hand, emotionally healthy individuals are in contact with their real selves, in that they are able to appreciate who they actually are; with their strengths and weaknesses; and with their ideal selves, or what they would ideally like to see in themselves. In addition, there is no insurmountable gulf between these contacts. On the other hand, mentally ill individuals can no longer reconcile the conflict between real and ideal selves, and they often end up either rejecting all ideals or living in an idealized fantasy of themselves and the world. It has been said that neurotics build castles in the sky; psychotics live in them. Ego psychologists have also used political metaphors to characterize the development of mental illness. Whereas in a healthy democratic psychological state each drive and interest is represented in consciousness, in an authoritarian (or neurotic) state, only a few of the interests are expressed at the expense of the others; in an anarchic or psychotic state, all sorts of drives run rampant.

Most psychodynamic theorists assume that symptom disorders are most likely to develop in individuals with preexisting personality disorders, which make them vulnerable. The stresses of the various developmental stages overwhelm the diathesis or vulnerability of those with personality disorders, in particular, the rigidity of such maladaptive patterns. However, symptom disorders may also be initial reactions that become generalized and entrenched in a person if they are not resolved in a timely manner. Alternatively, a particular symptom disorder (e.g., posttraumatic stress disorder) may develop independently of whatever personality disorder an individual also has.

Thus, it is important to analyze the mental illnesses as processes, often involving the social environment and the personality, which tend to become detached from the original precipitating issue. These processes sometimes become internalized as an endogenous psychological or even biological process, one that seems to take on a life of its own. When this happens, the original causes, perhaps involving both personality and social conditions, are no longer relevant. At the same time, other current social relationships and conditions may perpetuate the condition or provide avenues for its resolution. In this respect, the complex systems view complements the psychodynamic view by emphasizing the multiplicity of ways that the various adaptive and dysfunctional processes interact, making a minimum of assumptions about which systems and processes may be salient for a particular person.

D. Cognitive

In the mid-twentieth century, the central paradigm in psychology shifted from the behavioral to the cognitive. No longer were the inner workings of the mind regarded as an off-limits black box; instead, interest shifted to the role of internal representations (i.e., schemes or models) and to the various mental modules, each with its particular information-processing tasks. The cognitive sciences, which developed from academic psychology and disciplines such as linguistics and artificial intelligence, have typically focused on a "wide range of processes by which the recognized patterns are compared, associated with information already in memory, transformed in simple or complicated ways, and organized into responses" (Guastello, 2001, p. 13). Perhaps because the fields of emotion, personality, and behavior have been of secondary or even peripheral interest to most cognitive psychologists, applications to theories of psychopathology have been meager. Practical applications of psychopathology in the human services have also been limited, restricted largely to cognitive therapy, as developed by such popular theorists as Albert Ellis (2008) and Aaron Beck (1976).

The central concern of cognitive therapy is dysfunctional mental schemes or representations (sometimes referred to as schemata), which are often-unconscious attitudes and assumptions about the self and the social world. For Aaron Beck, mental illness arises out of these maladaptive schemata of systematic and entrenched biases that cause individuals to regularly misinterpret social relationships. The schemes come to be organized into cognitive styles characterized by chronic and systematic errors in reasoning and misinterpretations of socially agreed-on realities (see Shapiro, 1965). Pretzer and Beck (cited in Millon & Davis, 2000) identified core beliefs

associated with particular types of personality disorders and their associated interpersonal strategies:

- Antisocial personality disorder: "Others are patsies" (predatory
  strategy).
- Dependent: "I need people to survive" (help eliciting).
- Narcissistic: "I am above the rules" (competitive).
- Histrionic: "I can go by my feelings" (exhibitionistic).
- Schizoid: "Relationships are messy" (autonomous).
- Paranoid: "Goodwill hides a hidden motive" (defensive).
- Avoidant: "People will reject the real me" (withdrawal).
- Compulsive: "Details are crucial" (ritualistic). (Millon & Davis,
  2000, p. 52)

The anxious person habitually misinterprets problems in daily living as
dire threats. In contrast, depressed individuals typically overgeneralize
losses, considering them irredeemable, ubiquitous, and the story of one's
life. Whereas cognitive therapists, such as Aaron Beck (1976), have highlighted the role of schemes, others have explored the impact of dysfunctional thought processes. Silvano Arieti (1974), for instance, studied schizophrenic thought and proposed that it is characterized by overinclusiveness
and concretization, in which vague feeling may be perceptualized and loose
or eccentric, and by inappropriate associations.

Since the early 1990s, cognitive psychologists have moved away from
the exclusive focus on cognition as an abstract, disembodied type of information processing and toward an attempt to understand it in the larger
context of biological and social relationships as an embodied and contextu-
alized understanding. Thus, there have been increasing efforts to integrate
knowledge of emotion, neurophysiological processes, and evolution into the
cognitive approach.

One such approach is Jerome Wakefield's (1992) theory that mental illness is a type of harmful dysfunction. By "harmful" he means that mental
illness have consequences that are socially judged as detrimental. By "dysfunction" he refers to the inability to perform a natural or evolutionarily
evolved mental function, often involving the implementation of a behavior
in a developmentally or evolutionarily inappropriate manner. Cognitivists
have typically argued that the human mind is modular in that it represents
the operation of loosely connected mental functions, each with a fairly specialized purpose (e.g., decision making, motor coordination, detecting danger). It has been pointed out that Wakefield believes that "the concept of
a disorder is at the interface of the constructed social world and the given

natural world" (Quinsey, 1998, p. 267), and that in formulating this principle, Wakefield attempts to reconcile the constructivist approach with a realist and functionalist approach to mental illness. It is not enough for a condition to be socially labeled as a mental illness or to depart from evolved patterns of function; it must be both to qualify as a mental illness.

Many other cognitive psychologists have attempted to anchor their theories of mental illness in an evolutionary context. This effort is known as the field of evolutionary psychology, and it draws heavily from ethology, or the study of animal behavior. This field's fundamental notion is that humans have been evolving various cognitive and behavioral patterns for hundreds of thousands of years since before the advent of civilization, and that many of these patterns persist, often in inappropriate ways. For instance, the predominant behaviors among prehistoric hunter gatherers, in which males roamed about in search of prey and women stayed close to the camp to tend the young and gather easily accessible roots and berries, are believed to underlie contemporary gender roles. Whereas traditional social scientists have viewed gender roles as outcomes of recent political, economic, or cultural structures and functions, evolutionary psychologists argue that the roots of gender roles lay in prehistoric and mammalian behaviors as they have been molded by countless generations of natural and social selection. Unfortunately, evolutionary psychologists rarely consider self-selection a meaningful part of this evolutionary process.

In general, many evolutionary thinkers tend to diminish the importance of culture and cognition, instead focusing on tangible behaviors and biological and physical conditions. Nonetheless, there have been renewed attempts to reconcile the two perspectives. Theodore Millon and Roger Davis (2000) are among the few who have attempted to integrate both evolutionary psychology and cognitive theory in an understanding of psychopathology. They argue that evolutionary theory may be a kind of linchpin that can bring about the integration of many current theories of psychopathology, such as the interpersonal, psychodynamic, biological, and cognitive. Both healthy and pathological behaviors can be understood in terms of their success or failure in fulfilling the following functions: survival, adaptation to the environment, reproduction, and conflict management. With respect to reproductive strategies, Millon and Davis point out that many behavioral patterns can be understood in terms of two key reproductive strategies that evolutionary biologists have identified: (1) the R-strategy, or the spawning of a large number of offspring with minimal investment in each one and (2) the K-strategy, consisting of restriction in the number of offspring but substantial investment in the protection and nurturance of a few. He suggests that some sex-typed patterns may correspond to these. For example, the behavior of males may be loosely associated with the first and that of females with the second. However, the association of these patterns with particular mental disorders remains speculative.

Cognitive theories of mental illness provide invaluable tools for understanding individuals' internal responses to the forces of natural and social selection—the ways that they represent them, make decisions, process information, and buckle under or rise to the challenges. Complex systems theory, in turn, provides a broader and richer context for conceptualizing the diverse and dialectical relationships. For example, it suggests that change happens not only because of scarcity and the conflicts engendered by environmental forces but also because of individuals' and groups' specific self-selections and the self-organization of cooperative and interdependent relationships between people.

E. Biological

Just as there is no prototypical form of mental illness, there are no unified theories that propose a common etiology or dynamics behind the diversity of mental illnesses. The traditional distinction between organic and functional, or psychologically based, mental illnesses is an artificial one, as all conditions can, to a greater or lesser extent, be linked with both physical and psychosocial factors. Some of these theories focus on the person as a whole and have a systemic orientation, whereas others are specifically intracranial, focusing on the structure or functions of the individual brain. Various intracranial theories have either a diffused or a specific cerebral locus.

Although most human service workers have historically been interested in psychologically based mental illnesses, there are various mental health conditions that have well-known physical causes and generally require medical interventions as well as supplemental psychosocial therapies. This is a broad group of biophysical conditions with associated psychiatric symptoms and known physical causes, such as intracranial infections, neurosyphilis, encephalitis, alcoholic psychosis, poison syndromes, brain trauma, nutritional deficiencies (e.g., thyroid and adrenal syndromes), intracranial neoplasms, and cerebral degeneration (e.g., presenile dementia, Alzheimer's disease, Huntington's disease, chorea).

Many other conditions have no single or well-understood physical cause, and so are classified on the basis of their symptoms, course, or impact on functioning. These include epilepsy as well as various different types of mental retardation and other developmental disabilities. This overall group of biophysically rooted mental illnesses manifests unique neurological, cognitive, and psychiatric symptoms, as well as more specially affective and

behavioral symptoms, including depression, anxiety, or inappropriate behavior. Functional mental illnesses may, at times, mask more fundamental
biophysical problems. But more commonly, it is suspected that many mental
illnesses indirectly reflect undetected minimal brain dysfunctions (MBDs),
too subtle for physical detection, that are compensated for with varying success through psychological means. Even when such MBDs can be confirmed,
disentangling the cause and effect is an intractable problem. Too often the
MBD assumption serves to mystify and deflect from everyday problems
and relationships.

Specifically, intracranial theories of functional mental illnesses have usually pursued some combination of genetic, morphological, and neurochemical explanations. Genetic explanations are often a favorite, yet even for those
with the severest of the mental illnesses, such as schizophrenia, genetic abnormalities account for no more than 30% to 50% of variation in rates of
the disorder. These figures are derived from studies of identical twins (with
the same genes) raised in different environments and from the rates of occurrence of schizophrenia between family members with various degrees of
relatedness. For example, first-degree relatives have susceptibility of 5% to
10%; for those with two schizophrenic parents, 40%; fraternal twins, only
10% to 15%; and identical twins, at most, 30% to 50% (*Harvard Mental
Health Letter,* 1995). Whereas particular genes for major mental illnesses
have been identified for some small subgroups of individuals with bipolar
disorder, none has been discovered for schizophrenia. Most do not believe
that a single gene will be discovered but suspect that sets of interacting
genetic instructions that create vulnerability will eventually be isolated for
various major mental illnesses.

Some theorists believe that structural abnormalities in the brain may be
responsible for major mental illnesses such as schizophrenia. Many suspect
that schizophrenia is linked to abnormal prenatal brain development, as
there is some evidence that, in the early stages of schizophrenic brain development, neurons fail to migrate to assigned positions in the cortex, typically
during mid-pregnancy. Others have suggested that early physical trauma,
even prenatal trauma, may be responsible for abnormal brain development.
Among the structural abnormalities that have been detected are enlarged
ventricles (cavities or open spaces) and a smaller-than-average hypothalamus, corpus callosum, and prefrontal cortex. Whereas the hypothalamus
mediates sensory input in the brain and is involved with controlling emotion, the corpus callosum is the link between the right and left halves of the
brain (see chapter 4).

One theory is that such structural abnormalities or other brain lesions
(breaks in neural connections) do not have an impact until the brain

becomes fully developed in late adolescence. During this phase, symptoms of the major mental illnesses, such as schizophrenia, often manifest for the first time. Autopsies of long-term schizophrenics indicate that there is significant shrinkage of total brain mass, some of which is associated with enlarged ventricles.

It has been hypothesized that there is a type of kindling process, often seen in epilepsy, in which overactivity in a limited part of the brain spreads and consumes the entire brain. The structural abnormalities and biochemical factors are believed to be responsible for the low levels of activities found in the prefrontal cortexes of people with schizophrenia and other major mental illnesses. The prefrontal cortex matures relatively late and is associated with abstract thought, decision making, and planning, all of which are difficult for people with schizophrenia (see *Harvard Mental Health Letter,* 1995).

A prevailing theory of the biological basis of schizophrenia is the dopamine hypothesis, or the idea that the symptoms of schizophrenia result from excess dopamine (see Javitt & Coyle, 2003). Dopamine is one of many of the neurotransmitters released in the synapses or gaps between neurons, either activating or inhibiting the adjacent neuron, thereby conveying and processing information. Several lines of evidence support this notion. Traditional antipsychotic drugs, the phenothiazines, block the dopamine D2 receptor cells. Thus, when dopamine fails to be absorbed in the target cell, information is blocked and excess dopamine accumulates between cells. Similarly, it has been found that the amphetamine drugs not only stimulate greater dopamine production but also produce many of the same positive symptoms, such as hallucinations and delusions, characteristic of schizophrenia. Although this theory fits well for those who have many positive symptoms, for those who have negative symptoms, such as autism, withdrawal, or flat affect, the phenothiazines have not proved very useful. A revision of the dopamine hypothesis suggests that negative symptoms may result from a scarcity of dopamine in the prefrontal cortex, while positive symptoms result from excess dopamine in the limbic system. However, evidence in support of this version of the theory has not been forthcoming.

An important clue to the etiology of schizophrenia has emerged in recent years and involves the illegal drug phencyclidine, or PCP or angel dust, the effects of which mimic both the positive and negative symptoms of schizophrenia (Javitt & Coyle, 2003). Physically, PCP interferes with glutamate, another neurotransmitter that is pervasive throughout the brain. More specifically, PCP blocks NMDA, a key glutamate receptor molecule. Dysfunction in the NMDA receptor is highly correlated with positive and negative symptoms, and with dopamine abnormalities. A possible link between genetic and biochemical explanations of schizophrenia is that genes that code for proteins known as dysbindin and neuregulin have been implicated in the dysfunction of NMDA receptors, and thus in irregularities with neurotransmitters.

Perhaps the most difficult part of working out a comprehensive theory of schizophrenia is disentangling the extent to which biochemical and structural abnormalities are primary or secondary to psychosocial processes, as well as how biological and psychosocial conditions interact and reinforce one another. This specifically requires understanding the role of psychosocial stresses and associated affects in triggering the development of the abnormalities of neurotransmitters and brain structures, such as the prefrontal cortex or corpus callosum.

IV. Integration and Assessment

A. Assessment as an Ongoing Process

The preceding sections have reviewed selected theoretical perspectives on mental illness, each of which has emphasized a discrete subset of explanations to the exclusion of others. The holy grail of assessment theory is the ideal of a biopsychosocial assessment, which includes even spiritual assessment. This is, however, much more easily said than done. Most human service professionals have limited time to conduct extensive interviewing and testing for the purposes of clinical assessment. Even if their time were not so limited, clients are mostly interested in immediate help and not necessarily in explaining their entire life story. But even if this were not an issue, most professionals lack the conceptual tools to understand the multitude of transactions between the individual and his or her various environments, and the multiple levels of analysis, from the existential to the biological. Many have also subscribed to the ideal that assessment should be done during the beginning phase of work rather than be integrated throughout treatment, from beginning to end.

These challenges are not insurmountable, especially if professionals make creative use of an interpersonal helping process that involves careful listening and a collaborative exploration of clients' complaints. This means simultaneously exploring and understanding a client's currently presented dilemma, what it means, how it is experienced, and its various symptoms and signs—all while listening with the third ear, which means listening for the client's central strivings, values, dreams, aspirations, and fears. Mental health professionals then need to entertain alternative hypotheses about what is going on and about the most relevant dynamic processes, whether these involve biological, psychodynamic, family, or other larger systems.

A particularly important part of assessment is understanding the degree to which current behavioral difficulties have become internalized as mental illnesses, independent of current circumstances. Rarely are conflicts entirely independent of current social realities or a simple reenactment of an early trauma. Current difficulties often stimulate and aggravate prior unresolved conflicts, which in turn interfere with the individual's ability to resolve a current difficulty. Similarly, it is also important to determine whether the presenting problem represents the aggravation of a preexisting personality disorder or biological vulnerabilities or whether it is simply a response to overwhelming stresses.

B. Developmental Context

Several of the themes introduced at the start of this chapter are particularly relevant to the assessment process. Mental illness always occurs in a developmental context. Typically, unresolved issues and all their unmet needs, dysfunctional and generalized moods, and cognitive distortions accumulate in a snowball-like fashion, overwhelming the person and often at key developmental transitions. Likewise, there may be a regression back to earlier modes of functioning. Thus, understanding mental disorders requires an understanding of their developmental context.

C. Implications of Complex Systems for Assessment

Mental illness is also associated with psychic fragmentation. The various centers of the personality, including different drives and feelings, become progressively cut off from one another. Psychological conflict replaces harmonious functioning, feelings are dissociated from their associated thoughts, or confusion and generalized dissociated affect lead to a sense of disempowerment, indecisiveness, and apathy. Along with the various bifurcations and other splits that may come to punctuate the mind, there may develop a pathological synchronization (e.g., the cycling of moods as seen in the bipolar disorders) (Sabelli, Carlson-Sabelli, Patel, Levy, & Diez-Martin, 1995). This may be because feedback loops between the relevant psychic structures become impoverished, only able to react in homeostatic negative feedback loops, something like the household thermostat, or interrupted entirely. A central theme in the application of complex systems to psychopathology is the notion that it is illness, not health, that is most closely associated with equilibrium, and that health thrives at far-from-equilibrium conditions (see theory example 8.1).

Thus, mental illnesses are conditions of disordered external and internal feedback loops. They involve breakdowns in the balance between external relatedness, which in its extreme, leads to conformity, and internal integration of the various aspects of the self. Ken Wilber (2000) characterized this as the balance between communion and agency: communion with the larger social world and its systems, and the ability to experience oneself as a free agent, with a sense of self, of self-efficacy, and autonomy. Feedback loops involve not only transactional flows of information with the external world but also the ability to engage in internal dialogue and to develop a coherent narrative of the self. Feedback loops exist on multiple levels, with information and influences flowing from the physical and biological worlds to the psychological and social, and back again. Furthermore, feedback loops are not just simple regulatory transactions but positive transactions, even those involving strange attractors (see chapter 2), which generate the novel patterns required for problem solving, creativity, and change.

The assessment of mental illnesses means considerably more than their identification and categorization; it requires the development of a set of dynamic hypotheses about the client's struggles, placed in the contexts of their development and their various environmental challenges and opportunities. It rests on both the phenomenological exploration of the client's experiences and the professional's direct observations of various signs and symptoms. The accumulation of knowledge about these areas has been referred to as the social study, but the mere collection of the many facts about a person's condition, using an agency's assessment protocol, is not the assessment itself. The assessment is rather the understanding generated from this process, the formulation of the forces that precipitated the current crisis and those that maintain the status quo, the provision of possibilities for resolution, and the dynamic interaction of all of these. Exhibit 8.5 provides a sample outline for such an assessment, which is typically written up in a structured narrative format. Attached to this may be the DSM-IV-TR diagnoses, organized into the five axes, as well as treatment goals, a clinical intervention plan, and plans for ancillary services and follow-up.

In actual practice, the mental health professional may or may not be able to explore all these areas. In a crisis intervention or brief treatment unit, he or she may obtain only a fraction of this information. In these contexts, it is important to maintain an easily accessible record system for use on the multiple occasions that clients will use the service, one that includes information on the interventions (including psychotropic drugs) that have worked or failed to work during previous episodes. It is the presenting problem,

THEORY EXAMPLE 8.1: PSYCHOGEOMETRY AND THE CONFLICT THEORY OF AFFECTS

The psychiatrist Hector Sabelli and his colleagues (Sabelli, Carlson-Sabelli, Patel, Levy, & Diez-Martin, 1995) have applied complex systems theory to the study of psychopathology, focusing on the dynamic interrelationships among anger, fear, depression, and crime. They have used process theory and methodology to test the traditional conflict notion of noncontradiction that opposing forces in the psyche must conflict and balance one another rather than be either synergic or antagenic. As Sabelli states of the philosophic perspective, "Conflict is the father of all things, and harmony their mother."

THE CONFLICT THEORY OF AFFECT: Their work tests the theory that affective processes are best understood not so much as the dynamic conflict between fight-and-flight responses but as the integration of fight, flight, and surrender responses. The three reactions, ubiquitous in intraspecies relationships, and the related interpersonal orientations are summarized in the table here.

Conflict Theory of Affect

Innate Responses to Conflict	Fight	Flight	Surrender
Subjective Component	Anger	Fear	Sorrow
Pathological Manifestation	Rage	Anxiety	Depression
Interpersonal Orientation	Moving against others	Moving away from others	Moving toward others

Sabelli et al. (1995) theorize that, while normal individuals are able to integrate these responses, using each as is appropriate, pathological manifestations involve a splitting and thus considerable instability as the individual either cycles between these or suppresses less dominant patterns. They take exception to Freud's view that depression represents a displacement of anger against the lost object to the self.

TEST OF THE THEORY: The researchers tested their theory through daily measurements of anger, fear, and sorrow of sixteen normal and thirty-three adult outpatients for between thirty-five and seven hundred

THEORY EXAMPLE 8.1 (CONTINUED)

days. They found that anger, fear, and depression were positively correlated for both depressed and nondepressed subjects. Specifically, they found that depressed subjects experienced more anger than did controls but that anger and depression were not as highly correlated as with the controls (.31 versus .70). They also used various phase portraits (see chapter 2) to study the psychogeometry of such affective states, two of which are illustrated here. The figure on the left shows a normal subject, and the figure on the right shows a bipolar individual.

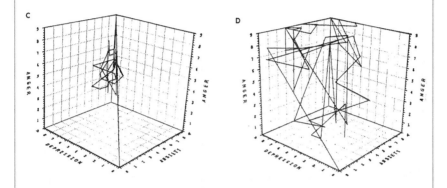

CONCLUSIONS: Sabelli et al.'s (1995) study supported three conclusions: (1) anger, fear, and depression are usually correlated but partially separated in pathological states; (2) there is a possible association of chaotic mood variability and depression; and (3) there is a possible association of the blunting of emotions with sociopathy. Perhaps one of the most significant conclusions was this: "criminals, but not normals, showed equilibrium patterns is at variance with the notion of health as equilibrium and illness as disorder."

as put forward by both the client and any referring parties, that will guide the assessment process, especially because any historical material should be elicited only to the extent that it flows from the presenting problem. The assessment process is an integral part of treatment, not a detached diagnostic phase at the end of which the client receives the verdict. Listening, clarifying, asking occasional questions, providing support, and collaborating to develop a plan are all integral parts of this initial phase. The client's ability

EXHIBIT 8.5: OUTLINE FOR INDIVIDUAL CASE ASSESSMENT

I. Psychosocial study

The following information is obtained from various sources: direct individual, family, or group interviews, as well as current and past medical records; staff observations; or standardized instruments, sometimes arranged with other professionals. Client logs or journals can be helpful in collecting needed information on symptoms or interactional patterns.

A. Presenting problem: Nature of crises or breakdown and current situation. Why did it happen now and in the manner it did? Who has sought help for who and what? What triggered application? How does the client/applicant perceive current difficulties? What is the overall precipitant(s)?

B. Symptomatology: Identify major signs and symptoms and the contexts in which they arise. What are primary and secondary gains from these symptoms? What patterns do they exhibit? Who reported these symptoms and to what extent can these reports be substantiated? What dangers and risks are there for the patient and others?

C. Salient environmental factors/current situation: e.g., housing, neighborhood conditions, income, employment and career problems, vocational capabilities and needs, education, medical facilities, religious institutions, legal and social agencies involved or available. Look at both primary and secondary supports which might be mobilized. Consider resources such as insurance or veteran's benefits. Consider cultural conflicts and supports, in particular, the fit of client's spiritual, religious, and/or philosophical commitments and beliefs with relevant environments. In general, look at environmental stresses, supports, and opportunities.

D. Medical or biological and psychiatric conditions and their history: Previous diagnoses, hospitalizations, causes and sequelae, experience with various forms of treatment—what interventions have or have not worked in the past? History of substance abuse, retardation, learning disabilities, child abuse or neglect, and other victimization, etc.? Experience with psychopharmacological treatment—benefits, side effects, 'compliance,' and other issues.

E. Family status and relationships: What strengths has the family mobilized in supporting the identified patient? Also, identify interactional patterns and roles which may have contributed to presenting and diagnosed problems. Which supports can be mobilized?

EXHIBIT 8.5 (CONTINUED)

Include here information on individual or family history relevant to presenting problems.

F. Psychological strengths, conflicts, and deficits: What kind of personality does this person have, and to what extent do their complaints and symptoms reflect complications of these patterns, whether they are strengths or weakenesses? Specific areas to be considered include:

(i) **Superego:** Type of demands, standards, harshness or permissiveness, guiding ideals, values, principles

(ii) **Ego functions:** Perceptual, judgmental, reality-testing capabilities, self-image, impulse control, ability as an executant, thought processes, identifications, capacity for guilt, defenses, general intelligence, creativity, adaptability, and activities of daily living (ADLs)

(iii) **Libidinal qualities/drives:** Narcissism, dependence, residuals of early developmental crises, capacity for mature love relations, ambivalence, aggressiveness, sexual immaturities, unresolved attachments and hostilities (e.g., regarding parents).

Consider conflicts among ego, id, and superego and environment, as well as early deficits in the development of any of the basic psychological functions, especially the ways these functions self-organize to generate the current issues.

II. Assessment

Systemic or ecological formulation: How have the foregoing individual characteristics and social conditions interacted dynamically to produce the symptoms and/or problems identified? Summarize only the most crucial facts, possible etiological and aggravating factors, major themes, and most salient needs, including personality and family interactional patterns. Consider how the particular combination of the client's motivations, capacities, and opportunities created the problem and present possible avenues for its resolution.

Notes: Additional sections on diagnosis, intervention goals, and treatment plan are often included.

to engage in such an interactive interpersonal process provides invaluable information about key personality and problem-solving patterns.

Depending on the understanding that results from this process, mental health professionals may discover that the presenting problem is primarily situational, involving unusual challenges, or reflects more deeply internalized patterns of dysfunctional thought, feeling, or behavior that have reoccurred on multiple occasions. Either way, if the client lacks the ability for such insight, it may be necessary to focus on the situational aspects of the problem until a time that the client can develop such insight and problem ownership. A situational focus can involve pragmatic problem solving or environmental manipulation (e.g., legal assistance, change of environment) or emotional support, as well as help setting goals, partializing tasks, and rehearsing and reviewing behavior. As the problem continues to recur, the client may then begin, with the therapist's help, to see that it can no longer be blamed on a particular partner, boss, or other situation. Early in family systems therapy the focus is often on efforts to help clients understand the dysfunctional transactions that they are involved in; only later is the focus on identifying, owning, and working on the individual or psychological issues that contribute to dysfunctional family relationships.

Perhaps one of the most important applications of complex systems theory in assessment and intervention is the idea that the goal is usually not to return clients to their former levels of functioning, as this can well mean perpetuation of their current difficulties (this would be like trying to reassemble Humpty Dumpty). Rather, the goal is often to facilitate new directions and to develop new competencies and new and different patterns of functioning based on all that can be learned from the current crisis.

V. Summary

The chapter begins by placing mental illness in its larger societal context: a barometer of a society's quality of life. It considers mental illnesses the result of exacerbated developmental impasses and problems of daily living. In doing so, it distinguishes emotional disorders from the major mental illnesses, primarily based on the extent that the latter have become internalized and partially separated from immediate environmental influences. The introduction also identifies several crosscutting themes that have been associated with most mental illnesses, such as problems of integration, equilibrium, control, relatedness, sense of self, and time competence. The complex systems perspective has led to a reframing of these criteria, such as by suggesting that mental illnesses may represent not so much a lack of integration and equilibrium but rather the wrong kind, as well as a failure to capitalize on the complexity of information processing to solve the increasingly difficult problems of contemporary life.

The chapter then reviews several approaches to the phenomenological study of mental illness, beginning with first-person accounts, the external second-person observation of patterns of signs and symptoms of mental illness, and the analysis of their functions. The major thrust of the chapter is an overview of several theoretical perspectives for understanding the etiology and dynamics of various mental illnesses.

The chapter concludes with a review of the application of the various theories of mental illnesses to the assessment process. It emphasizes the limitations of traditional assessment protocols and highlights the need to integrate assessment into the larger treatment process. It also urges assessing the various mental illnesses in their developmental context and considering the extent to which they have become internalized as relatively independent processes.

For Further Reading

Baron-Cohen, S. (Ed.). (1997). *The maladapted mind: Classic readings in evolutionary psychopathology.* Hove, U.K.: Psychology Press.

Beutler, L. E., & Malik, M. L. (Eds.). (2000). *Alternatives to the DSM.* Washington, DC: American Psychological Association.

Guastello, S. J. (2000). Nonlinear dynamics in psychology. *Discrete Dynamics in Nature and Society, 6,* 11–29.

Javitt, D. C., & Coyle, J. T. (2003, December). Decoding schizophrenia. *Scientific American, 290,* 48–55.

Kaplan, B. (Ed.). (1964). *The inner world of mental illness.* New York: Harper & Row.

Livesley, W. J. (2001). *Handbook of personality disorders.* New York: Guilford Press.

Lopez, S. R., & Guarnaccia, P. J. (2000). Cultural psychopathology: Uncovering the social world of mental illness. *Annual Review of Psychology, 51,* 571–598.

Mandell, A. J., & Selz, K. A. (1995). Nonlinear dynamical patterns as personality theory for neurobiology and psychiatry. *Psychiatry, 58,* 371–390.

Millon, T., & Davis, R. (2000). *Personality disorders in modern life.* New York: Wiley.

Sabelli, H.C., Carlson-Sabelli, L., Patel, M., Levy, A., & Diez-Martin, J. (1995). Anger, fear, depression and crime: Physiological and psychological studies using the process method. In R. Robertson & A. Combs. (Eds.),

Chaos theory in psychology and the life sciences (pp. 65–88). Mahwah, NJ: Erlbaum.

Tschacher, W., Scheier, C., & Grawe, K. (1998). Order and pattern formation in psychotherapy. *Nonlinear dynamics, psychology, and life sciences,* 2(3), 195–215.

PART III

The Systemic Context

CHAPTER 9

Small Groups and Their Processes

Never doubt that a small group of thoughtful, committed citizens can change the world.

—MARGARET MEAD

I. Introduction

A. Significance and Evolutionary Context

Whereas the preceding chapters focused on individual behavior, this chapter introduces its social context, specifically the role of small groups of people who come together to pursue a common interest. This may be for the purposes of personal change or for pursuing a political agenda, with or without the assistance of human service professionals. Groups are among the most fundamental of the building blocks of the institutions and communities that constitute the social environment. It is through groups that individuals are socialized, and often subjected to social control. Likewise, it is through groups that individual preferences become elaborated and amplified and are able to affect the greater society. In this spirit, Margaret Mead's epigraph to this chapter represents an optimistic assessment of the potential of small groups. Yet for each such statement in the literature, there are at least as many that highlight the limitations of groups. For instance, Frederick Nietzsche (1886/2008) complained, "In individuals, insanity is rare; but in groups, parties, nations and epochs, it is the rule."

Such contradictions are expected anytime phenomena as complex as small groups are treated as discrete structures, with defined, fixed functions. However, when small groups are considered as loosely coupled dynamic systems that serve multiple purposes, practitioners are then in a better position to appreciate both their strengths and limitations. Many groups exemplify the adage that the whole is greater than the sum of the parts; that groups perform better than the sum of the efforts of their members. However, some groups fail to achieve such synergy and can impede individual productivity or growth. The question of what distinguishes such groups is perhaps the pivotal issue in the study of small groups, a central theme of this chapter.

Small groups, however, are only one of the many possible supports for individuals. The field of evolutionary psychology has shown that a key feature that accounts for human success is the ability to come together in groups. Evolutionary psychology has stressed the many advantages of sociality over individual action. Forsyth (1996) emphasizes "benefits [of groups] in terms of reproduction (i.e., finding mates), avoiding predation, gathering food, social facilitation, division of labor, and the like. Like ants, termites, baboons, and dogs, we gather in groups because the advantages we accrue" (n.p.). Although humans have evolved the ability to take advantage of the benefits of group membership, this is no guarantee that benefits will materialize. Cooperative action is a hallmark of many groups. Nonetheless, the role of competition cannot be minimized, whether between members and/or between groups. Both cooperation and competition are dynamic processes that can lead to positive synergies of group experience or, conversely, to stagnation and oppression. The power of groups lies, in part, in their ability to capitalize on self-selection and self-organization, two of the central features of groups, which can account for observed patterns of cooperation and competition.

B. Definitions

The term *group* in its most generic sense connotes merely two or more real or abstract objects that share some important characteristic. However, in the human services, *small groups* generally refers to collections of between two and twenty persons who periodically come together to achieve some valued purpose (e.g., companionship, development of social skills, or some practical work, such as case reviews or political advocacy). Schein (1972) defined the small group as "any number of people who (i) interact with one another, (ii) are psychologically aware of one another and (iii) perceive themselves to be a group" (p. 81). Small groups typically involve face-to-face interactions in scheduled meetings, but such features of the small group are becoming less universal with the development of Internet discussion groups and chat rooms. The individuals involved may be clients, patients, members, workers, or administrators, to mention a few examples. The variety of groups, with their many purposes, activities, and participants, is discussed in the next section, but here it is sufficient to note that small groups are distinguishable sets of individuals who interact to achieve valued ends, however well or vaguely defined. Small groups are, thus, different from crowds, communities, institutions, and populations.

The aim of this chapter is to review what is known about small-group dynamics, both in general and from the perspective of complex systems theory—it is not to provide a primer on how to conduct groups. After discussing the range of groups typically encountered in practice, as well as the background of this field, the chapter considers the range of purposes and functions that groups are called on to address, as well as the dynamics of group development, and particularly several of the stages that groups often move through. Only then does the chapter take up the structure of small groups. It concludes with an overview of some of the major concepts from complex systems theory—such as chaos, entrainment, self-organization, and bifurcation theories—which have been used to understand the group experience. The chapter specifically introduces the role of the social environment in some of its most immediate transactions with individuals, whereas the subsequent chapter explores a specific and more pervasive form of a naturally occurring small group, the family. Although many of the examples of groups discussed in this chapter are intentional groups organized by human service professionals, many of the ideas covered also apply to naturally occurring groups.

C. Types of Groups

The range of groups that human service professionals encounter challenges the skills of even the most accomplished. Most professionals tend to focus on a few fashionable genres (e.g., therapy, psychoeducation) and to ignore the rest, especially many naturally occurring groups. To complicate matters, there is no universally agreed-on typology of the various kinds of groups. Nonetheless, several dimensions have been commonly identified and provide useful distinctions. Many authors distinguish between task groups (e.g., committees, work teams) and socioemotional or process groups (e.g., support or therapy groups). Closer analysis blurs this distinction, revealing that nearly all groups serve both functions, though one typically dominates and obscures the other. Another critical distinction is between primary and secondary groups. Primary groups are naturally occurring, such as families or friendship groups. Secondary groups are those typically organized by professionals. In the gray area between these are self-help groups.

Arrow, McGrath, and Berdahl (2000) recently proposed a particularly useful typology of groups in *Small Groups as Complex Systems,* one of the first books to analyze groups from a complex systems perspective. Arrow identifies two key dimensions. First is the extent to which a given group is organized internally out of the felt needs of its members or externally as a result of outside demands or circumstances. Second, groups vary according to the extent to which their development is emergent or planned. These two dimensions, illustrated in figure 9.1, are used to define four basic types of groups. Externally prompted emergent groups are known to as circumstantial groups, such as a group of people in a bus or plane crash who are forced

FIGURE 9.1: MAJOR TYPES OF GROUPS, BASED ON DIMENSIONS OF GROUP FORMATION SPACE

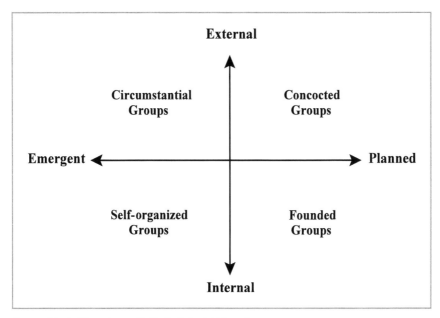

Source: Adapted from Arrow, McGrath, & Berdahl (2000).

to work together to survive until help arrives. Many groups encountered in the human services are also externally prompted but planned; these are concocted groups. Such groups include most treatment groups, committees, and task forces, which usually originate in external considerations and are intentionally and somewhat planfully developed. Those groups that develop spontaneously on the basis of member needs are self-organized groups (e.g., many self-help groups). Finally, groups that develop out of member initiative but in a planful manner are founded groups. For example, a small group of community organizers who develop an advocacy association may constitute such a group.

Perhaps one of the most useful features of Arrow et al.'s typology is that it highlights the larger social context of groups, how they serve social needs, and at the same time how they are called on to serve the immediate needs of their members. While the authors place self-organized groups in a single quadrant (emergent/internal), self-organization is a broader dynamic that takes place in other circumstances but less obviously so. For instance, in concocted groups, self-organization also takes place but is inhibited, and perhaps occurs only in the later stages of the group.

Several other distinctions that overlap with the preceding are useful for assessing groups and planning interventions. Some groups are strictly time limited (e.g., six sessions), whereas others are ongoing. Time limits help ensure a consistent membership and focus activities, though ongoing groups may be needed in an environment with members entering and exiting at different times, such as a psychiatric unit. Groups also differ on the basis of commitment asked from members. Committed groups require members to promise regular attendance or other activities, whereas noncommitted or low-demand groups make it easy for members to drop in and out, providing them with maximum leeway. Group organizers walk a fine line in judging the level of commitment that they can of a given population; the lack of required commitment may undermine the group process, or members may balk at the costs of overly stringent demands. Another key dimension is the extent that a given group is homogeneous or heterogeneous with respect to member characteristics, such as goals, issues, or features such as personality patterns, problem-solving styles, or demographics (e.g., age, sex, race). Group organizers need to balance the need for cohesiveness and a sense of commonality with the need for a diversity of perspectives and life experiences, and the point of optimal balance varies dramatically according to the purposes of the group and the individuals involved in it.

Various typologies have been proposed for specific group genres, such as treatment and task groups. Bates, Johnson, and Blaker (2003) suggest that treatment and other groups fall into the following categories: small-group instruction, group activity (e.g., task groups), group guidance, group counseling, T-groups (a type of self-awareness training group), sensitivity training groups (e.g., encounter groups), marathons, and psychotherapy groups. In contrast, Sundstrom, De Meuse, and Futrell (1990) focus on work groups and hypothesize that there are four primary types: (1) advice and involvement teams (e.g., committees, review panels, quality review circles, advisory boards), (2) production or service teams, involving groups that produce products or services (e.g., a diagnostic and pupil services team), (3) project and development teams, involving professionals who produce a onetime or unique product (e.g., community needs assessment, plan to address homelessness), (4) action and negotiation teams, which conduct critical tasks (e.g., an executive team, a team of union negotiators).

It is apparent that the group experience constitutes a strikingly varied picture, one that challenges the professional to vary, in a similar manner, his or her strategies for group assessment and facilitation. And given both the importance of groups for individual and social functioning and the variety of their uses, it is not surprising that considerable efforts have been made over the past century to study them. To this topic we now turn.

D. History of Group Dynamics

The field of group dynamics originated as an offshoot of social psychology at the start of the twentieth century (see Pepitone, 1981). Two textbooks, by Charles Cooley (1902) and William McDougall (1908), introduced the social psychology of groups. Whereas Cooley focused on the role of small primary groups in linking and integrating people with society as a whole, McDougall emphasized the evolutionary origins of human gregariousness, of a herd instinct, which he considered the basis for the formation of groups. As such, he highlighted individual psychological traits in the formation and functioning of groups. Also at this time, Norman Triplett (1898) conducted what is considered the first social psychological experiment that stimulated an extended body of research on the power of groups to facilitate performance and problem solving (see exhibit 9.1).

The field of group dynamics has also been traced to the human relations school of organizational research, prominent from the 1920s through the 1950s. The Hawthorne studies revealed the impact of experimental attention in enhancing work morale and performance and have been credited with stimulating the study of group dynamics. But more important was the work of Kurt Lewin (1935), whose field theory of change—unfreezing, changing, and refreezing problematic social structures—promoted the analysis of individual behaviors in terms of the current social situation, giving social psychology in general and group dynamics in particular a major boost. In 1944 Lewin founded the Research Center for Group Dynamics at the Massachusetts Institute of Technology. Shortly thereafter he became involved with group dynamics training for the Connecticut Interracial Commission, and out of this experience, he developed T-groups, or the laboratory method. Initially, small discussions developed into his training or T-groups. By 1950 the National Training Laboratories (NTL) was established and began promoting the use of T-groups, thus contributing to the development of the encounter group movement in the 1960s (Yalom, 1995). Also during this period, a few psychoanalysts, such as Wilfred Bion (1959), started using groups as a means of psychotherapy. Bion emphasized the role of unconscious assumptions, such as those involving fight or flight, dependency, and the need for pairing, in molding group behaviors. However, beginning in the 1950s and through the 1970s, the field of group dynamics was largely eclipsed by the cognitive science revolution, which emphasized individual problem solving, often on an unconscious level.

McGrath identified several of the major themes of group research, each characteristic of different schools of researchers (see Arrow et al., 2000). These schools involved the study of groups as systems for influencing

EXHIBIT 9.1: SOCIAL FACILITATION: DO GROUPS IMPROVE PERFORMANCE?

The sports psychologist Norman Triplett conducted one of the first experiments in social psychology in 1898. Triplett, a bicycling enthusiast, had observed that bicyclists performed better in races than when timed by mechanical devices or during solo racing. Triplett tested a number of explanations for this effect with forty pairs of schoolchildren who were asked to play a simple game both alone and in pairs. The experiments documented the superior effects on performance when others are present. This was found to be the case both with audiences and when individuals worked together.

Although subsequent experiments replicated Triplett's initial findings, exceptions have been identified. For instance, Floyd Allport (1920) conducted a series of experiments in which subjects were asked to think of word associations or cross out vowels in newspaper articles or to perform multiplications, while both alone and in group settings. He found that although quantity of output often increased under observational conditions, quality sometimes decreased.

Because of such contradictory findings, interest in the social facilitation impact of groups and social observation declined in the 1940s and 1950s. But in 1965, Robert Zajonc reignited interest by distinguishing between the impact of dominant and nondominant responses. Whereas dominant responses have been mastered and regularly used, nondominant responses are infrequently performed. In reviewing Allport's research, he concluded that the studies that demonstrated social facilitation involved dominant responses of well-rehearsed or instinctual behaviors such as bicycling or eating rapidly. Studies that had identified exceptions to social facilitation typically involved novel, complex, and unrehearsed undertakings, such as solving mathematical problems or composing poetry.

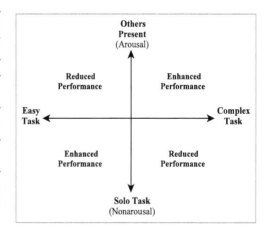

members (e.g., Lewin), systems for patterning interactions (e.g., Bion), systems for performing tasks (e.g., Tripplet, Hawthorne studies), means of improving self-understanding (e.g., NLT), holistic and sociotechnical systems, informal work units that affected work performance, and the result of interactions between intra- and intergroup processes. Throughout this history, there has been a progressive broadening of the focus from the psychological to internal group dynamics and to the larger system involving the interplay among environmental demands, group processes, and members' psychological characteristics. For example, the approach to groups as "intact, holistic, sociotechnical systems," originating in the work of the Tavistock Clinic in London, viewed "groups as intact systems, consisting not only of a collection of members but also of the tools, resources, and technology available (or imposed on them)" (Arrow, McGrath, & Berdahl, 2000, p. 17). The inputs and outputs of groups, including physical resources and human service technologies, establish both constraints and opportunities that affect internal group functioning.

More recent lines of group research have viewed groups as information-processing systems involving the acquisition, storage, processing, generation, and use of information; conflict-managing and consensus-seeking systems, or interest-or-perspective-blending systems; systems to motivate, regulate, and coordinate member activities; team units in work organizations; and vehicles to improve the learning and adjustment of members. In addition, a recent area of work is the function of groups in identity formation, through the identification of in-groups and out-groups, and in general the constructions that individuals are supported in developing about themselves and others. This work has drawn heavily on social identity and social categorization theories.

II. Functions of Groups

A. Overarching Functions

How a group actually operates is, in part, an outcome of the functions that it is called on to perform, both by the larger social environment and by the members themselves. *Function* has many meanings (see chapter 2). In the study of groups, it refers to the transformations, work, or other outcomes that the group is expected to produce, either explicitly or implicitly. Society and group members may or may not be able to articulate what the functions are, but close analysis of people's expectations and of the advantages and other outcomes associated with groups, provide clues about the functions.

The types of groups discussed in the foregoing section also provide important clues. The most important is the distinction between socioemotional and task groups. Socioemotional groups provide a sense of belonging, socialization, social support, and the like—all advantageous outcomes and expected functions of many groups. Similarly, task groups perform identifiable work. They conduct research projects, write reports, make decisions, or conduct diagnostic assessments, all of which are important functions that convert the input of people's time, ideas, efforts, and resources into potentially valuable products—but they often serve covert functions (e.g., killing a proposal by studying it to death, detracting attention from other more important issues.)

B. Curative Factors

The often-cited advantages or curative effects of groups are also a gauge of their social functions. Small groups are called on to perform a variety of complex tasks, ones that may also involve the need to build cohesiveness and consensus. Many groups in social service and educational settings facilitate the exchange of information, learning, and skill development in a way that maximizes knowledge internalization or retention. Other groups in the human services aim to provide social support and to maintain individuals at a sufficiently stable level to provide time for the possible solution of more enduring problems. Closely related with the social support function is that of networking—groups help connect people and facilitate needed interpersonal or practical exchanges. Other groups primarily serve a social control function of checking up on members and keeping them out of trouble (e.g., probation groups). Many therapy groups specifically focus on growth, both emotional and interpersonal. Still others seek to perform existential or spiritual functions to help people come to terms with their mortality or to feel a connection and trust in a higher power. Irving Yalom (1995), who has written what is probably the most widely read book on group psychotherapy, has identified twelve curative factors that support group treatment, ones that reflect the functions that the groups serve (see exhibit 9.2). These factors include most of those already mentioned, as well as catharsis or ventilation, development of insight, instillation of hope, opportunities for altruism, reenactment and resolution of painful family conflicts, and provision of guidance and models for people to identify with.

C. Typologies of Functions

A few theorists in the field of group dynamics have ventured to propose exhaustive typologies of group functions. Donelson Forsyth (1996) created

EXHIBIT 9.2: CURATIVE FACTORS IN GROUP TREATMENT FROM THE RESEARCH OF IRVING YALOM

After extensive research involving group observation, interviews, and Q-sorts, Irving Yalom (1970) identified the following list of curative factors in treatment groups:

- **Interpersonal learning:** Feedback from others on behavior and communication, and help in learning new behaviors
- **Catharsis:** Opportunity to ventilate, to express strong and painful feelings regarding one's life situation or other group members
- **Cohesiveness:** A sense of connection with the group, no longer being alone, being accepted
- **Insight:** Learning that one's reactions and behaviors may have more to do with one's background than the immediate situation, and developing awareness of underlying attitudes and feelings, especially those that complicate relationships
- **Interpersonal output:** Opportunity to practice new roles and behaviors in the context of the group; learning how to approach others
- **Existential awareness:** Developing perspective on life, on its injustices and on mortality; ability to focus on important things, and eschew trivialities.
- **Universality:** Learning that "we are all in the same boat," that one's seemingly unique struggles may be shared by many others.
- **Instillation of hope:** Encouragement through seeing that others in the group have been able to confront their problems
- **Altruism:** Opportunity to help others and think less about one's self provides self-respect
- **Family reenactment:** Being in the group provides opportunities to relive and rework dysfunctional family patterns within a more accepting atmosphere
- **Guidance:** Receipt of practical suggestions on life's problems from either group leader or other members
- **Identification:** Finding models of respected individuals that one can emulate

five categories: (1) belonging, (2) intimacy, (3) generativity, (4) stability, and (5) adaptability. Belonging refers to the provision of opportunities for developing a sense of cohesiveness and for networking. Intimacy focuses on quality of relationships, particularly on developing warm and loving relationships. Generativity refers to task accomplishment and productivity. Stability refers to continuity, and adaptability provides opportunities for problem solving and creativity. Belonging and intimacy have been referred to as maintenance functions; generativity, as a group task function; and stability and adaptability, as task maintenance functions. One can break up these functions into three, five, or twelve parts, but the important point is that the development, conduct, and assessment of any group requires an ability to identify the interplay—sometimes conflicting and sometimes synergetic— between the diverse outcomes or functions that both the social environment and the group members expect to see emerge.

III. Group Process

The study of group dynamics is the study of how groups change and evolve, including the forces that drive groups and the means by which forces generate various patterns of relationship and activity. There are multiple lenses through which group processes can be viewed, such as cohesion, patterns of interaction and communication, decision making, leadership, conflict and power, and the processes and stages of group development. The critical forces involve the functions identified in the prior section, specifically the ways that these become transformed into the expectations and hopes of the founders of the group and its members. However initial expectations transform, new interests inevitably emerge depending on the group's interactions and intermediate outcomes.

A. Cohesion

One of the most critical factors in the early stages of small groups is the level of group cohesiveness. This has been a central focus of group research, with questions about the causes, manifestations, and outcomes of cohesiveness. Cohesiveness is similar to the notion of relationship in individual therapy, and it has been simply defined as the "attractiveness of a group for its members" (Yalom, 1995, p. 48). It involves mutual understanding, acceptance, congruence in regard to basic expectations, and an identification with the purposes and membership of the group. Cohesiveness is evidenced by the openness of members and the level at which they engage in the work of the group. Unless members know one another before the start of the group, cohesiveness develops only over time; it is an outcome of early dynamics and a necessary, though not always sufficient, condition for successful outcomes, whether the fulfillment of socioemotional needs or the accomplishment of specific tasks. Cohesiveness has also been shown to reduce group dropout and turnover.

Cartwright and Zander (1968) found four interacting sets of conditions that influence the level of cohesion that can develop in a group: (1) the needs of members for affiliation, recognition, status, and security; (2) the various incentives available, whether tangible or intangible, such as recognition or networking opportunities; (3) the members' expectations of those benefits, including their assessment of the costs associated with membership; and (4) their comparison of the current group with other groups, with respect to the foregoing benefits and costs. As such, Cartwright and Zander argue that cohesion is not merely an outcome of interpersonal processes, empathy, and understanding but also a result of a variety of pragmatic and status considerations of each member.

B. Patterns of Interaction and Communication

The immense variety in groups, individuals involved, and leadership styles complicates the characterization of patterns of group activity. There is considerable overlap between interpersonal interaction and communication. Although communication, by definition, is interactive, with a little imagination, one can think of behavioral interactions with minimal communication, at least of formal variety. For instance, a member has a reaction to medication and starts to sweat profusely and becomes ill; this leads other members to decide to discontinue the group. While secondary communication is probably going on, behaviors manifest that have minimal communicative intent but an impact nonetheless.

On its most fundamental level, communication involves three stages: (1) encoding some meaning into a message (i.e., converting thoughts and feelings into a verbal statement); (2) transmitting the message, often in the context of random noise; and (3) decoding by the receivers, or interpreting the statement and translating it into meanings (Toseland & Rivas, 2001). The purpose of a communication may be to understand others, to find out where they stand in relation to others, to persuade others, to gain or maintain power, to impress others, to develop relationships, to hurt others, or to find solutions to common problems, to mention a few examples. Most group communications involve both verbal and nonverbal and intentional and nonintentional dimensions.

The encoding process consists of multiple and intricate internal processes and decisions about both the content and means of communication, and it is usually based on incomplete knowledge of what others will understand and how they will respond. It involves the interplay of denotation and connotation, between the interlacing of the literal meaning of words with various implications, often built on social context and shared histories. Connotations may be intended and conscious, semiconscious, or entirely inadvertent, especially when members are from markedly different cultural groups.

Decoding or interpreting the messages is likewise a complex task involving the construction of internal models or theories about the intent of the speaker. The models are often based on incomplete and subtle cues, and they require difficult decisions about the most relevant contexts for interpreting a message. In addition, communication is complicated by language barriers, foreign accents, speech and hearing problems, and impaired vision. Poor eyesight may make it difficult to tell who is being addressed or to appreciate nonverbal cues, all of which combine to make the process of communicating a fragile one that requires frequent clarification. The lack of visual cues is especially important in the functioning of online groups. Thus, communication is best thought of as an interactive, iterative transaction in which members approximate meaning over successive statements rather than transform input into output in a simplistic and linear manner.

Groups vary in the extent to which activity revolves around the designated leader. Often early in many groups, there is interaction only between each member and the leader; in contrast, interchanges may take place primarily among members. This is influenced not only by the personality and facilitation style of the leader and the expectations of the group but also by the perceived power of the leader. Figure 9.2 depicts several common interactional patterns. The leader-centered group is typically characterized by the maypole pattern in which each member interacts only with the leader. Some classes and therapy groups use a round-robin approach in which each participant takes turns talking or presenting. With the hot-seat approach, selected members intensely interact with the rest of the members, perhaps through questioning, confrontation, or participants' personal disclosures. The free-floating pattern involves fluid interactions, determined by the perceived needs of the moment rather than by some preset plan. While many groups start out with a maypole arrangement, they often move to round-robin, hot-seat, or another semistructured pattern, and then to a free-floating arrangement as group members become more comfortable with one another.

Interactional patterns have also been studied in relation to the types of roles and messages that are exchanged. David Kantor and William Lehr

FIGURE 9.2: TYPES OF INTERACTIONAL DYNAMICS IN SMALL GROUPS

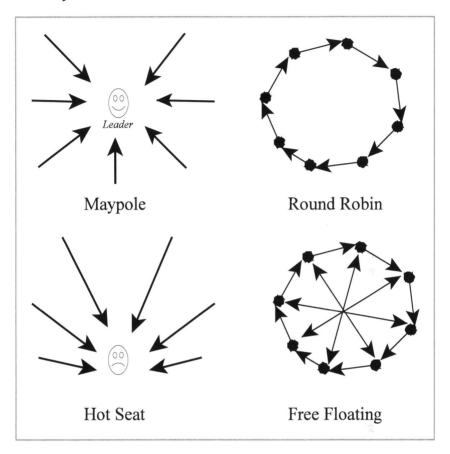

(1975) proposes a four-player model in which each interactional sequence can be decomposed into some combination of actions of members who alternatively function as mover, opposer, follower, or bystander. These are not roles in the formal sense, as they are constantly changing; the same person may function in each capacity in the course of a single group session. Chiu (2000) extends this model to propose that each statement has three dimensions: (1) an evaluative component that is supportive, critical, or unresponsive to the preceding communication; (2) the invitational dimension, which may encourage follow-up through a question and thus bring closure to the discussion through a command; and (3) the knowledge dimension, which contributes new information, repeats old information, or does not contribute any discernible knowledge (see figure 9.3).

Another method of analyzing communications between group members

FIGURE 9.3: THE RELATIONSHIP BETWEEN CORE COLLABORATION
ROLES AND THE STRATEGIES FOR IMPLEMENTING THEM

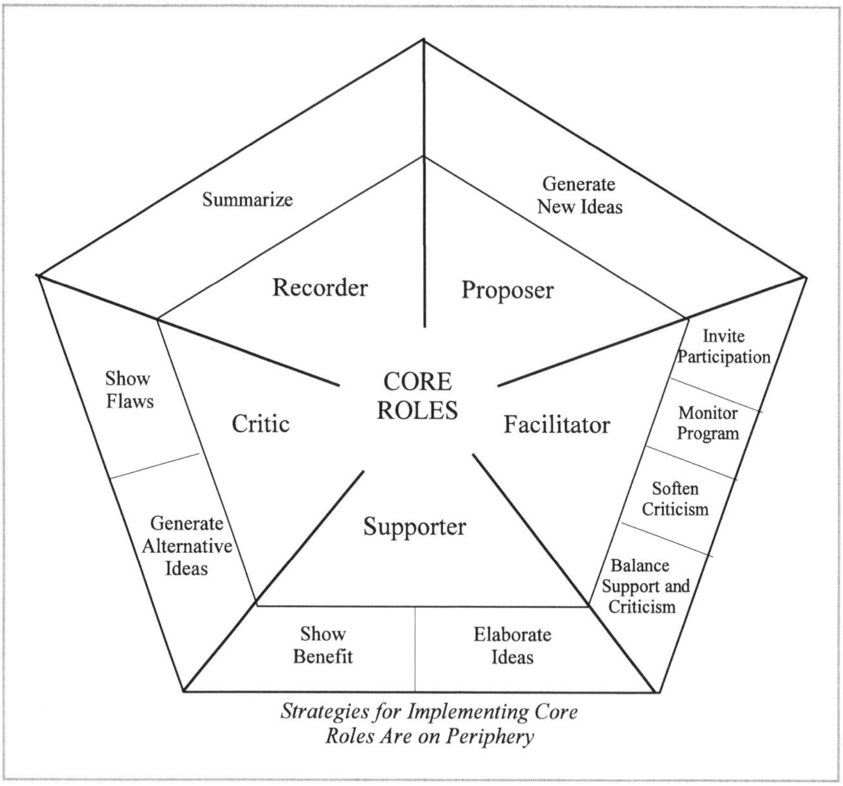

Strategies for Implementing Core
Roles Are on Periphery

Source: Chiu (2000).

was developed by Stephen Guastello (1998). In his research on online
groups, Guastello coded for nine different types of communication: (1) re-
questing information, (2) giving information, (3) reducing tension, (4) clarifying responses, (5) gatekeeping, (6) initiating, (7) following, (8) harmoniz-
ing, and (9) unclassified. Group members, thus, are assumed to have a wide
repertoire of possible approaches to the group experience. However, some
individuals may be able to vary their approach according to a variety of considerations, and others may have a limited repertoire of responses, perhaps
based on personality or other considerations. An important dimension in
the analysis communication patterns is metacommunication, or communication about communication. It is proposed that at the same time that each
statement has a manifest or literal meaning, it also conveys connotations
or implications about the speaker's feelings about current relationships. A

therapist asks how a client feels, and thereby discloses his or her expectation that it is part of the client's role to be confiding in the therapist.

C. Decision Making and Problem Solving

A group's pattern of communication and interaction is the matrix in which decisions are made and problems solved. Both individuals and groups engage in these activities; the extensive body of research and theory on these topics was reviewed in chapter 7. Both formal and informal procedures become intertwined, especially in small groups. Some small groups, such as advisory boards or review panels, are set up to make decisions and, if possible, to develop consensus. Although their procedures may be technical, legal, rational, or bureaucratic, with designated roles for individuals to undertake specific reviews or determinations or to provide ratings, usually informal procedures also are an important part of the work. Among the best-known informal procedure is caucusing, in which subgroups meet to chat in the hall or over coffee, often laying the groundwork for a consensus decision or perhaps planting the seeds for conflict. For this reason, the assessment of decision making in task groups requires an appreciation of the dynamics of the larger social environment and of the history of relationships among members. Many cynically regard the functioning of task groups as a kind of window dressing, as a way to formalize decisions that emerge from the environment in which these groups are embedded.

Therapy and support groups, in contrast, are usually based on the notion that individuals and those involved in their significant outside relationships are the ones who need to decide how to solve their own problems. The purpose of the group is to support and facilitate these individual decisions. In many such groups, the institution or group leader makes decisions about membership and meetings; however, the more decisions that can be turned over to the group, the more likely it is that the group will develop cohesiveness. Thus, groups vary in their ability to establish their own norms and to function as their own gatekeepers. A challenge of the group leader is to accurately gauge the group's interest and ability to govern itself. This is a decision that depends on the capacities of the individuals involved (e.g., children, residents of a nursing home, adults in an outpatient psychotherapy group, professionals working on a community task force).

D. Leadership

A group's ability to develop cohesiveness and fulfill its functions is partly contingent on its leadership. In many cases, a leader is assigned or sometimes imposed on the group, but in other cases, leaders emerge from the group's members. There have been many ways to characterize leaders and how they function. Consider, for example, the distinctions among authoritarian, democratic, and laissez-faire leaders. Whereas democratic leaders are selected by the group and to a greater or lesser extent elicit group input into key decisions, the laissez-faire leader takes a much less active role and largely expects the group to be self-governing. The communication style of leaders has also been characterized as varying from the instrumental to the expressive, with the former focusing on pragmatic issues and tasks and the latter paying closest attention to the socioemotional needs of the group and relying on informal relationships. The success of any of leadership and communication style rests on its congruence with the immediate group and the larger environment in which the group exists. The leader often must represent the group to the institutions or community that the group is part of. A key to leaders' success is the ability to correctly assess the needs and abilities of the group and to vary their leadership style accordingly. Often this involves assuming a more active role in early stages, with the ability to assume a backseat facilitative role as group relationships cohere and then to take a more directive role should crises develop.

E. Conflict and Power

Conflict can mean many things, helpful and harmful, in a group. A key distinction is between cognitive and interest conflict. People may have different or even conflicting beliefs, values, or styles of thinking or relating but still have a commonality of interests. Alternatively, they may be similar cognitively but have seemingly conflictual interests, perhaps for respect, promotion, or the exercise of some individual right. Different interests are not conflictual if the key parties conceive of ways to achieve all interests, albeit in different situations. This is referred to as a non-zero-sum game, in which one person's gain is not regarded as a loss for the next person. In contrast, in a zero-sum game, the available payoffs are viewed as a fixed pie, and a larger slice for one person means a smaller one for the next person. When this is the case, there is a considerably enhanced risk of conflict.

In its extreme, conflict can be arguing, unconstrained strife, fighting, and even violence, but when positive social norms and an underlying commonality of interests constrain conflict, then it can manifest as no more than mild interpersonal competitiveness. One factor that may tip the balance from polite competitiveness to more pernicious forms of conflict is when one participant believes that another has violated fundamental rules of respect and fair play or has engaged others, especially outsiders, in manner

FIGURE 9.4: CONFLICT MANAGEMENT STRATEGIES

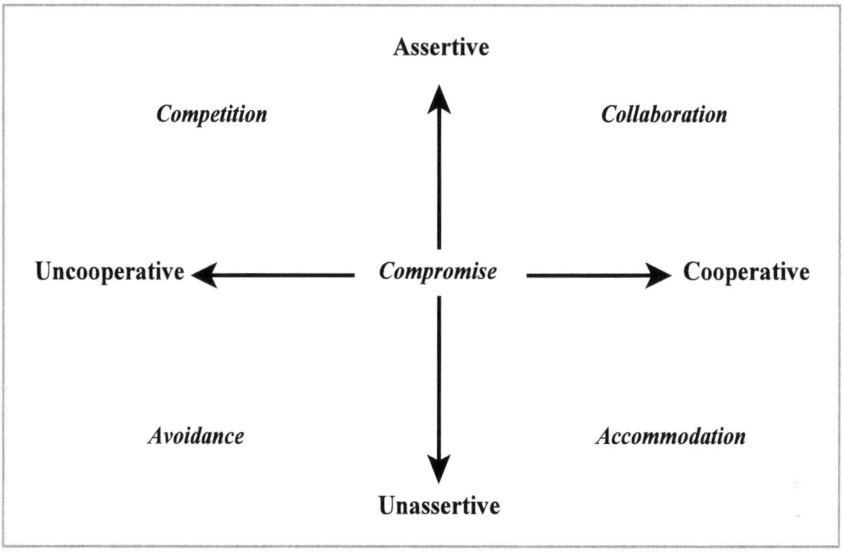

Assertive

Competition   *Collaboration*

Uncooperative ◄──────── *Compromise* ────────► Cooperative

Avoidance   *Accommodation*

Unassertive

Source: Ruble & Thomas (1976).

that unfairly imbalances the situation, thus making the playing field no longer level.

Ruble and Thomas (1976) hypothesize two key dimensions that under-lie a group's competitiveness and conflict. A key dimension is the level of assertiveness, or the ability to make beliefs and wishes known in a clear and nonthreatening manner. The other, cooperativeness, is the ability to get along with others. Those who are assertive and cooperative demonstrate the ability to collaborate, whereas those who are nonassertive and coop-erative are accommodative (see figure 9.4). In contrast, those who are as-sertive and noncooperative demonstrate competitiveness, and those who are neither assertive nor cooperative are avoidant. Although this typology describes individuals, in many instances groups come to demonstrate such collective behaviors.

Power is closely related to conflict, and if not managed correctly, it can unbalance groups and exacerbate conflict. Power can mean many things, but in its most fundamental sense, whether or not it is exercised, it refers to the ability to achieve desired ends. Power may be pragmatic, involving financial resources, control of budgets, hiring and firing, or the like. It may be formal or informal. Or it may involve personal characteristics of an individual, such as persuasiveness, knowledge, likeability, or the confidence they inspire in others. Wagner and Hollenbeck (1997) identified five types of power that are relevant to groups: (1) reward, or the provision of valued incentives; (2) coercive power, often involving threats and sanctions; (3) legitimate power, which derives from norms, values, and especially formal position and authority; (4) referent power, which is otherwise known as charismatic power; and (5) expert power, derived from expertise, knowledge, skill, or education. The ways in which these various forms of power coexist and amplify or suppress one another constitute a complex and multifaceted relationship. The actual exercise of power is called influence. Some people may have substantial power but exercise it only in unusual, critical situations, whereas others may have only modest power but actively attempt to use it. This activity may increase the person's power or, conversely, deplete it, depending on the person's attempt. The exercise of power in a competitive way may generate a win but often not without significant costs, whereas the more restrained exercise of power in a collaborative style potentially empowers not only the person exercising it but others as well.

The assessment of group dynamics involving conflict and power also raises the question of the relationship between intra- and intergroup conflict and power, and the trade-offs that exist between these. Extra- or intergroup conflict may carry over into the group, or vice versa. Similarly, one level of conflict may defuse the other. Conflict between two work teams may actually generate cohesiveness in the team, or conflict between members may circumvent intergroup conflict.

F. Group Development: Process and Stage Theories

One of the ways theorists have sought to understand group dynamics is by understanding their stages of development. However, other theorists have rejected such efforts as misguided and instead have sought merely to identify generic processes that drive development. Such processes typically emerge from the underlying assumptions and interactional rules of group members and manifest in such a wide variety of lines of group activity and development that it is impossible to characterize any discrete stages. Thus, the two main approaches to understanding group development are process and stage theories.

Examples of three process theories are discussed here. One of the earliest theories is that of Wilfred Bion (1959), who adapted a psychoanalytic method for group psychotherapy. He believed that the unconscious assumptions, which typically fall into three categories, of a group's members drive group process and its development over time. Some groups are dominated by the assumption of dependence: it is necessary to depend on someone, usually a strong leader. Some groups are pervaded by the fight-flight assumption: others, particularly strangers, are dangerous and need to be either confronted or avoided. In contrast, other groups are characterized by pairing: is necessary to pair with another person to cooperate (e.g., believing that having a child will solve all problems). These assumptions roughly parallel the interpersonal orientations that Karen Horney (1950) has proposed (see chapter 6). Whereas dependence and pairing manifest in the proclivity to move toward others, the fight-flight assumption may manifest in movement against or away from others. Although groups usually settle on one of these assumptions, Bion does not preclude the possibility that more than one may operate in a group. When this happens, particularly complex dynamics can emerge. In contrast to Bion's theory of the impact of unconscious assumptions, Donelson Forsyth (1997) attempts to draw inductively from empirical research. Specifically, he attempts to adapt the personality orientations from the five-factor model (see chapter 6) to groups. He argues that his five group functions—inclusion, intimacy, generativity, stability, and adaptation—are the basis for five of six group processes that operate across time. Specifically, he explains them in the following terms:

Inclusion (big-five factor: extraversion): The tendency for individuals to come together, develop cohesiveness, and develop relationships is a central dynamic that drives the development of groups, regardless of what other processes also take place.

Intimacy (big-five factor: agreeableness): In the context of developing inclusive relationships, groups also have a propensity to generate strong bonds of affection, either as a side effect or as an outcome.

Generativity (big-five factor: conscientiousness): Some groups perform more practical tasks than others, particularly those that are not conveniently accomplished on a solo basis. The drive to accomplish practical tasks and to achieve pragmatic outcomes is a recurrent process in many groups that becomes intertwined with other lines of developmental activity.

Stability (big-five factor: neuroticism): Groups tend to maintain a sense of equilibrium, a feeling of continuity and of predictability. Stability is related to the social-support function of groups.

Adaptation (big-five factor: *openness to experience*): Many groups support exploration, problem solving, and creativity, thus helping members adapt to changing conditions.

Power (Forsyth added this process, which he felt personality researchers had not addressed): He argues that groups are an arena for the exercise of power and the resolution of issues of status and influence, of questions about who calls the shots and of who controls what. Power also involves the dynamics of leadership and competition.

These group processes are meant to reflect lines of dynamic activity that may parallel one another, but it is more likely that they continually interact. Although one line may be more or less prominent, some tend to manifest more at the beginning, middle, or end of a group. They are not stages but rather component processes. The implementation of the associated functions through these lines of dynamic activity is influenced by the larger context of the group, the demands and resources impinging on it, the personality predisposition of the members (e.g., where each falls in the five dimensions of personality), and the ways that members deal with power and influence.

Marshall Poole (1981, 1983; Poole & Roth, 1989) proposes a similar model of three developmental tracks. He argues that groups jump back and forth between tracks of group task, manifest topic, and relationships. He compares the tracks to the intertwined strands of rope; each is present throughout the development of any group, albeit in alternating ascendency. The topic track concerns the development of the actual subject or agenda of the group over time, whereas the relation track deals with the interpersonal relationships among group members. The task track consists of the actual work of the group, whether or not this involves the designated topics or relationships. For example, in a therapy group, the group task may be to achieve self-understanding or to develop better interpersonal skills, but the actual topics of discussion may be much more specific, such as skills for negotiating conflicts with spouses or how to deal with anger. Poole also introduced the notion of break points, or points at which there is a shift from one track to another or a break in the process, such as changed conversations or adjournment.

In contrast to the process models of group development, stage theories assert that there are set stages that most groups go through, however indistinct the transition from one to the other. Notwithstanding slight variations, there is remarkable unanimity among these theorists (for examples from three of the best-known stage theorists—Bernstein [1965], Fisher [1970], and Tuckman [1965]—see table 9.1).

Each theory begins with a group formation stage, variously referred to as preaffiliation, orientation, or forming. The central issue for the group is deciding who is in and who is out, and each member commits to or aborts his

TABLE 9.1: SELECTED STAGE THEORIES OF SMALL-GROUP DEVELOPMENT

BERNSTEIN	FISCHER	TUCKMAN
PREAFFILIATION, IN/ OUT: Struggle of members to decide whether to join in.	ORIENTATION: Members orient themselves to each other and the task.	FORMING: Members learningabout each other, with relationships characterized by dependence and deference.
POWER AND CONTROL, UP/DOWN: Resolution of hierarchy and control issues,often with challenge to leader.	CONFLICT: Tension around tasks and relationships	STORMING: Characterized by competition and conflict in the personal-relations dimension and organization in the task-functions dimension.
INTIMACY, TOWARD/ AWAY: Decisions about closeness and how much to share.	EMERGENCE: The group settles on a system for being and working together.	NORMING: Personal relations characterized by cohesion,and acknowledgment of each member's contributions, along with community building and maintenance.
DIFFERENTIATION: Decisions on roles, specialization, who is responsible for what.		PERFORMING: Not reached by all groups. People work both independently and in subgroups, or as a total unit.
SEPARATION: Decisions of when and how to terminate.	REINFORCEMENT: Members support their new modus operandi through mutual and positive verbal reinforcement.	ADJOURNING: Termination of task behavior and disengagement from relationships. Mutual recognition.

Source: Bernstein (1965, p. 37);Tuckman (1965, p. 63).

or her engagement in the group. The decision involves orientation, and dependence, deference, and the need to achieve a sense of comfort and understanding of the group, its task, and the other members typically characterize interpersonal style. This may range in time from a single session to no more than two or three meetings. As soon as members feel oriented, comfortable, and committed to the group, issues of power and control emerge, often including competitiveness and conflict. This stage, involving the resolution of up-down issues of status and control, has been aptly referred to as storming. Simultaneous with the struggle for control are the planning and negotiation about the goals and modus operandi for any task, whether practical (e.g., conducting a study) or less tangible (e.g., clinical work). For these reasons, most group workers encourage the explicit discussion of issues such as goals, methods, rules, division of labor, and the nature of various roles (e.g., group leader, members). But no matter how careful a group leader is in attempting to explicitly resolve these issues, a competitive or extraverted member usually presents a significant challenge to the leadership, often between the third and sixth meeting. The response to and resolution of this challenge is particularly critical for the future quality of relationships in the group.

Once the group has survived the storming phase of group conflict, it often moves into a phase of relative intimacy in which members settle into their negotiated roles and begin to resolve questions about how close they wish to be with one another, how much they wish to share, and how specifically they wish to work with one another. Tuckman (1965) called this stage norming, as it involves the development of specific norms for interaction. Fisher (1970) called it emergence, as this is time that the work and relationships of the group gel.

The latter stage of emergence is also a time of differentiation, according to Bernstein (1965), and performing, according to Tuckman (1965). Differentiation refers to the development of specializations, of either tasks or roles. The division of labor, particularly in task groups, is associated with performance and is often one of the most productive phases of group activity. But this assumes that the prior stages—inclusion, control, and intimacy—have been successfully achieved. Fisher's (1970) emergence stage is followed by a phase of reinforcement, in which members support one another through mutual and positive verbal reinforcement.

Reinforcement completes Fisher's stages, but both Bernstein and Tuckman point out that there is often a final termination phase of separation or adjourning. This involves not only decisions about when and how to end the group but also an assessment of the experience and tasks achieved, mutual recognition, and emotional disengagement from the group. These stages are not formally identified stages but general tasks, with typical issues, that any given group may or may not successfully navigate. They are, in this sense, similar to Erikson's (1963) epigenetic stages of personal development, in that successful resolution of one stage lays the foundation for the next.

IV. Group Structure

It is often said that structure follows function. Group structures develop out of functions that have emerged in patterns of dynamic activity as a result of repeated interchanges and relationships. These crystallize into predictable structures (e.g., subgroups, roles, norms), which in turn both constrain and establish the platform for future group activity. Structure, when it involves groups, is primarily the structure of relationships, how boundaries are maintained, who talks to whom, and the rules that govern such interchanges. Larger groups, especially task groups such as governing boards, may have formal structures such as systems of subcommittees as well as informal structures. But most groups, especially support and therapy groups, have minimal internal structure of a formal variety. Their leadership structure and the group boundaries constitute a kind of formal structure. For the most part, the structure that emerges is an informal one that involves subgroups, alliances, and the like.

A. Triads and Other Subgroups

Subgroups may range from general friendship groups to more rigidly defined cliques and teams. These may involve dyadic or triadic relationships, or relationships with greater numbers of participants. Of particular importance are triads. Many people can effectively manage a relationship with one other person, but it is more difficult to maintain a balanced relationship with two others—figuring out how to address the subgroup, when to jump in, how to manage potential jealousies. The addition of only one person to a relationship adds considerable complexity, requiring greater empathy, self-confidence, and cognitive complexity on the part of each person involved. For many people, this comes naturally, especially if they have had a successful adolescence and have developed strong peer-to-peer interpersonal skills. It is said that successful group workers tend to come from families with many siblings.

Thus, triads are the proving ground and building blocks of group relationships. They are the bridges from dyadic to group relationships, ones that some never manage to cross. When triads flounder, various phenomena emerge, such as triangling or triangulation, a pernicious pattern of relationships that undercuts both dyadic and group relationships. Murray Bowen

(1978) was among the first to identify this phenomenon, regarding it as the tendency of individuals in a difficult relationship with another person to pull in a third person, often as an ally, which often destabilizes and inflames an already-difficult relationship. Two members of a couple in conflict both air their complaints with a group leader, and each expects the group leader to side with him or her and set the other straight. If the group leader is not careful, he or she will inflame and destabilize the relationship further.

A special version of triangulation is when one person plays victim in relation to a persecutor (real or imagined) and engages a third person as rescuer. The rescuer may overreact, making the persecutor into a new victim and the victim the persecutor, and so on, with the roles often switching around (see figure 9.5). But even when triangulation does not happen so overtly, many people are unable to negotiate the dynamics of third parties entering a difficult dyadic relationship. Being able to maintain a healthy triad is a special skill. Many groups develop an informal structure of loosely defined and shifting dyads, triads, and larger subgroups, which may represent positive relationships that help structure the group. However, when subgroups become overly rigid and disconnected from the larger group, perhaps characterized by in- and out-group attitudes, the structure becomes counterproductive. Important clues to the existence of such sub-groups can be found in the seating arrangements that group members select.

FIGURE 9.5: TRIANGULATION: SHIFTING RELATIONSHIPS IN THREESOMES

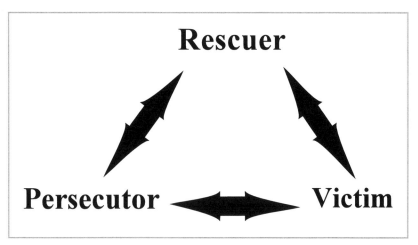

Note: Triangulation or triangling involves the tendency for individuals to be recruited into a rescuer, persecutor, or victim role, and then to see these roles periodically switched (e.g., the rescuer becomes a victim, the victim a persecutor, etc.).

B. Roles

Much of the structure of a group is subtler than the overt organization of subgroups, and it involves the roles and norms that govern behavior. Formal roles (e.g., facilitator, member) and informal roles (e.g., timekeeper, sage, clown, taskmaster) represent sets of social expectations about who does what, in relation to whom, when, and how. A fairly traditional definition of roles is that they are "pattern[s] of behavior organized around the specific rights and duties belonging to a defined position in a social structure" (Germain, 1999, p. 131). Examples include a mother in a family, a supervisor in a workplace, or a therapist in a therapy group. People enter groups with general expectations based on prior experiences and with roles that are iteratively enacted, negotiated, and refined through the group experience. The expectations and roles, along with their associated rules, self-organize into a group structure, with its distinctive patterns of work, communication, and subgroups.

There are various typologies of roles in small groups. For instance, Chiu (2000) proposes that the most common are those of facilitator, proposer, supporter, critic, and recorder. She defines a facilitator as one who "invites group participation, monitors the group's progress, and promotes group harmony" (p. 28). Although formal roles may be defined, many roles—such as proposer, supporter, or critic—shift frequently and can be assumed by the same person. Particularly valuable, especially in task groups, is the role of recorder, who takes minutes. This role is especially important in task groups and for those that meet infrequently, since it provides for a kind of collective group memory and thus better continuity.

C. Norms

In contrast to roles, norms are more specific rules that usually apply to particular situations. They may be prescriptive or proscriptive, defining what needs to done or what is unacceptable. Groups may have norms about membership eligibility, dress, attendance, confidentiality, acceptable discussion topics, dispute resolution, or decision making. Some of these may be discussed and mutually agreed on; others are unspoken and assumed. Norms that have to do with membership, attendance, confidentiality, and group focus are best defined explicitly. Norms that have to do with decision making vary dramatically depending on the type of group. Especially in work groups, its important establish a standard about which decisions will be made by consensus, by majority voting, or by other means. What types of decisions, if any, can the group leader or a subgroup veto? Group leaders need to be careful to help groups sort out what is within the purview of the group to decide on, and which kinds of decisions are in the domain of the individual member, leader, or larger institution or community.

Norms also vary in the range of their application: do they apply to everyone or only to some people, such as newcomers? Some norms may be fastidiously enforced while others are regarded as loose guidelines. Especially in the early stages of a group and for new members, uncertainty about norms tends to have a disquieting and in some cases a silencing effect. Members may be afraid to overstep their bounds. Thus, discussion and clarification of the ground rules of activity, if successfully conducted, tends to stimulate group process. The operation of rules through group process is a powerful illustration of self-organization.

V. Small Groups as Complex Systems

Traditional descriptions of group processes treat the small group as a system, with input, intervening processes, and output. The inputs are the members and the leadership, as well as associated resources, information, and societal expectations and constraints. The leader or spontaneous activities of members may drive transformations. And outputs, such as changed people with new skills and attitudes or tangible work products, complete the transformation, typically one that serves to restore or maintain social equilibrium. In contrast, treating groups as complex systems introduces additional dimensions that permit a far more varied array of dynamical outcomes. The dimensions include multiple levels of analysis, not just the individual level. The resulting patterns of interaction may involve many of the phenomena reviewed in chapter 1: creative or dysfunctional forms of self-organization, development of chaotic dynamics, bifurcation or splitting, and frequently a type of entrainment. Typically, group interactional patterns settle on one or a few strange attractors. One theorist observed that "groups appear to stammer on the edge of chaos" (Bütz, 1997, p. 179).

A. Levels of Analysis

Systems include subsystems. Organizational and community systems include many small-group systems, which in turn include subgroups and individuals. For this reason, some authors (Arrow et al., 2000) have distinguished among the contextual dynamics, or the larger environment that directs and constrains global and local dynamics; the global dynamics, or transformations of the group as a whole; and the local dynamics, or the activities of the constituent individuals and other elements. Groups typically begin as collections of individuals who develop global characteristics as a group the more that they interact. These patterns typically develop from the bottom up; nonetheless, significant top-down influences from the environment often modify such patterns. Thus, the key interactions take place between individuals; among the group, community, and institutional environment; within each subgroup; and within each individual.

B. Networks and Group Relationships

Most researchers consider the key elements of a group system to be the individuals involved. However, Arrow et al. (2000) point out that the situation is actually more complicated. Group networks include three elements: (1) people who join the group, (2) intentions—the hopes, aspirations, and expectations of key parties—embodied in group projects, and (3) resources, including the group's technologies. All three elements become linked in a "functional network of member-task-tool relations" that Arrow et al. call the "coordination network" (p. 50).

All three elements become input to the group. It is not just people who are the input, but people with specific struggles, attitudes, experiences, and skills. Most important, they are people with particular hopes, aspirations, and fears regarding the group experience, and these serve to energize the group or deplete its vitality and cohesiveness. Other inputs include the expectations of sponsors, administrators, group leaders, and significant others in members' lives. These expectations may represent welcome challenges, as may be the case with many task forces or committees, or burdensome demands that the group may prefer not to deal with. Other inputs are the particular issues and problems that group members bring, as well as the skills, knowledge, and interventions of the leader, whether expertise in a substantive area, in resolving problems, in conducting role-plays, or in facilitating insight in members. Unlike a simple physical system in which the inputs may be simple and fairly discrete, both the inputs and the group members have multiple levels of meaning and activity. Diverse and simultaneous streams of people, ideas, information, feelings, resources, and technologies feed into and are transformed through the small-group experience.

C. Complexity in Dynamic Processes

The intervening processes in small groups take place in the context of the preexisting or newly developed relationships and have several nearly universal characteristics: they are iterative, interactive, and nonlinear (see Bütz, 1997; Guastello, 1998; McClure, 1998). They are iterated, or repeated many times, which often is a process of gradual approximation. I explain something that is not understood, I add some facts, rephrase it, and find that I am still not understood, and so I add a few final clarifications. Relationships, by definition, are interactive, even when they seem to be a one-way street. Feedback comes both verbally and nonverbally in the absence of overt communications. In addition, communication is inherently nonlinear. Although some messages may presuppose that material is communicated in a necessary logical sequence, usually it is necessary to loop back and clarify the initial idea once the details have been shared. Whether the work of the group is simply providing emotional support or organizing a political campaign, two of the most critical parts of group process are the relationships discussed, and within them, the various transactions or feedback loops that take place within or among the various dyads, triads, other subgroups, and the group as a whole.

D. Self-Organization

Relationships and their associated transactions typically exhibit self-organization, in that the group settles into distinctive patterns of global activity. These may include recurrent conflict, self-congratulatory activity, or a pattern of domination by two or three members, with others afraid to speak up. These patterns of activity never repeat exactly but rather evidence the characteristics of strange attractors (see chapter 2), in which activity may follow a general sequence but never repeat in the same way. Few groups are so regular as to be governed by periodic attractors. Point attractors are particularly rare, as they eventually result in complete stasis and immobilization.

E. Bifurcation

A common group process is bifurcation or splitting (Guastello, 1998; McClure, 1998). As some parameter increases, say, an atmosphere of perceived risk, a single process splits into two subprocesses, and this bifurcation repeats itself as the parameter increases further, quickly resulting in a chaotic situation. In this example, the development of two subprocesses may involve the breaking up of a general discussion into two subconversations, and eventually by everyone trying to speak at once. The group leader needs to carefully monitor this occurrence and very quickly determine what drives it: Anxiety involving some risk? Anger over someone's inappropriate behavior? The parameter controlling this activity may not always be obvious and may require some exploration once the immediate situation has been resolved (see McClure, 1998).

F. Phase Locking

Another common process in many groups is variously referred to as phase locking, entrainment, or slaving (McClure, 1998). This is the tendency for multiple parallel processes to exhibit a type of synchronization. Phase locking was first observed in some clock shops, where it was observed that the ticking of clocks seemed to automatically synchronize over time. It has also been observed that menstrual cycles of women who live together fall into sync with one another. Similarly, in groups, the mood, activity, and patterns of thinking and relating eventually become a global pattern, one that may provide for a degree of cohesiveness but also may, in its extreme, create a pattern of groupthink (see chapter 7) in which the group loses its ability to consider diverse views and unfavorable data. Nonetheless, phase locking is often not so extreme and is often punctuated by periods of bifurcation and chaotic activity. McClure (1998) points out that change in groups is often second-order change. Certain control parameters change, ones that may be fundamental rules of the group or perhaps its assumptions. Such changes may cause group process to re-form around an alternative dynamic attractor, perhaps after a period of bifurcation.

G. Understanding Complexity in Groups

An understanding of group process and the complex transformations that they go through to produce the outcomes of interest requires an empathic understanding of the motivations, abilities, and opportunities of members. It also requires an ability to take a broader view of the patterns of relationships and work that emerge in groups, of the forces that drive and constrict them, and an appreciation of the strategic importance of group facilitation. Successful intervention in many cases needs to be only minimal, perhaps a particularly incisive and well-timed question or observation. It may, however, occasionally entail major structural interventions. An appreciation of the immense complexity of small groups requires that the group leader not only rely on the rational analysis of groups but also supplement this with empathic, creative, and intuitive forms of problem solving.

VI. Summary

Small groups are treated in this chapter as some of the fundamental building blocks of society, including its institutions and communities. Small groups permit the aggregation of individual preferences and their expression in the larger society, and they perform important socialization and social-control functions. The use of small groups needs to be considered in an evolutionary context, as small groups confer multiple advantages on the individuals involved. One of the key issues is determining when and how those advantages actually take place, and why it is that groups sometimes fail to provide such benefits.

Groups perform multiple functions that can be classified as socio-emotional and task related. The range of groups developed parallels, in a rough fashion, many of the functions and advantages of groups. Groups vary from primary, naturally occurring groups, such as the family, to various secondary groups, such as psychotherapy or psychoeducational groups. Groups also vary on the basis of whether they are externally or internally generated, and whether they are emergent or planned.

This chapter emphasizes that group structure emerges out of the formal and informal functions that groups are expected to fulfill and the ways that these functions become expressed through the processes of group activity and development. The analysis of groups, of their functions, processes, and structures, thus needs to be based on an understanding of their larger social context, of the institutional, community, political, and cultural forces that act on them. Critical areas of group process include the development of cohesiveness, patterns of communication and interaction, decision making, leadership, conflict and power, and development.

An important approach to understanding group process is the stages and lines of group development. Many groups develop along fairly well-understood stages; for instance, one theorist has suggested that these involve forming, storming, norming, performing, and adjourning (Tuckman, 1965). Group structure is considered a kind of crystallization of recurrent dynamic processes in groups. Three types of structure are considered: subgroups, roles, and norms. Subgroup structure is the most easily identified and often involves either dyadic (i.e., two-way) or triadic (i.e., three-way) relationships. Particular attention is paid to triads, including some of the dysfunctional triadic relationships known as triangulation. The structure of a group's roles and norms is no less important.

The final section reviews key concepts from complex systems theories, introduced in chapter 1, relevant to small groups. It makes the point that the transactional and iterative processes are those between members, as well as those among multiple levels of analysis (e.g., local, global, and contextual dynamics). In addition, the relationships also involve the resources of the group, including their technologies and tasks, in addition to the individuals involved. Some of the most relevant complex systems concepts for small groups include those of self-organization, bifurcation, phase locking, second-order change, and strange attractors.

For Further Reading

Arrow, H., McGrath, J. E., & Berdahl, J. L. (2000). *Small groups as complex systems: Formation, coordination, development, and adaptation.* Thousand Oaks, CA: Sage.

Bütz, M. R. (1997). *Chaos and complexity: Implications for psychological theory and practice.* Washington, DC: Taylor & Francis.

Chiu, M. M. (2000). Group problem-solving processes: Social interactions and individual actions. *Journal for the Theory of Social Behavior, 30*(1), 27–49.

Guastello, S. J. (1998). Creative problem solving groups at the edge of chaos. *Journal of Creative Behavior, 32*(1), 38–57.

McClure, B. A. (1998). *Putting a new spin on groups: The science of chaos.* Mahwah, NJ: Erlbaum.

Pepitone, A. (1981). The science of group dynamics: Lessons from the history of social psychology. *American Psychologist, 36,* 972–985.

Toseland, R. W., & Rivas, R. F. (2001). *An introduction to group work practice* (4th ed.). Boston: Allyn & Bacon.

Yalom, I. (1995). *The theory and practice of psychotherapy* (4th ed.). New York: Basic Books.

CHAPTER 10

Families as Complex Systems

VIII. Complex Systems and the Family
IX.   Summary

Families have always shown remarkable resiliency, or flex-
ible adjustment to natural, economic, and social challenges.
Their strengths resemble the elasticity of a spider web, a
gull's skillful flow with the wind, the regenerating power of
perennial grasses, the cooperation of an ant colony, and the
persistence of a stream carving canyon rocks. These are not
the strengths of fixed monuments but living organisms. This
resilience is not measured by wealth, muscle or efficiency
but by creativity, unity, and hope. Cultivating these family
strengths is critical to a thriving human community.
                                                    —BEN SILLIMAN (1995, P. 1)

I. Introduction

The previous chapter pointed out that small groups are among the fundamental building blocks of society. This chapter, in contrast, focuses on families, a particular type of naturally occurring group. Families can be defined
formally in terms of the nuclear and extended family as "one or more people
living in the same household who are related by birth, marriage, or adoption" (U.S. Census Bureau, 2000). They can also be defined more broadly
to include other enduring and committed relationships, such as cohabiting
partners. In either case, it is clear that the functioning of the family has mo-
mentous consequences for both the individual and social institutions. The
family is an enduring nexus of relationships that serves multiple functions
for its members and for society, including procreation, socialization, support, and links with societal institutions and culture.

As important as families may be, they are only one of several levels of
analysis. Individuals can blame neither their successes nor failures on the
family. Resilient families, as described so eloquently in the opening quotation, do not always produce healthy people. Conversely, severe dysfunction
in families does not always lead to the individual breakdown of its members.
Biological endowment, peer relationships, social supports, and a range of
other conditions also make decisive contributions to individual behavior.

As in the foregoing chapter on small groups, this chapter concentrates on
theories and research pertinent to the functioning and dynamics of families.
Of particular importance is the development of families, which parallels and

forms a context for individual development. Family systems theory in the past twenty years has only partially moved from the older cybernetic equilibrium models to ones that embrace the reality of ongoing change. Families can either flounder or thrive at far-from-equilibrium conditions and within immensely complex environments.

The purpose of this chapter is not to explore in depth the implications of family theory for intervention and therapy. Nonetheless, one such implication needs to be mentioned here: recent developments in family theory severely undercut the assumed importance of the confrontation and destabilization of dysfunctional families that has been so central to traditional family therapy approaches. Instead, the chapter stresses the importance of support, collaboration, and empowerment in work with families. To the extent that self-organization occurs in families, therapeutic interventions that rely on external carrots and sticks become less important than facilitating families' natural capacities for mutual support and proactive problem solving. This chapter emphasizes the power of self-selection, of the ability of individuals and families to select and pursue their own solutions despite external roadblocks, notwithstanding the forces of social selection that operate within and beyond the family.

II. Background

The study of family dynamics has developed across several fields. On the one hand, family sociology and social psychology have both contributed substantially to the academic study of healthy families. On the other hand, the field of family therapy, which emerged from several of the human service professions, has generated an impressive body of theory concerned primarily with the study of dysfunctional families, often those whose members exhibit severe psychopathologies, such as schizophrenia or personality disorders (see Yerby, 1995). For example, social work has a long history of family work, which goes back to one of its founders, Mary Richmond (1917), who regarded the family rather than the individual as the primary unit of intervention. As the founder of psychosocial casework, Richmond emphasized the role of multiple environments in family functioning. However, she did not have the benefit of a theory of dynamic systems, which Ludwig Bertanlanffy first introduced in the mid-1940s (see chapter 1 and exhibit 10.1).

The emphasis of the early family theorists, characterized as the first cybernetics, was on understanding the feedback loops that families use to maintain equilibrium and resist change (Pincus, 2001). Feedback loops are recurrent transactional patterns that are often governed by a set point, or

EXHIBIT 10.1: TIMELINE OF THE DEVELOPMENT OF FAMILY SYSTEMS THEORY

1945 Bertanlanffy publishes *General Systems Theory.*

1945 Murray Bowen at Menninger Clinic and Carl Whitaker at Emory initiate work with families.

1948 Whitaker organizes conferences on schizophrenia.

1950 Gregory Bateson begins his work at Palo Alto, California.

1951 Ruesch and Bateson publish *Communication: The Social Matrix of Society;* Bowen conducts experiments with residential treatment of mothers and children at Yale.

1952 Bateson receives a Rochefellow grant for study of community at Palo Alto.

1954 Bateson conducts research on communication in families with schizophrenic members; Bowen conducts research at the National Institute of Mental Health.

1957 Don Jackson publishes "The Question of Family Homeostasis"; Nathan Ackerman starts the Family Mental Health Clinic with Jewish Family Services of New York; and Boszormenyi-Nagy launches the Family Therapy Department at EPPI in Philadelphia. 1959 Don Jackson starts the Mental Health Research Institute.

1961 John E. Bell publishes *Family Group Therapy;* Ackerman and Jackson start the journal *Family Process.*

1963 Jay Haley publishes *Strategies of Psychotherapy.*

1964 Virginia Satir publishes *Conjoint Family Therapy.*

1965 Nathan Ackerman launches the Family Institute (now the Ackerman Institute); Salvador Minuchin is appointed director of the Philadelphia Child Guidance Clinic.

1967 John Watzlawick and colleagues publish *Pragmatics of Human Communication.*

1971 Nathan Ackerman dies.

1972 Bateson publishes *Steps to an Ecology of Mind.*

1974 Minuchin publishes *Families and Family Therapy;* Watzlawick and colleagues publish *Change.*

1976 Haley publishes *Problem-Solving Therapy.*

1980 Milton Erickson and Gregory Bateson die.

1981 Lynn Hoffman publishes *Foundations of Family Therapy.*

1982 Carol Gilligan publishes *In a Different Voice;* the Family Therapy Network is founded by Richard Simon.

1988 Kerr and Bowen publish *Family Evaluation;* Virginia Satir dies.

1990 White and Epston publish *Narrative Means to Therapeutic Ends;* Murray Bowen dies.

1992 Family Institute of New Jersey organized by Monica McGoldrick.

1995 Carl Whitaker and John Weakland die; Jay Haley and Salvador Minuchin retire; and Family Studies Inc. renamed the Minuchin Center.

some rule or expectation about what is or is not acceptable behavior (see chapter 1). Whenever a family member exceeds the permissible boundaries around this set point (e.g., by attempting to marry a person of a different race, class, or religion), other family members may repeatedly react to maintain the desired level of homogeneity. Early family therapists regarded a system as any entity whose parts covary with one another and that maintains equilibrium in an error-activated way (Hoffman, 1981).

Murray Bowen and Carl Whitaker initiated some of the earliest clinical work and theory development in the late 1940s in their work with families with members suffering from schizophrenia. Bowen was known for hospitalizing not only the identified patient but also his or her family, given the assumption that family dynamics were integral to the psychopathological condition. Perhaps the most renowned contributions of the 1950s was Gregory Bateson's research on communication patterns among families with schizophrenic members (see Bateson, Jackson, Haley, & Weakland, 1956). Bateson organized the Mental Health Research Institute in Palo Alto, California, in collaboration with Jay Haley, Don Jackson, Virginia Satir, and John Watzlawick. However, it was John E. Bell whom many regard as the father of family therapy. He was one of the first to engage the family as a group rather than just the identified patient. It was in 1953 that Bell first reported his work to a group of psychologists, and in 1961, he published *Family Group Therapy*, perhaps the most highly regarded contributions to the field.

One of the more significant outcomes of this early research was double-bind theory. In this theory, when one family member, such as a parent, gives mixed messages (e.g., "You're damned if you do and damned if you don't") there are profound implications for the other family members who are subject to such communications. Specifically, a mixed message is transmitted when there are conflicting injunctions on two levels of communication (e.g., verbal and nonverbal) and the recipient is not permitted to acknowledge or otherwise escape from the conflict. The content of the injunctions may vary widely, but it typically involves issues of anger or separation. For example, "You've got to become more independent" and "Something terrible will happen [i.e., someone will die] if we don't stick together."

It was believed that dysfunctional families, which could not deal with conflict, engaged in excessively vague communication, and thus created numerous double binds that tended to lead to schizophrenia. It was acknowledged that double binds happen in many social contexts, not just the family. However, despite numerous attempts to empirically test this theory over the years, results have been equivocal (Koopmans, 1997). Double-bind theory was a central initiative of the early communications school of family treatment, associated with Bateson's Mental Health Research Institute, but it was also part of a larger body of research on the impact of social labeling, associated with Erwin Goffman (1959), Thomas Szasz (1960), and Ronald Laing (1961).

By the 1960s, interest in family dynamics had broadened considerably to include an array of dynamical patterns. In 1960, Bateson's colleague John Weakland proposed a version of the double-bind theory involving three-party interactions (Hoffman, 1981). Out of this emerged various theories of triadic (or three-way) interactions, such as the persecutor-victim-rescuer triangle discussed in chapter 9 of this book. At about the same time, second cybernetics emerged (Pincus, 2001), which broadened the understanding of feedback loops to include not just negative, or deviating-controlling, transactions but also positive, or deviation-amplifying, transactions.

The second cybernetics also focused on multiple system levels, of systems nested in systems. Jay Haley (1959) attempted to redefine schizophrenia as a conflict of groups and suggested that the condition was a name for behavior that emerges out of conflict between warring family triangles. When an individual cannot deal with conflict, he or she often defends against it with ambiguity. Perhaps one of the most interesting dynamics is scapegoating, a way of relocating a family split or conflict to a single individual, such as an adolescent who is acting out. It had been assumed that whenever families ask for help for a symptomatic member, they attempt to maintain family equilibrium by projecting the systemic problems onto that person. It has been observed that success in treating a symptomatic individual merely displaces the pathology elsewhere in the family. At the same time that interest in family systems has continued to grow, development of the underlying theory and research has languished.

There have been attempts to correct the earlier assumptions about the impact of dysfunctional families, such as the assumption that certain schizophrenogenic mothers are responsible for their offspring's schizophrenia because of such traits as their coldness or aloofness. Along with this there has been an enhanced focus on family strengths and resiliency in an effort to integrate an understanding of normal family dynamics with more clinically based work on dysfunctional families. Others have attempted to deconstruct families through a narrative approach, which involves a focus on the culture of families and the stories that structure and guide their development.

III. Crosscutting Assumptions and Concepts

There are several assumptions that characterize the array of approaches to family systems, and those assumptions can guide and inform understanding while creating blind spots to alternative explanations. Among the least controversial of these assumptions is that families are a fundamental influence in life. Yet in recent decades, studies in areas as diverse as genetics, peer relationships, and cultural and economic systems have highlighted some of the limitations of the role of families. The assumption that history repeats itself emphasizes that the transmission of family influences happens not only within generations but also over multiple generations. Family systems theorists generally assume that a central dynamic in families is the tension between the needs for separateness and connectedness; that the inherent instability of this conflict is a central motivating factor in family life. Finally, family systems theorists usually assume that the sources of distress originate in family relationships and only then become internalized in individuals—not the other way around. As influential as family dynamics are, this may be an unnecessary assumption, as it minimizes the possibilities of individuals having an impact on the larger pattern of family relationships.

A. Interaction

Family relationships are understood as the global pattern of relationships that self-organize out of innumerable discrete interactions. Thus, analysis of family dynamics entails the analysis of multiple interactions or transactions. Interactions may be as simple as a critical look and cynical comment between two people, or they may be complex sets of sequential behaviors on the part of an entire family. This may be exemplified by the confession of a family secret, followed by rapt attention, angry questioning, and the mobilization of practical and emotional supports. Such interactions involve both behaviors and communications, intended and unintended. Such interactions are typically conceptualized in terms of the feedback loops (positive, negative, or a combination of those) discussed in previous chapters.

Symptoms are understood only in this larger context. For example, one researcher concluded, "A suicide attempt is not an outcome, but an event embedded in a more complete and complex pattern of interaction in some families" (Chamberlain, 1995, p. 1). Chamberlain (1995) found that suicide can occur in situations of extremely positive or extremely negative feedback. Another example is Gottman's (1993) cascade theory of marital dissolution, which hypothesizes that cascades occur when the number of negative communications dramatically exceeds the number of positive communications. This sets into motion negative attributions, distancing, a recasting of the entire history of the marriage, and finally divorce (Ward, 1995). A

key notion relevant to cascade theory is that of the incremental approximation of a goal as a result of repeated transactions. For instance, an explanation is given, feedback is received, the unheard part of the message is
restated, and this is repeated until the message is successfully conveyed or
perhaps rejected.

B. Communication and Metacommunication

One the most important kinds of interaction is communication. Family
system theorists emphasize that communication, both intended and unintended, constantly occurs on multiple levels. Family members attempt to
convey information not only through their speech but also through their
tone of voice, physical posture, eye contact, position, and actions. All of
these may support, modify, or contradict the overt message. Some of the
information conveyed may be regarded as metacommunication, or communications about the communication process itself, including the desired
relationship.

Matthijs Koopmans (1998) emphasizes the importance of communication in the self-regulation of families and in the maintenance of consistent
feedback patterns. In contrast, Jay Haley (1959) points out that, particularly
in families with schizophrenic members, levels of communication are habitually confused, which severely inhibits interpersonal learning. These conflicting messages and resulting double binds serve to confuse and mystify.
The double bind theory is the basis of the notion of serial or transactional
disqualification, which Haley (1959) first proposed and Sluzki, Beavin, Tarnopolsky, and Verón (1967) later developed. This involves the marginalization of family members and the inhibition of initiative and healthy problem
solving. Sluzki et al. categorized the various types of disqualification as eva-
sive changes of subject; sleight of hand, whereby the response to an issue
is so confused that it is missed; and status disqualifiers, when an issue is
minimized because the speaker presents him- or herself as in a position of
superior knowledge. Nonverbal disqualifiers include stonewalling, silence,
and emotional cutoffs. Wynne, Ryckoff, Day, and Hirsch (1958) identified
particular examples of disqualification involving multiple and conflicting
levels of communication, such as pseudomutuality, pseudohostility, and the
rubber fence. Pseudomutuality refers to the tendency of some families to
use a facade of mutuality for the purpose of masking conflicts; in contrast,
pseudohostility involves the use of superficial splits and constant arguing
to maintain distant relationships. The rubber fence refers to the shifting
and inconsistent boundaries that were believed to characterize families with

members suffering from schizophrenia. Expressed emotions are not as they would seem to be in such families, and even the presumed permeability of family boundaries may be illusory and highly restraining.

C. Levels of Change

Just as communication involves multiple levels, so does change. Magorah Maruyama (1968) differentiated between the maintenance of form (morphostasis) and its change (morphogenesis). Closely related is the distinction between first-order and second-order change. First-order change is merely a change in behavior or communications, which may or may not mean a fundamental morphogenetic change. What Maruyama, and many family theorists, are most interested in is second-order change, or change in the underlying rules, beliefs, or values that govern external interactions and communications. These rules are often much more difficult to change. They may involve social norms concerning permissible behaviors or modes of communication, who talks to whom, and in what way. They may involve the basic values and associated criteria for decision making. These tend to be tacit, unacknowledged, and thus more resistant to change than external patterns. Second-order change, thus, consists of changes in the rules of the game, in the underlying set points, permissible boundaries, and corrective actions that govern the negative and positive feedback transactions that occur in families.

D. Family Culture

The family systems field has increasingly focused on family culture, viewing families as "continuous entities with rules, beliefs, and values that shape and are shaped by individual members over time" (Yerby, 1995, p. 339). Unlike a focus on individual rules, the focus on family culture involves the larger system of rules, beliefs, and values that endures over time. It is not enough to identify a particular rule, but rather it is necessary to identify the aggregate effect of the system of rules that governs family life.

A manifestation of family culture are family paradigms, a concept introduced by Reiss (1981), who applied Thomas Kuhn's notion of scientific paradigms to families. For Reiss, the key dimensions of family paradigms vary between families, typically by the degree to which the family believes that the world is ordered and predictable, the degree to which the family believes that social opportunities are accessible to each member, and the extent to which the family relates new events to its own history. Family paradigms involve the ways that a family conceives of what a family is and might be, and thus are a critical component of the particular system of rules and beliefs that operate in a particular family environment.

Closely connected, and in a sense a consequence of certain types of family paradigms, are family secrets. Forbidden or taboo thoughts or behaviors are often a consequence of certain types of rigid family paradigms that perpetuate the suppression and festering of emotional wounds, ones that, like psychiatric symptoms, both express and hide important longings and fears.

E. Attempts at Integration

There have been several recent attempts to bring together the diverse strands of family systems theory. For example, the Finnish family theorist Jarl Wahlström (2007) classifies family systems theories into those that describe information processing, describe how families use language, and describe patterns of action and communication. This is similar to Pincus's (2001) 5-R model, which argues that it is necessary to understand the following five dimensions:

1. Rules: These may apply to individuals or groups and are the principles that govern action and communication.
2. Roles: These may be either generic (e.g., parent, son) or specific (e.g. peacekeeper, clown).
3. Relationships: Relationships form when rules and roles interact between two or more family members.
4. Realities: Pincus (2001) defines realities as "shared, family-relevant cognitive structures or schemes" (p. 143).
5. Response: The pattern of family functioning that results from the interaction of the foregoing rules, roles, relationships, and realities.

Pincus suggests that family systems result from the self-organization of the interactions of the first four of these Rs to collectively generate the fifth R, the response pattern. He suggests that the five Rs permit an understanding of how bottom-up personality factors and top-down cultural factors come together to account for patterns of family interaction.

Figure 10.1 shows an application of Pincus's perspective and how family dynamics in the central circle are nested in the larger social systems. Here, realities are assumed to include multiple external environments (e.g., work, recreation, neighborhood) that modify, for better or for worse, the feedback

FIGURE 10.1: INTERRELATIONSHIP OF KEY CONCEPTUAL ELEMENTS OF FAMILY SYSTEMS

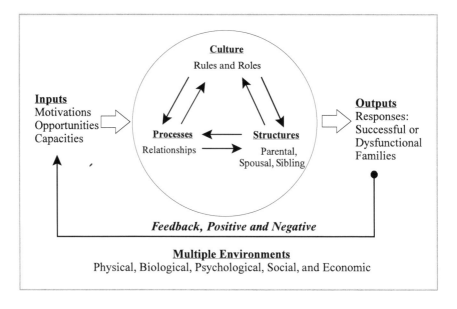

loops that connect a family's outputs with its inputs. In each family there are innumerable feedback loops that involve its relationships; its internalized culture as contained in its rules, realities, and paradigms; and its established structures, such as the parental or child subsystems.

IV. Functions and Strengths of Families

A. Functions

Therapists who take the family systems perspective have traditionally been interested in dysfunctional families, but investigators in the fields of family sociology and social psychology have been much more interested in the roles of families in the larger society and their strengths. Functionalists are primarily interested in understanding the standard ways in which families contribute to society. There are any number of such functions that have been identified (see Horwitz, 2002). Most traditional lists, at a minimum, include the regulation of sexuality, the facilitation of procreation, and the primary socialization of children. Many of these lists also include the following functions:

- Economic and especially nonmarket production
- Protection and support (including emotional support) of family members, especially children
- Linkage with the larger society
- Maintenance of boundaries and privacy vis-à-vis larger society
- Provision of a sense of meaning and purpose
- Mediation of conflict
- Problem solving and information processing

Families carry out a range of social functions and expectations such that they mirror and represent the larger society while also buffering and protecting members from the unsavory aspects of society. Thus, analysis of families cannot be restricted to purely intrafamily processes; it also must consider the inputs (e.g., tangible financial or material factors, or intangible cultural, emotional, and informational resources) and, most important, the outputs, especially with respect to the successful or unsuccessful performance of social functions.

B. A Normative Model of Family Functioning

Among the best known of the social psychological models of normative family functioning is the equilibrium or cybernetic model of David Kantor and William Lehr (1975). Their model is specifically known as the distance-regulation model because it concerns the ways that families regulate internal relationships. Kantor and Lehr observe that "family systems are constantly engrossed in the task of regulating traffic in accord with their goals" (p. 64). In this cybernetic-like model, they make active use of the metaphor of a thermostat, which includes various set points as defined by "targets or goals made by two or more people who are systematically bound in a social-biological arrangement" (p. 18). They also emphasize information processing, commenting that families are "organizationally complex, open, adaptive, and information processing systems" (p. 10). Yet Kantor and Lehr also argue, "It is almost impossible to overstate the importance of family meaning regulation in a society that is intellectually concerned with the meaning or meaninglessness of existence" (p. 52).

The distance-regulation model consists of several key components: target dimensions, access dimensions and mechanisms of family process, the subsystems of the family and their interfaces, three family-process types, and the interaction system of four player parts. The target dimensions consist of goals involving affect, power, or meaning, the same motivations and goals identified in several preceding chapters of this book. They assume that all individuals are driven by interests in certain types and combinations of feelings or subjective states; control, efficacy, or power; and knowledge or meaning. In contrast, the access dimensions involve the arenas or means for achieving the target dimensions of space, time, and energy. Every goal, whether of a child seeking affection or a parent trying to achieve control, necessarily involves considerations of physical and psychological space, available time, and the resources and energy to navigate through spatial and temporal structures to attain the desired end. Actions are performed through access dimensions and in relation to the target dimensions. Actions are carried out in the various subsystems of the family (equivalent to the notion of family structure). Kantor and Lehr categorize the subsystems into family unit, interpersonal, and personal; or the system of the whole, subgroups, and individual person. Each system and subsystem has particular boundaries that help define the access dimensions of space, time, and energy.

For Kantor and Lehr (1975), the family system is primarily an action system that consists of players' multiple strategies and associated feedback loops. They define a strategy as "purposive patterns of moves toward a target or goal" made by two or more family members (p. 18). Possible roles for family members are mover, follower, opposer, and bystander.

C. Family Resiliency

In recent years there has been a growing interest in the notion of family resiliency (see chapter 6). Froma Walsh (2003), of the University of Chicago, has pointed out that resilience involves more than simply handling stress but also the capacity for growth. Resiliency is the ability to bounce back in the face of adversity. Indeed, models such as Kantor and Lehr's provide a basic understanding of the various feedback loops that enable this kind of adaptability in families. Walsh argues that it is important to think about adaptability in the larger context of human ecology and development, as well as social systems change. In contrast to many clinicians who are interested in the dynamics of chronically dysfunctional families, others have occasionally emphasized an idealized view of the family. The astute family worker, however, recognizes both as possibilities. Such workers are slow to jump to conclusions and are interested in why some families can achieve a kind of relational synergy that is greater than the sum of its parts. Conversely, such workers are concerned with why the strengths of individuals in other families seem to cancel one another out. Important clues to this conundrum are found in the study of family development, to which we now turn.

V. Family Development

Just as there are stages in the life cycle of individuals, there are also stages in the development of the family. Family stages of development demonstrate considerable variation and levels of achievement, especially considering the types of family units. Family development theory assumes that family behavior is a direct result of past experiences of the family, that families develop in predictable ways, and that families perform specific functions based on the family's stage of development (Friedman, Bowden, & Jones, 2002). Many researchers have settled on models that depend on certain well-defined markers, such as the birth of the first child or the last child leaving home.

A. Couple and Marital Development

Several of the stage theories begin with a stage of coupling, which includes the partners' courtship and evolving marital relationship. Individuals may be attracted to potential mates because they envision the possibility of re-creating their family of origin. Conversely, individuals from unhappy backgrounds may seek mates that they hope will correct deficiencies in a parent of the opposite sex; for example, an individual may have as a high priority avoiding marriage with a distant or abusive partner. On the whole, research has shown that individuals often marry others of similar intelligence, values, interests, and personality characteristics. A related issue in the study of marital relationships is complementarity, as in the popular notion that opposites attract (e.g., a dominant man and a passive woman being attracted to each other). Psychoanalysis had initially endorsed this theory of the complementarity of need (Winch, 1958). However, there have been few theories in the social sciences as soundly repudiated as that of Winch (Gottman, Murray, Swanson, et al., 2002). This repudiation of Winch's work does not to say that partners do not, sometimes complement one another, but that relationships emerge out of complex combinations of both similar and opposing characteristics.

Most studies of marriage involve fairly nonsystemic theories or extrapolations from case studies. However, recent research on marital relationships has demonstrated the possibilities of rigorous time-series analyses that focus on long term and nonlinear patterns of marital development. Gottman et al.'s (2002) provocatively titled *The Mathematics of Marriage* reports the most outstanding examples. They attempt to mathematically model marital dissolution and found support for the notion that "(1) unhappily married couples appear to engage in long chains of reciprocated negativity, and (2) there is a climate of agreement created in the interaction of happily married couples" (p. 17). They were able to show that in healthy marriages the ratio of positive to negative communications is about 5 to 1, and in unhealthy marriages, only about .8 to 1 or less, a ratio that was highly predictive of divorce (see also Fredrickson & Losada, 2005). Other phenomena associated with ailing marriages are the following:

- Triumph of negative over positive affect
- Negative affect reciprocity (relates with inability to self-sooth)
- Demand-withdrawal pattern
- Negative behaviors, or "four horsemen of the apocalypse": (1) criticism, (2) defensiveness, (3) contempt, and (4) stonewalling or listener withdrawal, particularly with men (p. 22).

Gottman et al. also found several mechanisms implicated in failed marriages. One was emotional inertia and withdrawal. They commented, "Even before being influenced, the uninfluenced set-point is more negative" (p. 142). Thus, when conflict begins, partners induce each other to become progressively more negative. Over time, such dysfunctional patterns become structurally embedded in the marriage, and any semblance of a positive steady state is lost.

Gottman et al. propose the core triad of balance theory, which involves certain cascades of marital breakdown (figure 10.2). The core triad refers to the interactive effects of three dimensions. First is P-space, or the surplus of positive over negative behaviors in the marriage (in previous research they had found that this was one of the factors most predictive of divorce). Second is Q-space, which refers to the overall perception of the partner and the well-being of the marriage. Third is the physiological response to conflict, such as diffuse physiological reactivity (DPA) or the inability to self-soothe, which, like the Q-Space, aggravates the effects of an unfavorable ratio of positive to negative interactions. An unfavorable collective impact of the three dimensions—the core triad of balance—generates emotional flooding and negative attributions. The crumbling marriage causes a negative halo effect, not a positive one, in which each partner is prompted to reflexively interpret the other's behaviors in the most unfavorable light. This leads to emotional cutoffs and distancing, which in turn induce partners to begin to recast the marriage as a mistake or failure. By the time the cascade of negative behaviors, physiological responses, attributions, distancing, and negative conclusions has reached a crescendo, divorce is often close at hand. Unfortunately, Gottman et al. (2002) hardly considered the impact of

FIGURE 10.2: CASCADES OF MARITAL DISSOLUTION: CORE TRIAD OF BALANCE THEORY OF GOTTMAN AND COLLEAGUES

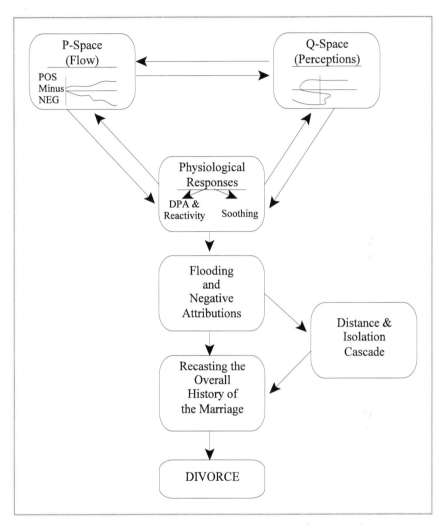

Source: Adapted from Gottman, Murray, Swanson, Tyson, & Swanson (2002, p. 253).

particular events, such as the birth of the first child, major disabilities, the death of a child, and unemployment, among other environmental impacts. Nonetheless, their model is unique in that it is a truly dynamic model, based on extensive research and multivariate data analyses with some of the most current nonlinear modeling techniques.

In a revision of the theory that focuses on the repair of dysfunctional marriages, Gottman et al. (2002) also hypothesized that friendship is the foundation of successful marriages, and that there are several elements essential to the creation of positive affect in a nonconflictual relationship. One such element is an "emotional bank account," in which a couple builds up a reservoir of trust, respect, and caring. This enables positive sentiment override, or a positive balance in the emotional bank account, which permits the partners to view each other's negative behaviors in a positive light. This also contributes to the successful regulation or management of conflict, something that is much more important than conflict resolution. Finally, the authors stress the importance of couples developing shared symbolic meanings that provide a common framework for the ongoing relationship.

B. Traditional Stage Models

Most theories of family development are less analytical than descriptive. One of the traditional and best-known family development theories is Duvall's (1957) eight-stage model:

1. Married couples with no children
2. Childbearing families in which the oldest child is younger than thirty months
3. Families with preschool children, with the oldest child between two and a half and six
4. Families with school-age children, with the oldest child between six and thirteen
5. Families with teenagers, with the oldest child between thirteen and twenty
6. Families with young adults, beginning when the oldest child leaves home and ending when the youngest child leaves home.
7. Middle-aged parents, including the beginning of retirement and empty nesters
8. Aging family members, beginning with the partner's retirement and ending at death

Ellen Galinsky (1987) proposes a more in-depth, six-stage characterization of the stages of parental development:

1. Image-making stage: During pregnancy, parents form and re-form images of the anticipated birth and plan for the new family.
2. Nurturing stage: At this time, parents adjust their expectations to their actual experience, a process that occurs from the time of the

baby's birth to a toddler's use of the word *no* at about the age of eighteen to twenty-four months. This is a time of both attachment and of questioning. Parents question their priorities and the use of their time.

3. Authority stage. Between the age of two to four or five years, the parents develop their style for handling discipline and authority.

4. Interpretive stage. During the child's preschool years, including preadolescence, the most salient task is interpretation, especially as it pertains to the self-concepts of the child and the parents. Parents also need to develop ways to interpret the outside world for their children.

5. Interdependent stage. During the teenage years, families must often rework the original solutions to the earlier stages, especially the authority stage, as well as finding new and more equal ways to relate with their children.

6. Departure stage. At this time, the central task is for parents to evaluate their children's new independence but also the entirety of their parenting experience.

As families age, the individual developmental trajectories of children and parents often become linked. Children frequently struggle with issues that stimulate parents' memories, feelings, and reactions associated with the corresponding stages in the parents' own upbringing. For instance, a child's effort to separate may stimulate a defensive or empathic response from a parent that depends on how successful the parent was in separating at a similar age in his or her life. It is not unusual for parents to attempt to live out their own unfulfilled aspirations through children. This may give the parents a second chance to work through earlier unresolved conflicts, but the phenomenon can hinder the child's own development.

Research on family development is still in its infancy. Just as the understanding of processes of individual development is hamstrung by immense variability, so is family development. Much of the theory and research has focused on the traditional nuclear family. This research has done well in elucidating development with the subgroup, but alternative types of families, such as those without children, blended families, or gay or lesbian families, have been neglected. In addition, there has emerged only recently a literature on development in elderly families, with or without adult children (Yerby, 1995). Family stage theories assume a greater level of stability or equilibrium within stages than is justified, often neglecting the possibility of multiple and alternating patterns of functioning (Gottman et al., 2002).

Finally, it needs to be noted that many of these theories are skewed toward the experience of middle-class families and give short shrift to the role of the larger sociocultural environments.

VI. Family Structures and Types

A. Typologies Based on Membership and Relationship

Emerging out of the ongoing functioning and development of families are the structures that define the various family types. There have traditionally been two approaches to the characterization of the different kinds of family structures: one based on membership and the other based on the kind of relationships between the members. At the most basic level, families usually fall into one of the several categories described in exhibit 10.2.

Families also vary in the types of relationships that members have with one another. One of the first typologies was that of Salvador Minuchin (1967), which was based on his study of families of delinquent boys. He distinguishes between disengaged families and enmeshed families. Disengaged families have "an atomistic field; family members have long moments in which they move as in isolated orbits, unrelated to each other. They act as parts of a system so loosely interlocked that it challenges the clinician's notion that a change in one part of a system will be followed by compensatory changes in other parts" (Hoffman, 1981, p. 72).

In contrast, enmeshed families have little internal structure and few boundaries. They are often characterized by high levels of expressed emotion, in which there is little restraint, overstimulation, few opportunities for dyadic relationships and other subgroups, constant attributions of feelings and thoughts, and few opportunities for members to express individual feelings or viewpoints. The healthy family is believed to fall someplace in the middle of this continuum. The enmeshed-disengaged continuum has become the most popular approach to the description of family structure and types. One such example is illustrated in figure 10.3, which shows Beaver's cross-sectional model of family types (see Hoffman, 1981). Beaver combines Minuchin's disengaged-engaged, or centrifugal-centripetal continuum, with that of levels of family functioning, along the horizontal axis. Whereas families that function on a low level, with poor boundaries and confused communications, usually are found at the extremes and rarely in the middle, highly functioning families are usually located closer to the middle of the continuum. This model also serves to relate individual pathology with family type, suggesting that sociopathic offspring are associated with disengaged

---

EXHIBIT 10.2: MAJOR TYPES OF FAMILIES

1. **Nuclear:** Two parents and one or more children
2. **Single-parent:** One caretaker, and one or more children
3. **Extended:** A nuclear or single-parent family, with one or more relatives living in the home or in close proximity, and regularly involved
4. **Blended or reconstituted:** Typically a remarriage, where one or both partners brings children from their previous marriage into a new home (also called an amalgamated family)
5. **Cohabitation partnership:** Typically involves two unmarried individuals living together, gay or straight, with or without children (often in a common-law marriage)
6. **Cross-generational:** Families with three or more generations in the same household, either aged parent(s) of the partners or grandchildren
7. **Same-sex parent:** Gay or lesbian partnerships, married or unmarried, with children
8. **Joint/shared custody:** Two divorced parents living apart, with children commuting back and forth, or with out-of-home parent highly involved in caretaking
9. **Substitute care:** Families in which the children are present on a provisional basis, such as in foster care or guardianship (does not include families with adopted children)
10. **Community families:** Families with multiple caretakers and children, typically involved in a communal living arrangement with shared parenting responsibilities (e.g., some kibbutzim in Israel)
11. **Commuter:** Families living apart, for example, with husband and wife living in separate cities because of work responsibilities, and only visiting weekly or monthly

---

families, and those with process forms of schizophrenia often come from enmeshed families. However, this remains only a hypothesis, as efforts to link individual pathology with particular family structures have generally been inconclusive.

Other typologies focus on power relationships. For example, Kantor and Lehr's (1975) three family types parallel the family political arrangements of authoritarian, anarchist, and democratic regimes. Some have attempted to define more process-oriented typologies, such as Lynn Hoffman's

FIGURE 10.3: OVERVIEW OF BEAVER'S CROSS-SECTIONAL MODEL OF FAMILY TYPES

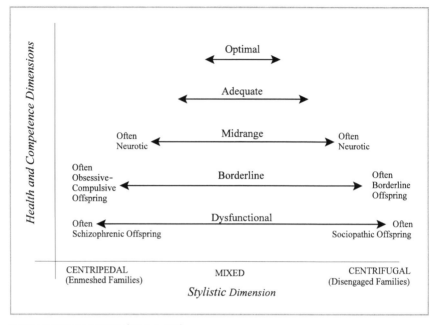

Source: Beaver & Hampson (2002, p. 555).

(1981) spiral platters of family organization, pointing out that families often shift among multiple states of quasi equilibrium or, in the language of complex systems, between alternative basins of attraction or strange attractors.

B. Use of Genograms

One of the more useful approaches to understanding family structure, more than locating the family in a typology such as the foregoing, is the use of the genogram. A genogram is a type of family-tree diagram that lays out the essential relationships and events pertinent to the structure of a particular family. Figure 10.4 provides a summary of the key symbols and other conventions used in drawing genograms. The diagrams are used extensively in assessment, as they facilitate the location of central conflicts, problematic relationships, or intergenerational patterns that otherwise are easily overlooked. There are several commercial computer programs that practitioners can use to draw such diagrams.

FIGURE 10.4: CHARTING INTERGENERATIONAL FAMILY PATTERNS: USE OF THE GENOGRAM

Drawing a genogram, either by hand or through the use of a graphic computer program, facilitates the identification of key patterns in the identification of intergenerational family dynamics. Common symbols and examples are as follows:

Depicting Individuals:

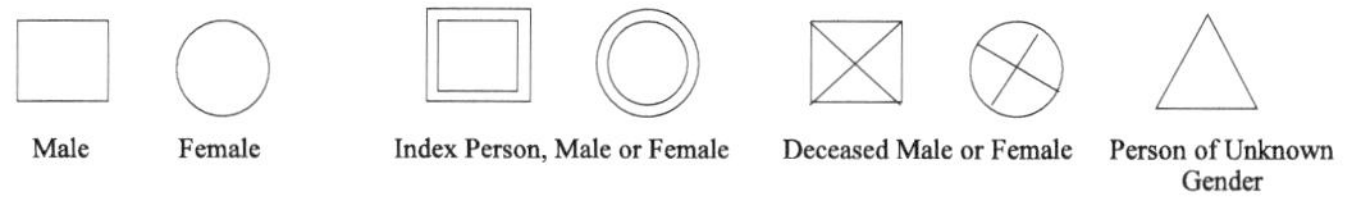

| Male | Female | Index Person, Male or Female | Deceased Male or Female | Person of Unknown Gender |

Couple Relationships:

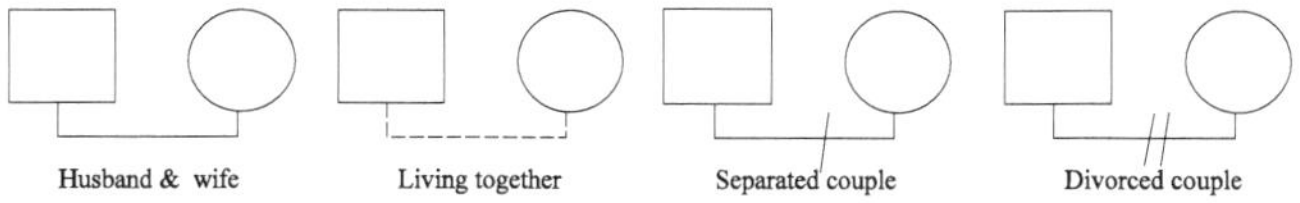

Husband & wife | Living together | Separated couple | Divorced couple

Parent-Child Relationships:

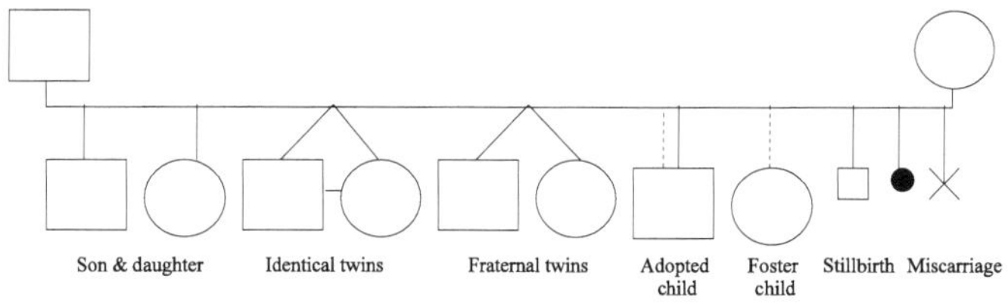

Son & daughter | Identical twins | Fraternal twins | Adopted child | Foster child | Stillbirth | Miscarriage

Children, and other persons, are listed from oldest to youngest, left to right

Other Relationships:

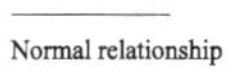

Normal relationship

The relationships below can be superimposed on the family relationships listed above. They may be horizontal, vertical, or diagonal in orientation.

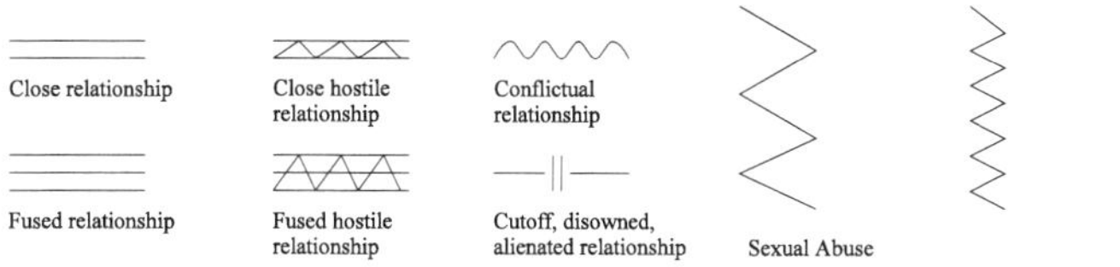

Close relationship | Close hostile relationship | Conflictual relationship

Fused relationship | Fused hostile relationship | Cutoff, disowned, alienated relationship | Sexual Abuse

Example of a Genogram:

The above symbols are integrated into a multi generational chart, depicting the most salient facts of the family organization. Additional information, such as age, location, relevant dates, and other notes, can be inserted in the chart. This is a small example; most charts usually contain considerably more detail.

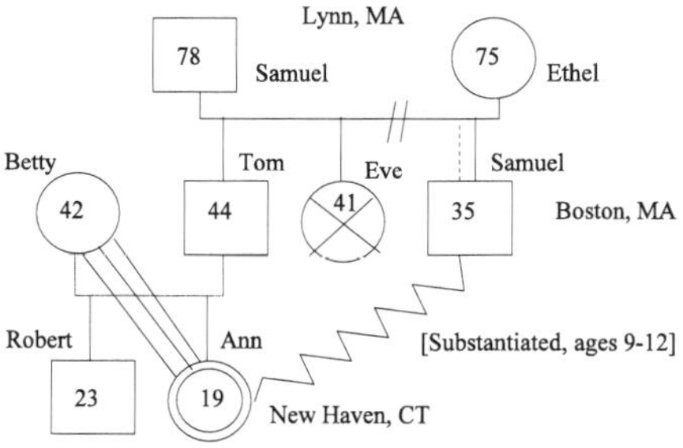

Lynn, MA

78 Samuel — 75 Ethel

Betty 42 | Tom 44 | Eve 41 | Samuel 35 | Boston, MA

Robert | Ann | [Substantiated, ages 9-12]

23 | 19 | New Haven, CT

VII. Approaches to Family Systems

Most theories of family systems are also therapeutic models or approaches; in fact, it is often not possible to separate these. Because most contemporary family systems theorists have evolved unique blends of perspectives derived from their predecessors and from their own ideas, there has been considerable overlap in the approaches. For this reason, there are no universal typologies of family systems approaches. Gurman and Kniskern (1991), however, have proposed a frequently cited one. They classified family systems approaches into the following categories:

- Structural family therapy (e.g., Colapinto, Minuchin, & Minuchin, 1989; Minuchin, 1974)
- Conjoint family therapy (e.g., Satir, 1998)
- Contextual therapy (e.g., Boszormenyi-Nagy, 1991)
- Strategic therapy (e.g., Madanes, 1981)
- Brief therapy
- Milan systemic therapy (e.g., Boscolo, Cecchin, Hoffman, & Penn, 1987)
- Narrative therapy (e.g., Freedman & Combs, 1996).

This section, however, departs from this typology to briefly review several of the most popular approaches. It does not attempt an exhaustive description of any one of them.

A. The Communications School

The background section of this chapter discussed the seminal contributions during the 1950s of several theorists associated with the Mental Research Institute at Palo Alto, California, such as Watzlawick, Jackson, Bateson, Haley, and Satir. A central theme of this school is the centrality of communications, or the idea that the family system is a multilevel system of communicative feedback loops. Bateson's (1972) application of Bertrand Russell's theory of logical types was applied to understand family dysfunction, much of which was viewed as resulting from excessive ambiguity, mind reading, and especially disavowed conflicts between messages sent on different levels (e.g., verbal and nonverbal). These scholars introduced the notion of metacommunication (i.e., communication about communication) and the relationship at hand. Double-bind theory was quickly elaborated into the theory of triangles, which became a central element in the analysis of family structure.

The preceding perspective was then refined and amalgamated with other clinical theories. Wynne et al. (1958) integrated the perspective with psycho-analytic thinking, coining terms such as *pseudomutuality* and *pseudohostility* to characterize the "strangely unreal quality of positive and negative emotions" (Hoffman, 1981, p. 35) in dysfunctional families, or the ways that feeling is expressed in an inauthentic manner. Wynne et al. focused on the dynamic interplay among the various triangles in the family, between the alliances and splits, as a means of maintaining equilibrium.

Virginia Satir (1972, 1978) combined communications concepts with those from humanistic and transpersonal psychology, to create an important offshoot of the communications school (see profile 10.1). She explains that her approach, referred to as conjoint family therapy (1963), works with personal experiences and aims to help family members experience the value of the individual. She believed that therapists needed to employ multiple levels of communication to convey the relational qualities found in families and to bring about change in them. The approach draws on various feeling and communicative exercises and games, such as family sculpture. It emphasizes the management of difference as the challenge that gets most families into trouble. Her approach has also been referred to as a human-validation process model, which entails open communications, enhancement of self-esteem, encouragement of growth, and transformation of extreme rules into useful and functional rules.

Jay Haley (1987) developed another offshoot of the communications approach that has been variously referred to as strategic, paradoxical, or problem-solving therapy. Haley studied with the master hypnotherapist Milton Erickson and, on the basis of this work, he developed an integration of pragmatic problem-solving and creative techniques to engage clients through the use of paradoxical instructions (e.g., prescribing symptoms) and strategic attempts to defocus from the identified patient. Haley's 1973 book *Uncommon Therapy* has become a classic, illustrating his theories and techniques with a rich and provocative array of clinical vignettes.

B. Bowenian Theory

Murray Bowen (b. 1913–d. 1990) developed one of the most influential approaches in the family systems field. Bowen began his career at the Menninger Clinic in the 1940s and became involved with a five-year research initiative at the National Institute of Mental Health (NIMH) in Bethesda, Maryland, which involved hospitalizing families of schizophrenic individuals for extended periods. He then left NIMH in 1959 for an appointment in the Department of Psychiatry at Georgetown University Medical Center,

PROFILE 10.1: FAMILY SYSTEMS
PIONEER: VIRGINIA SATIR, 1916–
1988

Virginia Satir, born in Wisconsin in 1916, has come to be known as the mother of family systems therapy and the Columbus of family therapy. She developed the Satir model, which emphasizes personal growth and self-acceptance. She regarded therapy as able to help individuals and families not only deal with pain and difficulties but also achieve inner joy and happiness (see Andreas, 1991).

Even as a young child she was fascinated with families: she is reported to have said, "I'd be a children's detective on parents." She earned a master's degree in social work from the University of Chicago's School of Social Service Administration and later worked at the Dallas Child Guidance Center and the Illinois State Psychiatric Institute. Satir worked closely with the Bateson group in Palo Alto, California, helping to start the Mental Research Institute there and organizing one of the nation's first training programs in family therapy.

Satir conducted numerous trainings in family treatment over the years and authored a dozen books. Among the best known are *Conjoint Family Therapy* (1964), *Peoplemaking* (1972), and *The New Peoplemaking* (1998). She is known

> "I believe the greatest gift I can conceive of having from anyone is to be seen by them, heard by them, to be understood and touched by them."
> —VIRGINIA SATIR

for her human validation process model, which features four pivotal goals in family treatment: (1) open communications, in which clients are encouraged to share their perceptions; (2) enhancement of self-esteem, in which family decisions emerge out of individual needs; (3) encouragement of growth, differences are accepted and regarded as opportunities for change; and (4) transformation of extreme rules into functional rules. Her work drew on various techniques, including hypnotherapy and Eastern forms of meditation, such as deep breathing and visualization. She paid careful attention to the therapeutic relationship, including eye contact and touch, and in general, to engaging clients on whatever level they are on. She was renowned for her warmth and empathy, clarity as a communicator, and insight into issues of self-esteem and psychological functioning.

PROFILE 10.1 (CONTINUED)

In 1977, Satir organized the Avanta Network educational foundation referred to as the Avanta Network (see Avanta–The Virginia Satir Network, 2005). Avanta sponsors workshops that use the Satir model, including various exercises that Satir developed. It has branches in eighteen countries and is committed to the notion that enhancing the quality of individual lives can facilitate world peace. Virginia Satir passed away in 1988.

and he later founded the Georgetown Family Center. He drew on diverse intellectual traditions, not only communications theory and psychoanalytic thought but also sociological and evolutionary theory. He believed that anxiety and the desire to avoid a sense of emptiness were central in the etiology of dysfunctional relationships, and in general complicate life through the overreactivity that they engender. This reactivity, he believed, was the source of difficulties that many have differentiating their thoughts from their feelings, as well as from those of others, and thus acting rationally. Confusion between thoughts and feelings affects both psychological and social functioning, creating a type of pseudoself, especially prevalent when individuals fail to emotionally differentiate or separate from their family of origin.

Murray Bowen (1978; see also Kerr, 2003) is best known for eight concepts that he either developed or adapted to his theoretical perspective. First, the best known is the notion of the differentiation of the self, or the ability to be inner-directed and to have a clear sense of boundaries while also maintaining relationships with others. Second, like other family therapists, Bowen emphasized triangular relationships. He argued that triads are more stable than dyads, as they can accommodate greater stress by shifting it around the three two-way relationships of the triad. When the stress becomes too great to control in one triangle, it is often shifted to other connected triangles that one or another member is simultaneously a part of. Nonetheless, he acknowledged that triads still demonstrate some instability. Triangles can be healthy or dysfunctional; in either case, they are critical elements of the larger social structures.

The third idea is that of the nuclear family emotional system, which concerns several fundamental relationship patterns that control where problems manifest in a family. The patterns apply to single-parent, stepparent, and traditional nuclear family configurations. The first of the four patterns Bowen identifies takes place when stress induces the marital partners to externalize difficulties, projecting them onto the partner and his or her perceived inadequacies. The partners try to control each other and resist the other's efforts at control, thus creating a conflictual marriage. Another dysfunction in the nuclear family emotional system takes place when problems primarily manifest in one partner, creating the scenario of the underadequate or overadequate marital relationship. A common dysfunction takes place when the couple assumes a united front and focuses exclusively on a child experiencing anxiety or difficulties, thus creating a projection system that may result in a scapegoated child. The fourth pattern in the nuclear family emotional system that Bowen identifies is *emotional distancing,* which occurs when family members withdraw to protect themselves from the underlying intensity of emotions, thus leading to considerable isolation and loneliness.

Fifth, the concept of the multigenerational transmission of family experience is the idea that initially minor variations in levels of differentiation in a family become amplified over multiple generations. This transmission happens through a number of means, ranging from intentional socialization on the part of parents to unconscious imitation on the part of offspring. Supporting this transmission is the effect of a common genetic endowment. For example, the diverse children of a family, some with higher and some with lower levels of differentiation from their parents, often marry individuals of similar levels of differentiation—this process over time amplifies differences among branches of the family.

Sixth, Bowen specifically proposed that intergenerational transmission often occurs through a three-step projection process. In the first step, parents focus on a child out of the fear that something is wrong. In the second step, parents find imagined evidence in their child's behavior for the worst of their fears. In the third step, the parent acts toward the child in a way that confirms and reinforces the dysfunctional and feared behavior.

Another means of multigenerational transmission is emotional cutoff. Often when relationships become too intense or problematic, one or more individuals may precipitously cut off their emotions and then do the same with the relationship. For example, an angry partner may walk out of an argument or move out of the home. In many instances, this has the effect of relieving the immediate anxiety, but it causes the issues to go unresolved, and thus become replicated in new relationships.

Bowen was very impressed with the research of the psychologist Walter Toman (1961), concerning the impact of sibling position. Seventh, Bowen thus emphasized the role of sibling position in development and behavior. Toman believed that people who grow up with the same sibling position function in similar roles. For instance, eldest children often gravitate toward leadership positions and are usually more conservative, whereas youngest children tend to be innovators.

The eighth tenet of Bowen's theory is the societal emotional process. Bowen observed that most of the foregoing dynamics also apply to nonfamily social groups, including institutions and communities. He pointed out that such institutions, as well as society as a whole, goes through alternative periods of progression and regression, of differentiation and conflict. For instance, he argued that a regressive pattern began unfolding shortly after World War II and worsened during the 1950s and 1960s. This manifested in the growth of crime, an increasing divorce rate, a more legalistic attitude, greater divisions between racial groups, less principled decision making by leaders, and a preoccupation with rights over responsibilities.

C. Structural and Systemic Therapy

In the structural approach to family therapy, as developed by Salvador Minuchin (1967, 1974), the central concern is changing behavior, specifically the structure of relationships and alliances. Often the therapist is interested in strengthening the parental subsystem, thus reinforcing its boundaries. One of the most important tasks in the beginning phase involves the therapist joining with the family. Once accomplished, the therapist is expected to challenge the family's characteristic ways of doing things, of their established equilibrium, and then move to help the family restructure their relationships.

D. Symbolic-Experiential and Narrative Approaches

Closely related to Minuchin's approach is the Milan school of systemic therapy. Two of the best-known members of this groups, Luigi Boscolo and Gianfranco Cecchin (Boscolo et al., 1987), also expanded on the work of the communications school, specifically strategic approaches to family systems. They are interested not so much in first-order change of behaviors and symptoms but in the second-order change of the underlying rules governing them. Boscolo et al. (1987) introduced the notion of news of difference, suggesting that it is the newfound awareness of difference among family members that motivates much change. One of the roles of the therapist in this approach is to ferret out information on family differences through dialogue and questioning. They reject the notion of an initial assessment by an expert system involving clinicians. Instead, they promote a partnership, emphasizing curiosity and the co-construction of new directions. Thus, they created a social constructivist orientation with the first-generation applications of cybernetic theory, emphasizing meaning making through a symbolic-interactionist approach.

A more radical and explicitly atheoretical approach to symbolic-experiential therapy is that promoted by Carl Whitaker (see Napier & Whitaker, 1978). His approach calls for the minimization of negative forms of anxiety, or the fear of being overwhelming by the breakdown of defenses, and enhancing positive anxiety which involves the awareness of not living up to one's potential. Like the others who argue for symbolic-interactionist approaches, Whitaker emphasizes the therapist's active use of his- or herself in interaction with the client family. Specifically, Whitaker (1975) characterized this as a kind of "psychotherapy of the absurd" in which the therapist attempts to unbalance or interfere with the families' rigid, pseudomutual, closed, or ritualistic forms of organization. He has urged the therapist to "screw it up so [the family] can't enjoy the way it is going anymore, they'll work out ways of making a more adequate and effective methodology of living which will give them more enjoyment" (Neill & Kniskern, 1982, p. 221). He referred to this process as a type of contrapuntal dialogue.

Another variation of the symbolic-interactionist or experiential approach is narrative therapy. The followers of this approach believe that life events emerge from an underlying story, one that gives meaning to events or fails in this regard. Change is sought by helping the family to discover and tell this story. The approach is not only interactive but also interpretive, and it attempts to understand the interrelationship of the family's meanings and stories and those of the larger culture. Followers of the narrative approach believe that family systems are linguistically co-constructed by participants and the larger world and that the development of knowledge about these systems is a reflexive process, a dialectic that transpires between the knower and the participant (Freedman & Combs, 1996).

E. Other Approaches

There have been many other approaches to intervention in family systems, but few of these have been well developed or widely implemented. In fact, there have been attempts to apply just about every model of individual therapy to families, such as psychoanalytic, object relations, and feminist models. Approaches such as focal family therapy (Bentovim & Davenport, 1992), contextual family therapy (Anderson & Hargrave, 1990), or brief family therapy (Berg & Gallagher, 1989) appear to be simply a repackaging of the perennial concepts of strategic problem focus or the role of the environment, as if these represented new or innovative contributions. For instance, focal therapy was developed for working with families with members who struggle with schizophrenia. The approach calls for the identification and definition of a focal issue, the targeting of behavior and attitudes that require some focal change, and the implementation of a range of specific techniques referred to collectively as focal family therapy.

There are also a range of behavioral and psychoeducational approaches to family therapy. *Psychoeducation* is a broad term that describes several approaches to family skills training, such as elements of behavioral parent training and a combination of instruction and experiential exercises in other defined problem areas. The approaches emphasize systematic problem solving, open communication, anger management, and conflict resolution. One of the more promising and better researched of the approaches is family psychoeducation, developed by Gerald Hogarty (Anderson, Reiss, Douglas, & Hogarty, 1986), which is oriented toward supporting families with schizophrenic members. One of its goals is to help such families control levels of expressed emotion, which is known to be associated with schizophrenic relapse.

F. Critiques of Family Systems Theories

As popular and intuitively plausible as many of the family systems theories are, there are a range of criticisms that have been lodged against the approaches. Criticism typically involves their focus, issues of diversity, epistemological limitations, and most important, a naive view of equilibrium and change. Although recent theorists have addressed most of these concerns, many in the human services continue to actively draw on the earlier generations of family systems theory that the critiques were directed at.

Several have lamented the focus and scope of family systems theories from several different perspectives. On the one hand, there is the complaint that family systems minimize internal psychological functioning and experience. On the other hand, some criticize the approach as ignoring the larger system issues, of the impact of the institutional, community, and sociocultural environments in mediating between the inputs and outputs of families. A related concern is the tendency of some to create a split between the individual and family perspectives (Yerby, 1995). Family theorists typically assume that the most critical dynamical processes involve the overall patterns of family functioning, and that these may become internalized into the psychological functioning of the individuals or may spill over to the over environment. As long as this is merely an assumption, one may easily fall prey to a kind of family reductionism and ignore alternative dynamic processes, such as the possibility that problems in a child's cognitive functioning tax the larger family system, thus contributing to relationship problems in it. Others have criticized the scope of family systems theory as ignoring older families and those without children, especially because the interest in the nuclear family with young children has dominated the field (Yerby, 1995).

Critiques concerned with diversity, especially as it pertains to race, sex, and socioeconomic status, have been especially pronounced in recent years. These often arise from the disproportionate focus on middle-class nuclear families, although there are significant exceptions, such as Salvador Minuchin, who has been particularly interested in low-income families. Nonetheless, feminist authors have interpreted the emphasis on clear boundaries and differentiation, especially by theorists such as Minuchin and Bowen, as male oriented and nonrelational. Some consider the analysis of family structure to ignore gender, to be essentially patriarchal. More generally, the tendency of some family theorists to ignore the larger environment is viewed as minimizing the powerful roles of social injustice and other inequities in family functioning. A related criticism is that changing the focus from a scapegoated family member to the larger system could unduly absolve individuals, such as an abusive father, of responsibility for their actions, thus perpetuating victimization in the family.

Family systems theorists have also been criticized because their approach to knowledge building may be either too theoretical or metaphorical and insufficiently empirically grounded (Pincus 2001) or overly restricted, thus ignoring a multiperspectival approach that includes transrational ways of knowing. Along these same lines, some have expressed skepticism about defining family problems merely on the basis of the privileged position of the researcher or clinician (Yerby, 1995). The reality is that in the family therapy field, there is a considerable diversity of approaches that range from the more empirically grounded methodologies of Kantor and Lehr to the social constructivists and antiempirical, antitheoretical stance of a Carl Whitaker.

Finally, there is the issue of how both family theorists and therapists understand stability and equilibrium. As noted earlier, most of the traditional approaches were based on a cybernetic model that assumed that the primary problem was overly set negative feedback loops that maintain existing pathology. Various criticisms have been leveled against this assumption. Family systems often have multiple steady states that they alternate between, only some of which may be dysfunctional. Knowing about the existence of such steady states or attractors says nothing about what maintains them. Most important, it does little to clarify how families change, for better or worse. It is suggested that the distinction between stability and disequilibrium is a continuum, though one that may have sudden, catastrophic points of discontinuity.

It has been pointed out that approaching a system, such as a family, with a simplistic understanding of its overall tendency to maintain equilibrium has substantial implications for outside change agents, such as human service professionals. Doing so puts family therapists in an adversarial position against the families that they are expected to work with (Wile, 1993, quoted in Gottman et al., 2002). Practitioners, thus, begin with the assumption that they must find ways to counter family's efforts not to change, to challenge them using carrots, sticks, or trickery. Wile contends, "Ackerman deliberately charms, ridicules, and bullies family members; Haley and Watzlawick, Weakland, and Fisch strategically manipulate them with paradoxical instructions; Jackson and Weakland tactically place them in therapeutic double binds; Haley systematically browbeats certain partners to fail to do the tasks he assigns them; Minuchin and his colleagues 'frontally silence' overbearing wives to 'rock the system'" (p. 168, citations excluded).

The notion of partnering with families, supporting their resiliency and other strengths, and building on their aspirations for change and growth is a foreign notion. Instead, many regard challenge and response, and the inducement of conflict and crisis, as the royal road to change. Yet some of the most important contributions of complex systems theory, including self-organization and autopoieses, all support a more collaborative strategy, and it is this subject that the chapter will now turn to.

VIII. Complex Systems and the Family

Although the application of systems theory to understanding families is far from new, it has only been in the past few decades that the field of family systems has begun to update its theoretical base. The most significant contribution of the complex systems field is the redefinition of family structure, with its seemingly stuck interactional patterns, in terms of process. For example, nonlinear dynamics has introduced the concept of the attractor, specifically the strange attractor, that exhibits chaoticity (or elements of chaos). These patterns may appear temporarily fixed and repetitious, but they actually never repeat themselves and are acutely sensitive to initial conditions. Perhaps for a few weeks or a few years, a circular transactional pattern in a family will appear to be repetitious. But as certain parameters or fundamental conditions change, there is often a dramatic shift to an entirely new pattern, a new basin of attraction, perhaps followed by a change back to the original condition but more likely by an entirely new one. Lynn Hoffman hypothesized a spiral typology of family interactional patterns that suggests that families experience multiple points of dynamic equilibrium.

Matthijs Koopmans (1998) argues that "this approach allows us to more effectively address one of the outstanding questions in the field, namely, how self-regulatory behavior can contribute to structural transformation of the family system" (p. 133). Typically, it is not necessary to eradicate or excise apparently dysfunctional family structures through either confrontation or trickery but rather to change the fundamental rules or parameters governing the behaviors. Such apparently modest impacts may result in fundamental changes in behavioral patterns, especially when such efforts are supported through positive feedback loops and sensitivity to initial conditions. Thus, identifying key feedback loops, helping families reconsider and renegotiate the rules that govern the feedback relationships, and finding ways to reinforce and reintegrate these changes is a key strategy of family work.

The criticism that family systems theory unduly exonerates key individuals for responsibility for change and tends to blame the victim is no longer valid in a complex systems perspective. The possibilities for dramatic change originating from anyone in the family do not speak to the ethical and moral issues involved. The ability to change, whether oneself or others, is a very different issue from a respect for the rights of others, involving human dignity and safety, or from the question of the responsibility for change. One task of family systems work is helping those involved in such complex situations sort out the individual issues (i.e., internalized dysfunctional patterns) from the external interactional patterns that camouflage and either buffer or aggravate the impact of various individual behavioral patterns.

Interactional patterns involving bifurcation, nucleation, and positive feedback loops, when driven by rules that generate chaotic patterns, may contribute to the seemingly out-of-control cascades of family disintegration observed in practice settings. To the extent that these processes operate in a given family, it becomes critical to understand the initial stress on the system. These patterns may, for example, involve the shift from a two-person to a triangular relationship with the birth of a child. They require an understanding of the larger sociocultural and psychological conditions and attitudes that generate the emotional vulnerabilities that aggravate and fuel family crises. These may originate, for example, with the entry or exit of a family member to the system (e.g., birth, adoption, doubling up of an extended family).

Bifurcation is the splitting of processes and the failure to coordinate or integrate the resulting subprocesses. This is exemplified by emotional cutoffs, splits between home and work life, the father-son and mother-daughter subgroups in a family, or rational and intuitive approaches to problem solving.

The splits may or may not become problematic, but when there is a regressive accumulation of such splits, out-of-control cascades of dysfunctional behaviors often result.

A similar process is exemplified by the nucleation or the seeding of initial conflicts or solutions, often through self-selective decisions that establish pathological or healthy precedents and rules. These rules, when repeatedly enforced, may lead to the incremental accumulation of suspicion and enmity, or conversely, trust and love. Each dynamic, such as self-selection, bifurcation, and nucleation, has been observed for many years, but it has been only recently that we have developed the concepts, metaphors, and mathematical tools to understand them.

One of the most significant contributions of complex systems theory to the study of families that has emerged is the understanding of self-organization. Pincus (2001) argues, "By nesting the general components of different family system theories within a self-organized framework, one may predict that the evolution of the 5-Rs ... in families is likely to follow a meta-pattern in which the system moves toward greater complexity and flexibility as it evolves, a point that is made in Koopmans's (1998) discussion of family change patterns" (p. 150).

As natural groups, families are inherently self-organizing, in healthy or unhealthy ways. Conflict, especially when incited from without, is rarely needed to stimulate change. Change is always happening, whether slowly or furiously. Rather than function as task makers, human service professionals are usually more effective when they function as midwives with families, supporting natural processes of problem solving and giving a nudge here or there. Understanding the dynamics of self-organization, including the central role of self-selection, the impact of interactional rules, the flow of energy and resources (whether emotional or concrete), and the balancing act of living at the edge of chaos are all essential to the successful midwifery of family work.

IX. Summary

This chapter has reviewed both traditional and current approaches to the understanding of family systems. It has sought to consider the family in the context of the psychological and biological functioning of its members, as well as in relation to the larger sociocultural systems that families are embedded in. Although traditional approaches have focused on highly dysfunctional families, often believed to produce members with serious mental illnesses, contemporary approaches have increasingly emphasized the resilience of families, and their ability to support members, solve problems, and continue to develop over time.

Most family systems theorists subscribe to assumptions involving the centrality of family influence, the notion that history repeats itself in family development, that much of family life involves the tension between separateness and connectedness, and that distress usually originates in the external pattern of family relationships that become internalized. Concepts and themes that characterize most family systems theorists are interaction and specifically communication, multiple levels of change, family culture, and family process and structure. Although change can involve alterations in external patterns of behavior and communication, what many are most interested in is change in the underlying rules that govern these phenomena, especially the underlying system of rules, attitudes, and culture that, in aggregate, self-organize to create the observed patterns of behavior. There have been diverse efforts to integrate these diverse strands, for example, Pincus's 5-R model, which considers rules, roles, relationships, realities, and families' responses to the foregoing.

The chapter concludes with a review of some of the key ideas from complex systems theory that are useful for either understanding either family dysfunction or healthy functioning. Notions of nucleation, bifurcation, and positive feedback loops are applied to understanding regressions in family functioning, whereas the creative aspects of self-selection and self-organization are emphasized as avenues to cohesive problem solving. But it is also pointed out that any of the complex systems concepts discussed can be used to understand both regressive and constructive processes of family development. One of the benefits of complex systems theory is that it reframes static family structures into dynamic terms, thus permitting a better understanding of the types of changes that continue to happen in families or ones that may be possible.

For Further Reading

Bowen, M. (1985). *Family therapy in clinical practice.* New York: Aronson.
Freedman, J., & Combs, G. (1996). *Narrative therapy: The social construction of preferred realities.* New York: Norton.
Gottman, J. M., Murray, J. D., Swanson, C. C., Tyson, R., & Swanson, K. R. (2002). *The mathematics of marriage: Dynamic nonlinear models.* Cambridge, MA: MIT Press.

Haley, J. (1959). The family of the schizophrenic: A model system. *Journal of Nervous and Mental Disease, 129*(4), 357–374.

Harris, S. M. (1996). Bowen and symbolic experiential family therapy theories: Strange bedfellows or isomorphs of life? *Journal of Family Psychotherapy, 7*(3), 39–60.

Hoffman, L. (1981). *Foundations of family therapy: A conceptual framework for systems change.* New York: Basic Books.

Kantor, D., & Lehr, W. (1975). *Inside the family: Toward a theory of family process.* New York: Harper.

Koopmans, M. (1998). Chaos theory and the problem of change in family systems. *Nonlinear Dynamics, Psychology, and Life Sciences, 2*(2), 133–148.

Minuchin, S. (1974). *Families and family therapy.* Cambridge, MA: Harvard University Press.

Napier, A. Y., & Whitaker, C. A. (1978). *Family crucible: The intensive experience of family therapy.* New York: Harper & Row.

Pincus, D. (2001). A framework and methodology for the study of nonlinear, self-organizing family dynamics. *Nonlinear Dynamics, Psychology, and Life Sciences, 5*(2), 139–173.

Satir, V. (1998). *The new peoplemaking.* Mountain View, CA: Science & Behavior Books.

Walsh, F. (2003). Family resilience: A framework for clinical practice. *Family Process, 42*, 1–18.

Ward, M. (1995). Butterflies and bifurcations: Can chaos theory contribute to our understanding of family systems? *Journal of Marriage and Family, 57*, 629–638.

Yerby, J. (1995). Family systems theory reconsidered: Integrating social construction theory and dialectical process. *Communication Theory, 5*, 339–365.

CHAPTER 11

The Dynamics of Organizations

Organizations are living systems, not machines, because they are made up of people. As innovators in a living system, we must learn to think more like gardeners than mechanics. When we view the organization as a living system, our perspective becomes one of how to provide the right environment or context for the organization to fulfill its purpose.
—ANDREW PAPAGEORGE (2004, P. 21)

I. Introduction

A. Levels of Analysis

This chapter takes a further step in the direction initiated in the previous chapter, on family dynamics. It explores the role of organizations in individual and small-group behavior. It introduces a new level in the application of complex systems theory, sometimes referred to as mezzosystems. Microsystems include individuals and sometimes small groups and families, and macrosystems include state and national policy systems. The mezzo level of analysis falls midway on this continuum and includes the study of local organizations and communities. Just as small groups and families are the building blocks of society, organizations and communities are larger modules, or substructures, of society. This is, however, a traditional and overly simplified view, as organizations and communities are regarded as largely unchanging environmental units, with both good and bad consequences for the individual. It is a view that minimizes the role of larger systems as dynamic agents in their own right, solving problems, making decisions, fulfilling social functions, and sometimes even pursuing long-term goals.

Indeed, observers often experience the processes involved in organizational systems as so glacially slow that it seems to be a misnomer to refer to them as dynamic processes. Nonetheless, organizations and communities are better considered self-organizing streams of interrelated activities than discrete entities. When viewed from a distance, a stream may be perceived as a fixed structure, but close up it is a pattern of continuous change, of ever-changing input, transformation, and output.

B. The Entanglement of Organizations and Communities

The conventional equilibrium model of organizations and communities has another limitation. It assumes a simple hierarchy of systems and, thus, of authority. Individuals are embedded in families and groups, groups in organizations, organizations in communities, communities in societies, and so forth. Although there are many variations on this theme, the message is the same: social causation is a one-way street, from top down, whether natural or intentional, healthy or unhealthy. However, if individuals and small groups can also affect larger systems, then the resulting feedback loops are considerably more complicated, which results in entangled hierarchies (Hofstader, 1979; see chapter 1). Just like the M. C. Escher drawing in an earlier chapter, the smaller embedded systems sometimes come to encompass and control the larger systems that they are a part of. The boundaries between levels become blurry. This is often thought to be dysfunctional. An example is when a child who is said to be "parentified" tries to take over the role of a lost parent. It can also occur in a creative relationship, such as when a chief executive is required to report to a constituency that has elected him or her. A common assumption is that organizations are the building blocks of communities. However, observation also reveals that organizations not only are embedded in communities but also cut across them. Conversely, some communities may be embedded in organizations and cut across organizational boundaries.

Organizations and communities are interdependent and interpenetrating. They exist in a dynamic tension that involves both cooperation and competition. Such overlap can be dysfunctional but also integrative. Communities are loosely structured and naturally occurring social systems in which freedom and autonomy are optimized. In contrast, organizations are more intentional and structured social systems in which responsibility and mutuality are emphasized. In reality, both types exist on a continuum and represent different and complimentary types of social systems. Organizations give communities structure, while communities are the life that surrounds, energizes, and gives organizations their vitality. Most individuals function, either simultaneously or in alternation, within several organizations and communities as they move through a typical day. The multiple points of overlap of organizations and communities in the lives of average people form an interlocking mosaic of structured processes, which constitutes the social landscape (see figure 11.1).

The traditional hierarchical vision of social systems also atomizes social reality into discrete structures. Brown and Duguid (2005) observed, "The reorganization of the workplace into canonical groups can wittingly or unwittingly disrupt these highly functional non-canonical—and therefore often invisible communities" (n.p.). Any simplistic overemphasis on attaching individuals to discrete groups such as organizations and communities risks obscuring the complex interdependencies that the same people have within the larger mosaic of groups, communities, and organizations that they are also part of.

FIGURE 11.1: THE MEZZO-STRUCTURE OF SOCIETY AS AN INTERLOCKING MOSAIC OF ORGANIZATIONS AND COMMUNITIES

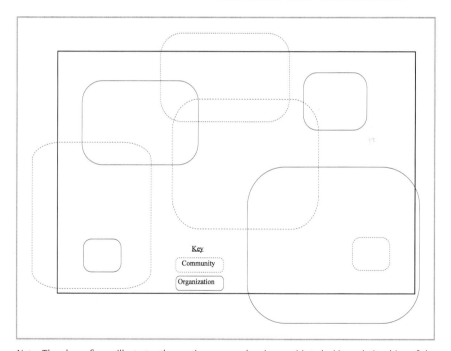

Key
Community
Organization

Note: The above figure illustrates the continuous, overlapping, and interlocking relationships of the multiple communities and organizations, both large and small, that constitute the social environment. In some cases communities are included within organizations, and in other cases, the opposite is the case; typically, organizations and communities overlap.

C. Social Institutions

Both organizations and communities develop, are maintained, and dissolve in the context of the larger society that they constitute and are a part of. Sociologists typically define society as an organized collective that is stable and patterned (i.e., with social structures). A social structure is made up of a combination of institutions, statuses, roles, and groups. Institutions are regarded as groups with consistent rules and relationships intended for the regulation of social activities and realization of core human values. In addition to the social welfare system, other major social institutions include the economy, government, family, education, religion, and medicine (Macionis, 2005).

Although the term *institution* sometimes also refers to a large bureaucracy, in this context, institutions are neither organizations nor communities. Institutions may be organizations and communities, but more fundamentally, they are the set of cultural memes—the fundamental ideas, practices, and protocols—that diverse social structures and processes implement and replicate. In a sense, institutions are the next higher level in the social hierarchy, within which organizations and communities are nested. However, even here, it would be remiss to minimize the complex entanglements and feedback loops linking the levels.

The focus of this and the next chapter is on several emerging theories of organizations and communities, especially as they incorporate insights from the study of complex systems. They involve the intermeshing of bottom-up and top-down processes, and the self-organization of patterns of cooperation and competition. This chapter regards organizations as parts of the environment, part of the essential context of individual human behavior. They provide essential supports and opportunities, as well as stresses and challenges, that affect individuals and are, in turn, molded by the cumulative impact of the people that pass through or interact with them.

D. The Problem of Altruism, Cooperative Social Action, and the Prisoner's Dilemma

A classic problem in social thought is the question of how cooperative social action, particularly altruism, is possible given apparently pervasive self-interest. Cold rational calculation too frequently seems to transform self-interest into unremitting and ruthless competition. This dilemma has been studied in many contexts, but one of the most famous and perhaps most revealing is game theory, specifically, the game of the prisoner's dilemma (see exhibit 11.1). In recent years it has been demonstrated that, although the rational outcome for any single play in this game involves snitching on one's partner, when the game is repeatedly played—or iterated—it can be shown that cooperative action leads to substantial payoff (see Axelrod, 1997). In the real world, interactions are iterated or repeated; people remember the outcomes of previous interactions and anticipate the outcomes of future events. A short-term vision of social relationships as isolated interactions may result in the conclusion that cutthroat competition is the most rational outcome. However, recent analyses have demonstrated that in the larger spatial and temporal context of society, with its repeated interactions, social support and altruism are more rational than the pursuit of short-term, immediate payoffs. Organizations and communities are built on the assumption that cooperative action is rational, yet they also incorporate and often encourage some degree of competition within or between systems. A central part of the assessment of either type of system involves a careful analysis of the underlying values, rules, and protocols that govern the various kinds of cooperation and competition. Much of the activity of the systems can be understood in terms of how they facilitate cooperation and regulate competition, and the interplay between the two.

Organizations are a source of solutions and the root cause of many problems; however, they have a monopoly on neither. They are a pervasive presence in contemporary society and provide a range of opportunities for human service professionals to work as part of multidisciplinary teams. They are extensions of individual problem-solving strategies, which dramatically amplifies both their flaws and their genius. Most organizations, in the human services and beyond, are complex systems, and they are increasingly understood in such terms.

E. Definitions

So, what are organizations? According to Scott (1992), "Organizations are collectivities oriented to the pursuit of relatively specific goals and exhibiting relatively high formalized social structures. . . . Most analysts have conceived of organizations as social structures created by individuals to support the collaborative pursuit of specified goals" (p. 22). Similarly, Barnard (1938) defines organizations as involving "that kind of cooperation among men that is conscious, deliberate, purposeful" (p. 4). March and Simon (1958) contend that "organizations are assemblages of interacting human beings . . . the largest assemblages have a semblance of a coordinating system [and] high specificity of structure and coordination (vs. diffuse and variable) between

EXHIBIT 11.1: THE PRISONER'S DILEMMA

THE PROBLEM: How is it possible for people to cooperate and engage in altruistic action when rational calculations of payoffs suggest that one may be better off acting out of self-interest, at the expense of others?

THE GAME: The prisoner's dilemma has been most frequently studied through variations in the outcomes associated with a hypothetical game involving two prisoners under interrogation (see Axelrod, 1997).

THE SCENARIO: Two partners in crime have been apprehended for a crime that merits a jail sentence of between zero and five years, depending on the mitigating circumstances, especially the willingness of the prisoner to confess and implicate his or her partner. The prisoners are interrogated separately, and neither can know what the other will decide to do. If both cooperate—neither confessing nor snitching on the other—then both receive an intermediate sentence of three years. If both confess and implicate the other, they each receive a one-year sentence. However, if only one remains loyal and one defects, then the defector is rewarded with a dropped sentence, and the loyal partner gets the maximum for failing to confess or implicate the partner. Thus, in this scenario, if both actors are rational, both will decide to defect and neither will gain anything. However, if both irrationally decide to cooperate, both would knock two years off of their maximum sentence.

APPLICATION: This rather artificial and highly simplified scenario is a metaphor for the problem of cooperation in a wide variety of contexts. The benefits are fully realized only when all decide to cooperate and when there are no defectors or free riders. In contrast, when a few or

Prisoner's Dilemma: Payoff Matrix

Prisoner A Prisoner B	COOPERATE	DEFECT
Cooperate	Reward for Mutual Cooperation $R^a = 3$; $R^b = 3$	Sucker's Payoff and Temptation to Defect $S^a = 0$; $T^b = 5$
Defect	Temptation to Defect and Sucker's Payoff $T^a = 5$; $S^b = 0$	Punishment for Mutual Defection $P^a = 1$; $P^b = 1$

EXHIBIT 11.1 (CONTINUED)

none invest resources, time, or energy in an endeavor, and others take advantage the situation, maximum social costs are incurred, at least by investors. There are, however, a variety of possible investments and costs, as well as alternative rules for interacting, many of which may result in payoffs for cooperation other than those depicted in this game. Of particular importance is the situation in which the prisoner's dilemma, or a variation, is repeated multiple times, providing the possibility of players rewarding or punishing their partners in subsequent interactions. It has been shown that in such iterated versions of the game, several different interactional rules (e.g., tit for tat) result in long-term cooperation.

organizations" (p. 4). In a sense, organizations are special types of large enduring groups, ones in which formal instrumental relationships dominate and that are committed to achieving specific social or private goals.

The study of organizations and their management is an extensive field, one that cuts across many disciplines and professions, including business, sociology, social and industrial psychology, economics, and the various human service professions. There are several important distinctions, the most critical of which is between management and organizational dynamics and structure. Whereas academic disciplines, such as sociology, are mainly interested in understanding the phenomenon of existing organizations, applied fields such as business or social work are more concerned with management issues and questions of how to intervene and make organizations more effectively achieve some designated purpose. However, to achieve the latter, a solid grounding in theory and research on organizational dynamics is vital.

F. Organizations and the Systems Perspective

As complex systems, organizations exemplify several of the dynamics previously discussed. On the most basic level, they represent the transformation of input, via intervening processes, into output. Input can be funds, tangible resources, new staff, clients, information, or public expectations. The intervening processes are all the paths and other means through which the input is transformed (e.g., money allocated, resources assigned, staff and clients brought together, information analyzed and disseminated). Output includes money spent, discharged clients, graduating students, public relations campaigns or press releases, and even the organization's garbage and toxic wastes. Particularly important are the relationships, practices, technologies, and complex and iterative feedback loops used to orchestrate transformations. It may be tempting to reduce organizations to a simple linear sequence of input, transformation, and output. Complexity, however, enters into the picture with diverse feedback loops, with all their unpredictability, as well as the multiple possible levels of analysis. There is feedback within levels and between levels (e.g., between individuals and their departments). For this reason, multiple perspectives and approaches to understanding organizations have been developed and will be briefly introduced in the sections that follow. This will be done first through a discussion of some of the historical approaches, and then through a consideration of contemporary and emerging theoretical paradigms.

II. Some History

A. Origins

Although formal organizations date back to antiquity—to ancient Egypt, Rome, and China—it has been only since the late 1800s that they have become a subject of academic study. The Industrial Revolution brought with it the substitution of machine power for human power, spawning resource accumulation, capital growth, and a concern for achieving efficiencies of scale. Organizations, especially industrial enterprises, became larger, more specialized, and more pervasive. Models of authoritarian administration, borrowed from traditional agrarian societies, were amplified and rationalized in the new organizational models. These involved centralization, rigid hierarchies, and increasing specialization, including that among owners, workers, and managers. The ethos of the scientific revolution, when translated into the culture of the workplace, engendered a pervasive and thoughtless scientism that was often used to rationalize oppressive organizations. These approaches were called by various names, such as *scientific management* and even *scientific charity*.

B. Scientific Management

Of particular historical relevance is the scientific management approach of Frederick Winslow Taylor (1856–1915), who attempted to apply the scientific method to the study of work processes so as to determine the "one best way" to organize them. Taylor's (1977) approach also emphasized the scientific selection of personnel, the active use of financial incentives, and functional foremanship, which refers to a strictly enforced split between the planning and supervision of work and its execution. The preeminent value that scientific management sought to realize was economic efficiency, or the problem of converting a minimum input into optimal output and profit. Although the problem of worker motivation had become intractable at the apex of the Industrial Revolution, for Taylor this was a problem of simply matching workers to jobs and providing an optimal schedule of economic incentives, typically involving performance-based payments. Henri Fayol (1949), a contemporary of Taylor's, took a broader view of management, regarding it as the orchestrated execution of five essential elements: (1) planning, (2) organizing, (3) command, (4) coordination, and (5) control. Yet his approach was a traditional mechanistic model that relied on external control, even though the model preferred incentives over sanctions. Close supervision of individual interests were central to Fayol's view.

C. Weber's Bureaucratic Model

The best known of the early organizational theorists was the German sociologist Max Weber (b. 1864–d. 1920), who developed the traditional bureaucratic model (see Weber, 1946). The term *bureaucracy* now has a decidedly negative connotation, usually referring to ossified organizations mired in needless procedures and paper pushing. But for Weber, bureaucracy represented an ideal type of organization, one characterized by efficiency and impartiality. For Weber, the ideal bureaucracy entailed the following:

- A well-defined hierarchy or chain of command
- Clear division of work, to maximize benefits of specialization
- An unambiguous system of rules defining the rights and responsibilities of workers and managers
- Defined procedures for the work of the organization
- Impersonality of interpersonal relations
- Selection and promotion based on technical competence rather than nepotism or other subjective considerations

During his time, Weber's model was a substantial step forward for both industry and the public civil service. Yet over the years, many shortcomings in the approach have emerged. For example, it largely ignores the complexities of worker motivation, assuming that all are equally motivated by financial incentives or controlled by sanctions. Its principles are often inconsistent and lack empirical validation. It does not take into account differences between various kinds of routine and professional tasks, changing environments, or a wide range of uncertainties that preclude a clear definition of roles and procedures.

D. Human Relations School

It is perhaps not coincidental that the first major departure from classical organizational theory occurred at the onset of the Great Depression, an economic failure that cast doubt on industrial models of organizational design. What has come to be referred to as the human relations school of organizational design emerged out of a series of experiments conducted in the Hawthorne Western Electric plants in Illinois between 1927 and 1933 (see Dessler, 1980). The researchers were interested in determining the impact of alternative levels of illumination on worker productivity, assuming such physical factors to be of central importance. They discovered no clear pattern. In each experiment, worker output was enhanced regardless of lighting levels. This led the researchers to the conclusion that the physical environment was less important than psychosocial conditions, especially the fact that researchers were taking an interest in and observing worker performance. This effect is similar to what is referred to as the placebo effect in the context of treatment research, and its basis is the idea that the provision of some imagined benefit or placebo—if only a fake pill or some care and attention—is often sufficient to stimulate considerable improvement in a condition of concern. The Hawthorne experiments stimulated interest in a wide variety of problems in the area of organizational behavior, typically those involving motivation, morale, teamwork, and compliance with organizational goals. The classical theorists assumed that if an organization provided the right kind of supervision and economic incentives, compliance with organizational goals would follow automatically. In contrast, those in the human relations school assumed that the primary task was to provide sufficiently flexible supports and structures, based on the needs of the workforce, and then appropriate goals, tasks, and motivation would follow.

Since this initial interest, the human relations model has faced many critiques, most of which involve its excessive focus on small systems and social and psychological factors. Organizational theorists have pursued a broad range of approaches that attempt to integrate this small-system perspective with, on the one hand, structural, environmental, technological, and strategic considerations, and on the other hand, an even more in-depth understanding of individual psychological processes. Many of these efforts—especially the former—have attempted to develop contingency theories that hypothesize that particular organizational designs and practices depend on the type of strategic goals, information, technology, and the larger environment. These more contemporary approaches are briefly discussed in the following sections. Many such models emphasize a greater decentralization and flatter organizational structures, reliance on teams or cost centers, and maximum flexibility.

E. Impact of Information Society

The previously noted changes are integrally linked with the transition from the industrial to the postindustrial economy, or the information economy or society. In the information society, the most predominant activity is the production, analysis, and sharing of information, and the use of that information to add value to a full range of products and services. In agrarian and industrial societies, the cost of information is at a premium, and managers and other elites monopolize its exploitation. However, in contemporary societies, the cost of information has been dramatically reduced as a result of increased education, computerization, and the Internet. Because of this, traditional bureaucratic models are becoming increasingly dysfunctional, which forces some degree of decentralization. However, this has often failed to keep pace with rising expectations for participation in governance and decentralized control in many organizations.

III. The Organizational Landscape

A. Diversity of Organizations

Organizations are pervasive. In the United States they number in the millions, ranging in size from small partnerships and clubs to multinational corporations and mammoth governmental agencies. Examples of the latter include the U.S. Department of Health and Human Services, which employs hundreds of thousands of individuals and has a budget larger than the economy of many countries. In 2004 there were 1,397,263 nonprofit organizations in the nation, up by 28.8% from 1,084,897 in 1996 (National Center for Charitable Studies, 2003). Because of this organizational diversity, there have been no commonly agreed-on typologies for all organizational types, but typologies have been developed for particular sectors, such as religious or health-care organizations, or based on particular features, such as legal status.

B. Legal Statuses

Probably the broadest cut that can be made is between public and private organizations. Public organizations—typically established through the legislative process or occasionally through public regulations—are supported primarily through tax receipts and are directly accountable to the executive branch and indirectly to the voters. In contrast, private organizations are established when one or several charter members decide to work together, almost always incorporating their collective enterprise through state laws and supporting the efforts through funds generated from the sale of goods or services, donations, or grants or contracts with public or private organizations. Their staff members are directly accountable to the owner, a board of directors, the membership, or some combination, depending on the particular legal arrangements; they are only indirectly accountable to their broader constituencies.

Two major types of private organizations are those incorporated for profit and nonprofit organizations (sometimes called not-for-profit), often educational or human service organizations. The Internal Revenue Service (IRS), an agency of the federal government, grants status as a nonprofit organization in the United States. The IRS has been assigned this responsibility because nonprofit status entails a decision as to tax-exempt status, which is based on an official recognition of the organization's educational, charitable, or scientific purpose. For many such organizations, the ultimate governing authority rests with a board of directors that can reelect itself. But for others, such as professional associations, authority rests with the membership from which a board of directors is elected according to the association's bylaws.

C. Mintzberg's Organizational Typology

One of the more commonly used typologies is Henry Mintzberg's (1979), which focuses on organizational design. This typology is based on alternative strategies for achieving internal coordination; the type of control and degree of centralization; and the configuration of five basic or functional parts of most organizations. Coordination strategies consist of some combination of direct supervision; standardization of work processes, outputs or products, and skills; and mutual adjustment, involving informal communications among workers. Closely related are five types of control, that range from the centralized to the decentralized, consist of the following:

1. Vertical and horizontal centralization, in which all power rests with the executives
2. Limited horizontal decentralization, in which power is shared with technical specialists
3. Limited vertical decentralization, in which managers of independent units or cost centers are delegated control
4. Vertical and horizontal decentralization, in which most authority is delegated to frontline workers
5. Selective vertical and horizontal decentralization, a combination of limited horizontal and limited vertical decentralization

In addition, each organization represents some configuration of the five types of functional parts or units: (1) the strategic apex, or executives, (2) the middle line, or middle managers, (3) the operating core, or frontline workers, (4) the "technostructure," or supporting specialists, and (5) the supporting staff, such as accounting, information technology, public relations, and the like. The typology is based on an organization's approach to control and coordination. Each type of organization can be imagined using alternative organizational charts with varying widths for the strategic apex, the middle line, and the operating core, as well as varying heights, representing the relative level of authority for upper management. The first two types—the simple structure or the machine bureaucracy are illustrative of small farm or traditional industrial organizations and have weak middle-management layers. However, the machine bureaucracy also includes a technostructure and support staff. The professional bureaucracy, divisionalized bureaucracy, and adhocracy—are more likely found in the human services, including private agencies, public human service divisions, and professional associations and private practices. The professional bureaucracy has a flatter operating core and relatively small technostructure and support staff, in contrast to the adhocracy, which includes many middle managers and virtually no operating core. The divisionalized bureaucracy is similar to the professional bureaucracy but has multiple hierarchical units embedded in its operating core (see Mintzberg, 1979).

D. People-Processing versus People-Changing Organizations

Yeheskel Hasenfeld and Richard English (1974) developed a typology more specific to the human services, which is based on predominant human service function and client type. The authors contend that all human service organizations have as their main purpose either people processing or people changing. People-processing organizations make determinations, assign statuses, or refer individuals. For example, a juvenile court or accrediting agency carries out these functions, though they may occasionally be involved in people changing. In contrast, people-changing organizations attempt to alter characteristics of individuals, whether their skills and knowledge, psychological adjustment, social relationships, or economic circumstances. The primary clientele of human service organizations is either normal-functioning or malfunctioning clients. Normal functioning clients might be students or perhaps their parents who attend a preventative psychoeducational program. Malfunctioning clients are those who exceed the commonly recognized bounds of normal behavior or functioning, such as individuals with schizophrenia, prisoners, or victims of child abuse. Table 11.1 outlines the four types of organizations that are defined by predominant functions and type of client, and provides examples of each. In some respects, this typology states the obvious. For many the obvious functions of human service organizations are not people processing, and the obvious clients are not usually considered normal functioning. In this respect, Hasenfeld and English's typology highlights the breadth and flexibility of human service organizations.

The remainder of this chapter focuses on human service organizations, though not exclusively. Human services are being delivered in an increasingly

TABLE 11.1: THE FUNCTION AND DOMAINS OF HUMAN SERVICE ORGANIZATIONS

| | | Predominant Functions | |
		PEOPLE PROCESSING	PEOPLE CHANGING
TYPE OF CLIENTS	NORMAL FUNCTIONING	TYPE I University admissions office Employment placement service	TYPE II Public school YMCA
	MALFUNCTIONING	TYPE III Juvenile court Diagnostic clinic	TYPE IV Prison Hospital Mental health clinic

Source: Adapted from Hasenfeld & English (1974, p. 5).

broad array of organizational contexts, including industry, unions, and even the military. Even when services are not provided in such settings, clients often work in such organizations.

IV. Frames for Analyzing Organizational Dynamics

Understanding always takes place in a context, with emphasis on certain foreground activities or entities and others relegated to the background or periphery of attention. Somewhere between the center of the stage and back-stage are the curtains of awareness, and these are the frames that help us de-fine and interpret what is at center stage. We may frame the prospects of some initiative by saying that there is an 80% chance of success—which sounds fairly promising—or a 20% chance of failure, a definite cause for concern. In general, framing is defining and interpreting an issue, and establishing its relevant context and boundaries. It is this metaphor of framing that Bolman and Deal (1997) use to suggest that each group of theories or frames contrib-utes important insights but that none is complete in itself—only through multiple perspectives are organizational problems most effectively solved. Bolman and Deal group frames into the following areas: classical or structural, human resources, political, and symbolic. Each frame has a central metaphor, key concepts, style of leadership, and leadership challenge (see table 11.2).

A. Classical or Structural Frame

The classical or structural frame regards dynamic processes as secondary or derivative of set patterns of organization. The structural is a decidedly mechanistic approach, with the factory as its central metaphor. The classical administrative theorists such as Frederick W. Taylor (1977) and Max Weber (1946) were among the greatest proponents of this frame. Supporters of this view emphasize formal organizational charts, lines of authority, and well-defined policies and procedures. A central assumption is that there is a single optimal or best fit among an organization's goals, environment, technologies, and administrative structures and practices. There also is an assumption of considerable constancy and clarity of what the goals, environments, and technologies are, and that cause-effect or means-ends relationships are well understood. Decision making and problem solving are attempted through exclusively rational means. Jobs are broken down into specialized tasks, with considerable burden of control and coordination placed on the management structure. Some defend the use of this approach in industrial contexts; however, few overtly support its use in human services. Yet the classical or structural

TABLE 11.2: BOLMAN AND DEAL'S FOUR FRAMES FOR ANALYZING ORGANIZATIONAL DYNAMICS

	Frame			
	STRUCTURAL	HUMAN RESOURCE	POLITICAL	SYMBOLIC
Central metaphor	Factory or machine	Family	Jungle	Carnival, temple, theater
Key concepts	Rules, roles, goals, policies, technology, environment	Needs, skills, relationships	Power, conflict, competition, organizational politics	Culture, meaning, metaphor, ritual, ceremony, stories, heroes
Leadership	Social architecture	Empowerment	Advocacy	Inspiration
Leadership challenge	Attune structure to task, technology, environment	Align human and organizational needs	Develop agenda and power base	Create faith, beauty, meaning

Source: Bolman & Deal (1997, p. 15).

frame has had considerable influence in many human service agencies, especially many large public human service and health-care institutions.

B. Human Resource Frame

In contrast, the human resource frame views people as the heart of the organization, and is thus concerned with the needs of employees and clients and with fitting organizational goals, tasks, technologies, and administrative arrangements to the motivations, interpersonal styles, and capabilities of staff and clients. This frame takes a considerably less instrumental approach than does the classical or structural frame, as its central metaphor is the family. The empowerment of workers and enhancement of organizational morale and climate are central. Considerable emphasis is placed on small-group process, team building, decision making, and loyalty. In this respect, the human resource frame is a powerful antidote to the excesses of the structural frame, as it compensates for its impersonality. In many respects, the structural and human resource frames represent a bifurcation of organizational thinking and practice. In human service organizations these models may compete, coexist, or interfere with one another, and enclaves in formalistic structures are carved out to implement the human resource frame.

An example of a human resource theory is Douglas MacGregor's theory Y (see Dessler, 1980). MacGregor contends that what distinguishes personnel practices in traditional hierarchical and more humanistic organizations are the underlying assumptions of managers about their employees and their motivations. The traditional set of assumptions, which he calls theory X, is that people dislike work and can be expected to minimize efforts, are motivated by financial incentives, and prefer to be told clearly what to do. Thus, close monitoring and supervision is required. In contrast, other managers hold a different set of assumptions, or theory Y: people have an inherent desire to work if conditions are favorable, are motivated by not only external incentives but also loyalty to coworkers and clients, and find intrinsic satisfaction in work. Those who hold these assumptions tend to provide supervision and worker supports and emphasize training, work teams, the recognition of worker achievements, and the like. Greater emphasis is placed on participatory management.

C. Political Frame

Unlike the human resource frame, especially MacGregor's theory Y, the political frame assumes a still-different pattern of human motivation, one premised on the desire for control or dominance. Particularly relevant are concepts of power, conflict, competition, and politics. This frame assumes that resources are scarce and that organizational life is a zero-sum game (e.g., if one person succeeds in getting a larger slice of the pie, the next person must accept a smaller piece). Its central metaphor is the jungle, where there is relentless and often-cutthroat competition in an environment with minimal rules. It emphasizes the dynamics of clashing interest groups, though it acknowledges the role of compromise and coalition building. Its politics is one of jobs and organizational control. Under this frame, leadership often means identification of constituencies, alliance building, and advocacy for collective interests. Its central leadership challenge is to build and maintain its power base, develop its agendas, and co-opt or squash possible challenges when necessary. While some see this framework as cynical, others consider it realistic. Although the model has made definite contributions, it is deeply rooted in social Darwinism: self-organization, mutual support, synergistic cooperation, and the development of a shared consciousness are obscured or relegated to a secondary role.

D. Symbolic Frame

Bolman and Deal's (1997) fourth frame is the symbolic one. Its central concern is with organizational culture, including the shared meanings, philosophies, and narratives of a given group. The authors use the carnival, temple, or theater as metaphors, but they also emphasize that each organization develops distinctive metaphors as a part of its cultural traditions. Leadership here is inclusive, visionary, and inspirational, ideally addressing the challenges of lack of loyalty or faith, meaninglessness, and alienation. The symbolic frame assumes that when organizations are able to develop a viable culture, problems of less-than-optimal structures, poor morale, or conflicting interests are easily resolvable. Harvey Cox (1969), in his book *Feast of Fools,* comments on the central importance of symbolism: "Our links to yesterday and tomorrow depend also on the aesthetic, emotional, and symbolic aspects of human life—on saga, play, and celebration. Without festival and fantasy, man would not really be a historical being at all" (p. 13). This frame is perhaps the least used of the four, yet it provides a critical basis for moving among the other frames and integrating their applications. According to Bolman and Deal (1997) the cultural frame is most useful when objectives and information are uncertain, when causal relationships are unclear, and when there is substantial cultural diversity.

E. Emerging Perspectives on Organizations

There are several other emerging perspectives on organizations. Perhaps most important is that of information processing. Organizations are increasingly understood in terms of their ability to process information, to access and organize data, to solve problems, and to exchange information with other organizations in order to add value to products and services (see Weick, 1996). Central to this is organizational memory. Organizational structures, personal practices, political conflict and negotiation, and organizational culture all have dramatic implications for how information flows and is transformed. Likewise, the ways information is managed have substantial consequences for the existing power structures and organizational culture. With the information economy and computerization, networking, and the Internet, the information perspective has become central to many organizations, which we see in departments of information technology and the title of chief information officer. Another emerging perspective, closely aligned with the political frame, is the evolutionary perspective (see Murmann, Aldrich, Levinthal, & Winter, 2003), which emphasizes the role of scarcity, chance, competition, and social selection. Of particular importance is the application of the concept of coevolution to organizational change, or the idea that organizations adapt to one another and then continuously re-adapt as competitors flourish or flounder. It is to this topic of organizational development and change that we will now turn.

V. Organizational Change and Development

As are individuals, families, and groups, organizations are continuously changing, emerging, adapting, and growing or disintegrating. Similarly, there are ongoing debates as to whether such changes can be described in terms of standard paths or stages. Theories of the organizational life cycle tend to be global and highly generalized, and thus offer limited guidance on points of leverage. In contrast, specialists, particularly organizational consultants, have proposed various theories of intentional or planned organizational change. Unfortunately, many of these are not grounded in an understanding of how organizations naturally change and assume static structures. For example, Kurt Lewin (1951), often regarded as the father of organizational change theory, theorized that organizational change involves three stages: (1) unfreezing, (2) change, and (3) refreezing. Lewin, in the spirit of equilibrium theory, considered frozen structures the norm.

Many organizational change theories reflect a division between those who subscribe to evolutionary theories and those who are committed to models that emphasize human intention and planning, sometimes referred to as teleological theories (Kezar, 2001). On the one hand, there are those who focus on organizational environments, competition between and within organizations, and a deterministic process of gradual adaptation to changing conditions and conflicts. In this model, missions, goals, and long-term plans are rhetorical exercises with little relevance to day-to-day responses to encountered threats and opportunities. On the other hand, many theorists emphasize the role of leadership, rational planning, and management in the pursuit of internally developed goals. In this approach, the external environment is merely a pale backdrop to the strategic work of the organization.

Yet there are other models that represent efforts to reconcile or move beyond the limitations of the evolutionary and teleological models. Adrianna Kezar (2001), in her comprehensive analysis of organizational change theories, places these into six primary groups: (1) evolutionary, (2) teleological, (3) life cycle, (4) political, (5) social cognition, and (6) cultural theories of organizational change (see table 11.3).

Life-cycle theories are cyclic models that draw on the metaphor of human growth, maturity, and decline. For example, one cyclic theory characterizes

TABLE 11.3: OVERVIEW OF THEORIES OF ORGANIZATIONAL CHANGE

TYPE OF THEORY	WHY CHANGE OCCURS	PROCESS OF CHANGE
Evolutionary	External environment	Adaption; slow, gradual; nonintentional
Teleological	Leaders; internal environment	Rational, linear, purposeful
Life Cycle	Leaders guiding individual's natural growth	Natural progression; result of training and motivation; altering habits and identity
Political	Dialectical tension of values, norms, or patterns	First order followed by occasional second order, negotiation and power
Social Cognition	Cognitive dissonance; appropriateness	Learning; altering paradigms or lens; interconnected and complex
Cultural	Response to alternations in the human environment	Long-term, slow; symbolic process; nonlinear; unpredictable

Source: Kezar (2001, p. 57).

OUTCOMES OF CHANGE	KEY METAPHOR	EXAMPLES OF THEORIES
New structures and processes; first order	Self-producing organism	Resource dependency, strategic choice; population ecology
New structures and organizing principles	Change master	Organizational development, strategic planning; reengineering; TQM
New organizational identity	Teacher	Developmental models; organizational decline; social psychology of change
New organizational ideology	Social movement	Empowerment; bargaining; political change; Marxist theory
New frame of mind	Brain	Single-and double-looped learning; paradigm shifting; sensemaking
New culture	Social movement	Interpretive strategy; paradigm shifting; processual change

organizational change, especially as applied to boards of directors, as a progression from entrepreneurship to collectivity, formalization and control, and finally elaboration of structure (Lynall, Goldman, & Hillman, 2003). These theories attempt to balance a focus on organizational environments with the internal logic of organizations' internal unfoldment. In such a model, managers actively facilitate successful transitions between phases. For example, a typical life-cycle model includes the following four stages:

1. *Emergent:* These organizations are characterized by fragile management, few subsystems, and limited resources but often are innovative and adaptable.
2. *Launch or growth:* Organizations that have crystallized their design, settled on their program or service mix, and are positioned for growth.
3. *Consolidated:* Such organizations have determined their mission and strategy, developed policies and procedures, increased efficiency, and moved toward greater sustainability.
4. *Mature:* These independent organizations often develop the ability to creatively manage and adjust goals to changing internal and external conditions and challenges.

Mature or established organizations face formidable problems and do not always successfully adapt. A leading organizational theorist, Philip Selznick (1996), put forward the idea of organizational institutionalization, based partly on notions of moral hazard and asymmetric information flows. He contends that as organizations age, their goals increasingly focus on the survival and glorification of the organization. He comments that "to institutionalize is to infuse with value beyond the technical requirements of the task at hand" (p. 271). This is often referred to as goal displacement, when, for example, an organization loses sight of enduring goals that pertain to the development of a quality product or service and replaces those goals with short-term ones that pertain to personal or organizational survival, or simply the repetition of some familiar process or procedure. Means become or displace ends. Thus, there ceases to be any basis for adjusting those means to better achieve goals under changing conditions.

The political or dialectical models emerge out of the neo-Marxist perspective and emphasize conflict and negotiation between polarized interests, especially those involving financial and class interests (see chapter 2). Change is viewed as a function of power relationships, often involving such managerial skills as agenda setting, networking and forming coalitions, and bargaining and negotiation (Kotter, 1985). These approaches deemphasize rational problem solving and instead call on a wide variety of transrational skills, including intuition, charisma, persuasion, and the like.

An emerging area involves models of organizational change based on social cognition. These are a direct outcome of the development of the cognitive sciences and its emphasis on the role of mental representations or maps. Such models have also involved social constructivist and phenomenological approaches to organizations, which suggest that the most critical processes of change involve the ability of groups of people to negotiate a shared set of ideas about the nature of their social and organizational realities.

In contrast to teleological models, which emphasize the role of rational planning, cultural models instead focus on the role of the unconscious and a wide variety of cultural meanings, philosophies, norms, and even rituals in creating a shared inner context for organizational change. In such models, change occurs in response to changing cultural environment that is simultaneously external to the organization but typically shared by its members.

Each model has distinctive assumptions about why and how organizations change and the outcomes of such change. Environmental theories emphasize chance and environmentally induced conflict and selection of the most successful or adaptive organizations. This competition typically results in new structures or processes. In contrast, teleological theories focus on the rational planning activities of managers, which may result in improved structures, processes, or organizing principles. Life-cycle theorists suggest that change occurs because of the relatively modest role of managers in facilitating transitions, which often results in new organizational identities. Political models suggest that change arises from conflict between material interests, often reflected in the tension of opposing values, which results in new organizational ideologies. The social cognition models emphasize cognitive dissonance as a key reason for change, which then results in new learning and the alteration of shared mental maps, and only secondarily actual functioning. Cultural theorists also emphasize responses to the changing environment, but that environment is an inner environment of shared meanings.

All six approaches to organizational change acknowledge a role of the environment as well as of the individuals and groups involved with an organization. They differ in the extent that they view one or the other as the primary motivator of change. They also hold contrasting views on whether the contribution of the individuals involved is rational or draws more broadly on various mental functions, including the unconscious, persuasion, and the development of shared meanings and culture. Extreme varieties of the evolutionary, environmentalist position negate the role of human choice. They instead focus on selection on the part of the social environment, regardless of whether key players' have planned or decided on their selection.

Attempts to integrate the polar positions of the evolutionary and teleological theorists, as well as the other theories, have resulted in several perspectives on how the dimensions interact. A common denominator of such efforts is self-organization, whether this involves political accommodation, sensemaking, or cultural evolution, often either driven or responded to by some combination of environmental conditions and individual choices.

VI. Organizational Learning

A. Theories of Collective Cognition

The developing appreciation of the complexity of organizational systems has brought with it skepticism about traditional models of change, including evolutionary, political, and even teleological approaches. It has also brought with it a greater recognition that change is ubiquitous and continuous. Thus, it is not surprising that in the past decade there has developed an interest in the phenomenon of collective cognition, or how organizations learn, remember, and continuously solve problems and adapt to changing conditions. Researchers have pursued several lines of work in this area such as retention learning mechanisms (Moorman & Miner, 1997), communities of practice (Wenger, 1998) (see chapter 12) and the incorporation of knowledge in communities of practice (Brown & Duguid, 2005), distributed or organizational memory (Wegner, Erber, & Raymond, 1991), and structures of collective mind or cognition (Weick & Roberts, 1993). A common theme in these approaches is that learning is an incremental process of successive approximation and improvisation, one that entails "repeated acts of translation that convert ideas into useful artifacts that fit purposes at hand, or repeated acts of learning that enlarge, strengthen, or shrink the repertoire of [organizational] responses" (Weick & Quinn, 1999, p. 377). The recent interest in organizational learning is an important elaboration of the information-processing paradigm.

B. Technical versus Social Perspectives

A central question is, What constitutes a learning organization? How do you know one when you see one? According to Easterby-Smith, Araujo, and

FIGURE 11.2: PATH DIAGRAM OF ORGANIZATIONAL LEARNING: SINGLE AND DOUBLE LOOP

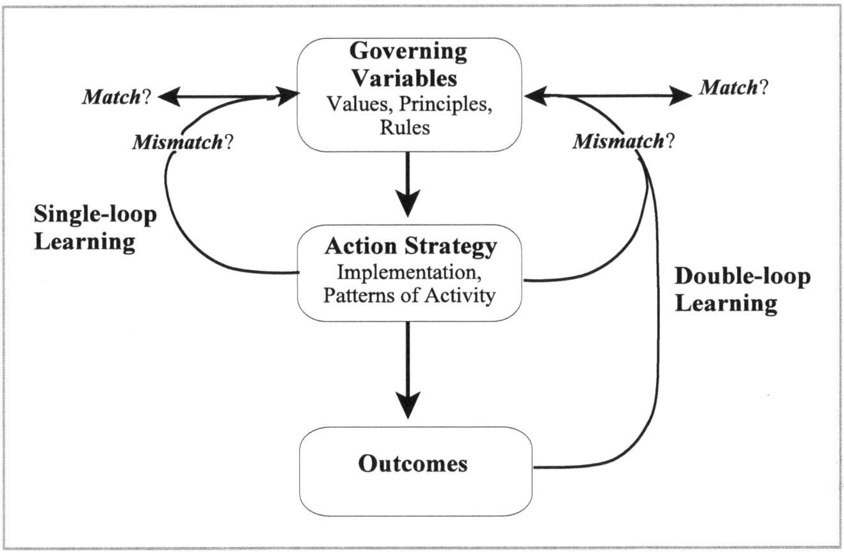

Source: Argyris (1999, p. 68).

Burgoyne (1999), there are two predominant answers to this question, the technical and the social. The technical view is that organizational learning is a type of information processing that often uses well-defined protocols of data collection, research, and formal decision-making, based on both qualitative and quantitative data, typically data obtained in the public domain.

One of the earliest and most influential concepts from this approach is Argyris and Schön's (1974) distinction between single- and double-loop learning (see figure 11.2). The more routine processes of single-loop learning involve the continuous adjustment of action strategies on the basis of their outcomes, whereas double-loop learning refers to not only routine learning but also its occurrence in the context of adjustments in the parameters governing that action—the underlying values, goals, philosophies, or action rules or principles—out of which the action strategies emerge. Double-loop learning, while less frequent and often more arduous or even painful, allows for considerably enhanced flexibility and successful problem solving.

The social perspective involves the less well defined and multiple ways that individuals and groups develop organizational frames and interpret information at hand, including political accommodation, intuition, and the application of culturally rooted ethical principles and values.

C. Organizational and Transactional Memory

An area of interest for those who take a social perspective is organizational or transactional memory (Wegner et al., 1991), which refers to the idea that memory is not only an attribute of individuals but also of social systems. Various people and groups, given their job descriptions, roles, or personal characteristics, are expected to remember different types of information or to know how to access different types of information, and to provide this to the large organization whenever called on to do so. Many who take the social perspective view organizational learning as a type of social construction in which learning occurs when groups of individuals can successfully construct a shared vision of the world, whether or not that vision is functional or true.

VII. Attempts at Theoretical Integration

A. Contingency Theories

The development of organizational theories can be characterized by their proliferation and the recurrent efforts to reconcile these models. Classical theorists assumed that there was a best way to structure organizations, such as through hierarchy, differentiation, and the separation of policy from its implementation. In contrast, for several decades now, the prevailing approach to this problem has been contingency theory. There are actually multiple contingency theories—those concerned with leadership, technology, organizational design, decision making, personnel management, or some combination of those. The common denominator is an effort to quantify one or a combination of factors for which particular management responses are considered optimal. Such theories attempt to identify combinations of environmental and technological conditions that suggest whether to pursue particular organizational designs or personnel practices. The two most commonly cited dimensions of the environment are complexity and stability (Duncan, 1972; Lawrence & Lorsch, 1967; Thompson, 1967). Complexity in this context refers to the number of factors that must be considered in decision making, and stability refers to the extent that factors stay the same over time.

One review of the research on contingency theory concluded that more uncertain and complex environments indicate the need for a more decentralized, organic structure (Dessler, 1980). Although much valuable work has been conducted using contingency theory, a major limitation is that the results tend not to be cumulative. Individual studies identify combinations of three to five factors associated with outcomes of interest, but these tend to be done in different contexts and with different measures. Perhaps for this reason, as far back as 1975, Pennings concluded that there was little support for the idea that effective organizations designed their structures in line with environmental contingencies. Others have sought to remedy this problem by hypothesizing that organizational success is contingent on an environmental goodness-of-fit and on an internal fit or the coherence of an organization's constituent parts. Specifically, Baird and Meshoulam (1988) have proposed that there are two strategies that need to be balanced to maximize organizational effectiveness: (1) an external fit in which the department's design, systems, and management approach must fit the organization's environment and stage of development, and (2) an internal fit in which the features of the organization need to complement one another. Baird and Meshoulam's model, thus, incorporates both external and internal fit.

B. An Application of Complex Systems Theory: Chaordic Organizations

In recent years, large networks of organizations have developed with increasing interdependencies among them (e.g., the Internet, financial institutions, international regulatory bodies, social service systems). This trend has undercut the classic command-and-control models of organizations as well as contingency theories of hypothesized linear relations between limited numbers of variables. The analysis of organizational and interorganizational networks has increasingly come to rely on complex systems theory. Such networks are viewed as often decentralized collectivities of autonomous agents (individuals or organizations) that, with sufficient balance between order and chaos (i.e., the edge-of-chaos phenomenon), self-organize to generate highly adaptive systems. Dee Hock (1999), the founder of Visa, the largest private financial institution in the world, was a pioneer of the application of complex systems to organizations. From his experience with Visa, Hock coined the term *chaordic organizations* to refer to networked organizational systems that successfully capitalize on decentralized structures and self-organization. Hock (1999) proposes the following definition: "Chaord (kay´ord) 1: any autocatalytic, self-regulating, adaptive, nonlinear, complex organism, organization, or system, whether physical, biological or social, the behavior of which harmoniously exhibits characteristics of both order and chaos. 2: an entity whose behavior exhibits patterns and probabilities not governed or explained by the behavior of its parts. 3: the fundamental organizing principle of nature and evolution. Chaordic (kay´ordic)

1: anything simultaneously orderly and chaotic. 2: patterned in a way domi-nated neither by order nor chaos. 3: existing in the phase between order and chaos" (p. 30).

Chaordic organizations, Hock contends, rely on shared decision mak-ing, with decisions originating at any point in the system. They empha-size lateral, rather than hierarchical, relationships among colleagues. They also successfully integrate both top-down and bottom-up processes, as well as competition and cooperation. He points out that while information is centralized, power is decentralized. Hierarchy is used not to concentrate decision making and authority, but to manage participation of autonomous agents. Perhaps one of the most important insights of Hock's theory of cha-ordic organizations, derived from complexity theory, is that "purpose and principle, clearly understood and articulated, and commonly shared, are the genetic code of any healthy organization. To the degree that you hold pur-pose and principles in common among you, you can dispense with command and control. People will know how to behave in accordance with them, and they'll do it in thousands of unimaginable, creative ways. The organization will become a vital, living set of beliefs" (see Hoffman, 2002, n.p.).

This is an application of the idea that particular types of shared decision rules constitute an essential source of the adaptive self-organizing processes. Such shared decision rules probably need to be reflected in both the infor-mal and often unspoken culture of the organization and in the explicit and formal rules and protocols that guide its everyday activities. The successful emergence of a workable system of shared rules, values, and understand-ings is now supported by the proliferation of electronic modes of real-time communication, cell phones and text messaging, e-mail, and the Internet. These developments dramatically undercut the viability of classical organi-zational designs.

C. Leadership in Diverse Conditions

Such integration and decentralized adaptability, as evidenced by chaordic organizations, does not happen magically or always from the bottom up; it sometimes also involves top-down processes. For this reason, Jeffrey Gold-stein (1997), who has been a central figure in the application of complex systems theory to organizations, has emphasized the importance of leader-ship. However, Goldstein carefully distinguishes different types of leader-ship that are possible and even needed within different types of systems. He distinguishes between the type and source of structure in an organization and contends that the resulting leadership emerges out of combinations of the two dimensions (see table 11.4). Structure may be either hierarchical or

TABLE 11.4: A CONTINGENCY THEORY OF LEADERSHIP FROM COMPLEX SYSTEM THEORY

| | | Type of Structure | |
		HIERARCHICAL	PARTICIPATORY
SOURCE OF STRUCTURE	SELF-ORGANIZED	Informal Leadership	Emergent Networks
	EXTERNALLY IMPOSED	Command and Control Stucture	Imposed Teams

Source: Goldstein (1997).

participatory, and the source of structure may be externally imposed or self-organized. Traditional leadership is found in hierarchical organizations that impose structure, otherwise known as a command-and-control bureaucracy. However, traditional hierarchical organizations may sometimes allow for a degree of self-organization, and when they do, informal leadership may emerge, among either people designated as managers or frontline staff. In contrast, organizations that have imposed or designed forms of structure may attempt to encourage participation, often through the designation of teams, whether quality circles or total quality management (TQM) teams. Occasionally, though, organizations may not impose structure and instead encourage participation. When they do, there is the greatest likelihood that emergent networks, or chaordic organizations, will arise, with distributed and informal forms of leadership.

Leadership is generally distinguished from management in that proactive, executive, and perhaps even visionary qualities are incorporated. Such leadership stands in contrast with the often-reactive focus of much of middle-level management, which is more involved with maintenance and repair functions. Leadership often incorporates management tasks, but it also serves a more truly integrative function when it attempts to build on an organization's history and resources not only to solve immediate problems but also to work toward realizing its longer-term visions. A precondition for doing this is the success of leaders in integrating bottom-up input with top-down efforts at coordination in the interests of successful organizational learning and problem solving.

The complex systems perspective has come to incorporate several approaches to learning, and it draws on contingency theory, such as Goldstein's approach to understanding the integrative functions of leadership. A source of its effectiveness in reconciling several diverse strands of theoretical thought is its placement of organizational dynamics and change at the center of attention, in contrast to organizational functions and structures. It assumes no single engine of change, acknowledging the respective roles of chance and social selection, competition and conflict, self-organization, co-operative action, and intentional and rational planning. To the extent that it assumes that change is ever present, it suggests that the primary role of the change agent involves not so much external intervention but rather redirection and facilitation of changes already under way. Weick and Quinn (1999) go so far as to propose that under such a paradigm, change agents do not function according to the traditional Lewinian injunction to unfreeze, transition, and refreeze organizational structures. Instead, they may sometimes work to temporarily freeze or reflect dynamics through maps, schemes, and stories; to rebalance or reinterpret the forces and patterns involved; and to unfreeze or resume improvisation, translation of the stories to new contexts, and ongoing learning. Rather than function as the prime mover that creates change, in this alternative paradigm, the change agent functions as a sense maker that engages, facilitates, and redirects change.

VIII. Summary

This chapter introduces the mezzo level of complex systems analysis to problems involving organizations. It considers organizations a special type of large ongoing group, one in which formal instrumental relationships dominate and one that is committed to achieving specific social or private goals. Organizations are embedded in communities and may include communities in them; as such, they represent one component of entangled social hierarchies. Both organizations and communities are located in and actualize various social institutions, such as the family, church, government, and education. Both organizations and communities face the problem of balancing cooperative and competitive relationships. Organizations generally are concerned with maximizing cooperation and interdependence, whereas many communities in the United States place a premium on freedom and autonomy.

The chapter reviews two emerging areas: organizational change and organizational learning. Theories of change reviewed include the evolutionary, teleological, life cycle, political, social cognition, and cultural. The point is made that the complex systems perspective includes each of these, viewing organizational change as ongoing, and that when such an approach is taken, the role of the change agent becomes one of facilitation and rebalancing rather than of unfreezing and external intervention. Organizations are also discussed in terms of their ongoing ability for memory, learning, and problem solving.

The chapter concludes with a discussion of selected efforts to integrate the plethora of competing theories, including traditional contingency theories, as well as the application of complex systems and chaos theory—specifically, Dee Hock's theory of chaordic organizations. It also reviews an application of the idea of self-organization to the development of a kind of contingency theory of organizational leadership.

For Further Reading

Axelrod, R. (1997). *The complexity of cooperation: Agent-based models of competition and cooperation.* Princeton, NJ: Princeton University Press.

Bolman, L. G., & Deal, T. E. (1997). *Reframing organizations: Artistry, choice, and leadership.* San Francisco: Jossey-Bass.

Dooley, K. J. (1997). A complex adaptive systems model of organizational change. *Nonlinear Dynamics, Psychology, and Life Sciences,* 1(1), 69–97.

Easterby-Smith, M., Burgoyne, J., & Araujo, L. (Eds.). (1999). *Organizational learning and the learning organization.* London: Sage.

Goldstein, J. (1997). Riding the waves of emergence: Leadership innovations in complex systems. In C. Lindberg, P. Plsek, & B. Zimmerman (Eds.), *Edgeware: Complexity resources for health care leaders* (pp. IX17–IX36). Cranbury, NJ: Curt Lindberg.

Hock, D. (1999). *Birth of the chaordic age.* San Francisco: Berrett-Koehler.

Kezar, A. J. (2001). *Understanding and facilitating organizational change in the twenty-first century: Recent research and conceptualizations.* San Francisco: Jossey-Bass.

Weick, K. E., & Quinn, R. E. (1999). Organizational change and development. *Annual Review of Psychology,* 50, 361–386.

CHAPTER 12

Community Theory, Dynamics, and Assessment

A healthy social life is found only, when in the mirror of each soul the whole community finds its reflection, and when in the whole community the virtue of each one is living.

—RUDOLF STEINER

I. Introduction

A. Issues

Steiner's comment in the epigraph on the interdependency of the individual and his or her community, on the need for each to contain within itself a reflection of the other, captures an evolving conception of this relationship. At the foundation of the community is a mutuality of consciousness, of loving awareness, between individuals and their social environments. Unlike families, small groups, or even organizations, the notion of community is notoriously difficult to define. Raymond Williams (1976) points out that the term's ambiguity arises out of its reference to matters of "direct common concern" (pp. 65–66)—a community of mutual interests—as well as to various modes of organization (e.g., a university community) that actualize those common interests. He also observes that it always has a positive connotation, with an associated warmth and closeness, in contrast to the coldness and distance of formal organizations or the state.

The concept of community is charged with a range of values rather than a narrow focus on instrumental relationships. The literature on communities reflects this sense, as it highlights the many benefits and positive functions of communities. This perspective also contains within it a fundamental problem with how communities are understood. There appears to be a much more limited understanding, both in the professional literature and in the general public, about how communities actually function and the required inputs for achieving the idealized benefits of communities. For this reason, there is a lack of consensus about individuals' responsibilities for realizing community ideals. Human service professionals typically see individual clients and too often rely on secondhand reports of their relevant communities. As such, human behavior is decontextualized. This chapter aims to reintroduce these contexts, both the supports and the opportunities that may exist, as well as their destructive aspects, in the hope that readers will consider community building a central strategy for use in the human services.

B. Definitions

The term *community* has been part of the English language since the fourteenth century. It originated from the French and Latin words that involve the notion of things being held in common. The Latin word *cum,* meaning "together," and the word *munus,* meaning "a gift," were combined to form the word *community,* which literally refers to a coming together or sharing of gifts. Thus, the notion of community goes beyond simple interdependency and exchange to include the idea of voluntary and caring exchange. It is not surprising that many definitions of community emphasize a group that one feels one belongs to and that one shares important things with. Increasingly, it has come to connote social collectivities in which egalitarian relationships and consensus decision making are emphasized. Others, such as Roland Warren (1973), define community in terms of its functions, as "that combination of social units and systems which perform the major social functions having locality relevance" (p. 9). Examples of communities include small towns, neighborhoods in larger cities, or large groups of individuals identified with a common interest, whether it be stamp collecting, a religion, an ethnic identity, or a profession. Some communities may be as small as several dozen practitioners within a large organization. Or occasionally in times of crisis, a large metropolitan area or even a nation can be experienced as a community, although this tends to be the exception. The examples illustrate the ambiguous and shifting nature of community boundaries that often depend on changes in the consciousness of shared values and interests.

Human service practitioners work not only to enhance the competencies of individuals but also to build the communities they work with. This chapter will therefore review key developments in theory and research on communities as an essential part of the multiple social environments that individuals continuously interact with. It expands on the previous chapter on organizations in that it explores a type of social system in which organizations are not only embedded but also often enlivened. At the beginning of the previous chapter, the case was made that organizations and communities are in many respects entangled hierarchies, commingled to form complex systems. Although communities consist of both instrumental and psychosocial components, the latter are often predominant and should be understood broadly to include interpersonal, political, and cultural dimensions. This chapter will begin with the subject of community as a value, including its benefits and functions, as well as community types. It then turns to the more difficult task of understanding how community networks actually function and, finally, the major societal trends that affect communities and how community systems are assessed in practice.

II. Community as a Value: Benefits and Functions

A. Community Values

The functioning of communities as complex systems is partly based on the underlying values and perceived benefits that motivate people to take part in these kinds of associations. Whether these values and ideals are successfully realized is an open question, but their content and spirit represent a critical foundation for community building. The literature has continuously emphasized the importance of community characteristics such as trust, tolerance, and reciprocity (Smith, 2009). Trust in the context of communities has been defined as "the confident expectation that people, institutions, and things will act in a consistent, honest, and appropriate way" (Smith, 2009), yet not uncritically and without appropriate protections. Closely related are tolerance and respect for differences, an openness to learning from one another (Walzer, 1997), and even the celebration of diversity. Another critical element of community as a value is reciprocity. Robert Putnam (2000) characterizes reciprocity in these terms: "I'll do this for you now, without expecting anything immediately in return, and perhaps without even knowing you, confident that down the road you or someone else will return the favour" (p. 134). Reciprocity is the embracing of feedback, of exchange, of interdependency. Valuing community means valuing the regular give-and-take upon which it is built.

B. Preconditions for Community Functioning

The values of trust, tolerance, and reciprocity have been defined in a variety of terms, one of which involves the following critical preconditions for community life (Occidental College, 2006):

Social contact. Physical and social opportunities for social reciprocity are of critical importance.

Shared values. Examples may be a common interest in raising families, sharing a religious faith, or the academic life in a university community. The development of value statements and other cultural or artistic expressions of these values can be of critical importance in the identification of shared values.

Communication. Reciprocity and exchange must have a means of realization, including a common language and avenues of communication, whether this involves e-mail, telephone, curbside and other ad hoc discussions, or formal meetings.

Self-regulation. Communities need to be supported by norms involving individual responsibility and mutuality in holding one another accountable to commitments made.

Member involvement. As with all other systems, effective functioning presumes that communities are energized by not only necessary resources, the interest, motivation, and commitments of its members to actualize their shared values.

Shared physical environment. Although this usually means shared common physical spaces [e.g., meeting rooms, parks, town halls], it also involves a shared temporal environment. It is not enough to share space, if at entirely different times. Shared spatial and temporal environments can also mean shared means of community on the Internet, for example, through common websites, chat rooms, or the like.

Sense of belonging. Effective communities involve not just a utilitarian engagement but also a feeling of belonging, of connection and mutual being, that is fulfilling and engaging beyond all practical considerations. People feel esteemed not just for what they might contribute but also for their very existence.

Lists of preconditions, such as the preceding, are useful not only for assessing problems in existing communities but also for planning community-building initiatives. These may involve towns or neighborhoods, but they often involve communities within or centered on particular organizations, such as psychosocial clubhouses, nursing homes, a university dormitory, or a public housing development.

C. The Psychological Sense of Community

A related approach to the study of such preconditions has used the psychological sense of community, which many believe is one of the most critical preconditions for healthy community life. In 1974, the psychologist Samuel Sarason formulated the concept of the psychological sense of community and emphasized its importance in individual identity and self-esteem. McMillan and Chavis (1986) developed the "sense of community," defining it as "a feeling that members have of belonging, a feeling that members matter to one another and to the group, and a shared faith that members' needs will be met through their commitment to be together" (p. 9). They say that it has four elements: membership, influence, integration and fulfillment of needs, and shared emotional connection. McMillan and Chavis attempt to operationalize membership by identifying a community system's boundaries, emotional safety, sense of belonging and identification, personal investment of the participants, and common symbol system. Influence is the ability of members to influence one another and the group. There must, in short, be a sense of efficacy and empowerment. The third element—integration and fulfillment of needs—presumes that the group serves specific psychological, social, or practical needs, that it must create an "an economy of social trade" (p. 322). These authors emphasize their fourth element of emotional connection and identified each of its components from the body of community research:

1. *Contact hypothesis.* Greater personal interaction increases the likelihood that people will become close.
2. *Quality of interaction.* This involves the extent of closure, clarity, importance, mutuality, and respect of interactions.
3. *Closure to events.* Ambiguous interaction and unresolved tasks inhibit group cohesiveness.
4. *Shared valent event hypothesis.* Increased importance of a shared event (e.g., a crisis) facilitates a group bond.
5. *Investment.* Beyond boundary maintenance and cognitive dissonance, the community becomes more important to someone who has given more time and energy to it.
6. *Effect of honor and humiliation on community members.* Someone who has been rewarded in front of a community feels more attracted to that community; someone who has been humiliated feels less attracted to that community.
7. *Spiritual bond.* The authors admit that this quality is difficult to describe but maintain that it is "present to some degree in all

communities" (p. 14) and give the example of the concept of soul in the formation of a national African American community in the United States.

McMillan and Chavis theorize that their five attributes of membership (i.e., boundaries, emotional safety, sense of belonging and identification, personal investment, common symbol system) interact in a "circular, self-reinforcing way, with all conditions, having both causes and effects" (p. 15). Similarly, others see the psychological sense of community as an outcome or side effect of a well-functioning community. McMillan and Chavis propose several heuristic formulas to characterize the dynamics involved with the development of a sense of community or shared emotional connection:

Shared emotional connection = contact + high-quality interaction.

High-quality interaction = (events with successful closure – ambiguity) × (event valence × sharedness of the event) + (amount of honor given to members – amount of humiliation). (p. 15)

D. Social Capital

Community as a value, preconditions of community life, and sense of community are all examples of what has been termed *social capital.* This idea has been around for many years and was first introduced by Lydia Hanifan (1916) in relation to rural school community centers during the early years of the twentieth century. It has recently been popularized by one of the leading community theorists, Robert Putnam. Whereas Hanifan (1916) defined social capital as "those tangible substances [that] count for most in the daily lives of people" (p. 130), Putnam (2000) comments, "Whereas physical capital refers to physical objects and human capital refers to the properties of individuals, social capital refers to connections among individuals—social networks and the norms of reciprocity and trustworthiness that arise from them. In that sense social capital is closely related to what some have called 'civic virtue.' The difference is that 'social capital' calls attention to the fact that civic virtue is most powerful when embedded in a sense network of reciprocal social relations. A society of many virtuous but isolated individuals is not necessarily rich in social capital" (p. 19).

The World Bank (2009) has used the notion of social capital in many of its social development initiatives. Other contributions have been advanced by Jane Jacobs (1961), with respect to urban life and neighborliness; Pierre Bourdieu (1984), in relation to social theory; and James S. Coleman (1988), in his work on the social context of education (see Smith, 2001). A central idea is that some communities, because of their history, culture, and other norms and relationships, are able to build up a reservoir of goodwill, trust, and working relationships, and that this social asset is one of the most important because of its ability to solve problems and to achieve sustainable development. According to the World Bank (2009), there is increasing evidence "that social cohesion is critical for societies to prosper economically and for development to be sustainable." Social capital is also being applied to the study of problems of organizational maintenance and development (Cohen & Prusak, 2001; Smith, 2001).

Social capital has often been operationalized through an assessment of the extent that individuals engage with community associations and related activities. In French adult education, this has been referred to as "la vie associative" (Smith, 2001). Toynbee (1985) notes that this is a difficult phrase to translate into English "because it contains an idea or even an ideal which is not so apparent in Britain. It recognizes the importance of association in the widest sense of the word and the effect which this can have both on the life of the individual and on the life of a village, town, region or country. The 'life of the associations' or the 'associative life' are inadequate translations" (p. 33).

In the United States, as in Britain, there has been much concern over the quality of community life. For example, it has often been pointed out that there has been substantial decline in the active membership in associations such as parent-teacher associations, clubs, athletic teams, and other community groups. Putnam wrote about this phenomenon in his popular book *Bowling Alone* (2000), mentioning that there has also been an increase in individualized leisure activities.

There is an extensive body of research that has identified many practical benefits that accrue from a community's social capital (Putnam, 2000). A common finding is that there is a strong correlation between the possession of social capital and physical health. Putnam points out, "As a rough rule of thumb, if you belong to no groups but decide to join one, you cut your risk of dying over the next year in half. If you smoke and belong to no groups, it's a toss-up statistically whether you should stop smoking or start joining" (p. 331). He finds that regular attendance in community groups has the same impact as obtaining a college degree or more than doubling personal income. Civic relationships are almost as powerful as marriage and wealth in predicting life happiness.

Putnam (2000) also cites evidence to demonstrate that "child development is powerfully shaped by social capital. Trust, networks, and norms of reciprocity within a child's family, school, peer group, and larger community have far reaching effects on their opportunities and choices, and hence on their behavior and development" (pp. 296–306). Social capital also has a powerful impact on the physical cleanliness and safety of public spaces. Places with higher crime rates arise partly because people avoid participating in community organizations; do not volunteer to mentor younger people; and lack networks with family, friends, and neighbors. In addition, there is an emerging body of research that suggests that "where trust and social networks flourish, individuals, firms, neighborhoods, and even nations prosper economically" (pp. 319–325).

E. Functions of Communities

So far the focus of this section has been on the strengths and benefits of communities and their underlying attributes such as social capital. This is, however, an idealized and incomplete view, because it neglects both the necessary inputs and the role that outputs play in the larger social system. Roland Warren (1973) has promoted a functionalist perspective on communities. For example, he defines the community as "that combination of social units and systems which perform the major social functions having locality relevance" (p. 9). Specifically, he hypothesizes that communities perform the following functions: production, distribution, and consumption; socialization; social control; social participation; mutual support; and external linkage. For example, certain types of communities take on the function of converting uneducated children into responsible, productive, and civic-minded adults. Functionalism is beset with significant problems, including assumptions that society is a type of equilibrium-maintaining mechanism involving the external production of preset outcomes. Nonetheless, it does present a starting point for the analysis of complex community systems, one that needs to include but also move well beyond the identification of simple input-throughput-output functions.

F. Communitarian Theory

One response to the limitations of the idealized and the functionalist perspectives on communities has been the development in recent years of the communitarian movement. Communitarianism emerged during the 1980s, partly in reaction to disenchantment with liberal theory and practice. One of its central themes is that individual rights need to be more effectively counterbalanced with social responsibilities, and that individuals do not exist in isolation but are molded by and in turn mold the values and cultures of the communities they participate in. Communitarians argue that the individual and community define each other in interactive feedback loops, ones that are even tautological. They suggest that there is an unbalanced emphasis on rights in liberalism. Dominant liberal theories of justice, as well as much of economic and political theory, emerge out of liberalism's conception of the individual as a disembodied self, uprooted from cultural meanings, community attachments, and the life stories that form the identities of real human beings.

One of the founders of the communitarian movement is the Israeli sociologist Amitai Etzioni, who, along with Mary Ann Glendon and William Galston, developed the movement's platform in November 1991. The platform argues for devolving government services to their appropriate levels, pursuing new kinds of public-private partnerships, and developing national and local service programs. The platform begins with the following preamble:

> American men, women, and children are members of many communities—families; neighborhoods; innumerable social, religious, ethnic, work place, and professional associations; and the body politic itself. Neither human existence nor individual liberty can be sustained for long outside the interdependent and overlapping communities to which all of us belong. Nor can any community long survive unless its members dedicate some of their attention, energy, and resources to shared projects. The exclusive pursuit of private interest erodes the network of social environments on which we all depend, and is destructive to our shared experiment in democratic self-government. For these reasons, we hold that the rights of individuals cannot long be preserved without a communitarian perspective. (Communitarian Network, 2005)

For communitarians, the value of community transcends liberal theories of social justice. Ideologically, communitarianism can be placed at a low to moderate level in its emphasis on both personal and economic liberties. It instead favors community commitment and responsibilities (see figure 12.1). The question of the priority of the individual or community has had major implications for perennial ethical questions involving health care, abortion, multiculturalism, hate speech, and the like. Another closely related use of the term is ideological and has been referred to as responsive communitarianism, which Etzioni practices. This approach falls between the traditional Right and Left by emphasizing a balance of both and individual

FIGURE 12.1: COMMUNITARIANISM IN RELATION TO MAJOR POLITICAL ORIENTATIONS USING THE NOLAN CHART

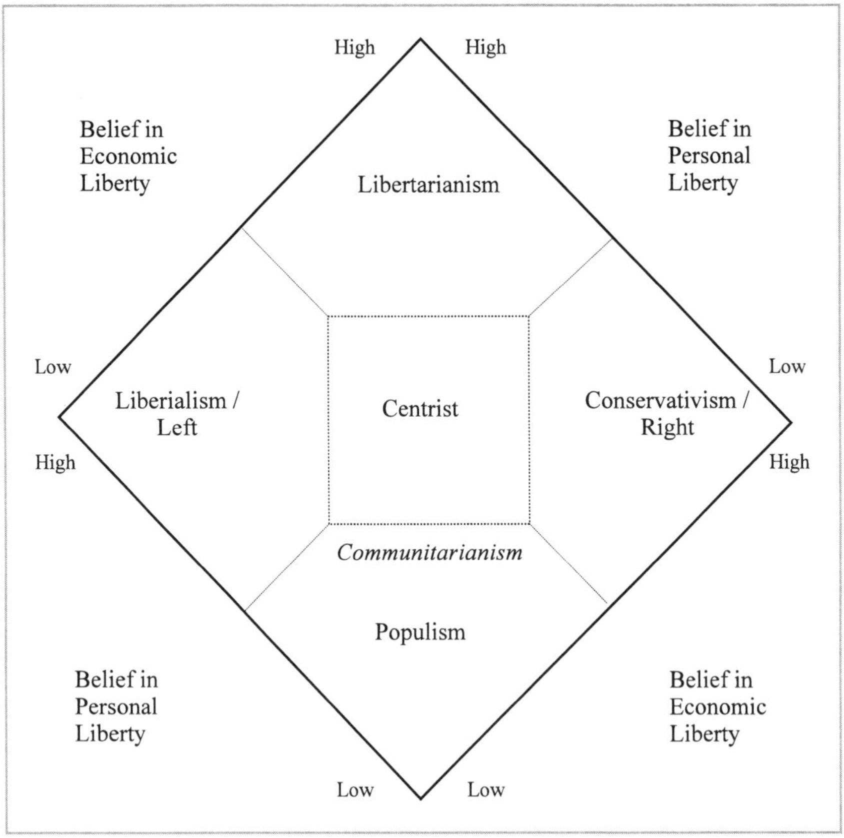

High   High

Belief in
Economic   Belief in
Liberty   Libertarianism   Personal
                                                  Liberty

Low   Low

Liberialism /   Centrist   Conservativism /
Left   Right

High   High

Communitarianism

Populism

Belief in   Belief in
Personal   Economic
Liberty   Liberty

Low   Low

Note: This figure illustrates the theory that political orientations can be characterized by a person or group's position on two dimensions: (1) The extent that they believe in personal liberties, and (2) the degree that they emphasize economic liberty. For example, someone who believes in economic liberties such as free trade and who is concerned about too many personal or social liberties (e.g., personal medical decisions) is often identified as conservative.

Source: Adapted from Nolan (1971).

responsibilities and communal rights. How we think about communities and define the balance of individual rights and responsibilities has substantial implications not only for community practice but also, more fundamentally, for our propensity and approach to participating in the communities that we are part of and those that we seek to develop (see Institute for Communitarian Policy Studies, 2009).

III. Types of Communities

Communities come in many sizes and shapes. Sometimes groups of hobby-ists, such as stamp collectors or cave explorers, are thought of as communities, especially when an interrelated array of such groups are considered. Self-help groups such as Alcoholics Anonymous or Gamblers Anonymous, political and spiritual groups, labor unions and professional groups, and Internet discussion boards are all examples of communities with varying degrees of cohesiveness and member identification. Online communities are usually better thought of as virtual communities.

A. A Classical Typology

The German sociologist Ferdinand Toennies (1855–1936) introduced one of the first typologies of communities. He based this typology on his theory that there are two kinds of human will: on one hand, there is the essential will (*Wesenwille*), which is a fundamental or organic drive that is focused on community well-being; on the other hand, he identified the arbitrary will (*Kürwille*), which is an individually oriented will that is instrumental, intentional, and goal directed. Toennies referred to some communities as gemeinschaft communities (often translated as "community"), based on the essential will and also referred to as locational communities, as prime examples are the traditional village or extended family. Here relationships are valued intrinsically, not as a means to an end. In contrast, Toennies (1957) used the term *gesellschaft* (translated as "society") to refer to communities that are based on arbitrary will, on instrumental purposes, and in which membership arises out of a shared purpose. These are also referred to as identificational communities.

B. Combinations and Variations

Most communities, however, display elements of each of these ideal types. Whereas a village-based community may be mainly a network of primary and noninstrumental relationships, situated at a particular time and space, there are usually a wide variety of instrumental associations that overlap and interpenetrate such communities. These may involve responses to governmental taxation, local governance, or religious associations. Similarly, in a professional community, practical considerations such as career and service advancement or exchange of new information or developments may be dominant. However, these should not obscure the possibilities for primary forms of identification, caring, and mutual support in such professional contexts. In an important sense, healthy communities require both dimensions and permit the flexible coexistence of multiple and overlapping subgroups that cooperate in supporting members and that compete for them and their resources. The ambiguity of the term *community*, especially when it involves networks of associations of varying sizes, highlights the community as emerging out of the collective consciousness of a people. Such an understanding of community is based on the recognition of mutuality and interdependence, one that constantly shifts from the local and particular to an extended recognition of common interests and aspirations.

There are several related kinds of community that are usually regarded as variations of gesellschaft or identificational communities. One is religious or ethnic communities, which have come to be dispersed through either migration or forced relocation, and these are known as diasporas, for example, the Jewish Diaspora. Another variation of the gesellschaft community is the virtual community on the Internet. These can involve Listserv discussion groups, online learning services, interactive encyclopedias (e.g., Wikipedia), gaming or music sites, and dating or employment services, to mention a few examples. Porter (2004) defines virtual communities as "an aggregation of individuals or business partners who interact around a shared interest, where the interaction is at least partially supported and/or mediated by technology and guided by some protocols or norms" (p. 3). Given the technological infrastructure that supports such community networks, they are remarkably free of the constraints of space and even time. While chat-room discussions may require scheduling at a particular hour, and for this reason are referred to as synchronous, many Internet interactions can happen over extended periods of time and thus are referred to as asynchronous. For example, those researching family history may respond to posts or comments that someone made several years earlier (with the hope that that person is still around and reading new posts). Several attempts have been made to characterize the major kinds of virtual communities, one of which is Porter's (2004) two-part typology: (1) member initiated and (2) organization sponsored. Member-initiated virtual communities are either social or professional in orientation, and organization-sponsored virtual communities arise out of the nonprofit, commercial, or governmental arenas.

IV. Dynamics of Communities

This section reviews several approaches to understanding how communities change. Both researchers and practitioners have been concerned with communities as contexts, targets, or agents of change (Coulton, 2004). Most practitioners in the human services regard communities as merely contexts within which they work with individuals, families, and small groups—and sometimes with organizations. For others, communities are sources of problems and thus the object requiring change. A minority of practitioners view communities as agents or partners in bringing about change in other systems, those on either the macro level or the micro level. But whichever is the practitioner's primary orientation, the foundation of each approach involves an understanding of how communities continuously change, for better or worse.

An understanding of the patterns of change and continuity in communities, including their official decision-making structures, financial and business interests, and socioeconomic profiles, are critical and recurring needs in the study of communities. All of these involve the need to understand communication patterns: who talks to whom, about what, and why. One of the foundations for understanding social systems is understanding their component networks and how they operate. The essential building blocks of any network are exchange and communication linkages, especially their component feedback loops. These may involve an exchange of gifts, information, money or goods, services, care, or respect, to name a few examples. Are these exchanges voluntary, contractual, or coerced? Are they simple or complex, involving multiple-stage exchanges? What are the rules governing them? For Herbert Simon (1969), communities were defined by frequency of social interaction, with their boundaries being marked by sparse interactions.

A. Traditional Approaches

There have been a variety of traditional approaches to study community dynamics. Anthropological, psychoanalytical, and sociological approaches have dominated the study of community. However, such disparate professions as social work, economics, cultural history, and political science have also made important contributions. Cutting across these disciplines and professions has been a diversity of theoretical frameworks that have guided this study, most notably human ecology, the development and application of constructed typologies (e.g., that of Toennies, 1957), action and leadership, and change and social problems (Poplin, 1972).

One of the more promising ways to classify approaches to the study of communities is that of Bernard (1973). On one hand, he argues that there are two ideological frameworks that motivate this research, and on the other hand, these ideologies inform four approaches. He contends that the two ideologies that involve capitalism and structural functionalism "constituted the encompassing matrix within which community research took place" (p. 15). The four analytical frameworks are the ecological, class, power structure, and rural-urban continuum. The *ecological approach,* derived from structural functionalism, attempts to understand community in geographic and land-use terms, both as a context and as an outcome of the underlying community relationships. The study of class and inequality of opportunity, both its economic and its cultural dimensions, derived in part from capitalist ideology and its failures. Political scientists, in contrast, have usually been more interested in decision making and power structures and have debated whether these are best characterized by elitist, pluralist, or dialectical theories. Finally, the study of the rural and urban dimensions of communities, of their gemeinschaft and gesellschaft characteristics, treated the community as a dependent variable, subject to broad social trends such as industrialization or bureaucratization. As much as each of these approaches has sought to unravel community dynamics, ultimately each has largely failed. Each has used a version of conflict theory that assumes that change happens simply as a result of the pushes and pulls, the competitions and collisions, of interests. They have assumed only a secondary role for coalition building, cooperative effort, and human aspirations, with the particular content and outcome of these conflicts largely an outcome of specific historical and material conditions and accidents. Most have failed to consider human aspirations, the impact of collective identities, and the ways that such self-selections have driven communities' efforts to self-organize.

B. Approaches to Intentional Community Change

Much of social change theory concerns global patterns in the development of societies and civilizations. Such global trends constitute the broader context for change as the human service professional encounters it on the community, organizational, and personal levels. Applications of social change theory to communities are less developed than are applications on the macro level (see chapter 2). Theory of the natural processes of community change is particularly undeveloped, but considerably better developed are theories that concern intentional or prescriptive community change. This may be because of the assumption of equilibrium: that communities, once formed, change little without intentional or planned efforts.

The area of community change and functioning that has been most extensively studied is that of political decision making. Political decision-making theory is one of the better-developed theories of change involving communities. However, it fails to account for change in other dimensions of communities, such as culture or structure. Much greater attention has been paid to identifying strategies of intentional change in communities. Reviewers of these theories have proposed several typologies. For example, James Midgely (1993) suggests that these theories fall into three general categories: (1) individualist, (2) collectivist, and (3) populist. Whereas individualist strategies involve personal change, competency building, and self-actualization, collectivist approaches most often involve organizational development as a means for strengthening communities. Populist strategies aim to mobilize strategic constituencies for facilitating structural changes in decision making or the distribution of resources.

Similarly, approaches popularly referred to as bottom-up involve such strategies as mass mobilization, social advocacy, or community organization to impact social control systems (e.g., governmental bodies) from the outside, and top-down strategies attempt to work with such systems to plan and administer social programs, develop better policies, and the like. Occasionally writers have proposed participatory or partnership models that combine the two approaches, and these call for government administrators to enter into partnerships with and advocate for key constituencies. A meta-theory of intentional community change would no doubt identify conditions that indicate top-down, partnership, or bottom-up strategies. Roland Warren (1973) touches on such an idea in his proposed principle of least contest: If possible, begin with a collaborative strategy involving work with key decision makers. If there is resistance and countervailing interests, then it becomes necessary to move to a campaign strategy, and when this fails, a strategy involving contest or overt conflict becomes necessary.

A more detailed breakdown of the strategies of community change has been proposed by Barry Checkoway (1995). His review of the literature identifies six major approaches: (1) mass mobilization, (2) social action, (3) citizen participation, (4) public advocacy, (5) public education, and (6) local services development (see exhibit 12.1). Unlike Midgely's typology or the traditional top-down or bottom-up categorization, Checkoway's strategies assume that community change must come from the outside, from the people, from the bottom up. The assumption is that existing power structures are inherently conservative and resistant to change, and thus they must be either externally influenced or sidestepped. While this may be the case, both theorists and practitioners of social change should carefully assess the possibilities of working within or with the prevailing power structure before foregoing such resources or resorting to conflict. The extent to which local, regional, or national power structures need change requires a similar assessment.

Exhibit 12.1: Major Strategies of Community Change

- **Mass mobilization:** This strategy aims to organize large groups of individuals around particular public issues so as to compel changes from existing power structures.
- **Social Action:** This is a more focused effort to build advocacy groups and take specific, well-planned actions to appeal issues and affect key decision makers, often on a longer-term, more targeted basis than with mass mobilization.
- **Citizen participation:** By involving citizens, consumers, and other critical groups in program planning and implementation, often through public hearings, committees, boards or other advisory groups, programs will better respond to the needs of their constituencies.
- **Public advocacy:** Unlike the more general strategy of social action, public advocacy usually represents clients or client groups in formal administrative, judicial, or legislative hearings, often involving appeals of claimed entitlements.
- **Public education:** This has been a strategy popular in Europe and in developing countries that involves a combination of practical and political education of the public, usually conducted in small groups through dialectical means. Paulo Freire pioneered this education for critical consciousness in Brazil; it is also referred to as conscientization, or building a public conscience.
- **Local services development:** This involves efforts to build services at the local level, sometimes through cooperatives and from a small-is-beautiful perspective.

Source: Checkoway (1995).

C. Social Network Theory

An increasingly popular approach to the study of communities is social network theory. The term *network* refers to a constellation involving at least two persons or other objects—or nodes—and a mapping of the transactions among nodes. For example, a network might include a person and his or her relationships with friends or coworkers, showing either the simple fact of the relationship or its direction (i.e., whether it is one way or two way). The content of these transactions may be concrete (e.g., money) or informational and affective (e.g., attraction, respect). The analysis of networks is valuable because it not only is an important way to conceptualize and describe social systems but also reveals strategic points of intervention. These could, for example, involve individuals who control the flow of information between critical subsystems or with outside communities. Network analysis is also a way to identify the social assets within a community, including their concentration in key subgroups. The more linkages that a person has in the social network, the more knowledge and power he or she likely has.

There have been thousands of studies that have analyzed a wide range of social networks. Data on networks is often collected through surveys that query respondents about their associations. This data is then plotted in network maps. One example is a study of sexuality in an American high school (Bearman, Moody, & Stovel, 2004), revealing the extensiveness of such relationships among the majority of students in this school (for a map of the sexual relationships, see figure 12.2). Network analysts have developed their

FIGURE 12.2: AN EXAMPLE OF THE APPLICATION OF NETWORK THEORY TO THE STUDY OF SEXUAL RELATIONSHIPS IN AN AMERICAN HIGH SCHOOL

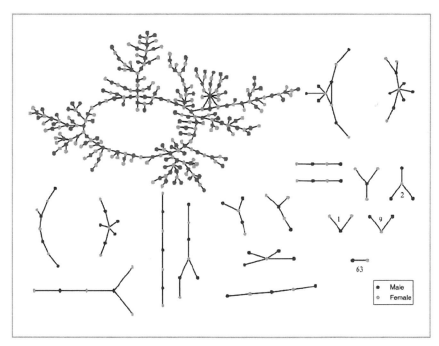

Note: Each dot represents a student; light dots, females; and dark ones, males. Each line connecting two dots represents a sexual relationship, past or present, between two students.

Source: Bearman, Moody, & Stovel (2004, p. 1).

EXHIBIT 12.2: KEY CONCEPTS USED IN SOCIAL NETWORK THEORY

1. **Degree centrality:** Network activity for a node is often evaluated through the notion of degrees, or the number of direct connections it has with other nodes. It is commonly assumed that the more connections one has, the better; however, this is not always so. A key question is where the connections lead to.

2. **Betweenness centrality.** Although an individual may not have many connections, the connections he or she does have may involve key groups; because of these, the individual can exercise particular influence.

3. **Closeness centrality.** A person may have few connections; however, the pattern of direct and indirect ties allows him or her to quickly interact with many other people in the network. Therefore, the individual is in a prime position to monitor information in the system and maintain a high profile in its operation.

4. **Boundary spanners.** Nodes that link one group with other groups have high network metrics. Boundary spanners play a more pivotal role than most of their neighbors whose linkages are merely local. They are in an excellent position to be innovators and information brokers, and to bring together different ideas and knowledge into novel products and services.

5. **Peripheral players.** Most people view the nodes on the periphery of a network as not very important. Yet peripheral nodes are often connected to networks that are not currently mapped.

6. **Network centralization.** This describes the disparity between the number of central nodes, including their betweenness and closeness, and the number of peripheral players. The greater is the preponderance of peripheral players, the more centralized is the network. Decentralized networks have fewer opportunities for failure because it is easier in such systems for roles to be shifted (Valdis, 2005).

own terms to describe such patterns, a few of which are summarized in exhibit 12.2 (Valdis, 2005). In recent years, several authors have attempted to extract from this body of knowledge some of the essential ideas, or propositions for which there is empirical support. Charles Kadushin (2004) identified thirteen such propositions (see exhibit 12.3).

Research on social networks has generated numerous findings, some of

EXHIBIT 12.3: BASIC PROPOSITIONS OF SOCIAL NETWORK ANALYSIS

PROPOSITION 1: PROPINQUITY. At all levels of analysis, nodes are more likely to be connected with one another, all else being equal, if they are geographically near to one another. For instance, people are more likely to be friends if they are geographically adjacent. Propinquity is sometimes defined as being in the same place at the same time (e.g., two individuals who study at the same university at the same time).

PROPOSITION 2: HOMOPHILY AND CONNECTIONS. In contrast, homophily is the sharing of common characteristics or experiences but not necessarily at the same time. This proposition states that the greater the homophily, the more likely two nodes are to be connected.

PROPOSITION 3: DISTANCE BETWEEN ANY TWO NODES. The distance between two nodes in a network is determined by four parameters: (1) the size of the first-order zone of nodes in the network; (2) the extent to which nodes in the network have overlapping members in their first-order zones; (3) barriers between nodes; and (4) agency exercised by the nodes.

PROPOSITION 4: MUTUAL REGULATION. Beginning with dyads (twosomes) and triads (threesomes) that involve two-way connections, some form of mutual regulation typically develops. Much of this regulation happens through triads, in which the third person may function as an observer, broker, or mediator. The addition of a third member to a dyad often complicates relationships and upsets the preexisting balance.

PROPOSITION 5: THE BALANCE HYPOTHESIS. In the case of three entities, a balanced state exists if all three relations are positive in all respects, or if two are negative and one is positive.

PROPOSITION 6: CENTRALITY. Where centrality and hence, independence are evenly distributed, there will be no leader, many errors, high activity, slow organization, and high satisfaction.

PROPOSITION 7: INFORMAL AND NAMED RELATIONS. 'Informal' or prescribed or non-instituted relations tend to be correlated with the formal or prescribed relationships.

PROPOSITION 8: STABILITY OF NAMED POSITIONS. Roles, statuses, or positions that have names are much more likely to have a longer life than roles or positions that have been ascribed to a structure as a result of network analyses.

PROPOSITION 9: WEAK TIES. Weak ties facilitate the flow of information from otherwise distant parts of a network. Individuals with few weak ties will be deprived of information from distant parts of the social system and will be confined to the provincial news and views of their close friends. Weak ties also serve to integrate social systems.

Exhibit 12.3 (continued)

PROPOSITION 10: CORES. Cores possess whatever attributes the network most values. Leaders are said to embody more of the norms and values of a community than their followers.

PROPOSITION 11: NETWORK POLARIZATION. This is a key process in social change. Whether it is a cause or an effect, the polarization or bifurcation of networks is critical to understanding conflicts associated with much social change.

PROPOSITION 12: SOCIAL CIRCLES. Members of social circles, especially core members, enjoy some characteristics of primary groups: social support and enforceable trust.

PROPOSITION 13: SOCIAL CAPITAL. The greater the number of intersecting social circles of which a node is a member, the greater is that node's social capital (all citations omitted).

Source: Adapted from Kadushin (2004).

which are counterintuitive. A well-known result is the so-called rule of 150, which states that the size of a genuine social network is limited to no more than about 150 members (this is also referred to as the Dunbar number) (see Dunbar, 1993). The rule came from cross-cultural sociological and anthropological research that indicated that the maximum size of a village in primitive societies (or an ecovillage) is about 150. Evolutionary psychologists have hypothesized that this number represents the limit of most humans to recognize members and track their emotional states and interrelationships in a group. It has also been suggested that it may have to do with economics and a limit to the ability to detect free riders. Detecting those who do not contribute their share to a community becomes an increasingly difficult task in larger groups, especially in those that rely on informal give-and-take.

Network analysis has become a key approach to understanding social systems and specifically communities, but its application is far from straightforward. One difficulty is determining the appropriate way to conceptualize the linkages as well as the identities of the nodes. Are we concerned with the relationships among individuals, families, or organizations? Which kinds of exchanges are we most interested in, for instance, economic exchanges, political tit-for-tat accommodations, social exchanges, frequency of communication, or respect or liking? How do these various kinds of exchange affect one another? Such questions illustrate the immense complexity of even apparently simple social systems. For this reason, the contribution of network theory is more in its ability to describe community systems and its heuristic value in generating dynamic hypotheses than in its actual ability to disentangle the complex dynamics of community systems.

D. Coevolution and Community Change

A classic problem in the understanding of human relationships and their development is why and how mutual support and altruism occurs (see discussion of the prisoner's dilemma, chapter 11). Traditional conflict theories, as well as classic explanations involving social Darwinism and evolutionary theory, emphasize the role of random variation, diversity, and the survival of the fittest, suggesting that it is simply the most adaptive arrangements of the individual that prevail. If this is so, it is very difficult to explain sacrifices on the part of individual for the larger group—for their families, organizations, communities, or nations—that may have a maladaptive value for the individual.

Two modifications of evolutionary thinking that have been used, often in conjunction with each other, to address this quandary are coevolution and multiple-level selection. Coevolution is a kind of evolutionary arms race. One species or group adapts to another, and the second group adapts to the first group's adaptations, and back and forth. Likewise, one individual, organization, or community adapts to another and, if successful, institutes this adaptation and others learn from it. Communities that learn successful ways to address problems, such as crime, are more attractive than those that fail to do so. However, the latter may learn from these innovations and surpass the original innovators. Coevolution represents a kind of nonlinear positive feedback loop that may create group- or community-level rewards. The rewards reinforce individual sacrificial behaviors that otherwise might be considered maladaptive if only in terms of the immediate consequences for the individual. An example may involve a whistle-blower who loses his or her job in the fight against white-collar crime. Although this behavior may be individually dysfunctional for the person's career, it may strengthen the community or attract greater resources, which indirectly help the whistle-blower over the long run or even his or her offspring.

These examples touch on the second dynamic mentioned: multiple-level selection. Evolutionary change does not happen only on the individual level or through the selection of the fittest individuals; it also happens through group-level cooperation and competition. This takes place at the family, organizational, and community levels. Communities that function most effectively through the optimal combination of cooperative and competitive behaviors thrive, with the benefits filtering down to individual members. Likewise, the benefits of individual growth and development diffuse into their communities.

E. Community Decision Making and the Ecology of Games

Chapter 6 reviewed several of the traditional perspectives on the dynamics of community decision making. Whereas the mainstream approach in the United States has been pluralism, which views decision making in terms of the conflict or competition of diverse interests groups, two alternative views have also been advanced. The elitist view is that there is a monopoly of power by an elite or elites, often ones that assiduously hide their ties and collusive methods to protect dominant political or economic interests. A variation of this view has it that there are specialty elites that convene around particular issues, such as welfare, infrastructure, or cultural interests. A third, but less prevalent, view is the dialectical-materialist position, which contends that decisions arise primarily out of divergent class interests, mainly those protective of capital investments. The extent of evidence for each of these theories has largely depended on the type of community examined.

Cornwell, Curry, and Schwirian (2003) have extended the understanding of community decision making through their attempt to apply the ecology of games to community decision making. Ecology, it will be recalled, is a geographically based study of the shifting interactions of populations with their various environments, through the evolution of a system of niches and adaptive, coevolutionary behavioral responses to these environments. Games are patterned and rule-governed protocols, characterized by structured decision points for the attainment of valued ends, usually within a competitive environment. An ecology of games, thus, refers to the shifting interplay and emergent system of games that key actors engage in to address issues of concern, or "the everyday business of the community—passing laws, shaping policy, building bridges—can be seen as an emergent series of outcomes that result from the intersection of a dynamic set of separate but interdependent personal interests and goals" (Cornwell et al., 2003, p. 123).

Cornwell et al.'s (2003) framework for analyzing the community ecology of decision-making games calls for identifying the actors, the games, and the issues. The actors of interest are those who not only have a stake in the issues of concern but also have the ability to influence the outcome; typically these are elected officials, business, and other formal and informal community leaders. Games, as patterned rule-based protocols for maximizing desired outcomes, can be identified in narrow or broad terms. These authors take the latter approach, citing examples of a political game, a banking game, a contract, and an ecclesiastical game. They recommend identifying actors' goals as the first step in discovering the games that are being played. Finally, a critical component of their framework involves the identification of the key decision issues, which they explain represent "junctions or crossroads in the constantly unfolding series of events that constitute community affairs. The essence of an issue is that it represents more than one possible course of action" (p. 124), which thus occasions the calling up of favorite games on the part of interested actors.

Drawing on network theory, the authors propose several simple qualitative and quantitative tools for the analysis of the pattern of games in a community. They point out that a critical dimension is the density of interconnections of the various actors and games. Unfortunately, they had not made the connection with developments in complex systems theory. One such development is the concept of the edge of chaos, which is defined by an intermediate level of interconnections in a community network. This can be quantified through a Lyapunov coefficient of close to 1 (see the glossary), below which is unremitting periodicity and above which is deterministic chaos. A main contribution of Cornwell and colleagues is the observation that games emerge as a critical link between actors and the issues and outcomes that they are concerned with, and the possibility of describing the changing spatial and social distribution and interaction of these games. Games shift from individual to individual, issue to issue, and represent a critical and dynamic component of community decision-making structures.

F. Communities of Practice

An important development in both organizational and community theory is that involving communities of practice (CoPs), a theory that Jean Lave and Étienne Wenger first proposed in 1991. Such communities are of special relevance to the professions, as they consist of "groups of people who share a concern or a passion for something they do and who interact regularly to learn how to do it better" (Wenger, n.d., para. 3). More specifically, Wenger (n.d.) points out that these are constituted by people who are engaged in "a process of collective learning in a shared domain of human endeavor: a tribe learning to survive, a band of artists seeking new forms of expression, a group of engineers working on similar problems, a clique of pupils defining their identity in the school, a network of surgeons exploring novel techniques, a gathering of first-time managers helping each other cope" (para. 2).

Communities of practice differ from social groups in that they focus on work tasks of common interest. Whereas practice networks tend to involve discussion of specific problems, CoPs also include an active process of learning around a variety of practice issues. Although CoPs may be located within particular organizations, they are semiautonomous because they are based on voluntary and nonhierarchical associations, ones that often transcend any particular department or organization. The study of CoPs developed out of several traditions, including cognitive theory and both constructivism and social constructivism, as well as the recent interest in embodied and situated learning.

There are two major types of CoPs: (1) self-organizing and (2) sponsored (Nickols, 2000). Self-organizing CoPs are also self-governing and usually emerge spontaneously as a result of the felt needs of a small group of colleagues. In contrast, sponsored CoPs are usually initiated by an organization, such as an association, company, or social agency. Whether a CoP is self-organizing or sponsored, the focus of such communities varies dramatically and might arise out of a profession such as nursing, law, medicine, or research; a work-related responsibility such as assessment or advocacy; a recurrent problem associated with a profession or organizational mission; or a general theme such as client engagement, evidence-based practice, or quality assurance. Often, CoPs operate through a combination of in-person and online contacts, for example, conferences, workshops, ad hoc meetings, Listservs, and chat rooms, to mention a few examples. Figure 12.3 traces the development of a typical CoP, illustrating examples of its major activities at each of the stages of development. These are not dissimilar to those of both organizations and communities, and they involve stages that Wenger (1998) refers to as potential, coalescing, active, dispersed, and memorable.

G. Communities as Complex Systems

That communities are systems, and complex ones at that, may not be controversial. However, communities are not merely simple input-output mechanisms for the processing of people and families, fulfilling standard social functions such as socialization, social control, production, and wealth distribution. The traditional conception of social systems is that structures determined by the family and other social institutions, such as the government, the church, and business, form the primary context that constrains and determines the nature of exchanges. In contrast, the complex systems perspective is based on the notion that the exchanges and feedbacks—whether these involve money, goods, services, ideas, or affection—are primary, and they ultimately determine the structures that emerge or are swept away.

FIGURE 12.3: STAGES OF DEVELOPMENT OF COMMUNITIES OF PRACTICE

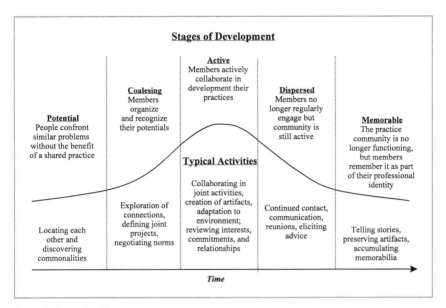

Source: Wenger (1998).

Several additional considerations highlight the inherent complexity of community systems. One is that these are multiple-level systems. These include physical systems involving a community's infrastructure: its streets, power lines, sewage, and in general its ecology, all of which are processes critical to determining the physical, aesthetic, and public health viability. Thus, this level has major implications for quality of life, social climate, and mental health of its members. These systems are also closely linked with the governmental and organizational systems that develop and maintain them, which in turn are linked with the tax and resource base of the community and especially with the historically evolved social contracts (e.g., the town charter, the U.S. Constitution and Bill of Rights) that constitute the foundations of the actual government systems. Nested within these systems are innumerable other systems involving particular organizations, families, and individuals, each with its particular physical, legal, technical, social, and psychological modes of operation. The entanglement of the levels, consisting of the multiple feedback loops, blurs their boundaries and creates inherent unpredictability. Seemingly unchanging structures represent relatively slow-moving dynamic processes, ones that are temporarily defined by simple periodic or even by strange attractors. The multiple levels of community systems involve a complexity of different types of exchange: the medium of exchange in community systems is communication (see Luhmann, 1990); in economic systems, primarily through money; and in natural systems, through matter and energy, whether water, electricity, or gas.

In the general systems perspective, the community as a system is defined by its boundaries, as if these were membranes surrounding the protoplasm in cells. Rather, the boundaries are simply regions of relatively low frequency, weak, filtered, or prohibited interactions. People interact frequently with those in their own towns but only occasionally with those in other towns. Frequent interactions permit relationships to evolve, say, from an acquaintance to a friendship and then to a business or an intimate relationship, and so forth. This evolution permits simple feedback loops ("Hi, how are you?" "Great," "See you later") to evolve into complex hypercycles, which consist of the linking of feedback loops into complex multiple-stage cyclical processes (see Smith & Stevens, 1999). While an in-depth conversation may illustrate this, better examples are considerably more involved, extending over multiple contacts, relationships, issues, and people.

A fractal nature distinguishes many complex community systems, specifically the recurrence of distinctive patterns on multiple system levels, on various scales or levels of magnification (see chapter 1). This is sometimes referred to as self-similarity, in which the distinctive signature of the system as a whole is evident in each of its parts. In biological systems, this may manifest as autopoiesis, or the ability of adaptive systems to self-replicate. Self-similarity may be one means through which systems attain and maintain coherence and integration. To the extent that each member can replicate and adopt the values and ideals of a community, the foundation is laid for a psychological sense of community. The phenomenon of self-similarity has also been considered a type of parallel process, in which issues, feelings, or interactive patterns of an individual become generalized to a group or organization; conversely, those of the larger community become replicated in the individual. In social work, this is sometimes thought of as the personal becoming the political—and the political, the personal. These shared ideas and patterns, which evolutionary psychologists also call memes, constitute the basis for a community's intersubjectivity, for its mutual understanding and support.

Just as self-organization is a critical foundation for understanding how communities evolve as complex systems, bifurcation is also a critical process. Bifurcation, it will be recalled, refers to the splitting of a single process into two processes and is the basis for understanding not only community fragmentation but more commonly, what was traditionally thought of as differentiation, or the specialization of function. It is these processes that over time lead to subgrouping and the formation of internal community structures. When bifurcation happens repeatedly and too frequently, leaving insufficient time for self-organization to occur, system coherence is lost. The result is that the community loses optimal balance between orderly and chaotic patterns. In such cases it is not unusual that the extrusion of disenfranchised groups takes place, causing discrimination, racism, or even genocide (see chapter 13).

V. Trends Affecting Communities

A. Social Development, Deindustrialization, and Servicetization

Communities are similar to other kinds of social systems in that they constantly interact both with their component systems, such as individuals, families, and organizations, and with changes in the broader social systems in which they are embedded. Traditionalists imagined a simple unilinear progression from agrarian, to industrial, and postindustrial societies, with particular communities positioned to experience either the benefits or the costs of these transitions. Beginning with the work of Daniel Bell (1973), the transition to postindustrial societies has been increasingly viewed as a transition to an information economy in which the principle engine of development is the ability of well-educated workforces to productively use information to add value to products and services. For example, industries that require fewer information-based technologies (e.g., heavy manufacturing, extraction) might relocate to less developed nations to minimize labor and other costs. Since the 1950s, developed nations have seen dramatic levels of deindustrialization, accompanied by a shift to services, a trend also known as servicetization (see Hudson, 1998). The development of services, ranging from fast-food restaurants and lawn care to child care and psychotherapy, has emerged partly out of increased labor-force participation, especially of women, resulting in the need for families to purchase a far wider range of services that they formerly provided themselves.

B. Technological Developments

Technological developments have driven deindustrialization and servicetization, often involving enhanced efficiencies that have accompanied automation, computerization, and the development of communications and networking. In coming years, the impact of nanotechnology—involving ultraminiature devices—and bioengineering may well eclipse these developments. A trend closely related to deindustrialization and serviceti-zation is continued urbanization. The ratio of the urban to rural population has been steadily growing. It has been projected that by 2015 more than half of the world's population will be urban. The population living in meg-acities—or urban centers containing more than 10 million inhabitants—is projected to double to more than 400 million (Central Intelligence Agency, 2000). Thus, the towns and other communities that make up these cities are expected to become increasingly interdependent. This will happen not only with respect to their external linkages but also in the complexity of internal organizations, groups, and individuals that they consist of, thus taxing their adaptive capacities to the limit.

C. Globalization

The trends involving deindustrialization, servicetization, and the devel-opment of the information economy are increasingly thought of in terms of globalization. Globalization is a broad trend, and a controversial one. Specifi-cally, it is regarded as including one or more of the following developments:

1. *Growing economic and social interdependency.* The once largely independent economies of nations have grown increasingly inter-dependent as a result of the increasing ease of free trade, brought about by deregulation, improved transportation and communica-tions, and finance.
2. *Increased economic specialization.* Because of enhanced interde-pendency, the economies of nations and regions are becoming more specialized. With a broader and more intensively competi-tive field, to survive many companies have had to narrow their fo-cus and outsource many of the tasks they traditionally performed to other localities, companies, or individuals.
3. *Growth of multinational and transnational corporations.* Although most organizations are still rooted in particular nations, this is becoming less frequent. As of 2000, there were an estimated fifty thousand multinational corporations, with nearly five hundred thousand affiliates (Central Intelligence Agency, 2000).
4. *Reduction of trade barriers and deregulation.* For several decades now, a major trend has been to encourage trade and free market competition through the minimization of trade barriers, such as duties and tariffs, often through the use of regional trade agree-ments and deregulation in other sectors, such as environmental protection.

5. *Resource fluidity.* The preceding trends have been associated with increased fluidity of capital investments and other resources, including labor. It has been noted that "the elements of globalization—greater and freer flow of information, capital, goods, services, people, and the diffusion of power to non-state actors of all kinds—will challenge the authority of virtually all governments. At the same time, globalization will create demands for increased international cooperation on transnational issues" (Central Intelligence Agency, 2000, para. 2). While this has made economies more responsive to changing local conditions, it has also introduced a new dimension of social instability.

6. *Privatization and outsourcing.* Whereas national governments have increasingly sought to delegate, often through contracting, a variety of responsibilities to private companies, private companies in turn have sought to outsource their work to other organizations and individuals, often to gain greater control over the performance of this work and to minimize overhead and fringe-benefit costs. Outsourcing has been local, but increasingly it is also international; for example, many customer service jobs in information technology are outsourced to India. Both these trends have manifested in commodification, marketization, and the corporatization of much economic activity. In health care and human services, there are recurrent efforts to redefine many services as commodities to be aggressively marketed.

7. *Deterritorialization.* Given the increasing interdependencies and the enhanced role of market forces, transnational corporations, and international regulatory bodies, many observers have noted a reduction in the power of national governments.

8. *Westernization and cultural homogenization.* Some commentators argue that increasing economic interdependencies especially Western imperialistic tendencies have brought with them the indiscriminate spread of Western culture. However, there has been considerable debate about the extent of this process, with many in developing and undeveloped nations insisting that social development, linked with globalization, need not and should not mean Westernization and the eclipse of local culture.

It has been argued that most of these approaches to globalization are merely different ways to think about or label the long-term impacts of modernization (Scholte, 2000). It is perhaps more accurate to regard these as extensions of modernization, ones that, in the aggregate, qualitatively change its meaning. Deterritorialization, or the growing irrelevance of the traditional territories or nation-states in particular, adds a fundamentally new element, though one that is still in its early stages. Similarly, the impact of the economic and technological dimensions of globalization on cultural changes, involving the spread and amalgamation of Western culture with local traditions, is also in its early stages.

Both approaches to globalization illustrate the operation of cultural lag, a phenomenon that Ogburn (1922) identified in the early years of the twentieth century as involving the tendency for economic and technological changes to outpace cultural changes, including the political and the social. This gap is central to much of the "clash of civilizations" (Huntington, 1996) that has manifested in various fundamentalist movements. These movements, and especially those in Islamic nations, have often viewed the modern and postmodern worlds as mortal threats. Because globalization has been conceptualized in so many diverse ways, it is not surprising that its impacts have been seen in such dramatically different lights, ranging from improvements in overall economic conditions to declines in the conditions and opportunities of the most impoverished. Homelessness, unemployment, migration and other forms of economic displacement, increasing income inequality, burdens placed on low-income families leading to increased abuse and neglect, and environmental degradation are a few examples of the costs of globalization, however great its overall benefits may be. Both urbanization and globalization have subjected local communities to massive stresses, mostly in terms of their fragmenting effects. The proliferating demands of gesellschaft, or interest-based communities that cut across geographic communities, challenge the ability of individuals to integrate the disparate strands of their lives within their local communities.

D. Demographic Shifts

Many trends are defined by changing demographics or population characteristics. Most notable has been population increase, although major strides have been made to bring population growth under control. Technological developments and increased efficiencies have regularly undercut predictions of resource scarcity resulting from population growth; nonetheless, diminishing available land, water, and fossil-fuel supplies represent a major threat to economic sustainability. In the early 1800s, Thomas Malthus predicted that the population would inevitably grow faster than food supplies. The failure of such classical predictions illustrate the challenges of operationalizing a systems perspective, which, for example, requires factoring in increasing technological achievements, including increasing investments in the development of alternative fuel supplies as the cost of fossil fuels rises.

A particularly important population trend is increasing longevity, otherwise known as the epidemiological transition. There has, however, been some concern about whether this will mean a decline in quality of life among the elderly. Continuing work on understanding the "age of delayed degenerative diseases" (Olshansky & Ault, 1986, p. 355) has led to an emerging consensus that improvements in both lifestyle and health care among older adults will more than compensate for the effects of degenerative diseases.

A more pressing concern is the increasingly unfavorable dependency ratio. This refers to the ratio in a community or nation of economically dependent individuals, including children, older adults, and the disabled, to the gainfully employed. The growing dependency ratio is increasingly threatening the economic viability of various pension funds and social security systems. Many of these systems make payments to beneficiaries from the contributions of current workers rather than from the retiree's own personal contributions, as is commonly assumed. Painful decisions about increasing contributions, delaying the age of retirement, or using means-tested benefits may weaken the sense of mutual support and of community that such systems engender when they function as they should.

E. Civil Society

Several community theorists have written about a trend involving the weakening of civil society. Societal alienation—traditionally known as anomie—has diminished the involvement of people not only in voting and in partisan political processes but also in speaking up in public forums on issues of public concern. The idea of civil society includes voluntary associations of all kinds: religious institutions, neighborhood groups, clubs, social agencies, unions, political parties, social movements, and families. It involves an active and informed citizenry that debates public issues, develops consensus, and drives the political processes. Jane Addams (see profile 12.1), one of the founders of social work and a developer of community organization as a central practice method, emphasized the development of a civil society through community building, and she demonstrated this through her development of Hull House in Chicago. Sirianni and Friedland (2009), of the Civics Practices Network, explain, "Civil society refers to that sphere of voluntary associations and informal networks in which individuals and groups engage in activities of public consequence. It is distinguished from the public activities of government because it is voluntary, and from

PROFILE 12.1: JANE ADDAMS

Jane Addams (b. 1860–d. 1935) is a founder of social work who brought the settlement house movement to America and a tireless advocate for peace and women's rights. In addition, Addams is regarded as the single most influential person in the development of community organization as a method of social work practice. In 1931, she received the Noble Peace Prize, the only social worker to have received the distinction.

Addams was from a large Quaker family, born September 6, 1860, in Cedarville, Illinois, to Sarah Weber Addams and John Addams. Her father was a prosperous miller, banker, state senator, and confidant of Abraham Lincoln. Her mother, a stern disciplinarian, became ill and died when Jane was three, and she subsequently grew very close to her father. Jane enrolled in the Rockford Female Seminary, where her father was a trustee, and graduated as valedictorian. It was not until two years later that she received her bachelor's degree, when the school became the Rockford College for Women. Over the next six years, she studied medicine but left the field because of her poor health. Over the next few years, Addams traveled to Europe for two years with her friend Ellen Gates Starr.

In 1888, while in London, Addams visited Toynbee Hall, a settlement house serving the low-income sections of East London. The experience inspired her to return to the United States to start a similar program. It was on the West Side of Chicago,

> "The good we secure for ourselves is precarious and uncertain until it is secured for all of us and incorporated into our common life."

at Polk and Halsted, that Addams leased an old mansion and named it Hull-House. The charter for the program committed it to "provide a center for a higher civic and social life; to institute and maintain educational and philanthropic enterprises, and to investigate and improve the conditions of the industrial districts of Chicago." It would do this through a variety of programs, including a public kitchen, a coffee house, a kindergarten, adult evening study programs, a gymnasium and swimming pool, discussion groups,

PROFILE 12.1 (CONTINUED)

an art studio, a book bindery, and an employment bureau. The programs quickly attracted thousands of local residents each year, and collaborated closely with such notable activists and social workers as Edith and Grace Abbott.

Addams later shifted her attention to national issues, specifically women's rights, the peace movement, and child welfare issues, including the establishment of the first juvenile court in Chicago and the fed-

> "Social advance depends much upon the process through which it is secured as upon the result itself."

eral Children's Bureau. She did this through her tireless lecturing, prolific writing, and appointments to leadership positions in various national and international organizations. These included the Chicago Board of Education, the National Conference of Charities and Corrections, the Women's Peace Party, and the International Congress of Women. In 1913, she was elected, second to Thomas Edison, the most useful American in a poll by *Independent* magazine, but in 1919, she was vilified as the most dangerous woman in America because of her opposition to the U.S. entry to World War I.

In 1931, Addams was awarded the Noble Peace Prize; however, she was unable to personally receive it because of the effects of a heart attack she had had a few years earlier. She died in 1935 shortly after learning she had cancer. Although she had eschewed marriage and family life, her legacies in the fields of social work and social activism, the settlement house movement, women's issues, and peace activism continue to this day (see Addams, 1910; Bettis, 2005; Davis, 1973; Lundblad, 1995).

the private activities of markets because it seeks common ground and public goods. It is often described as the 'third sector.' For democratic societies, it provides an essential link between citizens and the state. Its fundamental appeal since its origin in the Scottish Enlightenment is its attempt to synthesize public and private good" (para. 1).

Some have proposed that the decline of civil society in the West is due to the expansion of the government and corporate sectors, and the decline of the voluntary sector. It may also be due to the diversified allegiances that have accompanied diversified community and organizational structures, thus narrowing social concerns to only those perceived as directly and immediately affecting one's lifestyle and particularly real estate values (e.g., taxes, schools and competence testing, jobs).

F. Ethnic Relationships

Another trend, to be explored in greater depth in the next chapter, involves changing conceptions of ethnic identity. For much of American history, ethnicity was largely eclipsed by the myth of ethnic homogeneity, of the idealized vision of American society as a melting pot in which whatever residual ethnic identities immigrants brought with them soon merged into an American identity, for the most part, a white and Anglo-Saxon identity. By the 1960s, when the civil rights, women's, and ecological movements were launched, this vision had lost its allure, and in many quarters, a back-to-your-roots movement celebrated racial and ethnic diversity, highlighting differences and values that make each group completely unique, whether African Americans, Native Americans, Hispanics, or Asian Americans. By the 1990s, many came to consider this excessive, leading to a fragmentation of American society and eclipsing any common values or culture (Schlesinger, 1998). David Hollinger (2000), a historian at the University of California, has advanced a more recent understanding of the role of ethnicity. Hollinger proposes a postethnic perspective that emphasizes civic engagement and freely chosen affiliations over those defined by traditional ethnicities. He specifically rejects the assumptions that motivate what he calls the ethno-racial pentagon (e.g., exemplified by the five racial categories included on official census forms) and suggests that these are invalid as proxies for defining racial and ethnic backgrounds. Instead, he urges that individuals develop their own unique cultural and ethnic identity based on their mix of genetic and cultural influences, as well as personal identifications. To the extent that each person can develop his or her own identity, it is more likely that a common ground will be found and that separative ethno-racial particularism can be avoided. A core challenge in all community-building initiatives is to support diversity while discovering common values that cut across particular racial and cultural identifications so as to strengthen a sense of community and a commitment to mutual support.

VI. Community Assessment

A. The Task

The perception of a serious community need, problem, or issue is usually the motivation for a group or organization to undertake a community assessment. The hope is that such an assessment will answer basic questions about the extent and nature of the problem; help develop a consensus; and influence key decision makers, lawmakers, and funders. Such assessments, often referred to as needs assessments, are typically undertaken by a task force or committee, usually under the sponsorship of human service agency or association such as a community mental health board or a United Way, or an alliance of several such groups. Rarely are community assessments the project of a lone professional. These assessments may be relatively brief projects that last only a few months or they may span several years. Their focus may involve a global assessment of human service needs in the community or a focused examination of the need for a particular kind of program, such as a community center. More typically, the focus will entail several interrelated needs or issues, such as examination of a community's child-care needs, dissatisfaction with the school system, or a desire to solve the problem of homelessness or unaffordable housing.

B. The Concept of Needs

Traditional community assessments have often been thought of as needs assessments. They attempt to determine the absolute or overall need for a service or resource and to break this down into both the met need and the unmet need. They may also attempt to obtain information on perceptions of what is working or not working in the current system. In recent years, there have been numerous efforts to generalize and recast this traditional model. Perhaps the most important way has been to focus on community assets or strengths. This involves a careful inventory of not only physical assets but also human resources, those involving people's skills, their community spirit, and other less tangible assets. However, as important as it is to take a positive focus on assets, these need to be always considered in relation to the aspirations or goals of the community, the frustration of which ultimately define the needs and problems.

The traditional view of needs is that they are set or absolute. Needs assessments represent judgments that arise from both a population's goals and the awareness of the existence of a necessary means for their attainment. For example, even though a community may experience a transportation problem, not many would conclude that there is the need for teleportation devices, à la *Star Trek.* Usually we don't need things that don't exist. However, if someone invented a teleporter, then perhaps at first such a device would be viewed as a luxury. However, new considerations inevitably emerge, for example, wide usage, low cost, safety, and so on, that could lead people to conclude that teleporters are actual needs, or even necessities. Thus, needs are not absolutes but complex psychosocial constructs, and only one way to understand the concerns of a community. Is the primary

EXHIBIT 12.4: COMMUNITY ASSESSMENT: MAJOR METHODOLOGIES

1. **Use of existing data:** An immense amount of data is available from government sources, including census, employment, child welfare, and educational data. Although such data is relatively inexpensive, its location, preparation, and analysis can in themselves be major tasks. A strong feature of such data is that they can often be broken down by zip code or block level, which permits a fairly visual or spatial understanding of the location of needs. Occasionally, several time points are available, which allows for a dynamic view. Although some assessments may rely entirely on existing data, more typically an analysis of existing data files is a preliminary stage.

2. **Community surveys:** A common but expensive methodology is the survey (e.g., of community residents or some subgroup such as clients, service providers, or decision makers). The strongest surveys usually involve large numbers of randomly selected households, whereas surveys of clients or providers are often subject to such dramatic biases that their potential usefulness is negated. For example, providers almost always report high levels of need for the problems that they are regularly exposed to or the service methods that they are trained to or interested in providing. Such surveys can be conducted by mail, but usually better response rates are possible from telephone surveys.

3. **Focus groups and forums:** Focus groups are increasingly popular as a means of community assessments. The projects typically involve a series of onetime small-group discussions, so as to explore in depth people's perceptions of the needs, issues, or concerns of the assessment. Forums, in contrast, are sometimes conducted as community hearings in which the public is invited to provide testimony on the most pressing needs. Focus groups and forums are the weakest methodologies; however, they have many advantages in terms of the political and community organization dimensions, involving the building of a consensus and the development of a power base.

4. **Other methods:** Many other methods have been used in recent years, a few of which are mentioned here. Methods from the field of geographic information systems (GIS), involving mapping of data, are useful not only with existing data but also with community surveys, often in combination with one another. Concept

---

EXHIBIT 12.4 (CONTINUED)

mapping is an extension of the focus group, in which specialized software is used to elicit data from individuals and groups about their perceptions of the relationships among key concepts involved with a community effort (e.g., an assessment of children and family services). A rarely addressed issue in the human services, community decision-making processes, can be studied through snowball sampling methods in which one person refers the interviewer to another and so on until the field of possible respondents is exhausted. Finally, an emerging trend in community assessments involves "listening projects," in which trained interviewers go from house to house to hear the concerns of community residents, especially those who may be angry or oppressed. Such projects tend to focus more on healing, reconciliation, or mediation, and only secondarily on research or community assessment.

---

need among the homeless food, financial resources, better education and skills, new jobs, or housing? Community assessments, when done effectively, include the assessment of needs but also attempt to generate a common understanding of the dynamic systems that are relevant to both the problems and the possible solutions.

C. Methods

Methodologies for community assessments are varied and often hinge on the time and resources available rather than the actual requirements of the project. Their methodologies are often quick and dirty approaches to applied community research. However, to the extent that rigorous methods can be used, the legitimacy of the findings will be greatly enhanced, increasing the likelihood of the implementation of any recommendations. Often community assessments draw on a combination of several methods, often in a staged fashion, and these typically involve one or more of methods described in exhibit 12.4.

D. Areas of Assessment

Various paradigms, each with a distinct acronym, have been proposed as guides to the content of community assessments. Whichever paradigm is actually used, it is critical that a clearly defined purpose motivating the

EXHIBIT 12.5: COMMUNITY ASSESSMENT: PRIMARY AREAS OF CONCERN

I. Motivation/Concerns
Context and background enable understanding motivation:
- What are the agendas of the key organizations and players?
- Why now? What is triggering this effort?
- Are there immediate or long-term threats that must be addressed?

II. Context and Background
- **Community history and development:** What are the unique, dynamic pathways through which the community has arrived at its present position in regard to the issue(s) of concern?
- **Physical environment and infrastructure:** This may include real estate, utilities, transportation, communication systems, as well as its parks, recreation, resources for business, and the like.
- **Population:** Who are its residents? What are their demographic and ethnic characteristics? How are they organized?
- **Standard of living, quality of life, culture:** This can include the occupational profile of the community, the mix of socioeconomic classes, lifestyles, and spiritual and religious practices.
- **Inventory of key organizations and players:** This is a more focused question about the identity of the organization, groups, and individuals directly involved with the issue under consideration or potentially available for its resolution.
- **Available information:** What is believed and known about the problem, and what other information is available, either within the community or beyond it?

III. Opportunities: These involve existing resources or possible initiatives that might be taken advantage of, for example, a request for proposals, a national housing program such as Title VIII, or interest in the state legislature for repealing a discriminatory law.
- What resources—material, organizational, or psychosocial—exist in the community?
- What resources, including legal and financial, exist beyond the community that might be brought to bear on the problems of concern?

IV. Assets and Capacities: Unlike broader opportunities, assets and capacities are the more immediately available resources, whether material or immaterial, involving skills and attitudes, that can be mobilized to take advantage of the identified opportunities. These

EXHIBIT 12.5 (CONTINUED)

might involve available staff to be assigned to the initiative, the willingness of the community to volunteer, and the availability of specialized skills needed for the initiative.

V. **Organization:** Political and decision-making structures relevant to accessing the opportunities sought and bringing the available assets and capacities to bear on them.
  - Formal and informal decision-making structures
  - **Network structure:** Linkages, including subgroups of individuals and organizations and their interrelationships.
  - **Rules governing interactions:** What are the relevant norms, laws, and customs to consider in planning action?

assessment guide its actual design. This purpose will emerge from a combination of perceived problems or issues, anticipated solutions, and the values of participants. When a sponsoring agency is involved, it provides an initial mandate and parameters for the project, the details of which participants work out.

Lillian Ripple (1969) proposed that each assessment should consider motivations, opportunities, and capacities (MOCs). This paradigm is particularly useful, as it is one of few that emphasize the centrality of motivation. It is on the basis of the motivations that all other environmental and individual factors are considered, whether these involve opportunities or capacities. A more commonly used paradigm is that developed in the 1960s partly by Albert Humphrey at the Stanford Research Institute, which involves an assessment of an organization's or community's strengths, weaknesses, opportunities, and threats (SWOT). The SWOT paradigm distinguishes longer-term opportunities from threats, implying the importance of considering both proactive and reactive responses. Assessment involves consideration of the various groups affected, the formal and informal organizations and their decision-making processes, the physical and larger sociopolitical and cultural environments, and issues involved in both available and possible technologies pertinent to the problems examined. Each of the assessment paradigms has a somewhat different emphasis, either a subjective, psychosocial, and cultural focus or a more functional, even material, conception of the community. But whichever the focus, exhibit 12.5 outlines some of the most critical areas to consider in most community assessments.

It is of central importance that professionals involved in needs assessments and community building understand their target community's motivations, its assets and to take advantage of existing opportunities, and the rules that govern the action systems in the community. When they do so, they will be in an optimal position to determine how to best facilitate a community's preexisting efforts at problem solving and self-organization.

VII. Summary

This chapter has reviewed some of the central ideas in community theory from the perspective of complex systems. Much of the interest in communities has arisen from an idealization of their functions and benefits, which has obscured understanding of individuals' necessary inputs and dynamical patterns of functioning. Ideals and values associated with the notion of communities include trust, tolerance, and reciprocity. One of the most essential defining features of community is the subjective sense that such a commonality exists, something that has been referred to as the psychological sense of community. Communities also need to be analyzed not only in terms of unmet needs but also in terms of their assets or social capital, which include intangible relationships and attitudes among members. Nonetheless, communities also need to be considered in relation to the actual social functions that they are expected to perform, such as those that Roland Warren (1972) identifies: production-distribution-consumption, socialization, social control, social participation, mutual support, and external linkage.

The analysis of a community usually considers its type: whether it is organized in terms of primary relationships, geographically and temporarily localized, as is the case with the traditional rural village (gemeinschaft community), or as an identificational community, organized around particular interests, perhaps ones of a utilitarian nature (gesellschaft community). However, it should be remembered that most communities contain elements of each model, and many overlapping communities assume a wider variety of forms, whether these involve virtual Internet communities or an ethnic or religious diaspora.

Approaches to understanding community dynamics have ranged from traditional models, such as the structural-functional, ecological, inequality of opportunity, and urban-rural, to networking and complex systems. Networking has been of particular importance, as it provides the tools for mapping the many transactions between community participants. It has tended to be descriptive and has had only limited success as an explanatory theory. However, social networking theory has been successfully used in the study of community decision making, for example, through the study of the ecology of games that decision makers play. Another offshoot is the study of communities of practice, of groups of practitioners who come together to facilitate one another's learning and problem solving. Complex systems theorists have extended these approaches through the application of self-organization theory, which emphasizes the bottom-up emergence of communities based on particular interactional rules. Communities may also be understood through the operation of both periodic and strange attractors, and through bifurcation theory.

This chapter has considered the broader societal context and trends affecting communities and approaches to the assessment of communities. Trends of particular importance involve the transition to an information economy, involving deindustrialization and the development of services, and more generally, globalization, which involves the increasing integration of the world economy, which often occurs more quickly than the integration of organizational and cultural forms. While some communities have thrived on globalization, many have suffered acutely from growing income disparities and problems of access to mainstream economic opportunities. Human service professionals are increasingly called on to assist individuals not only in competency building but also in community building. An essential part of this involves the community assessment, which may be narrowly understood as a needs assessment or more broadly understood as an assessment of the community's motivations, opportunities, and capacities, with respect to both infrastructure and intangible social capital.

For Further Reading

Castells, M. (1996). *The rise of the networked society.* Oxford, U.K.: Blackwell.

Coleman, J. S. (1988). Social capital in the creation of human capital. *American Journal of Sociology, 94*(Suppl.), S95-S120.

Cornwell, B., Curry, T. J., & Schwirian, K. P. (2003). Revisiting Norton Long's ecology of games: A network approach. *City & Community, 2*(2), 121–142.

Fellin, P. (2001). *The community and the social worker.* Itasca, IL: F. E. Peacock.

Guimera, R., Danon, L., Diaz-Guilera, A., Giralt, F., & Arenas, A. (2003). Self-similar community structure in a network of human interactions. *Physical Review, 68,* 1–4.

Gwyther, B. (2000). *Social capital and communitarianism.* Paper presented at the conference Sociological Sites/Sights of the Australia Sociology Association.

Lave, J., & Wenger, E. (1991). *Situated learning: Legitimate peripheral partici-pation.* Cambridge: Cambridge University Press.

Lundblad, K. S. (1995). Jane Addams and social reform: A role model for the 1990s. *Social Work, 40*(5), 661–669.

Midgely, J. (1993). Ideological roots of social development strategies. *Social Development Issues, 15*(1), 1–13.

Putnam, R. D. (2000). *Bowling alone: The collapse and revival of American community.* New York: Simon & Schuster.

Scholte, J. A. (2000). *Globalization: A critical introduction.* London: Palgrave.

Smith, T. S., & Stevens, G. T. (1999). The architecture of small networks: Strong interaction and dynamic organization in small social systems. *American Sociological Review, 64,* 403–420.

Applications

CHAPTER 13

Diversity: Problems, Challenges, Opportunities

Injustice anywhere is a threat to justice everywhere. We are caught in an inescapable network of mutuality, tied in a single garment of destiny. Whatever affects one directly, affects all indirectly.

—Martin Luther King,
"Letter from Birmingham Jail," 1963

I. Introduction

This chapter introduces part IV of this text, which focuses on some key applications of human behavior theories by reviewing a subject of critical importance, one that cuts across all system levels, whether personal or social, and forms an essential context of professional practice in the human services. This is the subject of cultural diversity as it arises out of and affects the broader dimensions of personal and biocultural diversity. Its importance derives partly from the many ways that our overall understanding of and responses to people depend on how we perceive and think about their diversity. These responses include our personal reactions to others and our preferred helping strategies. This chapter specifically aims to move beyond politically correct themes by disentangling some of the diverse meanings expressed through and camouflaged by the notion of diversity and to explore its problems, challenges, and opportunities.

Expectations that human service professionals demonstrate cultural competence with various groups come from not only professional associations and accrediting bodies, such as the Council on Social Work Education, but, more important, from the diversification of American society itself. Data based on the 2000 U.S. Census illustrate these trends. Asians and Pacific Islanders constituted 3.7% of the U.S. population in 2000, but that percentage is projected to increase to 6% by 2020 and to 9% by 2050. Projected increases in the Hispanic population are particularly noteworthy, from 12.5% in 2000 to 17% in 2020, and to 24% by 2050. In contrast, only slight increases are expected for the African American population, from 12.1% in 2000 to a level 13% from 2020 through 2050. Similarly, the population of American Indians, at 0.7% of the population in 2000, will stabilize at about 1% of the population through 2050 (U.S. Bureau of the Census, 2000).

At the same time that the needs for cultural competence among professionals are increasing, both cultural and human diversity in general are threatened. For example, it has been reported that of the six thousand languages that exist in the world, half are in danger of extinction. The usage of these languages varies widely: 96% of the world's population speaks only 4% of those languages, and 90% of the languages are not even represented on the Internet. Another indicator of the threat to cultural diversity is the fact that five countries monopolize the world's entertainment and cultural industries, which include publishing and entertainment. An example is the field of cinema for which it has been reported that of the 185 countries in the world, 88 have never developed their own film industry (UNESCO, 2005).

A. Background

In an important sense, American history is a history of multiculturalism. The national motto of the United States, "E pluribus unum," first proposed by the Great Seal Committee in 1776, is usually translated as "Out of many, one." The motto has been interpreted in many ways, but most typically it has referred to the integration of the original thirteen colonies and their residents into a single nation. Since the original proclamations of the founding fathers, the original narrow conceptions of liberty, equality, diversity, and other ideals have been become legion. Much of American history has seen the gradual expansion and redefinition of those ideals; the abolition of slavery and the success of the suffragist (women's voting rights) movements are two of the most outstanding examples. Beginning with the 1790 census, each slave counted as only three-fifths of a person for the purposes of congressional apportionment. This history is one of alternations between, on the one hand, gradual liberalization and the inclusion of oppressed and indigent groups such as African Americans, women, and immigrants in mainstream society, and on the other hand, periodic backlashes, ranging from lynchings to the glass ceiling that affects working women. Underlying all of these struggles has been a profound ambivalence over the range of people who are allowed to be considered American citizens, and more generally the kinds of rights to which all humans are entitled.

The origins of the contemporary idea of multiculturalism are found in the 1960s and 1970s. In the United States, ethnic revival accompanied the civil rights and women's movements of that era. At the time, there was considerable disillusionment with the ideal of the American melting pot, the notion that each new group of immigrants would inevitably assimilate into mainstream American culture, which was mostly white and Anglo-Saxon. One of the earliest critiques of this ideal came from Nathan Glazer, who, along with

Daniel P. Moynihan (1963/1970), originally published *Beyond the Melting Pot: The Negroes, Puerto Ricans, Jews, Italians, and Irish of New York City* in 1963. Their central thesis was that American culture was failing to eradicate the distinctions among various religious, ethnic, and racial subcultures. Some view the myth of the melting pot as a device of the white-dominant culture to oppress and marginalize minorities, or even as an instrument of genocide. The ethnic revival of the 1960s celebrated the uniqueness of various ethnic groups (e.g., "black is beautiful"). It also stimulated the search for ancestral roots among "anyone who could recover that ancestral part of themselves that had not been homogenized" (Ravitch, 2000, 268).

However, the United States did not adopt multiculturalism as an official national policy. In Canada, it was officially implemented on the advice of the Royal Commission on Bilingualism and Biculturalism, set up partly in response to the aspirations of Quebec's French-speaking minority. The government of Pierre Trudeau enacted the Official Multiculturalism Act in 1971, which declared Canada a multicultural nation and provided funding to ethnic groups to help preserve their cultures. During the subsequent decades, Australia, Germany, and other countries adopted similar policies. In the United States, affirmative action laws were passed to require any organizations doing business with the federal government to ensure that designated minority groups were adequately represented in staff, client, and student populations; among contractors; and throughout operations. Court battles over the meaning and implementation of the civil rights legislation of the 1960s and affirmative action laws of the 1970s, such as the use of school busing to achieve educational integration, set the stage for the culture wars and identity politics that began in the 1970s.

The term *culture wars* is a label given to the confrontation between traditionalists and multiculturalists, especially in the context of curricular reform. This confrontation arose out of the identity politics of the many groups and movements concerned with sexual, racial, ethnic, and religious oppression. The groups sought to alleviate real or perceived injustices against them that were based on their identity. They promoted various strategies, ranging from the collaborative to the confrontational. Sometimes that meant a separatist approach, such as black nationalism, Irish nationalism, Hispanic nationalism, black separatism, white separatism, black supremacy, white supremacy, radical feminism, gay rights, masculinism, Zionism, Christian fundamentalism, Islamic fundamentalism, or disability rights. By the 1980s, the attraction of radical separatism had waned and been replaced by a recognition of the need for the diverse advocacy groups to collaborate with one another, if only because of the conservative populism of the Reagan administration. It is perhaps no coincidence that at about the same time, by the late 1980s and early 1990s, the language of multiculturalism and multicultural diversity began to be used on a widespread basis in the United States.

B. Defining Diversity

At the beginning of the twenty-first century, *diversity* has become one of the most commonly used, yet rarely defined catchwords. The dictionary definition reveals about as much as it obscures. *Diversity* is usually defined as the condition of being variegated or different. Synonyms from a thesaurus are only slightly more revealing: *diverseness, diversification, heterogeneity, heterogeneousness, miscellaneousness, multifariousness, multiformity, multiplicity, variegation, variety, variousness.* The broadest usage of the term comes from statistics and pertains to the variation or spread of values of a variable or characteristic of interest, such as age, race, or sex, in a given group. Most of the natural and social sciences have been dedicated to the task of describing and explaining the sources and effects of variation, whether this involves biology's interest in the biodiversity of living organisms or psychology's interest in understanding variations in child development, personality, and psychopathology.

Most typically, though, the multicultural movement has been interested primarily in cultural diversity. Sometimes the term *cultural diversity* refers to organizations, communities, societies, or nations that have many distinct cultural groups, often as a result of immigration. Central to many approaches to multicultural diversity is the idea that the groups are distinct, that they are of central importance in defining the identities of their members, and that a healthy society is one that protects and cherishes these differences. For others, it means the recognition of the complexity and pluralism of modern society, and the principle that no single cultural group can or should define the standards of goodness, beauty, truth, or justice. This pluralistic view is reflected in the U.S. Library of Congress (2008) classification in this definition: "The condition in which ethnic, religious or cultural groups coexist within one society." The concept of multiculturalism goes beyond the simple notion of variety and its celebration, however broadly or narrowly those might be defined. It also represents a vision of society as described by Parekh and Bhabha (1989): "Multiculturalism doesn't simply mean numerical plurality of different cultures, but rather a community which is creating, guaranteeing, encouraging spaces within which different communities are able to grow at their pace. At the same time it means creating a public space in which these communities are able to interact, enrich the existing culture and create a new consensual culture in which they recognize reflections of their own identity" (p. 27).

Parekh (2000) points out that what might be considered a multicultural perspective consists of the creative interplay of three complementary ideas: (1) the cultural embeddedness of human beings, (2) the pervasiveness of cultural pluralism, and (3) the variegated and multicultural dimensions of each constituent group. At the same time that many in the humanities and social sciences would prefer to restrict the meaning of the term to cultural diversity, others reject this approach, complaining that culture cannot be divorced from the hard facts of the biological and physical worlds. Instead they prefer the more inclusive notion of biocultural diversity. Yet there is concern about such a broadening of the term, for fear that it would dilute the importance of culture or obscure the specific injustices that minorities of color, women, and other historically oppressed populations have been subjected to.

The conservative commentator Thomas Sowell (1991) points out that the idea of culture itself faces this same controversy: culture is not only a historically created system of meaning, significance, and identity but also one that has been defined as a "system of beliefs and practices in terms of which a group of human beings understand, regulate, and structure their individual collective lives. It is a way of both understanding and organizing life" (Parekh, 2000, 143). In this broader sense, the notion of culture includes social organization and even modes of technology, but it still falls short of the even more expansive concept of biocultural diversity. This lack of definition reflects a lack of consensus about the kinds of diversity that are of greatest importance, and the values that inform our responses to diversity. It is to this latter topic that we now turn, in preparation for an exploration of the major types of diversity and our responses to them.

C. Diversity as a Value

As an umbrella concept, diversity has come to be vested with disparate priorities, aspirations, and passions. For some it may be a singular value, but for others it is more elaborate and grounded in multiple perspectives. Perhaps the most useful way to think about diversity as a value involves the question of whether it is a core value or an instrumental value. Any object, concrete or abstract, can be valued either as an end in itself or as a means to other ends. Most people value money as a means to other ends: supporting one's family, impressing others, or giving to charity; for these people, money is purely an instrumental value. However, some people covet money for its own sake, perhaps as an unexamined symbol of security or power. Whereas specific objects, such as money, are usually considered instrumental values, general ideals such as social justice, mutual support, freedom, and equality are regarded as core values. But what is a core value for one person may be an instrumental value for the next person, and vice versa.

Most values contain elements of both ends and means, and likewise with the value of diversity. Diversity may be promoted regardless of its consequences, as it may be cherished as constituting the very beauty of life. But many perceive diversity as a means to various other ends, whether justice for historically oppressed groups, improved social or even public relations, or enhanced problem solving. Thus, while any two people might agree on a definition of diversity, they may be miles apart with regard to the values they invest into the rubric of diversity. As a result, any efforts to engage a group, such as the staff of a social agency, in enhancing diversity or multicultural understanding are best grounded in a clear understanding of the diverse aspirations of all concerned, which may take considerable exploration to achieve.

Diversity is not an isolated value; it exists as part of a complex system of values and meanings, or more accurately, of personal and cultural systems of valuing. As a value, it has emerged in the context of the ongoing tension between the ideals of freedom and equality, especially in the United States and other democratic nations. In an important sense, it has represented an effort to resolve this tension. To the extent that people are allowed to exercise their various freedoms, they will inevitably make wise and unwise choices, and will either enjoy the fruits of their successes or suffer the pain of their failures. Even if people start out at equal positions with respect to resources and natural abilities, the impact of choice, chance, and history (see chapter 3) guarantees increasing inequality in outcomes as their lives develop. Thus, few people in the United States or other democratic nations seriously argue for equality of outcome, though many believe that the harshness of socioeconomic disparities needs to be mitigated through such means as progressive taxation, social security, and the human services.

Much less controversial is equality of rights under the law, or the idea that all are entitled to due process and equal protection of the laws, regardless of race, sex, and other considerations. Although there are winners and losers in the game of life, there should at least be a level playing field. However, this is easier said than done. In most societies children start at different points because they inherit the successes and failures of their parents in the form of the different environments they are born into. Even if they are born in a utopian commune, at a minimum they inherit their parents' genes.

As is the case with equality of outcome, equality of opportunity can never be completely realized. However, the social commitment to equality of opportunity is considerably greater than that for equality of outcome, espe-cially for children. Enhancing equality of opportunity unfortunately means sacrificing some freedoms, if for no other reason than the necessary redistri-bution of resources through taxation, expenditures, and other means.

In the United States, when push comes to shove, Americans have typi-cally preferred maximizing freedom and liberty—independence and auton-omy—over the various forms of equality, except perhaps equality under the law. Diversity as a value and as a philosophy attempts to preserve and cherish individual differences that result from individual and group histo-ries, and seeks to aggressively confront inequality, especially the inequalities of opportunities and of the application of laws. Multiculturalism asserts that people can freely enjoy their differences but in some sense be equal. This is in contrast with the stance of those living in monocultural environ-ments, such as that which is idealized as the American melting pot. This now-outmoded ideal declares that to enjoy equal opportunity and rights, and to enjoy the resulting freedoms, you must be sufficiently like others, if not in skin color, then at least in your values, attitudes, and behaviors.

These ideological positions illustrate how the meanings and values in-vested in the ideal of multicultural diversity exist only in the context of an individual's or group's overall philosophy. Key questions involve how one can resolve or manage the trade-offs between diversity and the related values of freedom, liberty, equality, and justice. What are the relevant types of diversity? Is there an optimal level of diversity? Is more diversity always better? What are healthy and unhealthy ways of responding to diversity or to the lack thereof? The following section more specifically explores the major approaches to diversity. This is followed by a discussion of the types of primary diversity that both clients and professionals regularly encoun-ter, that is, some of the major ways in which individuals vary. The chapter concludes by exploring the various forms of secondary diversity, that is, the healthy and unhealthy ways that individuals respond to primary forms of human diversity, including dynamic sequelae of interactions that emerge out of these responses.

II. Major Approaches to Cultural Diversity

Each of the major approaches to cultural diversity evolved during particular historical eras. Most of the stances continue to exist today, and their adher-ents often use similar terminology but intend very different meanings. Most commentators divide the approaches into several major categories: separat-ism, assimilationism, pluralism, multiculturalism, and postculturalism.

A. Separatist Models: Separate and Unequal

Separatist models are primarily of historical interest and are exemplified by societies in which de jure policies and the informal practices and culture of the time buttress systematic segregation. Examples of de jure policies include voting discrimination in many communities in the United States in the first half of the twentieth century and the recent South African system of apartheid (from 1948 to 1994). In the United States, the 1896 *Plessy v. Ferguson* Supreme Court case temporarily established that African Americans could be legally segregated in schools and in other ways. The Court found that treating minorities of color in a separate but equal fashion would not violate the Constitution. However, in 1954 the Supreme Court reversed this decision and found in *Brown v. Board of Education* that the infamous principle of separate but equal was inherently discriminatory, and thus unconstitutional under the equal protection clause of the Fourteenth Amendment. Yet many other laws remained, including the infamous Jim Crow laws that required discrimination in voting registration, education, access to public conveniences, employment, and the like. Examples of Jim Crow laws included requirements that African Americans use separate water fountains or sit in the back of buses. Various de facto forms of segregation (i.e., those implemented through informal and hidden practices) bolstered the de jure forms of discrimination, including redlining African American residential areas as ineligible for mortgages. Currently in the United States and in most other countries, only the most extreme separatists, such as neo-Nazis, adhere to this perspective.

B. Assimilationist Models: The Vision of the Melting Pot

Those who espouse an assimilationist perspective believe that new entrants to a society such as the United States should and inevitably do adopt the culture, language, and behaviors of the mainstream culture. This has been the expectation of many generations of Americans, most dramatically epitomized by Israel Zangwill, who in 1908 coined the term *melting pot* in a play he wrote:

> America is God's crucible, the great Melting Pot where all the races of Europe are melting and re-forming! Where you are melting and re-forming! Here you stand, good folk, think I, when I see them at Ellis Island, here you stand in your fifty groups, with your fifty languages and histories, and your fifty blood hatreds and rivalries. But you won't be long like that, brothers, for these are the fires

of God' you've come to—these are the fires of God. A fig for your feuds and vendettas! Germans and Frenchmen, Irishmen, and Englishmen, Jews and Russians—into the crucible with you all! God is making the American. (Zangwill, 1926).

Unlike contemporary multiculturalists, traditionalists who subscribe to the vision of the melting pot contend that the United States is not a nation of separate cultures, but that it is and should remain one nation built on a traditional Judeo-Christian set of values and on the cultural heritage of the West. It is assumed that the language, religion, and culture of immigrants are superficial and within a few generations will fall by the wayside. Assimilation was particularly encouraged during the mass immigration that took place around 1900 until as late as World War II.

Assimilation is often used synonymously with the term *acculturation,* though sometimes the latter refers to only the part of assimilation that has to do with formal culture rather than with language, legal integration, and the like. Similar terms are *socialization* and *enculturation,* but these are far more general and mainly refer to the induction of children into the ways of the dominant society or culture. Another increasingly popular term is *ethnoconvergence,* with which there is no implication that a dominant culture is absorbing a minority culture. Rather, two or more cultures grow more similar and converge through intermarriage and socialization. This is similar to transculturation, which more specifically refers to the exchange of cultural characteristics.

C. Pluralistic Models: Separate and Competing

After World War II, the dominant approach in the United States became one of pluralism: the idea that separate groups—cultures, races, ethnicities—continue to exist long after their entry into mainstream society. Each competes to contribute to the overall vibrancy of mainstream culture, but each maintains its own identity, however modified that might be by its participation in the larger society. The separate cultures are not considered necessarily equal. Each is regarded as having a place based on the quality of its contributions to the greater culture. Whereas many on the political right subscribe to the assimilationist position, more moderate Americans accept some version of this pluralist vision.

The pluralist perspective considers the diverse groups as representing only partially overlapping circles. Kottak and Kozaitis (1999) contend that pluralists regard ethnic boundaries as firm, cultural borders as static, and identities as fixed. They suggest that pluralists speak of "the Italians," "women," "Asians," "homosexuals," and "blacks," conveying a monolithic image of each group and ignoring the groups' internal diversity and fuzzy boundaries (Kottak & Kozaitis, 1999). They point out that pluralists believe that ethnic and racial differences should be allowed to exist, as long as they do not threaten mainstream values and norms. Pluralism emphasizes moral relativism and tolerance, and posits that the major task of intergroup relations is negotiating the respective contributions of each group to the cultural mosaic. It is this liberal pluralism that set the stage for the development of multiculturalism.

D. Multiculturalism: Separate but Cooperating

By the late 1980s, an alternative orientation toward racial and ethnic relations had emerged in the United States. Unlike both assimilation and pluralism, which assume the primacy of a single national culture, multiculturalism views any such culture as secondary or even fictional. It instead assumes that the central sources of identity reside in ethnicities, in cultures, and are intertwined with race: Cuban, French-Canadian, Navajo, West African. Hinman (1998) contends that the core idea of multiculturalism involves the identity argument, which consists of three parts: (1) to be happy, one's identity must be affirmed; (2) a central part of identity is racial (or ethnic) identity; and (3) society must act in such a way as to permit or even encourage the celebration of racial identity.

According to Kottak and Kozaitis (1999), multiculturalism differs from both assimilationism and pluralism by affirming a multiplicity of well-defined cultures, by accepting singular cultural transmission as the source of group formation, and by actively promoting democratization and equity among groups. Society is conceived of not so much as the community of various traditions blending into one heritage but as the coexistence of many distinct heritages and newly invented traditions within a single nation-state. It assumes conflicts and differences rather than the integration into any cohesive larger culture. Proponents of multiculturalism often favor aggressive compensatory versions of affirmative action, even those that set aside quotas of positions for people of designated minority groups for admissions into schools or jobs. Some argue for reparations for the descendants of people who were enslaved during the nineteenth century.

There have been several critiques of multiculturalism, from the radical left but more often from the right. For example, Matthew Jacobson, in his book *Whiteness of a Different Color: European Immigrants and the Alchemy of Race* (1999) contends that the celebration of ethnic difference can serve as a smokescreen for the maintenance of whiteness. Jacobson traces the beginning of the notion of whiteness to the 1920s. Prior to this time there were believed to be a variety of Caucasian races, such as Anglo-Saxons, Celts, Hebrews, Mediterraneans, and Slavs. This consolidation of white identity received a significant boost as a result of the civil rights movement of the 1950s and 1960s. Jacobson contends that this movement further polarized the organization of racial difference in the United States. This led to a further blurring of the earlier distinctions among white groups, especially as the various minority ethnicities came to be emphasized. Whether awareness is enhanced or obscured for the various Caucasian or minority ethnic groups, several commentators complain about the arbitrariness of how particular groups are defined, especially considering the substantial cultural sharing that goes on between the various groups. Whereas some, such as Arthur Schlesinger (1998), complain that multiculturalism is divisive and weakens any identification with a common national culture, others complain about the relativism of multiculturalists. Specifically, they complain about a reluctance to make judgments about alternative cultural beliefs and practices, whether this involves the practice of female genital mutilation by some West African groups or the many critically important contributions of Islamic civilization to Western culture, in art, architecture, and mathematics, including Arabic numerals and algebra. They contend that multiculturalists regard culture as a given, as a static set of set of beliefs and practices that define the individual.

E. Postculturalism: Overlapping

This final perspective was introduced in the 1990s by such people as David Hollinger (2000), who writes about postethnicity, and Eric Liu (1999), who coined the term *omniculturalism.* The common theme of these approaches is that identity emerges out of a fluid, dynamic intermingling of diverse cultures and histories, especially given the increasing rates of intermarriage. Although intermarriage of African Americans has increased only slightly, intermarriage among Hispanics and Asians has grown substantially. This perspective is consistent with complexity theory, and it recognizes the diverse and hybrid identities that arise in contemporary culture. The continuing difficulty in defining what it means to be Hispanic or Latino illustrates some of the ambiguities that result when competing criteria, such as national origin, language, or race, are used to define ethnicity (see exhibit 13.1). This perspective emphasizes the ways that individuals' diverse ancestral and personal histories combine to create entirely new identities. Hollinger argues that cultural identifications are essentially voluntary. The postethnic perspective diverges from multiculturalism mainly in its recognition that culture is not a fixed or monolithic entity but loosely coupled sets

Exhibit 13.1: Defining Ethnicity: Hispanics in the United States

Because ethnic identity is multidimensional, drawing on race, national origin, language, and religion, the definition of any group is subject to many interpretations and ambiguities, and this is perhaps no more effectively illustrated than with Hispanic ethnicity. The term *Hispanic* in the U.S. came into mainstream prominence when the 1980 U.S. Census asked respondents to identify if they were of "Spanish/Hispanic origin or descent." Hispanics now are the largest single minority group in the nation, representing 14.1 percent of the population in 2004, and the fastest-growing group: the population is projected to expand to 102.6 million, or 24 percent of the U.S. population by 2050. Almost half (49 percent) of the Hispanic population lives in California, Texas, and Arizona ("Hispanic American Demographics").

Hispanic status is commonly defined as including any person whose ancestors originated from Spain, the Spanish-speaking countries of Latin America, or former Spanish territories in what is now the U.S. Southwest. Yet the term *Hispanic* is controversial. Many consider *Hispanic* too general or even offensive. A popular misconception is that Hispanics are members of a particular race of brown-skinned people, whereas Hispanics may be either of Caucasian, African American, or even of Asian descent. The Spaniards who colonized most of Latin America were primarily of Western European origin but some were of Middle Eastern descent as well. The Hispanic designation also ignores the fact that a significant proportion of the populations of the Americas are of mestizo origin: a combination of Amerindian and European ancestry. Consider the estimated mestizo percentages of the populations of the following nations Colombia (61 percent), Ecuador (65 percent), El Salvador (90 percent), Honduras (90 percent), Mexico (60 percent), Nicaragua (69 percent), Panama (70 percent), Paraguay (95 percent), and Venezuela (64 percent) (CIA, 2009). Because almost two-thirds (64 percent) of U.S. Hispanics are of Mexican origin, many Hispanics in the United States also share the hidden biocultural legacy of the indigenous populations of Mexico, particularly the Aztec culture. Other Hispanics in the United States have a very different origin, which is revealed by DNA testing of Hispanic populations in the Southwest, which has shown that between 10 percent and 15 percent of men have a Y chromosome with origins in the Middle East (Kelly, 2004).

Related Terms

LATINO. The most frequent alternative self-designation for Hispanics is *Latino* (or *Latina*). *Latino* links the individual to Latin American countries,

Exhibit 13.1 (continued)

or countries in the Americas where the official and predominant language is Latinate: Spanish or Portuguese (and sometimes French). One area of confusion with the Latino designation is that several nations in the Caribbean, Central America, and South America (e.g. Guyana, Suriname, Belize) do not speak Latin languages, and thus are not considered by some to be part of Latin America.

CHICANO. This term is used by many Hispanics in the American Southwest who specifically trace their ancestry to Mexico (*Chicana* is the feminine form). Although the term is believed to be originally a contraction of *Mexicano,* there no agreement about its origin. By the 1960s and 1970s, the term had become an emblem of ethnic pride among persons of Mexican descent, especially those involved in organizing for immigrant and farm worker rights.

TEJANO. This term refers to people of Mexican descent who live in Texas (the feminine form is *Tejana*). They may also consider themselves part of the broader Latino, Hispanic, or Chicano groups.

NUYORICAN. This term is derived from the blending of *New York* and *Puerto Rican.* It includes all those in the Puerto Rican diaspora and their descendents who live in the New York City area.

CREOLE. The generic meaning of Creole is a people or a culture that is distinctive of a locality. Throughout Latin America, *Creole* usually refers to people of unmixed Spanish or Portuguese descent who were born in the New World.

MULATTO. This is a term of Spanish (or Portuguese) origin that refers to the offspring of persons of African and European ancestry. Many Americans of Mexican American, Puerto Rican, or Cuban origin identify themselves as mulatto. The term is also used in many other countries.

OTHER. Many Hispanics instead prefer designations defined by national origin, such as Cuban American, Puerto Rican, or Mexican American.

of beliefs, norms, and values that constantly combine, split, and recombine with other ones. Western culture itself represents a complex amalgam of Judeo-Christian, Greek, Roman, Anglo-Saxon, Continental, Islamic, Asian, and African influences. A recent work on the role of Anglo-Saxon culture in the United States, *Albion's Seed: Four British folkways in America* (Fischer, 1989), has documented that this purportedly monolithic culture is itself a complex group of loosely coupled subcultures: Puritan, Royalist, Quaker, and Borderer (or Scotch-Irish).

F. Discussion

Strategies to promote diversity, thus, can mean many things, ranging from pursuing a pluralist agenda to developing multicultural initiatives and adopting a postcultural perspective. The central challenge has been to decide how broad a range of populations to consider, and how to conceptualize the relationship of individual and group identities to the large culture, whether one of separation, competition, coexistence, integration, or some combination. Phillip Fellin (2000) pointed out that in social work education there have been three major approaches to defining diversity: (1) cultural pluralism, or the idea that all individual and group identities should be recognized and celebrated; (2) the population-at-risk approach, or the idea that the focus should be restricted to people of color and other traditionally oppressed groups, such as gays and lesbians, older adults, and the disabled; and (3) the notion that diversity should be restricted only to peoples or communities of color and ethnic minorities. There has been a tendency to confuse the broader phenomenon of diversity with the more specific issue of oppression. Although the two are intimately related, the relevance of diversity goes far beyond its implications for oppression. For many, the central concern of multicultural diversity has been to enhance minorities' numerical participation in the broader society.

A central question has been how to best implement multiculturalism, by simply increasing the numerical representation of oppressed groups in key social positions, by raising consciousness and intergroup relationships with the belief that the former will follow, or some combination of the two. Will change in the social structure—specifically greater minority participation— lead to a change in consciousness and the acceptance of differences, or is a change in consciousness needed first for any lasting changes in the social structure? What additional changes are required to support more inclusive structures and attitudes? William J. Wilson (see profile 13.1) has argued that, while remaining a central issue, the significance of race in the perpetuation of inner-city poverty has declined in recent years, and that greater attention needs to be paid to an array of social and economic supports.

III. Types of Diversity

This section explores a few of the most relevant types of primary diversity, which involves variations in personal and social characteristics. Cultural diversity is of central importance, but we will cover this only after we review biological diversity. First, we will briefly identify the major dimensions of

© William Julius Wilson, Lewis P. And Linda L. Geyser University Professor, Harvard University. Reprinted with permission

PROFILE 13.1: WILLIAM JULIUS WILSON, AMERICAN SOCIOLOGIST

William Julius Wilson (b. 1935–), one of the most influential sociologists in the United States, has played a decisive role in shaping contemporary debates on the role of race in urban poverty, placing it with an understanding of the systemic confluence of multiple economic and social forces.

Wilson, born in Derry Township, Pennsylvania, in 1935, was educated first at Wilberforce University (B.A., 1958) and Bowling Green State University (M.A., 1961), and he completed his Ph.D. at Washington State University (1966). After an initial appointment at the University of Massachusetts at Amherst, he taught at the University of Chicago from 1972 to 1996 and served as chair of its sociology department during his tenure there. In 1996, he was appointed a university professor at Harvard University's Kennedy School and director of its Joblessness and Urban Poverty Research Program. Wilson is perhaps best known for his spatial mismatch theory (1987), in which he proposes that globalization and deindustrialization have led to a diminution and displacement of low-income jobs from the inner city. He regards the decline of industrial jobs as a cause of not only high inner-city unemployment but also low marriage rates among young blacks, which thus results in high rates of single-parent families. He disputes the theories of Charles Murray that welfare is a cause of poverty among blacks and others who deemphasize environmental forces. In fact, his book *The Declining Significance of Race* (1978) is particularly controversial, as he argues that poverty among inner-city blacks cannot be blamed exclusively on the historical legacy of racism—though he is quick to argue that racism has played a key role. For example, he comments: "Affirmative action has to be combined with a broader program of social reform that would emphasize social rights: the right to employment, the right to education, the right to good health" (quoted in Early, 1996). Wilson has occasionally been mistaken as a conservative, despite the fact that in several of his books, such as *When Work Disappears: The World of the New Urban Poor* (1996), he takes liberal positions, such as his argument for expanded social welfare programs. In addition, his original use of terms such as *black underclass* gave some the impression that he favored a culture-of-poverty explanation

---

PROFILE 13.1 (CONTINUED)

of urban poverty. He has more recently disavowed that terminology and made it clear that he believes that the cultural dimensions of ghetto life are primarily the consequence, rather than the cause, of poverty.

William Julius Wilson has been a particularly productive scholar and influential in advising presidents on issues of race and urban poverty. He has been president of the American Sociological Association, and he received the prestigious MacArthur Fellows Program Award from 1987 to 1992 and the National Medal of Science in 1998.

---

diversity, its purview, relevant characteristics, and levels mandated by affirmative action. The final section of the chapter explores secondary forms of diversity, that is, the range of responses to naturally occurring diversity.

A. Major Dimensions

The diversity movement, including policies promoting diversity such as affirmative action, encompasses a wide variety of groups and activities. In the United States, affirmative action laws require equality of opportunity for employment, study, contracts, and other benefits for designated groups. The laws apply to federal employees, as well as staff, students, and clients in organizations that receive funds from the federal government. More broadly, diversity is often sought in any organizational or service context, such as boards of directors, special events, and in work assignments. Interest in diversity also goes beyond such contexts and often includes the expectation that oppressed and other diverse groups are adequately represented in entertainment, advertising, history books, and educational curricula at the primary, secondary, and higher education levels. Of particular relevance is the need to ensure that both concrete and soft human services, from income maintenance to counseling, are delivered through accessible, culturally competent, and linguistically appropriate means. Whether social workers, politicians, or newscasters are concerned, both written and spoken language is expected to be nonracist, nonsexist, and in general, culturally sensitive. Thus, although statistical or structural diversity is regarded as a minimum goal, the intent of the diversity movement goes far beyond such a narrow focus to include changes in underlying consciousness and social relations. Commenting on diversity in educational settings, Guerin (2005) states: "The impact of structural diversity depends greatly on classroom and informal interactional diversity. Structural diversity is essential but, by itself, usually not sufficient to produce substantial benefits; in addition to being together on the same campus, students from diverse backgrounds must also learn about each other in the courses that they take and in informal interaction outside of the classroom."

Another critical dimension involves the definition of the groups covered by affirmative action laws. In the United States, the Civil Rights Act of 1964 protects individuals from discrimination based on race, sex, religion, national origin, physical disability, and age. Discrimination based on gender includes pregnancy, childbirth, and related medical conditions. Other laws, such as the Americans with Disabilities Act of 1990, prohibit discrimination based on a physical or mental handicap by employers engaged in interstate commerce and state governments. In general, these laws cover initial employment, wages, promotions, working conditions, and termination. Although the groups targeted by these laws, such as minorities of color and women, have been those with the most widely publicized histories of discrimination and oppression, a wide range of other groups have come to be included in many diversity initiatives, such as gays, lesbians, transgender individuals, low-income people, immigrants, to mention a few.

Finally, a particularly important dimension of diversity is the level or goal of diversity that is mandated or sought. Some groups support the inclusion of historically oppressed groups in broader opportunities but insist that they should be included in a nondiscriminatory or color-blind manner and that standards for admission, employment, or services not be lowered for such groups. The usual argument is that while it may be acceptable to increase applications by minority applicants through recruiting, that actual consideration of those applications should never consider minority status. This is considered by many to be the weakest standard, and some people regard it as racist because it ignores historical discrimination. However, there are many members of minority groups who support this approach, because it is believed that preferential treatment through lowered standards undermines both their own self-respect and that of others. Those who favor color-blind affirmative action policies are often accused of tokenism, or of favoring the occasional hiring of a minority person simply to appear to be inclusive and nonracist.

For many, diversity and affirmative action mean preferential treatment for targeted groups through admission quotas, handicapping factors, or simply goals. Until the U.S. Supreme Court outlawed the use of quotas in 1978 in the *Bakke* decision, employers or schools could set aside a designated number of slots for admission under a relaxed standard. When that strategy was outlawed, interest turned toward assigning points for minority status, a form of preferential treatment that continues to be controversial. Such goals presumably do not lower entry standards. However, there may be preferential treatment in terms of recruitment for bringing the numbers up to some designated benchmark. What the benchmark should be has been a matter of dispute. What is the relevant benchmark? The proportion of the target population in the local area or in the state? Current or potential clients? The particular profession, all professions, or all workers? Thus, although diversity may seem to be a simple matter, there are various highly contentious issues involving its scope, the groups targeted, and the acceptable levels of diversity and minority representation.

B. Biodiversity: Layers of Diversity and the Question of Race

Variation in biological characteristics, of both populations and their environments, is pervasive and forms one of the most important contexts of cultural diversity, yet it is highly controversial. To what extent do variations depend on the underlying genotype, or genetic inheritance, and to what extent are they an outcome of the organism's phenotype, which manifests in characteristics, partly or wholly influenced by the environment? Linking the two is epigenetics, which refers to the systematic ways that the organism unfolds and through which genetic information is integrated with other forms of information to generate the phenotype through individual and collective developmental processes. Biological diversity, thus, can be analyzed in terms of the nested integration of several levels of developmental patterns. Brown (1988) has described these levels in the following terms:

- Phylogenesis pertains to the sequence of events involved in the evolutionary development of a species or taxonomic group of organism. An example is the evolution of *Homo sapiens* and the species' differentiation from other now-extinct hominid species, such as *Homo erectus* or *Homo africanus.*
- Ethnogenesis refers to the ways an ethnic group comes into being. One pattern of ethnogenetic development involves the branching off of an ethnic group as the result of its geographic isolation. Another pattern consists of the coming together of two or more ethnic groups (the melting-pot scenario) to create a homogeneous whole, perhaps under the dominant influence of a constituent group. For example, after the Moghuls' invasion and conquest of Baghdad in the twelfth century, the conquering Moghuls assimilated within a few generations into the local Arab population.

- Ontogenesis refers to the individual maturation and development (to be discussed in detail in chapter 5) that takes place within the contexts of phylo- and ethnogenesis.
- Microgenesis refers to the momentary, often biologically rooted, development of cognition, whether this involves affect, beliefs, or their expression through behavior. Evolutionary processes involving natural selection are used to explain the almost instantaneous development of particular thoughts, for example, through a type of neural Darwinism, or survival-of-the-fittest mental models. The theory of microgenesis has been used to explain language acquisition (Ohta, 2000). The American psychologist Jason Brown first proposed microgenesis, and he theorized that mental processes recapitulate evolutionary processes. Openness to diversity, as well as stereotypical and racist thinking, each can be understood as the bottom-up emergence of competing mental models of the relation of the individual to his or her social world.

Despite the wide range of ways in which humans biologically vary, those which have received the most attention have been the most visible traits, the ones associated with the greatest historical struggles (e.g., skin color, sex). For example, the concept of race has been notoriously difficult to define, and there has been no consensus on whether distinct races actually exist. W. E. B. DuBois (1903) elegantly stated this conundrum slightly more than a century ago: "The problem of the twentieth century is the problem of the color-line—the relation of the darker to the lighter races of men in Asia and Africa, in America and the islands of the sea."

Although few question the existence of different racial groups, the ways that the groups have been defined has continuously changed. For many years, the standard classification consisted of three to four major groups: Caucasoid, Negroid, Mongoloid, and sometimes Australoid. Five groups defined by the U.S. Census Bureau have replaced this now-archaic classification. Each decade these categories have been adjusted, some either combined or split. In the 2000 census, respondents were for the first time given the opportunity to check more than one category, which Hollinger (2000) referred to as the "racial pentagon": (1) white, (2) black or African American, (3) American Indian or Alaskan Native, (4) Asian, or (5) Native Hawaiian and other Pacific Islander, in addition to "other." For several decades now, Hispanics have been separated out in a separate question on ethnicity, recognizing that someone of Hispanic background can be white, black, or just about any other race. The constant revisions of the categories highlights the essential social basis of their definition. The social basis of race as a category is also suggested by the observation that in many societies membership in a minority racial group is assigned to a person with any discernible percentage of ancestry that group, even one-fourth or one-eighth, and not according to any percentage of ancestry from the dominant racial group. Historically in the United States, a person is considered African American if only one of his or her four grandparents is African American. Racial categories, thus, have never been objective biological classifications but shifting social constructions that are linked only loosely to biological traits. However, these categories have profound implications for individuals' rights, status, and roles in society.

There has never been consensus not only about the definition of racial groups but also about whether they exist in the first place. It has been reported that only a slight majority of physical anthropologists accept the notion of separate races. Anthropologists and biologists point out that there are no specific genes but rather a variety of genes that code for overall racial differences. All races share virtually all the same genes, but some genes have different effects in different groups (Gill, 2005). Yet it is also recognized that there are many physical differences, not only skin color but also type of hair, bone structure, and disease susceptibility. Such variations, however, are not categorical but rather continuous or "clinal." This means, for instance, that if one travels north from the equatorial regions, skin color changes gradually but not necessarily consistently. Many have cited Richard Lewontin's (1972) classic study in which he reported that most of the variation (84%) in racial characteristics is found within each racial group (i.e., between individuals of the same race), and only 10% of the variation is found between racial groups—an exceptionally weak basis for any classificatory system. Thus, any single characteristic such as skin color cannot reliably distinguish racial groups. The rejoinder to this conclusion has been that several characteristics in combination can permit reliable classifications.

Skin color, the most visible of the racial differences, does not represent the expression of separate genes per se but rather is controlled by genes present in all people. The yellowness or blackness of skin results from the expression of either of two kinds of the melanin skin pigment: phenomelanin and eumelanin, respectively. The operation of the enzyme tyrosinase controls the tone of both kinds of pigment.

The most common theory about the origin of the major skin color groups is that increased melanin has evolved to protect individuals in the tropics from excessive exposure to ultraviolet radiation (UVR). However, in recent years this theory has been modified to account for occasional variations in skin color that depart from a simple north-south gradation in UVR exposure. Jablonski (2004) and Chaplin (2004) have proposed a theory involving the nonlinear combination of two selective factors consisting of both the costs and the benefits in natural selection for UVR exposure. The costs involve the destructive breakdown of many compounds, of which vitamin B is the most important. However, UVR also provides for the beneficial synthesis of vitamin D. Thus, both Jablonski and Chaplin theorize that skin color evolves as a location-specific compromise between the requirement for skins light enough to maximize UVR penetration for vitamin D synthesis (especially in northern latitudes) but dark enough to minimize the breakdown of vitamin B (in equatorial regions).

Those who reject the concept of race do so on several grounds, not solely on the lack of variation accounted for by existing systems of racial classification. Loring Brace (2005) observes, "Every time we plot the distribution of a trait possessing a survival value that is greater under some circumstances than under others, it will have a different pattern of geographical variation, and no two such patterns will coincide." He points out that the geographic gradients in the distribution of racial features (referred to as "clines"), such as skin color or nose or eye shape, all vary independently of one another. Thus, the aphorism "There are no races; there are only clines" has become popular among biologists.

Proponents of this perspective argue not only that racial categories cannot be justified empirically but also that they mostly reflect social constructions. For instance, David Hollinger (2000) compares the current status of Hispanics with that of Jewish Americans. Jews, he notes, were once considered a separate race, but no longer. This change occurred not as a result of biological discoveries but rather because prejudices against Jews in the United States have come to be regarded as less destructive than those against Hispanics, whom some mistakenly believe constitute a separate race. What many people consider races Hollinger refers to as "communities of descent," or ethnic identities, as he believes that racial categories are defined on the basis of nothing other than ongoing prejudices of dominant groups.

Since the completion of the Human Genome Project in 2001, which mapped the human genetic code, major strides have been made in identifying the major genetic groups of humans, which are now referred to as "haplogroups." These are, in many respects, the true communities of descent. Haplogroups are broad groups—essentially the branches on the family tree of *Homo sapiens*. In contrast, haplotypes represent the leaves of the tree. In contrast, haplotypes are the subgroups that come under the various haplotypes. There have been several systems developed to define and name haplogroups and haplotypes. To standardize the categories, a group called the Y Chromosome Consortium has developed a new system to name the haplogroups and their subtypes. A haplogroup includes all the descendants of the

FIGURE 13.1: MIGRATION ROUTES OF MAJOR HUMAN HAPLOGROUPS

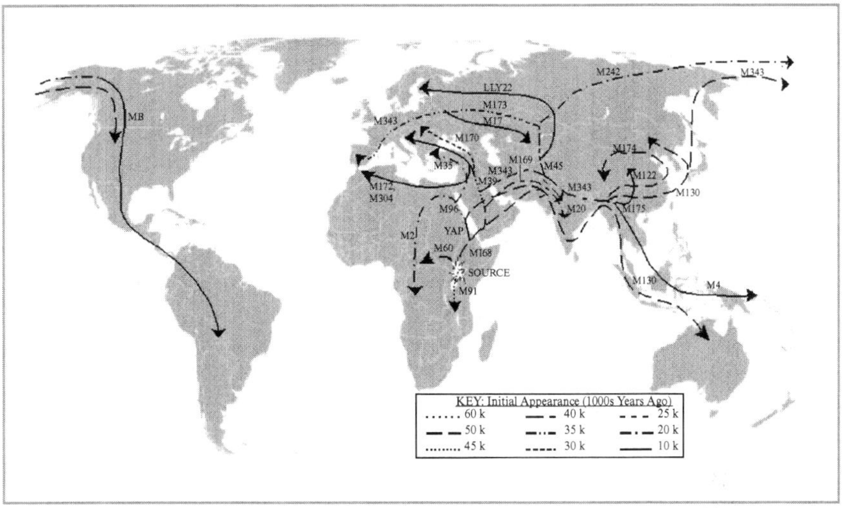

Note: The above represents the major pathways of migration taken by the various genetic groups of humans, based on analysis of Y chromosomes of the various human genetic haplogroups, originating in East Africa.

Source: Canuckguy et al. (2006; based on Stix, 2008).

individual who first showed a particular kind of mutation, referred to as the single nucleotide polymorphism (SNP). The mutations identify groups with a common ancestor far back in time. Because these mutations are extremely rare, they serve only to identify groups over a time span of tens of thousands of years. This consortium has defined eighteen major haplogroups, designated by the capital letters *A* through *R*, which represent the major categories of human biodiversity based on mutations in the Y chromosome. Each of these major haplogroups, which are sometimes called clades, usually have subgroups, or "subclades" (see figure 13.1). Use of haplogroups is potentially a very useful system: it has allowed tracking the historical periods during which the major human ethnic groups originated, as well as the resulting migrations. Humans today represent complex biological, social, and cultural integrations of these original eighteen haplogroups.

Human biodiversity, however, goes far beyond what many regard as racial or genetic variations. A wide range of human traits, especially physical traits such as physique, agility, strength, coordination, and susceptibility to particular diseases have been shown to be biologically and genetically rooted. For many years social scientists subscribed to the blank-slate theory: although physical characteristics might be genetically rooted, features of personality and mental functioning result purely from socialization. However, most studies now show that as much as 40% to 60% of variation in personality, as well as the occurrence of major mental disorders, is attributable to genetic differences (see chapter 5).

C. Biocultural Diversity

Given the difficulties of disentangling biological, psychosocial, and cultural sources of diversity, a recent trend has been to attempt to understand the sources of biocultural diversity. For many, ethnicity connotes merely the impact of culture. Most definitions of ethnicity, however, regard it as a composite of cultural and biological characteristics. Burkey (cited in Longres, 2000), for instance, identifies three factors that constitute ethnicity: (1) language, (2) culture, and (3) physical type. Similarly, Barker (1991) defines an ethnic group as "a distinct group of people who share a common language, set of customs, history, culture, race, religion, or origin" (p. 77). Thus, strictly understood, ethnicity involves both biological characteristics and cultural identity shared with other people of similar background.

Nonetheless, the notion of biocultural diversity goes beyond questions of ethnic diversity to include consideration of the biological diversity in plant and animal species. Recently, Loh and Harmon (2005) developed an index of biocultural diversity, which they define as the total variety exhibited by the world's natural and cultural systems. They calculate their index using three methods: (1) an unadjusted richness measure, (1) one adjusted for land area, and (3) one adjusted for the size of the human population. Using this index, they located three areas of exceptional biocultural diversity: the Amazon basin, central Africa, and Indo-Malaysia/Melanesia.

Two types of biopsychosocial diversity have been particularly controversial in recent years: intelligence and sexual preference. In their reviled 1994 book *The Bell Curve,* Herrnstein and Murray suggested that the observed difference in intelligence between whites and African Americans, about fifteen IQ points on average, is genetically based and a significant cause of many African Americans' low socioeconomic status and social problems. They argued, for example, for the legitimacy of the "G factor," the idea that there is an overall measure of general intelligence rather than multiple types, as Howard Gardner (1993) and others contend. In addition, they argued against the notion that systematic racial biases in testing can account for the observed differences. There have been many critiques of Herrnstein and Murray's analysis, one of which notes that they failed to control for differential levels of education as a part of socioeconomic status in their analysis of IQ differences in racial groups. In addition, a critique has noted that the they exaggerate the heritability of intelligence, placing it at about 60%, whereas more recent studies place it closer to 40% (Lemann, 1997). More important, Herrnstein and Murray are widely regarded as blaming the victims and discounting the role of historical patterns of racial oppression in observed racial disparities.

The debate on intelligence illustrates the difficulties in examining group differences. In one context an identified difference may be viewed as a benign trait defining the groups involved. In another context, it may be cause for special blame or admiration, or in still another context, an occasion for pity or humor. Too often dominant groups define these differences in ways that serve their narrow interests. For this reason, essential questions to consider when examining any claims about group differences are not only who is defining the differences and for what purpose, but also what is the extent of overlap in the distributions of such characteristics in each group. In addition, of critical importance is the reliability and validity of the characterizations, especially whether they are fine-grained enough to capture the different types of variations. For example, in the case of intelligence, does it consider the most important types of cognitive abilities? Figure 13.2 illustrates how a given characteristic, such as intelligence, may vary not only between but also within two groups so much that the group means provide

FIGURE 13.2: ILLUSTRATION OF EFFECT OF INTRAGROUP VARIATION IN COMPARISON OF INDIVIDUALS FROM TWO GROUPS WITH DIFFERENT AVERAGES

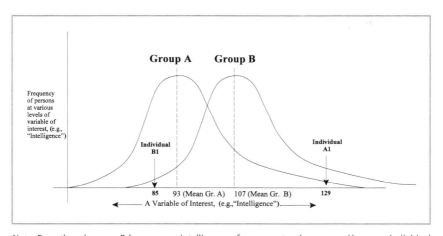

Note: Even though group B has a mean intelligence of 107, greater than group A's 93, an individual (A1) from group A may have a much higher intelligence from individuals from both groups, and likewise, an individual from group B (B1) can have an substantially lower IQ than not only his or her own group but also that of group A.

scant information to infer differences between any two individuals from the groups of interest.

The essential message here is not to ignore considerations of group differences for fear of stereotyping but to make sure that there is some clarity about the need to identify such differences. If there is such a need, then it becomes necessary to ensure that the determinations are reliable and valid, and not misused. In addition, it is critical to consider the ratio of within-and between-group variation. Historically, much biomedical research was done on samples of males, with little regard for whether the results could be generalized to females. New requirements in federally funded research have largely ameliorated this bias. However, progress has been slower with respect to ethnic minorities. Recently a new field has emerged to address this gap, ethnopsychopharmacology. This is based on the recognition that ethnic and cultural influences can modify an individual's reactions to medications. The field investigates cultural variations and differences that influence the effectiveness of the various psychiatric medications. Areas investigated range from genetic variations in drug metabolism to psychosocial and cultural practices that affect diet, medication compliance, the placebo effect, and choice of treatment methods (Lin, Anderson, & Poland, 1997).

A particularly sensitive area of biocultural diversity involves sexual preference, given the historic stigma that gays and lesbians have been subjected to as oppressed minorities. Because of stigma, such individuals have historically been largely invisible, and that continues to be the case, despite the fact that they constitute between 1% and 5% of the population (Bailey & Pillard, 1991). The often negative characterization of sexual preference has reflected the biases of the prevalent heterosexual communities.

Homosexuals have most often been stigmatized by the belief that their sexual preference either is a sinful moral choice or is symptomatic of psychopathology. Freud characterized male homosexuality in psychopathological terms as an outcome of overly protective mothers and distant, hostile fathers. It was not until 1972 that the American Psychiatric Association deleted homosexuality from its *Diagnostic and Statistical Manual of Mental Disorders.* Since then, there has been considerable debate about whether to regard homosexuality as a type of learned behavior, a biologically rooted preference, or some combination. Many in the gay and lesbian communities consider it biologically rooted, as something one is born with, yet there are others in the same communities who are reluctant to minimize social learning and even individual choice as factors. However these factors combine in a given individual, it is clear that sexual preference is an outcome of complex biopsychosocial processes.

In 1991, the neuroscientist Simon LeVay reported that he found key differences in the brains of homosexuals as compared to heterosexuals. Specifically, he discovered that clumps of neurons in the hypothalamuses of male homosexuals that control sexual behavior were about twice as large as those in heterosexual males. However, it was not clear whether this was a cause or consequence of the sexual preferences and behaviors of the individuals involved. Also in 1991, the psychologist J. Michael Bailey and Richard Pillard reported results from a study of identical twins raised separately: if one of the twins was gay, there was a 50% chance that the other was also gay; for fraternal twins, the rate was 20%, which provides strong support for a genetic explanation. However, the interpretation of results from such studies often fails to consider that the twins may not have had identical intrauterine experiences, given their different fetal positions. In fact, there is a growing school of thought that it is not so much genetics as differential exposure to high levels of male hormones in the early phases of intrauterine development, due to position in the womb, that controls the development of key parts of the brain, and eventually sexual preference. Although there is no consensus around any single theory, there is an emerging consensus that somehow sexual preference represents a complex epigenetic unfolding of genetic influences, triggered by hormonal and other intrauterine conditions, and later by other psychosocial conditions, such as cultural responses of caretakers. Thus, sexual preference is a prime illustration of the biocultural, and more specifically the biopsychosocial, diversity of humans. It illustrates our lack of understanding of this dimension, as well as the likelihood of multiple developmental pathways that result in a homosexual orientation.

D. Other Types of Diversity

Embedded in a community's biological diversity is its cultural diversity, including psychosocial variations of its members. Many of the sources of variation are not regularly considered part of cultural diversity (e.g., type of personality, cognitive style, character, type of family relationships). For example, there is a substantial empirical literature documenting systematic differences in cognitive styles and associated interactional patterns between Westerners and East Asians. Richard Nisbett (2003), a social psychologist from the University of Michigan, has spent the better part of his career researching culturally based patterns of cognition. He reports: "My research has led me to the conviction that two utterly different approaches to the world [Western and Eastern] have maintained themselves for thousands of years" (p. xx). The approaches, he explains, have fundamentally different views about social relations, the nature of the world, and characteristic thought processes. He notes that the approaches represent self-reinforcing, homeostatic systems. He also suggests that the philosophies of Aristotle and Confucius epitomize the approaches. Some of the main comparisons he draws between the modes of thought based on an extensive body of social psychological research are summarized in figure 13.3. Yet such variations can also have dramatic impacts on the extent to which individuals are discriminated against or persecuted.

Other types of diversity are unequivocally part of cultural diversity, such as political ideology and religious or spiritual orientation. Yet there is much confusion as to the extent and manner that communities should respond to those with minority, extremist, or intolerant positions. Such individuals may be discriminated against even by some groups that otherwise promote diversity. Actions on the part of the American Civil Liberties Union to assert the constitutional right of neo-Nazi groups to hold public marches illustrate some of the difficult choices that sometimes need to be made to protect diversity and freedom of speech. Variations in political and religious beliefs, and in the extent and type of disability, illustrate the distinction between a rights perspective that mandates nondiscrimination and a diversity perspective that promotes active steps toward inclusion. Whereas a nondiscrimination stance prohibits not hiring someone on the basis of a disability that is not relevant to the task under consideration, or a person who cannot be reasonably accommodated, a diversity stance seeks to actively promote respect, perhaps even by euphemistically redefining persons who are disabled as those who are differently abled.

IV. Sources and Functions of Diversity

This section will review selected theories about the sources and functions of diversity, primarily those involving cultural diversity. What one believes about the causes and functions of diversity, or the lack of it, largely determines one's response to it, a subject that the final section of this chapter takes up. Central to the concept of diversity is its relationship to the idea of systemic integration, coherence, or holism. Are these mutually exclusive, or do they supplement one another? What are the trade-offs, if any? One theorist asks, "How can we preserve diversity in the face of a threatened unity which serves the interests of the dominant group?" (Klaus, 2005). This section begins by discussing the interplay between the forces that generate diversity and those that bring about integration and convergence. It then presents a few examples of their application in the study of social and cultural phenomena.

FIGURE 13.3: THE GEOGRAPHY OF THOUGHT: COMPARISONS OF WESTERN AND EASTERN MODES OF THOUGHT

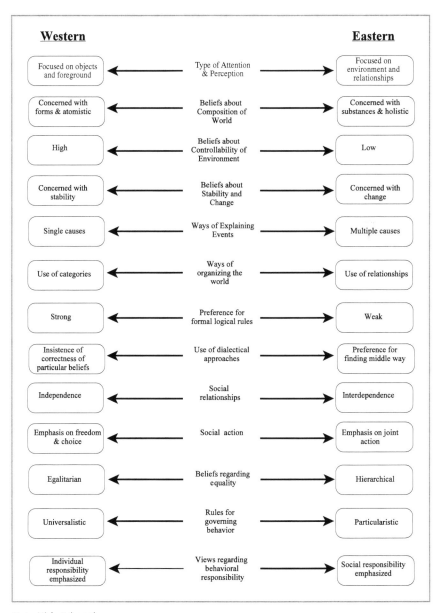

Note: Nisbett (2003).

A. Balance of Convergence and Diversification

Social change and history itself can be understood in terms of the interplay of forces of diversification and unification, of divergence and convergence, of the continuous splitting and remixing of human populations and cultures, like dough being kneaded. In times of social stress, scarcity, or persecution, human migrations occur to new promised lands, or at least ones that promise some safety. In the new lands, each group either merges with the indigenous population or develops a new but still separate identity and culture, sometimes assimilating with similar migrant groups. This complex biocultural splitting and recombining parallels the genetic recombination that takes place in marriage and procreation, ensuring an almost endless diversity of cultural, individual, and biological variations that fuel cultural development and any continuing biological evolution.

Some have characterized Western societies as monocultural. However, others emphasize their increasingly fragmentary character (Harvey, 1989; Smart, 1993), and it has been pointed out that there are no pure cultures as such. Any composite of cultures that develops appears to be, and in fact often becomes an integrated whole that results from the joining and separation of populations and, in general, their synthesis, which results in new cultures. Baker (1993) has suggested that much of cultural diversity and fragmentation can be understood on the basis of the ways that one individual's "centering and peripheralizing activities compete with the centering and peripherializing activities of others, for others are similarly trying to center their worlds" (p. 193).

B. Theories of Diversity

Theories that attempt to explain diversity usually focus on a particular type of diversity, or on oppressive reactions to diversity that are based on race, ethnicity, class, or sex. Furthermore, such theories differ according to their emphasis; for example, small-system conditions include individual and psychological factors, and larger-system conditions emphasize social structure, migration patterns, or economic opportunities.

Many oppressed groups experience a disproportionate level of poverty and, in general, low socioeconomic status. Most recognize poverty among African Americans as the legacy of historical patterns of enslavement and discrimination; however, there have been continuing controversies about the causes of poverty. These involve the question of whether people are poor because of a culture of poverty that involves dysfunctional attitudes transmitted from one generation to the next or because of historical and structural conditions.

The culture-of-poverty thesis is associated with Oscar Lewis, who first introduced the notion in his 1965 book *La Vida: A Puerto Rican Family in the Culture of Poverty, San Juan and New York.* Lewis attempted to portray low income people as those whose lives had been transformed through a unique culture of poverty. He emphasized how many low-income people live for the present day only and find it difficult to consider the future, and that they are primarily reactive rather than proactive. He argues that setting goals, planning ahead, and investing are not part of the culture of most poor. Lewis (1998) explains:

> The people in the culture of poverty have a strong feeling of marginality, of helplessness, of dependency, of not belonging. They are like aliens in their own country, convinced that the existing institutions do not serve their interests and needs. Along with this feeling of powerlessness is a widespread feeling of inferiority, of personal unworthiness. This is true of the slum dwellers of Mexico City, who do not constitute a distinct ethnic or racial group and do not suffer from racial discrimination. In the United States the culture of poverty of the Negroes has the additional disadvantage of racial discrimination. People with a culture of poverty have very little sense of history. They are a marginal people who know only their own troubles, their own local conditions, their own neighborhood, their own way of life. Usually, they have neither the knowledge, the vision nor the ideology to see the similarities between their problems and those of others like themselves elsewhere in the world. In other words, they are not class conscious, although they are very sensitive indeed to status distinctions. When the poor become class conscious or members of trade union organizations, or when they adopt an internationalist outlook on the world they are, in my view, no longer part of the culture of poverty although they may still be desperately poor. (p. 7)

Lewis has been severely criticized for blaming the poor for causing their own predicament, although he and others have denied this. In contrast, there are structural theories of poverty that, for instance, regard low-income and other marginal populations as a source for slack labor for times of economic expansion and as surplus workers in times of contraction, which needs to be maintained through welfare. Other structural theories emphasize changing economic patterns, such as deindustrialization or the impact of immigration.

My own research on variations in the size of homeless populations throughout the United States has revealed that economic trends, such as the development of the services sector of the economy, along with housing unaffordability and family fragmentation, are among the most powerful predictors homelessness levels, whereas levels of disability and the extent of human services accounted for exceptionally little variation (Hudson, 1998). However, the guiding intuition of many researchers has been that poverty is an outcome of the interplay of both individual and structural factors.

In one study that used data from the National Longitudinal Study to test Lewis's theory, the researchers found significant differences between the descendants of the lower class and those of the middle class with respect to both individual and large-system variables (Abell & Lyon, 1979). The authors interpreted the findings to support a theory of intergenerational transmission of income, occupational prestige, and IQ scores. They identified six predictors of educational, occupational, and financial achievement: race, region of the country, degree of urbanization, number of siblings, home reading material, and IQ. They also report that structural forces beyond individuals' ability to change explain two-thirds of the income gap between descendants of poor and middle-class individuals, thus a indicating a mixture of situational responses and cultural sources of poverty. Although they found that cultural behaviors are not the primary factors in the perpetuation of economic poverty, they nevertheless play an important secondary role.

Some accounts of the sources of diversity, particularly oppressive reactions toward individuals who do not share the characteristics of the social majority, emphasize the role of differential patterns of immigration (Longres, 2000). On the one hand, immigrants have often been welcomed as sources of cheap and low-skilled labor. On the other hand, they have been feared and excluded as threats to the economic interests and cohesiveness of established majority groups. The outcomes of this experience vary widely and include several of the previously discussed phenomena: assimilation, acculturation, amalgamation, and biculturalism. The congruence between immigrant and majority cultures; the extent of socioeconomic, racial, religious, and other differences, and the histories surrounding these; the economic and cultural contributions of the new group; and perceptions about the reasons for and legitimacy and legality of the immigration all influence the particular outcomes of immigration as they play out over several generations. Whereas some groups culturally assimilate, or even become amalgamated through intermarriage, others retain a strong group identity and culture, even protecting it through a separatist stance. Intergroup relationships are considered largely a function of the management of conflicts between majority and immigrant groups.

Other structural theories emphasize differential patterns of long-term historical development, ones that have been largely contingent on differences in physical environment. Jared Diamond, in *Guns, Germs, and Steel* (1997), identifies various differences among the environments and societies in Africa, the Americas, Eurasia, and Australia that account many of the current disparities in economic development across the continents. Unlike the original residents of the Americas, Africa, and Australia, those in Eurasia had access to far more species of animals for domestication and a wide variety of grains. This access allowed for the early development of agriculture, and thus the food surpluses that are required for development of cities as well as technology and culture (see chapter 2 and figure 2.2).

Patterns of similarity and difference between diverse ethnic groups can also be understood as a function of patterns of cultural transmission, which refers to the passing on of culturally relevant knowledge, skills, attitudes, values, symbols, and practical arrangements—including technology—from person to person or from culture to culture. In the field of complex systems research, Robert Axelrod (1997) has tested a variety of models of cultural transmission in which each person is regarded as encoding a designated number of cultural features that can assume different values. Whereas individuals in one society may adopt one of three represented religions, in another society individuals might select from among hundreds of religions represented in the social environment. Axelrod's simulations have demonstrated that the more similar individuals are, the higher the probability is that they will assume characteristics of their neighbors in remaining areas of difference. In general, he found that "local convergence can generate global polarization" (p. 148): as neighbors become more similar to one another, differences on the macro level tend to become more pronounced (Klemm, Eguiluz, Toral, & Miguel, 2005).

Thomas Sowell (1991) emphasizes cultural transmission as involving practical innovations, with the patterns determined by the dominance of ideas or innovations that serve fundamental human values in an evolutionary fashion: "cultural diversity, viewed internationally and historically, is not a static picture of differentness but a dynamic picture of competition in which what serves human purposes more effectively survives while what does not tends to decline or disappear."

C. Globalization and Diversity

The previous chapter introduced several trends in what has come to be known as globalization, such as the breaking down of trade barriers and greater fluidity in the flows of capital and in the migration of human populations. Currently there is an active debate about whether globalization is leading to greater cultural homogenization, especially in regard to the spread of Western culture, which is sometimes viewed as a type of cultural imperialism. Already in 1902, the Briton William Stead had published *The Americanization of the World,* in which he introduced the idea that American culture was encroaching on the rest of the world (Pells, 2002). It has been pointed out that as early as 1904 the World's Fair in St. Louis ignited an anti-American backlash overseas, as many exhibits tended to celebrate an alleged American cultural, political, and even ethnic supremacy. Alternatively, many argue that globalization is leading many back to their roots, if only as a reaction to the overwhelming social changes it brings with it. For instance, Thomas Friedman (2000), in *The Lexus and the Olive Tree,* argues that globalization is leading many to attempt to revive their indigenous cultures. Richard Pells (2002) makes a similar point: the appeal of U.S. culture for many around the world is the result of the United States' own diverse, immigrant population, which is able to produce entertainment, products, and services that naturally appeal to a transnational array of tastes and values. Richard Pells points out that this is something to be respected, not criticized as cultural imperialism: "in the end, American mass culture has not transformed the world into a replica of the United States" (p. B7). Instead, he claims that "America's dependence on foreign cultures has made the United States a replica of the world" (p. B7). Thus, globalization is a complex phenomenon with respect to its impact on diversity, which effectively illustrates Axelrod's belief that local convergence leads to global polarization. Because particular communities experience greater homogenization, there may well be greater global polarization, which one author goes so far as to characterize as a clash of civilizations (Huntington, 1996).

D. Functions of Diversity

Regardless of the causes of diversity or the dynamical processes through which it ebbs and wanes, the benefits and outcomes of diversity are of central importance in understanding why it exists and why it is so often suppressed. The functions that diversity serves in social relationships fall into several general groups. At the least, cultural diversity minimizes homogeneity, stagnation, and oppression. It provides for both improved competition and improved cooperation: better competition with a greater variety of players and better cooperation because of its egalitarian stance. A diverse social environment tends to be associated with individuals who can assume multiple perspectives, such as thinking divergently and outside the box, and thinking convergently, which are two essential parts of creative problem solving. The literature on creative personalities has demonstrated that these qualities develop when individuals have a capacity for relativism, complexity, and richness in their thinking (see chapter 7). Simonton (1997, as cited in Murray, 2003) found that highly talented children are more likely to come from rich, diverse, cultural environments than from culturally monolithic settings. Just as biodiversity usually supports evolutionary development, cultural diversity facilitates both cultural and personal development. However, an essential caveat is that the level of such diversity does not degenerate into divisiveness and overwhelm the ability of the individuals involved to integrate and learn from the resulting experiential diversity. Just as inclusive attitudes and divergent thinking may be an outcome of structural or statistical diversity, structural diversity presumes some level of development of the internal capacities for divergent and inclusive thought on the part of the individuals involved. The next section focuses on both the healthy and destructive ways that individuals and groups respond to primary diversity.

V. Responses to Diversity

This section moves to the subject of secondary diversity, involving the variety of individual and social responses to the array of physical and cultural differences, such as those defined by race, sex, age, or religion. Whether we view diversity and difference as opportunities or threats influences how we respond to them. The quality of the response is integral to all social relationships. If we view differences in others as errors, deviations, or violations of acceptable norms, then we will resent such people, view them as threats, and respond to them with destructive means. To the extent that individuals and groups are confident in their ability to learn, problem solve, and grow, they will, for the most part, welcome differences and novelty. This section will, therefore, review a few major responses to diversity, whether healthy, controversial, or dysfunctional and destructive.

It first needs to be said that the notion of response itself may be simplistic, unless responses are regarded as dynamical patterns of activity, of action and reaction, that develop in the context of multiple individual and societal systems. People respond not only to differences but also to other responses, whether past, concurrent, or anticipated. An initial response to a client—for example, a young white therapist's discomfort with and nonresponsiveness toward a newly assigned older African American client—may cascade into discriminatory behavior, leading the client to gravitate toward another more welcoming agency and to the subsequent homogenization of the clientele of the agency. Such discrimination might mean that the therapist makes referrals only for medication rather than attempt to provide counseling, or a combination of the two. Racist assumptions might involve the expectation that a low-income African American client does not have the capacity for enough self-reflection to benefit from psychotherapy. A further challenge in understanding patterns of response is that they are fraught with ambiguity. Was the young white therapist responding to the client's skin color, socio-economic status, behavior, lack of eye contact, a negative experience he or she had with another African American individual, or some combination of those? It is the exceptional individual who is sufficiently self-reflective to be fully aware of the basis of his or her actions in such situations. The responses themselves may also be ambiguous. For example, was the therapist being distant and unfriendly, or was he or she simply thoughtfully listening and reflective? Most likely, the ability of therapists to tolerate and grow from diversity as it arises in themselves is associated with the ability to welcome external diversity, and vice versa.

A. Healthy Responses

An individual's ability to find common ground with others assumes a lack of overresponse or oversensitivity to differences. It requires that the individual is able to recognize a commonality of interest and human experience regardless of readily visible differences involving skin color, ethnicity, age, sex, and the like. Yet it is critical that this recognition of an underlying commonality does not lead to the sweeping of differences under the carpet, of minimizing sometimes competing power; economic and status interests; or very real differences in personal abilities, assumptions, and perspectives. Thus, healthy responses involve openness, civility, and empathy combined with a respect for current differences, including recognition of the ambiguous, contextual, and constantly changing nature of those differences. They also involve a reluctance to make moral or other difficult judgments when they are not relevant and the demonstration of openness to diverse experiences and perspectives. Healthy responses may occur in first-time encounters between individuals of different ethnic backgrounds and may result in improved learning and creativity, better social relationships, and enhanced cultural competence on the part of human service professionals and organizations.

An area of considerable interest in diversity studies is the effect of first-time exposure of individuals to diverse groups. For instance, one study involving the effects of college roommate assignments examined the question of how white students assigned a roommate of a different race would differ from those randomly assigned someone of similar race or ethnicity. This and similar studies confirm the results from a large body social psychological research on social contact. Contact between groups has been found to have positive effects, but only when certain conditions are met: (1) equal group status in the immediate environment where the contact takes place, (2) participants' sharing of common goals and norms of intergroup cooperation, (3) authorities' visible endorsement of group equality, and (4) sufficient opportunities for group members to interact (Duncan, Boisjoly, Levy, Kremer, & Eccles, 2003). Outcomes found from such exposure include improved problem solving, better social relations, and greater support for social welfare policies that are supportive of indigent and minority populations.

Other studies involving healthy responses to diversity have led to the formulation of a variety of models of ethnic-sensitive practice (Steiner & Devore, 1983) and of both individual (Weaver, 1999) and organizational (CasaNet Resources, 2005) cultural competence. Steiner and Devore (1983) recommend preparing for a type of "active ethnic reality testing" (p. 63) in social work encounters by giving attention to ethnic facts, assumptions, or suppositions related to the anticipated encounter. Ethnic sensitivity, as these authors envision it, involves the following four areas of knowledge: (1) the ethnic reality of target populations, including their collective history and behavioral dispositions, (2) what persons with such an ethnicity are likely to assume in an encounter with a helping professional, (3) what persons with the practitioners' ethnic identity are likely to assume in similar circumstances, and (4) the ethnic reality, history, and behavioral dispositions of the practitioner, especially factors that affect his or her ability to engage the client in a helping relationship.

More recently, the focus of diversity studies in the helping professions has shifted from ethnic sensitivity to the stronger notions of cultural competence and culturally competent practice. The latter involves a set of practice skills, knowledge, and attitudes that must include five elements: (1) awareness and acceptance of difference, (2) awareness of one's own cultural values, (3) understanding of the dynamics of difference, (4) ability to adapt practice skills to fit the cultural context of the client or patient, and (5) development of cultural knowledge (Weaver, 1999).

Yet it is insufficient for individual practitioners to be culturally competent if their employer organizations are not able to demonstrate a type of collective cultural competence. A model for organizational cultural competence requires that the organization value diversity, conduct cultural self-assessments, be conscious of and manage the dynamics of difference, institutionalize cultural knowledge, and adapt services to fit the cultural diversity of the community served (Family Resource Coalition, 1995–1996).

B. Controversial Responses

Although most people can agree on the importance of cultural sensitivity and competence, as well as on the inhumanity of discrimination and racism, there are a range of individual, programmatic, and societal responses to diversity for which there is little agreement. Many of these controversial responses are associated with some of the diverse perspectives reviewed earlier in this chapter, such as biculturalism, acculturation, assimilation, and amalgamation. A central attitude underpinning some of the responses involves subtle forms of ethnocentrism, the idea that one's own culture, religion, or ethnicity represents a superior standard, perhaps a God-given one, that needs to be protected from defilement or even imposed on others. For example, some view the effort not to discriminate without preferential treatment, or reverse discrimination of minorities (a policy known as color blindness), as the most equitable policy. Yet others consider such color blindness to be inherently discriminatory and ethnocentric because it maintains the advantages of majority groups. Another example is the diverse forms of feminism that have evolved as responses to sexism. Some of these forms enjoy widespread support, but some of the more separatist or radical types remain controversial in most contemporary societies (see exhibit 13.2).

Although blatant forms of ethnocentrism receive little support, subtle variations can be controversial. In the early years of sociological study of intergroup relations, debates in this area revolved around two pivotal theories. On the one hand, Robert Park (1964), a member of the Chicago school of sociology, theorized that the cycle of race relations initially involved contact, followed by competition, which gave way to partial accommodations and eventually to a more complete assimilation of the minority group into the majority culture. On the other hand, William Newman (1973) proposed the conflict theory of community relations, which hypothesized that initial contact leads to competition, which results in the negotiation of dominant and subordinate status relations. He believed that, rather than moving on to accommodation and assimilation, competition and conflict were ongoing, leading to periodic realignments. Newman's theory can be viewed as a "stuck" version of the process that Park identified, one that never arrives at accommodation or assimilation. Both should be regarded as two of many possible outcomes of the initial encounter of two ethnic groups. Both theories maintain separation and conflict, and can be regarded as expressions of ethnocentrism.

Each of the perspectives identified earlier—biculturalism, acculturation, accommodation, and amalgamation—involve highly contentious responses to the diversity of individuals, and often responses involving large groups.

Exhibit 13.2: Responses to Diversity: The Varieties of Feminism

Feminism is a social movement concerned with the experiences of women, especially as they involve diverse forms of discrimination, oppression, and sexism. It has largely focused on limiting or eliminating gender inequality and promoting women's rights, interests, and aspirations in society, as well as celebrating their contributions. It is based on a variety of sometimes disparate theories, strategies, and groups directed toward these ends. Some of the branches of feminism include the following:

- **Egalitarian feminism.** The best-known version of egalitarian feminism is that promoted by Christina Hoff Sommers in her book *Who Stole Feminism* (1994). Her emphasis involves fundamental forms of legal equality, such as equal rights and equal opportunity. She has suggested: "Most American women subscribe philosophically to the older 'First Wave' kind of feminism whose main goal is equity, especially in politics and education" (1994, p. 22). In contrast, individualistic feminism holds that all humans have a moral or legal right to their own persons and property but not to any sort of affirmative action policies or privileges.
- **Gynocentric feminism.** This perspective places women at the center of one's view of the world and its culture and history, and it assumes the superiority of the female point of view. A major variation is cultural feminism, which contends that there are basic cultural differences between men and women, and that women's differences are special and should be celebrated. This approach acknowledges biological differences between men and women. Related is a popular stereotype of feminism, pop feminism, which emphasizes the expression of feminism in popular culture and is based on a widespread belief that most feminist doctrines are anti-male. Also related to gynocentric feminism are gender feminism and radical feminism, which emerged during the 1960s as part of second-wave feminism.
- **Variations based on belief in centrality of patriarchy.** In addition to radical feminism, these include anarcha-feminism and French feminism. Anarcha-feminism arose out of early-twentieth-century authors and theorists such as Emma Goldman (1931) and Voltairine de Cleyre (see Avrich, 1978)—it holds that the struggle against patriarchy is central to class struggle. French feminism is associated with the work of Julia Kristeva, Hélène Cixous, Luce Irigaray, Monique Wittig, and Catherine Clément (see Gayatri, 1981). It is a

Exhibit 13.2 (continued)

more philosophical and literary approach to feminism than many of the others. Its writings are effusive and metaphorical, less focused on political issues, and more concerned with an understanding of how the body is conceptualized.

- **Variations based on belief of centrality of capitalist oppression.** One such form is Marxist feminism, which is concerned with the dismantling of capitalism as a means of liberating women. A less radical variant is socialist feminism, which focuses more on actively reorganizing capitalist society so as to substantially ameliorate its destructive impact on women. Some proponents have critiqued traditional Marxism for its inability to definitively link patriarchy and classism.
- **Variations that reject biological differences.** Amazon feminism rejects the idea that any traits or predispositions of the genders are inherently masculine or feminine and promotes a vision of heroic womanhood. Similarly, psychoanalytic feminism contends that gender differences are purely a matter of childhood experiences and the stages of psychosexual development.
- **Segregationalist feminism.** Several approaches to feminism emphasize either the partial or temporary, or even complete, separation of the genders. Lesbian feminism or separatism holds that all women should become lesbians to most effectively support other women. Similarly, separatist feminism does not condone heterosexual relationships due to the purported pervasiveness and destructiveness of gender power disparities.
- **Other forms of feminism.** There are a wide variety of other forms of feminism, some based on race, such as Black feminism or womanism; culture, such as Asian feminism; philosophy, such as existential feminism, ecofeminism, or spiritual feminism; or historical or geographic experience, such as postcolonial feminism or third-world feminism (see PhilPapers, "Varieties of feminism").

Many view biculturalism, or the maintenance of separate identities with one's own and the majority culture, as divisive and fragmentary. A similar issue arises with acculturation, which involves the adoption of secondary group patterns in institutional and external relationships (e.g., in African American culture, this is known as the Uncle Tom or Oreo phenomenon: "black on the outside, and white on the inside"). Although many people now regard such assimilation as dysfunctional, there are some who imagine it to be a model of mental health. Assimilation is not just fitting in but instead represents a fairly complete abrogation of a minority culture in favor of a majority culture. Assimilation is often confused with amalgamation, which does not represent the submersion of one culture into another but a full integration or blending of the two, theoretically, on equal grounds. From many people's perspectives, this distinction misses the distinct possibility that at least one of these cultures is essentially lost. Although most people support the idea of cultural sharing and transmission of the best features of each culture, dramatic changes or even extinctions of cultures are as difficult to accept as are the extinctions of species. We know and can accept that all individuals eventually die, but it is particularly difficult to accept that cultures pass away, whether through assimilation or other means, especially as these events often appear to be avoidable.

Amalgamation, or the merging of cultures, is also controversial because it involves intermarriage, as well as substantial cultural transmission and sharing. By 1990, U.S. census reports revealed out-marriage rates for young Hispanic individuals, born in the United States, at about 33%; for Asian Americans, about 50%; and for American Indians, about 60%. However, for African Americans, by 2000, only 9.6% of African American men had married white spouses and only 3.8% of African American women had married white men (Hollinger, 2003). According to a Gallup poll (cited by Hollinger, 2003), 86% of African Americans, 79% of Hispanics, and 66% of whites indicated that they would accept the marriage of a child or grandchild to someone of a different race. The percentage of whites who opposed marriages between African Americans and whites declined from 35% in the 1970s to 10% by the 2000s. Overall, racial intermarriage has increased from less than 1% of all married couples in 1970 to more than 5% of couples in 2000.

Yet despite these dramatic changes, for many people intermarriage continues to be controversial. It used to be referred to as miscegenation, or a downgrading or "mongrelization" of a supposedly "superior" race by its mixing with "inferior" races, traditionally prohibited by law. Hollinger (2003) points out, "The very word 'miscegenation' was, after all, an American contribution to the English language. . . . Prior to the coining of this term during the Civil War, 'amalgamation' had been the word generally used to refer to the mixing of races." It has been hypothesized that the concern lay at the heart of the resistance to the civil rights movement (Moore, 1997):

> The Civil Rights Movement was not about equality, democracy or liberty; it was about miscegenation. So said many southerners who fought the movement at every turn. Selma, schools, and suffrage were a backdrop to the gut issue: namely whether or not blacks and whites should be allowed to intermarry. At the turn of this century,

writer and preacher Thomas Dixon wrote *The Klansman.* The novel provided the plot for D. W. Griffith's epic film *The Birth of a Nation,* which helped to revive the modern Ku Klux Klan. Dixon promoted the idea that civil rights organizations were formed in an effort to mongrelize the white race. According to Dixon, blacks were of a lower order than whites. It was only natural, in light of Darwin's then widely popular theory of "survival of the fittest," for blacks to desire sex with whites. The offspring of such unions would be a step up for blacks, and a step down for whites. Civil rights and integration meant one thing: intermarriage.

However, it has not been only majority groups that have sought to stop intermarriage. Some minority groups have regarded intermarriage as a type of fundamental disloyalty, even as a type of genocide. Thus, the particular secondary responses of individuals, whether involving separatism or amalgamation, to one another's primary racial and ethnic characteristics may elicit a range of tertiary reactions. This is especially the case when the individual's preferred response deviates too far afield from that of his or her key social groups.

Many of the same debates around diversity on both the individual and policy levels have also concerned programmatic responses to diversity. To what extent should there be specialized programs for particular minority populations? Would such separation be inherently unequal and discriminatory, or protective and respectful of the identity of the groups concerned? Alternatively, when minority groups are served in the context of mainstream social services, how can the services be made culturally and linguistically sensitive to their needs? One strategy that is sometimes used involves the matching of worker and clients on the basis of ethnicity. Stanley Sue (1988) has conducted extensive research on the cultural dimensions of psychological treatment. In one of his reviews on the research on ethnic matching of therapists and clients in psychotherapy, he reports mixed and inconclusive evidence on the outcomes of matching. In the review, he distinguishes between ethnic membership, which involves national or geographic ancestry, and cultural membership, which consists of current identifications with the group(s), including common values, attitudes, ideologies, and so on. He concluded that, whereas ethnic matching has no discernible effects, cultural matching is of considerable value in achieving positive outcomes.

In the United States, the population is too diverse in terms of its cultural and political perspectives for there to develop any coherent national policy supportive of diversity, as is the case in Canada. However, federal and state affirmative action laws, developed on the tail end of the civil rights movement, were developed to alternatively protect against discrimination or to promote diversity. These have become a lightning rod of debate. Besides the question of which groups should be protected by such laws, the central controversy has been whether they should simply protect against discrimination in such areas as hiring, promotion, and firing or should actively seek to remedy past discrimination and even promote diversity, even if discrimination narrowly defined is absent.

A closely related debate involves compensation and apologies for historic acts of injustice, oppression, and exploitation. Although most agree that such collective actions are needed, there is little agreement as to which instances of oppression should be covered, how far back historically these should go, and who should bear the costs of such reparations. While the U.S. government has moved toward compensating the Japanese people imprisoned during World War II, and the German government has compensated many survivors and families of the victims of the Holocaust, there is considerably less support for reparations for groups enslaved or persecuted prior to the memory of people who are still living.

C. Dysfunctional and Destructive Responses

Harmful responses to diversity may range from those that are subtle and easily overlooked to the catastrophic murder of populations, known as democide. They may be acts of either omission or commission by lone individuals, or they may be the institutionalized responses of entire governments or even societies. They may be directed against those with specific characteristics, such as a minority skin color or nationality, or against those with a wide range of stigmatized traits. Furthermore, dysfunctional reactions may be against primary indicators of diversity or against secondary responses to diversity, such as the actions of social workers who advocate for the rights of an oppressed population.

Subtle reactions of a harmful nature include social and emotional distancing, including unarticulated discomfort, fear, and suspicion in the presence of members of a minority group. An example is homophobia, a term coined by George Weinberg in 1972 to describe heterosexuals who have a "dread of being in close quarters with homosexuals" (p. 4). Closely related is insensitivity or ignorance of the cultures commonly encountered in everyday life. The effects of such insensitivity may include suspicion of minorities and tokenism, or the practice of including minorities to the least degree possible, thereby marginalizing their social participation. William Graham Sumner (1906) defined the ethnocentrism of many of these reactions as "this view of things in which one's own group is the center of everything, and all others are scaled and rated with reference to it" (p. 13). This is not to say that everyone is expected to be an expert in the full range of groups and cultures encountered, only that there is sufficient knowledge, sensitivity, and openness to comfortably interact and develop needed relationships, including the cultural competence required to fulfill those relationships. When this base does not exist, the individual risks lapsing into being judgmental and ethnocentric. Although such insensitivity may remain fairly contained and overlooked by most, it is the breeding ground for the emergence of more overtly harmful reactions such as prejudice and discrimination.

Prejudice and discrimination are two closely related concepts that unfortunately are often confused. Prejudice is a matter of attitudes, and discrimination is a matter of actions. Prejudice involves negative and emotionally charged prejudgments about other groups based on little or no information other than generalized group membership or superficial criteria. It may concern the motivations, capabilities, or potential contributions of minority groups (e.g., a police officer's assumption that a Hispanic man encountered on a lonely street in the middle of the night is up to no good, a high school guidance counselor's assumption that a low-income teenager will not go on to college or will be accepted only at a community college). An important point is that such prejudices often arise out of stereotypes or from socially shared and fallacious conceptions of those who are different (e.g., the assumption that Jews are "opportunistic"). Whereas stereotypes are socially shared misconceptions, prejudices arise out of stereotypes that become animated in individuals through emotions of dislike, hate, distrust, and the like. Some people may dispassionately hold stereotypes simply out of ignorance and lack of exposure to the stereotyped group; for others, stereotypes may give rise to prejudices.

Stereotypes and prejudices may or may not become expressed through discriminatory actions or practices. Newman (1973) defined discrimination as "any action of differential treatment toward a group or an individual perceived as a member of a group," and noted that the intent, whether overt or covert, is to create a disadvantage for that group or individual (p. 199). There are two types of discrimination. De jure discrimination involves legalized forms of disenfranchisement, for example, special requirements that complicate the ability of African Americans to register to vote. In contrast, de facto discrimination involves general practices that are not condoned by law—for example, the intake workers of a mental health clinic may exhibit the YAVIS syndrome (Schofield, 1964), where they accept for psychotherapy only young, attractive, verbal, intelligent, and sexy clients and refer others elsewhere, especially low-income or poorly educated members of minority groups. Key theories of the causes of discrimination include the projection of dissociated traits onto out-groups; frustration-aggression, or aggressive acting out under conditions of frustration; the need for authoritarian personalities to maintain at least the illusion of control; the role of discrimination in managing conflict and in maintaining status and resources for dominant groups; and the impact of childhood socialization.

An important type of discrimination is scapegoating. Scapegoating takes place when an individual or group discriminates against another individual or group through active blaming, recrimination, and negative typecasting, often to deflect responsibility for some failure and to place the burden of change or compensation on a particular party. For example, some people might blame all U.S. terrorism on Arab Americans, or they might blame a failed response to a hurricane disaster on a single incompetent administrator. Scapegoating can take place in dyadic relationships, but it is more typical in groups, families, organizations, and larger social systems. Those who are most at risk of being scapegoated are powerless out-groups already subject to existing stereotypes, though the impulse to scapegoat is not limited to any particular group. Scapegoating often uses the psychological mechanism of projection, or the tendency to see in others what one cannot acknowledge in oneself.

Of even greater severity than prejudice and discrimination are racism, sexism, ageism, and other isms of human oppression. These represent more ingrained and pervasive complexes or systems of stereotypes, prejudices, and discriminatory behaviors targeted at one or more out-groups. Racism, for instance, is rooted in an ethnocentric attachment to one's own race. It is associated with negative stereotypes of other racial groups driven by distrust, revulsion, and hate. In addition, it is acted out through discriminatory and persecutory behaviors, whether these involve informal practices or the use of formal legal and bureaucratic means to distance, depreciate, or disempower members of rejected racial groups. The *Oxford English Dictionary* (1998) defines racism as a "belief in the superiority of a particular race; prejudice based on this (racism), antagonism towards other races." Such beliefs, feelings, and behaviors tend to be deeply ingrained, long-term, and pervasive in the lives of such individuals or groups. This is not to say that racism, or any of the other isms, may not be sometimes hidden. However, the ability of racist people to hide these patterns from themselves or others tends to be temporary and limited in scope. Racism has existed throughout history, and virtually every racial and ethnic group has at some point been a victim of racism, particularly when a group represents disempowered minority populations (see exhibit 13.3).

Although racism is often considered an individual phenomenon, it is more typically an attribute of social groups, in which the various stereotypes,

EXHIBIT 13.3: AN ISLAMIC PERSPECTIVE ON WHITE RACISM

According to The Qur'an, all human beings are coloured, including those who self classify as "White." Therefore, by setting themselves off against or "distancing" themselves from "coloured" people, White Supremacists (Racists) are rejecting their God-given colouring. In this connection, it is significant to note that the Arabic verb *sha-th'a-na,* from which is derived the noun *ash-Shay'th'aan* ("The Satan"), means "to become distant." On this basis, it might be said that *ash-Shay'th'aan* refers to the aggressive, alienating (or "distancing") personality type among human beings and that White Supremacists (Racists) are examples of people who manifest this type.
                                                    —FROM SYED MUSTAFA ALI (2005)

prejudices, and discriminatory and scapegoating behaviors reinforce one another in the various members. Racism may also be a characteristic of institutions, otherwise known as institutional racism. This happens when formal practices, rules and norms, structures, and policies of organizations and other institutions systematically discriminate or otherwise harm particular racial groups. There may or may not be conscious intent or awareness of discrimination or harm on the part of the participants. In fact, the perpetrators often attempt to rationalize the effects as due to the deficiencies of the victims. An example of institutional racism is the practice of some banks to not issue mortgages in certain poor neighborhoods, known as redlining, because of high resident populations with poor credit ratings.

Institutional racism illustrates the role of the fundamental attribution error, one of the most important cognitive distortions identified by the field of social psychology. The fundamental attribution error is a pervasive error to overemphasize ingrained personal or character traits in the assessment of others' behaviors and to give short shrift to the less visible situational causes. It arises, in part, from the fact that people are more visible than their more diffuse environments. Most individuals see their own environments, and thus are much less likely to commit this error when considering their own actions.

One reason that majority group members tend to be oblivious to racism, and especially to institutional racism, is the invisibility thesis, or the theory that racism is often invisible to the majority for several reasons, including that they suffer less from it, they do not attribute their own failures to race, they do not always see the suffering that minority groups endure, and victims often hide the effects because of their sense of vulnerability.

When institutional racism is implemented on a national scale, through the system of law and government, it is apartheid, most infamously manifested in South Africa from 1948 to 1994. Colonialism also has typically been a manifestation of institutional racism, enforced through the subjugation of one group of people by a foreign power, usually of a different race.

Institutional racism often is a type of aversive racism, one that slowly, systematically, and silently disempowers minority groups. But even more severe are the blatant forms of racism manifested in ethnic conflict, persecution, terrorism, forced depopulation through rape and terror, and extermination. Examples include the lynchings of African Americans in the United States in the first half of the twentieth century, the attempted ethnic cleansing in Bosnia in the 1990s, the attempted depopulation of western Sudan by Muslim tribesmen in 2004, and the many catastrophic campaigns of genocide and democide by the Nazis, Stalinists, and other groups throughout the twentieth century. Rudolph Rummel (1994), who has spent his career researching such catastrophes, has coined the term democide to mean the murder of populations and distinguishes between several types of democide:

- *Genocide* is the killing of people by a government because of their group membership, particularly that based on race, ethnicity, religion, or language.
- Politicide is the murder of any person or people by a government because of politics or for political purposes.
- Mass murder, in contrast, is the indiscriminate killing of people by a government.

Rummel assiduously documented all known instances of democide during the twentieth century (up until 1989), ones that account for the systematic extermination of 169 million individuals (see table 13.1). Although democide is virtually unknown in the contemporary United States and the West, it nonetheless has instilled a debilitating fear that has become part of the collective memory of various groups, including African Americans, Jews, Cambodians, Armenians, and American Indians. A pervasive theme in Rummel's study of such events is reflected in the adage "power corrupts; absolute power corrupts absolutely." In his correlational analyses he reports that the extent of democide in a society is directly associated with the extent to which totalitarian regimes have developed. He concludes, "In theory and fact, democracies do not (or virtually never) make war on each other; the more democratic two regimes, the less likely violence between them; the more democratic a regime, the less its overall foreign violence; and the

TABLE 13.1: TWENTIETH-CENTURY MASS MURDERS: DEMOCIDES AND GENOCIDES (1900–1989)

Nations with Reported Mass Murders	PERIOD	Democide (in 1,000s) TOTAL KILLED	PERCENTAGE OF POPULATION[1]
TENS OF MILLIONS MURDERED	1900–87	128,168	0.18
USSR	1917–87	61,911	0.42
China, People's Republic	1949–87	35,236	0.12
Germany	1933–45	20,946	0.09
China (KMT)	1928–49	10,075	0.07
MILLIONS MURDERED	1900–87	19,178	1.63
Japan	1936–45	5,964	—
China (Mao–Guerrilla period)	1923–49	3,466	0.05
Cambodia	1975–79	2,035	8.16
Turkey	1909–18	1,883	0.96
Vietnam	1945–87	1,670	0.10
Poland	1945–48	1,585	1.99
Pakistan	1948–87	1,503	0.06
Yugoslavia (Tito)	1944–87	1,072	0.12
MILLIONS MURDERED (SUSPECTED)	1900–87	4,145	0.24
North Korea	1948–87	1,663	0.25
Mexico	1900–20	1,417	0.45
Russia	1900–17	1,066	0.02
UNDER A MILLION (TOP FIVE)	1900–87	14,918	0.26
China (Warlords)	1917–49	910	0.02
Turkey (Ataturk)	1919–23	878	2.64
United Kingdom	1900–87	816	—
Portugal (Dictatorship)	1926–82	741	—
Indonesia	1965–87	729	0.02
OTHERS	1900–87	2,792	.1
WORLD TOTAL	1900–87	169,202	.12

1. The percentage of the population killed for each of the designated years for the nation listed.
2. Rummel reports that the world yearly percentage is based on the 1944 world population.

Source: Rummel (1994).

more democratic a regime, the less its genocide and mass murder (which in this century has killed about four times the battle dead of all its foreign and domestic wars)" (1997, p. 23).

If these findings prove to be robust, they will support the notion that cultural competence and openness to diversity, the capacity for complex thinking that involves multiple perspectives, and an openness to bottom-up forms of emergence and self-organization, both on the individual level and the societal level, all represent powerful antidotes to socially condoned violence. The secondary reactions to diversity reviewed in this section, whether subtle or blatant, often represent the progressive and dynamic sequelae of cascading failures that can begin with seemingly simple breakdowns of understanding, empathy, and everyday problem solving.

VI. Summary

This chapter provides an overview of cultural diversity as it arises out of and affects the broader dimensions of personal and biocultural diversity. It begins by reviewing the background of the concept of diversity in American society and the ways that it has been broadened and redefined to include a progressively wider array of populations. It distinguishes between primary diversity, the natural variability of human beings; secondary diversity, the variability of responses to human differences; and tertiary diversity, the range of responses to others' responses. The introduction also explores diversity as a value; the question of whether it is a core or instrumental value; and its relationship with traditional American values of freedom and equality, including equality of opportunity, rights under the law, and outcome.

The chapter then turns to the major perspectives on diversity, both traditional and contemporary. After a brief discussion of the separatist approach, which contends that racial or ethnic groups can be separate but equal, the chapter explores the assimilationist stance, that is, the idea of American society as a melting pot in which new immigrant groups convert to dominant cultural ways within a few generations. In contrast, pluralism holds that new groups retain their culture and identity, and contribute to the dominant culture through competition. Multiculturalism is similar to pluralism in emphasizing the coexistence of multiple groups; however, it assumes that group ethnic identity is central to individual identity, and it more actively promotes mutual respect and the abolition of inequalities between groups. The most recent perspective, postculturalism, makes fewer assumptions about the role of ethnicity in defining individuals, instead emphasizing the fluid and evolving nature of cultural identity that develops in the context of substantial cultural transmission. This section concludes with a discussion of the chicken-and-egg conundrum of whether the goals of cultural diversity are best achieved first through structural changes involving better representation of minority groups, changes in the underlying consciousness, or both simultaneously.

The chapter then explores several types of diversity, questions of which groups are considered targets of diversity policies, and how the goals of such policies are defined. Of central importance is the question of race: is it a valid biological concept or primarily a social construction of cultures tied only loosely to biological traits. The section discusses Hollinger's notion that contemporary definitions of race are the outcome of majority group prejudices and perceptions of the history of oppression. In addition, the section summarizes recently biological formulations of the biodiversity of humans, especially the notions of haplogroups and haplotypes that describe the major genetic groups of humans and their unique patterns of development and migration. The chapter then considers several issues in the field of biocultural diversity, and questions of the relationship of intelligence with race and sexual preference.

The final section of the chapter explores the range of responses, both secondary and tertiary, of individuals and groups toward the existence of racial, gender, ethnic, and other types of differences. Whereas some of the responses have been particularly needed, such as the development of cultural sensitivity and competence, as well as institutional cultural competence, many are either controversial or manifestly destructive. Dysfunctional and destructive responses to diversity range from the subtle, such as emotional distancing, to the catastrophic, such as persecution, forced depopulation, and democide. In between are a range of phenomena, most notably stereotyping, prejudice, discrimination, racism, sexism, and other isms. Whereas stereotypes are mistaken and detrimental misconceptions, usually involving minority groups, prejudice builds on such misconceptions through feelings of dislike, revulsion, fear, or hate.

Discrimination typically takes prejudices to the next level, through unjust or hurtful actions directed against minority or other marginalized groups. Racism is a complex system of such stereotypes, prejudices, and discriminatory actions that is highly entrenched and pervasive. After reviewing the range of responses to human differences, the chapter observes that dysfunctional reactions to diversity, whether subtle or blatant, are progressive sequences of cascading failures that can begin with seemingly simple breakdowns of understanding, empathy, and everyday problem solving.

For Further Reading

Fellin, P. (2000). Revisiting multiculturalism in social work journal articles. *Journal of Social Work Education, 36,* 271–272.

Harvey, D. (1989). *The condition of modernity: An enquiry into the origins of cultural change.* Oxford: Oxford University Press.

Hollinger, D. A. (2000). *Postethnic America: Beyond multiculturalism.* New York: Basic Books.

Jacobson, M. F. (1999). *Whiteness of a different color: European immigrants and the alchemy of race.* Cambridge, MA: Harvard University Press.

Klemm, K., Eguiluz, V. M., Toral, R., & Miguel, M. S. (2005). Globalization, polarization and cultural drift. *Journal of Economic Dynamics and Control, 29,* 321–334.

Kottak, C. P. & Kozaitis, K. A. (1999). The multicultural society. In *On being different: Diversity and multiculturalism in the North American mainstream* (pp. 48–51). New York: McGraw-Hill.

Liu, E. (1999). *The accidental Asian: Notes of a native speaker.* New York: Vintage Books.

Nisbett, R. E. (2003). *The geography of thought: How Asians and Westerns think differently . . . and why.* New York: Free Press.

Rummel, R. J. (1994). *Death by government.* New Brunswick, NJ: Transaction.

Schlesinger, A. (1998). *The disuniting of America.* New York: Norton.

Sowell, T. (1991, May/June). Cultural diversity: A world view. *American Enterprise, 2,* 44–55.

Steiner, J., & Devore, W. (1983). Increasing descriptive and prescriptive theoretical skills to promote ethnic-sensitive practice. *Journal of Education for Social Work, 19*(2), 63–70.

Sue, S. (1988). Psychotherapeutic services for ethnic minorities: Two decades of research findings. *American Psychologist, 43,* 301–308.

Weaver, H. (1999). Indigenous people and the social work profession: Defining culturally competent services. *Social Work, 44*(3), 217–225.

Wilson, F. H. (2004). *Race, class, and the postindustrial city.* Albany: State University of New York Press.

Wilson, W. J. (1987). *The truly disadvantaged: The inner-city, the underclass, and public policy.* Chicago: University of Chicago Press.

CHAPTER 14

Helping Relationships and Generalist Practice in Complex Systems

*Social advance depends as much upon the process through
which it is secured as upon the result itself.*

—JANE ADDAMS

I. Introduction

This text now departs from its review of theories of human behavior applicable to both small and large systems and turn to the application of these theories in professional practice, in terms of both practice models and the ethical and spiritual dimensions that inform them. The extensive body of theory that is available to human service professionals has an even greater range of possible applications in the various professions, ones that a single chapter or book cannot possibly cover. Instead, this chapter will introduce an emerging conception of practice variously referred to as generalist or advanced generalist, as it is this approach that most effectively builds on the insights of complex systems theory.

A central concept of systems theory is the interdependency of systems— of people, groups, organizations, communities, and societies. To the extent that client problems cut across these systems, the methods that practitioners employ must also do the same. This represents an opportunity to improve practice, but it requires clarity about the principles and rules that should guide service planning. Developers of generalist models of practice, as well as the fields of best practices and evidence-based practice, have only begun to identify these rules (see O'Hare, 2005). It is said of social workers that their expertise is not in any substantive area, but in the helping process itself. Jane Addams's sage comment in the epigraph to this chapter about the importance of service process suggests that practitioners need to simultaneously consider not only the goals of practice or the questions of why but also the question of how through a careful matching of methods with desired outcomes that clients and their social workers collaboratively identify.

The approach of the current chapter is to present the generalist practice model from the ground up, from some of its historical roots through the incremental development of key concepts and methods, and most recently to

Figure 14.1: The Development of Advanced Generalist Practice Models, as Inclusive of Generalist, Professional, and Natural Helping Relationships

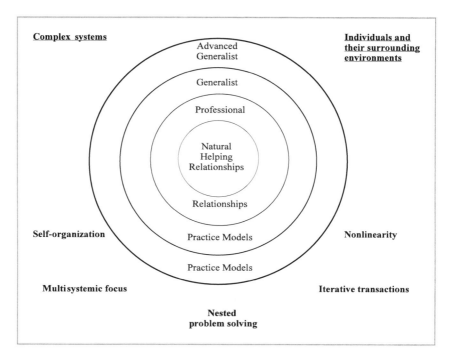

a conception of an advanced generalist practice based on complex systems theory. The chapter begins with an exploration of theory and research pertinent to helping relationships in general, whether voluntary or nonvoluntary, professional or nonprofessional, and then reviews the development of an integrative social work practice as the precursor to the more recent generalist models (see figure 14.1). Each human service profession has developed its own distinctive combinations of specialist and generalist methods, and in recent years, many such professions have promoted generalist models. Debates on these models have most typically concerned the question of whether there is a universal set of methods and skills, knowledge and values, that are necessary for practice, whatever problems or environments are involved.

One the most perennial of these issues is the centrality of interpersonal skills and relationship building to human service practice. Some argue that such skills are necessary and sufficient for professional practice: if a worker is sufficiently empathic and congruent with clients, that all else follows and that particular methods will not add much to the relationship in general or to an intervention specifically. However, the more common position is that empathy and relationship building are necessary but not sufficient conditions. This second position suggests that the development of working relationships with clients just gets one to the starting line and enables the use of a wide range of possible methods, such as role-play, group discussion, and community organization campaigns. If this second position is untenable, then any consideration of practice models, whether generalist or otherwise, is moot. And if one believes this, then the rest of this chapter can probably be dispensed with.

II. Dimensions of the Helping Relationship

A central problem in the social sciences is the question of human mutuality and altruism. Why do many people support and help one another in situations with no apparent self-gain or even considerable cost? Conversely, why do some people fail to support others even when it serves their self-interest to do so? What are the essential conditions for effective helping? Understanding why, when, and how people successfully support one another, as well as the dynamics of helping, may be one of the most important tasks for both the enhancement of professional human services practice and the success of nonprofessional, volunteer, and self-help initiatives. The range of theories that has been proposed on the dynamics of helping parallels the range of helping relationships that can be observed, as well as the motivations ascribed to them.

A. Motivations for Helping

Many theories emphasize the role of self-interest and argue that people engage in helping relationships because of the gains they expect, whether respect and status, economic benefits, a sense of control, or a means of reworking personal conflicts. These theories emphasize a kind of social economics, the idea that helping is simply another service or commodity that is exchanged on the open market (Foa & Foa, 1975). However, most individuals attempt to protect the value of the help they give by assiduously avoiding any impression of an overt sale or bartering. Help may be concrete— money, food, or shelter—or less tangible, such as services, information, caring, or recognition. In either case, the offering often exists in the context of some relationship. The trade-offs involved can be understood as guided by a mini-max strategy in which participants attempt to minimize costs while they maximize gains (Dixit & Nalebuff, 1991). An example is the attempt to reconcile the receipt of a necessary concrete service with the psychological discomfort of receiving and its associated obligations.

Some social psychologists understand helping relationships in terms of arousal or cost-reward theory (Piliavin, Dovidio, Gaertner, & Clark, 1982). This theory proposes that individuals attempt to minimize their own unpleasant emotions (e.g., fear, revulsion, pity, grief) when they see someone in need. The more dire the need and the greater the emotional connection, the more likely it is that the individual will help. In this context, helping the other becomes a means of helping oneself. Similarly, evolutionary psychology also proposes that motivations to help are a direct function of the possibility of self-gain, but more specifically of the degree of genetic link between those involved and the likelihood that the help given will perpetuate the giver's genes (see Dawkins, 1989). In contrast, others emphasize the possibility of helping as arising specifically out of compassion and empathy, even when the helper must make a substantial sacrifice (Dass & Gorman, 1997).

B. The Gift Relationship

In 1971, Richard Titmuss (b. 1907–d. 1973), whom many regard as the leading architect of the British welfare state, conducted one of the classic studies of altruism, *The Gift Relationship*. Titmuss studied the case of blood donations in both the United Kingdom and the United States, reasoning that blood donations are for the most part anonymous and involve some sacrifice and discomfort, and no apparent self-gain. He was particularly interested in comparing the impact of the U.K. system of entirely voluntary donations with the U.S. system, which involves a combination of voluntary donations and sales. He concluded that the British voluntary system was superior in efficiency, efficacy, quality, and safety. His data also demonstrated that in the mixed U.S. system, the blood itself tended to be of lower quality when sold. His study helped prevent the privatization of the blood service in the United Kingdom during Margaret Thatcher's administration.

Important clues to the question of motivations can be found in the circumstances associated with helping. A classic example is public attacks, and bystanders have been found to be more likely to help victims when there are fewer people around (Darley & Litane, 1968). One interpretation of this finding is that when many people are present, each bystander feels less of a sense of responsibility and a greater expectation that others will decide to incur the risks and costs of helping the victim. Similarly, when people are in a rush to get someplace, they are less likely to help strangers in need, no doubt because any help given will involve greater costs to that individual. In contrast, in other situations involving lesser dangers or costs to the helper, seeing others help influences people to help. Finally, helping behaviors are facilitated to the extent that the helper and the helped share common personal characteristics, whether race, sex, and age; socioeconomic class; or other features that reduce the sense of social distance (see Hudson, 1987). Personal characteristics found to be associated with helping include positive emotionality, empathy, self-efficacy, ability to self-monitor, and religious faith (see Bierhoff, Klein, & Kramp, 1991; Eisenberg, Fabes, Schaller, Carlo, & Miller, 1991; White & Gerstein, 1987). Thus, it is clear that helping relationships arise out of a wide range of motivations, ranging from the selfish, to the mutual, and to the selfless and even sacrificial, depending on both the support of the social environment and the psychological health of the helping individual.

The factors that influence helping behaviors are not necessarily the same as those that facilitate helping relationships, although there is some overlap. A study by Salem, Reischl, Gallacher, and Randall (2000) examined perceived helpfulness in the context of a self-help organization known as Schizophrenics Anonymous (SA). The study examined the roles of referent power, or influence based on a sense of identification, as compared to expert power, or influence based on knowledge and expertise, in accounting for the levels of perceived helpfulness of relationships among members of the group. Although members experienced higher levels of referent power with fellow SA participants, they also reported more expert power among their leaders and mental health professionals. The perceived helpfulness of the relationships was associated with both forms of perceived power, but most significantly, it was correlated with expert power and its interaction with referent power. The findings support the importance of perceived relationship quality and the power of perceived professional expertise in supplementing or enhancing the interpersonal relationship (Salem et al., 2000).

C. Psychotherapy Research

For years the field of psychotherapy theory and research has investigated the essential ingredients to helping relationships, whether of professionals or volunteers. The psychoanalytic tradition has regarded the professional relationship as a kind of laboratory for exploring and resolving issues in clients' lives, typically those involving earlier relationships. Psychoanalytic theory has emphasized the interpretation and resolution of client transferences. A transference happens when a client unconsciously carries over the patterns of feeling, thinking, or relating characteristic of an earlier relationship (e.g., with a parent) into the current therapeutic relationship. It then becomes the therapist's task to help the client understand and emotionally work through this behavior so it does not interfere with the client's current life. Transferences may be fleeting transference reactions, in which only some elements of prior relationships carry over, or they may be full-blown transference neuroses, in which the previous pattern is transferred as a whole, often resulting in regression to earlier developmental stages and reenactment of the associated behaviors in inappropriate contexts. Some people in the psychoanalytic tradition instead emphasize the analysis and resolution of countertransferences, involving the transferences of the therapist that interfere with the client's progression. In the psychoanalytic paradigm, the quality of the helping relationship is considered extremely important but rarely a sufficient condition for a successful outcome. Instead, it is the expertise of the therapist in clarifying, interpreting, and facilitating the client's exploration and healing that is of central importance. Other psychotherapeutic traditions, such as behavioral, deemphasize the role of the relationship and place primary emphasis on the technical contributions of the therapist (e.g., implementation of a behavioral desensitization program for a client with a phobia).

Perhaps one of the most popular yet controversial contributions of psychotherapeutic research to understanding helping relationships is that of Carl Rogers (b. 1902–d. 1987) and those, such as Roger Carkhuff, who have continued this line of research. Rogers (1965) was among the first to develop the field of psychotherapy research, using tape recorders and similar devices to analyze the micromovements of therapeutic process. Initially, this work showed little impact of therapy on the sought-after outcomes, beyond the impact of spontaneous remission. Most therapies arising from various theoretical orientations showed equally modest results. However, further analysis of the data led Rogers to conclude that three fundamental characteristics differentiated effective and ineffective therapists: (1) empathy, (2) congruence, and (3) unconditional positive regard. Empathy is the ability to share in another's feelings, thoughts, and perceptions, and often (though not necessarily) experience some compassion for that person. Rogers (as cited in Brazier, 1996) later defined congruence in terms of the therapist's demonstrated authenticity. He reported, "It has been found that personal change is facilitated when the psychotherapist is what he is, when in the relationship with the client he is genuine and without 'front' or facade, openly being the feelings and attitudes which at that moment are flowing in him. We have coined the term 'congruence' to try to describe this condition. By this we mean that the feelings the therapist is experiencing are available to him, available to his awareness, and he is able to live these feelings, be them, and able to communicate them if appropriate" (p. 61).

Unconditional positive regard, in contrast, involves the ability to feel esteem for the client, no matter what problems or behaviors he or she demonstrates. As a humanistic psychologist, Rogers was committed to the notion that each person has an inherent tendency to actualize his or her potential and that the role of the therapist was therefore somewhat passive, involving active listening and facilitation of this underlying process. The research that Rogers and his colleagues has engendered has led many to conclude that the essential qualities for helping relationships are personal rather than therapeutic techniques, and that these qualities are the necessary and sufficient conditions in both professional and nonprofessional relationships. It has led many to conclude that professional training is not as important as simply having one's heart in the right place (see Brazier, 1996).

Roger Carkhuff (1984) replicated Rogers's findings but went even further to emphasize the universality of empathy, congruence, and unconditional positive regard in all types of helping relationships. He concluded, for instance, that lay trainees function at least as well as professional trainees, and that professional trainees actually function worse after their first year of training because of a loss of congruence or authenticity in their relationships with clients, which may be due to their reliance on "highly elaborate, highly cognitive systems" (Carkhuff, 1984, p. 10). Carkhuff suggests that as clients converge on the level of personal functioning of their therapists, trainees gravitate toward the level of functioning of their trainers.

Later in his research, Carkhuff (cited in Brazier, 1996) broke down Rogers's therapeutic conditions into two dimensions of eight factors: (1) the responsive dimension is a function of empathy, respect, and specificity, whereas (2) the initiative dimension derives from the role of genuineness, self-disclosure, confrontation, immediacy, and concreteness. While Rogers emphasized responsive qualities of the therapist, Carkhuff attempted to incorporate some of the more pragmatic features of behavioral interventions into his theory. These may involve the role of the therapist in taking initiative and even directing change, whether through his or her own self-disclosure, confrontation, or other types of input. Carkhuff also emphasized the importance of clients' exposure to these conditions of change, specifically during life crises, when they are most open to change. Other interpretations of this body of research abound, for example, van Ryn and Heaney (1997) proposed, "These literatures combine to establish the bases for proposing two essential components of effective helping relationships: (1) providing unconditional acceptance and positive regard for clients, and (2) sharing power and control through participatory processes" (p. 683).

The study of the characteristics and preconditions of helping relationships may cause some to question the value of professional practice, but it also provides professionals with important insights into the facilitation of a range of such relationships, whether they involve volunteers or self-help groups or families. If nothing else, such studies have established that professionals have no exclusive franchise on helping. The findings of this line of research are consistent with the insights of those who assume a spiritual perspective on helping, such as Ram Dass (also known as Richard Alpert) and Paul Gorman (1997) who together deplore the role of professional warmth: "Denial, abstraction, pity, professional warmth, compulsive hyperactivity: These are a few of the ways in which the mind reacts to suffering and attempts to restrict or direct the natural compassion of the heart" (p. 64). They go on to point out, "The most familiar models of who we are— father and daughter, doctor and patient, 'helper' and 'helped'—often turn out to be major obstacles to the expression of our caring instincts; they limit the full measure of what we have to offer one another. But when we break through and meet in spirit behind our separateness, we experience profound moments of companionship. These, in turn, give us access to deeper and deeper levels of generosity and loving kindness. True compassion arises out of unity" (p. 20).

D. The Professions and Helping Relationships

As much as one might like to emphasize the voluntary, spontaneous, and even spiritual dimensions of the helping process, services require both time and other concrete resources, as well as specialized bodies of knowledge and skill. Thus, professional relationships become channeled into and constrained by the legal, fiscal, and contractual relationships needed to support them, ones that involve economic exchange and are guided by the knowledge and values of the profession involved. Traditional sociologists of the professions have identified the hallmarks of professions as involving a particular type of social sanction or mission, a body of knowledge, extensive training, an ethical code, the notion of careers committed to public service, and often a professional association.

The professions involve the systematic application of knowledge to the solution of socially valued problems, using validated methods in an ethical framework and a socially sanctioned field of responsibility. In recent years, however, such lists of features of the professions have become less fashionable, no doubt because of many people's questions about the legitimacy of the professions. Some view professions as exclusive franchises that protect the economic interests, power, and status of elite groups while disempowering others. George Bernard Shaw (1911/2008) epitomized this view when a character in one of his plays protested that professions are "conspiracies against the laity" (p. 36). The human service professions have not been exempt from such attitudes, and some go so far as regarding them as welfare programs for workers who cannot make an honest living otherwise.

At the same time that many have questioned the legitimacy of the human services, there have been concerted efforts for several decades now to develop the means of ensuring that value is indeed added to the personal qualities that workers bring to their professional work. For many years this trend has manifested in such developments as a concern for accountability and demonstrating outcomes, or implementing the practitioner-researcher model. In more recent years, the movements involving best practices, empirically based practice, or evidence-based practice (EBP) have flourished, all in an attempt to demonstrate professional effectiveness and to improve it. Similarly, others have sought to better define professional practice through an explication of its underlying methodologies. In social work, integrated, generalist, and advanced generalist models have been increasingly emphasized.

A central tension that has permeated efforts to define models of professional practice has been the question of whether the worker's primary obligations are toward the individual or toward society as a whole. The conflict has many resolutions, each with its subtleties, relative priorities, and operational rules. For example, many social workers believe that their primary obligation is to the individual client, with exceptions made only in well-defined cases involving suspected child abuse or neglect, imminent harm to self or others, orders of the court, and the like. Other exceptions to the primacy of service to clients arise out of agency policies and funding constraints.

The tension between serving the individual and serving society is loosely reflected in the contrasting experiences of human service workers in the public and private sectors. In the public sector, which is more frequently involved with involuntary clients, there is a greater awareness and sense of the primacy of the worker's obligations to society, often as represented by workers' public agency employers. Practice in these settings (e.g., child welfare, youth services, state mental health) is more tightly constrained by the awareness of the rights and responsibilities of workers, sometimes to the point of being bureaucratic and legalistic. In contrast, private agencies that serve a greater proportion of voluntary clients see a type of practice informed more by the spirit of voluntarism and awareness of a gift relationship, with less emphasis on the contractual rights and obligations inherent in the worker-client relationship. There is a more direct sense of responsibilities to clients, whose interests are typically considered primary rather than secondary to the larger social good.

Conflicts involving social versus individual, public versus private, and involuntary versus voluntary dimensions form the essential context of professional practice in most of the human services. Whether professional practice in the human services involves psychotherapy, outreach, case management, administration, or policy development, such practice represents an amalgam of, on the one hand, negotiated contracting with clients and their surrounding systems, and on the other hand, the spirit of person-to-person empathic and even selfless work with others. Whereas the former can lead to bureaucratic disengagement, the latter can devolve into directionless interpersonal sharing, rescue fantasies, and what has become known as compassion fatigue. Although professional practice honors the potency of human relationships and associated helping processes, it also respects the need to apply empirically validated helping methods to the achievement of defined outcomes.

III. The Generalist Practice Model: The Approach of Social Work

Just as the human service professions as a whole have struggled to define the value they add to natural helping processes, social work has also sought to define its unique contributions among the professions. Various fields also use many of the methods used in social work, whether case management, psychotherapy, crisis intervention, administration, or policy development. What is it that elicits the question, Is there a social worker on the premises? Pincus and Minahan (1973) attempted to answer this question in their definition of the profession's core purposes: "The purpose of social work is to (1) enhance the problem solving and coping capacities of people (2) link people with systems that provide them with resources, services, and opportunities, (3) promote the effective and humane operation of these systems and (4) contribute to the development and improvement of social policy" (p. 9).

As reasonable as this definition may seem, any such thumbnail definitions are invariably lacking, if only because of their generality. General definitions not only fail to answer the question of what is distinctive but also leave the impression that just about anything goes. The dark and often-unacknowledged shadow of the generalist is the dilettante, the jack-of-all-trades, master of none.

A. Background

Efforts to define social work date back more than a hundred years. During the late 1800s and early 1900s, two branches of social work emerged. One involved the settlement house movement, initiated in the United States by Jane Addams (see figure 12.4), which emphasized community building and organization, education, and the development of a variety of social policies targeted at the major social problems of the era. The other branch of the profession, which developed out of the charity house movement, was concerned with providing casework support to individuals and families and was often preoccupied with problems of differentiating the deserving from the undeserving poor through the application of principles of "scientific charity." It was out of this second movement that Mary Richmond (1917) defined the field of social casework in her classic work, *Social Diagnosis*. She characterized her individual and family approach as consisting of the "betterment of individuals or families, one by one" (p. 25). In doing so, she laid the seeds for a microlevel version of generalist practice, as she noted that, "in essentials, the methods and aims of social work were the same in every type of service" (p. 5).

This notion of generalist practice was developed further during the 1920s by a group of social agency administrators who met to attempt to define and standardize social work practice. Their work culminated in the Milford Conference in 1928, when they formally concluded that "a common generic casework practice existed that superseded any of the specializations based on a particular problem or practice" (Schatz, Jenkins, & Sheafor, 1990, pp. 218–219). Eventually, this report was the basis for identifying the following eight elements of social work practice:

1. Knowledge of the typical deviations from accepted standards of social life
2. The use of norms of human life and human relationships
3. The significance of social history as the basis for particularizing the human in need
4. Established methods of study and treatment of humans in need
5. The use of established community resources in social treatment
6. The adaptation of scientific and formulations of experience to the requirements of social case work
7. The consciousness of a philosophy that determines the purposes, ethics, and obligations of social case work
8. The blending of the foregoing into social treatment. (National Association of Social Workers, 1974, p. 15)

Despite efforts to define a common base of social work practice, which typically emphasized direct service to the exclusion of indirect methods, social work developed during subsequent decades as a loosely affiliated network of practitioners concerned with particular methods or populations, such as group work, psychiatric social work, or oncological social work. These developments were finally addressed in 1958 when the diverse social work groups merged into the National Association of Social Workers (NASW), a development that dramatically weakened the influence of specialty groups. That same year, Harriet Bartlett (1958) published a paper in which she argued that social work was defined not by any single element, but by the combination of its values, purposes, sanction, knowledge, and methods. However, it was in the next few years that several authors added critical elements to this list. In 1959, the Boehm Curriculum Study (Boehm, 1959) proposed that social functioning is the goal of social work. Boehm was among the first to suggest that the primary concern of social work is the social interaction between people and their environments. Shortly thereafter, William Schwartz (1961) pointed out that social work's most distinctive feature is its mediation between the individual and society.

The next major thrust in the development of generalist models came about as a result of the 1974 decision by the Council on Social Work Education (CSWE) to accredit bachelor of social work (BSW) programs. The CSWE defined the purview of baccalaureate education to be generalist practice. It thereby established the BSW as the central standard for entry-level professional social work education. At this same time, master degree programs in social work, such as at the University of Chicago's School of Social Service Administration, started introducing curricular tracks that involved integrated or coordinated methods. Although generalist practice flourished at the undergraduate level, graduate education adopted such models considerably more slowly as they competed with the more popular clinical and other special method concentrations. Generalist models at first were introduced only as new schools emerged.

Generalist practice involves the foundations of social work. Thus, the major challenge at the graduate level was to define what was advanced about these models. Since the mid-1980s there have been a few dozen graduate programs that teach advanced generalist practice, sometimes as a separate course or concentration and other times as a unifying theme for an entire graduate program.

B. Core Elements of Generalist Practice

Generalist practice is still largely regarded as "a practice perspective in search of a conceptual framework" (Schatz et al., 1990, p. 217). Its three most commonly cited features are (1) a focus on the person-environment relationship, (2) a multimethod and multilevel approach, and (3) the use of the steps of the problem-solving or planned intervention process. Other less consistently cited features include its roots in systems or ecosystems theory; its implementation through various professional roles; the strengths perspective; and its emphasis on self-determination, empowerment, and social justice. Rarely mentioned is the broad approach to integrating diverse ways of knowing, including empirical evidence, practice wisdom, and the use of theory. Most authors usually define generalist practice in terms of two or three of these dimensions and rarely consider its broader array of features. For example, Gibbs (2003) suggests that "the generalist model of practice has two central features. First, it is problem-solving centered, rather than methods-driven . . . and, second, it uses the person-in-environment configuration for assessment and intervention, giving practice a holistic emphasis throughout the entire problem-solving process" (p. 234).

1. SELF-DETERMINATION

The remainder of this section will now turn to a discussion of what is meant by these features, beginning with client self-determination and with the practice principle that directs the worker to begin where the client is at. Although this may seem to be a simple and obvious rule, the adage masks enormously complex issues, such as determining not only who the client is, whether an individual is asking for help, the client's family, and the employing agency but also where the client is at. Once the primary client has been identified, the question turns to what he or she is most concerned about and asking for, especially when the client may be confused, conflicted, or under pressure to not to fully disclose the nature of the presenting problem or the motivation for seeking service. Sometimes brief discussion is sufficient to clarify these matters, but often this takes considerably more extended exploration. Thus, respecting client self-determination and engaging clients around an understanding of their motivations is a critical beginning point of social work, whether micro or macro, but often it is a beginning point with an indeterminate location.

The concept of salient need, first introduced by Frances Scherz from Chicago's Jewish Family and Community Services, has been proposed as a means of resolving this uncertainty (see Chapman, n.d.) and of identifying a beginning point for the work. A salient needs is that concern, need, or interest of the client that is most current, pressing, and of greatest strategic value in addressing the wider array of problems that may be present. A homeless person may have concrete physical and mental health issues, but there is usually one need—emergency shelter, food, or medical attention—that is of the most pressing and strategic need, that provides an entry point for engaging the client and attending to the other needs. The salient need is likely to be but not necessarily what the client is asking for. Chapman (n.d.) argued that "the salient need of the client system, whether an individual, family, or small group, is that which leaps out from the matrix of facts and inferences as if crying to be recognized. It is a conceptual link in a chain made up of client, worker, problem, and situation. Once identified, it becomes the focusing, directing searchlight" (p. 4).

2. Strengths Perspective

Generalist practice is also strengths based. Understanding client strengths and their various capacities—psychological, interpersonal, vocational, or otherwise—can take place only in relation to their motivations and presenting problems. Strengths are strengths only when they promise to resolve some actual living dilemma; otherwise, they are simply traits. A strengths perspective and a problem focus are two sides of the same coin, the value of which can be synergistically realized only by applying strengths to relevant problems of concern.

3. Role of the Environment

A third area of central concern in generalist practice is the environments that clients face, not only as a source of problems—of victimization, marginalization, deprivation, or confusion—but also as a source of opportunities and supports for confronting these same problems. Only by understanding the complexities of the environments that clients deal with is it possible for workers to fully appreciate the dual and changing functions of environments in both supporting and complicating clients' lives. These complexities include interactions between these environments, between the family and the workplace, or among the larger community, economic, and cultural environments, as well as the ways these relationships complement or undercut one another. Are workplace pressures spilling over into the home, which may or may not be successfully buffered by friendship or religious supports? Understanding the complex structures of environmental opportunities provides the essential context for assessing clients' relevant strengths and capacities in relation to particular problems.

4. Systemic Assessment

Achieving a meaningful focus in the helping relationship is a perennial concern of both novice and experienced professionals, one that directly ties in with the assessment process that is concerned with clarifying the most salient problem. This clarification is often achieved through a consideration of motivation, capacity, and opportunity, the classic triad of the assessment process introduced by Lillian Ripple (1969). This calls for identifying the point of intersection of the client's motivation and capacity to achieve valued

FIGURE 14.2: ASSESSMENT AS A PROCESS OF IDENTIFYING
THE STRATEGIC JUNCTURE OF CLIENT AND ENVIRONMENTAL
MOTIVATIONS, CAPACITIES, AND OPPORTUNITIES

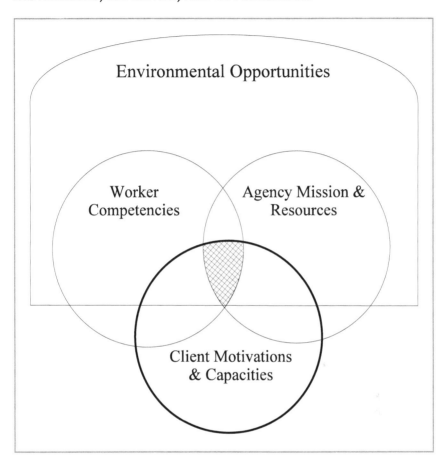

Environmental Opportunities

Worker Competencies

Agency Mission & Resources

Client Motivations & Capacities

Note: The above Venn diagram illustrates the critical intersection (cross-hatched area) of client motivation and capacities, on one hand, with the opportunities in inherit in both the immediate service system and the larger environment, on the other hand. It is at this point of overlap that there is the greatest synergy and the maximum opportunity for creative growth and change on the part of the client. The ideas in the above have been adapted from the work of Ripple and Alexander (1956) as well as the contributions of the functional school of social casework.

ends, both the mission of the sponsoring agency and the interest and skills that the worker brings to the relationship, as well as other environmental resources and supports (see figure 14.2). Of primary importance is the client's motivation—what is he or she asking for? How does he or she see the problem? Understanding the client's struggles, yearnings, struggles, and fears is no small task, as the client often has an incomplete understanding of these. Also, the mission of the sponsoring agency, including its capabilities and supports, is of some importance. For example, the mission of schools is first and foremost education, and thus schools are generally able to assist only partially with complex psychosocial struggles, and usually only to the extent that they directly interfere with academic learning. To overstep these limitations potentially undercuts the authenticity and quality of the helping relationship. For this reason, when professionals work for human services or other organizations, they need to be aware of the history, mission, and policies of these institutions and be able to interpret them to their clients.

Just as virtually all forms of professional practice are grounded in the assessment process, so is generalist social work practice. The content and processes of assessment vary dramatically from one field of practice to another. However, an essential feature of assessment in the generalist model is that it is based on an understanding of systems, and thus, is holistic. This is not to say that, in many brief forms of service, the holistic ideal can be fully attained but that such comprehensive assessments are done to the extent that the relationships, resources, and context require and permit.

Assessments sometimes end with categorical or descriptive accounts of client issues, as exemplified by psychiatric diagnoses or the traditional social history. But their real value lies in their ability to also identify the dynamic interrelationships between multiple factors, especially the various positive and negative feedback loops that perpetuate or aggravate current problems, or conversely, provide avenues for their resolution.

5. Goodness-of-Fit Between Person and Environment

Assessment is structured not only by the careful consideration of client motivations, capacities, strengths, and environmental opportunities but also by goodness of the person-environment fit. This focus has been interpreted in multiple ways. Helen Harris Perlman (1957) emphasized that it involves a person-problem-environment assessment. This is especially true given that most problems that bring clients to professionals involve a lack of goodness-of-fit between the person and his or her environment. Others emphasize the transactional nature of this fit, that the assessment involves determining whether change is needed in the transactions themselves, in the environment, or in the individual. And still others, such as Lawson and Alameda-Lawson (2001), emphasize the task of boundary spanning as a central means of addressing the lack of goodness-of-fit that plagues many individuals. Boundary spanning may be accomplished through various roles, for instance, those of the conferee or mediator.

Three potential pitfalls have often accompanied the thoughtless application of the goodness-of-fit concept. First, many assume that the client is only the person, but this client may actually be any system, such as a family, organization, or community, and its goodness-of-fit with its environments. As stated previously, it is important that professionals avoid thinking about environments as singular and monolithic. We relate with many environments, and when thought of in this way, environments cease to be overwhelming, mysterious, and unchangeable. Finally, for many the goal of human life is not the achievement of goodness-of-fit with the environment, or simply fitting in. Happiness, fulfillment of human potential, and the achievement of other core values usually require some degree of congruence with supportive environments, but attempting to unthinkingly help clients to achieve such fit in impossible and oppressive environments would represent a disservice, for example, in many institutions, ghetto communities, or racist cultures. Goodness-of-fit must be assessed in relation to the client's and the profession's values, and it is better conceived of as a means rather than an end. While some relationships are ends in themselves, others are instrumental means to a variety of other ends. When understood in this broader perspective, optimizing the goodness-of-fit and relationships with relevant environments is an essential part of assessment and intervention.

6. WORKER-ENVIRONMENT RELATIONSHIP

The concern with the client-environment relationship highlights a related feature of generalist practice: the focus on the worker-environment relationship. Just as there is a client system, which may or may not be the same as the target system, the change agent system and the broader action system may or may not be the same. The change agent system refers to the worker and his or her immediate system, whereas the action system also includes the broader array of community or collateral resources that may be brought to bear on the client and/or target system (Pincus & Minahan, 1973). A precursor of the generalist practice model, the functionalist school of social casework, developed at the University of Pennsylvania beginning in the 1930s (see Smalley, 1970), emphasized the use of agency sanction or mission to guide and focus work. The practices of an individual professional or department are synergistically enhanced when they are in harmony with the overall agency mission. In addition, the coherence achieved in the change agent system is further strengthened when the roles that the professional assumes are consistent with both the mission and the needs of clients. For this reason, several social work theorists have portrayed generalist practice as the integrated application of a wide range of possible roles on the part of the worker. Hernandez, Jorgensen, Judd, Gould, and Parsons (1985), for instance, characterize these roles as conferee, enabler, broker, mediator, advocate, and guardian. Each can be assumed in the context of either direct or indirect forms of social work practice (see table 14.1).

7. MULTILEVEL APPROACH

One of the most commonly mentioned features of generalist practice is that it involves multiple systemic levels and multiple crosscutting dimensions. The idea that it is multilevel refers to one of two things. On the one hand, some conceive of generalist practice primarily in terms of direct or clinical practice and urge that problems that manifest in larger systems, such as the family or community, be addressed to the extent that they impinge on particular cases. On the other hand, some are clearer that practice can start with concerns on the individual or larger system levels, whether or not there needs to be transitions between the levels. The client may be an agency, community group, or other large entity and not an individual person or family. A worker, for instance, may advocate for or plan changes in rules and regulations that affect the population of a state's welfare recipients without becoming involved with individual cases.

The multiple dimensions involved in assessment can also mean many things. The dimensions sometimes refer to multiple levels of analysis, such as the biological, psychological, social, and cultural levels that are generally relevant to each systemic level. They can refer to multiple perspectives, for example, the individual or collective, or the subjective or objective. Often multiple dimensions involve the many ways that people can vary, for example, with respect to their personalities (extraverted or introverted, right or left brain dominance).

8. MULTIMETHOD APPROACH

Gale Wood and Ruth Middleman (1989) propose a structural model of social work consistent with generalist practice and that provides a useful typology of major social work methods. They view structural or generalist practice as defined by the two dimensions. One is the type of action system, whether involving direct work with beneficiaries or indirect work with others on behalf of the target system. The other is the type of target population, whether involving work with individuals and small groups, case by case, with populations as a whole. The two dimensions define four major types of practice: (1) interpersonal practice, or direct work with small systems (e.g., psychotherapy), (2) social treatment, involving indirect work on behalf of small systems (e.g., certain types of case management or parental guidance), (3) community practice, involving direct work with populations (e.g., community organizing), and (4) policy practice, consisting of indirect work on behavior of populations at risk (e.g., social administration, policy

Table 14.1: Examples of Service Methods Used with Selected Roles and System Types

Client Systems

Role	INDIVIDUAL	FAMILY	SMALL GROUP	ORGANIZATION	COMMUNITY
CONFEREE	Counseling	Family therapy, parental guidance	Group therapy	Supervision/ consultation	Consultation
ENABLER	Modeling	Family life education	Skill training, psycho-education	Organizational development	Social planning/community education
BROKER	Casework, case manager	Information provision	Self-help	Network development	Community needs advocacy
MEDIATOR	Help with decison making	Divorce, custody mediation	Intergroup mediation	Third-party peacemaking	Community conflict resolution
ADVOCATE	Case advocacy	Case advocacy	Education	Grant writing/ program development	Policy advocacy/bargaining
GUARDIAN	Individual protective services	Family protective services	Mandated group therapy	Controlling	Individual legal action

Source: Adapted from Hernandez et al. (1985, p. 32).

TABLE 14.2: MULTIMETHOD DIMENSIONS OF GENERALIST PRACTICE, AS ILLUSTRATED BY THE SIMULTANEITY AND STRUCTURAL MODELS

Action System \ Target Population	SMALL SYSTEMS (INDIVIDUALS, FAMILIES, GROUPS)	LARGE POPULATIONS (COMMUNITIES)
DIRECT WORK WITH TARGET SYSTEM(S)	INTERPERSONAL PRACTICE Work with clients on their own behalf	SOCIAL ACTION Work with clients on their own behalf and others like them
INDIRECT WORK WITH OTHERS, ON BEHALF OF TARGET SYSTEM(S)	SOCIAL TREATMENT Work with others on behalf of clients	POLICY PRACTICE Work with others on behalf of populations-at-risk

Note: This chart represents a consolidation of the language from two virtually identical models, the structural and simultaneity models.

Source: Adapted from Jackson, Macy, & Day (1984, p. 21). See also Wood & Middleman (1989).

development) (see table 14.2). Wood and Middleman point out that any given setting may use two or three of these approaches, usually either interpersonal, social treatment, and community organization, or policy practice, community organization, and social treatment, with the starting point usually involving one of these areas followed by activity shifted into related modalities as needed. For example, a policy planner with a state oversight agency may use participatory planning to engage in some community-organizing activities as needed. Wood and Middleman propose several principles for selecting the appropriate level and type of practice. An example is the need to first attempt to resolve environmental problems before assuming that a psychological problem exists.

Although generalist practice is often described as a multimethod approach, it is usually with the proviso that a systemic or multidimensional assessment guides the selection of methods. The rationale is that human problems are diverse and overlapping, and thus usually require a variety of methods. Practitioners who are specialists in a single method (e.g., psychotherapy) are liable to see all problems as psychological problems and inappropriately apply their favorite method. The multidimensional and multimethod dimensions of generalist practice, however, pose a problem of determining the rules or principles by which transitions are made between levels and methods. It is easy enough to boast that one does what works best. But there are often competing considerations, for example, conflicts between empirical evidence, the various preferences of the clients, the inclinations and skills of the worker, requests by legal authorities, and professional values. When this is the case, it may not always be clear how to reconcile the considerations. A careful and detailed assessment certainly helps in this regard, but it rarely is definitive with respect to which intervention is indicated.

9. PROBLEM-SOLVING PROCESS

Finally, a key part of generalist practice is the use of steps of the problem-solving process. More recently, these have been referred to as the steps of planned intervention. In other contexts, they are known as the steps of rational problem solving (see chapter 7). In social work, a typical breakdown of these steps is as follows: engagement, assessment, planning, implementation, evaluation, termination, and follow-up (Kirst-Ashman & Hull, 2006). Other listings include goal setting and contracting under planning. Many tend to assume that the steps apply only to individual-level practice. Increasingly, though, generalist theoreticians emphasize that the steps are applicable to multiple system levels, albeit with alternative terminologies. Instead of assessment, one might conduct a community needs assessment; instead of an evaluation, one might undertake a policy analysis. Any listing of steps and stages is always a gross simplification, often done only for didactic purposes. Such generalities gloss over the extent to which the stages overlap with one another and loop back, either at intermediate stages or after termination. They also create the impression that practice is an interventionist or technocratic undertaking in which the professional assesses or treats a passive client rather than as a collaborative undertaking conducted at the wish of the client and under the leadership of the professional.

In most settings only a limited range of methods are typically used, with only one or a few system levels. Agency practices, policies of funding bodies, client expectations, and the staff training all constrain the range of methods and levels used, simplifying the decision-making process. Nonetheless, Gibbs, Locke, and Lohmann (1990) pointed out, "The generalist orientation is particularly valued because it lacks assumptions about problem cause or location and allows interventions to be shaped by holistic assessment, rather than driven by predetermined methods" (p. 235). On the one hand, many funding and regulatory bodies have attempted to standardize and even deprofessionalize service, eliminating any complexity that requires advanced training and licensing. On the other hand, many in the professions have avidly sought to protect professional autonomy. This has been done partly through broadening the scope of decision making; in the fields in which this has occurred, it has required graduate education and advanced generalist models of practice. It is to this topic that we will now turn.

IV. Advanced Generalist Practice: Distinctive Features

A defining feature of professional practice is that it is at a level regarded as advanced and specialized. In the human services, this is often interpreted as requiring the completion of a graduate degree (e.g., MSW, MSN, MS), though some bachelor's degrees (e.g., BSW) are considered the professional entry level. This raises the question of how generalist practice can be advanced and specialized, a question that many have floundered in answering. In social work, attempts to answer this question have typically involved distinguishing between foundation and advanced practice, which may or may not be generalist. Advanced practice is most typically regarded as involving the application of the foundation generalist skills to a particular field or method of practice. During a master's degree program, often in the final year, students are typically required to successfully complete a concentration of courses focused on a particular method (e.g., community organizing or group work, a particular population such as the developmentally disabled or people with medical problems, a particular field of practice such as mental health or child welfare). Some master's degree programs organize all of their offerings around the notion of advanced generalist practice, and fewer programs offer a concentration in this area. In either case, advanced generalist practice is usually distinguished from the beginning or foundation generalist model, taught both in the BSW and in the first year of many MSW programs (see exhibit 14.1).

The dimensions of practice listed in exhibit 14.1 do not represent sharp distinctions. They are continua that instead represent gradations of practice sophistication. Whereas the advanced generalist who earns an MSW may be more accomplished in most of these areas than someone who has earned only a BSW, it takes many years of education, training, and experience to truly achieve an advanced level of competence. For some, models of practice, including the advanced generalist, are regarded with much skepticism because they are viewed as abstractions removed from the realities of everyday practice. However, the final dimension described in exhibit 14.1—evidence-based practice—is a particularly important feature of advanced generalist practice.

Evidence-based practice is perhaps the most recent incarnation of various practices and models, such as the promotion of accountability,

EXHIBIT 14.1: CRITERIA THAT DISTINGUISH ADVANCED GENERALIST FROM FOUNDATION GENERALIST PRACTICE

- **Concurrent specialization:** What is considered advanced is the application of the generalist skills to a particular problem, population, or field of practice, for example, developmental disabilities, older adults, or community health.
- **Complexity:** The areas of application are regarded as more complex than with generalist practice. This complexity often consists of a wider variety of actors and systems and a resulting wider variety of methods than the beginning practitioner is prepared for. Complexity also involves multiple and simultaneous interactions governed by poorly understood rules.
- **Ambiguity and conflict:** The problems addressed with these models are ill defined and often involve a wider variety of areas of conflict than beginning professionals are trained to address. For example, instead of a simple conflict between an employee and an employer, there may also be conflicts between employees and between administrative staff that exacerbate the focal conflict.
- **Risk:** The risks inherent in the more complex, ambiguous, and/or conflictual systems is more acute than the beginning professional can safely address. These risks may involve suicidal or homicidal clients, the possible failure of a major employer or social agency, or the permanent placement of a child in an adoptive home or his or her return to biological parents. This is not to say that inadequately prepared workers often find themselves forced to make such determinations.
- **Multisystemic and multidimensional:** Advanced generalist practice involves not only multiple levels and methods but also multiple systems and dimensions of practice. A worker may need to coordinate interventions of education, child welfare, and mental health systems on behalf of a child and his or her family. While doing so, he or she must consider the systems from multiple perspectives—from that of the client, a group, or the community—and consider objective and scientifically based perspectives.
- **Leadership:** Most of the preceding elements require that the advanced generalist practitioner function in a leadership position, perhaps as a team leader, supervisor, consultant, or educator. Leadership requires considerably more than executing formal roles of considerable responsibility; it requires the ability to bring key

EXHIBIT 14.1 (CONTINUED)

people together, to inspire them, and to optimize each person's areas of expertise.

- **Grounded in theory:** Given the nature of the problems confronted,
  the advanced generalist must be able to draw from a wider array of
  theories and to creatively integrate their insights into person- and
  problem-specific formulations involving the dynamic functioning
  of relevant systems. Such formulations are often hypothetical and
  require vigilant use of objective observations, on the part of the
  practitioner and the profession.

- **Evidence based:** The greater ambiguity and complexity of problems requires a broader, more systemic, and critical incorporation
  of research and other forms of evidence into practice. Whereas
  beginning practitioners do well in gaining familiarity with basic
  findings in their field of practice, advanced generalists develop the
  ability not only to more critically understand and adapt their findings in a individualized manner but also to produce new research
  in collaboration with others.

outcomes assessment, data-based practice, empirically based practice, and
the practitioner-researcher model. Perhaps its simplest definition is that it
consists of practice based on the best available evidence (O'Hare, 2005).
O'Hare specifically defines evidence-based practice as "the planned use of
empirically supported assessment and intervention methods combined
with the judicious use of monitoring and evaluation strategies for the purpose of improving the psychosocial well-being of clients" (p. 6). In contrast,
Gibbs (2003) emphasizes that this approach derives from the posing of key
questions: "Placing the client's benefit's first, evidence-based practitioners
adopt a process of lifelong learning that involves continually posting specific questions of direct practical importance to clients, searching objectively
and efficiently for the current best evidence relative to each question, and
taking appropriate action guided by evidence" (p. 6).

The central idea behind evidence-based practice is that practitioners are
accountable for using methods based on the best evidence available and
have an ethical responsibility to convey any uncertainty, possible negative
side effects, and costs of their interventions to their clients and others concerned. The use of theoretical models provides only general parameters for
intervention decisions based on global conceptual, philosophical, and ethical

considerations. More detailed guidance as to what will likely work in a particular context, with particular clients, derives from the empirical literature or studies that the practitioner might undertake. But even after both theory and research are considered in practice decision making, ambiguities and conflicts still persist. It is then that collaborative decision making with the client, including intuition and other transrational ways of knowing, assume particular importance in professional decision making. Just as the same theory may be consistent with several strategies, multiple interventions may be equally effective, and neither is always sufficient to inform the countless everyday decisions of the practitioner.

Evidence-based practice emphasizes the use of research throughout the problem-solving process, including the tasks of assessment, setting goals, planning interventions, and evaluating both the process and the outcomes of interventions (see table 14.3). According to O'Hare (2005), evidence-based practice "emphasizes outcome research to help guide the initial choice of intervention, and monitoring and evaluation methods to facilitate optimal implementation" (p. 5). Similarly, Gibbs (2003) emphasizes its process dimensions, noting that its major steps consists of the following:

1. Becoming motivated to apply evidence-based practice
2. Converting information needs into well-formulated answerable questions
3. Tracking down with maximum efficiency the best evidence with which to answer the question
4. Critically evaluat[ing] evidence for its validity and usefulness
5. Applying results of evidence appraisal to policy practice
6. Evaluating performance
7. Teaching others to do the same. (pp. 8–9)

On the one hand, there are those who contend that clients have a right to be treated with evidence-based methods, and that without validated research, the possibilities for clients to provide truly informed consent and engage in self-determination is compromised. Nonetheless, the extent and adequacy of the scientific knowledge base available for evidence-based practice is still in its infancy. Practitioners regularly confront both global decisions and day-to-day operational choices for which the evidence does not exist, is inaccessible, or otherwise fails to provide practical guidance. Furthermore, the evidence may be consistent with more than one theory; thus, extrapolations to unique cases may be precarious. However, when combined with theory, the values and ethics of the profession, and the reflective use of

Table 14.3: Examples of Integration of Empirical Evidence in the Stages of the Problem-Solving Process

ENGAGEMENT	• Use of census data in identifying groups requiring outreach efforts • Easy availability of accurate and useful resource information for clients in crisis
ASSESSMENT	• Use of rapid assessment instruments in determining type and extent of needs and problems, including psychopathology • Standardized interview protocols • Review of research on selected populations-at-risk to understand possible concerns, problems, dynamics • Community needs assessments and resource inventories
GOAL SETTING	• Use of evaluation or other intervention research (e.g., literature reviews and metaanalyses), to ascertain possible outcomes that can be realistically expected • Qualitative research on the values, cultures, and aspirations of selected client groups, (e.g., use of focus groups)
INTERVENTION PLANNING	• Evaluation research, and its various reviews, in assessing promising intervention methods, their effectiveness and drawbacks • Use of descriptive surveys in assessing the availability of various service alternatives within a given area
CONTRACTING	• Review of results of psychotherapy process studies to determine optimal approaches to contracting • Policy Delphi studies as a means of developing consensus among stakeholders
INTERVENTION	• Use of rapid assessment and monitoring instruments in tracking changes in problem status over course of treatment • Process studies of impact of particular techniques • Client satisfaction surveys and focus groups
EVALUATION AND TERMINATION	• Use of single-subject studies in assessing effectiveness of interventions implemented

the self in the helping process, the worker is in a particularly strong position to address the complexities of advanced generalist practice reviewed earlier in this section. Yet as far as the ideal of advanced generalist practice goes, this practice model has largely failed to fully capitalize on the insights that are now being developed in the field of complex systems theory, and it is to this final subject that this chapter will now turn.

V. Advanced Generalist Practice and Complex Systems

Just as generalist practice is based on the assessment of relevant systems, advanced generalist practice is increasingly grounded in the assessment of complex systems. Thus, it has come to incorporate complex systems theory. This means many things, including a recognition of the pervasiveness of far-from-equilibrium conditions and multiple equilibria. It means a rejection of the artificial distinctions between structure and process, form and function. It means not only the simple recognition of diverse system levels neatly or not-so-neatly pancaked on top of one another but also their active interconnections, and most important, the nesting of local action systems within global action systems, often in entangled ways that obscure the operation of simple local activity rules and practice principles.

A. Multisystemic Focus

It has been pointed out that the traditional view of the social environment as merely a singular structural context for practice serves to mystify the environment and portray it as unchangeable. GlenMaye, Lewandowski, and Bolin (2004) pointed out that traditional models "tend to reify social systems as things in themselves . . . , when in fact it is the interactions that define system boundaries. . . . Such reifications may contribute to workers' reluctance to intervene at larger system levels, since those systems are viewed as structures rather than as dynamic systems defined by their transactions, interactions, and qualities of communication between individuals" (p. 120).

Many large social systems, such as organizations and communities, appear to be static and unchanging. They are often characterized by the use of diverse mechanisms that minimize the sharing of information and the formalization of relationships. Although boundaries are often symbolically defined, relatively infrequent interactions primarily define the practical boundaries between any two systems. Formal structures are merely the residue of prior dynamic processes, ones that continue to change in such a slow and incremental manner that they are imagined as set entities. Such slow-moving processes create the impression that they are merely the shell or form, and that the functions, processes, and work of the systems are altogether separate. General systems theory was based on this unfortunate simplification; however, complex systems theory rejects any fundamental distinction between structure and process, form and function. The distinctions represent different perspectives rather than different realities.

B. Iterative Transactions and Strategies of Approximation

Complex systems theory directs practitioners to be attuned to process, and especially to the patterns of transaction between key actors on multiple system levels. This involves several dimensions and requires especially close attention to the iterative character of the patterns. This means that each transaction, each feedback loop, takes off from and transforms the output of the previous transaction. This often takes places in a highly unpredictable manner, one that exhibits extreme sensitivity to initial conditions, a defining feature of chaos. When this is the case, detailed and long-term intervention planning becomes impossible and must be replaced by a strategy of successive approximation to desired ends, involving the successive adjustments of actions to intended consequences, as well as the underlying rules that govern those actions. The successive approximations of actions is simply the gradual adjustment of practitioners' responses. An example is the successive questioning, paraphrasing, and commenting by the worker, based on the quality of the client's communications. Although such practice-based flexibility in the human services has a long history, in recent years it has been compromised by many people's interest in standardizing practice, often to minimize costs and liabilities through the use of detailed assessment protocols. Successive approximation also refers to the gradual adjustment and renegotiation of the rules that govern actions: "Please feel free to ask me any questions that you would like," or "We need to be more careful to consult with each other before taking action." Such strategies of successive approximation require a clear understanding of what it is that the worker seeks to approximate (e.g., engagement in counseling, vigilant decision making on the part of a client, commitment in an organization to a common strategy of community action). In addition, strategies of approximation preclude not long-term planning but only overly detailed planning that interferes with day-to-day practice and such strategies of iterative, successive approximation. Some of the efforts hit dead-ends, which requires more fundamental efforts at reassessment and comprehensive planning.

C. Nonlinearity

Another implication of complex systems theory for practice is an understanding of nonlinearity. Recall from chapter 1 that linear thinking involves the assumption that inputs produce outputs in a predictable or tit-for-tat fashion. For example, many assume that if one doubles the number of counseling sessions, the benefit will double, or if an agency's budget increases by 50%, then the number of clients served can increase by 50%. In contrast, there are several aspects of nonlinearity, which is characteristic of interactive service relationships. There may be a saturation point, or a point of diminishing returns, when benefits cease to increase with increasing inputs. One may be successful when mildly encouraging a client to act in a more productive manner, but with more persistent reminders, the client may become resistant and act out further. Conversely, there may be little positive benefit from low levels of service provision until a critical threshold is reached, but when a comprehensive package of services is in place, the client may enter a positive feedback loop that leads to successful problem resolution. Thus, factoring in nonlinearity, a key question becomes, What is the critical level or the right mix of services? Clients are helped to discover optimal balance in their lives—between immediate well-being and long-term gains, between care of self and of others, between sharing and listening—instead of living by a philosophy of more is better.

D. Nested Problem Solving

The concept of hierarchical complexity suggests not only that there are multiple levels of systems that each need to be understood but also that some of these are nested in others in nonobvious ways. Communities are nested within nations, organizations nested within communities, agencies nested within communities, and so forth. This nesting is often entangled: organizations cut across multiple communities, families negotiate multiple community environments, and these nested relationships often are convoluted and circular. An agency is considered part of a community and responsive to the community's needs. Yet if it is a particularly large and powerful agency, the community may also be part of the agency, depend on it, and respond to its needs. Relationships that are both nested and entangled have both positive and negative consequences. They can ensure a degree of responsiveness and reciprocity, but sometimes at the expense of coherence, predictability, and integration.

The primary implication of nested systems is that the helping system itself is multilevel and nested. The individual worker is employed by or embedded in a program, which is part of an agency, which in turn is embedded in community and national service and policy systems. Thus, problem solving itself is fundamentally a nested process. The steps of planned intervention—engagement, assessment, goal setting and contracting, intervention planning, intervention, and evaluation and termination—take place on the worker level, in the agency and community systems as a whole, and at the professional level. If this is the case, then a critical implication of complex systems theory is that the steps of planned intervention at each level need to be coordinated and systematically linked. This process of nested problem solving is a central and integrative component of advanced generalist practice.

Figure 14.3 illustrates nested problem solving, how all efforts at problem solving are ultimately embedded in the relationship between the individual worker and society, and more specifically in his or her profession. The professional engages the respect of a profession, often during the educational process; assesses its problems, needs, and opportunities; sets goals; imagines a career and some mix of professional roles; and sets about to implement this lifelong intervention. In the job-hunting process, the professional engages the interest of a social agency; assesses its problems, environments, and opportunities; and with a little luck, contracts with one such agency to delivery some mix of services, the plan for which might be described in a formal job description. Nested in this planned intervention are the worker's efforts to engage a range of groups, families, and/or individuals.

The larger intervention, symbolized by the worker's contract with the employing agency, forms the context for multiple nested cycles of problem solving with each group and individual. The agency context and action system has the power to energize or undercut the many mini-problem-solving cycles that the worker engages in each time he or she takes on a new client. The assessment of a family, for instance, forms an essential context for the assessment of individuals within that family; the goals for work with the family, thus, need to be linked with the goals for each individual.

Nested problem solving means not only that the worker intervenes on more than one level (e.g., individual and family) but also that the steps of the problem-solving process on each level are coherently linked. An example is a school social worker who is assigned to three schools in three different communities. Although many such workers have traditionally failed to individualize their services to the local service environment, nested problem solving requires that the worker assess and plan for the specific mix of services that each school needs, whether clinical, social treatment, or community organization services, and then seek agreement with the employer and

FIGURE 14.3: THE NESTING OF PROBLEM SOLVING WITHIN MULTIPLE SYSTEM LEVELS

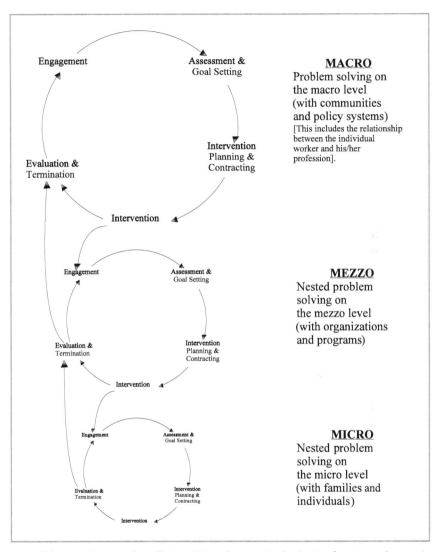

Note: Although only one cycle is illustrated in each successive level going from top to bottom, in actuality, multiple minicycles are usually embedded in each level. In addition, for lack of space, only three levels are illustrated here, whereas there can often be several levels within the macro, mezzo, and micro catagories. For example, on the micro level, an assessment and intervention plan may be worked out with a family, and within that context, successive individuals assessments and plans established for several of its individual members.

responsible administrators for the service plan for each school. This service plan, which may be summarized in a one- or two-page memorandum, then becomes a key tool, a contract and guide, for engaging in a similar process with any groups, families, or individuals served.

Nested problem solving suggests a flow of information from macro- to microlevel problem solving. Yet the links also go the other way. Workers learn the needs of their clients and advocate for changes in their agencies and communities, including in their professional role. Administrators and policy researchers may survey workers or clients to identify unmet needs and promising interventions. Just as treatment plans are modified on the basis of the client's response to the planned interventions, so are job descriptions modified or replaced according to the worker's successes and failures, which may result in reassignment, promotion, or simply the tweaking of job responsibilities based on the cumulative experience from assignments. Similarly, career goals and employing organizations may also be modified on the basis of the outcome of repeated employment successes and failures or simply disengagement.

E. Self-Organization

To the extent that advanced generalist practice draws on the insights of complex systems theory, it incorporates an understanding of self-organization, both the self-organization that individual clients and larger systems engage in and that which takes place in helping systems. In either case, such self-organization may be functional or dysfunctional. Recall from earlier chapters that self-organization theory has identified several important dynamic processes that clarify some of the sources of self-directed organizational activity. First is the dissipative flow of energy and information through a collection of related individuals or other agents, stimulating interaction among the component parts. Second, these interactions then become structured by evolving local activity rules. Third, in certain instances these rules bring about their structural coupling into larger units. Fourth, evidence suggests that the rules and subsequent coupling result in a balance between order and chaos, or the edge-of-chaos phenomenon. Last, the system is then best able to capitalize on the random fluctuations and diversity within its boundaries, amplifying these into novel and adaptive structures or behavioral patterns (Hudson, 2005).

Understanding self-organization, including its preconditions, dynamics, and the ways that it may be functional or dysfunctional, is a foundation for knowing when and how to intervene to facilitate, or even to control, such processes. Engaging clients, helping them clarify their needs and goals, and establishing conditions for self-help by drawing on family and community support networks are among the many social work values that are consistent with self-organization theory. However, self-organization theory suggests that attention be paid to the flow of energy—whether enabling information, physical resources or money, or a sense of enthusiasm—through a system and to understanding the rules governing the use of this energy. Such rules might involve unconscious assumptions that people make about themselves or others, the norms for interacting, or formal rules and laws governing a community or policy system. The theory also suggests that the combination of the flow of energy and certain rules increases interactions among formerly isolated parts, leading to interdependency and structural coupling, which may involve helping as well as destructive relationships. If we draw on an expanded version of self-organization theory as suggested here, then we need to also observe for top-down control processes, and either strengthen or encourage them.

Self-organization theory often favors bottom-up strategies and suggests that the social work adage "Start where the client is at" is of particular importance. However, it does not exclude top-down approaches or external intervention, for example, that which might be needed in a child protective setting. If self-organizing processes are understood as sometimes including the dynamics of conscious self-selection, even that which is nonlocal, then the approach may prove a particularly valuable part of social work's theoretical base (Hudson, 2005). Advanced generalist practice, in its ongoing assessment of complex human relationships, is thus attuned not only to the impact of the various environments on individuals but also to the possibilities of self-organization in the human and social systems of concern, as well as its impact on the environment.

VI. Summary

This chapter introduces the application of human behavior theory to the understanding of helping relationships and to an emerging approach to practice with the human service professions. A perennial issue introduced in the first part of the chapter is the controversy about whether empathic relationships are prerequisites to effective helping, or whether they might be also sufficient conditions. The work of Carl Rogers and Roger Carkhuff is reviewed, especially as it has provided some understanding of the necessary conditions for helping relationships, ones that involve empathy, emotional congruence, and positive regard.

The central part of the chapter focuses on the profession of social work, which has struggled to define what it adds to the natural helping process and its distinctive contribution to the helping process. The discussion focuses on the continuing efforts to formulate a model of generalist practice. Most agree that generalist practice minimally involves a focus on the person-environment relationship, its multimethod and multilevel approach, and the use of the steps of the problem solving or planned intervention process. There are, however, several additional features central to generalist practice: a commitment to promoting client self-determination, including the idea of starting where the client is at; a focus on client strengths and capabilities; and assessment based on an understanding of systems, including professional and other action systems.

Advanced generalist practice is an approach that requires the application of generalist practice to an area of specialization (e.g., mental health, child welfare, problems with relatively high levels of complexity, ambiguity, conflict, and risk and that involve multiple systems and multiple dimensions). Given the greater difficulty of the problems addressed, advanced generalist practice typically entails leadership roles and a more systematic incorporation of both theory and empirical evidence in the formulation of assessments and intervention plans.

The final part of the chapter discusses the interface between advanced generalist practice and complex systems theory. In addition to considering multiple system levels, complex systems theory suggests the importance of understanding the often-convoluted relationships between systems and system levels, identified as entangled hierarchies in previous chapters. Complex theory builds on the traditional emphasis on transactions in the social sciences. It also recognizes their iterative or repeated character and the idea that series of transactions, with the output of one becoming the input of the next, are often the basis for strategies of successive approximation in both human and specifically professional relationships. Iterative transactions are also typically nonlinear. Self-organization suggests a more facilitative rather than interventional role for the practitioner, and nested problem solving requires the systematic coordination or nesting of microlevel problem-solving efforts in mezzo- and macrolevel problem-solving strategies.

For Further Reading

Dass, R., & Gorman, P. (1997). *How can I help: Stories and reflections on service.* New York: Knopf.

GlenMaye, L. F., Lewandowski, C. A., & Bolin, B. L. (2004). Defining complexity: The theoretical basis of advanced generalist practice. In A. W. Roy

& F. J. Vecchiolla (Eds.), *Thoughts on an advanced generalist education: Models, readings, and essays* (Chap. 7). Peosta, IA: Eddie Bowers.

Kirst-Ashman, K. K., & Hull, G. H. (2006). *Understanding generalist practice* (4th ed.). Belmont, CA: Thomson-Brooks Cole.

Markland, D., Ryan, R. M., Tobin, V. J., & Rollnick, S. (2005). Motivational interviewing and self-determination theory. *Journal of Social and Clinical Psychology, 24*(6), 811–831.

O'Hare, T. (2005). *Evidence-based practices for social workers.* Chicago: Lyceum Books.

Rogers, C. R. (1965). *Client-centered therapy.* London: Constable.

Schatz, M. S., Jenkins, L. E., & Sheafor, B. W. (1990). Milford redefined: A model of initial and advanced generalist social work. *Journal of Social Work Education, 26*(3), 217–231.

Titmuss, R. M. (1971). *The gift relationship: From human blood to social policy.* New York: Vintage Books.

Wood, G. G., & Middleman, R. R. (1989). *The structural approach to direct practice in social work.* New York: Columbia University Press.

CHAPTER 15

Values, Ethics, and Spirituality in the Human Services

No man is an Island, entire of itself; every man is a piece of
the Continent, a part of the main; if a clod be washed away
by the sea, Europe is the less, as well as if a promontory were,
as well as if a manor of thy friends or of thine own were;
any man's death diminishes me, because I am involved in
Mankind; And therefore never send to know for whom the
bell tolls; It tolls for thee.

—JOHN DONNE

I. Introduction

The previous chapter on models of advanced generalist practice reviewed some of the ways that theory and research inform practice decisions, as well as their limitations in this regard. This chapter moves beyond those models to other foundations of practice, those involving the values, strategies of ethical decision making, and spirituality of both clients and practitioners. These constitute some of the most universal foundations of professional practice; they guide the selection of theories through a dialogue between human service professionals and their clients, employers, and funders around the selection of interventions. Advanced generalist practice not only is evidence based but also represents a critical integration of the best values and principles of all parties directly or indirectly involved in the professional relationship.

This review of the role of values, ethical decision making, and spirituality in practice builds on the entirety of this text. Choice and intention, which are also fundamental features of consciousness, characterize both living and social systems. Central to human development is the development of moral thought, a subject that is also central to the study of personality and states of subjective well-being. The study of decision making, problem solving, and creativity is also the study of the application of values and ethical principles. Difficulties in problem solving, particularly those that result in psychopathology, too often represent breakdowns of the ability to hold internalized guiding ideals and to recognize the human interdependency that the epigraph of this chapter speaks of. A central subject of this chapter, therefore, lies at the intersection of motivation and meaning: supporting clients in developing, discovering, and implementing their most fundamental values and ideals. Meher Baba (b. 1894–d. 1969) commented, "Modern psychology has done much to reveal the sources of conflict, but it has yet to discover methods of awakening inspiration or supplying the mind with something which makes life worth living" (1967, p. 65).

The ethical and spiritual dimensions of the human services are situated in the context of two pervasive and interlocking trends: modernism and globalization. The earlier trend involving industrialization, bureaucratic rationalization, and the development of secular society—collectively referred to as modernism—is epitomized by overspecialization and even social fragmentation. Most relevant here is the split between, on the one hand, scientific and secular society, and on the other hand, faith-based groups, with the increasing marginalization of the latter. Modernism reached its apex in the first half of the twentieth century, and since then the increasing challenges to its limiting assumptions, those involving materialism, atomism, rationalism, and relativism, have inspired multiple efforts to develop a more holistic worldview, ranging from postmodernist philosophies, such as existentialism and the ecological and green movements, to a variety of spiritual orientations, ranging from the evangelical to the mystical and activist. Some of these responses, such as religious fundamentalism, are responses to the clashes between traditionalist and modernist cultures, whereas others represent the interpenetration and resulting integration of divergent traditions. Globalization and cultural integration are gradually supplanting cultural fragmentation, brought about by modernism, but not without substantial conflict and stress. Cultural integration has stimulated efforts to combine the best of multiple religions and spiritual perspectives involving a type of spiritual syncretism.

The many resulting conflicts, such as the culture wars (see chapter 13) and the blending of cultures and spiritual perspectives have led to considerable academic interest in the study of values, ethics, and spirituality. This includes a reemergence of branches of philosophy that were considered bygone until recently. Axiology, the study of values; epistemology, or the study of knowledge; ontology, the study of the nature of being; and metaphysics and cosmology, the study of the origins, nature, and fate of the universe, have all emerged as either subjects in their own right or as parts of existing professions, including the human services.

The study of values, ethics, and spirituality is fraught with subjectivity and ideology. Attempts to compensate for such subjectivity typically draw from a range of discipline-specific methods that bolster critical thought, including phenomenological analysis, grounded theory, ethnographic methods, and traditional quantitative survey and quasi-experimental techniques. Those who analyze ethical and spiritual issues in practice or study them through formal research projects need to carefully differentiate between the diverse claims that individuals and groups make, which Jürgen Habermas (1979, as cited by Chilton, 2009) characterized in the following terms:

A. *Truth:* I am reporting the objective truth.
B. *Truthfulness:* I am reporting my own experience (as accurately as I can, anyway).
C *Rightness:* I am reporting something meaningful to us both.

Clarity about the nature of pronouncements on values, ethics, and spirituality has the advantage of focusing dialogue on those things that fall within individual or collective experience (points B and C) and deemphasizing absolute pronouncements about things that can not be verified (point A).

II. Values as Living Processes

A. Definitions

The term *value* has multiple and ambiguous meanings. It is most typically used as a noun, in reference to an assessment by either an individual or a group of something of worth or some ideal. The term comes from the Latin *valere,* which means "to be strong, to prevail, or to be of worth" (Meinert, 1980, p. 5). Yet it has an even more generic meaning, referring to the information that results from any measurement of a quality or quantity of interest. For instance, one value of the variable of religion may be Christian, or a value for the variable of age may be forty-nine. However, Frederic Reamer's (1995) definition captures the more common meaning: "Values . . . are generalized, emotionally charged conceptions of what is desirable; historically created and derived from experience, shared by a population or a group within in; and they provide the means for organizing and structuring patterns of behavior" (p. 11). Individuals and groups may value many things, both concrete and abstract, ranging from money and status, comfortable homes, well-manicured lawns, and productive employment to beauty, truth, justice, mutual support, and freedom. In this sense, values are relatively fixed or enduring cognitive entities, priorities and criteria that lie at the heart of motivation and decision making.

Although most people regard values as fixed entities, as enduring priorities, there is little consensus about how to identify a person's or a group's values. Are these evidenced by spoken rhetoric, by feelings experienced when certain values are invoked, by intended actions or by those that are actually carried out? For some, all of these indicators consistently point in the same direction. The value of human respect may be reflected by general pronouncements, use of nonstigmatizing language, and practical advocacy on behalf of marginalized people. But many values present a mixed picture, including general identifications and feelings that are yet to be implemented in any consistent or meaningful way. Some individuals may even talk and act in contradictory ways, and it is these phenomena that reveal that values are not singular mental priorities but living processes, or complex social and psychological systems.

Chapter 6 pointed out that motivations are themselves complex systems, with a constant interplay between conscious and unconscious mental assessments, conclusions about the feasibility of certain ends, their rewards, and perceived skills and behavioral patterns. Likewise, what most people think of as set values are rather reflections of ongoing cognitive, emotional, and behavioral processes involving the emergence and adoption of new dreams and ideals, their clarification and the emotional investment in them, the development of skills supportive of their realization, the formation of links with others with similar predispositions, and engagement in problem-solving activities and other behaviors that support their realization. As certain values are attained or become irrelevant, others rise to take their place. In this sense, values are not just nouns but also verbs: living processes that go on within and between people. The information encoded as values is even represented biologically in the nervous system, but it is poorly understood. Only recently has some progress been made in clarifying the neural mechanisms involved. The study of the interface between values, when represented in the brain, and economic choices has come to be termed *neuroeconomics* (see exhibit 15.1).

B. Types of Values

In many traditions values are primarily evidenced through prohibitions, or "thou shall not's." In Western cultures positive values are often not explicitly expressed, partly because of the emphasis on individualism. For example, in the psychoanalytic tradition, values are regarded as rooted in the superego, which is assumed to act only in a prohibitive rather than a permissive manner. It was only neo-Freudians and self-psychologists who recognized some of the positive, permissive, and energizing functions of values in the formation of internalized guiding ideals (e.g., Kohut, 1971). In the psychoanalytic tradition, values are regarded as primarily unconscious, although self-aware individuals may become at least partially conscious of their values. In recent years the distinction between instrumental values and core values has been recognized. Instrumental values are things that are valued as means to other ends. In contrast, core values are considered intrinsically valuable, in the here and now, regardless of their consequences. For most people, money is an instrumental value, and fairness, love, and

EXHIBIT 15.1: A NEUROLOGICAL BASIS OF VALUE? RESEARCHERS CLAIM NEUROLOGICAL MECHANISMS ARE ASSOCIATED WITH ECONOMIC CHOICE

A recent issue of *Nature* reported that two Harvard University researchers identified specific neurons in the brains of macaque monkeys that encode food preferences. It has long been known that particular neurons respond to various features of objects, such as hardness, color, or edibility. In this recent study, Padoa-Schioppa and Assad (2006) identified particular neurons in the orbital frontal cortex (OFC) of the monkeys that represented, in a common metric, their preference for various foods. They eliminated the possibility that the neurons were encoding particular features of the objects, actions needed to secure them, or ways to communicate their preferences. Padoa-Schioppa reported, "The neurons we have identified encode the value individuals assign to the available items when they make choices based on subjective preferences, a behavior called 'economic choice.'" He contends: "This result has broad implications for possible psychological models of economic choice. . . . It suggests that economic choice is, at its essence, a choice between goods as opposed to a choice between actions—such as reach to the right to take the apple or to the left to take the orange."

The study, thus, has contributed to the emerging field of neuroeconomics. The results set the stage for better understanding of conditions known as choice-deficit disorders (e.g., eating disorders, compulsive gambling, substance abuse) that display abnormal propensities to make certain choices. As is the case with many studies, this research raises at least as many questions as it answers. How is the information on preferences encoded into the neurons? How is it changed? Are abstract or general values, such as justice, love, and freedom, likewise correlated with specialized neurons; are there additional layers that aggregate many concrete preferences into a general value; or are there entirely different mechanisms through which such values are encoded and processed in the human brain?

human dignity are examples of core values. A critical point is that the same value, say, diversity, may be a means to an end for some; for others, it may be something to be sought regardless of its consequences.

C. Individual and Social Values

Although many people think of values as primarily individual, an extensive body of social science research and theory is based on the notion that values are social and cultural, held in common by groups and societies but expressed in a variety of ways by individuals. A complex systems perspective, in contrast, emphasizes the interplay between individuals and larger groups: groups have a massive impact on the socialization of individuals, especially the young, to hold common values, and individuals introduce new values or redefine or repudiate existing values. It is the exceptional individual who is able to step outside of a tradition and introduce entirely new perspectives, such as Anwar Sadat, the Egyptian president who successfully led his nation to a peace treaty with Israel, one that went against the professed values of most of those in his social environment (Sheehy, 1991).

D. Professional Values

Researchers who have examined the question of whether professional groups have common values report mixed results. For example, some of those who have studied the values of social workers have concluded that such professionals hold few values in common; that is, their values reflect the values of the larger population. Others, such as Ann Abbott (1988), have reported that although social work values may not be dramatically different from those of the larger population or other professional groups, social workers nevertheless share a distinctive or core set of values. Abbott used factor analysis to analyze the agreement or disagreement of hundreds of social workers with 121 value statements (e.g., "Those in need of long-term care should be maintained in the community as long as possible," p. 151). Through this analysis, she identified four primary or core values held by most social workers:

- *Respect for basic rights:* All those values directly pertinent to life, liberty, and the pursuit of happiness, including the value of human life and human dignity, justice and procedural rights, and fundamental rights, such as those involving control of one's body, and in general, direction of one's own life.
- *Sense of social responsibility:* This involves one's sense of mutuality and interdependence with others, the notion that one is responsible not only for one's own actions but also for supporting the welfare of others to the extent possible. This has also been referred to with the Greek term *charitas*.
- *Commitment to individual freedom:* This value includes the freedoms of speech, assembly, and religious freedom, and various other political, economic, and cultural types of freedom.

• *Support of self-determination:* This final value builds on individual freedoms and emphasizes the support for more active use of these freedoms in individual decision making, whether this be through voting, participation in the governance of social agencies, or facilitation of the active choices of clients in taking advantage of social and economic opportunities (pp. 25–28).

Depending on the level of experience of the social workers and on the particular professional comparison group used, Abbott's research reveals a mixed picture. For example, seasoned social workers had significantly higher scores on all of the values than did similarly seasoned business professionals, but there was no significant difference in scores compared with those in the field of psychology. In addition, social workers' sense of social responsibility and individual freedom scored significantly higher than those working in medicine, education, and nursing, whereas the only difference with lawyers was social workers' greater sense of social responsibility. Nonetheless, although there are statistically significant differences between professions, the extent of the differences is extremely modest, and there is considerable overlap between the value orientations of these groups. The greatest single difference involved the value of social responsibility, for which social workers had a mean score of 38.2 and those in business had a mean score of 30.4. Thus, it is clear that while any professional group has its own unique profile of values, the stated values are only minimally predictive of the actual choice of profession or of the profession's effects on its members. This suggests that values should be considered in terms of not only stated positions on the issues of the day but also the extent to which behavior reflects those stances.

E. Values as a Basis for Understanding Human Behavior

The evolutionary psychologist Stephen Pinker (1997) emphasizes the importance of understanding goals, which are closely linked with values, through an example of a young man who sets off across town to visit his mother. There are many possible analyses of this man's psychosocial history, family relationships, financial situation, competing commitments, and urban traffic patterns in attempting to understand his travel behavior, but none of these analyses can compete with the specific understanding generated by simply asking, "Why are you taking this trip today?" His answer may not tell the entire story (e.g., does he want to care for her, or perhaps is he desperate to borrow some money?), but it dramatically narrows the field of possible explanations. Likewise, values and their associated processes are powerful explanatory constructs, especially when they can be articulated, but they also leave much unsaid.

III. Ethical Decision Making

Values primarily concern ends, but the focus of ethics is the acceptable means to achieve those ends. Ethics are the standards of conduct that guide decisions and actions, and they are often based on responsibilities and duties derived from core values. Ethics, thus, define the permissible parameters of behavior of both individuals and groups. Jane Addams (1905) once commented, "Action indeed is the sole medium of expression for ethics." (p. 273). It is through ethical action that values may be realized.

Ethical action is typically understood as guided by various ethical injunctions, such as "Act towards others as you would expect them to act toward you," "Obey the law," or "If you cannot accept it, then attempt to change it." Although in many contexts these propositions are communicated informally or by word of mouth, many of the human service professions have codified and published them in their codes of ethics (e.g., the National Association of Social Workers). The problem is that many rules, often broadly framed, derive from different groups and cultures, are subject to interpretation, and often conflict with one another. For instance, ethical principles affirmed through international treaties usually prohibit torture of prisoners, but some government officials may argue that torture is permissible if it involves the prevention of terrorism. Because of such a simplistic, rule-based approach to ethics, many have argued that the focus should be on the process of ethical decision making, on those skills and principles that support the analysis of complex ethical dilemmas, and on the development of coherent resolutions. Ethical dilemmas are conflicts between two or more equally compelling ethical principles in a situation where core values are at stake and the resolution of which is not obvious. Rushworth Kidder suggested that ethics concern the balance of right versus right. Of course, what may be an ethical dilemma for some may not be a dilemma for others.

A. Approaches to Ethical Decision Making

Socially shared principles and systems intended to support their application and the resolution of conflicts characterize ethical decision making. Ethical decision making involves informal practices, such as consultation, and formal processes, both quasi-legal and legal, involving mediation and adjudication. Professional ethics committees, research review committees, and hospital bioethics panels are a few such examples. In recent years, the field of applied ethics—which has developed out of the once-separate fields of medical, business, legal, philosophical, and professional approaches to ethics— has emerged in support of efforts to facilitate ethical decision making.

B. Cultural Dimensions and Hypernorms

There are unresolved issues involving the social dimensions of ethical decision making, such as the extensiveness of ethical norms across cultural and national boundaries. One school of thought is that all ethical principles are specific to particular cultures and contexts. What is considered bribery in one context is regarded as the cost of doing business in other places. In recent years, several theorists have developed the integrative social contracts theory (Donaldson & Dunfee, 1994, 1999). Among other things, this theory proposes that when fundamental values are not at stake, individuals seek to abide by local ethical norms, engaging in ethical decision making relativistically. However, the theory also hypothesizes that when fundamental values are at stake, individuals give priority to hypernorms, or norms that concern abiding to norms. These are characterized as "principles so fundamental to human existence that . . . we would expect them to be reflected in a convergence of religious, philosophical, and cultural beliefs" (Donaldson & Dunfee, 1994, p. 265). They are sets of "standards to which all societies can be held—negative injunctions, most likely, rules against murder, deceit, torture, oppression, and tyranny" (Walzer, 1994, p. 10). A recent study by Spicer, Dunfee, and Bailey (2004) examined the extent to which American businesspeople working in the United States and in Russia drew on local or universal standards in their responses to a series of vignettes involving ethical dilemmas. The study found that in situations that threaten only local norms, the positions of local and foreign businesspeople were significantly different, whereas with those involving hypernorms, there was little divergence of positions between local residents and foreigners. One still-undeveloped part of the theory is an adequate system for defining and operationalizing a comprehensive listing of hypernorms.

Likewise, transpersonal theorists have often emphasized the possibility of universal values and ethical norms. For instance, Ken Wilber (2000) proposes grounding ethics in the consideration of three types of values: (1) ground, (2) intrinsic, and (3) extrinsic. All beings and things, he argues, have ground value (what deep ecologists call "intrinsic value") in that each being and thing is a radiant manifestation of the divine; exists in its own right; and in this respect, is of equal value to all other entities. In contrast, he regards the intrinsic value of a being as the value of "its own particular wholeness, or its own particular depth" (p. 354). In short, the more evolved, complex, and conscious a being is, the greater is its intrinsic value, because the more of the "Kosmos" (which Wilber defines as the physical, psychological, and spiritual cosmos) is enfolded within its being. Thus, a human has greater intrinsic value than a crayfish, and a crayfish has more than an amoeba, but all three have equal ground value. Wilber goes on to point out that, because each "holon," or each being, is not only a whole but also an interdependent part of a larger system, it also has extrinsic or instrumental value to the extent that it supports others, and both their ground and intrinsic values. The three types of value logically entail both rights and responsibilities of all living beings in relation to one another. Replacing a unidimensional conception of intrinsic value with such a tripartite concept of value provides a basis for balancing and ultimately simplifying some of the seemingly insoluble ethical conflicts that emerge from the simplistic application of traditional values involving equality and equity.

C. Ethics and Social Theory

Ethical decision making is grounded not only in universal values, as well as socially shared norms and hypernorms, but also in various ethical theories deriving from a range of philosophical and spiritual perspectives. While some people adhere to particular theories, most attempt to integrate several of the following:

- *The utilitarian approach:* Decisions made on the basis of this framework maximize positive outcomes and minimize harm, however these might be defined. The approach focuses on consequences and on achieving the greatest balance of good over harm for the greatest number of people. It attempts to be pragmatic but can easily devolve into a tyranny of the majority over minorities, who must bear the brunt of many policy decisions. It sidesteps many difficult issues, such as the balance of different types of benefits, the importance of individual and group rights, and the equal distribution of benefits.
- *The rights approach:* A focus on rights represents an effort to correct some of the deficiencies of the utilitarian approach. Some ethicists propose that ethical action is that which most effectively protects and respects individual rights. It is concerned not only with outcomes but also with process. Its central concern is avoiding harm to

individuals and deprivation of their liberty, and its secondary concern is to maximize the common good. Rights include due process of law, freedom of religion and of speech, the right to consent to medical procedures, and so on. This approach assumes that the common good follows from the maximum protection of rights.

- *The fairness or justice approach:* For some people the preeminent principles are those that involve equality and equity. Aristotle and other Greek philosophers emphasized the importance of treating all equally (at least all who are considered citizens). If literal equality is not possible, then people should at least be treated equitably or fairly, such that rewards and punishments are given out on the basis of some defensible principle, such as the value of their contributions, the risks they take, or the heinousness of their crimes.
- *The common good approach:* Another approach, also promoted by some ancient Greek philosophers, is that ethical action promotes the quality of community life and relationships. This goes beyond the bean counting of the utilitarian approach to consider the quality of relationships. Proponents of this perspective suggest that the quality of a society can be determined by the way it treats its most vulnerable members. The approach goes beyond the utilitarian approach in considering society as a collective of individuals to emphasize the conditions central to the welfare of all, whether social welfare programs, public education, or universal health care.
- *The virtue approach:* The virtue approach emphasizes fundamental virtues such as honesty, thrift, fidelity, truth, and beauty. To the extent that actions embody such virtues, they are considered inherently ethical. For some, the virtue approach is spiritually grounded in the notion that humans are created in the image of God and that ethical actions are those that approximate such divine qualities. Similarly, for some humanists, ethical action actualizes the highest human potential. This perspective emphasizes process and the quality of actions in the here and now, and it discounts judgments made on the basis of distant outcomes (Velasquez, Andre, Shanks, & Meyer, 2006).

On the basis of the preceding theories, ethicists have identified various tests or criteria that should be satisfied before it can be concluded that a particular decision is ethical. Several of these can be either as general criteria for qualitative judgments or incorporated into a structured instrument for assessing the degree to which an individual is confident in a particular decision

---

Exhibit 15.2: Examples of Ethical Tests

The following are examples of tests or ethical criteria often used in the analysis of ethical dilemmas. In general, the assumption is that the solution chosen is the one that best satisfies all criteria. A central problem is weighting. For example, what if one alternative meets all criteria at a high level but completely fails a critical test (e.g., fairness) and another meets all criteria but only at minimal levels. Which one is chosen?

1. **Relevant information test:** Has all relevant information concerning the alternatives and their consequences been obtained?
2. **Involvement test:** Have all key parties been consulted or involved in this decision?
3. **Consequential test:** Have the likely outcomes of key alternatives been identified? If so, with what level of confidence?
4. **Fairness test:** Would key stakeholders perceive the proposed solutions as fair?
5. **Institutional values test:** Does the proposed solution respect the values of any organizations involved in its implementation?
6. **Universality test:** To what extent can the principles involved in the proposed solution be applied universally to like situations?
7. **Light-of-day test:** How would this proposed solution be seen by significant others (e.g., family, colleagues, supervisors) if its details become widely known?
8. **Legal test:** Is the proposed solution legal? How has this been determined?

Notes: The eight generic tests identified here are summarized from a survey of Doug Wallace and Jon Pekel, Twin Cities consultants in the Fulcrum Group.

(see exhibit 15.2). These include the relevant information and involvement tests to determine whether all available information and participants have been consulted. In the spirit of the utilitarian approach, the consequential test examines whether all consequences have been understood and accepted (see Wallace & Peckel, 2006). The fairness test is concerned with whether each participant agrees that results are fair or equitable. The universality test asks whether the envisioned solution upholds widely held values. In contrast, the light-of-day and legal tests are more concerned with whether the proposed solution will be viewed as acceptable in the immediate political, cultural, and legal environment. Although this list of tests provides a useful guide, it is not foolproof. One might rate an alternative as high on all tests except for the consequential test, and thereby engender considerable confidence in the option under consideration. However, there might be unanticipated consequences with horrendous outcomes, such as considerable loss of life. For this reason, some recommend considering worst-case scenarios and conducting sensitivity analyses on the impact of being wrong about the underlying assumptions of unknown circumstances.

D. Process Models of Decision Making

Finally, several models have been proposed that emphasize the process of ethical decision making. Reamer and Conrad (1995, as cited by National Association of Social Workers, 2009) apply a model of rational decision making to ethics, emphasizing the need for thorough deliberation and consultation. Although, for the purpose of simplicity, they present their recommended steps in a linear or sequential fashion, they clearly recognize that such decisions are developed in an interactive and iterative manner.

1. Determine whether there is an ethical issue or/and dilemma. Is there a conflict of values, or rights, or professional responsibilities?
2. Identify the key values and principles involved. What meanings and limitations are typically attached to these competing values?
3. Rank the values or ethical principles which—in your professional judgment—are most relevant to the issue or dilemma. What reasons can you provide for prioritizing one competing value/principle over another?
4. Develop an action plan that is consistent with the ethical priorities that have been determined as central to the dilemma. Have you conferred with clients and colleagues, as appropriate, about the potential risks and consequences of alternative courses of action? Can you support or justify your action plan with the values/principles on which the plan is based?
5. Implement your plan, utilizing the most appropriate practice skills and competencies. How will you make use of core social work skills such as sensitive communication, skillful negotiation, and cultural competence?
6. Reflect on the outcome of this ethical decision making process. How would you evaluate the consequences of this process for those involved: Client(s), professional(s), and agency [or agencies]?

Many decisions are fairly simple, straightforward applications of one or a few commonly accepted rules. However, many involve several competing principles and multiple stakeholders, whose interests, rights, and responsibilities may not be clearly defined. It is these decisions that call for more sophisticated models. Kristen Swain (2006) has proposed one such model that incorporates the six stages of moral development as identified by Kohlberg (see Swain, chap. 5). In this model, the preferred alternative is the one that best fulfills criteria associated with the higher stages of moral development, such as those that emphasize the social contract (stage 5), and especially universal rights and principles (stage 6). The model begins with the careful definition of the dilemma and identification of stakeholders; moves on to the development of a system for examining alternatives and an application of moral development theory; and concludes with comparison, decision, implementation, and the monitoring of results (see figure 15.1).

FIGURE 15.1: THE APPLICATION OF MORAL DEVELOPMENT THEORY TO ETHICAL DECISION MAKING: SWAIN'S COMPREHENSIVE JUSTIFICATION MODEL

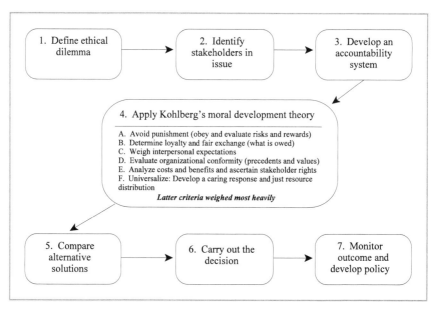

Note: Swain (2006) points out that more complex models are needed when (1) one is confronted with ambiguous problems; (2) the stakes are high, or (3) there's a need to comprehensively consider all known options for all the known stakeholders. Her proposed model involves a series of decision criteria that roughly correspond to Kohlberg's six stages of moral development (Kohlberg & Gilligan). She argues that the optimal solution doesn't necessarily meet all the criteria, but instead is the one that best meets the criteria associated with the higher stages of development.

IV. Spiritual Dimensions of Human Behavior

Attempts to define values and ethics reveal that these are often embedded in spirituality, a subject that we will now turn to. The human services have their roots, on the one hand, in the naturalism and materialism that motivated the development of the sciences, including psychology and the social sciences, and on the other hand, in the major religious traditions. In recent years, the development of a broader understanding of spirituality, which encompasses formal religion yet reaches beyond it, has minimized the historical split between these two realms of human experience and activity.

A. Definitions of Spirituality and Religion

Spirituality is generally understood as a person's or group's relationship with their highest or deepest values, and how those values are understood, experienced, and lived in everyday life. It includes beliefs about the purpose of life, as well as its origins, its place in the universe, and destiny. Until the 1960s the term *spirituality* was associated with spiritualism, but since the 1960s the term has been dramatically redefined. It is often associated with the recognition of an inner force, the human spirit, at the root of motivation and creativity. Émile Durkheim (1965) characterized this inner life as a transcendent religious force that is actualized "in and through" the individual person so that it becomes "imminent in them. . . . [T]hey feel it present and active within them" (p. 253). Edward Canda (1988), a contemporary writer on spiritual issues in social work, similarly defined spirituality as "the human striving for a sense of meaning and purpose through moral relations between people and ultimate reality" (p. 30). He argues that spirituality should not be limited to the nonphysical world but is a part of loving relationships between people, as well as part of the interplay between human limitations and suffering.

In contrast, definitions of religion usually emphasize the formal doctrinal and ritual dimensions of organized religious groups, but sometimes they also touch on the theme of an inner spiritual life. Durkheim (1965), for instance, defined religion as "a unified system of beliefs and practices relative to sacred things, that is to say, things set apart and forbidden—beliefs and practices which unite into one single moral community called a Church, all those who adhere to them" (p. 62). Stark and Glock (1968) proposed a multidimensional typology of religion involving the doctrinal, the intellectual, the ethical-consequential, the ritual, and the experiential. The assessment of the religious orientation of any particular individual or group, thus, needs to consider the extent that it emphasizes received doctrines, intellectual exploration, the application of religious and ethical principles in everyday life, the enactment of rituals, or the inner experience of communion with an all-embracing reality. Stark and Glock (1968) broke down the ritual dimension into devotional and public ritual, and emphasized that their distinction of religion along multiple dimensions was not the same as distinguishing religions. Yet the notion of religion as multidimensional is not without controversy, as some believe that this minimizes the idea that each religion needs to be taken as an integral whole.

B. Pervasive Role of Spirituality

In the various human service professions, work with clients around spiritual or religious issues has often been treated as taboo. In both the United States and Western Europe, this reticence to consider spirituality is usually attributed to both the impact of modernism, with its accompanying scientific naturalism, and the strict separation of church and state. Yet in the United States, the vast majority of Americans are affiliated with religious traditions, and data indicate that, for many people, spirituality plays a central role in their lives. Andrew Greeley (1987) reported that most Americans have acknowledged having had mystical experiences. One study reported that almost four-fifths (79%) reported having had peak or ecstatic experiences (Davis, Lockwood, & Wright, 1991). In another study, Hardy (1979) obtained from more than four thousand survey respondents personal accounts of their religious experiences. Close to one-fifth reported a sense of certainty or enlightenment (19%) or visions (18%); one-ninth, a sense of purpose behind events (11%); and fewer respondents mentioned contact with the dead (8%), voices (7%), exaltation or ecstasy (5%), and telepathy (4%).

Thus, there are probably few, if any, areas of human behavior that are not either overtly or covertly influenced by an individual's or a group's spirituality. On the one hand, the strengths and resiliency of many, including their care for others, their fortitude, or even their sense of humor, can be directly traced to their spiritual beliefs and experiences. On the other hand, much psychopathology has been associated with immature, rigid, or narcissistic religious or spiritual beliefs. The profile of an individual's spirituality—involving his or her particular beliefs; ethical principles; rituals; and inner experiences of understanding, love, and a sense of efficacy and interconnection with the larger world—is both a cause and a consequence of the individual's developmental trajectory. The interplay between a person's spirituality and his or her developmental trajectory results in that person's distinctive motivational dispositions and personality, as well as his or her patterns of problem solving and decision making.

C. The Relationship Between Psychology and Spirituality

Psychology, and more generally the human services, has had a love-hate relationship with spirituality. This is reflected through several prototypical stances taken toward spirituality. For many people, this relationship has been one of conflict, with each seeming to offer mutually exclusive explanations of human behavior. The position of conflict has usually led to an enforced separation: human service professionals are socialized not to concern themselves with matters of faith. This position often assumes a type of agnosticism about matters of faith. In contrast, some people within the various human service professions have taken a more active stance in attempting to explain spiritual and religious phenomena in psychological or even physical terms. Whereas Freudians often take a stance of psychological reductionism that attempts to explain religious sentiments as reflecting an inappropriate carryover into adulthood of unresolved issues in the individual's early relationship with parents, evolutionary psychologists have attributed the notion of a divine force to the action of the so-called God gene (Hamer, 2005). A less common stance regards psychological conflicts and dynamics as masked expressions of spiritual struggles. For instance, the psychological dynamics involved with personal identity formation are viewed as either the explicit or the implicit effort to realize a spiritual self (e.g., Taylor, E., 1999). Still others prefer to think of psychology and spirituality as being in dialogue, each contributing a different interpretive frame for understanding human experience. In this stance, both realms partially overlap and potentially enrich one another.

There are also a variety of combinations of the previously mentioned perspectives. One might, for instance, believe that all psychological drives and conflicts are spiritual ones at root, yet be reluctant to actually use spiritual terminology to describe these issues. Starting where the client is at may preclude active discussion of the spiritual dimensions of the client's presenting problems. Yet in other instances, dialogue about the spiritual dimensions of problems may be called for, such as when the client consciously struggles with such issues. The term *psychology* originally referred to a kind of science of the soul when it began as a subdiscipline of theology in the sixteenth century. Psychology was later treated as a subdivision of anthropology, or the science of people, which also included somatology, or the science of the body (Vande, 1986).

After a considerable hiatus in attention to the spiritual dimensions of human behavior, some of the most respected figures in the history of psychology, such as William James, Gordon Allport, Erich Fromm, Viktor Frankl, Abraham Maslow, and Rollo May, rediscovered the role of spirituality in

TABLE 15.1: STAGE THEORIES OF MORAL AND SPIRITUAL DEVELOPMENT

	KOHLBERG: MORAL DECISION MAKING
Infancy	
Early Childhood	Preconventional: punishment and obedience
Middle Childhood	Preconventional: Instrumental exchange
Older Childhood	Conventional: Interpersonal relations/conformity
Adolescence	Conventional: Social order/laws
Early Adulthood	Postconventional: Social contract/utility
Middle Adulthood	
Older Adulthood	Postconventional: Universal rights/principles

Note: The combination of several stages in a single cell in the bottom part of each column connotes uncertain or exceptional progression.

FOWLER: FAITH	WILBER: CONSCIOUSNESS
Primal Faith: Trust in the universal or God	Sensoriphysical: Body-oriented awareness
Intuitive-projective faith: Creative fantasy	Preoperational: Fantasy-emotional centeredness
Mythic-literal faith: Loyalty to community and representational beliefs	Late preoperational: Symbolic representational thinking
Synthetic-conventional faith: Personalized peer referenced beliefs	Concrete-operational: Autonomous but comformist
	Formal-operational: Sophisticated rationality
Individuative-reflective faith: Critical reflection	Vision-logic: Holistic inclusivity
	Psychic: Communion with world
Conjunctive Faith: Complex and pluralistic	Subtle: Communion with divinity
Universalizing faith: Nonjudgmental, transcendent, and inclusive	Causal: Formlessness, no separation
	Nondual: Union

everyday life. Abraham Maslow (1963), for instance, argued that once individuals are able to find satisfactory solutions to "prepotent" needs involving physical safety, security, self-esteem, and social inclusion, they are able to progressively address their needs for self-actualization and self-transcendence. Yet others have criticized this as simplistic, ignoring considerable data on the active spirituality of many children as well as on individuals undergoing major economic deprivations such as homelessness.

D. Stage Theories of Spiritual and Faith Development

Several theorists have sought to understand the development of spirituality, whether defined narrowly as faith or more broadly as involving various states of consciousness. Carl Jung (1921/1971) characterized this process as one involving individuation, which he believed most commonly began in the second half of life. He explained that it entailed the reconciliation and integration of split off and unconscious aspects of the personality, such as the shadow, anima, and animus, with the conscious ego. James Fowler (1996), a Christian theologian, conceived of this process as one of faith development, and he incorporated elements of Piaget's genetic epistemology and Kohlberg's stages of moral development (see table 15.1). He defines faith broadly, as a "pattern of our relatedness to self, others, and our world in light of our relatedness to ultimacy" (1996, p. 21). Faith, he believes, serves to ground ego functioning as well as moral decision making in the individual's relationship with whatever it is that he or she conceives of as of ultimate significance. He conceives faith development as progressing from fantasy and a mythic-literal understanding of religion during childhood to a conventional faith grounded in the attitudes of peers and, for some adults, to an individuative-reflective faith involving critical reflection. A few adults are believed to progress to either a conjunctive or a universalizing faith that is nonjudgmental, transcendent, and inclusive. Others, such as Ken Wilber (2000), have drawn on Eastern mystical traditions and envisioned spiritual growth as a movement from the pre-egoic to the egoic and trans-egoic levels of awareness, to increasing levels of integration, culminating in what he terms *unitary consciousness*.

Depending on how one conceives of spirituality—whether as a relationship with the divine, inner experiences, attitudes of faith, or exemplary moral actions—stage theories of spiritual development take wildly divergent forms. Thus, any of these models should be regarded as suggestive of possible avenues of the development of individuals. Just as is the case for stage theories of adult development, theories of spiritual development confront such an immense diversity of developmental patterns that it has been suggested that this kind of growth is more like that of a bush than a tree, that there are no typical patterns, and that it often proceeds in multiple directions. Nonetheless, when such development takes place, it is usually conceptualized as involving at least one and often several of the following transitions:

- From dependence to independence to interdependence
- From control of others to self-control
- From taking to giving and taking, to giving
- From gaining experience for oneself (e.g., happiness, excitement, spiritual experiences) to a focus on sharing and giving of experience
- From an external to an internal frame of reference
- From a reactive to a proactive stance
- From information to knowledge to understanding and wisdom
- From a sense of meaninglessness to a sense of meaningfulness
- From seemingly directionless change to purposeful, systematic, unfolding and spiritual growth
- From fragmentation to integration and coherence
- From a limited to a shared sense of self, to selflessness

This process can be understood as a multilinear or multicyclical one, that is, one consisting of multiple lines of development and repeated transactions between the individual and his or her relevant environments. It involves the progressive internalization and distillation of understanding obtained through a range of life stages and experiences. Erik Erikson's (1963) identification of trust, autonomy, industry, identity, intimacy, generativity, and integrity as the result or residues of successfully negotiated life stages represent some of the multilayered foundations for spiritual growth.

There may, in addition, be special mechanisms that facilitate spiritual growth. In some traditions, it is believed that the individual needs to develop a type of spiritual ego, or a provisional psychological scaffolding to permit self-reflection and the internalization of any understanding gained. Just as ego psychologists such as Hartman emphasized the development of neutralized energy under the control of consciousness, Don Stevens (1995) has proposed the development of a "neutral plateau" (p. 95) that facilitates nonreactive reflection. This contrasts with many people's experience of overdetermined psychological functions that often manifest in feelings of compulsion, being driven, or otherwise being unable to gain self-control, whether this involves self-destructive habits, worry, or depression.

E. Role of Spirituality in Psychological Functioning

Spirituality can serve multiple functions in the facilitation of problem solving and personal growth, as well as in the oppression of the self and others. William James (1905) hypothesized that there are four different types of religion: (1) supernormal, (2) normal, (3) neurotic, and (4) psychotic. He distinguished between healthy-minded and sick-souled religiousness. The healthy-minded usually are able to ignore the evil in life and focus on the good. He cited Walt Whitman and the "mindcure" religious movement as examples of healthy-mindedness in *The Varieties of Religious Experience*. In contrast, those with a sick-souled religiosity demonstrate little compassion and trust, are punitive toward themselves and others, and evidence little flexibility or initiative in problem solving. A common mistake in the assessment of the role of a person's spirituality in functioning and growth is to assume that if the person is functioning well, then his or her spirituality can be only a positive force; conversely, if the person is experiencing difficulties in functioning, such as mental illness or substance abuse, then his or her spirituality has not served well. In fact, in the first case, the person may do well despite a rigid or archaic spirituality; in the second case, it may prevent more serious decompensation and facilitate recovery. Just as a person with exemplary personal strengths and faith may develop cancer, such a person may also develop a serious mental illness, perhaps due to an unusually severe confluence of personal stresses and biological vulnerabilities. When this happens, the contents of the unconscious—whether unresolved personal feelings carried over from childhood; anger or depression; or internal coping resources, such as faith, insight, or a sense of bliss—may emerge into consciousness, as the integrative capacities of the ego are temporarily disabled.

The importance of understanding client spirituality and its role in resolving or complicating the problems that come to the attention of human service professionals cannot be overemphasized. A central part of this calls for understanding of what spirituality means to an individual or group client: Does it involve participation in a particular religious or spiritual community? Observance of certain rites and rituals? Adoption of a particular theological or philosophical perspective? Living according to particular ethical standards? The experience of communion with a higher reality? Canda and Furman (1999) present a useful paradigm for understanding a person's spiritual propensity, which they define as involving both the degree and the manner that a person expresses spirituality (see figure 15.2). They regard spiritual propensity as consisting of two dimensions: the extent of its religious expression and its intrinsic realization. The first dimension describes

FIGURE 15.2: TYPES OF SPIRITUAL PROPENSITY

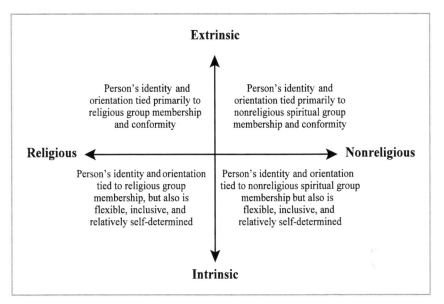

Source: Canda & Furman (1999, p. 274).

those whose spirituality is tied to a particular religious group or is expressed through nonreligious means. The second dimension characterizes those whose spirituality is merely expressed externally through religious or non-religious involvementsor those who are "able to apply spiritual principles flexibly in daily life and who are relatively self-determined in spiritual deci-sion making," regardless of external affiliations (p. 274). Understanding cli-ent spirituality is different from its assessment or evaluation, which implies a comparison with some normative standard. Particular caution needs to be taken in avoiding comparative evaluations involving the worker's personal standards or some imagined social norms. If any comparison is done, it should be only with the client's own standards and ideals, and only in a holistic and empathic manner (i.e., one that recognizes the complex and changing nature of the client's experience). Any comparison also needs to be done with an understanding of the client's ability to form ideals in the first place, ones that motivate growth rather than stifle it.

F. Healthy Aspects of Spirituality

There is an accumulating body of research that has documented the impact of religion and spirituality in the prevention of various conditions

(Larson, Larson, & Koenig, 2000). Benson (1992) reviewed close to forty studies that provided persuasive evidence that people with a strong spirituality are less prone to substance abuse. Similarly, research has shown that spiritual commitment is associated with fewer problems with alcohol (Hardesty & Kirby, 1995), or conversely, those who do not have a strong religious commitment are more likely to abuse alcohol (Gartner, Larson, & Allen, 1991). Lindgren and Coursey (1995) reported that 83% of psychiatric inpatients noted that spiritual belief had a positive effect on their illness. This was partly because it created feelings of being cared for and being connected with a larger reality. Larson et al. (2000), who reviewed much of Lindgren and Coursey's research, concluded that spiritual commitment enhances recovery from depression, serious mental or physical illness, and substance abuse; helps prevent suicide; and reduces overall health risks.

There is also considerable evidence of substantially positive effects of spirituality on mental health (Myers, 1992). However, there is less agreement about the reasons for this effect. Two of the most commonly cited reasons are the connection of the individual to a larger community of similarly inclined individuals and the creation of a sense of meaning and purpose, of a comprehensive narrative that links an individual's life with a community's core values and beliefs. Whereas for many people religion is merely external conformity to a system of beliefs, norms, practices, and rituals, for other people, spirituality connotes direct communion with a transcendent reality, whether this is sought as a goal or experienced as a side effect of a spiritual way of life. Maslow (1962) referred to these as peak experiences (see exhibit 15.3), which he described as

- Very strong, deep experiences, akin to ecstasy
- Deep sense of peacefulness and tranquility
- Feeling in tune with or in harmony with universe
- Feeling of deeper knowing or profound understanding
- Sense of ineffability, of the indescribability of the experience

In his classic work *Variety of Religious Experience* (1905), William James attempted to provide criteria to distinguish genuine spiritual experiences from pathological states. The first that he mentions is ineffability: "The handiest of the marks by which I classify a state of mind as mystical is negative. The subject of it immediately says that it defies expression, that no adequate report of its contents can be given in words" (p. 380). Next he cites their noetic quality. He explains that although they are similar to states of feeling, mystical states are marked by states of knowledge or insight; as he explains, "They are illuminations, revelations, full of significance and

---

Exhibit 15.3: Peak Experience: A First-Person Account of Spiritual Experience

I remember the night, and almost the very spot on the hill-top, where my soul opened out, as it were, into the Infinite, and there was a rushing together of the two worlds, the inner and the outer. It was deep calling unto deep,- the deep that my own struggle had opened up within being answered by the unfathomable deep without, reaching beyond the stars. I stood alone with Him who had made me, and all the beauty of the world, and love, and sorrow, and even temptation. I did not seek Him, but felt the perfect unison of my spirit with His. The ordinary sense of things around me faded. For the moment nothing but an ineffable joy and exaltation remained. It is impossible fully to describe the experience. It was like the effect of some great orchestra when all the separate notes have melted into one swelling harmony that leaves the listener conscious of nothing save that his soul is being wafted upwards, and almost bursting with its own emotion. The perfect stillness of the night was thrilled by a more solemn silence. The darkness held a presence that was all the more felt because it was not seen. I could not any more have doubted that He was there than that I was. Indeed, I felt myself to be, if possible, the less real of the two.

—Quoted in William James,
Varieties of Religious Experience (1902, p. 42)

---

importance, all inarticulate though they remain; and as a rule they carry with them a curious sense of authority for after-time" (pp. 380–381). James also mentions two other criteria, which he considered less critical: the experience's transiency and passivity. He claims that such experiences are almost always transient; that they can rarely be experienced for longer than an hour or two. They are also characterized by a sense of passivity, that they come from beyond, that they happen to the individual, and they are in no way creations of the individual's mind. There is a sense that something objectively real is apprehended, more real than everyday experience.

Closely related with peak experiences is the phenomenon of pit or nadir experiences. These are experiences that typically begin with feelings of profound despair, alienation, or fragmentation, yet may give away to a peak experience of bliss, insight, or recognition of an alternative reality. May (1986) pointed out that transpersonal psychology has often been criticized for ignoring the reality of suffering. Pit experiences can also be profoundly transformative, especially when they involve the dissolution of underlining dysfunctional beliefs and assumptions, perhaps ones involving distrust, self-blame, and alienation. Sometimes pit experiences culminate with a peak experience.

G. Spiritual Crises

Pit or nadir experiences have also been thought of as spiritual emergencies. Two of the leading figures of the transpersonal psychology movement, Stan and Christina Grof, distinguished spiritual emergence from spiritual emergency. They observed that when spiritual emergence or unfolding happens precipitously or dramatically, crisis may ensue, and the result may be a spiritual emergency, often involving some combination of spiritual growth and psychopathology. They explain, "People who are in such a crisis are bombarded with inner experiences that abruptly challenge their old beliefs and ways of existing, and their relationship with reality shifts very rapidly. Suddenly they feel uncomfortable in the formerly familiar world and may find it difficult to meet the demands of everyday life. They can have great problems distinguishing their inner visionary world from the external world of daily reality. Physically they may experience forceful energies streaming through their bodies and causing uncontrollable tremors" (Grof & Grof, 1989, p. 35).

The Grofs have proposed several diagnostic criteria for spiritual emergencies. The primary criteria are ecstatic mood, a sense of newly gained knowledge, perceptual alternations, and any one of several themes related to mythology and the history of religion. These may involve death, being dead, meeting the dead, or meeting death; rebirth, including a new identity and name; journeying or being on a mission; encountering spirits, either demonic or helpful; and cosmic conflict and the emergence of a new age. Of special importance is the theme of divine love and union with God. Prognostic signs of a positive outcome include the absence of conceptual disorganization, good pre-episode functioning, acute onset during a period of three months or less, stressful precipitant to the psychotic episode, and a positive exploratory attitude toward the experience. In addition, the person is not at major risk for homicidal or suicidal behavior.

A limitation of the Grofs' conceptualization of spiritual emergency is that it does not distinguish between emergencies that take place at various developmental stages. In contrast, Roberto Assagioli (1965), the founder of psychosynthesis, hypothesizes that such crises may be dynamically precipitated by ordinary life events or may represent reactions to intense inner experiences and spiritual awakening:

- Crises preceding the spiritual awakening, such as disillusionment with one's usual pursuits or a sense of the unreality and emptiness of ordinary life.
- Crises caused by spiritual awakening: Assagioli explains that "the opening of the channel between the conscious and the superconscious levels, between the ego and the Self, and the flood of life, joy, and energy which follows, often produce a wonderful release," but in many cases, one may be overwhelmed by its "suddenness and intensity" (p. 43).
- Reactions to the spiritual awakening. These occur somewhat later than the foregoing reactions and can involve a wide range of conditions, including self-doubt, or difficulty in assuming the responsibilities of everyday life.
- Phases of the process of transmutation. Assagioli explains that this is like the problem of an engineer who needs to rebuild a railway station without disrupting the usual traffic, and that its difficulty is likely to produce a variety of psychological troubles, such as exhaustion, insomnia, emotional depression, aridity, mental agitation, and restlessness, as well as a variety of physical symptoms and disorders.

H. Spirituality and Psychopathology

Other theorists have recognized that spiritual and psychopathological experiences may be intermixed and have suggested criteria for distinguishing between the two. Lukoff (1995) proposed that two new categories be added to the *Diagnostic and Statistical Manual of Mental Disorders,* suggesting the need for a differentiation between mystical experiences with psychotic features and psychotic experiences with mystical features (see figure 15.3). On the basis of their experience working with an ultra-Orthodox Jewish population in Israel, Greenberg and Witzum (cited in Lukoff, 1985) likewise proposed criteria to distinguish between conventional religious beliefs and experiences arising from psychotic symptoms.

- Psychotic experiences are very personal and may involve special messages from religious figures.
- The details of psychotic experiences exceed accepted beliefs (e.g., they are more intense than normative religious experiences in their religious community).
- The person in a psychotic episode may be terrified by the experience rather than excited by it (fear rather than bliss predominates).

FIGURE 15.3: RELATIONSHIP BETWEEN MYSTICAL AND PSYCHOTIC EXPERIENCES

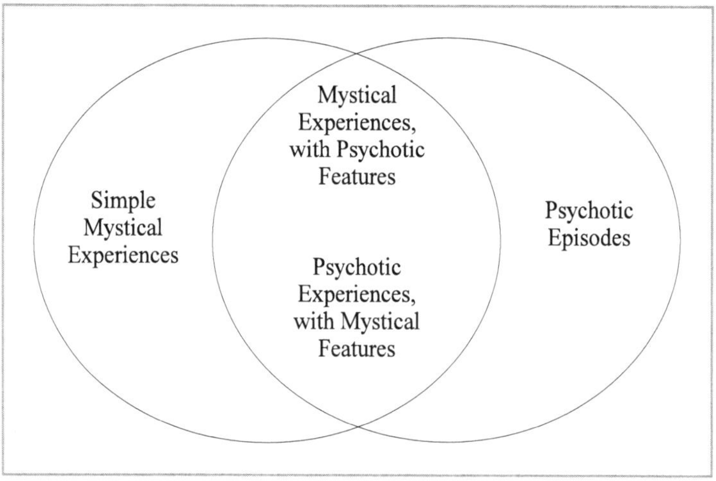

Source: Lukoff (1985).

- The person in a psychotic episode is preoccupied by the experience and can think of little else—preoccupation with the experience rather than the subject or object of the experience.
- The onset of the experience is associated with deterioration of social skills and personal hygiene.

Although Lukoff's distinction to date has not been included in the *Diagnostic and Statistical Manual of Mental Disorders,* in its most recent edition the manual has included several *V* codes for other conditions requiring clinical attention, one of which is "V-62.89—Religious or spiritual problem," which "can be used when the focus of clinical attention is a religious or spiritual problem. Examples include distressing experiences that involve loss or questioning of faith, problems associated with conversion to a new faith, or questioning of spiritual values that may not necessarily be related to an organized church or religious institution" (American Psychiatric Association, 2000, p. 741).

For others, spiritual beliefs and experiences are inherently dysfunctional and limiting of the individual. In *Totem and Taboo* (1913), Freud developed the notion of the Oedipus complex, which consists of unresolved sexual feelings of a son toward his mother and competitive hostility toward his father, and he theorized that religiosity emerges in some of the earliest stages of human development. He then developed his theory of religiosity in *The*

Future of an Illusion (1927), and later he examined biblical history in *Moses and Monotheism* (1939) in light of his theory of psychosexual development. Freud argued that religion functions as a fantasy structure that must eventually be outgrown for maturity to occur. He regarded the idea of God as an outgrowth of an unresolved paternal transference, and religious belief as essentially infantile and neurotic. As much as professionals might like to advance particular interpretations of the role of spirituality in psychological and social dynamics, that is not their job. Rather, they need to support clients in finding their own solutions that are meaningful to them within their own philosophical or spiritual traditions.

V. Spirituality and Professional Practice

The role of spirituality in the human services is not limited to understanding client behavior; it also extends to the understanding of professional practice, particularly its motivating impulse. Unlike the occupations in which the primary motivation is often economic, that of making a living, in the human services the ideal of public service plays a pivotal role. Human service professionals often forego competitive compensation so as to engage in a meaningful activity that promises to be of benefit to others (e.g., counseling people with emotional problems, teaching, caring for the physically ill, building stronger communities).

The notion of public service connotes placing others' interests first and supporting those interests through ethical action involving the best knowledge and skill possible. Professional service also suggests an extended commitment, not only to a particular job but also to a career involving higher education, continued training, and advancing positions and expertise. This kind of direction reflects what was traditionally was thought of as a type of mission or calling. In the East, this has been regarded as an expression of a person's dharma, or the unique path or way that an individual takes in fulfilling his or her potential. The concept of dharma is a broad one and has multiple meanings, one of which entails the concrete activity of charity or almsgiving. The principle of dharma has been said to include the mission of "protecting or salvaging the lowly, the oppressed." It involves the ideal of selflessness, not self-abasement, but a relationship with a deeper, broader, and shared sense of self, beyond the limits of individual identity. It involves a recognition of interdependency, of a synchronicity and simultaneity of interests, rather than a sense of the separateness of individual beings. In many respects, this is a foreign concept in a culture that emphasizes competition and looking out for No. 1.

This is not to suggest that the ideal of selfless service is often realized in practice. Many other motivations attract individuals to the human services. These may involve rescuing others, sometimes thought of as symptomatic of codependency. They may involve a latent interest in working out one's own problems, one's unresolved relationships, through clients, perhaps to impel others to act out one's own pathology. This could involve an attempt to compensate a sense of guilt over previous relationship failures or to vicariously reexperience unresolved trauma in an attempt to master it. It may involve the effort to bolster self-esteem, to control others, or to meet unfulfilled personal needs for closeness and relationships through a captive audience, or simply to obtain a sense of recognition and status. Although many professionals share some of these tendencies, for most these needs are worked through and the worker is able to approximate the ideals of the profession. A key indicator that such needs are not being successfully worked through is an excessive focus on helping or serving others that is not tempered by the recognition of the mutuality of the helping relationship, by the understanding that the professional also substantially benefits from the opportunity to work with others. When such humility does not temper practice, the ideal of service and helping may devolve into a narcissistic and oppressive objectification of clients. Although the human services are sometimes thought of as the exclusive province of helping relationships, such relationships may just as well be realized in other fields, including business, the sciences, or the arts. A safe assumption is that no single occupation or profession has an exclusive franchise on helping relationships, and in none excludes the possibility of helping relationships.

Thus, it is important for professionals to understand the spiritual propensities and beliefs of clients that often form the basis of their difficulties and attempted solutions. It is equally important that professionals understand the spiritual and existential basis for their own work. It is especially critical for professionals to understand the admixture of spiritual and personal issues that motivate their own desires to change others' behavior. When a sense of urgency to intervene and change a person compromises and replaces the ability to simply be present with a person, there is a clear indication that unresolved personal issues have obscured the spiritual foundations for responding to the complex problems that clients present to human service professionals.

VI. Summary

This capstone chapter explores the role of values, ethical decision making, and spirituality in understanding human behavior, specifically, the ability to discover meaning and to realize this meaning in daily life. The chapter treats both values and ethics not as abstract objects, but as living processes, intimately involved with motivation, decision making, and problem solving. The chapter also discusses several contrasting ways of thinking about values, for example, the treatment of values as ideals and the understanding of values as levels of valuation.

The section on values also explores professional values in the human services. It discusses the question of whether human service professions, such as social work, have unique values or whether they share the values of the larger society. The research of Ann Abbott is reviewed, which shows that although there are proclivities to hold certain values, no one profession uniquely holds those values. The values that her study examined involved respect for basic rights, the sense of social responsibility, individual freedom, and self-determination.

Next, the chapter explored ethical decision making as a way to resolve conflicts between competing values and principles, between right versus right. Several approaches to such decisions were presented, beginning with some of the major philosophical stances: the utilitarian, rights, fairness, justice, and virtue approaches. The question of whether all ethical decision making is local and situation specific or whether there are universal standards is discussed. Research suggests that when universal values are not at stake, standards are culture specific, whereas people draw on hypernorms in situations of fundamental human rights. The section discusses several useful ethical tests, such as the consequential, fairness, and light-of-day tests. It also reviews selected process models of ethical decision making, specifically Reamer and Conrad's problem-solving approach and Swain's model, which draws on Kohlberg's developmental stages of moral decision making.

The chapter then considers spirituality, distinguishing it from religion. It defines spirituality as a person's or group's relationship with their highest or deepest values, and how those values are understood, experienced, and implemented in everyday life. It discusses the ambivalent relationship that psychology and the human services have had with spirituality, including enforcement of a complete split between the two realms, attempts to reduce one to the other, or facilitation of a dialogue between the two. In recent years there has been growing interest in spiritual and religious diversity as an essential element of practice in the human services.

Where chapter 5 considered the stages of moral development, this chapter extended the material and presented several theories of the stages of faith and spiritual development, specifically, those of James Fowler and Ken Wilber. It then explored the role of spirituality in psychological functioning, both its positive and its negative contributions. The section cites the work of

William James, who hypothesized that there are four different types of individual religiosity: supernormal, normal, neurotic, and psychotic. The chapter considers the role of peak and specifically spiritual experiences as well as their essential characteristics, such as their ineffability and noetic quality. It then discusses spiritual crises, or pit experiences, and finally Lukoff's work in distinguishing mystical from psychotic experiences. The section also discusses the work of Roberto Assagioli, who points out that spiritual crises vary considerably on the basis of whether they precede, accompany, or follow spiritual awakening. The chapter concludes with a discussion of spirituality and professional practice, particularly, motivations for entering helping relationships. It emphasizes the importance of workers having full understandings of their own motivations in undertaking such work.

For Further Reading

Abbott, A. A. (1988). *Professional choices: Values at work.* Silver Spring, MD: National Association of Social Workers.

Canda, E. R., & Furman, L. D. (1999). *Spiritual diversity in social work practice: The heart of helping.* New York: Free Press.

Carpendale, J. I. (2000). Kohlberg and Piaget on stages and moral reasoning. *Developmental Review, 20,* 181–205.

Dass, R., & Gorman, P. (1997). *How can I help? Stories and reflections on service.* New York: Knopf.

Fowler, J. W. (1996). *Faithful change: The personal and public challenges of post-modern life.* Nashville, TN: Abingdon Press.

Freud, S., & Krug, S. (2002). Beyond the code of ethics, part I: Complexities of ethical decisionmaking in social work practice. *Families in Society: The Journal of Contemporary Human Services, 83*(5–6), 474–482.

Grof, S., & Grof, C. (1989). *Spiritual emergency: When personal transformation becomes a crisis.* Los Angeles: Tarcher.

Larson, D. B., Larson, S. S., & Koenig, H. G. (2000, October). Research findings on religious commitment and mental health. *Psychiatric Times, 17*(10), 25–54.

Lindgren, K. N., Coursey, R. D. (1995). Spirituality and serious mental illness: A two-part study. *Psychosocial Rehabilitation Journal, 18*(3), 93–111.

Reamer, F. G. (1995). *Social work, values, and ethics.* New York: Columbia University Press.

Taylor, E. (1999). *Shadow culture: Psychology and spirituality in America.* Washington, DC: Counterpoint.

Glossary

Accommodation. Jean Piaget's term for the adaptation of existing mental representations or maps to novel situations or to the creation of new representations.

Adhocracy. One of Henry Mintzberg's organizational types that involves changing, flexible, and often-overlapping work teams designed to respond to changing needs.

Allopoietic systems. Complex systems that lack the ability to learn and adapt and that operate through preset decision rules or algorithms.

Archetype. An ideal example, prototype, or primordial image. Much of Carl Jung's psychology was based on the notion of the archetype, a fundamental pattern of thought that derives from collective human experience. He proposed that archetypes operate through the personal unconscious, animating thought and psychological functioning. They manifest recurrently in dreams, myths, and literature (e.g., the Madonna-child motif, superman, pilgrimage).

Assimilation. Jean Piaget's term for the taking in or adapting of one's perceptions and environment to existing mental representations. In diversity studies, *assimilation* is an immigrant group's adoption of the culture of the new society.

Attractors. Dynamic patterns that a system usually settles into, typically expressed through graphs in nonlinear dynamics and chaos theory. The patterns exhibit some degree of structure that is fixed and predictable or only approximately repeating within general bounds (i.e., strange attractors).

Autopoietic systems (or autopoiesis). Self-organizing and self-regulated systems that can alter internal instructions to adapt to new conditions and to self-produce and replicate.

Avolition. A mental state involving a pervasive lack of desire, drive, or motivation. Avolition is one of the four negative symptoms of schizophrenia, where it is frequently encountered. The other symptoms are flat affect, alogia, and anhedonia.

Axiology. A branch of philosophy concerned with the study of values.

Bifurcation. A splitting of a dynamic process into two subprocesses. "The term bifurcation is commonly used in the study of nonlinear dynamics to describe any sudden change in the behavior of the system as some parameter is varied. The bifurcation then refers to the splitting of the behavior of the system into two regions: One above, the other below the particular parameter value at which the change occurs" (Hilborn, 1995, p. 13).

Biocultural diversity. Cultural diversity (e.g., ethnicity, language, religion) considered in the context of biological characteristics and the overall diversity in biological environment, or biodiversity.

Blindsight. A rare neurological condition in which the subject experiences blindness, but nevertheless has access to information gained through sight, for example, the location of specific objects.

Bureaucratic rationalization. The systematization of decision making and other procedures in organizational settings with the aim to ensure fairness, accountability, and transparency.

Chaordic. Dee Hock's term for organizations and other systems that can creatively capitalize on edge-of-chaos phenomena involving a particular combination of chaos and order.

Chaos theory. The study of dynamic processes that exhibit three features: (1) sensitivity to initial conditions, in which small differences in initial conditions typically lead to dramatically different results, (2) patterned processes, in which behaviors are repeated only within general bounds, and (3) nonrepeating processes, in which exact trajectories are never repeated.

Coevolution. The concurrent evolution of multiple individuals or species based on the mix of their ongoing cooperative or competitive relationships and that may incite a kind of evolutionary arms race.

Coherence theory of truth. The idea that truth involves systems of propositions that are consistent among themselves, with some foundational principles, or with greater society.

Complex systems. Defined by Varela and Coutinho (1991) as systems formed by a large number of discrete elements that are highly interconnected in nontrivial forms.

Conation. That part of the mind that involves the will and ability to form intentions.

Consciousness. In this book, a sense of existence or awareness accompanied by some level of knowledge, feeling, and intention (there is no generally agreed-on definition). The awareness or sense consists of the ability to recognize, register, or otherwise apprehend something, either an aspect of self or an aspect of some object or objects, or other state, whether material or immaterial.

Correspondence theory of truth. The idea that what is true is what best corresponds with or mirrors an external reality.

Cross-catalysis. In chemistry, catalysis is the effect of some substance to stimulate or expend a chemical. Cross-catalysis happens when the resulting products of two or more different processes stimulate or energize each other. In recent years cross-catalysis has been a metaphor for interlocked social or psychological processes that stimulate one another.

Cultural lag. A theory proposed by William Ogburn that attempts to explain problems in social development as a function of the gap between cultural and technological development.

Culturally competent practice. A set of practice skills, knowledge, and attitudes that must include five elements: (1) awareness and acceptance of difference, (2) awareness of one's own cultural values, (3) understanding of the dynamics of difference, (4) ability to adapt practice skills to fit the cultural context of the client or patient, and (5) development of cultural knowledge (Weaver, 1999).

Cybernetics. The science or study of control or regulatory mechanisms in both human and machine systems, such as computers. Norbert Wiener coined the term, made popular by his 1948 book *Cybernetics or Control and Communication in the Animal and the Machine.* He based the term on the Greek word *kybernetes,* meaning "steersman" or "governor."

Decalage. A gap in the level of development of various abilities. Jean Piaget's idea of horizontal decalage is the tendency for people to rely on the most highly developed abilities during a given period of development to scaffold development of other less developed abilities. Vertical decalage is the partial appearance of a new cognitive structure during a stage before the time at which it is ordinarily encountered.

Deduction. Logical reasoning that involves inferences from general propositions to specific conclusions. For example, obesity is defined as a person being 30% or more over the ideal body weight. Johnny is 40% over his ideal body weight. Therefore, Johnny is obese.

Deep ecology. A broad, holistic approach to the study of ecology that includes psychological, social, cultural, and spiritual dimensions of ecology, as well as purely physical, biological, and behavioral dimensions.

Democide. The murder of any person or people by a government, including genocide, politicide, and mass murder (Rummel, 1994).

Diaspora. A dispersed community or ethnic group that originated from a common land and continues to maintain cultural identification and traditions.

Diathesis. A predisposition or area of vulnerability that individuals have to certain types of stress, which may result in the development of various conditions, such as mental illness. The term *risk factor* is more commonly used.

Discrimination. Unfair, unjust, and/or malicious actions on the part of a dominant group toward a minority group, which results in the deprivation of rights, liberties, or entitlements. Discrimination is typically based on prejudices and stereotypes.

Dissipative structure, system, or process. An open system that operates at far-from-equilibrium conditions and that exchanges energy or matter with its environment. Such systems are often characterized by the spontaneous appearance of novel structures. Ilya Prigogine originally used the term to refer to nonequilibrium open systems.

Double-loop learning. Learning that consists of changing or developing new values, goals, philosophies, or action rules or principles, in contrast to simply learning new behaviors or habits.

Downward causation, or back action. The influence of a system as a whole on its component parts.

Ecomap. Graphic representation of an individual's interrelationships with his or her most important individuals, groups, institutions, and other environmental entities (see figure 1.4).

Ecosystems theory. The application of systems theory to the study of populations and their relationships with their environments.

Elitism, theory of. theory of political and community decision making in which decisions are assumed to be the outcome of collusion between small groups of high-status decision makers. In plural elitism, multiple elites are involved only when issues arise pertaining to their particular areas of interest.

Emergence. Minimally, the development of novel properties of systems that, when considered as a whole, cannot be explained or predicted given the characteristics of the component parts or precursor systems.

Entrainment (also slaving, or phase locking). The tendency of periodic patterns, when sufficiently replicated, to create a threshold effect that then spreads to other systems (Gleick, 1987). It involves the naturally occurring synchronization of the rhythms of the processes of multiple objects or persons.

Entropy. A law based on the second law of thermodynamics that states that all energy tends to flow from heterogeneous and organized states toward maximum homogeneity and disorganization—from the least probable to the most probable.

Epigenetic. Anything that develops or unfolds in a biological manner, with each final function or ability reflected in an underlying plan (often genetic) that is implemented in approximately predetermined phases as the appropriate conditions come into play.

Epiphenomena. Phenomena considered incidental, derivative of a more fundamental reality, and a type of illusion, or at least an emergent characteristic of the more fundamental material (e.g., some consider consciousness an epiphenomenon of brain processes).

Epistemology. The study of knowledge that has been traditionally a branch of philosophy but is increasingly a part of many professional disciplines. Epistemology is concerned with questions of what can be known and how knowledge is best developed.

Equifinality. The fact that systems often accomplish the same ends or produce the same outputs through widely divergent means, including both inputs and intervening processes.

Equilibration. From Piaget's developmental theory, the balancing of demands of adaptation to the external environment, including accommodation and assimilation, with the demands of maintaining internal coherence or organization.

ERTAS (Extended Reticular Thalamic Activating System). A system of brain structures that many theorists believe is central to understanding consciousness.

Ethnology. Another term for cultural anthropology, or the study of societies in terms of their shared understandings based on social transactions.

Ethnocentrism. The attitude that one's own culture, religion, or ethnicity is a superior standard, perhaps God given, that needs to be protected from defilement or even imposed on others.

Ethnoconvergence. The process of multiple cultural or ethnic groups becoming like one another or merging through such means as cultural transmission or intermarriage.

Etiology. The study of the origins or causes of medical and psychiatric conditions, usually involving the earliest discernible conditions that initiate a cascade of events that eventually results in a condition. Such causes can be genetic abnormalities, traumas, toxic substances, environmental deprivation, or some combination of those.

Eudaemonic. Pertaining to the inner self or spirit.

Eustress. A term Hans Seyle coined for stress that is healthy and that represents an achievable challenge.

Evolutionary drivers. Laws, principles, or forces that function to direct and/or energize the evolution of new physical, biological, or social forms.

Evolutionary epistemology. The study of knowledge building in the context of evolutionary processes, often emphasizing competition among theories and survival of the fittest. The philosopher Karl Popper first promoted the idea.

Existential phenomenology. A type of radical empiricism that attempts to describe phenomena purely in terms of direct experience and eschews the use of theory.

Fallibilism. Karl Popper proposed this approach to knowledge building as an alternative to verificationism and inductivism in particular. Knowledge is developed not through the inductive accumulation of observations and subsequent generalization but through active efforts to falsify hypotheses and theories using both observation and critical reasoning.

Feedback loops. Reciprocal, interactive, or two-way relationships that either maintain stability or amplify minor influences to create major, unpredictable changes. They may involve intentional communications or purely biological or physical transactions.

Feminist epistemology. An approach to epistemology that studies both how traditional approaches to knowledge building systematically oppress women and the identification of alternative approaches.

Field theory. Karl Lewin's theory that the understanding of human behavior requires understanding the total field, or "lifespace," of that behavior, before examination of underlying behaviors.

fMRI (functional magnetic resonance imagery). A recently developed technique that allows the visualization of activity in the brain and other parts of the body as it actually takes place.

Fractals. Abstract visual representations of some of the iterative mathematical calculations used to characterize chaotic processes (see figure 1.7).

Functionalism. A group of theoretical approaches from such fields as sociology, psychology, and anthropology that attempts to understand its subject (e.g., groups, individuals, psychological functioning) in terms of the role, job, or effect they perform or have on the larger system that they are part of. In mathematics a function is a formula that relates an input with an output (see definition of structural functionalism herein for the sociological version).

Gaia hypothesis. A theory proposed by James Lovelock (1979) that hypothesizes that Earth's biosphere functions as a single, interdependent organism to actively transform its physical environment.

Gemeinschaft. Communities, sometimes referred to as locational communities, which are based on primary relationships between family and neighbors, such as in rural villages. Relationships are valued intrinsically, not as a means to an end.

General systems theory. A theory developed by Ludwig von Bertalanffy in the 1940s that focuses on understanding the ways that systems maintain equilibrium, using information theory, cybernetics, and various other approaches.

Genocide. The systematic killing of people by a government because of their membership in a racial, ethnic, or linguistic group (Rummel, 1994).

Gesellschaft. Coined by Ferdinand Toennies (1957), the term refers to communities based on instrumental purposes and in which membership arises out of a shared purpose. They are sometimes referred to as identificational communities.

Goal displacement. A phenomenon observed in many organizations when, for example, enduring goals involving the development of a quality product or service are lost sight of and replaced with a concern for personal or organizational survival, or simply the repetition of some familiar process or procedure. Means become or displace ends.

Group (or small group). Distinguishable groups of individuals who interact to achieve valued ends, however well or ambiguously defined. Thus, small groups are different from crowds, communities, institutions, and populations.

Haplogroup. All the descendants of the individual who first showed a particular kind of mutation, or single-nucleotide polymorphism. Such mutations define groups with a common ancestor far back in time. Because the mutations are extremely rare, they are useful only for identifying groups that have developed over a time span of tens of thousands of years. Haplotypes are subtypes of haplogroups.

Hard problem of consciousness. The difficulty of understanding the subjective qualities, or qualia, of consciousness, how is it that one experiences a sense of existence, and the unique qualities of experience.

Heisenberg uncertainty principle. A proof in quantum physics that demonstrated the impossibility of knowing both the position and the momentum (or other pairs of attributes) of a particle simultaneously, thus demonstrating fundamental limits to human knowledge.

Hermeneutics. Traditionally, the interpretation of and dialogue about the meaning of religious texts and, as a result of dialogue, the continual updating of interpretations (or theories). Social constructivists have used the metaphor of hermeneutics to describe the processes of interpretation, dialogue, the use of narratives in knowledge building, and psychotherapy.

Heuristic. First, as an adjective, it refers to the ability of a theory or activity to generate new hypotheses, theories, or avenues of research. Second, as a noun a heuristic is a simplified rule of thumb, trick of the trade, or other similar aide to professional decision making.

Hierarchical complexity, or hierarchization. A principle of organization found in many complex systems, such as the brain, in which there are multiple levels, each nested within progressively more encompassing forms of organization.

Holarchy. Introduced by Ken Wilber, the idea that naturally occurring structures are organized by a hierarchy of holons, which are parts that are simultaneously wholes. Every living being or holon is both a part and a whole, and consists of systems of holons on finer levels of organization.

Homunculus. An imaginary "little man," or center of consciousness, that some believed was centered at a specific location in the brain to observe and control its activity. The metaphor, proposed by René Descartes, is now only spoofed.

Hypernorm. A core norm or standard of behavior that governs when to adhere to a given norm and, alternatively, when to invoke more universal norms as guides.

Hypothetical-deductive approach. A prevailing conception of the scientific method that involves the formulation of theories and hypotheses, deduction of consequences that should follow, the systematic testing of predictions or consequences using empirical methods, and the revision of original theories and hypotheses given the outcomes of the tests.

Incompleteness proof. Kurt Godel's proof that demonstrated that it is possible to have a complete mathematical system or a consistent one, but not both at the same time.

Inductivism. An approach to knowledge building, specifically to logical inference, which relies on the simple accumulation of observations and the generalization of patterns from such observations, without preliminary theories or hypotheses.

Institutionalism. A term with diverse meanings depending on the context. Irving Goffman, who studied the debilitating effects of total institutions (e.g., mental hospitals, nursing homes, prisons) on their long-term residents used the term to refer to a syndrome of passivity and hopelessness that often develops in such environments. In political science, institutionalism is an approach that regards political parties as having some ability to adapt and as being molded by their own original ideology and subsequent history. *Institutionalism* also is used to mean the uncritical acceptance of the role of institutions in social life.

Intersubjectivity. A widely used term with several meanings; however, it most often refers to the process of two or more persons coming to agreement about a set of meanings or about the way some reality is framed.

Iteration. Not only the general processes of repetition, feedback, or approximation but also a mathematical technique of feeding back the results of an equation, one that describes a relationship, into a repeated calculation of the same equation for subsequent periods.

Knowledge base. In the human service professions, the body of theory, empirical research, practice wisdom, and procedures widely recognized and used in a given profession.

Lamarckism. A theory advanced by the French biologist Jean-Baptiste Lamarck on the heritability of acquired characteristics, or the notion that an organism can develop characteristics during its lifetime and pass these on to its offspring.

Libido. A term used in the psychoanalytic tradition that refers to sexual energy or tension.

Logical positivism. An approach to knowledge building that says that only statements that referred to observed realities can be regarded as meaningful; thus, ideas in ethics, metaphysics, and religion are regarded as meaningless.

Logical types, theory of. A theory, advanced by Bertrand Russell, which attempted to find way to avoid paradox by forbidding statements that refer to themselves. The theory proposes that in any logical or mathematical system, statements should be clearly distinguished from one another on the basis of their hierarchical reference to other statements. Statements of a more general logical type cannot refer to themselves but only to those of a lower type, typically, those that are more concrete.

Lyapunov coefficient. A statistical index from nonlinear dynamics that indicates how stable or chaotic a time series or system is. If it is less than 1, the system is stable and predictable. If it is close to 0, it is at the edge of chaos. If it is more than 0, it may fulfill the criteria for deterministic chaos and for being nonrepeating.

Means-ends analysis. An approach to problem solving used in areas as diverse as information technology, management, social work, and engineering. It involves first describing or understanding the current state of a problem, the goal, and the difference between the two. This in turn is used to define a means to be implemented for achieving the goal. Once the means is implemented, the current state and goal are again compared, and the process is iteratively repeated until the goal is achieved.

Memetics and memes. A recent approach, introduced by Richard Dawkins, to evolutionary epistemology that studies the transmission and replication of ideas or memes among individuals and societies and emphasizes the role of social selection in knowledge and cultural development.

Meta-analysis. A set of statistical and research methodologies to aggregate the results of a collection of similar research studies.

Metacognition. An approach to problem solving that involves the ability to step back from a difficult problem and to think about the approach to that problem. When a direct solution cannot be found, sometimes the problem solvers need to analyze their efforts at problem solving. In short, it is the ability to think about thinking.

Metacommunication. Communication about communication. The exchange of information about the communication process itself and, in general, the relationship of the communicators. This may be fully conscious but is often an unconscious and indirect exchange of information, positive or negative, about the preferred relationship among those speaking.

Microtubules. Protein structures in cells that are believed to have structural, regulatory, and information-processing functions. Evidence has accumulated that these structures are central to understanding consciousness.

Mindfulness. The practice of living fully in the present and accepting life as it is, with a heightened yet tranquil state of awareness. Mindfulness originated in the Buddhist tradition but has been applied in recent years to diverse fields.

Model. A term with many meanings, most of which involve a fairly specific operational rendition of a theory. Models typically reflect how a general theory functions in practice or how it might be applied to a particular problem.

Moral hazard. The possibility that an unintended side effect of insurance—and various forms of social welfare and social support—is to encourage people to purposely engage in risky behavior, given the expectation that compensation, medical care, or other forms of support are forthcoming.

Motivation. Complex psychological functions that serve to energize and direct goal-directed behavior. Motivation may serve underlying biological drives and other needs, and it typically has multiple dimensions, including the biological, psychological, and social.

Multifinality. The possibility that the same system inputs may lead to widely divergent, multiple outcomes.

Mutual aid, theory of. An early theory of evolution that Peter Kropotkin proposed that it is not so much competition but cooperation between individuals and species that drives evolution.

Natural selection. The theory of Charles Darwin that suggested that evolutionary changes are driven by the operation of differential environmental conditions, in conjunction with variation from genetic mutation and recombination, in selecting new successful adaptations.

Negentropy. The idea that as energy flows toward disorder (entropy) it also creates greater order in the process.

Neurological correlates of consciousness (NCCs). The discovery of NCCs is a goal of consciousness studies, especially for those working in the neurosciences.

Neuronal gating. The function of various brain structures in regulating the activation of neurons, by limiting their activity, directing it, or bringing them into synchronization, through any one of several means.

Neurotransmitters. Complex molecules that are released in the gaps or synapses between neurons and transmit information from one neuron to the next creating either an excitatory or an inhibitory effect. There are many different types of neurotransmitters, each serving specific functions.

Node. From network theory, centers or units that are connected to one another (e.g., individuals, families, organizations, any number of other types of entities).

Nonlinear dynamics. In dynamics, or the study of how systems change, changes that involve nonproportional effects of an input variable on an output. Most such systems involve iterated or repeated application of certain rules of transformation.

Nonlocality. Causal connections between systems that are spatially or temporally disconnected and rely not on local interactions but on some type of synchronicity. A phenomenon observed in quantum physics that many have hypothesized is relevant for understanding coincidences, simultaneous cultural developments, or psychic phenomena.

Nucleation. A concept that originated in chemistry and refers to the initiation of physical changes at discrete points in a system, for instance, the formation of bubbles or crystals. More generally, it refers to the seeding of development and change, the formation of the initial informational conditions that govern the subsequent growth or evolution of the system.

Optimization. An approach to problem solving that involves the iterative effort to adjust one or more input values to maximize outcomes of interest.

Orch-OR theory. The theory of orchestrated objective reduction, proposed by Stuart Hameroff and Roger Penrose, as a means of addressing the hard problem of consciousness through the application of quantum theory, quantum computation, and microbiology.

Outsource. The practice of companies, including governmental and social agencies, of transferring responsibility for a good or a service to outside individuals or organizations. This may be done through a wide range of purchasing, contracting, and fee-for-service arrangements.

Norms. In contrast to roles, somewhat more specific rules, usually applying to particular situations. They may be prescriptive or proscriptive, defining what needs to done or what is unacceptable.

Paradigm. Broad systems of belief that are often not consciously held. They usually inform a more delimited area of activity, such as scientific investigation, law, or human services.

Phenomenology. Originally a philosophical movement introduced by Edmund Husserl that focused on the study of conscious experience, bracketing off assumptions, theories, and considerations of an objective reality to the extent possible. Since then, phenomenology has been applied as a methodology in numerous fields such as psychology and sociology.

Pluralism, theory of. The theory of political and community decision making that holds that decisions are a function of the interaction, involving both conflict and compromise, of multiple interests and groups, with no single party dominating the process.

Politicide. The murder of any person or people by a government as a result of their politics or for political purposes (Rummel, 1994).

Practice wisdom. Typically regarded as the body of practice principles, rules of thumb, and tricks of the trade that are a central part of a profession's culture and typically passed down from supervisor to supervisee, and from colleague to colleague.

Pragmatic epistemology. An approach to knowledge building introduced by

William James and John Dewey that emphasized the successful application of knowledge in problem solving as a critical criteria for its validity. They believed that the world is never passively perceived but is understood only through its active manipulation.

Prejudice. Negative and emotionally charged prejudgments made about other groups on the basis of little or no information other than generalized group membership or superficial criteria.

Prepotency. Associated with the motivational theory of Abraham Maslow, the tendency of some motivations to become salient only after others have been met.

Psychoneuroimmunology. A relatively new field of research involving the many interactions between psychological and neurological functioning and the body's immune system, for example, the possibility that states of anxiety and depression may suppress immunity to disease.

Psychosynthesis. An alternative approach to psychoanalytic psychotherapy developed by Robert Assagioli, which seeks to provide clients with active help in setting goals, integrating diverse elements of experience, and strengthening the will rather than simply self-understanding.

Pygmalion effect. The impact of social expectations on individual performance, often observed in experiments involving teachers and students.

Racism. Attitudes that are rooted in an ethnocentric attachment to one's own race, negative stereotypes of other racial groups that are animated by distrust, revulsion, and hate, and are acted out through discriminatory and persecutory behaviors, whether informal practices or the use of formal legal and bureaucratic means to distance, depreciate, or disempower members of rejected racial groups.

Reductionism. From philosophy, a practice in many fields to attempt to explain complex, multidimensional phenomena in simplistic terms, reducing them to a single type of explanation. For example, psychological reductionism may attempt to explain social relationships simply in terms of psychological motivations; economic reductionism may try to explain economic decisions purely in terms of rational calculations of individuals or organizations. Another example is biological reductionism.

Resiliency. The ability to recover from trauma or other difficulties, to bounce back.

Salient need. In social work, the concern, need, or interest of the client that is most current, pressing, and of greatest strategic value in addressing the wider array of problems that may be present.

Scapegoating. When an individual or group discriminates against another individual or group through active blaming, recrimination, and negative typecasting, often to deflect responsibility for some failure and place the burden of change or compensation on a particular party.

Schemes (also known as schemata, schemas, or mental maps). Mental representations or constructions that are mentally organized sets of related knowledge.

Self-organization. The spontaneous development of order in a system, with little or no control from external sources, often through cumulative effect of the rules governing local interactions.

Self-selection. The propensity of humans to select themselves for particular relationships, activities, occupations, or life courses before, in lieu of, or in conjunction with the selections of the environment, either through social or natural selection.

Self-similarity. A property of fractals and complex systems in which similar patterns are found to naturally occur on many system levels, or levels of magnification, though not necessarily in precisely the same manner.

Sensemaking. The combination of processes required to arrive at principled and informed understanding and decision making. It may entail searching for documents that are relevant for the task at hand and then, in an interactive and dialectical manner, interpreting and reframing meanings until they are coherent and useful.

Servicetization (or servicization). The shift of economic activity in contemporary society from extractive industries and manufacturing to the provision of services to individuals and organizations, broadly understood as ranging from personal care (e.g., laundry, hairdressing) to professional services (e.g., legal, therapeutic, design).

Set point. In cybernetics and general systems theory, a standard that controls or switches feedback processes on or off depending on the divergence between an actual state of the system and some standard, ideal, or set point. Illustrated by the setting of a desired temperature on a home thermostat. Set points are common not just in electrical or mechanical systems but also in biological and social systems, albeit in many other forms. Set points may, for example, consist of optimal levels of hydration, body heat, activity, or intimacy.

Situatedness. In Varela's theory of embodied action, the many ways that consciousness is embedded with and interacts with the body and the larger social, cultural, and physical environments to form an essential though changing part of its functioning.

Social capital. The reservoir of goodwill, trust, working relationships, and other psychosocial and cultural strengths of a community that can be drawn on in community problem solving and ongoing development.

Social constructivism. A theory of knowledge building that rejects the notion of truth as correspondence to an external reality and instead analyzes it in terms of what knowledge communities subscribe to, or its viability.

Social Darwinism. A philosophy, introduced by Herbert Spencer, that applied Darwin's theory of natural selection to society, suggesting that virtually any kind of mutual support or social welfare serves only to perpetuate unfit individuals and degrade the human race.

Social institutions. Organizations and communities but, more fundamentally, the set of cultural memes, the fundamental ideas, practices, and protocols, that become implemented and replicated through diverse social structures and processes, from small groups to national policy systems. Examples of common social institutions are the family, church, economy, and government.

Social welfare system. The institutional and social systems that transfer cash, goods, or services to people who need support because of physical or mental illness, poverty, age, disability, or other defined circumstances. This includes natural helping systems, such as families, religious groups, and work organizations such as unions and professional associations; the formal systems of income transfer (e.g., income maintenance, progressive taxation); and the formal human services.

Spiritual syncretism. The integration of old and new elements, whether beliefs or practices, from diverse religious and spiritual traditions to develop and adapt existing practices to changing conditions.

Standard Social Science Model (SSSM). A term coined by Tooby and Cosmides to refer to a pervasive orientation in the social sciences in which social development is viewed as proceeding largely independently of or, at most, under only very general constraints of biology, and that behavior is best understood in terms of environment and social learning.

Structural coupling. The linkage of lower-order systems through feedback loops to create higher-order systems.

Structural functionalism. An early sociological approach to the study of society that emphasized the examination of the relationships of parts and wholes and focused on the functions of social institutions. Its central idea is that social systems are best understood in terms of the functions or needs that they fill.

Synapse. A gap between neurons, specifically, between the dendrites and axons, across which signals are passed, most commonly through neurotransmitters (e.g., dopamine, serotonin) and less often through direct electrical or quantum-tunneling connections. The nature, type, and operation of synapses control information flow between the various parts of the brain and nervous system, and thus have dramatic implications for the type of consciousness experienced, the capacity for problem solving, and the kinds of mental illnesses that might be encountered.

Tacit knowledge. Unarticulated, preconscious knowledge that is nonetheless accessible.

Tautology. A circular logic. If A, then B. If B, then A. A definition is said to be *tautological* if one term is defined in terms of itself (e.g., "A tautology is a statement that is tautological"). Although tautologies are usually to be avoided, it has been argued that many cultural systems (e.g., law) consists of meanings, rules, and principles that define one another ultimately in circular terms.

Technostructure. One of the dimensions of organizational structure that includes the structure of technical specialists, including the supporting infrastructure, such as information systems, research and development facilities, and related social and physical systems needed to support the implementation of technology in accomplishing an organization's objectives.

Teleology. The belief that natural processes are shaped or directed toward some end, purpose, or design.

Temperament. "Constitutionally based individual differences in reactivity and self-regulation, influenced over time by heredity and experience" (Clark & Watson, 1999, p. 399).

Theory. A formal and informal conceptual framework with which we organize our beliefs and knowledge in a communicable, testable, and potentially useful manner.

Transrational. Approaches to knowledge development that emphasize the importance of alternative forms of knowing, such as intuition, tacit knowledge, and dialogue, and deemphasize traditional rational and empirical methods.

Triangulation. The simultaneous use of both quantitative and qualitative methodologies to enhance the validity of a study. In family and group dynamics, triangulation also refers to dysfunctions that develop in relationships involving threesomes. For example, this might involve the roles of victim, persecutor, and rescuer that shift among players as the dynamics evolve, or it may simply involve the destabilization of a couple's relationship when a third party becomes inappropriately involved. Sometimes this second meaning of triangulation is also called triangling.

Value. A reference to an assessment by an individual or a group of something of worth or of some ideal.

Verificationism. A school of thought that takes as its point of departure the principle of verification—for a proposition to be meaningful, it must be empirically supported—proposed by A. J. Ayer in *Language, Truth and Logic* (1936).

Worldview . Very general perspectives, often expressed in philosophies and religions, of the world, the purpose of life, and humankind's place in it.

Zone of proximal development. A term used by Lev Vygotsky to refer to partially developed abilities that still require the support of a more experienced mentor or teacher for continued development.

Appendix: Quantum Approaches to Consciousness

I. Introduction

Perhaps more than any other issue, it has been the hard problem of accounting for qualia, the subjective aspects of consciousness, that has motivated many investigators to look at consciousness in light of the new physics, specifically quantum theory. The neurosciences have been based largely on assumptions of classical Newtonian physics. This nowantiquated paradigm assumes that it is only physical reality that has any meaningful existence, and that this reality can be objectively observed and understood when reduced to its basic elements, with the help of science and mathematics. It minimizes—some say, banishes—the role of consciousness. And very important, it envisions the world in atomistic terms, as changing only through the local interactions of its component building blocks. Many have concluded that this view—especially the minimized role of the observer or of the consciousness—is what underlies the many difficulties in solving the hard problem of consciousness.

As an alternative, quantum theory is attractive for several reasons. It is regarded as a more general master theory, within which Newtonian mechanics is a special case. It is far more predictive than Newtonian mechanics; in fact, its predictions are the most accurate in the history of science, as they are consistently correct to nine or more decimal places. But it also demonstrates that no measurement or understanding of a phenomenon is independent of the observer, of the consciousness of one who studies it. Thus, some understand that quantum theory establishes that consciousness is an integral aspect of reality, not simply an epiphenomenon of physical processes, a kind of secretion of the brain. Although parts of quantum theory are considered deterministic, quantum theory as a whole is probabilistic, leaving open the possibility of free will. Moreover, both the theory and associated experiments in the field of quantum mechanics demonstrate that the world cannot be understood through a dichotomous logic or local atomistic interactions; rather, it consists of multiple simultaneously existing realities, and ones that involve nonlocal causal connections that transcend time and space as commonly understood in the classic view. These features of the theory make it an ideal candidate for solving the binding problem, as well as understanding human volition and the subjective aspects of consciousness. But before reviewing a few of the applications of quantum theory to the study of consciousness, this appendix first introduces a few of the central concepts of the theory.

II. Quantum Theory

Quantum theory was first introduced in the 1920s in an attempt to resolve anomalies in thermodynamics and a long-standing debate between advocates of the particle and the wave theories of matter and energy. Electromagnetic and other forms of energy could be explained alternatively as patterns of particles or waves. Early quantum theorists demonstrated that it was not a choice between either of these concepts, but that both were simultaneously true: physical reality demonstrates both wavelike and particlelike characteristics. This, it was found, depends on the nature of the measuring devices used. If one looked for particles, they would be found, and if one looked for waves, they would be found. The initial pioneers also reformulated the model of the atom. Previously, the atom was regarded as a miniature solar system, with electrons orbiting the nucleus. Now, the electrons (and other particles) were treated as clouds of probabilities. The equations governing particles showed that they are undefined, in multiple states, within a loosely defined area or cloud, until they are observed, at which time they randomly manifest as discrete particles at specific locations, without physical movement between the locations. Quantum theory received its name from the fact that the manifestations, or quantum jumps, occurred in discrete or quantified orbits or states, depending on the energy involved and the presence of other particles. The finding that particles are in multiple or superposed states simultaneously, until they are observed, has now been repeatedly demonstrated through double-slit experiments in which even single photons simultaneously pass through two separated slits in a barrier to create an interference pattern, in the same way that populations of particles and waves do when they pass through the separate slits.

One of the early breakthroughs of quantum physics was Werner Heisenberg's (1927) discovery of the uncertainly principle. Heisenberg proposed and verified a simple equation governing all subatomic particles that demonstrates that it impossible to know with certainty both the location and the momentum (as well as other variables) of a particle at the same time: the more exactly one knows one piece of information (e.g., location), knowledge of other variables (e.g., momentum) becomes increasingly uncertain. This is not just a matter of measurement error or uncertainty but is a problem of superposition, where the particle is in multiple states—locations, energies—simultaneously. The Heisenberg uncertainty principle explains electron tunneling, or how under certain circumstances when electrons meet a barrier they are annihilated and then almost simultaneously remanifest on the other side. Perhaps because quantum theory includes the effects of observation and captures in its mathematical equations phenomena such as uncertainty and superposition, it paradoxically represents a remarkably precise science, permitting computerization, nuclear power, lasers, and many other technologies that underlie the current information economy.

A few of the central notions of quantum theory, such as superposition and nonlocality, may be central to understanding consciousness. Nonlocality is a type of superposition in which particles or other objects affect one another regardless of temporal or spatial distances or any conceivable physical interaction. Since the inception of quantum theory, nonlocal relationships between particles has been one of the theory's central predictions. Such relationships Einstein found particularly objectionable, calling them "spooky action at a distance." In a classic article by Einstein, Podolsky, and Rosen (1935), the authors proposed an experiment to test the prediction of nonlocality. In the 1960s, Bell (1964) offered a mathematical proof of nonlocality, but it was not until 1982 that existing technology permitted an experimental test. Aspect, Grainger, and Roger (1982) were the first of many to experimentally confirm nonlocality and also disprove alternative explanations that hidden variables might be involved. Specifically, he examined the case of pairs of photons that become entangled and then separated, yet retained an instantaneous ability to covary in their spin, with no possibility of any physical connection between them. A common interpretation is that when particles are entangled, they are actually the same particle, manifesting at different points in time and space.

Counterintuitive phenomena from quantum physics, such as superposition, have been extensively debated. One of the founders of quantum physics, Erwin Schrodinger, stimulated much of this debate with his proposed thought experiment concerning a cat (see Gribbon, 1985). Imagine a closed box, inside of which is a particle-emitting source. The particle has a 50–50 chance of being emitted. Also in the box is a Geiger counter that registers such an emission. If the particle is emitted, the Geiger counter, which is attached to a food dispenser, causes poisoned food to drop into a dish and kills an adjacent cat. If not, wholesome food is released and the cat lives. Quantum physics demonstrates that the particle, until observed or measured, is in all locations allowed by the Schrodinger equation at the same time, emitted and not emitted. If this is so, the cat should be simultaneously dead and alive until someone opens the box, at which time the particle will be emitted or not emitted, and the cat either dead or alive. Although quantum theory demonstrates a bizarre world on the level of microphysical processes, most of these anomalies do not manifest on the macrophysicial level that we observe in our everyday life, where cats are either alive or dead, but not both.

How can this contradiction between an experimentally verified theory and common sense be resolved? Most physicists are content to use mathematics for practical purposes and not worry about the interpretation and some of the more bizarre implications. Another approach, which has now been almost universally rejected, has been to assume that with superposed phenomenon, the multiple states are simply mathematical possibilities or artifacts with no superposition on either the micro- or macrophysical levels. However, it has been amply demonstrated that multiple superposed states can have real physical effects. Another minority but increasingly popular position among physicists is that superposition not only is real but also governs both microphysical and macrophysical phenomena. This has been referred to as the multiple universes interpretation, and it suggests that there is an unimaginably large collection of universes, each slightly different from the next (see Deutsch, 1997). There are innumerable variations of you and me in many of these universes. Although this interpretation resolves the mathematical contradictions, most reject it because of its implausibility.

Most scholars believe that there is some kind of split, so that microphysical phenomena are superposed, but then in our macrophysical world, there is some kind of reduction or collapse of the multiple states to a single, consistent, noncontradictory reality. But so far no one has been able to adequately define where this split is made, or how and why it happens. Proposals involve a given level of complexity, the presence of sufficiently conscious beings, the presence of chaotic and irreversible processes, the size of the system, or some objective physical process. Roger Penrose (1994), for example, theorizes that gravity operates between the multiple realities or dimensions, and that the larger a superposed system becomes, the more quickly it will collapse to a single coherent reality in the dimensions we are familiar with.

Although a small system of atoms or molecules may collapse in not much less than a second, something as large as a dead and an alive cat would collapse to a single reality in nanoseconds or less. Penrose has proposed a space-based experiment to verify this theory, but it is yet to be conducted. Thus, although there is a developing acceptance of the existence of such a split—below which multiple superposed realities exist and above which they are somehow reduced or collapsed to a single reality—how or why this collapse happens remains an open question. Penrose points out that while basic quantum-superposed processes, governed by the Schrodinger equation, are deterministic, the phenomenon of collapse is neither deterministic nor random.

An anticipated application of quantum theory is quantum computation. Researchers have developed algorithms and programs based on the rules of quantum mechanics. These programs capitalize on the superposition of states, using the various superposed possibilities for massively parallel computations. The approach draws on the notion of qubits instead of bits, as is the case with digital computers. Instead of a bit assuming the value of 1 or 0, a qubit can assume multiple values at the same time, such as 1, 0, 1; and 0, 0, 0; and so on. Some of the initial applications expected are search algorithms and code-breaking programs that capitalize on the tremendous power of quantum computation to factor the large numbers on which many encrypted codes are based. Each time a new technology is developed, it has been often observed, the metaphors of the new technology have been applied to understanding the human brain. At first, the brain was considered a hydraulic system; later, a kind of digital computer; and increasingly, a massively parallel electro-optical quantum computer. Thus, quantum theory, particularly the notions of nonlocality, superposition, and collapse, are beginning to assume a pivotal position in a number of approaches to the study of consciousness, as it is hypothesized that quantum computation, including nonlocality and superposition, may provide a possible solution to the binding problem, difficulties in understanding memory and vision, volition, and the subjective aspect of consciousness.

III. Initial Approaches

Since the early years of quantum theory, physicists such as John von Neumann and David Bohm have noted the possible relevance of quantum theory to an understanding of consciousness. The apparent effect of human observation on the behavior of particles brought about an abiding intuition that consciousness may be a fundamental aspect of the physical world, or even that the physical world itself may be an expression of consciousness. In the 1970s authors such as Fritzof Capra, in his popular book *The Tao of Physics* (1975), speculated on the relevance of quantum theory. But this remained speculation and philosophy until the 1980s, when several developments in related fields started revealing some of the specific ways that quantum processes, involving superposition and nonlocality, might be associated with conscious experience. These included developments in microbiology, the study of the brain, and Richard Feynman's suggestion about the possibility of quantum computation in the early 1980s.

Several of the initially proposed theories by physicists, such as Amitai Goswami (1995) from the University of Washington, and Henry Stapp (1993), from the University of California at Berkeley, involved global states of brain superposition. Stapp suggested that conscious states correspond to activity in large portions of the brain that are superposed, and that upon collapse, these states generate successive moments of conscious experience. He explains that the central idea of his theory is that there are, similar to events in measuring devices, quantum reductions in the brain that bring about experience. Each state corresponds to a large-scale pattern of neural activity that is experienced as the basis for that initiated by that pattern.

Unfortunately, these theories did not identify the specific biological processes involved. But a more formidable problem is demonstrating that superposition can take place on such a large scale. Although there is little debate that superposition is relevant to microphysical systems, even systems of large proteins, it is unclear how extensive the systems can be.

One of the earliest biological mechanisms proposed that might support nonlocal and superposed states of consciousness is the ion pumps associated with the propagation of electrical charges in neurons. Herbert Frohlich (1968), a founder of superstate physics, formulated a model of a system of coupled molecular oscillators in a heat bath supplied with energy at a constant rate. When the energy exceeds a given level, a condensation of the whole system of oscillators happens in a manner similar to a Bose-Einstein condensate. This creates a coherent, nonlocal, superposed state in the system. The most critical feature of Bose-Einstein condensates is that the component parts not only behave as a whole but also actually become the whole. An analogy for this is a group of dancers all moving as a harmonious whole (Zohar, 1990). While Bose-Einstein condensates were predicted for many years, it was not until 1995 that their existence was experimentally verified.

Quantum processes have also been identified in several other locations relevant to the neurological correlates of consciousness. Evan Walker (2000) is renowned for his discovery of gap junctions between neurons. In most of the synaptic junctions that link successive neurons, the major mechanism involves the release of complex molecules called neurotransmitters that serve to either stimulate or inhibit the firing of the connected neuron. However, Walker discovered that between 5% and 15% of neurons are connected by gap junctions that involve direct electron tunneling between cells. Electrons, when they arrive at the synapse, disappear and reemerge on the other side of the boundary. The almost-instantaneous speed of these connections permits assemblies of such interconnected neurons to function as single units, unimpeded by the relatively slow speed of neurotransmitters used in ordinary synapses. Thus, this process potentially supports the spread of superposed processes to sufficiently large systems of neurons to make plausible a connection with conscious experience. Recent studies of such gap junctions have found that they are particularly prevalent in the pathways that connect the thalamus and cortical regions, ones that traditional researchers believe are critical to understanding consciousness (Micevych & Abelson, 1991).

Perhaps the most important system within which superposed processes of quantum computation may take place is the microtubules of each cell (see figure A.1). These are complex systems of proteins initially believed to serve only a structural function, but more recently they have been shown to transmit and process information, essentially to serve as a kind of intracellular nervous system. Two Japanese investigators, Mari Jibu and Kunio Yasue (1995), have hypothesized that, of the many ways that microtubules process information, the most important may take place within the cores of these hollow cylindrical structures. When they become sufficiently stimulated, the proteins emit a type of coherent light called superradiance, similar to the light from a laser, into the core. This superradiance then can not only pass through their hollow cores but also jump from one microtubule to the next through the related process of self-induced transparency, in which the coherent or laserlike light creates a kind of transparency within the surrounding protein structures. The photons in such coherent beams are in a state of nonlocal superposition. Although the existence of superradiance and self-induced transparency is established, their relevance to consciousness and mental information processing is yet to be verified.

IV. The Orch-OR Theory

Probably the best-developed application of quantum theory in consciousness studies is that proposed by Stuart Hameroff, an anesthesiologist at the University of Arizona, and Roger Penrose, a mathematical physicist at Oxford University (Hameroff, 1994; Hameroff & Penrose, 1994, 1996). They

FIGURE A.1: SCHEMATIC DIAGRAM OF LAYOUT OF MICROTUBULES
AND ASSOCIATED MAP STRUCTURES WITHIN NEURONS

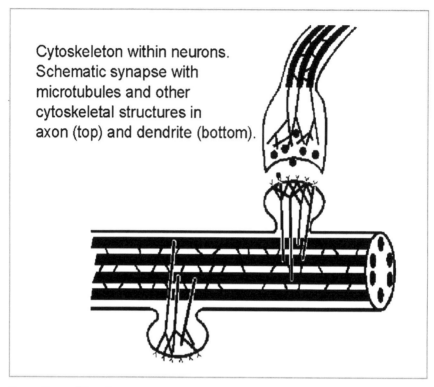

Cytoskeleton within neurons.
Schematic synapse with
microtubules and other
cytoskeletal structures in
axon (top) and dendrite (bottom).

Source: Hameroff (1997).

refer to their approach as the Orch-OR theory because of two of its central
ideas. The most critical is objective reduction (OR), a particular perspective on how the collapse of superposed quantum states happens. This is of
central importance because they propose that the pulses of consciousness
noted by traditional researchers such as Francis Crick, are associated with repeated collapses of superposed information states in tiny protein structures
within each neuron. They propose that unconscious mental processing is
associated with classical neural and intraneural information processing and
that preconscious thought is associated with the activity of these structures
while they are in superposed states. They also propose that consciousness
is specifically associated with the recurrent collapsing, or reduction to a
classical state, of the preconscious superposed informational states. This reduction is said to be objective because it does not rely on either an external
observer or on interference from environmental heat activity. Instead, if the

reduction does not occur as a result of one of the other causes, it will inevitably come about because of the objective effects of quantum gravity, or the operation of gravity on the microphysical level, governed by equations worked out by Penrose. Penrose proposes that gravity operates between superposed states, and when these states become sufficiently massive, gravity forces a selection of one of many of the superposed states to become actualized. This process of collapsing of alternative informational states—say, three alternative images of a face—into a single state or image is neither deterministic nor random. Instead, it is based on some yet-to-be-defined inner logic, involving an element of choice. But most important, it generates or is associated with a pulse of awareness.

The "Orch" part of the Orch-OR theory refers to Hameroff and Penrose's proposal that this is an orchestrated process involving a system of multiple sites representing a coherent set of information, such as an image or thought. This basic level of information processing, they suggest, involves not so much the connections between neurons but rather the processes inside of them. Perhaps the most significant contribution of the theory is their identification of the specific structures within cells that are most likely to support such processes. Inside each cell is a system of protein tubes, or microtubules, which perform structural and informational tasks (see figure A.2). Although these are in all cells, they are particularly extensive and stable in neurons. The results of these computations are orchestrated partly by protein structures calls MAPS, which connect the microtubules, as well as a variety of other structures and processes. It is hypothesized that when microtubules go into superposition, this happens simultaneously across entire assemblies of cells, perhaps as many as twenty thousand connected through the gap junctions that Evan Walker identified (see figure A.3). Although Hameroff and Penrose do not negate the important functions of neuronal connections and larger brain structures, they suggest that it is at this intracellular level that decisions are made that control the firing of individual cells and the functioning of the larger structures. They do not dispute many of the ERTAS theories reviewed earlier (see chapter 4). Rather, they argue that they are incomplete, that there is a much finer grain of organization and functioning associated with the subjective aspect of consciousness, its sense of wholeness and depth, qualia, and volition.

So far no one has been able to design a direct test of the Orch-OR theory; however, considerable evidence has been cited in the literature to support it. Recent tests with functional magnetic resonance imagery have identified superposed states within the microtubule structures (Richter, Richter, & Warren, 2000). It is well known that, despite the absence of a nervous system, single-celled organisms use their microtubules (e.g., cilia) to swim, to

FIGURE A.2: DIAGRAM OF A MICROTUBULE AND AND ITS
COMPONENT PROTEIN TUBULIN

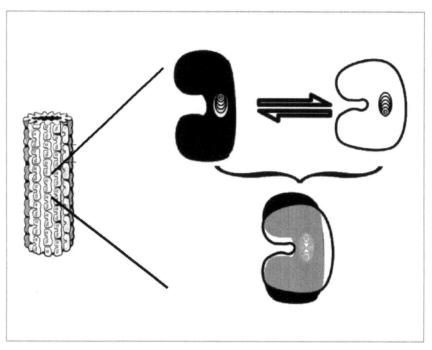

Note: On the left is a section of a cylindrical microtubule. On the top right is a schematic of a protein dimer, the building block of the microtubule. This is shown in two alternative conformations or shapes, which are controlled by the position of two electrons in their center. On the bottom right is shown the quantum superposition of these two conformations.

Source: Hameroff (1997).

avoid barriers, to seek out food, and apparently to solve simple problems. A common property of most anesthetics is that they disable the microtubular structures, whereas psychedelics intensify their activity. Alzheimer's disease is associated with the deformation of the microtubular structures in cells. Key questions involve the specific mechanisms by which any purported information processing, and especially the outcomes of the recurrent collapsing of information states, affects the larger structures that we know are implicated in consciousness.

Probably the major critique of the Orch-OR and similar theories is the problem of environmental heat interference (see Seife, 2000). It is known that superposed states are highly sensitive to heat interference; when this happens, the collapse may occur much too quickly to permit any meaningful information processing or feedback to larger systems. However, Hameroff

FIGURE A.3: CONSCIOUSNESS AND THE PROCESS OF QUANTUM SUPERPOSITION WITHIN SYSTEMS OF MICROTUBULES

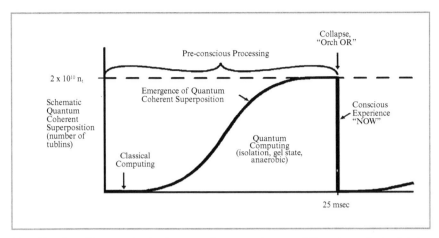

Note: The above illustrates the development of superposed states within systems of microtubules. Over the course of about one-fortieth of a second (25 msec) progressively more tubulins enter into superposed informational states; within each there may be alternative lines of preconscious cognition. When sufficient tubulins enter superposition, a collapse or reduction to a single state or line of cognition occurs, resulting in a pulse of consciousness.

Source: Hameroff (1997).

and Penrose counter by pointing out that the microtubules are protected by membranes of ordered water that insulate the superposed states. Others, such as Jeffrey Satinover (2001), hypothesize that the quantum states remain at a very localized level, but through positive feedback loops, involving sensitivity to initial conditions, their effects are amplified to the scale of neurons and larger brain structures. Another argument in support of such theories is that evolutionary processes of natural selection and self-organization would have inevitably capitalized on the massive adaptive advantages of intracellular quantum computational processes. A major advantage of such intracellular theories of quantum microtubular information processing is that they may address the binding problem, that of integrating separated elements of conscious experience. This may be because of the presence of an enormously increased estimate of the informational capacity of the brain, by many orders of magnitude compared to the traditional connectionist models, but also nonlocality or simultaneous relationships between particles and information states that have developed quantum entanglements but are physically separated.

References

Abbott, A. A. (1988). *Professional choices: Values at work.* Silver Spring, MD: National Association of Social Workers.

Abell, T., & Lyon, L. (1979, August). Do the differences make a difference? An empirical evaluation of the culture of poverty in the U.S. *American Ethnologist, 6,* 602–621.

Addams, J. (1905). *Democracy and social ethics.* London

Addams, J. (1910). *Twenty years at Hull-House.* New York: Macmillan.

Agre, G. P. (1983). What does it mean to solve problems? *Journal of Thought, 18,* 96.

Ahead 4 Health. (n.d.) Retrieved April 2004 from http://www.leeds.ac.uk/ahead4health/whatis.htm.

Ahl, V., & Allen, T. F. H. (1996). *Hierarchy theory, a vision, vocabulary and epistemology.* New York: Columbia University Press.

Ajzen, I. (1991). The theory of planned behavior. *Organizational Behavior and Human Decision Processes, 50,* 179–211.

Albin, S. (1997, June). *Building a system dynamics model.* Cambridge, MA: MIT System Dynamics in Education Project, MIT.

Alexander, C. (1999). The Origins of Pattern Theory and the Future of the Theory, And The Generation of a Living World. Retrieved June 24, 2009, from http://www.patternlanguage.com.

Alexander, C. (2003). *The nature of order* (Vols. 1–4). Oxford: Oxford University Press.

Alexander, C., Ishikawa, S., & Silverstein, M. (1977). *A pattern language.* Oxford: Oxford University Press.

Ali, S. M. (2005). *Racism: A Quranic perspective.* Retrieved April 2006 from http://www.quranicteachings.co.uk/racism.htm.

Allen-Meares, P., & Lane, B. A. (1987, November). Grounding social work practice in theory: Ecosystems. *Social Casework, 68,* 515–521.

Allied Media Corporation. Hispanic American demographics. Retrieved June 25, 2009, from http://www.allied-media.com/Hispanic Market/Hispanic demographics .html.

Allport, F. (1920). The influence of the group upon association and thought. *Journal of Experimental Psychology, 3,* 159–182.

Allport, G. W. (1937). *Personality: A psychological interpretation.* London: Constable.

Allport, G. W., & Odbert, H. S. (1936). Trait names: A psycholexical study. *Psychological Monographs, 47*(1), 171–200.

American Psychiatric Association. (2000). *Diagnostic and statistical manual of mental disorders* (4th ed., text rev.). Washington, DC: Author.

Anderson, C. M., Reiss, D. J., & Hogarty, G.E. (1986). *Schizophrenia and the family.* New York: Guilford Press.

Anderson, E. (2002). Feminist epistemology and philosophy of science. *Stanford Encyclopedia of Philosophy.* Retrieved December 2001 from http://plato.stanford.edu/ntries/feminism-epistemology/.

Anderson, W. T., & Hargrave, T. D. (1990). Contextual family therapy and older people: Building trust in the intergenerational family. *Journal of Family Therapy, 12*(4), 145–158.

Andreas, S. (1991). *Virginia Satir: The patterns of her magic.* Palo Alto, CA: Science and Behavior Books.

Antonovsky A. (1993). The structure and properties of the sense of coherence scale. *Social Science and Medicine, 36*(6), 725–733.

Appelbaum, R. P. (1970). *Theories of social change.* Chicago: Markham.

Argyris, C. (1999). *On organizational learning.* Oxford: Wiley-Blackwell.

Argyris, C., & Schön, D. (1974). *Theory in practice: Increasing professional effectiveness.* San Francisco: Jossey-Bass.

Arieti, S. (1974). *Interpretation of schizophrenia.* New York: Basic Books.

Arieti, S. (1976). *Creativity: The magic synthesis.* New York: Basic Books.

Arieti, S. (1978). *On schizophrenia, phobias, depression, psychotherapy, and the farther shores of psychiatry: Selected papers of Silvano Arieti.* New York: Brunner-Mazel.

Armstrong, D. M. (1981). The nature of mind. In *The nature of mind and other essays* (pp. 55–67). Ithaca, NY: Cornell University Press.

Arnold, M. L. (2000). Stages, sequences, and sequels: Changing conceptions if morality, post-Kohlberg. *Educational Psychology Review, 12*(4), 365–383.

Arrow, H., McGrath, J. E., & Berdahl, J.L. (2000). *Small groups as complex systems: Formation, coordination, development, and adaptation.* Thousand Oaks, CA: Sage.

Arthur, W. B. (1990, February). Positive feedbacks in the economy. *Scientific American, 92*–99.

Aspect, A., Grangier, P., & Roger, G. (1982). Experimental realization of Einstein-Podolsky-Rosen-Bohm gedankenexperiment: A new violation of Bell's inequalities. *Physical Review Letters, 49,* 91.

Assagioli, R. (1965). *Psychosynthesis.* New York: Penguin Books.

Avanta–The Virginia Satir Network. (2005). *The Unfolding Self.* Retrieved April 2005 from http://www.mts.net/~gomori/avanta.html.

Avrich, P. (1978). *An American anarchist: the life of Voltairine de Cleyre.* Princeton, NJ: Princeton University Press.

Axelrod, R. (1997). *The complexity of cooperation: Agent-based models of competition and cooperation.* Princeton, NJ: Princeton University Press.

Baars, B. J. (1988). *A cognitive theory of consciousness.* New York: Cambridge University Press.

Baars, B. J., Newman, J., & Taylor, J. G. (1998). Neuronal mechanisms of consciousness: A relational global workspace framework. In S. Hameroff, A. Kaszniak, & J. Lauakes (Eds.), *Toward a science of consciousness II: The second Tucson discussions and debates* (pp. 269–278). Cambridge, MA: MIT Press.

Baba, M. (1967). *Discourses.* San Francisco: Sufism Reoriented.

Bailey, J. M., & Pillard, R. C. (1991). A genetic study of male sexual orientation. *Archives of General Psychiatry, 48,* 1089–1096.

Bailey, K. D. (1990). *Social entropy theory.* Albany: State University of New York Press.

Bailey, K. D. (1994). Talcott Parsons, social entropy theory, and living systems theory. *Behavioral Science, 39,* 25–45.

Bailey, K. D. (1997). The autopoiesis of social systems: Assessing Luhmann's theory of self-reference. *Systems Research and Behavioral Science, 14*(2), 83–100.

Baird, L., & Meshoulam, I. (1988). Managing two fits of strategic human resource management. *Academy of Management Review, 13*(1), 116–126.

Bakan, D. (1968). *Disease, pain, and sacrifice: Toward a psychology of suffering.* Chicago: University of Chicago Press.

Baltes, P. B., Lindenberger, U., & Staudinger, U. M. (1998). Life-span theory in developmental psychology. In W. Damon & R. M. Lerner (Eds.), *Handbook of child psychology* (Vol. 1, pp. 1029–1043). New York: Wiley.

Bandura, A. (1977). *Social learning theory.* Englewood Cliffs, NJ: Prentice Hall.

Barbour, I. (1974). *Myths, models, and paradigms.* New York: Harper & Row.

Bargh, J. A., & Chartrand, T. L. (1999). The unbearable automaticity of being. *American Psychologist, 54*(7), 462–479.

Barker, R. L. (1991). *The social work dictionary.* Silver Springs, MD: National Association of Social Workers.

Barnard, C. I. (1938). *The functions of the executive.* Cambridge, MA: Harvard University Press.

Baron-Cohen, S. (Ed.). (1997). *The maladapted mind: Classic readings in evolutionary psychopathology.* Hove, UK: Psychology Press.

Bartlett, H. M. (1958). Toward clarification and improvement of social work practice. *Social Work, 3,* 3–9.

Bartos, O. J. (1996). Postmodernism, postindustrialism, and the future. *Sociological Quarterly, 37*(2), 307–325.

Baruss, I. (1986–1987). Metaanalysis of definitions of consciousness. *Imagination, cognition and personality, 64*(4), 321–329.

Bates, J. E. (1989). Concepts and measures of temperament. In G. A. Kohnstamm, J. E. Bates, & M. K. Rothbart (Eds.), *Temperament in childhood* (pp. 3–26). New York: Wiley.

Bateson, G. (1972). *Steps to an ecology of mind.* London: Intertext.

Bateson, G., Jackson, D. D., Haley, J., & Weakland, J. (1956). Toward a theory of schizophrenia. *Behavioral Science, 1,* 251–264.

Baum, R. F. (1986). *Doctors of modernity: Darwin, Marx and Freud.* Peru, IL: Sherwood Sugden.

Bearman, P. S., Moody, J., & Stovel K. (2004, July). Chains of affection: The structure of adolescent romantic and sexual networks. *American Journal of Sociology, 100*(1), 44–99.

Beck, A. T. (1976). *Cognitive therapy and the emotional disorders.* New York: New American Library.

Behe, M. J. (1996). *Darwin's black box: The biochemical challenge to evolution.* New York: Simon & Schuster.

Bell, D. (1973). *The coming of post-industrial society.* New York: Basic Books.

Bell, J. S. (1964). On the Einstein-Podolsky-Rosen Paradox. *Physics, 1,* 195–200.

Benson, P. (1992). Religion and substance use. In J. F. Schumaker (Ed.), *Religion and mental health* (pp. 211–220). New York: Oxford University Press.

Bentovim, A., & Davenport, M. (1992). Resolving the trauma organised system of sexual abuse by confronting the abuser. *Journal of Family Therapy, 14,* 29–50.

Berg, I., & Gallagher, D. (1989). Solution focused brief treatment with adolescent substance abusers. In T. Todd & M. Selekman (Eds.), *Family treatment of adolescent substance abusers* (pp. 93–11). New York: Grove Press.

Bernard, J. (1973). *The sociology of community.* Glenview, IL: Scott, Foresman.

Bernstein, S. (Ed.). (1965). *Explorations in group work.* Boston: Boston University.

Bertalanffy, L. (1950). *General systems theory.* New York: Braziller.

Bertalanffy, L. (1974). General systems theory and psychiatry. In S. Arieti. (Ed.), *American handbook of Psychiatry* (Vol. 1, 2nd ed., pp. 1095–1117). New York: Basic Books.

Berzonsky, M. D. (1993). A constructivist view of identity development: People as postpositivisit self-theorists. In J. Kroger (Ed.), *Discussions on ego identity* (pp. 169–203). Hillside, NJ: Erlbaum.

Bettis, N. (2005). Jane Addams, 1860–1935. Women's intellectual contributions to the study of mind and society. Retrieved May 2005 from http://www.webster.edu/~woolflm/janeadams.html.

Beutler, L. E., & Malik, M. L. (Eds.). (2000). *Alternatives to the DSM.* Washington, DC: American Psychological Association.

Bierhoff, H. W., Klein, R., & Kramp, P. (1991). Evidence for the altruistic personality from data on accident research. *Journal of Personality, 59,* 263–280.

Binswanger, L. (1946). The existential analysis school of thought. In R. May, E. Angel, & H. F. Ellenberger (Eds.). *Existence* (pp. 37–91) New York: Basic Books.

Bion, W. R. (1959). *Experiences in groups.* London: Tavistock.

Blasi, A. (1995). Moral understanding and the moral personality: The process of moral integration. In W. Kurtines & J. Gewirtz (Eds.), *Moral development: An introduction* (pp. 229–254). Boston: Allyn & Bacon.

Blasi, A. (1998). Loevinger's theory of ego development and its relationship to the cognitive-developmental approach. In P. M. Westenberg, A. Blasi, & L. D. Cohn (Eds.), *Personality development: Theoretical, empirical, and clinical investigations of Loevinger's conception of ego development* (Chap. 1). Mahwah, NJ: Erlbaum.

Boehm, W. W. (1959). *Objectives of the social work curriculum of the future* (Vol. 1). New York: Council on Social Work Education.

Boeree, C. (1997). Personality theories: Erik Erikson. Retrieved November 2003 from http://www.ship.edu/~cgboeree/erikson.html.

Bohm, D. (1996). *Wholeness and the implicate order*. London: Routledge.

Bolman, L. G., & Deal, T. E. (1997). *Reframing organizations: Artistry, choice, and leadership*. San Francisco: Jossey-Bass.

Bomben, K. D. (2002). Scientific truth. *The Skeptic*. Retrieved June 27, 2009, from http://www.skepticfriends.org/forum/showquestion.asp?faq=15&fldAuto=64.

Boscolo, L., Cecchin, G., Hoffman, L., & Penn, P. (1987). *Milan systemic family therapy: Conversations in theory and practice*. New York: Basic Books.

Boszormenyi-Nagy, I. (1991) Contextual therapy. In A. S. Gurman & D. P. Kniskern (Eds.), *Handbook of family therapy* (Vol. 2) (pp. 133–158). New York: Brunner-Mazel.

Bourdieu, P. (1984). *Distinction: A social critique of the judgement of taste*. London: Routledge & Kegan Paul.

Bowen, M. (1985). *Family therapy in clinical practice*. New York: Aronson.

Bowlby, J., & Ainsworth, M. D. (1991). An ethological approach to personality development. *American Psychologist, 46*, 333–341.

Brace, L. C. (2000). Does race exist? *Nova Online*. Retrieved March 2006 from http://www.pbs.org/wgbh/nova/first/brace.html.

Bragg, E. (1996). Toward ecological self: Deep ecology meets constructionist self-theory. *Journal of Environmental Psychology, 16*, 93–108.

Brazier, D. D. (1993). *The post-Rogerian therapy of Robert Carkhuff*. Amida Trust, Occasional Paper. Retrieved October 2006 from http://www.amidatrust.com/article_carkhuff.html.

Brenner, M. H. (1973). *Mental illness and the economy*. Cambridge, MA: Harvard University Press.

Brinkerhoff, M. B., & Jacob, J. C. (1999). Mindfulness and quasi-religious meaning systems: An empirical exploration within the context of ecological sustainability and deep ecology. *Journal for the Scientific Study of Religion, 38*(4), 524–542.

Brinton, C. 1952. *The anatomy of a revolution*. New York: Knopf.

Broce, G. (1973). *History of anthropology*. Minneapolis: Burgess.

Brown, J. (1988). *The life of the mind*. Hillside, NJ: Erlbaum.

Brown, J. S., & Duguid, P. (2005). *Organizational learning and communities-of-practice: Toward a unified view of working, learning, and innovation*. Providence, RI: Institute of Management Sciences (now INFORMS).

Brown, K. M. (1999). *Theory of reasoned action/theory of planned behavior*. Community and Family Health, University of South Florida, Tampa.

Bruffee, K. A. (1993). *Collaborative learning*. Baltimore: Johns Hopkins University Press.

Buchanan, B. (1997). Values, systems and consciousness. *Noetic Journal, 1*(1), 6–8.

Bütz, M. R. (1997). *Chaos and complexity: Implications for psychological theory and practice*. Washington, DC: Taylor & Francis.

Calvin, W. H. (1999). Ephemeral levels of mental organization: Darwinian competitions as a basis for consciousness. In S. Hameroff, A. L. Kaaszniak, & D. Chalmers (Eds.), *Tuscon III consciousness proceedings* (pp. 297–308) Cambridge, MA: MIT Press.

Çambel, A. B. (1993). *Applied chaos theory: A paradigm for complexity*. San Diego: Academic Press.

Campbell, D. T. (1974). Evolutionary epistemology. In P. A. Schilpp (Ed.), *The philosophy of Karl R. Popper* (pp. 412–463). LaSalle, IL: Open Court.

Campbell, J. H. (1985). An organizational interpretation of evolution. In D. J. Depaw & B. H. Weber (Eds.), *Evolution at a crossroads: The new biology and the new philosophy of science*. Cambridge, MA: MIT Press.

Cancer Prevention Research Center. (n.d.). Transtheoretical model: Detailed overview of the transtheoretical model. Retrieved March 2002 from http://www.uri.edu/research/cprc/TTM/detailedoverview.htm.

Canda, E. R. (1988, Winter). Conceptualizing spirituality for social work: Insights from diverse perspectives. *Social Thought, 14*(1), 30–46.

Canda, E. R., & Furman, L. D. (1999). *Spiritual diversity in social work practice: The heart of helping*. New York: Free Press.

Canuckguy. (2006). BlankMap-World6.svg. Retrieved August 2009 from http://commons.wikimedia.org/wiki/File:BlankMap-World6.svg.

Capra, F. (1975). *The Tao of physics: An exploration of the parallels between modern physics and Eastern mysticism*. Boston: Shambala Publications.

Carew, R. (1979). The place of knowledge in social work practice. *Journal of Social Work, 19*(3), 349–364.

Carkhuff, R. (1984). *Helping and human helations* (2 vols.). Amherst, MA: Human Resource Development Press.

Carling, A., & Nolan, P. (1998). Historical materialism, natural selection and world history. *Historical Materialism, 6*, 215–264.

Carpendale, J. I. (2000). Kohlberg and Piaget on stages and moral reasoning. *Developmental Review, 20*, 181–205.

Carson, R. (1962). *Silent spring*. New York: Houghton Mifflin.

Carter, R. (2002). *Consciousness*. London: Weidenfeld & Nicolson.

Cartwright, D. & Zander, A. (Eds.). (1968). *Group dynamics*. New York: Harper & Row.

CasaNet Resources. (1995–1996, Fall/Winter). *What is cultural competence? Family Resource Coalition's Report on culture and family-centered practice*. Retrieved May 2006 from http://www.casanet.org/library/culture/competence.htm.

Caspi, A. (1987). Personality in the life course. *Journal of Personality and Social Psychology, 53*, 1203–1213.

Caspi, A. (1998). Personality development across the life course. In W. Damon &

R. M. Lerner (Eds.), *Handbook of child psychology* (Vol. 3, pp. 311–388). New York: Wiley.

Caspi, A. & Silva, P. A. (1995). Temperamental qualities at age 3 predict personality traits in young adulthood: Longitudinal evidence from a birth cohort. *Child Development, 66,* 486–498.

Cassel, R. N. (2001). Comparing the dynamics of second and third force psychology. *Education, 122*(1), 131–134.

Castells, M. (1996). *The rise of the networked society.* Oxford: Blackwell.

Central Intelligence Agency. (2000, December). *Global trends 2015: A dialogue about the future with nongovernment experts.* Retrieved September 2005 from https://www.cia.gov/news-information/cia-the-war-on-terrorism/terrorism-rela ted-excerpts-from-global-trends-2015-a-dialogue-about-the-future-with-nongov ernment-experts.html.

Central Intelligence Agency. (2009). *World Fact Book.* Retrieved June 25, 2009, from https://www.cia.gov/library/publications/the-world-factbook/.

Chalmers, D. J. (1995a). Facing up to the problem of consciousness. *Journal of Consciousness Studies, 2*(3), 200–219.

Chalmers, D. J. (1995b, December). The puzzle of conscious experience. *Scientific American, 273,* 80–86.

Chalmers, D. J. (1996). *The conscious mind: In search of a fundamental theory.* New York: Oxford University Press.

Chamberlain, L. (1995). Chaos and change in a suicidal family. *Counseling and Values, 39*(2), 117–129.

Chaplin, G. (2004). *American Journal of Physical Anthropology, 125,* 292–302.

Chapman, M. (n.d.). *"Salient need"—A casework compass.* Chicago: Jewish Family & Community Services.

Chatterjee, P. (1996). *Approaches to the welfare state.* Silver Springs, MD: National Association of Social Work Press.

Checkoway, B. (1995). Six strategies of community change. *Community Development Journal, 30*(1), 2–20.

Chilton, J. (1992, April). Validity claims of spirituality. *University of Minnesota Interdisciplinary Team for Spirituality.* Retrieved April 2007 from http://www .d.umn.edu/~schilton/Articles/Spirit.html.

Chiu, M. M. (2000). Group problem-solving processes: Social interactions and individual actions. *Journal of the Theory of Social Behavior, 30*(1), 27–49.

Chomsky, N. (1959). A review of B. F. Skinner's Verbal Behavior. In J. A. Fodor & J. J. Katz (Eds.), *The structure of language: Readings in the philosophy of language* (pp. 547–578). Englewood Cliffs, NJ: Prentice Hall. (Original work published in *Language, 35,* 26–58).

Clark, L. A., & Watson, D. (1999). Temperament: A new paradigm for trait psychology. In L. A. Pervin & O. P. John (Eds.), *Handbook of personality* (2nd ed., pp. 399–423). New York: Guilford Press.

Clark, M. C., & Caffarella, R. S. (1999). Theorizing adult development. *New Directions for Adult and Continuing Education, 84,* 3–7.

Cloninger, C. R. (1986). A unified biosocial theory of personality and its role in the development of anxiety states. *Psychiatric Developments, 3,* 167–226.

Cohen, D., & Prusak, L. (2001). *In good company: How social capital makes organizations work.* Boston: Harvard Business School Press.

Cohen, I. L. (1984). *Darwin was wrong.* Greenvale, NY: New Research.

Cohen, M. D., March, J. G., & Olsen, J. P. (1972). A garbage can model of organizational choice. *Administrative Science Quarterly, 17,* 1–25.

Cohen, M. S., Adelman, L., & Thompson, B. B. (2000, March). *Experimental investigation of uncertainty, stakes, and time in pilot decision making.* Arlington, VA: Cognitive Technologies.

Cohn, M. L. (1969). *Class and conformity: A study in values.* Homewood, IL: Dorsey.

Coie, J. D., & Dodge, K. A. (1998). Aggression and antisocial behavior. In W. Damon & R. M. Lerner (Eds.), *Handbook of Child Psychology* (Vol. 3, pp. 779–861). New York: Wiley.

Cole, M. (1996). *Cultural psychology: A once and future discipline.* Cambridge, MA: Harvard University Press.

Coleman, J. S. (1988). Social capital in the creation of human capital. *American Journal of Sociology, 94*(Suppl.), S95–S120.

Communitarian Network. (2005). *Position paper.* Retrieved October 2005 from http://www.gwu.edu/~ccps/platformtext.html.

Compton, B. R., & Galaway, B. (1994). *Social work processes.* Pacific Grove, CA: Brooks/Cole.

Comte, A. (1876). *System of positive polity.* London: Longman, Green.

Cooley, C. H. (1902). *Human nature and the social order.* New York: Scribner's.

Copleston, F. (1974). *History of philosophy* (Vol. 1). New York: Doubleday.

Cornwell, B., Curry, T. J., & Schwirian, K. P. (2003). Revisiting Norton Long's ecology of games: A network approach. *City & Community, 2*(2), 121–142.

Coser, L. (1956). *The functions of social conflict.* Glencoe, IL: Free Press.

Costa, P. T., & McCrae, R. R. (1980). Influence of extraversion and neuroticism on subjective well-being: Happy and unhappy people. *Journal of Personality and Social Psychology, 38,* 668–678.

Costa, P. T., & McCrae, R. R. (1992). *Revised NEO personality inventory (NEO-PI-R) and NEO five factor inventory (NEO-FFI) professional manual.* Odessa, FL: Psychological Assessment Resources.

Coulton, C. (2004). *The place of community in social work practice research: Conceptual and methodological developments* (Aaron Rose Lecture). New Orleans: Society for Social Work Research.

Cowan, R., & Rizzo, M. J. (1996, February). *The genetic-causal tradition and modern economic theory.* London, ON: University of Western Ontario and New York University.

Cox, H. (1969). *Feast of fools.* Cambridge, MA: Harvard University Press.

Crick, F. (1984). Functions of the thalamic reticular complex: The search light hypothesis. *Proceedings of the National Academy of Sciences, 81,* 4586–4590.

Crick, F. (1994). *The astonishing hypothesis: The scientific search for the soul.* New York: Scribner's.

Crick, F., & Koch, C. (1990). Towards a neurobiological theory of consciousness. *Seminars in the Neurosciences, 2,* 263–275.

Csikszentmihalyi, M. (1990). *Flow: The psychology of optimal experience.* New York: Harper & Row.

Csikszentmihalyi, M. (1998). Creativity and genius: A systems perspective. In A. Steptoe (Ed.), *Genius and the mind: Studies in creativity and temperament* (pp. 39–64). Oxford: Oxford University Press.

Csikszentmihalyi, M. (1999). Emerging goals and the self-regulation of behavior. In R. S. Weber (Ed.), *Perspectives on behavioral self-regulation: Advances in social cognition* (pp. 107–118). Mahwah, NJ: Erlbaum.

Czikszentmihalyi, M. & Sawyer, K. (1995). Creative insight: The social dimension of a solitary moment. In Robert J. Sternberg & Janet E. Davidson, (Eds.), *The nature of insight.* Cambridge, MA: MIT Press.

Dahrendorf, R. (1964). Toward a theory of social conflict. In A. Etzioni & E. Etzioni (Eds.). (pp. 98–111), *Social change.* New York: Basic Books.

Damasio, A. (1999). *The feeling of what happens: Body and emotion in the making of consciousness.* New York: Harcourt, Brace.

Damasio, A. (2003). *Looking for Spinoza.* New York: Harcourt.

Darley, J., & Latane, B. (1968). Bystander intervention in emergencies: Diffusion of responsibility. *Journal of Personality and Social Psychology, 8,* 377–383.

Darwin, C. (1900). *Origin of the species by means of natural selection of the preservation of favored races in the struggle for life* (Vol. 2). New York: D. Appleton. (Original work published 1859).

Darwin, C. (1977). "Essay of 1844." In P. H. Barrett (Ed.), *The collected papers of Charles Darwin* (2 vols.). Chicago: University of Chicago Press. (Original work published 1844).

Darwin, C. (1986). *The works of Charles Darwin: Vol. 10. The foundations of the Origin of the Species: Two Essays Written in 1842 and 1844* (P. H. Barrett & R. B. Freeman, Eds.). London: Pickering.

Darwin, C. (2007). *The descent of man.* New York: Penguin Books. (Original work published 1871).

Dass, R., & Gorman, P. (1997). *How can I help: Stories and reflections on service.* New York: Knopf.

Davis, A. F. (1973). *American heroine: The life and legend of Jane Addams.* New York: Oxford University Press.

Davis, J., Lockwood, L., & Wright, C. (1991). Reasons for not reporting peak experiences. *Journal of Humanistic Psychology, 31*(1), 86–94.

Dawkins, R. (1986). *The blind watchmaker: Why the evidence of evolution reveals a universe without design.* New York: Norton.

Dawkins, R. (1989). *The selfish gene.* Oxford: Oxford University Press.

De Bono, E. (1967). *New think: The use of lateral thinking in the generation of new ideas.* New York: Basic Books.

Deci, E. L., & Ryan, R. M. (2000). The "what" and "why" of goal pursuits: Human needs and the self-determination of behavior. *Psychological Inquiry, 11*, 227–268.

Degler, C. N. (1991). *In search of human nature: The decline and revival of Darwinism in American social thought.* New York: Oxford University Press.

De Hoyos, G., & Jensen, C. (1985, October). The systems approach in American social work. *Social Casework, 66*, 490–497.

DeLamater, J., & Friedrich, R. (2003). Normal sexual development. *Journal of Sex Research, 39*, 10–14.

Dennett, D. (1991). *Consciousness explained.* Boston: Little, Brown.

Derlega, V. J., Winstead, B. A., & Jones, W. H. (Eds.). (1991). Personality: An introduction. In *Personality: Contemporary theory and research* (p. 3). Chicago: Nelson-Hall.

DeRoos, Y. S. (1990, June). The development of practice wisdom through human problem-solving processes. *Social Service Review, 64*(2), 276–287.

Dessler, G. (1980). *Organization theory: Integrating structure and behavior.* Englewood Cliffs, NJ: Prentice Hall.

Deutsch, D. (1997). *The fabric of reality.* London: Penguin Books.

Devaney, R. L. (1989). *An introduction to chaotic dynamical systems* (2nd ed.). Reading, MA: Addison-Wesley.

Devaney, R. L. (1992). *A first course in chaotical dynamic systems: Theory and experiment.* Reading, MA: Addison-Wesley.

Diamond, J. (1997). *Guns, germs, and steel: The fates of human societies.* New York: Norton.

Diener, E., Suh, E. N., Lucas, R. E., & Smith, H. L. (1999). Subjective well-being: Three decades of progress. *Psychological Bulletin, 125*, 276–302.

Dixit, A., & Nalebuff, B. (1991). *Thinking strategically.* New York: Norton.

Donaldson, T., & Dunfee, T. W. (1994). Towards a unified conception of business ethics: Integrative social contracts theory. *Academy of Management Review, 19*(2), 252–284.

Donaldson, T., & Dunfee, T. W. (1999). *Ties that bind: A social contracts approach to business ethics.* Cambridge, MA: Harvard Business School Press.

Donkin, W. (1969). *The wayfarers.* San Francisco: Sufism Reoriented.

Dooley, K. J. (1997). A complex adaptive systems model of organizational change. *Nonlinear Dynamics, Psychology, and Life Sciences, 1*(1), 69–97.

Drover, G., & Schragge, E. (1977). General systems theory and social work education: A critique. *Canadian Journal of Social Work Education, 3*(2), 28–39.

Du Bois, E. B. (1999). *The souls of black folk.* Chicago: A. C. McClurg. (Original work published in 1903).

Duke, M. P. (1994). Chaos theory and psychology: Seven propositions. *Genetic, Social and General Psychology, 120*(3), 267–287.

Dunbar, R. I. M. (1993). Coevolution of neocortical size, group size and language in humans. *Behavioral and Brain Sciences, 16*(4), 681–735.

Duncan, G., Boisjoly, J., Levy, D., Kremer, D., & Eccles, J. S. (2003, September). *Empathy or antipathy? The consequences of racially and socially diverse peers on attitudes and behaviors.* Retrieved October 2006 from http://www.jourdan.ens

.fr/piketty/fichiers/enseig/ecoineg/articl/Duncanetal2003.pdf. Duncan, R. B. (1972). Characteristics of environment and perceived environmental uncertainty. *Administrative Science Quarterly, 17*, 313–327.

Durkheim, É. (1964a). *The division of labor in society.* New York: Free Press.

Durkheim, É. (1964b). *The rules of sociological method.* London: Collier-Macmillan. (Original work published 1895).

Durkheim, É. (1965). *Elementary forms of religious life.* New York: Free Press.

Duvall, E. M. (1957). *Family development.* Philadelphia: Lippincott.

Early, G. (1996, September/October). William Julius Wilson [Interview]. *Mother Jones, 2.*

Easterby-Smith, M., Burgoyne, J., & Araujo, L. (Eds.). (1999). *Organizational learning and the learning organization.* London: Sage.

Edelman, G. M. (1989). *The remembered present.* New York: Basic Books.

Ehrenwald, J. (1984). *Anatomy of genius: Split brains and global minds.* New York: Human Sciences Press.

Einstein, A., Podolsky, B., & Rosen, N. (1935). Can quantum-mechanical description of physical reality be considered complete? *Physical Review, 47*, 777–780.

Eisenberg, N., Fabes, R., Schaller, M., Carlo, G., & Miller, P. (1991). The relations of parental characteristics and practices to children's vicarious emotional responding. *Child Development, 62*(6), 1393–1408.

Elder, G. H., & Shanahan, M. J. (2006). The life course and human development. In R. E. Lerner & W. Damon (Eds.), *Theoretical models of human development: Vol. 1. The Handbook of Child Psychology* (6th ed., pp. 665–715). New York: Wiley.

Eliasmith, C. (Ed.). (1998). *Dictionary of philosophy of mind.* St. Louis: Department of Philosophy, Washington University in St. Louis. Retrieved February 21, 2009, from http://philosophy.uwaterloo.ca/MindDict/emergence.html.

Ellis, A. (2008). *Theories of personality: Critical perspectives.* New York: Sage.

Eriksen, C. W., & St. James, J. D. (1986). Visual attention within and around the field of focal attention: A zoom lens model. *Perception and Psychophysics, 40*, 225–240.

Erikson, E. (1950). *Childhood and society.* New York: Norton.

Erikson, E. (1963). *Childhood and society.* New York: Norton.

Erikson, E. (1968). *Identity, youth, and crisis.* New York: Norton.

Etzioni, A. (1967, December). Mixed-scanning: A "third" approach to decision-making. *Public Administration Review, 27*, 385–392.

Eysenck, H. J. (1970). A dimension system of psychodiagnostics. In A. R. Mahrer (Ed.), *New approaches to personality classification* (pp. 69–207). New York: Columbia University Press.

Fauconnier, G., & Turner, M. (2002). *The way we think: Conceptual blending and the mind's hidden complexities.* New York: Basic Books.

Fayol, H. (1949). *General and industrial management* (Constance Storrs, Trans.). London: Sir Isaac Pitman.

Feingold, A. (1994). Gender differences in personality: A meta-analysis. *Psychological Bulletin, 116*(3), 429–456.

Feldman, M. (1998, February 28). Re: Rethinking quantitative social research. Statistical consulting newsgroup. Message posted to news://sci.stat.consult.

Fellin, P. (2000). Revisiting multiculturalism in social work journal articles. *Journal of Social Work Education, 36,* 271–272.

Fellin, P. (2001). *The community and the social worker.* Itasca, IL: F. E. Peacock.

Festinger, L. (1957). *A theory of cognitive dissonance.* Evanston, IL: Row Peterson.

Field, R. (2002). John Dewey (1859–1952). *The Internet encyclopedia of philosophy.* Retrieved April 2002 from http://www.iep.utm.edu/d/dewey.htm.

Fischbach, G. D. (1992, September). Mind and brain. *Scientific American, 267,* 48–57.

Fischer, D. H. (1989). *Albion's seed. Four British folkways in America.* New York: Oxford Press.

Fishbein, M., & Ajzen, I. (1975). *Belief, attitude, intention, and behavior: An introduction to theory and research.* Reading, MA: Don Mills.

Fisher, B. A. (1970). Decision emergence: Phases in group decision making. *Speech Monographs, 37,* 53–66.

Flake, G. W. (2000). *The computational beauty of nature: Computer explorations of fractals, chaos, complex systems, and adaptation.* Bradford, MA: Bradford Books.

Flavell, J. H. (1979). Metacognition and cognitive monitoring: A new area of cognitive-developmental inquiry. *American Psychologist, 34,* 906–911.

Flexner, A. (2001, March). Is social work a profession? *Research on Social Work Practice, 11*(2), 152–165. (Original work presented at the National Conference on Charities and Correction, 1915).

Foa, U. G., & Foa, E. B. (1975). *Resource theory of social exchange.* Morristown, NJ: General Learning Press.

Fodor, J. (1983). *The modularity of mind.* Cambridge, MA: MIT/Bradford Press.

Fogel, R. W. (2000). *The fourth great awakening and the future of egalitarianism.* Chicago: University of Chicago Press.

Ford, M. (1992). *Motivating humans: Goals, emotions, and personal agency beliefs.* Thousand Oaks, CA: Sage.

Forsyth, D. R. (1996). Why so social an animal? Retrieved December 2004 from http://www.has.vcu.edu/psy/faculty/fors/function.html.

Forsyth, D. R. (1997, November 1). *Why groups? The big six model of group functions.* Paper presented at the 20th Annual Meeting of the Society of Southeastern Social Psychologists, Chapel Hill, NC.

Forsyth, D. R. (2006). *Group dynamics* (4th ed.). Pacific Grove, CA: Brooks/Cole.

Fowler, J. W. (1996). *Faithful change: The personal and public challenges of postmodern life.* Nashville, TN: Abingdon Press.

Franken, R. (1994). *Human motivation.* Pacific Grove, CA: Brooks/Cole.

Frankl, V. (1993). *The pursuit of meaning.* San Francisco: Harper & Row.

Fredrickson, B. L., & Losada, M. F. (2005). Positive affect and the complex dynamics of human flourishing. *American Psychologist, 60*(7), 678–686.

Freedman, J., & Combs, G. (1996). *Narrative therapy: The social construction of preferred realities.* New York: Norton.

Freud, S. (1895). *Project for a scientific psychology.* London: Hogarth Press and Institute of Psycho-Analysis. (Original work published in 1957 in J. Strachey (Ed.). *The standard edition of the complete psychological works of Sigmund Freud*).

Freud, S. (1913). *Totem and taboo. The complete psychological works of Sigmund Freud* (Vol. 13, pp. 1–161). London: Hogarth Press.

Freud, S. (1927). *The future of an illusion* (J. Strachey, Trans.). New York: Norton.

Freud, S. (1955). *Moses and monothesism.* New York: Vintage Books.

Freud, S. (1959). *Collected papers* (Vol. 4). New York: Basic Books.

Freud, S. (1990). *Beyond the pleasure principle.* New York: Norton. (Original work published 1920).

Freud, S. (2009). *On creativity and the unconscious: The psychology of art, literature, love, and religion.* New York: Harper Perennial Modern Thought. (Original work published 1958).

Freud, Sophie, & Krug, S. (2002). Beyond the code of ethics, part I: Complexities of ethical decisionmaking in social work practice. *Families in Society: The Journal of Contemporary Human Services, 83*(5–6), 474–482.

Friedman, M., Bowden, V., & Jones E. (2002). *Family nursing: Research, theory, and practice* (5th ed.). New York: Prentice Hall.

Friedman, T. (2000). *The Lexus and the olive tree.* New York: Anchor Books.

Frohlich, H. (1968). Long range coherence and energy storage in biological systems. *International Journal of Quantum Chemistry, 2,* 641–649.

Fromm, E. (1947). *Man for himself.* New York: Rinehart.

Fukuyama, F. (1989, Summer). The end of history? *National Interest,* 3–18.

Galatzer-Levy, R. M. (1995). Psychoanalysis and dynamical systems theory: Prediction and self similarity, *Journal of the American Psychoanalytic Association, 43*(4), 1085–1113.

Galinsky, E. (1987). *The six stages of parenthood.* Reading, MA: Addison-Wesley.

Gambrill, E. (1999). Evidence-based practice: An alternative to authority-based practice. *Families in Society: The Journal of Contemporary Human Services, 80*(4), 341–350.

Gardner, H. (1985). *The mind's new science: A history of the cognitive revolution.* New York: Basic Books.

Gardner, H. (1993). *Multiple intelligences: The theory in practice.* New York: Basic Books.

Gardner, H. (1999). *Intelligence reframed: Multiple intelligences for the twenty-first century.* New York: Basic Books.

Gardner, H., Krechevsky, M., Sternberg, R., & Okagaki, L. (1994). Intelligence in context: Enhancing students' practical intelligence for school. In K. McGilly (Ed.), *Classroom lessons: Integrating cognitive theory and classroom practice* (pp. 105–128). Cambridge, MA: MIT Press.

Gartner, J., Larson, D. B., & Allen, G. (1991). Religious commitment and mental health: A review of the empirical literature. *Journal of Psychology and Theology, 19*(1), 6–25.

Gayatri, C. S. (1981). French feminism in an international frame, in C. Gaudin (Ed.), *Feminist readings: French texts/American contexts* (pp. 154–184). Yale French Studies No. 62. New Haven, CT: Yale University Press.

Germain, C. B. (1999). *Human behavior in the social environment: An ecological view.* New York: Columbia University Press.

Germain, C. B., & Gitterman, A. (1980). *The life model of social work practice.* New York: Columbia University Press.

Getzel, J. W. (1964). Creative thinking, problem-solving, and instruction. In E. R. Hilgard (Ed.), *Theories of learning and instruction: 63rd Yearbook of the National Society for the Study of Education* (pp. 240–267). Chicago: University of Chicago Press.

Getzel, J. W. & Csikszentmihalyi, M. (1976). *The creative vision.* New York: Wiley.

Gibbs, L. E. (2003). *Evidence-based practice for the helping professions: A practical guide with integrated materials.* Pacific Grove, CA: Thomson-Brooks Cole.

Gibbs, L. E., & Gambrill, E. (1999). *Critical thinking for social workers.* Thousand Oaks, CA: Pine Forge Press.

Gigerenzer, G. (2007). *Gut feelings: The intelligence of the unconscious.* New York: Viking.

Gill, G. W. (2005). Does race exist? *Nova Online.* Retrieved May 2006 from http://www.pbs.org/wgbh/nova/first/gill.html.

Gillen, J. (2000). Versions of Vygotsky. *British Journal of Educational Studies, 48*(2), 83–199.

Gilligan, C. (1998). Remembering Larry. *Journal of Moral Education, 27*(2), 125–140.

Glaser, B. (2002). Conceptualization: On theory and theorizing using grounded theory. *International Journal of Qualitative Methods, 1*(2), 1–31.

Gleick, J. (1987). *Chaos: Making of a new science.* New York: Penguin Books.

GlenMaye, L. F., Lewandowski, C. A., & Bolin, B. L. (2004). Defining complexity: The theoretical basis of advanced generalist practice. In A. W. Roy & F. J. Vecchiolla (Eds.), *Thoughts on an advanced generalist education: Models, readings, and essays* (Chap. 7). Peosta, IA: Eddie Bowers.

Goffman, E. (1959). *The presentation of self in everyday life.* Garden City, NY: Doubleday.

Goldberg, P. (1983). *The intuitive edge: Understanding intuition and applying it in everyday life.* Los Angeles: Tarcher.

Goldman, E. (1931). *Living my life.* New York: Knopf.

Goldstein, H. (1999). The limits and art of understanding in social work practice. *Families in Society: The Journal of Contemporary Human Services, 80*(4), 385–395.

Goldstein, J. (1995). Emergence as a construct: History and issues. *Emergence, 1*(1), 49–71.

Goldstein, J. (1997). Riding the waves of emergence: Leadership innovations in complex systems. In C. Lindberg, P. Plsek, & B. Zimmerman (Eds.), *Edgeware: Complexity resources for health care leaders* (pp. ix17–ix36). Cranbury, NJ: VHA.

Goleman, D. (1995). *Emotional intelligence.* New York: Bantam Books.

Gomory, T., & Thyer, B. (2001). Special point/counterpoint on the role of theory in research on social work practice. *Journal of Social Work Education, 37*(1), 9–66.

Gore, A. (1992). *Earth in balance.* New York: Plume Books.

Gorgias. (2008). *Microsoft Encarta Online Encyclopedia.* Retrieved December 2002 from http://encarta.msn.com/encnet/refpages/search.aspx?q=Gorgias.

Goswami, A. (1995, March). *The self-aware universe: How consciousness creates the material world.* Los Angeles: Tarcher.

Gottman, J. M. (1993). A theory of marital dissolution and stability. *Journal of Family Psychology, 7,* 57–75.

Gottman, J. M., Murray, J. D., Swanson, C. C., Tyson, R., & Swanson, K. R. (2002). *The mathematics of marriage: Dynamic nonlinear models.* Cambridge, MA: MIT Press.

Gould, S. J. (1989). *Wonderful life: The Burgess shale and the nature of history.* New York: Norton.

Gould, S. J. (1997, July). Kropotkin was no crackpot. *Natural History, 97*(7), 12–21.

Gould, S. J, & Eldredge, N. (1977). Punctuated equilibria: The tempo and mode of evolution reconsidered. *Paleobiology, 3,* 115–151.

Gray, J. A. (1991). The neuropsychology of temperament. In J. Strelau & A. P. Angleitner (Eds.), *Explorations in temperament* (pp. 105–128). New York: Plenum Press.

Greeley, A. (1987, January/February). Mysticism goes mainstream. *American Health,* 47–49.

Green, D. W. (1996). *Cognitive science: An introduction.* Oxford: Blackwell.

Gribbon, J. (1985). *In search of Schrodinger's cat: Quantum physics and reality.* New York: Bantam/Doubleday.

Grof, S., & Grof, C. (1989). *Spiritual emergency: When personal transformation becomes a crisis.* Los Angeles: Tarcher.

Grotevant, H. D. (1987). Toward a process model of identity formation. *Journal of Adolescent Research, 2,* 202–223.

Guastello, S. J. (1995). *Chaos, catastrophe, and human affairs: Applications of nonlinear dynamics to work, organizations, and social evolution.* Mahwah, NJ: Erlbaum.

Guastello, S. J. (1998). Creative problem solving at the edge of chaos. *Journal of Creative Behavior, 32*(1), 38–57.

Guastello, S. J. (2001). Nonlinear dynamics in psychology. *Discrete Dynamics in Nature and Society, 6,* 11–29.

Guilford, J. P. (1967). *The nature of human intelligence.* New York: McGraw-Hill.

Guimera, R., Danon, L., Diaz-Guilera, A., Giralt, F., & Arenas, A. (2003). Self-similar community structure in a network of human interactions. *Physical Review,* 68, 1–4.

Gurin, P. (2005). Expert report of Patricia Gurin. Gratz, et al. v. Bollinger, et al., No. 9775321 (E.D. Mich.). Grutter, et al. v. Bollinger, et al., No. 9775928 (E.D. Mich.). In *The compelling need for diversity in higher education.* Ann Arbor: University of Michigan.

Gurman, A. S., & Kniskern, D. P. (Eds.). (1991). *Handbook of family therapy* (Vol. 2). New York: Brunner-Mazel.

Gwyther, B. (2000). Social capital and communitarianism. TASA (The Australian Sociological Association) 2000 Conference—Refereed Papers. *Sociological Sites/Sights.* Retrieved June 27, 2009, from http://www.tasa.org.au/members/docs/conference.

Habermas, J. (1979). *Communication and the evolution of society.* Boston: Beacon Press.

Haken, H. (1988). *Information and self-organization: A macroscopic approach to complex systems.* Springer Series in Synergetics. Berlin: Springer-Verlag.

Halasz, M. F. (1995). Nonlinear dynamics in behavioral systems. *American Psychologist, 50,* 107–108.

Haldane, J. B. S. (1932). *The causes of evolution.* London: Longmans, Green.

Haley, J. (1959). The family of the schizophrenic: A model system. *Journal of Nervous and Mental Disease, 129*(4), 357–374.

Haley, J. (1973). *Uncommon therapy.* New York: Ballantine Books.

Haley, J. (1987). *Problem solving therapy.* San Francisco: Jossey-Bass.

Hall, C. S., & Lindzey, G. (1978). *Theories of personality,* New York: Wiley.

Hall, J. A. (1984). *Nonverbal sex differences: Communication accuracy and expressive style.* Baltimore: Johns Hopkins University Press.

Hall, T. D. (1995). Influence of Malthus and Darwin on the European elite. Leading Edge Research Group. Retrieved March 2002 from http://www.cco.net/~trufax/avoid/manifold.html.

Hallinan, M. (1997, February). The sociological study of social change. *American Sociological Review, 62,* 1–11.

Hamer, G. H. (2005). *The God gene: How faith is hardwired into our genes.* New York: Anchor Books.

Hameroff, S. R. (1994). Quantum coherence in microtubules: A neural basis for emergent consciousness? *Journal of Consciousness Studies, 1*(1), 91–118.

Hameroff, S. R. (1997). Quantum computing in microtubules: An intra-neural correlate of consciousness? *Cognitive Studies: Bulletin of the Japanese Cognitive Science Society, 4*(3), 67–92.

Hameroff, S. R. (1998). "Funda-Mentality": Is the conscious mind subtly linked to a basic level of the universe? *Trends in Cognitive Sciences, 2*(4), 119–127.

Hameroff, S. R., & Penrose, R., (1996). Orchestrated reduction of quantum coherence in brain microtubules: A model for consciousness. In S. R. Hameroff, A. Kas:zniak, & A. C. Scott (Eds.), *Toward a science of consciousness: The first Tucson discussions and debates* (pp. 507–540). Cambridge, MA: MIT Press.

Hanfling, O. (1981). *Logical positivism.* New York: Columbia University Press.

Hanh, T. N. (1995). *Living Buddha, Living Christ.* New York: Riverhead Books.

Hanifan, L. J. (1916). The rural school community center. *Annals of the American Academy of Political and Social Science, 67,* 130–138.

Hardesty, P. H., & Kirby, K. M. (1995). Relation between family religiousness and drug use within adolescent peer groups. *Journal of Social Behavior and Personality, 10*(2), 421–430.

Hardy, A. C. (1979). *The spiritual nature of man: A study of contemporary religious experience.* Cambridge: Clarendon Press.

Harris, S.M. (1996). Bowen and symbolic experiential family therapy theories: Strange bedfellows or isomorphs of life. *Journal of Family Psychotherapy, 7*(3), 39–60.

Hartman, A. (1995). Diagrammatic assessment of family relationships. *Families in Society, 30*(1), 111–122.

Hartmann, H., Kris, E., & Lowenstein, R. M. (1949). Notes on the theory of aggression. In *Psychoanalytic study of the child* (pp. 3–4). New York: International Universities Press.

Harvard Mental Health Letter. (1995, June). Schizophrenia update. Cambridge: Harvard Medical School.

Harvey, D. (1989). *The condition of modernity: An enquiry into the origins of cultural change.* Oxford: Oxford University Press.

Hasenfeld, Y., & English, R.A. (1974). *Human service organizations.* Ann Arbor: University of Michigan Press.

Hawkinshire, F. B., & Liggett, W. A. (1990). Lewin's paradigm of planned change: Theory and application. In S. Wheelan & E. Pepitone (Eds.), *Advances in field theory.* Newbury Park, CA: Sage.

Hayles, N. K. (1990). *Chaos bound: Orderly disorder in contemporary literature and science.* Ithaca, NY: Cornell University Press.

Haynes, S. N. (1995). Introduction to the special section on chaos theory and psychological assessment. *Psychological Assessment, 7*(1), 3–4.

Headey, B. W., & Wearing, A. J. (1992). *Understanding happiness: A theory of subjective well-being.* Melbourne: Longman Cheshire.

Hearn, G. (1979). General systems theory and social work. In Francis J. Turner (Ed.), *Social work treatment: Interlocking theoretical approaches.* New York: Free Press.

Hearn, G. (Ed.). (1969). *The general systems approach: Contributions toward an holistic conception of social work.* New York: Council on Social Work Education.

Hebb, D. O. (1949). *The organization of behavior: A neuropsychological theory.* New York: Wiley.

Heiby, E. M. (1995). Chaos theory, nonlinear dynamical models, and psychological assessment. *Psychological Assessment, 7*(1), 5–9.

Heisenberg, W. (1927). On the perceptual content of quantum theoretical Kinematics and mechanics. *Zeitschrift für Physik, 43,* 172–198. (J. A. Wheeler & W. Zurek (Trans.) (1983). *Quantum theory and measurement.* Princeton, NJ: Princeton University Press).

Hernandez, S. H., Jorgensen, J., Judd, P., Gould, M., & Parsons, M. (1985). Integrated practice: An advanced generalist curriculum to prepare social problem specialists. *Journal of Social Work Education, 21*(3), 28–35.

Herrnstein, R. J., & Murray, C. (1994). *The bell curve: Intelligence and class structure in American life.* New York: Free Press.

Heylighen, F. (1993). Epistemology, introduction. In F. Heylighen, C. Joslyn, & V. Turchin (Eds.), *Principia Cybernetica Web Brussels: Principia Cybernetica.* Retrieved November 2002 from http://pespmc1.vub.ac.be/EPISTEMI.html.

Heylighen, F. (2001). Bootstrapping knowledge representations: From entailment meshes via semantic nets to learning webs. *Kybernetes, 30*(5/6), 691–725.

Hilborn, R. C. (1995). *Chaos and nonlinear dynamics.* New York: Oxford University Press.

Hinman, L. M. (1998). *Ethics: A pluralistic approach to moral theory* (2nd ed.). Fort Worth, tX: Harcourt Brace.

Hirshfield, D. R., Rosenbaum, J. F., Breiderman, J., Bolduc, E. A., Faraone, S. V., Snidman, N., Reznick, J. S., & Kagan, J. (1992). Stable behavior inhibition and its association with anxiety disorder. *Journal of the American Academy of Child and Adolescent Psychiatry, 31,* 103–111.

Hispanic. (2005, October 8). *Wikipedia: The free encyclopedia.* Retrieved October 8, 2005, from http://en.wikipedia.org/wiki/Hispanic.

Hock, D. (1999). *Birth of the chaordic age.* San Francisco: Berrett-Koehler.

Hock, D. (2005). Chaordic commons. Retrieved October 2005 from http://www.chaordic.org/.

Hoffman, L. (1981). *Foundations of family therapy: A conceptual framework for systems change.* New York: Basic Books.

Hoffman, M. (2002, Fall-Winter). Transformation by design: An interview with Dee Hock. *Englighten Next Magazine,* no. 22. Retrieved October 2005 from http://www.enlightennext.org/magazine/j22/.

Hofstadter, D. R. (1979). *Gödel, Escher, Bach.* New York: Basic Books.

Holland, J. H. (1998). *Emergence: From chaos to order.* Reading, MA: Perseus Books.

Hollinger, D. A. (2000). *Postethnic America: Beyond multiculturalism.* New York: Basic Books.

Hollinger, D. A. (2003, December). Amalgamation and hypodescent: The question of ethnoracial mixture in the history of the United States. *American Historical Review,* 1363–1390.

Horney, K. (1950). *Neurosis and human growth.* New York: Norton.

Horwitz, S. (2002, January). The functions of the family in the Great Society. Unpublished Paper, St. Lawrence University, Canton, NY.

Hudson, C. G. (1987). An empirical model of state mental health spending. *Social Work Research & Abstracts, 23* (1), 3.

Hudson, C. G. (1988, Winter). Socioeconomic status and mental illness: Implications of the research for policy and practice. *Journal of Sociology and Social Welfare, 15*(1), 27–54.

Hudson, C. G. (1998). *An interdependency model of homelessness: The dynamics of social disintegration.* Lewiston, NY: Edwin Mellen Press.

Hudson, C.G. (2000a, Spring/Summer). At the edge of chaos: A new paradigm for social work? *Journal of Social Work Education, 36*(2), 215–230.

Hudson, C.G. (2000b). From social Darwinism to self-organization: Implications for social change theory. *Social Service Review, 74*(4), 533–559.

Hudson, C. G. (2004, Fall). The dynamics of self-organization: Neglected dimensions. *Journal of Human Behavior in the Social Environment, 10*(4), 17–38.

Hudson, C. G. (2005). Socioeconomic status and mental illness: Tests of the social causation and selection hypotheses. *American Journal of Orthopsychiatry, 75*(1), 3–18.

Hudson, C.G. (In press). Validation of a model for estimating state and local prevalence of serious mental illness. *International Journal of Methods in Psychiatric Research.*

Hudson, J. D. (1997, September). A model of professional knowledge for social work practice. *Australian Social Work, 50,* 3.

Huntington, S. P. (1996). *The clash of civilizations: Remaking of world order.* New York: Simon & Schuster.

Hy, L. X., & Loevinger, J. (1996). *Measuring ego development.* Mahwah, NJ: Erlbaum.

Inglehart, R., & Baker, W. E. (2000). Modernization, cultural change, and the persistence of traditional values. *American Sociological Review, 65,* 19–51.

Institute for Communitarian Policy Studies. (2009). Washington, DC: George Washington University. Retrieved October 2005 from http://www.gwu.edu/~ccps/index.html.

Jablonski, N. G. (2004). *Annual Review of Anthropology, 33,* 585–623.

Jackson, E. C., Macy, H. J., & Day, P. J. (1984). A simultaneity model for social work education. *Journal of Education for Social Work, 20*(2), 17–24.

Jackson, E. C., Macy, H. J., & Jackendorff, R. (1987). *Consciousness and the computational mind.* Cambridge, MA: MIT Press.

Jacobs, J. (1961). *The death and life of great American cities.* New York: Random House.

Jacobson, M. F. (1999). *Whiteness of a different color: European immigrants and the alchemy of race.* Cambridge, MA: Harvard University Press.

Jacobson, M. J. (2000). Problem solving about complex systems: Differences between experts and novices. In B. Fishman & S. O'Connor-Divelbiss (Eds.), *Fourth International Conference of the Learning Sciences* (pp. 14–21). Mahwah, NJ: Erlbaum.

James, W. (1892). The stream of consciousness. In *Psychology* (Chap. 11). Cleveland: World.

James, W. (1904). Does "consciousness" exist? *Journal of Philosophy, Psychology, and Scientific Methods, 1,* 477–491.

James, W. (1997). *The meaning of truth.* New York: Prometheus Books. (Original work published 1909).

James, W. (1997). *Varieties of religious experience* (reprint ed.). New York: Touchstone Books. (Original work published 1905).

Janis, I. (1982). *Groupthink: Psychological studies of policy decisions and fiascos* (2nd ed.). Boston: Houghton Mifflin.

Janis, I., & Mann, L. (1977). *Decision making: A psychological analysis of conflict, choice, and commitment.* New York: Free Press.

Javitt, D. C., & Coyle, J. T. (2003, December 15). Decoding schizophrenia. *Scientific American, 48–55.*

Jaynes, J. (1976). *The origin of consciousness in the breakdown of the bicameral mind.* Boston: Houthton Mifflin.

Jefferson, L. (1948). *These are my sisters.* Tulsa, OK: Vickers.

Jibu, M., & Yasue, K. (1995). *Quantum brain dynamics and consciousness.* Amsterdam: Benjamins.

Jonassen, D. H. (1997). Instructional design models for well-structured and ill-structured problem-solving learning outcomes. *Educational Technology, Research & Development, 1,* 65–94.

Jones, D. (1999). Evolutionary psychiatry. *Annual Review of Anthropology, 28,* 553–575.

Jordan, J. V. (Ed.). (1997). *Women's growth in diversity: More writings from the Stone Center.* New York: Guilford Press.

Jordan, J. V., Kaplan, A., Miller, J., Striver, I., & Surrey, J. (1991). *Women's growth in connection: Writings from the Stone Center.* New York: Guilford Press.

Jung, C. G. (1922). *Collected works of C. G. Jung.* (21 vols., rev. ed.). Princeton, NJ: Princeton University Press.

Jung, C. G. (1923). On the relation of analytical psychology to poetic art (H.G. Baynes, Trans.). *British Journal of Medical Psychology, 3,* 219–231.

Jung, C. G. (1963). *Memories, dreams, reflections* (Recorded and edited by A. Jaffé; R. & C. Winston, Trans.). New York: Vintage Books.

Jung, C. G. (1971). *Psychological types; or, The psychology of individuation.* Princeton, NJ: Princeton University Press. (Original work published 1921).

Jung, C. G. (1977). *The symbolic life* (Vol. 18, H. Mead, M. Fordham, & G. Adler, Eds.). London: Routledge & Kegan.

Kadushin, C. (In press). *Making connections: An introduction to social network theory.* Oxford University Press.

Kagan, J. (1998). Biology and the child. In W. Damon & R. M. Lerner (Eds.), *Handbook of child psychology* (Vol. 1, pp. 177–236). New York: Wiley.

Kagitcibasi, C. (1996). *Family and human development across cultures: A view from the other side.* Hillsdale, NJ: Erlbaum.

Kahn, A. J. (1973). *Shaping the new social work.* New York: Columbia University Press.

Kahneman, D., Slovic, P., & Tversky, A. (1981). *Judgement under uncertainty: Heuristics and biases.* Cambridge: Cambridge University Press.

Kantor, D., & Lehr, W. (1975). *Inside the family: Toward a theory of family process.* New York: Harper.

Kaplan, B. (Ed.). (1964). *The inner world of mental illness.* New York: Harper & Row.

Kaplan, D., & Manners, R. A. (1972). *Cultural theory.* Prospect Heights, IL: Waveland Press.

Kauffman, S. (1990). *The origins of order*. New York: Oxford University Press.

Kauffman, S. (1995). *At home in the universe: The search for laws of self-organization and complexity*. New York: Oxford University Press.

Kavanagh, D. J. (1992). Recent developments in expressed emotion and schizophrenia. *British Journal of Psychiatry, 160*, 601–620.

Kearsley, G. (2003). Explorations in learning and instruction. Stanford University. Retrieved May 24, 2009, from http://www.stanford.edu/dept/SUSE/projects/ireport/articles/general/Educational;%20theories%20Summary.pdf.

Kelly, D. (2004, December 5). DNA clears the fog over Latino links to Judaism in New Mexico. *Los Angeles Times*.

Kerr, M. E. (2003). *One family's therapy: A primer on Bowen therapy*. Washington, DC: Bowen Center for the Study of the Family.

Kessler, R. C., Chiu, W. T., Demler, O., & Walters, E. E. (2005). Prevalence, severity, and comorbidity of 12-month DSM-IV Disorders in the National Comorbidity survey replication. *Archives of General Psychiatry, 62*, 617–709.

Kezar, A. J. (2001). *Understanding and facilitating organizational change in the twenty-first century: Recent research and conceptualizations*. San Francisco: Jossey-Bass.

King, L. A., & Napa, C. K. (1998). What makes a life good. *Journal of Personality and Social Psychology, 75*(1), 156–165.

Kirst-Ashman, K. K., & Hull, G. H. (2006). *Understanding generalist practice* (4th ed.). Belmont, CA: Thomson-Brooks Cole.

Klaus, P. J. (2005). Summation lecture: CalState Eastbay. Retrieved January 2006 from http://class.csueastbay.edu/anthropology/claus/.

Klein, W. C., & Bloom, M. (1995). Practice wisdom. *Social Work, 40*(6), 799.

Klemm, K., Eguiluz, V. M., Toral, R., & Miguel, M. X. (2005). Globalization, polarization and cultural drift. *Journal of Economic Dynamics and Control, 29*, 321–334.

Kobasa, S. C., & Maddi, S. R. (1977). Existential personality theory. In R. J. Corsini (Ed.), *Current personality theories* (pp. 243–276). Itasca, IL: Peacock.

Koestler, A. (1976). Bisociation in creation. In A. Rothenberg & C. R. Hausman (Eds.), *The creativity question* (pp. 108–113). Durham, NC: Duke University Press.

Koestler, A. (1989). *The act of creation*. New York: Arkana.

Kohut, H. (1971). *The analysis of the self*. New York: International Universities Press.

Kohut, H. (1977). *The restoration of the self*. New York: International Universities Press.

Koopmans, M. (1997). *Schizophrenia and the family: Double bind theory revisited*. New York: York College, City University of New York.

Koopmans, M. (1998). Chaos theory and the problem of change in family systems. *Nonlinear Dynamics, Psychology, and Life Sciences, 2*(2), 133–148.

Kottak, C. P., & Kozaitis, K. A. (1999). The multicultural society. In *On being different: Diversity and multiculturalism in the North American mainstream* (pp. 48–51). New York: McGraw-Hill.

Kotter, J. P. (1985). *Power and influence: Beyond formal authority.* New York: Free Press.

Krippner, S. (1994). Humanistic psychology and chaos theory: The third revolution and the third force. *Journal of Humanistic Psychology, 34*(3), 48–61.

Kris, E. (1952). On preconscious mental processes. In E. Kris. (Ed.), *Psychoanalytic explorations in art* (pp. 310–318). New York: International Universities Press.

Kropotkin, P.A. (1972). *Mutual aid: A factor of evolution.* London: Allen Lane. (Original work published 1902).

Kuhn, T. S. (1970). *The structure of scientific revolutions* (2nd ed.). Chicago: University of Chicago Press.

LaBerge, D. (1995). *Attentional processing: The brain's art of mindfulness.* Cambridge, MA: Harvard University Press.

LaBerge, D. (1998). Defining awareness by the triangular circuit of attention. *Psyche 4*(7), 149–181.

Laing, R. D. (1961) *The Self and Others.* London: Tavistock.

Lamarck, J.-B. (1809). *Philosophie zologique* (Hugh Elliot, Trans. (1984). *Zoological philosophy: An exposition with regard to the natural history of animals.* Chicago: University of Chicago Press).

Lang, C. (2003). Predictive deduction: Expanding the arsenal of science. Retrieved August 2003 from http://philosophy.wisc.edu/lang/pd/pdo.htm.

Langer, E. J. (1997). *The power of mindful learning.* Reading, MA: Perseus Books.

Larson, D. B., Larson, S. S., & Koenig, H. G. (2000, October). The once-forgotten factor in psychology: Research findings on religious commitment and mental health. *Psychiatric Times, 17*(10), 18–23.

Lasch, C. (1978). *The culture of narcissism.* New York: Norton.

Laszlo, E. (1996). *Evolution: The general theory.* Cresskill, NJ: Hampton Press.

Lave, J., & Wenger, E. (1991). *Situated learning. Legitimate peripheral participation.* Cambridge: Cambridge University Press.

Lawrence, P. R., & J. W. Lorsch. (1967). *Organization and environment: Managing differentiation and integration.* Boston: Harvard University Graduate School of Administration, Division of Research.

Lawson, M., & Alameda-Lawson, T. (2001). What's wrong with them is what's wrong with us. *Journal of Community Practice, 9*(1), 77–97.

Leading Edge Research Group. (1995). Key figures, philosophies in the rise of materialistic scientism and the church of scientism. Retrieved March 2002 from http://www.trufax.org/avoid/scienus.html.

Leary, T. (1957). *Interpersonal diagnosis of personality: A functional theory and methodology for personality evaluation.* New York: Ronald Press.

Leighninger, R. D. Jr. (1977, Fall). Systems theory and social work: A reexamination. *Journal of Education for Social Work, 13*(3), 44–49.

Lemann, N. (1997). The bell curve flattened. *Slate.* Retrieved May 2006 from http://www.slate.com/id/2416.

Lerner, R. M. (2006). *Handbook of child psychology: Vol. 1. Theoretical Models of Human Development.* New York: Wiley.

LeVay, S. (1991, August), A difference in hypothalamic structure between hetero-sexual and homosexual men. *Science, 253*, 1034–1037.

Levin, M. (1998, July). Squaring the circle: An ingenious attempt to explain racial differences in achievement. *American Rennaissance, 9*(7). Retrieved June 27, 2009, from http://www.amren.com/ar/1998/07/#article1.

Levinson, E. A. (1994). The uses of disorder: Chaos theory and psychoanalysis. *Contemporary Psychoanalysis, 30*(1), 5–24.

Lewin, K. (1935). *A dynamic theory of personality.* New York: McGraw-Hill.

Lewin, K. (1951). *Field theory in social science: Selected theoretical papers* (D. Cartwright, Ed.). New York: Harper & Row.

Lewin, R. (1992). *Complexity: Life at the edge of complexity.* New York: Macmillan.

Lewis, H. (1982). *The intellectual base of social work practice.* New York: Haworth Press.

Lewis, O. (1965). *La vida: A Puerto Rican Family in the culture of poverty San Juan and New York.* New York: Vintage Books.

Lewis, O. (1998, January). The culture of poverty. *Society, 35*, 7.

Lewontin, R. C. (1972). The apportionment of human diversity. In T. Dobzhansky, M. K. Hecht, & W. C. Steere (Eds.), *Evolutionary biology* (Vol. 6, pp. 381–398). New York: Appleton-Century-Crofts.

Li, T. Y., & Yorke, J. A. (1975). Period three implies chaos. *American Mathematical Monthly, 82*, 985–992.

Lin, K. M. (1983). *Hwa-byung:* A Korean culture-bound syndrome? *American Journal of Psychiatry, 140*, 105–107.

Lin, K. M., Anderson, D., & Poland, R. E. (1997). Ethnic and cultural considerations in psychopharmacotherapy. In D. Dunner (Ed.), *Current Psychiatric Therapy II* (pp. 75–81). Philadelphia: Saunders.

Lindblom, C. E. (1950, Spring). The science of muddling through. *Public Administration Review, 19*, 79–88.

Lindgren, K. N., & Coursey, R. D. (1995). Spirituality and serious mental illness: A two-part study. *Psychosocial Rehabilitation Journal, 18*(3), 93–111.

Liu, E. (1999). *The accidental Asian: Notes of a native speaker.* New York: Vintage Books.

Livesley, W. J. (2001). *Handbook of personality disorders.* New York: Guilford Press.

Loh, J., & Harmon, D. (2005). A global index of biocultural diversity. *Ecological Indicators, 5*, 231–241.

Longley, J., & Pruitt, D. G. (1980). Groupthink: A critique of Janis's theory. In L. Wheeler (Ed.), *Review of Personality and Social Psychology* (Vol. 1, pp. 74–93). Beverly Hills, CA: Sage.

Longres, J. F. (2000). *Human behavior and the social environment* (3rd ed.). Pacific Grove, CA: Brooks/Cole.

Lopez, S. R., & Guarnaccia, P. J. (2000). Cultural psychopathology: Uncovering the social world of mental illness. *Annual Review of Psychology, 51*, 571–598.

'Lorenz, E. N. (1963). Deterministic nonperiodic flow, *Journal of the Atmospheric Sciences, 20*, 130–141.

Lorenz, E. N. (1972). Predictability: Does the flap of a butterfly's wings in Brazil set off a tornado in Texas? Paper presented at the AAAs Convention of the Global Atmospheric Research Program, MIT, Cambridge, MA.

Lorenz, E. N. (1993). *The essence of chaos.* Seattle: University of Washington Press.

Lovelock, J. E. (1972). Gaia as seen through the atmosphere. *Atmospheric Environment, 6*(8), 579–580.

Lovelock, J. E., & Margulis, L. (1974). Atmospheric homeostasis by and for the biosphere: The Gaia hypothesis. *Tellus, 26*(1), 2–10.

Loye, D., & Eisler, R. (1987). Chaos and transformation: Implications of nonequilibrium theory for social science and society. *Behavioral Science, 32,* 53–65.

Lu, L. (1999). Personal or environmental causes of happiness: A longitudinal analysis. *Journal of Social Psychology, 139*(1), 79–90.

Luhmann, N. (1986). The autopoiesis of social systems. In F. Geyer & J. van der Zouwen (Eds.), *Sociocybernetic paradoxes: Observation, control and evolution of self-steering systems* (pp. 172–192). London: Sage.

Luhmann, N. (1990). *Essays on self-reference.* New York: Columbia University Press.

Lukoff, D. (1985). Diagnosis of mystical experiences with psychotic features. *Journal of Transpersonal Psychology, 17*(2), 155–181.

Lundblad, K. S. (1995). Jane Addams and social reform: A role model for the 1990s. *Social Work, 40*(5), 661–669.

Lux, K. (1990). *Adam Smith's mistake: How a moral philosopher invented economics and ended morality.* Boston: Shambhala.

Lynall, M., Golden, B. R., & Hillman, A. J. (2003). Board composition from adolescence to maturity: A multitheoretical view. *Academy of Management Review, 28,* 416–443.

Maccoby, E. E., & Jacklin, C. N. (1974). *The psychology of sex differences,* Stanford, CA: Stanford University Press.

Macionis, J. J. (2005). *Sociology.* Upper Saddle River, NJ: Prentice Hall.

Madanes, C. (1981). *Strategic family therapy.* San Francisco: Jossey-Bass.

Maddi, S. R. (1994). *Wellness lecture series.* Oakland: University of California/HealthNet.

Maddi, S. R. (1996). *Personality theories: A comparative analysis.* San Francisco: Brooks/Cole.

Maddi, S.R. (1999a). Comments on trends in hardiness research and theorizing. *Consulting Psychology Journal: Practice and Research, 51*(2), 67–71.

Maddi, S.R. (1999b). The personality construct of hardiness: I. Effects on experiencing, coping, and strain. *Consulting Psychology Journal: Practice and Research, 51*(2), 83–94.

Maddi, S. R., & Khoshaba, D. M. (1994). Hardiness and mental health. *Journal of Personality Assessment, 63*(2), 265–274.

Magill, R. S., & Clark, T. N. (1975). Community power and decision making: Recent research and its policy implications. *Social Service Review, 49*(1), 33–45.

Mahler, M. S., Pine, F., & Bergman, A. (1975). *The psychological birth of the human infant.* New York: Basic Books.

Malinowski, B. (1944). A scientific theory of culture. Chapel Hill: University of North Carolina Press.

Malthus, T. R. (1971). *An essay on the principle of population or a view of its past and present effects on human happiness.* Reprints of Economic Classics. New York: Kelley. (Original work published 1798).

Mandel, D. R. (1995, February). Chaos theory, sensitive dependence, and the logistic equation. *American Psychologist,50,* 106–107.

Mandell, A. J. (1980). Statistical stability in random brain processes: Possible implications for polydrug abuse in the borderline syndrome. In N. K. Mello (Ed.), *Advances in substance abuse: Behaviorial and biological research* (Vol. 2, pp. 1–90). Greenwich, CT: JAI Press.

Mandell, A. J., & Selz, K. A. (1995). Nonlinear dynamical patterns as personality theory for neurobiology and psychiatry. *Psychiatry, 58,* 371–390.

March, J. G. & Simon, H. A. (1958). *Organizations.* New York: Wiley.

Marcia, J. E. (1966). Development and validation of ego identity status. *Journal of Personality and Social Psychology, 3,* 551–558.

Margulis, L. (1981). *Symbiosis in cell evolution.* San Francisco: Freeman.

Markič, O. (1999). Emergent properties. Retrieved December 2001 from http://ciiweb.ijs.si/dialogues/r-markic.htm.

Markland, D., Ryan, R. M., Tobin, V. J., & Rollnick, S. (2005). Motivational interviewing and self-determination theory. *Journal of Social and Clinical Psychology, 24*(6), 811–831.

Marrow, A. J. (1969). *Practical theorist: The life and work of Kurt Lewin.* New York: Basic Books.

Maruyama, M. (1963). The second cybernetics: Deviation-amplifying mutual causal processes. *American Scientist, 51,* 164–179.

Marx, K., & Engels, F. (1932). *The communist manifesto.* New York: International.

Marx, K., & Engels, F. (1959). *Das elend der philosophie.* (As quoted and translated in Ralf Dahrendorf, *Class and class conflict in industrial society.* Stanford, CA: Stanford University Press).

Maslow, A. H. (1943). A theory of human motivation. *Psychological Review, 50*(4), 370–396.

Maslow, A. H. (1971). *The farther reaches of human nature.* New York: Viking.

Maslow, A. H., & Lowery, R. (Eds.). (1998). *Toward a psychology of being* (3rd ed.). New York: Wiley.

Masters, W., Johnson, V., & Kolodny, R. (1982). *Human sexuality.* Boston: Little, Brown.

Mattingly-Scott, M. (2003). Retrieved April 2004 from http://home.t-online.de/home/scott/problem_solving.html.

Maturana, H. R. & Varela, F. J. (1987). *The tree of knowledge: The biological roots of human understanding.* Boston: Shambhala.

May, R. (1986). Transpersonal. *APA Monitor, 17*(5), 2.

May, R. M. (1976). Simple mathematical models with very complicated dynamics. *Nature, 261,* 459–467.

McCarthy, P. (2003). Subjective conscious experience: The real problem for materialism. Retrieved February 2003 from http://www.damaris.org/dcscs/readingroom/2000/experience.htm.

McClure, B. A. (1998). *Putting a new spin on groups: The science of chaos.* Mahwah, NJ: Erlbaum.

McDougall, W. (1908). *An introduction to social psychology.* London: Methuen.

McLaughlin, B. (1992). The rise and fall of British emergentism. In A. Beckermann, H. Flohr, & J. Kim (Eds.), *Emergence or reduction?* (pp. 49–93). Berlin: de Gruyter.

McMillan, D. W., & Chavis, D. M. (1986). Sense of community: A definition and theory. *American Journal of Community Psychology, 14*(1), 6–23.

Meacham, J. (1997). Autobiography, voice, and developmental theory. In E. Amsel & K. A. Renninger (Eds.), *Change and development* (pp. 43–60). Mahwah, NJ: Erlbaum.

Meinert, R. G. (1980). Values in social work called dysfunctional myth. *Journal of Social Welfare, 6*(3), 5–16.

Merriam-Webster dictionary (11th ed.). (2003). Springfield, MA: Merriam-Webster.

Merriam, S. B., & Caffarella, R. S. (1999). *Learning in adulthood: A comprehensive guide.* San Francisco: Jossey-Bass.

Merry, U. (1995). *Copy with uncertainty: Insights from the new sciences of chaos, self-organization, and complexity.* Westport, CT: Praeger.

Merton, R. K. (1957). *Social theory and social structure* (rev. ed.). New York: Free Press.

Merton, R. K. (1968). *Social theory and social structure* (rev. ed.). New York: Free Press.

Meyer, E., & Covi, L. (1960). The experience of depersonalization: A written report by a patient. *Psychiatry, 23,* 215–217.

Micevych, P. E., & Abelson, L. (1991). Disbribution of MRNAs coding for liver and heart gap junction protein in the rat central nervous system. *Journal of Comparative Neurology, 305,* 96–118.

Midgely, J. (1993). Ideological roots of social development strategies. *Social Development Issues, 15*(1), 1–13.

Miller, J. (1955). Toward a general theory of the behavioral sciences. *American Psychologist, 10,* 513–531.

Millon, T. (1969). *Modern psychopathology.* Philadelphia: Saunders.

Millon, T., & Davis, R. (2000). *Personality disorders in modern life.* New York: Wiley.

Mintzberg, H. (1979). *The structuring of organizations.* Upper Saddle River, NJ: Prentice Hall.

Minuchin, S. (1967). *Families of the slums: An exploration of their structure and treatment.* New York: Basic Books.

Minuchin, S. (1974). *Families and family therapy.* Cambridge, MA: Harvard University Press.

Miramontes, O. Complexity and social behavior. Retrieved February 11, 2009, from http://scifunam.fisica.unam.mx/mir/comp_soc.html.

Mjøset, L. (2002). Understanding of theory in the social sciences. ARENA Working Papers, Department of Sociology and Human Geography, University of Oslo.

Moore, M. (2005). Sex, miscegenation, and the intermarriage debate. *New Voices.* Retrieved May 2006 from http://www.shmoozenet.com/jsps/index.html.

Moorman, C., & Miner, A. S. (1997). The impact of organizational memory on new product performance and creativity. *Journal of Marketing Research, 34*(1), 91–106.

Morris-Suzuki, T. (1988). *Beyond computopia.* London: Routledge Kegan Paul.

Moshman, D. (1999). *Adolescent psychological development: Rationality, morality, and identity.* Mahwah, NJ: Erlbaum.

Mullen, B., Anthony, T., Salas, E., & Driscoll, J. E. (1994). Group cohesiveness and quality of decision making: An integration of tests of the groupthink hypothesis. *Small Group Research, 25,* 189–204.

Murmann, J. P., Aldrich, H., Levinthal, D., & Winter, S. (2003, March). Evolutionary thought in management and organization theory at the beginning of the new millennium. *Journal of Management Inquiry, 12*(1), 1–19.

Murray, C. (2003). *Human accomplishment: The pursuit of excellence in the arts and sciences.* New York: Harper Collins.

Myers, D. G. (1992). *The pursuit of happiness.* New York: Avon Books.

Myers, D. G. (2002). *Intuition: Its powers and perils.* New Haven, CT: Yale University Press.

Mystica. (2003). Intuition. Retrieved March 2004 from http://www.themystica.com/mystica/articles/i/intuition.html.

Naess, A. (1973). The shallow and the deep, long range ecology movements: A summary. *Inquiry, 16,* 95–100.

Nagel, T. (1974, October). What is it like to be a bat? *Philosophical Review, 83*(4), 435–450.

Nakamura, J., & Csikszentmihaly, M. (2001). Catalytic creativity: The case of Linus Pauling. *American Psychologist, 56*(4), 337–341.

Napier, A. Y., & Whitaker, C. A. (1978). *Family crucible: The intensive experience of family therapy.* New York: Harper & Row.

National Association of Social Workers. (1974). Silver Spring, MD: Author. (Reprinted from American Association of Social Workers. (1929). *Social case work generic and specific: A report of the Milford conference.* New York: Author).

National Center for Charitable Statistics. (2003). Nonprofit statistics. Retrieved August 2005 from http://nccs.urban.org/.

Neill, J., & Kniskern, D. (Eds.). (1982). *From psyche to system: The evolving therapy of Carl Whitaker.* New York: Guilford Press.

Nelson, J. (1993). Testing practice wisdom: Another use for single system research. *Journal of Social Service Research, 18*(1–2), 65–82.

Neugarten, B. (1985). Adaptation and the life cycle. *Counseling Psychologist, 6,* 16–20.

Newman, J. (1996). Thalamocortical foundations of conscious experience. Denver: Colorado Neurological Institute. Retrieved January 2003 from http://www .phil.vt.edu/assc/newman/default.html.

Newman, W. (1973). *American pluralism: A study of minority groups and social theory*. New York: Harper & Row.

Nickols, F. (2000). Communities of practice resources. Retrieved June 2005 from http://home.att.net/~discon/KM/CoPs.htm.

Nisbett, R. E. (2003). *The geography of thought: How Asians and Westerns think differently . . . and why*. New York: Free Press.

Nolan, D. (1971). Classifying and analyzing politico-economic systems. *Individualist,* 1457–1462.

Nordby, S. (2001, August). An essay on Edward de Bono. Retrieved February 2004 from http://members.aol.com/svennord/ed/debono.htm.

North Carolina, Health and Human Services, Division of Social Services. *Family Services* (Vol. 1, Chap. 8). Retrieved June 2009 from http://info.dhhs.state.nc .us/olm/manuals/dss/csm-60/man/CS1407-03.htm.

O'Hare, T. (2005). *Evidence-based practices for social workers*. Chicago: Lyceum Books.

Occidental College. (2006). Community development. Retrieved February 2006 from http://departments.oxy.edu/orgl/Manual/Community.htm.

Ogburn, W. F. (1922). *Social change*. New York: Huebsch.

Ogryzko, V. V. (1997). A quantum-theoretical approach to the phenomenon of directed mutations in bacteria (hypothesis). *Biosystems, 43*(2), 83–95.

Ohta, A. S. (2000). Rethinking interaction in SLA: Developmentally appropriate assistance in the zone of proximal development and the acquisition of L2 grammar. In J. P. Lantolf (Ed.), *Sociocultural theory and second language learning* (pp. 51–78). New York: Oxford University Press.

Olshansky, S. J., & Ault, B. A. (1986). The fourth stage of the epidemiologic transition: The age of delayed degenerative diseases. *Milbank Quarterly, 64*(3), 355–391.

Oxford Dictionary of English. (1998). Oxford: Oxford University Press.

Packard, N. (1988). *Adaptation toward the edge of chaos*. Technical Report CCSR-88-5, Center for Complex Systems Research, University of Illinois.

Padoa-Schioppa, C., & Assad, J. A. (2006, April 23). Neurons in the orbitofrontal cortex encode economic value. *Nature, 441,* 223–226.

Pajares, F. (2002). Biography, chronology, and photographs of William James. Retrieved April 2004 from http://www.emory.edu/EDUCATION/mfp/jphotos .html.

Papageorge, A. (2004). *GoInnovate!* Cardiff, CA: GoInnovate.

Parekh, B. (2000). *Rethinking multiculturalism: Cultural diversity and political theory*. New York: Palgrave.

Parekh, B., & Bhabha, H. (1989, June). Identities on parade. *Marxism Today,* 24–29.

Park, R. E. (1964). *Race and culture*. New York: Free Press.

Parlett, M. (1991). Reflections on field theory. *British Gestalt Journal, 1*(2), 68–91.

Parsons, T. (1951). *The social system*. Glencoe, IL: Free Press.

Pells, R. (2002, April 12). American culture goes global, or does it? *Chronicle of Higher Education*, B7.

Pennings, J. M. (1975). The relevance of the structural contingency model for organizational effectiveness *Administrative Science Quarterly, 20,* 393–410.

Penrose, R. (1994). *Shadows of the mind: A search for the missing science of consciousness* Oxford: Oxford University Press.

Pepitone, A. (1981). The science of group dynamics: Lessons from the history of social psychology. *American Psychologist, 36,* 972–985.

Perlman, H. H. (1957). *Social casework: A problem-solving process.* Chicago: University of Chicago Press.

Peters, M. (2000). Can there be a test for consciousness? *Cogito, 1*(2), 39–44.

PhilPapers. Varieties of feminism. Retrieved July 2006 from http://philpapers.org/browse/varieties-of-feminism.

Piliavin, J. A., Dovidio, J. F., Gaertner, S. L., & Clark, R. D., III. (1982). Responsive bystanders: The process of intervention. In V. J. Derlega & J. Grzelak (Eds.), *Cooperation and helping behavior: Theories and research* (pp. 279–304). New York: Academic Press.

Pincus, A. L. (1994). The interpersonal circumplex and the interpersonal theory: Perspectives on personality and its pathology. In S. Strack & M. Lorr (Eds.), *Differentiating normal and abnormal personality* (pp. 114–136). New York: Springer.

Pincus, A., & Minahan, A. (1973). *Social work practice: Model and method.* Itasca, IL: Peacock.

Pincus, D. (2001). A framework and methodology for the study of nonlinear, self-organizing family dynamics. *Nonlinear Dynamics, Psychology, and Life Sciences, 5*(2), 139–173.

Pinker, S. (1997). *How the mind works.* New York: Norton.

Pintrich, P. R. (1999). An achievement goal theory perspective on issues in motivation terminology, theory, and research. *Contemporary Educational Psychology, 25,* 92–104.

Poertner, J. (2001, May 23–25). Linking child welfare and child outcomes. In *Proceedings of the Fourth Annual National Forum of Services Training and Evaluation Symposium* (pp. 95–113). Berkeley: University of California, Berkeley.

Polanyi, M. (1966). *The tacit dimension.* Garden City, NY: Doubleday.

Poole, M. S. (1981). Decision development in small groups I: A comparison of two models. *Communication Monographs, 48,* 1–24.

Poole, M. S. (1983). Decision development in small groups II & III: A study of mutiple sequences in decision making. *Communication Monographs, 50,* 206–232, 321–341.

Poole, M. S., & Roth, J. (1989). Decision development in small groups V: Test of a contingency model. *Human Communication Research, 15,* 549–589.

Poplin, D. E. (1972). *Communities: A survey of theories and methods of research.* New York: Macmillan.

Popper, K. R. (1959). *The logic of scientific discovery* (Logik der Forschung, Trans.). London: Hutchinson.

Popper, K. R. (1974). *Conjectures and refutations: The growth of scientific knowledge.* London: Routledge. (Original work published 1963).

Popper, K. R. (1990). *A world of propensities.* Bristol, UK: Thoemmes Antiquarian Books.

Popper, K. R. (1974), *Conjectures and refutations: The growth of scientific knowledge.* London: Routledge. (Original work published 1963).

Popper, K. R., & Eccles, J.C. (1977). *The self and its brain.* Berlin: Springer.

Porter, E. (2004). A typology of virtual communities: A multi-disciplinary foundation for future research. *Journal of Computer-Mediated Communication, 10*(1), 3.

Powell, R. R. (n.d.). History of personality theory. Retrieved October 2003 from www .armchair_academic.homstead.com/HistoryPer-ns4.html.

Prigogine, I. (1996). *The end of certainty: Time, chaos, and the new laws of nature.* New York: Free Press.

Prigogine, I., & Stengers, I. (1984). *Order out of chaos.* New York: Bantam Books.

Prince, R. (1989). Somatic complaint syndromes and depression: The problem of cultural effects on symptomatology. *Mental Health Research, 8,* 104–117.

Prochaska, J. O., Velicer, W. F., DiClemente, C. C., & Fava, J. L. (1988). Measuring the processes of change: Applications to the cessation of smoking. *Journal of Consulting and Clinical Psychology, 56,* 520–528.

Pulkkinen, L., & Caspi, A. (Eds.). (2002). *Paths to successful development: Personality in the life course.* Cambridge: Cambridge University Press.

Putnam, R. D. (2000). *Bowling alone: The collapse and revival of American community.* New York: Simon & Schuster.

Quigley, C. (1979). *The evolution of civilizations: An introduction to historical analysis* (rev. 2nd ed.). Indianapolis, IN: Liberty Fund.

Quinsey, V.L. (1998, July). Review of S. Baron-Cohen (Ed.), (1997). *The maladapted mind. Classic readings in evolutionary psychopathology.* Hove, UK: Psychology Press. *Evolutionary and Human Behavior, 19,* 265–271.

Radcliffe-Brown, R. (1952). Structure and function in primitive society. New York: Free Press.

Radin, D. (1997). *The conscious universe.* New York: Harper Collins.

Ravitch, D. (2000). Multiculturalism: E pluribus plures. In S. Steinberg (Ed.), Race and ethnicity in the United States: Issues and debates (pp. 267–276). Malden, MA: Blackwell.

Reamer, F. G. (1995). *Social work, values, and ethics.* New York: Columbia University Press.

Reamer, F. G., & Conrad, A. P. (1995). *Professional choices: Ethics at work* (Video). National Association of Social Workers.

Reiss, D. (1981). *The family's construction of reality.* Cambridge, MA: Harvard University Press.

Richards, R. (1996, Spring). Does the lone genius ride again? Chaos, creativity, and community. *Journal of Humanistic Psychology, 36*(2), 44–60.

Richards, R. (1998). Everyday creativity. In H. S. Friedman (Ed.), *Encyclopedia of Mental Health* (Vol. 1, pp. 619–633). San Diego: Academic Press.

Richards, R. (2000–2001). Millennium as opportunity: Chaos, creativity, and Guilford's structure of intellect model. *Creativity Research Journal, 13*(3–4), 249–265.

Richmond, M. (1917). *Social diagnosis.* New York: Russell Sage Foundation.

Richter, W., Richter, M., & Warren, W. S., Merkle, H., Andersen, P., Adriany, G., et al. (2000). Functional magnetic resonance imaging with intermolecular multiple-quantum coherences. *Magnetic Resonance Imaging, 18,* 489–494.

Riesbeck, C. K., & Schank, R. (1989). *Inside case-based reasoning.* Mahwah, NJ: Erlbaum.

Rifkin, J. (1981). *Entropy: A new world view.* New York: Bantam Books.

Ripple, L. (1969). *Motivation, opportunity, and capacity: Studies in casework theory and practice.* Chicago: University of Chicago, School of Social Service Administration.

Rivkin, M. C., & Hoopman, M. (1991). Moving beyond risk to resiliency: The school's role in supporting resilience in children. Minneapolis: Comprehensive Teaming to Assure Resiliency in Students, Minneapolis Public Schools.

Robbins, S. R. (1999). Theory, knowledge, and social work practice: Ongoing debates and fresh perspectives. *Families in Society, 80*(4), 325–326.

Robertshaw, J. E., Mecca, S. J., & Reick, M. N. (1978). *Problem solving: A systems approach.* New York: Petrocelli Books.

Robinson, R., & Yaden, D. B. (1993). Chaos or nonlinear dynamics: Implications for reading research. *Reading Research and Instruction, 32,* 15–23.

Rogers, C. R. (1965). *Client-centered therapy.* London: Constable.

Rogoff, B. (2003). *The cultural nature of human development.* Oxford: Oxford University Press.

Romig, J. (1997). *Sum ergo cogito: Development and learning—An educational and cognitive perspective.* Des Moines, IA: Drake University.

Roscoe, W. (Ed.) (1947). *The works of Alexander Pope, Esq.* (Vol 4). London: Longman, Brown.

Rosen, A., Proctor, E. E., Morrow-Howell, N., & Staudt, M. (1995). Rationales for practice decisions: Variations in knowledge use by decision task and social work service. *Research on Social Work Practice, 5*(4), 501–523.

Rosenthal, D. M. (1991). Two concepts of consciousness. In D. M. Rosenthal (Ed.), *The nature of mind* (pp. 197–203). Oxford: Oxford University Press.

Rosenthal, R., & Jacobson, L. (1992). *Pygmalion in the classroom: Teacher expectation and pupils' intellectual development.* New York: Irvington.

Ross, K. L. (2002). Foundationalism and hermeneutics. Retrieved October 2001 from http://www.friesian.com/hermenut.htm.

Rothbart, M. K. (1989). Temperament in childhood. In G. A. Kohnstamm, J. E. Bates, & M. K. Rothbart (Eds.), *Temperament in childhood* (pp. 59–73). New York: Wiley.

Ruble, T. L., & Thomas, K. (1976). Support for two-dimensional model of conflict behavior. *Organizational Behavior and Human Performance, 16,* 143–155.

Rummel, R. J. (1994). *Death by government.* New Brunswick, NJ: Transaction.

Rummel, R. J. (1997). *Power kills: Democracy as a method of nonviolence.* New Brunswick, NJ: Transaction.

Rutledge, M. D. (1995). Social Darwinism, scientific racism, and the metaphysics of race. *Journal of Negro Education, 64*(3), 243–252.

Ryan, R. M., & Deci, E. L. (1999). Intrinsic and extrinsic motivations: Classic definitions and new directions. *Contemporary Educational Psychology, 25,* 54–67.

Ryan, R. M., & Deci, E. L. (2001). On happiness and human potentials: A review of research on hedonic and eudaimonic well-being. In S. Fiske (Ed.), *Annual Review of Psychology* (Vol. 52, pp. 141–166). Palo Alto, CA: Annual Reviews.

Sabelli, H. C., Carlson-Sabelli, L., Patel, M., Levy, A., & Diez-Martin, J. (1995). Anger, fear, depression and crime: Physiological and psychological studies using the process method. In R. Robertson & A. Combs (Eds.), *Chaos theory in psychology and the life sciences.* Mahwah, NJ: Erlbaum.

Sahlins, M. D., & Service, E. (1960). *Evolution and culture.* Ann Arbor: University of Michigan Press.

Salem, D. A., Reischl, T. M., Gallacher, F., & Randall, K. W. (2000, June). The role of referent and expert power in mutual help. *American Journal of Community Psychology, 28*(3), 303–324.

Sarason, S. B. (1974). *The psychological sense of community: Prospects for a community psychology.* San Francisco: Jossey-Bass.

Satinover, J. (2001). *The quantum brain.* New York: Wiley.

Satir, V. (1964). *Conjoint family therapy.* Palo Alto, CA: Science and Behavior Books.

Satir, V. (1972). *Peoplemaking.* Palo Alto, CA: Science and Behavior Books.

Satir, V. (1998). *The new peoplemaking.* Mountain View, CA: Science and Behavior Books,

Schatz, M. S., Jenkins, L. E., & Sheafor, B. W. (1990). Milford redefined: A model of initial and advanced generalist social work. *Journal of Social Work Education, 26*(3), 217–231.

Schein, E. H. (1980). *Organizational psychology: Foundations of modern psychology.* New York: Pearson.

Schlesinger, A. M. (1998). *The disuniting of America.* New York: Norton.

Schofield, W. (1964). *Psychotherapy: The purchase of friendship.* Englewood Cliffs, NJ: Prentice Hall.

Scholte, J. A. (2000). *Globalization: A critical introduction.* London: Palgrave.

Schon, D. A. (1983). *The reflective practitioner: How professionals think in action.* New York: Basic Books.

Schuler, D. (2008). *Liberating voices: A pattern language for communication revolution.* Cambridge, MA: MIT Press.

Schultz, D. & Schultz, E. (2000). *A history of modern psychology* (7th ed.). Fort Worth, TX: Harcourt.

Schuman, S. P., & Schwarz, R. M. (1998). Using theory and research to improve your practice. In J. Spee (Ed.), *Proceedings, International Association of Facilitators* (pp. 90–94). Santa Clara, CA: International Association of Facilitators.

Schwartz, W. (1961). Between client and system: The mediating function. In R. B. Pernell & B. Saunders (Eds.), *Theories of social work with groups* (pp. 171–197). New York: National Association of Social Workers.

Scott, A. (1995). *Stairways to the mind: The controversial new science of consciousness.* New York: Springer-Verlag.

Scott, D. (1990). Practice wisdom: The neglected source of practice research. *Social Work, 35*(6), 564–568.

Scott, R. W. (1992). *Organizations: Rational, natural and open systems.* Upper Saddle River, NJ: Prentice Hall.

Searle, J. (1980). Minds, brains and programs. *Behavioral and Brain Sciences, 3,* 417–424.

Seife, C. (2000, February 4). Cold numbers unmake the quantum mind. *Science,* 786–789.

Seligman, M. E. P., & Csikszentmihalyi, M. (2000). Positive psychology: An introduction. *American Psychologist, 55*(1), 5–14.

Selznick, P. (1996, June). Institutionalism "old" and "new." *Administrative Science Quarterly, 41,* 270–277.

Shakun, M. F. (2001). Unbounded rationality. *Group Decision and Negotiation, 97*(118), 97–118.

Shapiro, D. (1965). *Neurotic styles.* New York: Basic Books.

Shaw, G. B. (1911). The doctor's dilemma. *Project Gutenberg.* Retrieved April 2003 from http://www.gutenberg.org/wiki/Main_Page.

Shear, J. (1996). The hard problem: Closing the empirical gap. *Journal of Consciousness Studies, 3*(1), 54–68.

Sheehy, G. (1991). *Pathfinders.* New York: Morrow.

Sheehy, G. (1995). *New passages: Mapping your life across time.* New York: Ballantine Books.

Sheffield, A. (1937). *Social insight in case situations.* New York: Appleton Century.

Sheldon, K. M., & Elliot, A. J. (1999). Goal striving, need satisfaction, and longitudinal well-being: The self-concordance model. *Journal of Personality and Social Psychology, 76*(3), 482–497.

Sheldon, K. M., Elliot, A. J., Kim, Y., & Kasser, T. (2001, February). What is satisfying about satisfying events? Testing 10 candidate psychological needs. *Journal of Personality and Social Psychology, 80*(2), 325–339.

Sheridan, J. E., & Abelson, M. A. (1983). Cusp catastrophe model of employee turnover. *Academy of Management Journal, 26,* 418–436.

Siebert, A. (1996). *Survivor personality.* Portland, OR: Perigee Books.

Simmel, G. (1964). *Conflict and the web of group affiliations.* New York: Free Press.

Simon, H. A. (1969), *The sciences of the artificial.* Karl Taylor Compton Lectures. Cambridge, MA: MIT Press.

Simon, H. A. (1986). Decision making and problem solving. In National Academy of Sciences (Ed.), *Research briefings 1986: Report of the research briefing panel on decision making and problem solving.* Washington, DC: National Academy Press.

Simonton, D. K. (1997). Sociocultural context of individual creativity: A transhistorical time-eries analysis. In *Genius and creativity: Selected papers* (pp. 3–28). Greenwich, CT: Ablex.

Siporin, M. (1980). Ecological systems theory in social work. *Journal of Sociology and Social Welfare, 7*(7), 507–532.

Sirianni, C., & Friedland, L. (2005). Social capital. *Civic Practices Network.* Retrieved October 2005 from http://www.cpn.org/ections/tools/models/social_capital .html.

Slater, E., & Slater, P. (1944). A heuristic theory of neurosis. *Journal of Neurology, Neurosurgery, and Psychiatry, 49,* 49–55.

Sluzki, C. E., Beavin, J., Tarnopolsky, A., & Verón, E. (1967). Transactional disqualification research on the double bind. *Archives of General Psychiatry, 16,* 494–504.

Smalley, R. E. (1970). The functional approach to social casework. In R. Roberts & R. Nee (Eds.), *Theories of social casework* (pp. 79–128). Chicago: University of Chicago Press.

Smart, B. (1993). *Postmodernity.* London: Routledge.

Smelser, N. J. (1968). *Essays in sociological explanation.* Englewood Cliffs, NJ: Prentice Hall.

Smith, M. K. (2001). Community. *Encyclopedia of informal education.* Retrieved September 2005 from http://www.infed.org/community/community.htm.

Smith, T. S., & Stevens, G. T. (1999). The architecture of small networks: Strong interaction and dynamic organization in small social systems. *American Sociological Review, 64,* 403–420.

Sober, E., & Wilson, D. S. (1998). *Unto others: The evolution and psychology of unselfish behavior.* Cambridge, MA: Harvard University Press.

Solms, M. (1997). What is consciousness? *Journal of the American Psychoanalytic Association, 45*(3), 681–703.

Sorokin, P. A. (1947). *Society, culture, and personality.* New York: Harper & Row.

Sorokin, P. A. (1962). *Social and cultural dynamics.* New Brunswick, NJ: Bedminster.

Sowell, T. (1991, May-June). Cultural diversity: A world view. *American Enterprise,* 44–55.

Spencer, H. (1874). *The study of sociology.* New York: Appelton.

Spengler, O. (1939). *The decline of the west.* New York: Knopf.

Sperry, R. W. (1966). The great cerebral commissure. In Stanley Coopersmith (Ed.), *Frontiers of psychological research* (pp. 60–70). San Francisco: Freeman.

Spicer, A., Dunfee, T. W., & Bailey, W. J. (2004). Does national context matter in ethical decision making? An empirical test of integrative social contracts theory. *Academy of Management Journal, 47*(4), 610–620.

Spitzform, M. (2000). The ecological self: Metaphor and developmental experience. *Journal of Applied Psychoanalytic Studies, 2*(3), 265–285.

Springer, S., & Deutsch, G. (1989). *Left brain, right brain.* New York: Freeman.

Spruill, N., Kenney, C., & Kaplan, L. (2001). Community development and systems thinking: Theory and practice. *National Civic Review, 90*(1), 105–117.

Spurgeon, A., Jackson, C. A., & Beach, J. R. (2001). The life events inventory: Re-scaling based on an occupational sample. *Occupational Medicine, 51*(4), 287–293.

Stapp, H. P. (1993). *Mind, matter, and quantum mechanics.* Berlin: Springer.

Stark, R., & Glock, C. (1968). *American piety: The nature of religious commitment.* Berkeley: University of California Press.

Stead, W. T. (1972). *The americanization of the world or the trend of the twentieth century.* New York: Garland. (Original work published 1902).

Steiner, J., & Devore, W. (1983). Increasing descriptive and prescriptive theoretical skills to promote ethnic-sensitive practice. *Journal of Education for Social Work, 19*(2), 63–70.

Stern, D. (1985). *The interpersonal world of the infant.* New York: Basic Books.

Stern, G. G. (1970). *People in context.* New York: Wiley.

Stevens, D .E. (1995). *Some results.* Jersey, UK: Companion Books.

Steward, J. H. (1964). A neo-evolutionist approach. In E. Etzioni-Halevy & E. Amitai (Eds.), *Social change* (pp. 131–139). New York: Basic Books.

Stix, G. (2008, July). Traces of a distant past. *Scientific American, 299*(11), 56–63.

Storr, A. (1998) *The essential Jung* (3rd ed.). London: Fontana.

Streufert, S., & Swezey, R. W. (1986). *Complexity, managers, and organizations.* Orlando, FL: Academic Press.

Sue, S. (1988). Psychotherapeutic services for ethnic minorities: Two decades of research findings. *American Psychologist, 43,* 301–308.

Sullivan, H. S. (1953). *The interpersonal theory of psychiatry* (H. S. Perry & M. L. Gawel, Eds.). New York: Norton.

Sumner, W. G. (1906). *Folkways: A study of the sociological importance of usages, manners, customs, mores, and morals.* Boston: Ginn.

Sundstrom, E., De Meuse, K. P., & Futrell, D. (1990). Work teams: Applications and effectiveness. *American Psychologist, 45*(2), 120–133.

Swain, K. A. (2006). *Beyond the Potter box: A comprehensive justification model.* St. Petersburg, FL: Department of Journalism and Media Studies, University of South Florida.

Szasz, T. S. (1960). The myth of mental illness. *American Psychologist, 15,* 113–118.

Tarter, C. J., & Hoy, W. K. (1998). Toward a contingency theory of decision making. *Journal of Educational Administration, 36*(3), 212–228.

Taylor, E. (1999). *Shadow culture: Psychology and spirituality in America.* Washington, DC: Counterpoint.

Taylor, F. W. (1977). What is scientific management? In M. Matterson & J. Ivancevich (Eds.), *Management classics* (pp. 5–8). Santa Monica, CA: Goodyear.

Tesser, A. (1995). *Advanced social psychology.* New York: McGraw-Hill.

Thelen, E. & Smith, L. B. (2006). Dynamic systems theories. In R. M. Lerner (Ed.), *Handbook of child psychology* (Vol. 1, pp. 258–312). New York: Wiley.

Theorist—Erik Erikson. Retrieved July 2003 from http://taracat.tripod.com/erikson .html.

Thomas, J. (n.d.). IBM Research Hawthorne. *A Pattern for Living Communication.* Retrieved February 2004 from http://diac.cpsr.org/cgi-bin/diac02/pattern.cgi/public.

Thomas, L. (1995). *The lives of a cell.* New York: Penguin Books.

Thompson, E. (1999). Human consciousness: Integrating phenomenology and cognitive science. Report to the Fetzer Institute on the Symposium held at Seasons, September 24–27, 1999.

Thompson, J. D. (1967). *Organizations in action.* New York: McGraw-Hill.

Titmuss, R. M. (1971). *The gift relationship: From human blood to social policy.* New York: Vintage Books.

Toennies, F. (1957). *Community and society:* Gemeinschaft und gesellschaft (C. P. Loomis, Ed.) Lansing: Michigan State University Press.

Toennies, F. (1964). Community and society: *Gemeinschaft und gesellschalft.* In E. Amitai & E. Etzioni (Eds.), *Social change.* New York: Basic Books, 54–62.

Toffler, A. (1990). *The power shift.* New York: Bantam Books.

Toman, W. (1961). *Family constellation.* New York: Springer.

Tooby, J., & Cosmides, L. (1992). Psychological foundations of culture. In J. Barkow, L. Cosmides, & J. Tooby (Eds.), *The adapted mind: Evolutionary psychology and the generation of culture* (pp. 119–136). New York: Oxford University Press.

Torre, C. A. (1995). Chaos, creativity, and innovation: Toward a dynamical model of problem solving. In R. Robertson & A. Combs (Eds.), *Chaos theory in psychology and the life sciences* (pp. 179–198). Mahwah, NJ: Erlbaum.

Toseland, R. W., & Rivas, R. F. (2001). *An introduction to group work practice* (4th ed.). Boston: Allyn & Bacon.

Toynbee, A. J. (1939). *A study of history.* London: Oxford University Press.

Toynbee, W. S. (1985). *Adult education and the voluntary associations in France.* Nottingham, UK: University of Nottingham Department of Adult Education.

Triplett, N. (1898, July). The dynamogenic factors in pacemaking and competition. *American Journal of Psychology, 9*(4), 507–563.

Tripodi, T., Fellin, P., & Meyer, H. J. (1969). *The assessment of social research.* Itasca, IL: Peacock.

Tschacher, W., Scheier, C., & Grawe, K. (1998). Order and pattern formation in psychotherapy. *Nonlinear dynamics, psychology, and life sciences, 2*(3), 195–216.

Tucker, D. (1981). Lateral brain function, emotion and conceptualization. *Psychological Bulletin, 89,* 19–43.

Tuckman, B. (1965). Developmental sequence in small groups. *Psychological Bulletin, 63,* 384–399.

Turchin, V. (1993). On cybernetic epistemology. *Systems Research, 10*(1), 3–28.

Turiel, E. (1998). The development of morality. In W. Damon & R. M. Lerner (Eds.), *Handbook of child psychology* (Vol. 3, pp. 863–932). New York: Wiley.

Tversky, A. (1972). Elimination by aspects: A theory of choice. *Psychological Review, 79,* 281–299.

Tyler, K. (1992). The developmental of the ecosystemic approach as a humanistic educational psychology. *Educational Psychology, 12*(1), 15–25.

U.S. Census Bureau. (2000). Dicennial census data. Retrieved April 2006 from http://www.census.gov/main/www/cen2000.html.

U.S. Department of Health and Human Services, Public Health Service. (n.d.).

Depression Guideline Panel: Depression in Primary Care (Vol. 3). Washington, DC: Agency for Health Care Policy and Research.

UNESCO. (2005). Cultural diversity in the era of globalization. Retrieved May 2006 from http://portal.unesco.org/.

Valdis, K. (2005). An introduction to social network analysis. Retrieved May 2005 from http://www.orgnet.com/sna.html.

van Ryn, M, & Heaney C. A. (1997). Developing effective helping relationships in health education practice. *Health Education & Behavior, 24*(6), 703–706.

Vande K. H. (1986). Dangers of psychologism: The place of God in psychology. *Journal of Psychology and Theology, 14,* 97–109.

Varela, F. J. & Coutinho, A. (1991). Second generation immune networks. *Immunology Today, 12,* 159–166.

Varela, F. J., Thompson, E., & Rosch, E. (1991). *The embodied mind: Cognitive science and human experience.* Cambridge, MA: MIT Press.

Velasquez, M., Andre, C., Shanks, S. J., & Meyer, M. J. (2006). Thinking ethically: A framework for moral decision making. Santa Clara, CA: Markula Center for Applied Ethics, Santa Clara University.

Velicer, W. F., Prochaska, J. O., Fava, J. L., Norman, G. J., & Redding, C. A. (1998). Smoking cessation and stress management: Applications of the transtheoretical model of behavior change. *Homeostasis, 38,* 216–233.

Visser, A. (1996), Case based learning: a virtual practice in dreams and realities. Papers from the Husita 4 Conference, June 11–14, 1996, Lapland, Finland.

Vroom, V. (1964). *Work and motivation.* New York: Wiley.

Vygotsky, L. S. (1962). *Thought and language.* Cambridge, MA: MIT Press.

Vygotsky, L. S. (1978). The role of play in development. In M. Cole, V. John-Steiner, S. Scribner, & E. Souberman (Eds.), *Mind in society: The development of higher psychological processes* (pp. 92–104). Cambridge, MA: Harvard University Press.

Wagner, J., & Hollenbeck, J. (1997). *Organizational behavior: Securing competitive advantage.* Upper Saddle River, NJ: Prentice Hall.

Wahba, M. A., & Bridwell, L. G. (1976). Maslow reconsidered: A review of research on the need hierarchy theory. *Organizational Behavior and Human Performance, 15,* 212–240.

Wahlström, J. (1997). Developments in family therapy: From systems to discourse. In P. Hawkins & J. Nestoros (Eds.), *Psychotherapy. New perspectives on theory, practice and research* (pp. 425–452). Athens: Ellinika Grammata.

Wakefield, J. C. (1992). Disorder as harmful dysfunction: A conceptual critique of DSM-III-R's definition of mental disorder. *Psychological Review, 99,* 232–247.

Waldrop, M. M. (1992). *Complexity: The emerging science at the edge of order and chaos.* New York: Simon & Schuster.

Walker, E. H. (2000). *The physics of consciousness.* Cambridge, MA: Perseus Books.

Wallace, D., & Peckel, J. (2006). Ethical checklist. Retrieved February 2007 from http://www.managementhelp.org/ethics/ethxgde.htm.

Wallas, G. (1926). *The art of thought.* New York: Harcourt Brace.

Walsh, F. (2003). Family resilience: A framework for clinical practice. *Family Process, 42*, 1–18.

Walzer, M. (1994). *Thick and thin: Moral arguments at home and abroad.* Notre Dame, IN: University of Notre Dame Press.

Walzer, M. (1997). *On tolerance.* New Haven, CT: Yale University Press.

Ward, M. (1995). Butterflies and bifurcations: Can chaos theory contribute to our understanding of family systems? *Journal of Marriage and Family, 57*, 629–638.

Warner, A. G. (1894). American charities: A study in philanthropy and economics. New York: Crowell.

Warren, K., Franklin, C., & Streeter, C. L. (1998). New directions in systems theory: Chaos and complexity. *Social Work, 43*(4), 357–372.

Warren, R. (1972). *The community in America.* Chicago: Rand McNally.

Waterman, A. S. (1993). Two conceptions of happiness: Contrasts of personal expressiveness (eudaimonia) and hedonic enjoyment. *Journal of Personality and Social Psychology, 64*, 678–691.

Watson, J. (1930). *Behaviorism* (2nd ed.). New York: Norton.

Weaver, H. (1999). Indigenous people and the social work profession: Defining culturally competent services. *Social Work, 44*(3), 217–225.

Weber, M. (1946). *Essays in sociology* (H. H. Gerth & C. Wright Mills, Trans. and Eds.). Oxford: Oxford University Press.

Weber, M. (1964). *The theory of social and economic organization.* New York: Free Press.

Wegner, D. M., Erber, R., & Raymond, P. (1991). Transactive memory in close relationships, *Journal of Personality and Social Psychology, 61*, 923–929.

Weick, K. E. (1996). *Sensemaking in organizations.* Newbury Park, CA: Sage.

Weick, K. E., & Quinn, R. E. (1999). Organizational change and development. *Annual Review of Psychology, 50*, 361–386.

Weick, K. E., & Roberts K. H. (1993). Collective mind and organizational reliability: The case of flight operations on an aircraft carrier deck. *Administration Science Quarterly, 38*, 357–381.

Weiner, B. (1974). *Achievement motivation and attribution theory.* Morristown, NJ: General Learning Press.

Wenger, E. (1998). *Communities of practice: Learning, meaning, and identity.* Cambridge: Cambridge University Press.

Wenger, E. (n.d.). Communities of practice: A brief introduction. Retrieved November 2005 from http://www.ewenger.com/theory/communities_of_practice_intro.htm.

Whitaker, C. (1975). The psychotherapy of the absurd. *Family Process, 14*, 1–16.

Whitaker, C. (1976). The hindrance of theory in clinical work. In P. J. Guerin (Ed.), *Family therapy* (Chap. 8). New York: Gardner Press.

White, I. W., & Gerstein, L. H. (1987). Helping: The influence of anticipated social sanctions and self-monitoring. *Journal of Personality, 55*, 41–54.

White, R. (1963). Ego and reality in psychoanalytic theory: A proposal regarding independent ego energies. *Psychoanalytic Issues, 3*(3). New York: International University, 511–525.

Wilber, K. (1995). *Sex, ecology, and spirituality.* Boston: Shambhala.

Wilber, K. (1997). An integral theory of consciousness. *Journal of Consciousness Studies, 4*(1), 71–92.

Wilber, K. (2000). *A brief history of everything.* Boston: Shambhala.

Williams, R. (1976). Society. In R. Williams (Ed.), *Keywords: A vocabulary of culture and society* (pp. 276–312). London: Fontana.

Wilson, E. O. (1975). *Sociobiology: The new synthesis.* Cambridge, MA: Harvard University Press.

Wilson, E. O. (1998). *Consilience: The unity of knowledge.* New York: Knopf.

Wilson, F. H. (2004). *Race, class, and the postindustrial city.* Albany: State University of New York Press.

Wilson, W. J. (1978). *The declining significance of race.* Chicago: University of Chicago Press.

Wilson, W. J. (1987). *The truly disadvantaged: The inner-city, the underclass, and public policy.* Chicago: University of Chicago Press.

Wilson, W. J. (1994). *When work disappears: The world of the new urban poor.* New York: Knopf.

Winch, R. F. (1958). *Mate selection: A study of complementary needs.* New York: Harper.

Wood, G. G., & Middleman, R. R. (1989). *The structural approach to direct practice in social work.* New York: Columbia University Press.

Woodruff, P., McManus, I., & David, A. (1995). Meta-analysis of corpus callosum size in schizophrenia. *Journal of Neurology, Neurosurgery, and Psychiatry, 58,* 457–461.

World Bank. (2000, June 23). The World Bank, the United Nations Development Programme and Club Economika 2000 organize a workshop on understanding and building social capital in Bulgaria. (Press release No. 2000/##/ECCBG).

World Bank. (2009). Social capital. Retrieved October 2005 from http://go.worldbank.org/130PMQKLXo.

World Health Organization. (2001). *World Health Report 2001: Mental health: New understanding, new hope.* Geneva: Author.

Wynne, L. C, Ryckoff, I., Day, J., & Hirsch, S. (1958). Pseudomutuality in the family relations of schizophrenics. *Psychiatry, 21,* 205–220.

Yalom, I. (1970). *The theory and practice of group psychotherapy.* New York: Basic Books.

Yalom, I. (1995). *The theory and practice of psychotherapy* (4th ed.). New York: Basic Books.

Yerby, J. (1995). Family systems theory reconsidered: Integrating social construction theory and dialectical process. *Communications Theory, 5*(4), 339–365.

You, Y. (1993). What can we learn from chaos theory? An alternative approach to instructional systems design, *Educational Technology Research & Development, 41*(3), 17–32.

Young, T. R. (2002). Postmodern phenomenology. *Red Feather Institute.* Retrieved November 2001 from http://uwacadweb.uwyo.edu/RED_FEATHER/lectures/025PostmodernPhenomenology.htm.

Young-Bruehl, E. (1994). *Anna Freud: A biography.* New York: Norton.

Yu, C. H. (2001). Misconceived relationship between logical positivism and quantitative methods. Paper presented at the Annual Meeting of the American Educational Research Association, Seattle, WA. Retrieved December 2001 from http://seamondey.ed.asu.edu/!alex/computer/sas/positivism.html.

Zajonc, R. (1965). Social facilitation. *Science, 149,* 269–274.

Zangwill, I. (1926). *The melting pot.* New York: Macmillan.

Zeira, A., & Rosen, A. (2000, March). Unraveling "tacit knowledge": What social workers do and why they do it. *Social Service Review, 74*(1), 103–123.

Zohar, D. (1990). *The quantum self.* New York: Morrow.

Zohar, D. & Marshall, I. (1994). *Quantum society: Mind, physics and new social vision.* New York: Quill.

Permissions Acknowledgments

Permissions are gratefully acknowledged for reprinting material from the following sources:

Figure 1.2 is reprinted with the kind permission of Dr. Jay Forrester, Massachusetts Institute of Technology.

The graphic in Theory Example 1.2 is reprinted with permission. From John E. Sheridan & Michael A. Abelson (1983). Cusp catastrophe model of employee turnover. *Academy of Management Journal*, 26, p. 421.

Figure 1.3 is reprinted with permission. M. C. Escher, "Waterfall" © 2008 The M.C. Escher Company–Holland. All rights reserved.

Figure 1.8 is reprinted by arrangement with Shambhala Publications Inc., Boston, MA (www.shambhala.com). From Humberto R. Maturana & Francisco J. Varela. *The Tree of Knowledge*, © 1987 by Humberto R. Maturana and Francisco J. Varela.

Figure 2.2 is used by permission of W. W. Norton & Company Inc. From Jared Diamond, "Figure 4.1: Factors underlying the broadest pattern of history," from *Guns, Germs, and Steel: The Fates of Human Societies*. Copyright © 1997 by Jared Diamond.

The photo from Profile 4.1 (pfMS Am 092, #18) is reprinted by permission of the Houghton Library, Harvard University.

Table 4.1 is reprinted with kind permission of Springer Science and Business Media. From J. Ehrenwald (1984). *Anatomy of genius: Split brains and global minds*, Human Sciences Press, p. 16.

Figure 4.1 is reprinted by permission of the artist, Carol Donner (Tucson, AZ).

Figure 4.3 is reprinted and adapted with permission. From G. M. Edelman (2001). *Bright air, brilliant fire: On the matter of the mind*. New York: Basic Books, Figure 12–4, p. 132.

Figure 5.1 is adapted and reprinted with permission. From David Moshman (1999). *Adolescent psychological development: Rationality, morality, and identity*. Mahwah, NJ: Lawrence Erlbaum Associates, Figure 8.2, p. 73.

The photo from Profile 5.1 is reprinted by permission of Ted Streshinsky/Corbis.

Table 5.3 is adapted and reprinted with permission. From L. X. Hy & J. Loevinger (1996). *Measuring ego development*, 2nd ed. Mahwah, NJ: Lawrence Erlbaum Associates, p. 4.

Figure 5.2 and Table 5.5 are reprinted with permission. From C. G. Hudson (2004, Fall). The dynamics of self-organization: Neglected dimensions. *Journal of Human Behavior in the Social Environment, 10* (4), pp. 17–38.

Figure 6.2 is reprinted with permission. From K. M. Sheldon & A. J. Elliot (1999). Goal striving, need satisfaction, and longitudinal well-being: The self-concordance model. *Journal of Personality and Social Psychology, 76*(3), p. 483.

Figure 6.3 is reprinted with permission. *Wellness lecture series* (p. 5), Oakland, CA: University of California/HealthNet. Copyright 1994 by Salvatore R. Maddi. Reprinted with permission.

The photo from Profile 6.1 is reprinted by permission of INTERFOTO/Alamy.

Table 6.1 is reprinted with permission. From P. R. Pintrich (2000). An achievement goal theory perspective on issues in motivation terminology, theory, and research. *Contemporary Educational Psychology, 25*, p. 100.

Table 6.2 is reprinted with permission of the author. B. Weiner (1974). *Achievement motivation and attribution theory.* Morristown, NJ: General Learning Press, Table 1, p. 6.

Figure 6.5 and Figure 8.2 are adapted and reprinted with permission granted by John Wiley & Sons. From Theodore Millon & Roger Davis (2000). *Personality disorders in modern life.* New York: John Wiley & Sons, pp. 8–9, 19–20, & Figure 1.5.

Figure 6.6 is adapted with permission. From A. L. Pincus (1994). The interpersonal circumplex and the interpersonal theory: Perspectives on personality and its pathology. In S. Strack (Ed.), Differentiating normal and abnormal personality (114–136). New York: Springer.

Figure 7.2 is adapted and reprinted with permission. From Carlos A. Torre (1995). Chaos, creativity, and innovation: Toward a dynamical model of problem solving. In Robin Robertson and Allan Combs, *Chaos theory in psychology and the life sciences.* Mahwah, NJ: Lawrence Erlbaum Associates, p. 183.

Exhibit 7.3 is reprinted with the permission of the author John Thomas. A similar version of this pattern appears in Douglas Schuler (2008). *Liberating voices: A pattern language for communication revolution.* Cambridge: MIT Press.

Figure 7.4 is adapted and reprinted with the permission of John Thomas. From Marvin S. Cohen, Leonard Adelman, & Bryan B. Thompson (2000, March). Experimental investigation of uncertainty, stakes, and time in pilot decision making. Cognitive Technologies, Arlington, VA.

Figure 7.5 is reprinted with permission. From Mihaly Czikszentmihalyi & Keith Sawyer (1995). Creative insight: The social dimension of a solitary moment. In Robert J. Sternberg & Janet E. Davidson, *The nature of insight.* Cambridge, MA: MIT Press.

Exhibit 7.5 is reprinted with permission from Susan Traiman, Business Roundtable.

Exhibits 8.1, 8.2, 8.3, and 8.4 are adapted with permission from the American Psychiatric Association, *Diagnostic and Statistical Manual of Mental Disorders, Text Revision* (4th ed.). Washington, DC: American Psychiatric Association, copyright 2000.

Table 8.2 is reprinted with permission. From A. Spurgeon, C. A. Jackson, & J. R. Beach (2001). The life events inventory: Re-scaling based on an occupational sample. *Occupational Medicine, 51*(4), Table 1, pp. 288–289.

The photo from Profile 8.1 is reprinted by permission of Mary Evans Picture Library/Alamy.

The graphs in Theory Example 8.1 are reprinted with permission. From Hector C. Sabelli, Linnea Carlson-Sabelli, M. Patel, A. Levy, & Justo Diez-Martin (1995). Anger, fear, depression and crime: Physiological and psychological studies using the process method. In Robin Robertson and Allan Combs (Eds.), *Chaos theory in psychology and the life sciences*. Mahwah, NJ: Lawrence Erlbaum Associates.

Figure 9.1 is adapted with permission. From H. Arrow, J. McGrath, & J. Berdahl (2000). *Small groups as complex systems: Formation, coordination, development, and adaptation.* Thousand Oaks, CA: Sage.

Figure 10.2 is adapted and reprinted by permission of The MIT Press. © 2002 Massachusetts Institute of Technology. From John M. Gottman, James D. Murray, Catherine C. Swanson, Rebecca Tyson, & Kristin R. Swanson (2002). *The mathematics of marriage: Nonlinear models.* Cambridge, MA: MIT Press, figure from p. 253.

Table 11.1 is adapted with permission. From Yeheskel Hasenfeld & Richard A. English (1974). *Human service organizations.* Ann Arbor: University of Michigan Press, p. 5.

Table 11.2 is adapted and reprinted with permission of John Wiley & Sons Inc. From Lee G. Bolman & Terrence E. Deal (1997). *Reframing organizations: Artistry, choice, and leadership.* San Francisco: Jossey-Bass, p. 15. Copyright © 1997 by Jossey-Bass Inc., Publishers.

Table 11.3 is reprinted with permission of John Wiley & Sons Inc. From Adrianna J. Kezar (2001). *Understanding and facilitating organizational change in the twenty-first century: Recent research and conceptualizations.* San Francisco: Jossey-Bass, p. 57, with permission of John Wiley & Sons Inc.

Table 11.4 is adapted and reprinted with permission of the author, with nonexclusive rights. From Jeffrey Goldstein (1997). *Riding the waves of emergence: Leadership innovations in complex systems.* Edware—Filing Cabinet (http://www.plexusinstitute.com/edgeware/archive/think/main_filing2.html).

Figure 12.1 is adapted and reprinted with permission. From David Nolan (1971). Classifying and analyzing politico-economic systems. *The Individualist.* © David F. Nolan, 1971.

Figure 12.2 is reprinted with permission. From P. S. Bearman, J. Moody, & K. Stovel (2004, July). Chains of affection: The structure of adolescent romantic and sexual networks. *American Journal of Sociology, 100*(1), 58.

Figure 12.3 is adapted and reprinted by permission of the author. From E. Wenger (1998, June). Communities of practice: Learning as a social system. *Systems Thinker.*

The photo from Profile 12.1 is reprinted by permission from the Library of Congress.

The photo in Profile 13.1 of William J. Wilson is reprinted with permission. © William Julius Wilson, Lewis P. and Linda L. Geyser University Professor, Harvard University.

The map in Figure 13.1 is reprinted by permission of Canuckguy.

Table 14.1 is reprinted with permission from the Council on Social Work Education. From S. H. Hernandez, J. Jorgensen, P. Judd, M. Gould, & M. Parsons (1985). Integrated practice: An advanced generalist curriculum to prepare social problem specialists. *Journal of Social Work Education, 21*(3), 28–35.

Table 14.2 is adapted and reprinted with permission from the Council on Social Work Education. From E. C. Jackson, H. J. Macy, & P. J. Day (1984). A simultaneity model for social work education. *Journal of Education for Social Work, 20*(2), 17–24.

Figure 15.1 is reprinted with permission of Kristen Alley Swain, Assistant Professor, Department of Journalism, University of Mississippi. From Kristen Alley Swain (2006). Beyond the Potter box: A comprehensive justification model. Department of Journalism and Media Studies, University of South Florida, St. Petersberg, FL.

Figure 15.2 is reprinted by permission of the authors. From Edward R. Canda & Leola D. Furman (1999). *Spiritual diversity in social work practice: The heart of helping.* New York: Free Press, p. 274.

Figure 15.3 is adapted and reprinted with the endorsement of *Journal of Transpersonal Psychology.* From David Lukoff (1985). The diagnosis of mystical experiences with psychotic features. *Journal of Transpersonal Psychology, 17*(2), 155–181.

Figures A.1, A.2, and A.3 are reprinted by kind permission of the author. From Stuart Hameroff (1997). Quantum computing in microtubules: An intra-neural correlate of consciousness? *Cognitive Studies: Bulletin of the Japanese Cognitive Science Society, 4*(3): figures 2, 7, & 10.

The quotation on p. 299 by Chris Lang is reprinted with permission from C. Lang (2003). [Website: http://philosophy.wisc.edu/lang/pd/pdo.htm].

The quotation on p. 311 is reprinted by special permission of the William Alanson White Psychiatric Foundation Inc. (Washington, DC). © The WAW Foundation.

"Preconditions for Community Functioning" on p. 462 is adapted and reprinted with permission from Kecia Baker, assistant dean, Occidental College.

The preamble to the Responsive Communitarian Platform, on p. 467, is quoted with permission of the Institute for Communitarian Policy Studies and Professor Amitai Etzioni.

The quotation on p. 533 from Oscar Lewis is reprinted by permission of Nel van der Werf, Springer Publishing. From O. Lewis (1998, January). The culture of poverty. *Society, 35*(7).

The quotation on pp. 543–544 is reprinted with permission of Josh Nathan-Kazis, *New Voices Magazine* (New York, NY). From M. Moore (2005), Sex, miscegenation, and the intermarriage debate.

Permission to revise and adapt sections from the following articles is gratefully acknowledged:

Hudson, C. G. (2000, Spring/Summer). At the edge of chaos: A new paradigm for social work? *Journal of Social Work Education, 36*(2), 215–230.

Hudson, C.G. (2000). From social Darwinism to self-organization: Implications for social change theory. *Social Service Review, 74*(4).

Hudson, C.G. (2004, Fall). The dynamics of self-organization: Neglected dimensions. *Journal of Human Behavior in the Social Environment, 10* (4), 17–38 (tables 1 and 2).

About the Author

CHRISTOPHER G. HUDSON is professor of social work at Salem State College, Salem, MA. After obtaining his bachelor and master degrees at the University of Chicago in the early 1970s, and practicing as both a community organizer and a clinical social work for several years, he earned his Ph.D. from the University of Illinois at Chicago in 1983. Since then, he has regularly taught in MSW programs and published extensively in professional journals on human behavior and mental health policy issues, including developments in complex systems and chaos theories. His books include *Dimensions of State Mental Health Policy* (Praeger, 1991) and *An Interdependency Model of Homelessness* (Mellon, 1998). Professor Hudson has been the recipient of numerous awards, including Researcher of the Year, awarded by the Massachusetts Alliance for the Mentally Ill; and the senior faculty scholar award from the William J. Fulbright Commission, which took him to Hong Kong, where he began writing this book.

INDEX

bifurcation
  in communities, 484
  definition of, 32
  in families, 422
  Feigenbaum constant, 32
  in groups, 386
  of organizational thinking, 443
  psychological conflict, 346
binding problem, 95, 150, 154, 638
Binswanger, Ludwig, 326–27
biocultural diversity, 508, 526
biocultural functionalism, 8
biodiversity, 521–25, 537
bioengineering, 485
Bion, Wilfred, 363, 376–77
biophilia hypothesis, 22
biopsychosocial assessment, 345
bipolar disorder, 325, 343
The Birth of a Nation, 544
bisociation, 293
Black, Max, 6
black box, 133, 179
black separatist movements, 506
blank slate theory, 164, 168, 186, 525
Blasi, Augusto, 199
blended families, 407, 409. *See also* family
blending, 293–95
blindsight, 158
blood donations, 558
Bobo doll experiments, 180
bodily-kinesthetic intelligence, 178
Boehm, Werner W., 566
Boehm Curriculum Study, 566
Bohm, David, 128, 641
Bolman, Lee G., 441–42, 444
Bomben, K.D., 86
Bono, Edward de, 262
borderline personality disorder, 184, 232, 324
Boscolo, Luigi, 417
Bose-Einstein condensates, 642
Bosnia, 549
Bourdieu, Pierre, 464
Bowen, Murray, 381, 393–94, 413, 415–16
Bowlby, John, 185–86
Bowling Alone, 465
Brace, Loring, 524
Bragg, Elizabeth, 22
brain structure, 144–45
  amygdala, 152
  axons, 149
  basal ganglia, 152, 169
  brain stem, 147, 152

cerebral cortex, 147–48
core consciousness and, 147–48
corpus callosum, 146
dendrites, 149
ERTAS (extended reticular thalamic activating system), 144, 152, 156, 159
evolution of, 157
hemispheres, 145–46, 152
hind, 147
hippocampus, 147–48, 152
hypothalamus, 147, 173
lesions, 343
limbic system, 147–48, 152
neurons, 149–50, 154–55, 644–45
pineal gland, 130
reticular activating system, 147
subcortical nuclei, 154
synapses, 149, 151
thalamus, 147–49, 152, 154
break points, 378
Brenner, Harvey, 329
brief therapy, 412
Brown, Jason, 522
Brown v. Board of Education, 511
Buchanan, Bruce, 141
bureaucracy, 65, 435, 455
bureaucratic model, 435
bureaucratization, 64
busing, 506
butterfly effect, 30. *See also* chaos theory, sensitivity to initial conditions
bystander effect, 558

Caffarella, Rosemary S., 164–65
Calvin, William, 60, 151
Campbell, Donald, 99
Camus, Albert, 96
Canada, multiculturalism in, 506
cancer, 173
Canda, Edward, 605, 612
Capra, Fritzof, 642
Carkhuff, Roger, 560–61
Cartwright, Dorwin, 369
cascade theory of marital dissolution, 396–97
case-based reasoning, 275, 280–81
casework, 392, 565
Caspi, Avshalom, 165, 168
catastrophe theory, 28–30
catharsis, 367
Caucasians, 215, 514
caucusing, 373
causes, types of, 92–93, 102, 106

Stone Center (Wellesley College), 197
stonewalling, 397, 404
strain, 220
strange attractors
    Carlos Torre's triadic model, 266
    family systems theory and, 410, 421
    feedback loops and, 347
    in human services, 39
    illustration of, 31
    personality disorders and, 324
    small groups and, 384
strategic therapy, 412
strategies of successive approximation,
    582, 588
stream of consciousness, pragmatism, 131
strengths perspective, 567–68
stress, 25, 329–30, 332
stress reaction, 220
structural coupling, 36
structural functionalism, 8, 471–72
The Structure of Scientific Revolutions, 97
subjective self, 188
sublimation, 243
substance abuse, 614
subsystems, 384
Sudan, 549
suicide, 396
Sullivan, Harry S., 221, 244, 338
Sumner, William G., 56, 545
superposition, 639–40, 642. *See also* quantum theory
superradiance, 643
superstate physics, 642
suppression, 242
surveys, 494
survival of the fittest, 55. *See also* Darwin,
    Charles; evolutionary theory; social
    Darwinism
Swain, Kristen, 604
SWB (subjective well-being), 214, 221. *See
    also* happiness
SWOT paradigm, 497
symbiotic phase, 185
symbolic-experiential therapy, 418
symbolic play, 170
symbolism, 444
Symposium on Information Theory (1956),
    133
symptom disorders, 315, 338. *See also*
    mental illness
symptoms, 313–15. *See also under* mental
    illness
system dynamics, 24

systems theory
    definition of, 4
    emergence, 5
    energy, 10–11
    hierarchy, 12
    holism, 4, 9, 530
    interdependence, 5
    internal structure, 12
    negative feedback, 14–15, 69
    positive feedback, 30, 69
    reductionism, 4
systems thinking, 264
Szasz, Thomas, 395

tabulae rasae, 164, 168, 186, 525
The Tao of Physics, 642
Tarter, C. John, 270
task difficulty, 231
task groups, 360, 366, 373. *See also* groups
Tavistock Clinic, 365
Taylor, Frederick W., 434–35, 441
technological development, 485
technostructure, 439
Tejano, 516
telic decentralization, 307, 327
temperament
    adaptation and, 217
    attention difficulties, 171
    childhood, 167, 170–71
    infant, 170
    personality and, 213
T-groups, 362–63. *See also* groups
Thanatos, 76, 184, 227, 249. *See also* Freud,
    Sigmund
Thatcher, Margaret, 558
theory
    assessment of, 112–15
    causes and, 106
    comparative framework, 112
    components of, 87
    constructivist notion of, 100–101
    criticisms of, 89
    data sources, 106
    deductive-nomological approach to, 100–101
    definition of, 86
    drawbacks of, 87
    in human services, 87, 89, 108, 115–16
    idealizing notion of, 100
    practice, 87, 89
    as process of thought, 89–90
    system levels, 88
    use in assessment, 90, 112
    uses in social sciences, 100–101